HARRY
EMERSON
FOSDICK

HARRY EMERSON FOSDICK

Preacher, Pastor, Prophet

ROBERT MOATS MILLER

New York   Oxford
OXFORD UNIVERSITY PRESS
1985

Library of Congress Cataloging in Publication Data
Miller, Robert Moats.
  Harry Emerson Fosdick.
  Bibliography: p.
  Includes index.
  1. Fosdick, Harry Emerson, 1878–1969.   2. Baptists—
United States—Clergy—Biography.   I. Title.
BX6495.F68M54   1985   286'.1'0924 [B] 84–7168
ISBN 0–19–503512–7

Printing (last digit): 9 8 7 6 5 4 3 2 1
Printed in the United States of America

David Wood Miller
Abigail Hood Miller
Amanda Kathleen Miller
"The Hope of the World"

Preface

In this century, which rapidly draws to a close, no American Protestant minister has exceeded the prominence of Harry Emerson Fosdick. This is simply a statement of historic fact. I believe that this Baptist preacher was not only vastly influential, but also that he was a great human being. This, of course, is a subjective judgment, and others who disagree will find in this biography considerable—though it seems to me not overwhelming—evidence to support their demurring position.

The explanation for this protean man's towering importance lies precisely in the myriad ways his long and eventful life (1878–1969) connected with major concerns, sacred and secular, of a whirling and calamitous age.

Fosdick believed that it was possible to be a Christian in the twentieth century without throwing one's mind away, and he wished to help others make this same discovery for themselves. Despite the epithet "heretic" volleyed at him by fundamentalist brethren who deemed him "modernism's Moses," he belongs within the evangelical tradition, warming and winning the hearts of millions; giving point to Rabbi Stephen S. Wise's thoughtful judgment: "Fosdick—the least hated and best loved heretic that ever lived."

At the same time, by keeping faith and reason in creative tension, he challenged the minds of millions and thereby merited a place in the pantheon of gifted Christian apologists. In this enterprise Fosdick believed the most formidable opponents of the faith to be the champions of secular humanism and scientific naturalism, such stern and honorable individuals as Walter Lippmann and Joseph Wood Krutch.

In a real sense, throughout his ministerial life Fosdick preached from a single text: though astronomies change the stars abide. It was his historic mission to be the faithful's guide to the new astronomies while convincing doubt-plagued souls that the stars abide. His mission was both to perplexed believers and to inquiring unbelievers. As a preacher his voice reached great audiences from pulpit and lectern and over the airwaves. As a beloved teacher he quickened the minds of several generations of Union Theological Seminary students. As author or editor of nearly fifty books and a thousand printed sermons and articles, he informed the thinking of much of literate America. The hymns he composed are still admired, notably "God of Grace and God of Glory." He was minister to strategic churches, the most famous being New York's Riverside Church, to this day closely identified with Fosdick's original pastorate and with the Rockefeller millions that made the "cathedral" possible.

Nor was this all. Fosdick was one of the pioneers of psychological pastoral counseling, a powerful and controversial clinical movement within American Protestantism; in this capacity he advised and comforted afflicted multitudes. It merits mention that the best-selling *On Being a Real Person* illuminates the whole genre of "power of positive thinking" works. Furthermore, he was up to his hips in the vast mental health movement, and he was the first minister publicly to support Alcoholics Anonymous, one of his early talks before the group eliciting the praise, "My God what a blast—what a shame that man ain't an alcoholic too!"

Moreover, because Fosdick, like John Wesley, took the world as his parish and because, like his hero Walter Rauschenbusch, he understood that we rarely sin against God alone, he was deeply involved in the secular scene and in that process he afflicted the comfortable. Though an ardent participant in World War I, he came to echo Walt Whitman, "I say God damn the wars—all wars: God damn every war: God damn 'em! God damn 'em!" Whitman's litany Fosdick judged a prayer, and not even Pearl Harbor compelled him to recant the conviction that war is man's supreme defiance of God's will for His children. The sin of racism also burned Fosdick's conscience, and although a child of racist times, in the end his commitment to racial justice was such that Dr. Martin Luther King, Jr., would say to him: "You are the greatest preacher and foremost prophet of the century, you are a 'Christian saint.'" In the area of economic justice Fosdick carried the Social Gospel banner into the midcentury. Furthermore, Fosdick was hit hard for his championship of civil liberties from the Great Red Scare of 1919 to the Great Fear of the McCarthy Era. He returned the blows, once thundering to economic royalists attempting to muzzle the pulpit, "I am speaking for multitudes of my brethren when I say, *'Before high God, not for sale!'* "

It was Fosdick's fate to live in an age when America seemingly slipped from its Apollonian moorings into a Dionysian sea of unrestrained urges. Seen by religious conservatives as a rebel, Fosdick in fact was no radical in the realm of culture, and there is much poignancy in this minister's attempt to come to terms with cultural modernism, from contraception to jazz to psychoanalysis.

Fosdick was the "most influential interpreter of religion in his generation," believed Ralph W. Sockman, proclaiming "the God of Grace and Glory for the living of these days." His influence was "tremendous," judged Reinhold Niebuhr, because "he not only resisted the claims of the obscurantists but affirmed the message of biblical faith in such a way as to prove its relevance to the experience of modern men, who, it must be noted were proved upon analysis to be real men with man's perennial needs, however modern they might be." One may acknowledge that Fosdick was not a brilliant systematic theologian and yet concur in Niebuhr's statement that "he profoundly influenced the theological climate of his day," for theology was the anvil upon which his ministry was hammered out. His three major books of Biblical scholarship may be dated, but they were enormously influential in their day.

To understand Fosdick's commanding position in twentieth-century religious history, it is crucial to recall his influence in the realm of homiletics. He was, for weal or woe, clearly the era's leading homiletician, and the example of his preaching guided the preparation and delivery of the sermons of much of the Protestant ministry. If plagiarism is the sincerest form of flattery, a less modest man would have been consumed by pride, for it was common to present him to a group of clergy with this introduction: "I give you Dr. Fosdick, whose sermons you have heard and preached." I am not here asserting the greatness of Harry Emerson Fosdick, but am arguing Albert C. Outler's correctness in terming the story of Fosdick's life the biopsy of an epoch.

As the nineteenth century drew to a close the great Scottish churchman, Marcus Dods, then near the end of his career, said: "I do not envy those who will carry the banner of Christianity in the twentieth century. . . . Yes, perhaps I do: but it will be a stiff fight." Although good men have questioned whether the banner Fosdick carried was in truth that of Biblical Christianity, no fair person will charge that he flinched from the fight as he perceived it. On the eve of entering the ministry Fosdick was sternly instructed by the veteran Baptist preacher, George C. Lorimer, "Young man, never you fear the face of mortal clay!" Whatever Fosdick's flaws, surely a failure of moral nerve was not among them—and even bitter opponents honored him for this.

Is it possible to write a biography of Fosdick of broad appeal without it being a shallow study? Is it possible to make Fosdick's life accessible without, however, engaging in hagiography? Is it possible to believe as I do that Fosdick was an admirable human being—a splendid husband, father, and friend—without penning one of those moist memorials that frequently masquerade as religious biography, with all tics and traumas piously veiled? I like to think that it is and that in aiming for a broad readership critical standards have not been lowered.

On the advice of friends I have made the dubious decision not to barnacle this narrative with citation footnotes. The historian Charles A. Beard once argued that the writing of history is an act of faith. My point here is that the *reading* of history is also an act of faith. Although I have a lot of reservations and trepidations about interpretations advanced in this study, I am as confident as a Christian with four aces (to borrow from Mark Twain) that the research is solid, exacting as it did over a decade from my life. Interested readers may now turn to the "Essay on Sources" to judge for themselves whether this patently hubristic statement is true. Shortly there may also be found a heartfelt if inadequate acknowledgment of those individuals and institutions who loaned a helping hand.

This, admittedly, is a big book, not for the faint of heart or short of wind. But it is emphatically not written primarily for professional historians. The quotations are numerous, but Fosdick had such a compelling way of phrasing things, at least for his generation, that I think they are justified; anyhow, it seems appropriate to permit a preacher to have his say in his own words.

A penultimate point of importance. I did not have the good fortune to know Dr. Fosdick or ever to hear him in person preach. This is not in any sense an official, family-authorized biography. The Fosdick children, Dr. Elinor Fosdick Downs and Dr. Dorothy Fosdick, did not instigate this study, and neither they nor I desired a commissioned work. At the onset the Drs. Fosdick did give the enterprise their unofficial blessing; they agreed to be interviewed and they supported my access to the archives of The Riverside Church and to the Fosdick Collection at the Union Theological Seminary. After that they maintained a hands-off policy, and I am deeply grateful to them for this. I do not consider myself a church historian or historian of religion, but rather a general historian of the twentieth-century United States. Doubtless this essentially secular background was a handicap in the writing of a number of chapters, especially those dealing with theology, Biblical scholarship, and preaching. On the other hand, my experience as a generalist may have strengthened those chapters concerned with cultural, social, and political matters. And so I lift, in this connection, the old racetrack gambler's prayer: "Dear Lord, let me break even. I need the money."

Fosdick's first volume of published sermons was entitled (at the publisher's insistence) *The Hope of the World*. In the advertisements the title appeared in bold type immediately under a picture of Fosdick and his name. An old comrade, William P. Merrill, pastor of the Brick Presbyterian Church, immediately clipped the notice and sent it to Fosdick with the comment: "Oh, Yeah? Who says so? My admiration for you is almost boundless. But I confess I'd stop short of this. Yours devotedly." Well, if anyone should challenge the dedication of this book to David, Abigail, and Amanda, "The Hope of the World," I like to think their mother, Carol Herter Miller, and I would not back down.

Chapel Hill, N.C. R.M.M.
September 1984 "Lord, I believe; help thou mine unbelief."
Mark 9:24

Acknowledgments

Winthrop S. Hudson, Grant Wacker, and Peter F. Walker read portions of the manuscript and I am grateful for their thoughtful criticisms. To demonstrate this gratitude I will not specify the chapters they read, thus absolving them of responsibility for the flaws that remained when I mulishly refused to accept all their suggestions. In attempting to understand Fosdick's mental breakdown as a youth, I turned for help to several psychiatrists and neurologists. Dr. J. T. Monroe, Jr., and Dr. John B. Thomas, in particular, reviewed the documentary evidence with painstaking care and shared their judgments with me. Because the final conclusions are mine, of necessity, I hope their professional reputations will survive being associated, with their permission, with the writing of Chapter Three. From time to time friends in the historical profession alerted me to items concerning Fosdick they chanced upon in their own researches, and I thank again Gerald Grob, William Ellis, Ralph Luker, Justus Doenecke, Philip Ensley, C. Allyn Russell, Leonard Sweet, Daryl Revoldt, Charles Harvey, Richard Havens, Stan Harbison, William Mc-Kee, and Eugene P. Link. Mr. Pat Russo, that quintessential urbane, generous New Yorker, made less lonely long evenings following long days of research.

Mrs. Ceci P. Long typed the final draft of the massive manuscript with meticulous care and unfailing personal graciousness.

Stephen S. Wilburn then of Oxford University Press gave early and sustained moral support at a time when the outcome of the enterprise was much in doubt in my own mind. My thanks to him (although he failed to keep an initial date to meet me under the clock at the Biltmore, later giving the *lame* excuse that he forgot the appointment because he was due to be married the upcoming weekend). Cynthia A. Read of Oxford University Press corrected errors, smoothed prose, and skillfully guided the manuscript to publication. Moreover, she is a swell, and long-suffering, luncheon companion. Oxford associate editor Joan H. Bossert and copy editor Andrew Yockers also performed their editorial responsibilities in a spiffy style.

My indebtedness to many other individuals will be mentioned in the "Essay on Sources."

And now a word about institutional support. The Faculty Research Council of the University of North Carolina at Chapel Hill partially underwrote the costs of research travel to places as distant as San Juan, Puerto Rico. A $1,000 grant from the American Philosophical Society helped make possible research trips ranging from Buffalo, New York, to Boothbay Harbor, Maine. A Kenan Leave from our university in the fall semester of 1974 made possible six sustained months of research in New York City, and a handsome $9,000 award from the Rockefeller Foundation, Humanities Division, sustained survival in that wicked and expensive town. The Rockefeller grant also made possible many later vacation months in New York and elsewhere. Thanks to a National Endowment for the Humanities Senior Summer Stipend I was freed from one summer of teaching to concentrate on writing, and thanks to my chairman, Robert Don Higginbotham, I was released from certain departmental duties in the fall of 1981 to press the writing.

This volume, as the reader knows, is dedicated to my children. This is, of course, a real tribute to their mother.

Contents

    Preacher as Husband, Father, and Friend   285

17. "Gladly Do We Teach": Thirty-eight Years as Union Semi-
    nary Professor   319

18. "And How Shall They Hear Without a Preacher?": The Con-
    ceptualization of Preachable Sermons   333

19. "Sweating Blood": The Preparation and Presentation of
    Preachable Sermons   351

20. "The Dean of All Ministers of the Air": Radio's "National
    Vespers Hour" Reaches Millions   379

21. "The Church Must Go Beyond Modernism": A Faith That
    Could Not Be Shaken   389

22. The Passing of Victorian America: A Minister's Response to
    the Disintegration of the Bourgeois Synthesis   418

23. The Passing of Protestant America: A Minister's Response
    to the Crashing of "A Righteous Empire"   441

24. Racial Justice: A Minister's Response to America's Deepest
    Sin   449

25. Social Justice: An Evolving Social Gospel from the Age of
    Rauschenbusch to the Age of Niebuhr   464

26. "Can Satan Cast Out Satan?": Does Pacifism Have a Place
    in a World of Hitlers and Stalins?   490

27. "And the War Came" and the Wars Continued: A Peace-
    maker in Wars Hot and Cold, 1941–1969   533

28. The Decision To Step Down, 1946: Saying Farewell to Riv-
    erside and Union   548

29. "Leisure Is the Time for Doing Something Useful": A Re-
    tirement of Activities and Accomplishment   555

30. "Awaiting the Day of New Beginnings"   567

    Essay on Sources   571

    Index   593

HARRY
EMERSON
FOSDICK

Chapter One

Young Harry of Western New York

I

Harry Emerson Fosdick was born on May 24, 1878, in a modest house in Buffalo, New York, and he died on October 5, 1969, in modern Lawrence Hospital, Bronxville, New York. A long time, ninety-one years, over half the epoch of the Republic since the Founding Fathers brought forth a new nation, separated these two scenes. The purpose of this opening chapter is not to chronicle the story of growing up in western New York a century ago, a story already engagingly related both by Fosdick and his brother in their respective autobiographies. Rather, the immediate purpose is to single out several central themes of Fosdick's adult life and to search for the roots of those themes in his childhood. This quest for continuities will entail moving from his youth forward in time and from his maturity backward in time to the early years.

II

The life of Harry Emerson Fosdick may be viewed as a continuing commitment to Christian service. Although the precise form of this service was not to be defined until his college years, the commitment itself was clearly made at age seven.

Early in 1886 the Reverend Albert Tennant stood in the pulpit of the small vine-clad red brick Baptist Church in the village of Westfield, New York, and preached on the nobility of the command, "Go ye therefore and teach all nations." Listening intently, a fuzzy-haired, blue-eyed,

seven-year-old boy experienced what Saint Paul called being strengthened with might by God's spirit in the inner man. Fosdick's testimony
given in the years of his maturity refers to "a definite experience of conversion," being "born again," receiving "the grace of God," having a
"tremendous emotional experience," and catching a "glimpse of the
Vision Glorious." There came to him, he recalled, "visions of possibilities not there before and a sense of direction and purpose in life." He
was determined to be a foreign missionary. More immediately, he was
set to make public profession of his faith, receive baptism, and unite
with the church—and this despite his parents' anxious appeals to wait,
for he was so young. On February 21 a stool was sunk in the baptistry
for the lad to stand upon, and he was immersed in Baptist fashion in the
name of the Father, Son, and Holy Ghost. Fifty years later Fosdick
looked "back on that independent little chap with a good deal of satisfaction. I like his spirit. He was making one of the first great decisions
of his life for himself, knowing even then that nobody else could make
it for him."

The decision to be a Christian missionary was in fact then being made
by thousands of young Americans, and if there is any uniqueness in
Fosdick's commitment, it is the tender age at which he made it. In that
very year the Student Volunteer Movement had its genesis in a conference at Mount Hermon School when one hundred of the participants
volunteered for overseas service. By the spring of 1887 over two thousand idealistic youngsters had enrolled in the great task soon to be defined by John R. Mott, "The Evangelization of the World in This Generation." It is not improbable that Fosdick was caught up in the fervor
of the times, swept away as were so many of his peers by a call to carry
Christ's saving gospel to "Ceylon's isle" where "every prospect pleases"
and "only man is vile."

If the missionary zeal pervading American Protestantism is the larger
setting for the decision triggered by Tennant's sermon, what had been
the personal religious experiences of this lad that resulted in his pledging
his life to Christ?

"I judge that from the beginning I was predestined to religion," Fosdick mused in his autobiography, and though considering his adult difficulties with the Presbyterians, there is an irony in the use of "predestined," one is at a loss to find a substitute term. He recalled experiencing
far back in his youth "hours of mystical insight, vague but moving compulsions of the spirit, at times involuntary and surprising, at times consciously sought in solitude." In such quiet hours he grew still and listened until, like the young Samuel in the temple, he cried, "Speak, Lord,
for thy servant heareth." One such awestruck hour came to him stand-

ing, boyish cap pulled off his head, before Munkácsy's painting, *Christ before Pilate*, at an exhibition in Buffalo. That religion was to Harry an early and serious concern is confirmed by the memories of his younger brother, Raymond, whose many admirable virtues did not include a plenitude of piety. There was, beyond question, an element of mysticism in Harry Fosdick without which his critical decision would be inexplicable. This mysticism, which led him on repeated occasions to term himself at heart a Quaker, remained until the end of his days.

The conscious experience of intense fear of divine wrath is often a prelude to conversion. The boy was racked by just such fear. "Fifty years ago," Fosdick reminisced in a sermon, "a boy seven years of age was crying himself to sleep at night in terror lest, dying, he should go to hell, and his solicitous mother, out of all patience with the fearful teaching which brought such apparitions to the mind, was trying in vain to comfort him." On other occasions Fosdick recalled that as a "little lad seven years old" he had cried himself to sleep "in a paroxysm of agony" and also that "when I was seven" I cried myself to sleep "in dread that I was going to hell." Though in *The Living of These Days* Fosdick suggests that the "thought of God became a horror" to him only after he had turned eight, the evidence is persuasive, taking Fosdick at his own word expressed elsewhere, that the fear *began* at age seven or earlier and continued several years at least.

If there is irony in Fosdick's employment of the term "predestined" for his religious calling, there is tragedy in the possibility that the mother, through no fault of her own and, indeed, because of the son's devotion to her, contributed to those nights of anguish. In 1885 Fosdick's mother had suffered a severe nervous breakdown that necessitated a family move from Buffalo to Westfield in the Chautauqua hills, where her parents, the Andrew Weavers, lived, as did grandfather John S. Fosdick. The children, Harry, Raymond, and Edith, were divided between the Weaver and Fosdick households. The mother "for many weeks could barely lift her head from the pillow." Understandably, the children were permitted to visit her only "once in a while." The cause of the breakdown, shrouded by time and the absence of medical records, may only be conjectured. Perhaps there was an inherited delicacy of constitution, as both her brother and sister died of tuberculosis. Perhaps she continued to grieve over the 1881 death from diphtheria of a five-month-old daughter, Ethel. Harry was expected to die also, his parents watching the signs of death creep over him. He was not yet three at the time and reports no personal memory of the sister's death or death's breath upon him. It is possible that these events, though unremembered in maturity, impressed themselves on the small child's unconscious mind. Perhaps the birth of the twins, Raymond and Edith, in 1883 overtaxed Amie Fosdick's limited strength. Financial debts were a relentless concern, forcing the family to move from a modest but decent house at 373 Pennsylvania Avenue to a shabby one at 26 Prospect Avenue just prior to the breakdown. Finally, "neurasthenia" was endemic in middle-class Victorian America, especially among women; in 1881 Dr. George Beard could entitle his study of the national malady, *American Nervousness*. At any rate, the fact is that Harry's mother collapsed in "nervous prostration," a nightmare for her that became also a nightmare for her sensitive, devoted seven-year-old son.

Let us review the personal crises of Harry's childhood that may have contributed to his conversion experience and decision to give his life to missionary work. One, the intense fear of divine wrath that darkened his sleeping nights. Two, the enormous sense of helplessness and powerful guilt feelings attending his mother's breakdown. What "bad" things had he done to cause her illness? What was he to do now that his mother had withdrawn from him? Would God forgive him if he pledged his life to the church? Three, did the coming of the twins three years earlier cause Harry to feel shut out, isolated, alone, leading him to seek in the church another home, another "father's house"? Finally, might not the death of Ethel and his own close brush with death at age three have added to the terror, helplessness, guilt, and isolation arising from the other crises? Harry's mystical nature and the general evangelical spirit of the age were in themselves perhaps sufficient to explain his conversion experience, but one senses that his childhood experience played a role as well.

Thus far we have sought to understand Harry's decision to pledge his life to Christ by reference to Tennant's evangelical sermon, the missionary spirit of the age, the boy's mystical nature, his experience of God's anger, and the bewilderment consequent upon his mother's breakdown. These things must now be related to the general religious environment of the home.

"Religion was a force in our family rather than a form, . . . vital and real," reminisced Fosdick. "Together my father and mother gave me religion. I caught it from them, for they both were deeply religious," he stated on another occasion. Brother Raymond remembered, "From our earliest days, religion was for us children a vital part of the air we breathed." There were morning prayers and bedtime prayers and mealtime blessings. The Bible was read and studied. Church attendance, Sunday morning and evening and Wednesday evening, was so natural a part of the children's lives that they never questioned it. Both parents were much involved in church affairs. For a period Harry pumped the church organ, dancing about, a parishioner recalled, like a "young monkey."

The parents' theology was evangelical, but the atmosphere of the home was not dour. The father was often heard to say that his chief reason for wanting to go to heaven was "so that he could get God off in a corner somewhere and ask him some questions." On another occasion the father said of a sanctimonious, self-advertised "Quaker evangelist" relative, whose family prayers were endless and embarrassingly personal, "Uncle John is no more of a Quaker than I am a Chinaman." The mother's Christianity, too, found its sources more in the Golden Rule, the Sermon on the Mount, and the Beatitudes than in rigid dogmas or moral structures. Fosdick spoke the simple truth when he said: "Ours was a Christian family, where religion was vital, personal, and real."

Although his parents may have had reservations about Harry's decision to join the church at the tender age of seven, they did not veto that decision. In fact fifteen days earlier the father wrote a letter to a university official with these significant concluding words: "I will only add that if my oldest boy (now in his eighth year and who I expect, will be baptized Feb'r 21) ever goes to college and, as I hope he may, to the Theological Seminary, he will go to Madison." There was, certainly, no parental opposition to Harry's early commitment to a life of Christian service.

III

The life of Harry Emerson Fosdick may also be viewed as a revolt against the Calvinist ethos, that historic, powerful Protestant force suffused with convictions of the depravity of man, the awful precariousness of human existence, and the pitiless judgment of a wrathful deity. We have witnessed already the torments gripping him at seven. They increased in intensity at nine. "Was Calvinism comfortable?" Fosdick later asked. "Predestination, the damnation of nonelect infants, the eternal torture chamber of hell—there was small comfort in that, and some of us in our boyhood were driven by it nearly to hysteria." At age nine he feared he had committed "the unpardonable sin" because blasphemous words floated through his mind. He knew he was forever lost. Did not the Gospel of St. Matthew promise that blasphemy against the Holy Ghost "shall not be forgiven . . . neither in this world, neither in the world to come." And reading in the Book of Revelation about the horrors of hell left him "sick with terror." The father once finding Harry so pale he thought him ill sought to comfort the lad by saying that everybody has sacrilegious thoughts that float through the mind, adding that while you can't prevent crows from flying over your head, you can prevent them from making nests in your hair. The father's comfort could not completely dispel Harry's anxiety. "All through my lusty youth," Fosdick later wrote, "I perjured my soul almost beyond redemption in collective expressions of a deep desire to 'Wash my weary feet / In the crystal waters sweet, / Over Jordan!'"

If neither parent frightened their children with damnation talk (and this is the testimony of both sons), in that era the smell of sulfur yet lingered in the air. When itinerant preachers heated up the population for a revival, Fosdick bitterly recalled, "all hell opened its yawning mouth to receive us." Even in the Fosdick home there were religious children's books of monstrous morality. Three typical passages from them:

> God is very angry with children who behave wickedly to their parents, and he often punishes them by letting them die while they are young, and sending their souls to hell.

> If you are sick, my little darling, pray to God. . . . Are you afraid lest God should send you to hell and let you burn forever and ever? Then you must pray to God to spare you.

> God will bind them [naughty children] in chains and put them in a lake of fire. There they will gnash their teeth and weep and wail forever. . . . They shall not have one drop of water to cool their burning tongues.

The handmaiden of this theology of terror was a dreary moralism. Fosdick remembered with resurrected wrath hearing perfervid sermons against drinking sweet cider, dancing the Virginia reel, and reading the novels of George Eliot. Innocent amusements were not proscribed in the Fosdick home; indeed the father taught the children to play cards and even encouraged them to attend dancing school. Yet Harry, "morbidly conscientious" by his own admission, faced "agonizing scruples" about what amusements were proper for a Christian, and once he refused his father's invitation to see Edwin Booth in *Hamlet*.

The evidence is persuasive that the adult Fosdick's liberal theology, with its central theme of God's love as revealed in Jesus Christ, is rooted in a reaction to the "devastating horror of hell" he had suffered as a youngster. At its thinnest (perhaps in the preaching of Henry Ward Beecher), this understanding of God as a gentle and loving parent bordered on a kind of "resolute coziness"; but to persons reared in a creed as angular and unloving as Calvinism, it was about the most relevant and liberating message they could have heard.

IV

The life of Harry Emerson Fosdick may be viewed as a rebellion against creedal sectarianism, his admirers employing such descriptions as "Fighting Rebel" and his enemies dubbing him "the Jesse James of the theological world." Nonconformity was in Fosdick's blood. Stephen Fosdick, the first of the clan in America, was expelled from a Congregational church in 1643 for reading Anabaptist books. The maternal great-grandfather, Jacob Blain, was driven from the ministry of his Baptist church for writing a book proving to his satisfaction that a literal burning hell was not a matter of perpetuity but that it lasted only about a thousand years or so, then God in his infinite mercy pardoned all. As boy and man, Fosdick never once repeated the Apostles' Creed; in the Baptist tradition in which he was nurtured, no formal creeds were ever used. Moreover, in 1887 the Fosdick family moved to the village of Lancaster, New York, for seven years. Because Lancaster lacked a Baptist church, the Fosdick children attended the Presbyterian Sunday School and the Methodist Young People's Meeting, and the family alternated between the two worship services. When in 1895 the Fosdicks returned to Buffalo, they renewed their Baptist connection, but the adolescent associations with Presbyterianism and Methodism helped make it possible for Fosdick later to state: "I can never recall being a devoted sectarian; alike the good and evil that I feared in organized Christianity were interdenominational."

"Few remembered impressions of my childhood are more clear," Fosdick judged, "than the family's insistence on our individual liberty and responsibility; we were supposed to think and to make decisions for ourselves, and the whole bent of our upbringing was toward independence and training in the use of it." Toward the end of Harry's adolescence, father and son began the habit of discussing religious ideas at the Sunday dinner table, prompted by the fact that the father, to supplement the family income, led the congregational singing in the First Baptist Church while the rest of the family went to a church nearer home. The sermons of the two ministers, one a liberal and the other a conservative, served as the basis of the discussions. Although the younger children and the mother contributed little, Raymond recalled that the discussions reached "such a pitch of excitement, that we could scarcely wait until the following Sunday to continue them." To be sure, Fosdick's intellectual revolt did not come until college, but his independence of spirit was nurtured in boyhood. In a tribute the son reflected upon his father's influence:

In the home I can recall yet the freedom with which he treated religion, his impatience with its shams, his independence of its bigotries and prejudices, his breadth of tolerance. Yet always I recall, too, the impression of religious reality and reverence which his life carried with it. If, through the upsets and turmoils of a generation whose rapid changes have stripped away so many of their faith, I have kept my assurance that while religions pass religion abides, I have most of all to thank what I experienced in my boyhood home.

In his comparative group study of the origins of Protestant liberals and conservatives born in the second half of the nineteenth century, William R. Hutchison discovered that liberals not only were recruited more heavily than conservatives from professional families, but also came to a much greater extent from the families of educators. Frank S. Fosdick was a teacher and principal. Hutchison found the liberals' home environment to be nonrepressive, with the religious influence of the father (unlike orthodox homes) as or more important than that of the mother. Such was the Fosdick home. Hutchison noted that the biographies of liberals "with surprising regularity speak of the influence of a kind of person almost entirely missing from the conservative chronicles— of a parent or uncle or close family acquaintance who was somewhat heretical or freethinking by family standards but was clearly more admired in that circle than accepted in the community." Harry Fosdick had just such an uncle, his father's half brother, Charles, who wrote adventure books for boys under the nom de plume Harry Castlemon. A striking figure with black eyes, broken nose, and long hair curling on his shoulders, who carried a Civil War bullet in his leg and bore a sabre cut across his head, he was seen as a man of mystery. As Raymond Fosdick put it, the uncle "had a flair for living and perhaps one or two rather conspicuous human frailties which shocked the pious pretensions of his contemporaries. And he refused to go to church."

In 1925 Harry Emerson Fosdick was forced from the pulpit of New York's First Presbyterian Church because he refused to assent to the Presbyterian creedal requirement. He consented to become minister of the proposed great Riverside Church only on the condition that it be a creedless, interdemoninational fellowship. As we can now see, this is surely an instance of the child being father to the man.

V

The roots and forms of Fosdick's mature religious faith are discernible in his early years. Yet his childhood and adolescent faith alone might have resluted in no more than a sincere or even effective life of Christian service. Indeed, a ministry of evangelism need not have required much beyond an earnest faith and a natural eloquence. However, as teacher and scholar, author and apologist, Fosdick lived in the House of Intellect as well as in the House of Faith, and it is important to explore the early intellectual influences that helped shape his thought and hone his mind.

Harry attended grade schools as the family migrations dictated: Buffalo Normal, Westfield Academy, and then Lancaster Normal. Although the Fosdicks continued to live in Lancaster until 1894, Harry commuted the seven miles to Buffalo to enter high school in 1891. His freshman year he attended the Clinton Street Annex where his father was principal. He then transferred to Buffalo High School ("Old Central") to complete the final three years.

A "Star Scholar" for all four years, Harry stood first in the 1895 graduating class of 149 pupils, winning the coveted Jesse Ketchum Gold Medal and the honor of delivering the commencement oration. His courses included many semesters of Latin and Greek, subjects taught by his father. Harry was later to judge that "more than any other single influence" the study of Latin "made possible such mastery of the English language as I possess," and that the "best way to gain a mastery of excellent English was thoroughly to know Latin and Greek." Of his teachers he recalled with special gratitude Arthur Detmers, who "used to take me up into his room and quietly read to me some of the loveliest things in the English speech," including Browning, Wordsworth, and Whitman; the two continued to correspond for years. Harry must have caught the attention of other teachers as well, for when he won an essay prize a classmate remembered, "Miss Karnes swelled with pride. You were the only pupil she called by his first name; the rest of us were 'Mister.' "

Harry was up to his hips in extracurricular activities. He debated and orated. Although he later reported repeatedly being "petrified with stage fright," one wonders if his tongue was really often tied. After all, he was elected vice president of the debating society and the senior class named him their "Prophet"—and generally prophets are not mute. Years later a former classmate heard him preach and after the service she greeted him with "Still shooting your face off, Harry, I perceive."

He was also a member of the high school Cadet Corps and loved it, having "a glorious time playing at war preparation," and he proudly recalled the day when he stepped smartly to the front as adjutant of the battalion. Fosdick correctly disassociated all the military drill from any thought of actual battle, for in truth the Corps, as the thousand other paramilitary organizations for adolescents in that era, was designed not to train boys to be soldiers but to be better boys. Indeed military models and military metaphors were not absent from the structure and vocabulary of a host of specifically Christian youth groups formed at that time.

Harry's high school graduation address, "The Turk in Armenia," resonates the era's drum-and-trumpet Protestantism, a time when muscular Christianity was approaching its zany zenith and when "pumping iron" matched prayer in importance in the development of Christian character. (One historian of the Chautauqua Movement has suggested that if Chautauqua had had a coat of arms, the appropriate symbol would have been a dumbbell.) Holding the humane thought that biographers have the dead at their mercy, only a few passages from Harry's plea to rescue the Christian Armenians from the Turks will be resurrected:

An investigating commission? Forsooth! What cares the wily Turk for a commission?

As centuries ago all christendom arose under the Lillies of France and the Lion of England to snatch from the Saracen the holy sepulcher, so to-day ought all the forces of civilization to rise in combined might and release from the oppressive control of the merciless Turk . . . thousands of living bodies, living souls, entangled in the depths of Mohammedan oppression.

As in the ears of the Roman senators Cato's voice rang again and again with the words, "Carthage must be destroyed," so to-day to the ears of the civilized world come voices from the hundreds of thousands of Turkey's martyred victims pealing forth with no uncertain sound, "Turkey must be destroyed, and the Crescent, significant of all the barbarous cruelty which has marked its sovereignty for ages, must bow before that symbol of all that is good, all that is pure, and that is humane, the Cross."

Before dismissing this rhetoric as a mild case of teenage hysteria, we should recall that Teddy Roosevelt was presently to call forth cheers from the *adults* assembled in Republican National Convention with the apostrophe, "We want either Perdicaris alive or Raisuli dead."

Orating, debating, marching, Harry also worked for the school paper, *The Calendar*, and in fact was momentarily editor in his senior year, resigning in February because, the paper reported, of the pressure of other unnamed duties, though he continued as an associate editor. The obverse side to the emerging muscular Christianity of the 1890s and the masculine ideal of the "strenuous life" trumpeted by Teddy Roosevelt was the lingering hold of the genteel tradition with its cracked teacup sensibility and cult of feeling. These two strains are not necessarily in contradiction, for the martial spirit is often infused with sentimentality. Anyhow, Harry's poems appearing in *The Calendar* mirror as perfectly the feminine side of late Victorian culture as his orations and essays mirror the masculine.

There is discernible a hint of sublimated adolescent sexuality in these poems. He must have known awakening erotic longings and inevitably he encountered schoolboy smut, which he reported not understanding but never forgetting. Whatever battles this chaste lad (in a later private letter he testified to his premarital chastity) may have fought in coming to terms with his sexuality, these struggles could not but have been exacerbated by the temper of the era in which he came of age. Never before had the custodians of culture been so obsessed with autoeroticism and never had the official warning against the practice of the "solitary vice" been so dire. The famous psychologist G. Stanley Hall recalled that in his youth when ministers dwelt on the "unpardonable sin" at least some listening lads thought of their "self-pollution." Anton T. Boisen, a founder of pastoral psychiatry who grew to manhood in the 1890s, remembered that the churches and "Ys" deliberately aroused a sense of guilt and the fear of hell in youngsters in order to control sexual conduct. The president of Union Theological Seminary, Dr. C. Cuthbert Hall, soon to befriend Harry, touted the value of the daily water douche as an aid to cooling adolescent ardor, and straining for the proper metaphor to describe the therapy, came up with "baptism." It would be pointless as well as painful to quote Harry's poetry; he himself later admitted it to be hopelessly "mid-Victorian and lush." However, it is important to note that muted echoes of the poems' sensibilities may be found in Fosdick's adult utterances; to the end of his days his moral code, although not that of a prig, remained close to Victorian values—or, as he would insist, Christian values.

When Harry attended the Buffalo high school, it was undergoing reform. One historian found the improvement "impressive," and if the decade began with widespread criticism of the schools, "it ended with praise from all quarters." The reformation may be credited largely to one man, Harry P. Emerson, who was elected superintendent of schools in 1892, a New Englander of honesty, ability, imagination, and political moxie who had for many years taught in the Buffalo schools and who was to remain as superintendent until 1916. He and Frank Fosdick had been college roommates, sustained their friendship, and Harry was named after him.

Harry's curriculum may seem narrow and rigid by today's standards, but the classical course of study he followed was not necessarily arid. It might be compared to a Scotsman's supper: plain and simple without hors d'oeuvres, wines, or pastry, but substantial and nourishing once gotten down. The boy acquired a lifelong habit of hard, sustained, systematic study. His education fired him with intellectual curiosity and a passion for learning.

The didactic philosophy of the era held that schools should not simply teach children, they should teach them what is right. Harry P. Emerson had himself asserted that morality was the end of all teaching, and it was a Protestant morality that was inculcated. To be sure, it was no longer quite true to say that the public schools were an unofficial auxiliary of the Protestant churches, but even as late as 1895 the old alliance between Protestant piety and national patriotism had not yet unraveled. The schools remained committed to the training of character with the genteel value system defining that character. The schools remained agencies for socializing the child in the interests of society ("culture factories" in the biting term of one historian), and the interests of society demanded a morally earnest, self-disciplined, sober, and industrious citizenry. Order in the individual and order in society were, of course, mutually reenforcing. For good or ill, or more precisely, good *and* ill, Fosdick's values and attitudes, though modified over the years, can be identified with the ethos pervading the public schools in the late nineteenth century.

The atmosphere of the home, of course, is as important to a child's intellectual development as formal schooling, and books read in the parlor were to Harry as much meat and drink as the meals served in the kitchen. "Around the green-shaded 'student lamp' we gathered every evening, each person with a book," remembered Raymond, giving point to his grandfather's hired man's charge that the Fosdicks were "the readingest dern family" he had ever seen. Harry read omnivorously, and widely, especially after a dying relative in Chicago willed his library of four hundred volumes to the Fosdicks. Apparently the parents exercised little censorship, or at least little remembered by the children; even Uncle "Harry Castlemon's" adventure stories were available from him—on loan. Two best-selling novels Fosdick reported reading, *John Ward, Preacher* and *Robert Elsmere*, were subversive of the regnant religious orthodoxy. The former pointed to the decay of Calvinism; the latter raised the question of scriptural authority and miracles—and it concluded with a resounding question mark.

Typical of the home's cultural atmosphere are the scenes of the father accompanying himself at the piano as he sang hymns in Latin, of the father and mother playing piano and flute duets, and of the father seated on the floor preparing charts to illustrate a Chautauqua lecture on the development of the alphabet while the mother sat at the table preparing a Chautauqua lecture on Madame de Staël. One detects a whiff of self-consciousness in the Fosdicks' pursuit of culture—a determined bookishness typical of their class and era. Even so, one finds their love of books, music, and ideas authentic and admirable. At least no one in that household ever suffered from intellectual anorexia.

VI

In our endeavor to probe young Harry's religious and academic experiences, we have alluded to possible parental influences. Now we must directly address the two individuals most important in his early life, his mother and father. On a hundred instances the mature Harry Emerson Fosdick recalled his parents in admiration and affection; not a single extant public or private expression carries a hint of disrespect or criticism.

Frank Sheldon Fosdick was born in Buffalo, March 11, 1851. His early education was obtained in a public school where his father was principal and his mother a favorite teacher. He attended "Old Central" High School and in 1872 was graduated from the University of Rochester, the first college-trained man in the family line. He continued his studies in later years, winning the M.A. degree from Rochester. In 1872 he embarked on a teaching career in Buffalo and for fifty-four years, until his retirement in 1926, he was to be associated with the schools of Buffalo, as grammar school principal, high school teacher, principal first of Clinton Street Annex and later of all high school annexes, and then in 1897 principal of the new Masten Park High School with which his name is most closely linked. His energies, interests, and ambitions thrust him into civic and professional societies such as the Masons, Buffalo Historical Society, National Education Association, and the American Philological Association (at one time he apparently was the only individual in Buffalo belonging to that organization).

This brief biography, of course, tells us little about the man. Nor is the fact that the University of Rochester conferred on him the honorary degree of doctor of laws and the University of the State of New York the honorary degree of doctor of letters and Princeton University the honorary degree of master of arts, especially helpful. Judgment of the man must be based on other, more personal, testimony.

When in 1937 *Time* carried a story on the careers of Harry and Raymond, a former Masten Park student penned a letter to the editors praising Frank Fosdick as "one of the wisest as well as the most loveable educators and leaders of youth" in Buffalo's history. The writer concluded, " 'Pop' Fosdick, as he was affectionately called by his 'boys and girls,' was one of the grandest men I have ever known. He left the firm imprint of his character on all who were privileged to come under his influence, and no matter to what heights his sons may rise, they will have difficulty in surpassing their father!" Another former student, who believed Frank Fosdick "the epitome of every virtue a man, a teacher, a principal of a school should possess," wrote him in sorrow when Masten Park burned down and received this thoughtful reply: "Fifteen years, the best of my life, I put into Masten Park High School, but Charles, I did not put them into a building, but rather into the lives of my boys and girls." Recalled another: "It is safe to say that if ever a man had the power to quicken the dead, it was Mr. Fosdick teaching Latin and Greek. . . . What human understanding and sympathy, what drollery, what shrewdness, what wit, and yet what a sense of justice he always showed to us poor lack-wits. Is it any wonder that a class recitation under his direction was the event of the day?"

Toward the end of his principalship, it was customary for former students, usually over one thousand strong, to gather on his birthday in the ballroom of Buffalo's Statler Hotel to show their affection; and on retirement in 1926, two thousand Mastenites came from far reaches of the country to tell him of their gratitude and present him with a purse, a "demonstration of love and civic esteem, which never before has been witnessed in Buffalo." Frank Fosdick died a year later. A memorial service was held at all the high schools in the city. Said the student speaker at rebuilt Masten Park:

> We have said that "Pop" was a man we respected and trusted above all others; a man whom we admired as the most ideal leader of young people. But *now*, we realize that what our hearts felt of respect and devotion to him as a Principal was, in reality, a *love* for a *fellow-classmate*. What more lasting and perfect love is there in the world than that which is held for a companion, a chum, who has fought life as you have, who understands you better than you do, who always had time for you when you sought advice or solace.

Said the individual speaking for the faculty:

> As an administrator and teacher, he made a record equalled by few men of his generation, but in addition to this success . . . he was in a large way a father and a friend to every teacher who has been privileged to work in Master Park. . . . Everyone looked to Dr. Fosdick for counsel, advice and sympathy in all the joys and sorrows of life. To all he was guide, philosopher, and friend.

At that time the Buffalo Board of Education passed a resolution changing the school's name to Fosdick-Masten Park "in memory of our beloved 'Pop.' "

Frank Fosdick's great gift was his ability to build pride in a boy or girl. Students knew that he cared. He emphasized encouragement more than censure. Regulations were not to his liking; that every boy was to be a gentleman and every girl a lady was, he once remarked, the only rule he wanted in his school. "A teacher must be one with his students," he affirmed. "More often than not he did all the things he considers wrong in modern youth in his earlier days. But he has forgotten them. He cannot, he must not, set himself up as a tin god on wheels." Invariably he was on hand at school athletic and social functions. He favored coeducation, holding that "boys without girls are barbarians and girls without boys are prigs." This does not mean that he ran a lax school. His appearance was commanding: muscular body and a strong face dominated by a heavy moustache and piercing brown eyes. If trouble arose, there was a special assembly, a few direct words from "Pop," concluding with, "Now I believe we understand each other." If a student betrayed a trust, Frank Fosdick could create on call, Harry related, a thunderstorm of indignation that was positively terrifying. On one instance after trouble with a wayward boy, he investigated the home conditions. Then he called the boy's father in and, shaking a clenched fist in his face, said, "You miserable scoundrel of a father, if you had a prize pup you would know more about him than you know about your son."

Are the qualities of Frank Fosdick the teacher and principal evident in Frank Fosdick the father? The story about the father told most frequently and fondly by Harry goes like this: Starting for work one morning, his father turned to his mother, who was waving good-bye, and said: "Tell Harry he can cut the grass today, if he feels like it." Then after a few steps he turned back and added, "Tell Harry he had better feel like it!" This incident suggests certain larger truths about parental-child relationships in the Fosdick home.

On the one hand, the spirit of the family was democratic and the rod did not reign. When family problems arose, a conference was called, the children were asked their opinions, and these opinions were treated with respect. Reminisced Harry, "When, seeking my father's advice, I asked him what he thought about something, nine times out of ten he threw the question back at me and asked what I thought myself." Again: "He wanted no rubber stamps among his children. Yes-yessing was his *bête noire*. And I doubt if any father in the world ever knew with quicker sensitiveness just when to keep his hands entirely off and let us steer ourselves." From the beginning the children "were trained for independence" and were treated as "valuable, responsible, independent" persons.

On the other hand, "Tell Harry he had better feel like it!" "The in-

tended product of Victorian didacticism," observed a thoughtful historian, "was a person who would no longer need reminding of his duties,
who would have internalized a powerful sense of obligation and could
then safely be left to his own volitions." The aim was to bend rather
than to break children's wills; to control rather than annihilate the self.
In the Fosdick home—as in many "moderate" Protestant homes, to employ Philip Greven's classification—internalized controls were stressed:
duty, conscience, shame, appeals to affection and honor and loyalty
rather than the external control of physical punishment. Harry himself
perfectly captured the mood, though without, it seems, comprehending
the significance, of this internalization:

> Some of us were so fortunate as to be reared in homes where we were
> trained to obey something not external to ourselves but within ourselves.
> Call it conscience or ideals or self-respect or a sense of honor or the voice
> of God—we were taught that within us was a central object of our right-
> ful loyalty. Some of us can recall with what insistence and skill our par-
> ents in every case of flagrant transgression that we can remember pushed
> back our sense of guilt from the consciousness of having broken a family
> rule to the feeling that we had violated something within ourselves. In the
> last analysis we were taught that the ultimate authority to be obeyed was
> inward; that codes and rules, parents and teachers were valuable only as
> they made this inward law visible and cogent; that the real shame lay in
> being untrue to oneself.

Money was scarce in the Fosdick household. The family budget was
the subject of many somber conversations around the kitchen table, in
which the children were included. Yet, Harry remembered, "I never had
it presented to me in my boyhood as a conceivable ideal that any man
should ever live for the sake of making money. We were supposed to
choose a vocation that we thought would make us serviceable to our
generation." Again: "In all my boyhood I do not recall that the idea of
living for the sake of money ever occurred to me. That was a conception
of life so alien to our home that it was not credible. To make the most
of one's self for the sake of others . . . from the first was the assumed
ideal, and anything else would have been unthinkable. This is the basic
thing my father did for me, not by what he said but by the whole tenor
and spirit of his life. Money-making was precluded as an end in living
and skilled service was exalted as the one durable satisfaction and worthwhile goal." An overwhelming sense of duty to God and man weighed
heavily on the Victorian mind, and children in such a household as that
of the Fosdicks were reared to lives of serious calling. One of Fosdick's
first major books, *The Meaning of Service*, was dedicated to Frank Shel-

don Fosdick, who "has illustrated in his life the meaning of service." We remember that even prior to Harry's baptism his father expressed in a letter the wish that he enter ministerial training. Considering the father's wish and the father's authority, an authority all the more powerful because exercised in an unauthoritarian manner, Harry was arguably not as free in the election of the ministry as he imagined.

Frank Fosdick's zest for life was boundless. His fine baritone voice filled the home with songs and humorous Artemas Ward stories. He taught his children to swim and fish, play cards and dance, build hencoops and tree houses. Asked at age seventy-four if his sons had shown early signs of greatness, he replied: "No. They were just like hundreds of other boys. I thank Heaven they weren't geniuses. I wouldn't have a genius in my family." Asked how he reared two such fine boys, he replied, "Many times I rolled on the floor with them when I would have preferred to be doing something else." His high spirits, the sons remembered, were contagious. Inevitably, from time to time Harry would bungle, and his comment then was likely to be, "Harry, you would lose your head if it were not screwed on." When the child was in a bad temper, the father's device was to say: "Where's Harry? You are not Harry. Harry has gone. Go find him. I want Harry!" And after one bitter youthful experience, Harry went to his father for help. "I do not recall what he said," the son reported, "except that he put his arm about me and promised to stand by me through thick and thin, so that whereas I came up depressed, I went down resilient and sure of victory."

Symbolic of the relationship between father and son is another story Fosdick was fond of telling: On the day he left for college he gave his house key to his father. But his father returned it, saying, "My boy, you keep the key, and you let it be a symbol to you as long as you live, that you can come home any time, from anywhere, and come in without knocking."

There is ample evidence to support the assertion that long after Harry left home the father remained for him an inner court of tribunal. At age sixty-five Fosdick could declare:

When I think of my own life, of its hair-breadth moral escapes, of all the thin ice I have skated over and almost gone through, of the forks in the road where to take the wrong turn would have been easy, I see that what has saved me is not simply private character, something merely individual to myself, but a deeper factor—the agelong heritage of Christian faith and life, namely, into which I was introduced in youth. . . . I have had a conscience with ethical standards at the heart of it, that in a crisis rose imperiously to command and restrain, but these standards came from my heritage.

In their maturity both Harry and Raymond helped their father financially. When their father retired the sons arranged that he would suffer no reduction of income, and they saw to it that their half sister, Ruth, received a college education. (Widowed in 1904, Frank Fosdick remarried in 1907. His second wife, Myrtilla Constantine, was a teacher at Masten Park High and many years his junior.) Gifts of money, of course, might be evidence only of a sense of dutiful obligation. More revealing is the fact that the sons clearly continued to enjoy the company of their father and took particular pains to see that some vacation time was spent together in Maine. More revealing still is the tone of the letters the mature Fosdick wrote to his father, a tone at once concerned, affectionate, and joshing. On learning that the father was unwell, Fosdick ordered him to behave and "do what your wife tells you," closing, "Of course, if necessary, Raymond and I can come up to Buffalo and sit on you, and we are not at all incapable of doing that." On another occasion of shaky health Fosdick wrote: "Allow me to bestow my filial advice upon you and counsel you to let Myrtie keep her hands on the brakes and pull hard whenever she feels like it, and don't you try to get a hot-box by running when the brakes are on, either." When his father purchased a third-hand Studebaker, Fosdick feigned horror, comparing the acquisition to putting dynamite in a child's hands or furnishing a deadly dagger to an innocent babe. "I sincerely trust, however, that when you stage your great accident, which I am sure will come, you will succeed in landing in some part of your anatomy other than the bare and unprotected crown of your head." At the height of the Fundamentalist/Modernist controversy, Fosdick dashed a note to his father: "I sincerely trust that you have not gotten weary of being the father of a heretic. You are such a blooming old heretic yourself that I do not think you have much to complain of."

Maybe Fosdick was not dissimulating—not even to himself—when he characterized his father as "my closest chum, my best friend, the best man I knew."

Frank Sheldon Fosdick died, after a brief illness, in Raymond's home, February 27, 1927. Harry was then pastor of the Park Avenue Baptist Church. It says something about the father's reputation that the four strongest members of the congregation, led by John D. Rockefeller, Jr., hastened to Buffalo to attend the funeral service.*

* Readers of my biography of the great Methodist minister, Ernest Fremont Tittle, will know that I do not believe all father-son relationships are happy.

VII

Saint Augustine anticipated Freud when he cried, "Give me other mothers and I will give you another world." Considering Fosdick's total devotion to his mother, it is not surprising that as an adult he should quote the Talmud: "Since God could not be everywhere, he made mothers." Harry grew to manhood when the cult of domesticity was at its apogee, a cult that elevated middle-class women above the "sordid" concerns of business and politics while concurrently assigning them, as wives and mothers, the guardianship of moral and cultural values. The home was their immediate sphere of influence and they were arbiters of family life, as countless fathers acknowledged when they admonished their children, "Remember your dear mother, and never do anything, think anything, imagine anything she would be ashamed of." Only recently have some historians come to the recognition that this exaltation of wifehood and motherhood was, paradoxically, liberating as well as repressive. As wives and mothers, it was believed, women would instill a "feminine" ethic of self-sacrificing love in their husbands and sons, thereby ultimately regenerating all society. The home was not merely "a haven in a heartless world" to which men retreated from the "real" world, it was a school for the reformation of males and the ultimate feminization of American culture—or so some read the scenario.

Amie Inez Weaver was born in Westfield on September 4, 1852. She was educated at the Westfield Academy. Tradition has it that Frank Fosdick, a swanky young college sophomore on vacation, spotted the sixteen-year-old girl standing under a syringa bush in her parents' yard. His heart was made prisoner by her loveliness, an exceptional loveliness, really, if old photographs do not lie. Three years later Frank and Amie were married in Westfield, and as they rode in a buggy to Buffalo, sixty miles away, the groom sang aloud as he always did when happy.

"What is monogamy?," the adult Harry Fosdick was to ask. "It is the kind of home I had, where my father and mother loved each other so deeply that they did not care to love anyone else in the same way at all, and so, across the years, threw around their children the security of a lovely and dependable home. That is monogamy." When Frank Fosdick said to his young son that even the Virgin Mary, or so it seemed to him, could not have been lovelier than his wife, perhaps this was Victorian gush (though Frank was too salty to engage in much gush). But it was just such expressions that made possible the son's recollection: "My father and mother loved each other and there was peace at home" and the home "was as secure as the orbits of the stars."

Amie Weaver Fosdick was beautiful, devout, and interested in the life of the mind, though not a college graduate. Her husband found her idealism "incorrigible," yet a farm-bred realism saved her from podsnappery. Gentle and sympathetic, her standards of duty and honor and truth were nonetheless uncompromising. "Duty for her was indeed the stern daughter of the voice of God," remembered Raymond; "She was a kind of divine judgment seat, where one faced the ultimate standards of character," in Harry's words.

Fosdick possessed a moral gyroscope, and it was his mother, more even than his father, possibly, who set that gyroscope spinning. "In the most perilous temptation that I ever faced in my young manhood," he reported, "when I came as near as ever I did going over the brink of a moral precipice, what do you suppose it was that saved me? All unbidden in my imagination's eye rose the figure of my mother." Again: "In my young manhood I faced a critical temptation. . . . What saved me was nothing scientific, nothing unscientific, but something deeper—the imagined face of my mother rose in mind with such dominant restraint that even yet, across nearly half a century, I can feel its power."

Two instances do not prove a case, so, let us firmly nail down the mother's moral influence. Repeatedly Fosdick referred to his mother's standards "which would not let me be satisfied with myself" or to "live with her on any cheap and easy terms." These standards embodied "the everlasting right as she saw it, not to be compromised, over against the wrong which she would never pretend was right." What would good mothers (like his) have done on discovering their son "wallowing in vice?" Fosdick gave the answer: "They would have borne upon their hearts the outrage of our sin as though they had committed it themselves. They would have gone with vicarious steps to the gateway of any hell we turned our feet toward and stood grief-stricken at the door until we came out. They would have put themselves in our places, lived in our stead, felt upon their innocence the burden of our guilt. They would have forgiven us but it would have turned their hair gray." Fosdick recalled being disobedient as a boy, to have spoken resentfully, and to have stormed in anger from the room. But by and by he stole back to the closed door to hear his mother sobbing: "She was bearing on her heart the burden of my disobedience and that is the most sobering thing in human life."

"Sobering," yes, and disconcerting. Fosdick understood the effectiveness of the child-rearing techniques of his mother and other good mothers, but he has nothing to say about the unintended cruelty of such techniques—or the quite possibly repressive psychic consequences. If the memory of his mother kept his moral gyroscope spinning evenly through-

out his life, this maternal influence perhaps had three less happy consequences. For one thing, it narrowed the passional, aesthetic, and cultural
experiences Fosdick permitted himself as an adult. In this Fosdick was a
child of his age, for mental hygienists of the late nineteenth century were
virtually unanimous in warning against all extreme emotions and experiences and in advising lives of balance, moderation, self-control—the
golden mean in all things. For a second thing, it gave to some of his
adult moral judgments a kind of avuncular predictability. For a third, it
made possible the deliverance of such dubious homilies as this passage
from a 1935 sermon:

> A Roman Catholic nun saw one of the girls she had helped to train
> throwing herself away in an illicit love affair. All efforts to dissuade the
> girl failed. Then the nun began flogging herself daily. Every day as that
> girl went on with her loose living she knew that her friend, the nun, alone
> in her cell, was flogging herself. That girl had to give in, for she found
> herself facing, until she no longer could endure it, the most tremendous
> moral force in the world.

Fosdick's interpretation of the nun's action would not be shared by many
psychotherapists.

Amie Weaver Fosdick died in 1904 at the early age of fifty-one leaving behind a family paralyzed with grief. Her husband gained what comfort he could from the fact that he was bearing in her stead the loneliness that she would have been compelled to bear had he gone first. Harry
determined to handle his sorrow in such a way that his mother would be
proud of him. Many years later in dedicating a volume to the mother's
memory he appropriated the lines:

> 'Tis human fortune's happiest height to be
> A spirit melodious, lucid, poised, and whole;
> Second in order of felicity
> To walk with such a soul.

A recent author dedicated his book, "To my mother who never made
me any more anxious than she had to." Is it fair to Harry's mother to
say that she never made him any more anxious than she had to by the
lights of the Victorian ethos she had to guide her?

VIII

As a child Harry was surrounded by love, but this does not mean that
he, or those he loved, escaped the terror and contingency of human

existence. His maternal grandfather and grandmother were divorced on grounds of incompatibility—a shocking affair in those days. Both Amie's sister and her brother died of tuberculosis—lingering deaths in the home, which Harry witnessed—the brother a pathetic skeleton gasping for breath in his last hour and crying "Air!" An infant sister died in 1881. Financial problems were relentless and debts endless, the father earning annually between $1200 and $1800 during Harry's youth, an income providing little margin for emergency expenses and none for luxuries. Both boys recalled seeing their mother weep because, having reduced the family's standards of living as low as she thought she could, she found she had to lower it still another notch. (It must be remembered, however, that in Buffalo in 1880 the average wage of all hands engaged in manufacturing was $412.97 per annum.) Although the mother recovered from her first nervous breakdown, her health was never again sturdy, and relapses followed. Harry at age ten was taken in his father's arms and sorrowfully informed that his mother would probably not live another year, surely a scarring experience for the boy. Later Harry was forced to drop out of college for a year because of his father's breakdown, resulting, it may be conjectured, from financial worries, the strains of assuming a broadened principalship, and concern over his semi-invalid wife.

However, it is probable that Harry escaped at least one source of abrasion normal to families with more than one child, sibling rivalry. He was five years older than the twins, Raymond and Edith. Consequently he moved in a different world of schools, chums, interests. As the eldest and perhaps favored, he had a "place" reserved for him in the family circle. Raymond's autobiography suggests that he and Edith spent much time in each other's company, as would be natural. Harry states in his autobiography that it was not until college that he began to appreciate his brother and sister and that earlier they had endured from him the "hardships of oversight and condescension that an older brother commonly practices." As adults Harry and Raymond were close, and the only distance separating Edith from her brothers was a physical distance, for she lived most of her adult life teaching in foreign lands. There is nothing to suggest that Harry looked back in anxiety at Ray's race to catch up with his older brother.

IX

To go further into the area and era of Fosdick's boyhood, having sought to establish parental influences, it remains to discover the additional influences on his angle of vision: his "progressive" political and social views, which always, however, stopped short of radicalism; and his life-long devotion (or bondage) to pre-twentieth-century cultural standards. As we probe Harry's social environment, we take as our text Lionel Trilling's warning, "We do well to accept civilization, although we also do well to cast a cold eye on the fate that makes it our better part to accept it."

X

Harry Emerson Fosdick was an "old stock" American. Stephen Fosdick came to Massachusetts from Suffolk, England, in 1635. The lineage came down from Stephen through John, Samuel, Samuel, Samuel, Solomon, John, Frank. All of these Fosdick men married women with English names (Shapley, Picket, Turner, Thorne, Blain, Weaver) excepting the third Samuel whose wife was of Irish descent. The travails, transgressions, and occasional triumphs of these earlier Fosdicks as they journeyed through life and through place, in 1819 to western New York, may be followed in Harry's autobiography and in Raymond's autobiography and his *Annals of the Fosdick Family*. It is to their credit that neither claimed for their ancestors in America national prominence or in more distant England heraldic distinction. Their mother, as we know, was a Weaver, and she, too, descended from an ancestor who came to Massachusetts in 1635 from England. Our intent is not to present further genealogical detail, but to ponder the implications of this statement made by Harry in an untitled sermon preached March 6, 1920, in New York:

> We are accustomed to say that in contradistinction to other nations we have no aristocracy in America. We *have* an aristocracy in America, and there are lots of us here this morning who belong to it. I mean there are many of us whose blood goes back to the first landing on these shores, whose forefathers helped to lay the foundations of this commonwealth, and by their sacrifices made the nation secure; and who, generation after generation have grown up here amid the practical opportunities and the educational privileges and the religious influences which this great country had thrown around her children. And now, today, we stand with such wealth, it may be such moral fibre, such intellectual capacity as ought, without any credit, to belong to those who have such an ancestry behind them, and all around us, on this island here, are the others,—weak, immature, who neither in themselves nor in their families behind them have had such chance.

He went on immediately to say that these immigrants in their "little Hungarys and little Syrias" should not be exploited by older Americans, but rather helped and uplifted. Fosdick, emphatically, was not a bigot, not a nativist, but he was of old stock. In his case "ancestry is destiny" in the single sense that from birth he was accepted as one of the senior partners in the American entreprise. Not being a black, a Catholic, an immigrant or an immigrant's son, he was under no compulsion to prove his right to membership in the national club. He knew the psychological security of belonging from birth rather than the insecurity of being a "stranger in the land." On the other hand, not being the scion of New England Brahmins or Southern cavaliers, he was under no strain to uphold a patrician name. "Sturdy pioneer stock" and "poor humble folk" are phrases used by Fosdick to describe his forebears.

To be sure, in Fosdick's boyhood approximately one third of Buffalo's total population was foreign-born; there had been a major influx of Polish immigrants in the 1880s and Italian immigrants in the 1890s. Nevertheless, very few immigrant children were enrolled in the public schools attended by Harry, and all the evidence suggests that his closest chums were of ethnic backgrounds similar to his own.

Raymond Fosdick's insistence that there existed no racial or religious or ethnic prejudices in the Buffalo of his boyhood does not wash. One need only recall that W. E. B. Du Bois and his fellow black intellectuals met in 1905 in Canada to form the famous Niagara Movement because they had first suffered exclusion from Buffalo hotels. Rather, it would seem truer to say that the Fosdick children were unaware of such prejudices because their closest eighborhood, school, and Sunday School associations were with children from a similar WASP heritage.

XI

Young Harry was largely sheltered from contact with the inhabitants of Buffalo's east side "Polonia." He knew few of the "swarthy, dirty and lazy" Italo-Americans, those "dregs of Society," to borrow descriptive terms from Buffalo's newspapers of that time. He knew nothing, probably, of the prejudice faced by the newer Jewish immigrants from eastern Europe, prejudice encountered not only from the city as a whole, but also from the older established Jewish families. The anti-Catholicism fueling the American Protective Association may have eluded him. If no black man in Buffalo's infinitesimal black population could hope "to become rated as a high-skilled worker, foreman, office-worker, or professional and managerial worker," this, too, was outside his consciousness. Of course the bordellos and saloons in the "infested district" were off limits to him. The thousands of arrests reported annually did not touch him. Despite the family's tight finances, he could have had little understanding of the "deep-rooted pauperism in the city." However, the desperation of the jobless in the depression of 1893 was too pervasive to escape notice, and all his life he remembered "those dreadful days when penury stalked the country."

In the span of Harry's youth Buffalo was transformed from a provincial town to a major city, "the easternmost of America's western cities." Yet it could never be said that Harry was a child of the city streets—a true urbanite—as was, say, Al Smith.

His heart and the heart of his boyhood lay elsewhere, in Lancaster and Westfield. Writing in old age to a boyhood friend, Fosdick judged, "I don't think any boy ever had a more typically American experience than I had in Lancester." He was right, provided one defines as "typically American" the experiences of fishing, splashing in the village swimming hole, berrying, soaping windows on Halloween, "borrowing" the Methodist church bell's clapper, sleigh rides, hayrick rides, and "seeing Nellie home." None of the "old gang" permanently went wrong, recalled Fosdick, and we may believe him. The home in Lancaster was primitive, with no inside toilet and no running water except the pump in the kitchen sink. Heating was by stoves. The boys' clothes were handed down from the father to Harry to Raymond. But these things do not mark the Fosdicks as poor and in themselves did not make it possible for Harry to identify with children growing up in the slums and ghettos.

If Harry's youth is more intimately bound up with the small suburb of Lancaster than with the city of Buffalo, one has the feeling that it is more intimately still rooted in the village of Westfield in the Chautauqua hills where he spent his seventh year and his first twenty summers. Again and again he recalled tramping "every inch of the country," camping "all over Chautauqua Lake," catching his first fish in the lake, "one of the loveliest places in the country." Significantly, Frank Fosdick lies beside his father in the Westfield cemetery "because this is where he belonged," stated Raymond.

The Chautauqua Movement had its beginnings in an assembly held four years before Harry's birth. In the 1880s and 1890s thousands came to the grounds for spiritual refreshment, intellectual stimulation, and cultural uplift. (William James exclaimed as he left the refined atmosphere, "O, for another Armenian massacre.") Although Fosdick's major ministries are associated with New York City, he never came to love that seething, sophisticated, electrifying metropolis, a city he never visited in his youth. Without exception, his adult references to Gotham are pejorative: "this wicked and uproarious city," "this wretched and sinful city," "this barbarous mass of asphalt and stone," to quote from various letters. Culturally Fosdick never left home; his heart remained in the Chautauqua hills. It is possible to conjecture that millions of Americans responded to the message he preached because he touched their Chautauquan sensibilities. After all, no less an American than Teddy Roosevelt praised Chautauqua as "the most American place in America."

XII

Although there was little in Harry's heritage or environment to permit him to get inside the minds of America's new immigrants manning America's dark "Satanic" factories, although his angle of vision was not that of Buffalo's Canal Street, it does not follow that his empathies were with the elite of Buffalo's Delaware Avenue. As there was a strain of religious nonconformity in the Fosdick tradition, so there was a strain of political and social dissent. The grandfather, John Spencer Fosdick, whom both Harry and Raymond remembered with a mixture of affection and holy awe, was a farm boy by birth, a village carpenter and a shoemaker, and later a teacher. He was a sturdy soul whose abolitionist fervor involved him in the dangerous work of the Underground Railroad. He was also a temperance crusader and lay preacher to prisoners. His two-year term as superintendent of schools was explosive. Ramming through reforms, including the introduction of German, and moderating the use of corporal punishment, he made so many enemies that he was not asked to run again. The *Buffalo Courier* carried his remark to a group of teachers who met to honor him on his departure: "I once heard a man say that he thought he had done his duty because he had made everyone mad. Tonight I can enjoy the same reflection." The maternal grandmother, too, was independent of spirit, both a temperance advocate and an early crusader of women's rights. Frank Fosdick, who loathed Bryan, was a loyal Republican, but his republicanism, one suspects, looked back to Lincoln not forward to, say, Coolidge. The adult Harry Emerson Fosdick's instincts were with the underdog. His name became associated with a galaxy of reform causes. This adult political and social liberalism is not inconsistent with his heritage and boyhood experiences.

Chapter Two

Colgate University:
Years of Doubt and Decision

I

The train eighteen-year-old Harry boarded in Buffalo in September 1895 sped him along the main line to Utica and then crawled like a caterpillar on the little branch line before reaching the village of Hamilton, New York. He arrived with "appreciative faculties awake, critical faculties asleep," eagerly anticipating his freshman year at Colgate University, a small Baptist school numbering (exclusive of the Academy and the Seminary) approximately 150 students and fifteen faculty. Five years later (a family crisis called him home for one year) he graduated, easily first in his class. He remained in Hamilton an additional year for seminary study. This was a crucial period in young Fosdick's struggle for self-identification.

II

The adult Fosdick lived by the written and spoken word. Like few others in American history, Fosdick's generation dealt in words; in this respect the era's culture and the man's capabilities were perfectly mated. He was "the most celebrated preacher of his day," in the widely shared judgment of Reinhold Niebuhr. "Dr. Fosdick is commonly regarded as the greatest public speaker in this country, and to be frank about it no one else is near him," affirmed Gerald Birney Smith. The pulpit, platform, and radio station were the settings of his triumphs. He was also a prolific author, and through the mediums of articles and books his written words reached additional millions. This protean man was in truth a professional speaker and writer. Unless it is realized that Fosdick was first of all a wordsmith, there can be no understanding of his long and successful career, for it was eloquence of voice and pen that sustained that career. At Colgate Fosdick honed the skills initially cultivated in the grades.

Every year without exception he carried courses in Rhetoric, Public Speaking, Orations, Debates, Logic, or Argumentation. The major professor in public speaking was Ralph W. "Tommie" Thomas. If some students found him "as empty of original ideas as a bass drum" and if he drilled them in the artificial gestures and inflections of the old-time orotund oratory, nonetheless, they learned the discipline of careful preparation and organization and to quiet the jimjams of stage fright. Fosdick later expressed gratitude for Thomas's emphasis on writing speeches in full and then insisting that the student "get the substance inside till it obsessed him"—a lifelong practice Fosdick followed.

Harry's speaking skills were sharpened in public debate and oration. In the end he cantered off with more prizes than any other student in Colgate's history. The centrality of debating and orating to college life of that time is attested by the fact that several prizes won by Harry carried purses of $40 and $60, sums almost exactly equal to a year's tuition. It is quite true, therefore, to say that Harry "talked" his way through college.

Unfortunately, Harry's high school penchant for martial topics and overheated language remained unchastened. The rip-roaring oration, "The Battle of Omdurman," perhaps derived from his love of Kipling. (His nickname "Fuzzy" owed equally to Kipling's poem "Fuzzy-Wuzzy" and to his own shock of kinky hair, which he hated.) His address celebrating Admiral Dewey's victory over the Spanish at Manila Bay contained about as many references to "Dewey, Duty, and Destiny" as the speeches of President McKinley. This is no surprise, inasmuch as Harry ardently supported that "War of Humanity" and served as first lieutenant in a company of students and villagers that drilled throughout the spring of 1898. Let the following extended quotation from the prize-winning declamation, "The Rough Riders," serve to illustrate both the mood and the manner of Fosdick's college oratory:

> Through heat and rain, through sickness and fatigue, regardless of social rank or moneyed aristocracy, they who had volunteered to serve their country, learned the lessons of obedient discipline, molding their individual strength into one mighty engine of war. It was the discipline that shall preserve America. East, West, North and South, the people of the earth are trooping to our shores. They come from lands of light and darkness, from homes of ignorance and culture. With every shade of racial

disposition and inherited habit, with every stamp of religious bigotry and fanatic hatred, they are pouring their incongruous, inharmonious mass into our commonwealth; and through the lowering clouds that overhang the nation's future, lightning possibilities dart menacing tongues. Unassimilated, undisciplined, the hordes of immigration throng our gates, more potent for evil than the invading armaments of a Napoleon, more pregnant with disaster than the hostile armadas of the world. Startled by the portentous imminence of dissolution, the anxious heart of the nation thrilled with deep, unutterable joy, at sight of this representative regiment of composite America, drawn to unity, molded into common effort, blended into an irresistible force, by the inspiration of a principle and the magic of discipline. For in that resistless flight from Guasimas to Santiago, they typified the hope of America, and the permanence of her democracy. From the broad edges of the world, thrusting their blind disunion on the nation's life, shall come all races, all ranks, all creeds, to be made one, one in purpose, one in spirit, one in sacrifice; and the educative discipline of civic growth in a land worth living and dying for, shall, with an inexorable seal, stamp them, citizens of the republic.

The Rough Riders were made of the stuff that makes America, were trained with the discipline that shall preserve America, and were laureled with the victory which is America's destiny. That was the glory of it all! New-forged and all untried, they bent themselves to break the throttle-grip of Spain upon the Cuban. All hot with their new enthusiasm, they struggled through the tangled swamp and tropic forest, where the wispy spirits of the fever lay, through jungled glens where Spaniards kept their ambush. On hands and knees, tearing their tardy way with sabres and naked fingers, undismayed by barriers, unwavering in the face of fire, unblanched by the crawling arms of pallid mist that brought the death, they threw their line, a slender, attenuated line of brown about the base of San Juan Hill.

Fosdick later apologized to a Colgate graduating class for this "shamelessly exuberant oration" and to the readers of his autobiography for this "shamelessly militaristic piece"; in light of his post-Versailles pacifism, we may accept and honor his regret. But several points merit pursuing.

Note the initial apprehension concerning America's pollution by hordes of invading immigrants and the final confidence of their assimilation, through educative discipline, and the implicit assumption that these new citizens of the Republic would bear the stamp of the older Anglo-Saxon or British-American model. Fosdick the man was a foe of all Ku Kluxers, bigots, and nativists, but his mature utterances also contained echoes of this early fear of the ungluing of America, this blindness to the positive values of cultural pluralism, this whiff of cultural arrogance.

Note, too, the impassioned prose, a prose that would be greatly moderated as the years passed but never totally discarded. As boy and man, Fosdick preached for a verdict; and to reach that verdict, he was quite capable of playing upon the emotions of his audiences.

Thirdly, doubtless "The Rough Riders" drew cheers from the listeners and the judges' prize because Harry sensed what they wished to hear. The mature Fosdick's appeal rested in part on a similar conscious understanding of the audiences' sensibilities; he, naturally, termed it "clairvoyance."

Finally, note the broad appeal of the oration. Fosdick the preacher once offered this advice: "Homiletics reduces itself to this: place the provender where everybody, from giraffes to jackasses, may be fed." As a college student Fosdick learned to cast a wide net, and in his maturity he continued to fling this net. Said Jesus, "Feed my lambs." Harry Emerson Fosdick did feed lambs—and also giraffes and jackasses.

Harry's pen was busy in ways other than writing out prepared orations and debating notes. His freshman year the college paper, *The Madisonenses,* carried a number of his signed poems, although he soon put aside the writing of poetry. His junior year he was editor of the college yearbook, *Salmagundi;* his senior year he was elected editor-in-chief of *The Madisonenses,* but he resigned this administrative office on condition that he should still write the editorials, which he sometimes did by his own admission "with more pertness than good taste."

As associate editor in charge of reviews in his junior year, Harry biweekly wrote three book reviews and a column entitled "With the Magazines," which summarized articles in the *Atlantic, Lippincott's,* and *Ladies' Home Journal.* These writings stand in happy contrast to the orations he was delivering concurrently. They are mature and restrained and stand up well even today. The reviews also show that outside the classroom Harry was reading heavily in contemporary political science, sociology, economics, and science.

As a man Fosdick had an uncanny capacity to write at different levels, from popular stuff for *Reader's Digest* and *Ladies' Home Journal* audiences to trenchant prose targeted at scholars. This knack for adjusting his writing to the purposes at hand he cultivated at Colgate. He also wrote rapidly and easily. The editors of *Salmagundi* found these revealing lines appropriate to their characterization of Harry: "I write my sketches in the dark, I do not have to think, I let my fingers chase the pen and the pen chase the ink."

III

The daughter of Hamilton's mayor, whom Harry dated, remembered vividly that Harry knew everyone, was into everything, and was universally liked by students, faculty, and older townspeople.* Rushed by three fraternities, he pledged Delta Upsilon, rooming part of his college career in the frat house and part in a boarding home. As a D.U. he served the chapter as recording secretary, vice president, president, and delegate to the 1899 national convention. Throughout his life he remained loyal to his old "brothers" and remained in communication with them.

When Raymond followed Harry at Colgate, he tried out for the track team, causing the coach to shake his head sadly and say, "You're just as rotten as your brother." If Harry scarcely starred in track and participated not at all in other sports, nonetheless, he was an ardent rooter as cheerleader, manager of the varsity band, author of his class yell, secretary of the advisory board of the Athletic Association, Colgate representative at a meeting of the New York State Intercollegiate Athletic Union, and author of rah-rah editorials extolling support of the athletic teams.

His Y.M.C.A. involvement fluctuated with the swing of his religious moods. Still, upon graduation he had served as "Y" secretary, chairman of both the membership and finance committees, and delegate to regional conferences.

When it is remembered that Harry managed the Press Club and participated in the Toastmaster Association and, finally, was honored by election to the presidency of the Student Association, it is clear that he was a Big Man on Campus. And it is equally clear that he ran hard to achieve that status. By harnessing talent and ambition in the service of the school, he both slaked his thirst for public recognition and met his parents' self-sacrificial values. The drive, indefatigability, and dutifulness that characterized the later man were evident in the Colgate youth.

But neither the boy nor the man was so driven or so obsessed with success to be incapable of setting aside time for fun. At Colgate Harry dated, and he danced the girls off the floor. He skated and tobogganed. He serenaded town girls and at frat parties swapped stories and puffed churchwarden pipes with professors. And with a pal one dark night in 1900 he "stole" and buried a bronze statuette of Mercury, initiating a class rivalry that became a Colgate tradition until it was abandoned years later when the intensity of the rivalry reached near-fatal proportions. One likes encountering this episode in the record because it sug-

---

* How one historian, Robert Clark, could describe Harry as an undergraduate as "quiet" is a mystery to me and not supported by the evidence.

gests that although Harry's eye was on the main chance, he was yet free spirited enough to risk possible dismissal by masterminding a prank.

One wart mars the attractiveness of this collegian's portrait. When Fosdick was at the height of his career, Methodist Bishop G. Bromley Oxnam heard him lecture and confided to his diary: "I fear I do Fosdick an injustice, but I always sense a certain cockiness in his approach to problems. There is a certain assumption of achievement about him." The evidence suggests that as a college student Harry was something of a legend in his own mind. This may be inferred from the following characterization of him in the college yearbook:

Salmagundi,	'97:	F-SD-CK:	"Himself his world and his own God"
Salmagundi,	'98:	F-SD-CK:	"Your nature is somewhat demonstrative"
Salmagundi,	'99:	F-SD-CK:	"Go to! Let us be a celebrated individual"
Salmagundi, 1900:		FOSDICK:	"Harry is a bright young man, and no one else is more willing to admit this than he himself"

In his autobiography Fosdick admits to a youthful cockiness and gracefully acknowledges having been set straight by his wise parents. We may anticipate here our later assessment that the youthful wart of high self-esteem never became disfiguring in proportion, but never did it entirely disappear. Emphatically, however, the wart was never the whole toad.

IV

Multifarious as were Harry's extracurricular activities, he must have hit the books fairly hard, for he made a splendid academic record, graduating *summa cum laude* and picking up a Phi Beta Kappa key and prizes in Latin, Greek, and English composition. Admittedly Colgate University was hardly a university at all, but a small college, and academic standards were perhaps less rigorous and competition less keen than at the nation's leading institutions. An impressive number of Colgate graduates went on to leadership in the professions, business, and public life, however, and it would not be fair to Fosdick, or to Colgate, to denigrate his academic achievements.

Ed Dunklee, who roomed with Harry in the D.U. house, told a story that is worth repeating and pondering. Dunklee recalled walking to class with Harry in the morning, being questioned on the assignment by his unprepared friend, and in the end seeing Harry make the better recitation. Fosdick possessed a quick, supple mind; a near-photographic memory; an ability to absorb the ideas of others and meld those ideas with his own. It was a mind admirably suited to his future role as interpreter and mediator and apologist. Fosdick said that he never would have made a great creative scholar and perhaps he knew, or thought he knew, that his mind was not of the very first order. But his intellectual equipment was certainly equal—and more than equal—to the career he proposed to follow.

V

Harry's Colgate experiences have been examined in a manner intended to help understand the foundations of his later career in the service of the Christian faith, but during these college years the foundations of his own faith were desperately shaken, and it is to these experiences of doubt, disbelief, and returning belief that we now turn. Our task is eased by the fact that, in his autobiography and in the essays "A Spiritual Autobiography" and "There Really Is a God" as well as elsewhere, Fosdick himself has narrated his spiritual pilgrimage. Our task is complicated, however, by the fact that these narrations sometimes contradict one another.

In the decade misnamed the Gay Nineties Anglican Bishop Hugh Miller Thompson told a college audience that the time in which they were living was "the most serious and sadly earnest age that the earth ever saw." "We have none of the frivolous unbelief or frivolous skepticism of the last century," Thompson observed. "Where doubt exists in the nineteenth century it is deeply and profoundly earnest." The spiritual battle Harry fought was deadly serious. Thousands of young people of his era struggled with similar lethal doubts, and in the end some retreated to the secure fortress of fundamentalism; some, perhaps sadly but proudly, joined the growing army of nontheistic humanists and scientific naturalists; and some, like Harry, "cheered as the relief column of liberal theology, bagpipes skirling, marched to the rescue of the threatened Christian regiment."

Fosdick reported that when he entered college he was deeply religious, untroubled by any doubts, unquestioning in his acceptance of orthodox dogmas. "The fundamentalists in later years have hated me plentifully," he wrote, "but I started as one of them." One wonders. Fosdick never spoiled a story in the telling of it, and one suspects that he exaggerated the orthodoxy of his early belief to heighten the drama of his break from it, just as one suspects that he may have overstated his childhood fears of damnation to strengthen the case against Calvinism's harshness. By his own testimony, as a youth he was uncommitted to any creedal subscription, unpledged to any sectarian loyalty, and he and his father had warmly discussed theological questions. In September 1895 Harry may not have been a religious rebel, but surely his religious experiences to that point had not frozen him into an unbreakable mold.

In one reminiscence Fosdock recalled experiencing during his freshman year "no disquieting premonitions of the explosion that was to follow"; in another he remembered that by the end of his freshman year "I had completely blown my top." The moment when the mounting doubts climaxed cannot be pinpointed more precisely than the year 1896.

One of the best-known stories about Fosdick stems from his freshman year when he announced that he had become a convinced believer in evolution. His father's response squelched the drama of the occasion: "Well, I believed that before you were born." The story may or may not be true because in one version Harry made the announcement by letter and in another version at the family dining table while home on vacation. Assuming that it is true, there is nothing in the story to flutter the dovecotes. Certainly in becoming "a convinced believer in evolution" Fosdick never went "the whole orang" in seeing evolution as purposeless, nonprogressive, and materialistic as did those who unflinchingly faced the implications of the Darwinian Revolution. Like most liberal Protestants, Fosdick accepted evolution without sacrificing belief in God as "the ultimate Arranger of the universe and a professor of taxonomy, to boot." Certainly he was not one of the handful of Calvinists who accepted Darwinism in substance precisely because of the perceived affinities of Darwinism with orthodox theology. In any case evolution did not become an explosive and divisive issue in American Protestantism until after World War I and then primarily as a symbolic issue of the differences between fundamentalism and modernism.

Completing his freshman year, Harry in the spring of 1896 returned to Buffalo to a home devastated by Frank Fosdick's nervous breakdown. Harry believed financial worries contributed to the smash and volunteered to drop out of school and lend a financial helping hand until his father recovered. The year passed: clerking in a bookstore for $6 a week, reading voraciously on the side, learning shorthand, teaching a Sunday School class, and playing with such old high school friends as were still in town.

It was during this difficult, lonely year, when surely his heart was with his new-found pals and mentors at Colgate, that the nineteen-year-old Harry experienced with renewed intensity the mystical feelings of his earlier youth—"indubitable experiences of spiritual reality," "hours of inner exaltation, with premonitions in them of truth to be seen and work to be done," experiences that "were self-sufficient, mystically complete in their own deep satisfaction." Years afterward he encountered and had existential understanding of Canon Streeter's sentence: "I have had experiences which materialism cannot explain." Is it significant, one wonders, that Harry's conversion experience at age seven came immediately after his mother's nervous breakdown and that these later mystical hours came to him with radical force following his father's nervous collapse? In the first instance, when threatened with a motherless home, did the boy seek the emotional security of another home, the church? In the second instance, when threatened with the loss of a loving father, did the youth seek solace in the flight-of-the-alone-to-the-Alone? This mystical element in his nature later led him into close fellowship with the Quaker mystic, Rufus Jones, and membership in the Wider Quaker Fellowship. The authority of personal experience was for Fosdick forever to be the primary authority.

Even as Harry was becoming aware of an inner center of spiritual satisfaction and resource, he began discarding the outward formulas of faith. As he recalled, perhaps once again exaggerating for effect, "I no longer believed the old stuff I had been taught. Moreover, I no longer merely doubted it. I rose in indignant revolt against it." In this mood he returned to Colgate in September 1897. Outwardly as blithe a soul as any sophomore, he delighted in flaunting his daring, newly acquired questioning spirit, much to the consternation of his pious schoolmates who noted his absence from church, prayer meeting, and "Y" gatherings. Inwardly, however, he was engaged in an intense struggle to achieve a coherent view of life—as he later phrased it, "underneath I was fighting the battle of my life." Was it possible to remain a Christian without rejecting all that nineteenth-century science and scholarship were disclosing about the universe and man, pre-Christian religions, and Christianity itself, especially the authority of scripture as interpreted by the new higher criticism? Because the old orthodoxy was not now for Harry a live option (if indeed it ever really had been), the real decision for him was between the New Theology and no formal, institutionalized religion at all.

The sophomore year ended but not the inner conflict, and at the start of his junior year he returned to college determined, he reported, to think "as freely as the wind that blows across the hills, . . . to follow truth wherever it might lead, into the Church or out of it." So far so logical, for it is certainly possible—it has happened often enough—for a person to chuck the institutional church and retain a religious faith. But it seems illogical for this young man gripped by mystical experiences to say to his mother as he left home to return to Colgate in September 1898: "I'll behave as though there were a God, but mentally I'm going to clear God out of the universe and start all over to see what I can find." These are not the words of a mystic who had known experiences materialism could not explain. More probably they are words invented by Fosdick in retrospect to explain and justify his generation's eager acceptance of the new liberal theology.

As the junior year progressed, Harry began having "the first wild doubts of doubt" about his questioning spirit. "There seemed to be a compass within me that turned toward religious faith and religious effort," he recalled. "No matter how I seized the needle, the instant I removed the influence of my will from it, it would always swing back to that same direction." He began using his reason to go beyond reason. And so he arrived at the end of his junior year convinced (as he rather grandly put it) that he wanted to make a contribution to the spiritual life of his generation; a teaching rather than a preaching ministry looming as the original possibility.

At Colgate today it is widely believed that this decision was reached one spring night while he was engaged in conversation with William Newton Clarke on the distinguished professor's porch. The decision jelled that summer when his father affirmed during an evening walk, "Harry, you know as well as I do, that you will never be happy out of the ministry." There is one concrete piece of documentary evidence that proves that Harry's decision could not have come later than November 1, 1899. On that date the clerk's record for the Wednesday Evening Prayer Meeting of the Lafayette Avenue Baptist Church in Buffalo reads: "On motion which was unanimously carried, Bro. Harry E. Fosdick was granted a license to preach the Word of God." Fosdick makes no mention of this event in any of his published writings.

In later years he made three apposite observations about the decision to enter the ministry. One, he believed that he did have an authentic call. Two, he admitted to much soul-searching, adding that it is not well to slip into the ministry too easily: "It is only men who take the ministry seriously enough to have to struggle over it who are likely to amount to anything." And three, preaching on the text, "One thing I know, that, whereas I was blind, now I see," he said:

> In my youth the time came when formal creeds to me were dust and ashes. I did not believe them. How could I go into the ministry? Yet, in the Christian gospel I did see something—only a little to be sure, but at least that much I personally saw—and now with gratitude I look back on the day when I made the greatest venture of my life: I can preach what I see—that was the way I had to start. God helping me, I said, I will never

preach what I do not see, but what I see I can say. It seemed so little to go on at first, because I saw so little, yet now an older man I am glad I humbly joined the great tradition of this blind man, his eyes just opening, much dark to him, much unsure, saying simply, One thing I know, one thing at least, once blind I see!

When Harry returned to Colgate as a senior and the rumor spread that he was headed for the ministry, the college community was surprised and amused, for of late his piety was not renowned. "Fosdick," remarked Professor Thomas, "I hear you are thinking of entering the ministry." "Yes," Harry answered, "that is true." "Well," Thomas said, "I have just one question to ask you. Has it ever occurred to you that a minister is supposed to be an exponent of the spiritual life?" Apparently Harry, always inordinately conscious of his image, took the hint, for he cut dancing from his social activities. On the occasion of one dance, as he stood against the gym wall silently observing the waltzers and two-steppers, a former girlfriend asked, "Harry, aren't you missing the dancing?" He replied, "Beth, you wouldn't believe it, but I'm not." Incidentally, the mild romance between this girl, Elizabeth Leland, and Harry ended without rancor because he was unprepared to make a deep commitment (as he suggests) and because she possessed sufficient self-awareness to know she was never cut out to be a minister's wife, which would mean, among other things, giving up dancing!

Our next task is to try to discern those men and ideas assisting Harry in his decision to enter the ministry. An obvious influence was the Colgate faculty. That Harry's battle ended with the reconstruction of his faith rather than the final destruction of it was due in some measure to his personal contacts with professors who were without exception Christians and, for the most part, not without intellectual respectability. They gave witness to the truth that it was possible to be both intelligent and a believer.

A particularly luminous moment came after a class meeting with Melbourne Stuart Reed, professor of philosophy, when one of the six students in the course broke the sober silence with the exclamation, "Fellows, there really is a God!"* Fifty years later Fosdick wrote, "I still stand in the light of that hour's affirmation." The tone of the student's cry, redolent of a Campus Crusaders rally, should not make us so queasy as to miss the central point: the Colgate faculty made it, if not impossi-

---

* Fosdick dates the incident from his senior year in "There Really Is a God" and from his junior year in "A Spiritual Autobiography" and "Something More in Education"; *The Living of These Days* relates the story without mentioning the year. The Colgate transcript and other evidence makes almost certain the incident occurred the spring semester of his junior year.

ble, then certainly more difficult for Harry to have remained permanently in the valley of doubt.

Lending an assist from a greater distance was John Fiske, whose writings tamed the idea of evolution and then leashed it to an optimistic theism, easing an entire generation's intellectual and spiritual transition to a Darwinian universe. Fosdick autobiographically acknowledges Fiske's help; moreover, Harry reviewed affirmatively in *The Madisonensis* Fiske's confident *Through Nature to God*, as he did other works dealing with evolution by such authors as David Starr Jordan.

It was, however, William Newton Clarke of the Hamilton Theological Seminary who more than any other individual on or off the Colgate campus made it possible for Harry to outflank his intellectual difficulties. Fosdick's testimony to Clarke's impact could hardly be stronger: "[He] was really my spiritual godfather . . . without whose influence I would never have gone into the Christian ministry at all." Fosdick paid this or a similar tribute to Clarke not merely on two or three occasions, but quite literally on a score or more of instances—in print, in utterance, in private letter, in interview. Later, Clarke would come from Colgate to New York City to preach Harry's ordination sermon in 1903 and much later the great organ at The Riverside Church was dedicated to the memory of Clarke, "Friend and instructor of Dr. Fosdick."

As an undergraduate Harry took no formal course work with Clarke. Yet occasionally the student and the unprepossessing, slightly crippled seminary professor chanced to meet on the campus to walk and talk together. As we know, if memories may be trusted, it was on Clarke's porch that Harry, whether tentatively or finally, opted for the ministry. At commencement Clarke remarked to a luncheon guest, "If Fosdick decides to enter the ministry, in twenty years he will be the leading preacher in the United States." Little wonder that Clarke asked Harry to return to Hamilton in the fall of 1900 to study with him at the seminary and little wonder that the youth accepted, considering his admiration for the theologian—acceptance being made financially possible by money awarded Harry for a prize-winning essay against vivisection.

As an undergraduate Harry had read Clarke's *An Outline of Christian Theology* published in 1898. This work became so widely used that it has been called virtually the *Dogmatik* of evangelical liberalism and Clarke has been labeled the most notable representative of Ritschlianism in America.* Taking full cognizance of the new developmental approach to the world, man, and revelation, Clarke distinguished between religious experience and the forms with which it was expressed in philoso-

---

* Albrecht Ritschl was a nineteenth-century German theologian; Ritschlian theology was a reaction to rationalism.

phy and theology, holding that the experience preceding the particular doctrinal formulations could and should be interpreted in the light of changing cultural conditions and advancing knowledge. As his famous illustration runs: we are sure that the stars are there, though astronomies change; that the flowers are real, though botany alters its explanations. This illustration Fosdick picked up and translated into his own famous phrase: "We must distinguish between abiding experiences and changing categories." Unfortunately, Clarke almost totally neglected ecclesiology, and it would be to the adult Fosdick almost equally a matter of disinterest.

Greatly as Harry admired Clarke, he hungered to know a wider world than the seminary at Hamilton could offer; so, with Clarke's blessing and thanks to a scholarship, in the summer of 1901 he set off for New York City to attend Union Theological Seminary.

VI

When Harry departed for New York he was still uncertain in his own mind as to the nature of his future ministry: Would it center on teaching, as he originally intended, or on preaching? The ultimate resolution was to follow both a teaching and preaching ministry and to unite the two with a third ministry, that of counseling. Harry's early inclination toward teaching would, of course, find fulfilment not only in the classroom and counseling study, but in the pulpit as well. As we shall see, when Fosdick later defined preaching as the "moving and effective communication of truth" or a "cooperative dialogue" between preacher and congregation or "personal counseling on a group scale" or "problem solving"—in a word, when he championed the "project method" of preaching, he was defining preaching from a pedagogical perspective. The inadequacy of such a definition from a theological perspective we shall duly note. It may well be that the nature of Fosdick's preaching, both its strengths and weaknesses, was determined by his early desire to follow his father and grandfather into the teaching profession and that any vocational tensions were resolved not only as a professor at Union and as a counselor, but also in the pedagogical design and delivery of sermons.

VII

Writing in 1953 to the president of Colgate, Fosdick declared, "I owe more to Colgate than I can ever express." Throughout his life Fosdick was always loyal, and this trait is clearly seen in his loyalty to Colgate. He served the university as trustee for decades. He served as president of the Alumni Association. He occasionally attended reunions and returned to deliver addresses. He was a member of the Half-Century Club and otherwise assisted in fund drives. For its part, Colgate repeatedly honored its most famous graduate, awarding Fosdick the honorary D.D. degree as early as 1914 and elevating him to Trustee Emeritus as late as 1956. At the time of his retirement, President Everett Case invited him to accept the Colgate post of "a quiet personal ministry to the students." The year after his death a portrait bust was unveiled in a prominent campus location. In 1961 the Harry Emerson Fosdick Chair of Philosophy and Religion was created, with Laurance, Nelson, and David Rockefeller contributing generously to the total endowment of $300,000. Most important, it was while a student that Harry formed his association with James C. Colgate, and it may be flatly stated that Mr. Colgate remained until his death Harry's oldest, closest, and wisest mentor.

All in all, Colgate University and Fosdick had every reason to be mutually grateful.

Chapter Three

Union Theological Seminary:
A Time of Personal Crisis
and Ministerial Training

I

In all of Fosdick's ninety-one years, there were none more decisive than the three following his journey to New York in the summer of 1901 to enter the Union Theological Seminary as a "middler" with first-year credit transferred from Hamilton. In this period he had his earliest contact with urban America's slums. He suffered a terrifying suicidal smashup and there came to him with full fury the stern Delphic injunction, "know thyself." Recovering, he completed his seminary studies handsomely and established a lifelong association with Union. He gained firsthand knowledge of both a prestigious downtown church and an isolated rural parish, and he won a call to a suburban church, his first permanent pastorate. And he married the woman who was to be his devoted companion for six decades.

II

Young Fosdick arrived in New York in the heat of early July, he later reported, "without money and without friends on an adventure the outcome of which either practical or theological I could not foresee." Happily, he had the assurance of a scholarship from Union and the seminary's president, Charles Cuthbert Hall, adopted the stray, permitting him (against the rules) to bunk in the seminary dormitory prior to the opening of fall classes. Also, thanks to a Colgate fraternity brother, he had a summer job working in the Vacation Daily Bible Schools and, as well, the promise of a winter job assisting at Mariners' Temple, a mission at Oliver and Henry Streets just off the Bowery.

This work put a little cash in his pocket and, more important for the long term, first put him in contact with East Side toughies and Bowery bums, kids accustomed to diving into the soiled waters of the East River rather than swimming in clear Chautauqua Lake and men accustomed to downing boilermakers rather than drinking in cool Chautauqua culture. Once he attempted to set up a basketball game, only to have a boy unclasp a knife and slash the ball to ribbons. He recalled a fellow missioner's moving exposition of the prodigal son's return, to which a cynical voice responded: "So! He put it over on the old man again!"

These experiences were significant for Harry's broader education. For one thing, they forced him to adopt a speaking style less florid and anodyne than his college oratory, a simpler more direct style that characterizes, though not completely, his later sermons. For another, his eyes were opened to the truth of Walter Rauschenbusch's dictum: "We rarely sin against God alone." This awareness had come to Rauschenbusch while ministering near New York's Hell's Kitchen where, he reported, "One could hear human virtue cracking and crumbling all around." Fosdick's concern for the underdog was sharpened in these months of association with New York's poor and disinherited.

III

With the arrival of September, Harry's summer work with the Bible School children ended and the Bowery mission work began. Concurrently he embarked on his seminary courses at Union and additional classes at Columbia in philosophy and epistemology. Never before had he known such emotional excitement, intellectual stimulation, physical depletion, or harrowing psychological challenge. In November the warning signals mounted: blurred vision, stomach spasms, pervasive fatigue, insomnia, suicidal thoughts. He seemed to be losing his mind and was gripped by a sense of utter helplessness to brake the descent into darkness. In panic he fled to Worcester, Massachusetts, hoping that a brief respite in the company of the woman to whom he had become engaged months earlier would set him to rights. Relief did not come. The flight continued to his home in Buffalo. The anxiety refused to abate. One dreadful day he placed a razor to his throat. Was this a gesture only? Or would Harry Emerson Fosdick's life have ebbed away from a slashed jugular that day early in 1902 if his father had not been there to cry, "Harry! Harry!"

Presently he found himself in The Gleason Sanitarium in Elmira, New York. This nationally recognized institution had been established in 1852 by Dr. Silas Gleason and his wife Dr. Rachel Gleason, "the almost divine Mrs. Gleason" in Mark Twain's words of praise. It specialized in "nervous diseases" and in the treatment then popular known as hydropathy. Harry was released four months later. His affluent future father-in-law underwrote a six weeks' convalescent trip to England. In Stratford-on-Avon he finally got two blessed long nights of untroubled sleep. The tide had turned. In September 1902 he returned to his studies at Union, carefully watching his step, but increasingly confident that the worst had passed. As we shall never know how close Fosdick actually came to suicide, so also we shall never be positive how close he came to being permanently incapacitated by mental illness.

In *The Living of These Days* and a cluster of letters and writings Fosdick is rather candid about this "most hideous experience," the "inner hell" of this "neurotic agony" and "melancholia," the "pit of utter despair" in which he found himself, this "terrifying wilderness" through which he traveled and when he "dreadfully wanted to commit suicide." His descriptions of the experience ring true as far as they go. Our purpose is to discover, as precisely as the record and conjecture permit, the exact nature of the trouble; second, the possible causes of the trouble; and third, the lasting consequences of the experience.

Fosdick appears to have suffered a severe neurotic reactive depression. It was a neurotic rather than a psychotic episode because he did not have the confusion of thought characteristic of a psychotic illness. His depressive thoughts were not irrational (as "I am the cause of the world's suffering"), and he was thinking lucidly enough to tutor his doctor's child while in the sanitarium. There is one passage in his autobiography ("It was not trouble that slew me but happiness—the excitement of the most exhilarating opportunity I had ever had") suggesting a manic attack. But manics usually stay in the situation in which they find themselves, doing rash and irresponsible things; instead, Fosdick turned for help in Worcester and Buffalo. Fosdick uses strong language to describe his illness, but the terms he employs do not indicate hallucinatory or delusional states.

The biographer must at certain points put down his money and take his choice, and this we now do. Fosdick did not suffer from schizophrenia or manic-depressive psychosis or organic brain damage. The term "neurasthenia," the catchall "diagnosis of fashion" among the genteel classes of that era, is unhelpful today. Rather, his was apparently a very severe case of reactive depression. Gastrointestinal symptoms, visual refractive problems, insomnia, fears of things out of control, suicidal impulses, all seem to point to intense anxiety.

Now to the etiology of the case. Two causative factors immediately suggest themselves because they appear so frequently in the biographies of young people, not the least being those who entered adulthood in the Victorian era. Neither, however, appear relevant to Fosdick's ordeal. Unlike many others, in 1901 Fosdick was neither racked by religious doubts nor torn between his inherited faith and scientific naturalism. As we have learned, his crisis of faith was confronted and resolved earlier, while at Colgate. There is nothing in the record to indicate that while at Union he knew either the absence of the experience of God or the experience of the absence of God. Nor can we discern in 1901 any serious anxiety occasioned by unresolved career decisions. He had settled earlier on a career in the Christian ministry, and there is no evidence that the decision was reopened in his mind by his Union studies.

Dismissing, as we must, these two possibilities, where do we now turn? Two possible contributing factors come to mind. Fosdick repeatedly admitted to never having been "nervously tough" and to having inherited a "delicate nervous constitution." The mother suffered from a series of nervous breakdowns, one at least, being very serious, and his father knew at least one breakdown. Certain types of mental illnesses do tend to run in families; this is especially true of depression. Perhaps there was in the Fosdick inheritance a genetic streak of recurrent depression. In the absence of medical records the point must be declared moot. However, it is important that Harry *thought* his inheritance included a history of mental breakdowns. He must have been fearful that he, too, might follow the paths of his parents, and this very fear made him vulnerable to that which did in fact overwhelm him.

In his autobiography Fosdick alludes to things that "got me down": the humid heat of the city, incessant work, lack of exercise, improper diet. In later letters he suggests that his troubles stemmed from neurological causes. In one instance he blames "the nerves of my stomach," which were calmed by "a very simple prescription." In another instance he writes that "my difficulty was triggered in part by astigmatism of the eyes which I lacked the common sense to have examined." Although Fosdick was candid in describing the terror of his experience, these *explanations* are not very perceptive, and, indeed, are clearly rationalizations. However heavily the medical profession in 1901 might have weighed these factors together with heredity as causing "neurasthenia," few today hold that they could be of more than minimal significance. Young people of twenty-three are not felled by "overwork" or "insufficient exercise" or a "trick stomach."

Thus far we have tentatively advanced two explanations for the breakdown. Now a word about the two possibly most significant causative factors. The first is his work with the Bowery population. Nothing in his boyhood or undergraduate years had prepared him for this strange, frightening encounter with New York's underside. Gently nurtured, cherishing Christian ideals and Victorian moral values, knowing only success as a leader in high school and college, easily and always moving his peers with his oratory, what a shock for Fosdick to come up against the Bowery citizens. Time and again his exhortations were hooted, his idealistic appeals cynically scorned, his best efforts unavailing. Probably, he was verbally assaulted as a prig; maybe on occasions he felt physically threatened. Many times he might have felt like fleeing or striking back and could permit himself neither. For the first time he comprehended (as the autobiography notes) why New York was called "a very hotbed of knavery, debauchery and bestiality." Fosdick never flatly states that he judged his work with the Bowery people a failure, but maybe for the first time he experienced less than total success, and, consequently, the first severe self-doubts.

A second significant causative factor: all his life great things had been expected of Harry Fosdick. Until 1901 he had more than met the high aspirations of his parents and teachers and the towering standards he set for himself, graduating, it will be recalled, first in his high school class and first in his Colgate class and first in the mind of his Hamilton seminary mentor. For Harry, doing well at Union was not simply something desirable, but a *must*; there was no alternative, at least none that was thinkable. He faced, in his own words, "alike the greatest opportunity and the stiffest competition" he "had ever met." Were his abilities equal to the challenge? Would his string of earlier triumphs be broken? Would he fail the test, bringing humiliation to his family and fiancée and shame to himself? He was alone in New York, his confidence already shaken by the harsh Bowery experience. And now came a confrontation with brilliant Union and Columbia professors and able, competitive peers. He studied under enormous stress. Increasingly doubts, which he sought to repress, haunted him. Anxiety mounted, depression deepened, and in his fear of losing control the therapeutic qualities of rest and dreaming were denied to him when needed most. Here are four extracts from Fosdick's later statements, the first from a 1928 sermon, the second from a 1938 sermon, the third from an undated letter, and the fourth from a 1958 letter:

> Why is it that in the adolescent and early college years you so often hear about emotional collapses, nervous breakdowns, and sometimes suicide? One commonly hears it said about a case like that, He was so beautifully brought up; he had so lovely a home; he had everything to live for; why? But that is precisely the reason. He had had so sheltered and beautiful a

youth that when at last he faced the responsibility of manhood and in particular the necessity of succeeding or failing on his own, he shrank back. He was afraid. He may never have said it to himself. He rationalized it, as the psychologists say, made up all sort of other explanations for it, but underneath he was afraid of the untried experiences of maturity.

Some time since, I spoke in the morning to a fine lad, a promising student whom I knew well. He seemed happy. He shot himself before noon, and the reason, as it came out, lay in this realm where our thought is moving. Lifted from the background of his family, finding himself here in New York on his own, seeing that he had to make the grade or be a failure, feeling that he did not have it in him, he mishandled that appalling sense of inferiority.

Another aspect of a nervous breakdown is this: you not only feel sick but you feel *humiliated*. If you had diabetes you would be ill, but it would not be compounded with humiliation so that you would be ashamed of yourself. This is one of the cruelest aspects of a nervous breakdown. Face it! Stand off from yourself and look at your plight as objectively as you can. The utterly unjustified sense of shame, self-contempt and humiliation should be shouldered off as much as possible. Don't wallow in it! Like a running fever, it is just part of your particular illness.

Generally the worst place for the victim [of a nervous breakdown] to live is with his or her family. The more you love anyone the more sensitive you are to him or to her. Even if all is smooth and sweet in your relationships you are acutely, sensitively conscious of every mood and especially of the effect of your nervous illness on the family. With strangers one can be apathetic and not care. The doctors put me in a sanatarium for four months to separate me from those I loved most. It was a good move.

And years later when a famous fellow clergyman had a breakdown, Fosdick advised him: "Don't let anyone tell you to pull yourself together because what you pull yourself together with is broke."

These may surely be seen as autobiographical references. Harry feared failure. He was humiliated by his inability to will himself back to health—to "pull himself together." And the company first of his fiancée and then of his parents intensified rather than moderated his sense of shame. Only after separation in a sanitarium and then in England did recovery slowly come.

There were at least three long-range consequences of Fosdick's ordeal. For one thing, in his hour of need God came to him redemptively, and the experience was as profound as his conversion at age seven. "I learned to pray," he recorded, "not because I had adequately argued out prayer's rationality, but because I desperately needed help from a Power greater than my own. I learned that God, much more than a theological proposition, is an immediately available Resource." Again, "I found God in a desert." Again, "I learned intake as well as output," discovering a new meaning in Paul's words, "In Him who strengthens me, I am able for anything." Repeatedly he asserted that his little devotional book, *The Meaning of Prayer*, "would never have been written without that breakdown."

For a second thing, Fosdick now placed a preaching ministry ahead of a teaching ministry. "It is doubtless too much to say that that agonizing experience made me a preacher," he observed, "but it was a catalyst that decided the issue. Until then I had intended to teach about religion rather than to preach the Gospel, but henceforth I wanted to get at people, real people, with their distracting, anxious, devastating problems."

Third, the ordeal both fueled his interest in pastoral counseling and gave him insight into the problems of others. As he later wrote to a troubled girl, "I went through a nervous breakdown once, during which my despair was so great that I went to get a razor to cut my throat. Now as I look back on that hideous experience, I count it one of the most valuable of my life. There are multitudes of people that I never could have helped if I had not gone through that. It was a more important part of my education than a whole lot of my scholastic training." He recalled that Walt Whitman, who was a nurse in the Civil War, said once, "I did not ask the wounded man how he felt. I felt myself become the wounded man." Fosdick added, "Something like that was the consequence of my nervous breakdown, and while it was the most hideous experience of my life, I have learned to be grateful for it."

IV

On his return to Union Fosdick found it hard going at first, studying a half hour, then to ease the mental strain and fatigue walking a half hour. In the end, on May 10, 1904, he was graduated *summa cum laude*, receiving a bachelor of divinity degree. He matched his high school and Colgate honors, winning an A-plus academic average. Considering his initial ordeal, it took considerable grit to reach such a triumphant conclusion. Nor was it only a matter of grim survival, for one student recalled Harry "laughing unto tears at Raymond Knox's wise cracks" as the group of pals walked back to the seminary from Mrs. Twitchell's dining room.

Union Theological Seminary, then located at 700 Park Avenue, by 1901 had severed its official ties with the Presbyterian Church, U.S.A., becoming interdenominational in both leadership and outlook. The great divorce was precipitated in the 1890s by the General Assembly's concern for the doctrinal orthodoxy of Presbyterian seminaries. Charges were brought against two Union professors. Charles A. Briggs was placed on trial for heresy ("Briggs bacillus") and suspended from the Presbyterian ministry in 1892; Arthur Cushman McGiffert withdrew from the Presbyterian ministry in 1900 to escape that fate.

In *The Living of These Days* Fosdick mentions by name seven of his Union professors. One of these was President Charles Culthbert Hall with whom he took Missions (A and B and C) and Spiritual Life. Though not one of the seminary's most brilliant minds, Hall was caring and approachable and beloved by the students. Remembered Fosdick, "He was the greatest specialist in personal friendship that I have ever known, and he was one of the most beautiful interpreters of spiritual life in his own character."

English Bible (two terms) and Christian Social Thinking were taken with Thomas Hall. Aflame with the new social passion and desperately concerned to make religion relevant to life, Thomas Hall also shared the sanguine mood of the era's liberal Christianity, and in his classrooms, Fosdick recalled, "optimism reigned" as Hall "talked beguilingly of the 'kingdom dream.' "

Fosdick learned Old Testament Hebrew from Francis Brown. A scholar of erudition and renown, awesome in appearance and manner (his nickname among the students was Jahweh), though identified with the newer liberal position, there was nothing mockingly iconoclastic in his critical approach to the Old Testament. As a student recalled, "He represented to us the battle, then on the firing line, of historical criticism; and we gained the conviction that, if a man of such scholarship held on to his supreme faith through the shaking of the foundations, God would surely survive, shorn of some of His ancient trappings perhaps, but still a reliable God." Not being a scholar of Hebrew, Harry found Brown's mediation especially necessary, and the continuing indebtedness is evident in Fosdick's famous *A Guide to Understanding the Bible*. Perhaps significantly, Brown became president of Union in 1908, the very year Fosdick joined the faculty.

James Everett Frame was Harry's mentor in New Testament studies and because Harry did know Greek his interest in the comparative studies of the Gospels was keen. A small, almost shy man, Frame's colleagues and students referred to his scholarship in such terms as "rigorous," "painstaking," "meticulous" with an "almost pathological passion for accuracy to the last detail." It says something about Fosdick's own scholarship that in later years it was to Jim Frame to whom he turned, more

than to any other Union colleague, for critical readings of his manuscripts. Frame helped Fosdick formulate his hermeneutical concept of
"abiding experiences in changing categories," first suggested by William
Newton Clarke.

Arthur Cushman McGiffert, whose *A History of Christianity in the
Apostolic Age* (1897) was branded by conservatives as "the most daring
and thorough-going attack on the New Testament that has ever been
made by an accredited teacher of the Presbyterian Church in America,"
was Harry's teacher in the History of Protestant Theology and Church
History (two terms). A brilliant lecturer and future president of Union,
McGiffert was the idol of students, including Harry. He had studied under the great German church historian, Adolf von Harnack, to whom
there are three explicit references in Fosdick's B.D. thesis*; and Fosdick's
essay, "What Is Christianity" is indebted to Harnack's book of the same
title. Later Fosdick recalled McGiffert terming the immanence of God
"the most characteristic religious doctrine of the nineteenth century";
indeed divine immanence was central to the New Theology, including
Fosdick's own developing position. Both Harnack and McGiffert stressed,
as Fosdick was to do, the moral much more than the doctrinal and emphasized the infinite value of the human soul and the claims of human
brotherhood.

Harry had only one course with William Adams Brown, entitled "The
Person and Work of Christ." Not a scintillating lecturer, nevertheless,
Brown was a prolific and clear writer. He and Clarke, to whom he was
heavily indebted, are correctly regarded as the two outstanding system-
atizers of the New Theology; Brown's *Christian Theology in Outline*
(1906) was especially influential in seminaries on both sides of the Atlantic. Fosdick in his autobiography stated that Brown's course was
"among the most thought provoking" of his seminary career, perhaps
because Brown was explicating ideas Fosdick had already received from
Clarke. Yet when interviewed by a Th.D. candidate, Samuel Robert
Weaver, Fosdick told the young investigator that his thought had *not*
been significantly influenced by Brown. Faced with these seemingly contradictory statements, we may only observe that Fosdick's thought is
close to Brown's, especially in their common experiential approach to
religion.

The seventh Professor specifically mentioned by Fosdick is George
William Knox, under whom he took courses in Ethnic Faiths, Missions,

---

* The thesis is entitled, "The Significance of Christ's Death in Christian Thought:
An Inquiry into the Reasons for the Pre-eminence of the Crucifixion in the Chris-
tian Consciousness," and we shall refer to it in our later discussion of Fosdick's
Christology.

The Christian Doctrine of Salvation, Theism, and as a postgraduate in 1906–1907, two terms in The Philosophy of Religion. Keen and tough-minded, a gripping lecturer, slight of stature and slightly lame, Knox's realism was a needed antidote to the prevailing idealism. He dismissed the current "through nature to God" immanentism as sub-Christian; warned his students that the twin vices of the ministry were laziness and conceit; and cautioned his classes, "Beware how you baptize evolution in terms of progress!" As Fosdick reported, "That clicked. I never escaped its peremptory challenge to the naive social hopefulness with which my optimistic generation had infected me." It was in Knox's classes that Fosdick reported that Schleiermacher* and Ritschl "became very vivid and real," with Ritschl being the greater influence.

Inside and outside the classroom Fosdick inevitably encountered philosophic Idealism, and if we may generalize from the fragmentary clues he dropped in later years, his thought moved away, though never totally so, from the prevailing Hegelianism and its stately vagueness. In 1939 he paid this tribute to Nicholas Murray Butler, his Columbia philosophy teacher: "Longer years ago than probably he or I like to think, he was a teacher of mine. He taught me Plato, and I bear him public witness that it stuck. For, during all these years since, as materialistic mechanism and instrumentalism have come up into the philosophy of the day, I never have been able to get away from the conviction that Plato was ever-lastingly right, and that there is still an eternal world of ideas and values." It follows, as he stated, that as a student Fosdick was uninfluenced by Comte or Dewey or later by Otto or Wieman. On the other hand, he reported being strongly attracted to the American Idealists Josiah Royce and later William Ernest Hocking. Refus Jones must be counted among the "romantic absolute idealists" and reading his *Social Law in the Spiritual World* (1904) was to Fosdick a "memorable event." Further, Fosdick also found appealing the personalistic idealism of the Methodist theologian, Borden Parker Bowne, whose volume *Personalism* (1908) became virtually the "party line" of American Methodism. Fosdick marked his personal copy with such expressions as "great" and "capital idea." Earlier, at Colgate, Fosdick had used Bowne's *Metaphysics* as a textbook.

Acknowledging this significant and enduring strain of Idealism in his thought, Fosdick specifically notes that this neo-Hegelianism was called into question and moderated by the pragmatism of William James, whose Gifford Lectures, *The Varieties of Religious Experience*, were published in 1902. On reading James, Fosdick reported, "I became in general a pragmatist"; and his later writings are deeply informed by

---

* Friedrich Daniel Ernst Schleiermacher, German theologian who opposed German rationalism and theological orthodoxy.

Jamesian empiricism. Appropriate to his admiration for James, Fosdick retained a lifelong sensitivity to the psychology of religion. Whether or not it is in fact possible to accommodate the American Idealism of, say, Bowne, and James's pragmatism, this is what Fosdick sought to do.

Finally, Harry's studies at Union augmented rather than diminished his earlier interest in comparative religions, and his writings reveal a more than amateur's understanding of the world's great religions.

A half-century after graduating from Union, on the occasion of the endowment of a chair in his name, Fosdick truthfully declared: "This seminary made my ministry possible. Over 50 years ago, I came here a confused and hungry student, wishing above all else to teach and preach the Christian gospel, but wondering how I could do it with intellectual integrity and self-respect. And here the doors were opened."

V

While still a student Harry had two pastoral experiences revealing of the developing man. In the summer of 1903 he assumed his first charge, that of the tiny Guide Board Presbyterian Church of Santa Clara, New York, a hamlet on the northwest fringe of the Adirondacks. He also preached at the little Episcopal Church of the Good Shepherd. It was a good summer, especially for someone recovering from the sort of ordeal he had recently experienced and after a winter of study. Boarding at the home of Widow Dimick, he preached a little, visited, tramped the hills, and fished the streams. His family joined him for part of the summer, as did his fiancée. Many years later a sixty-three-year old woman would write to Fosdick of her girlhood memories of him as a young visiting minister, "the *most wonderful guy*, a sincere friend, a thoughtful friend, a little girl ever had." In vivid and poignant detail the now dying woman recalled Fosdick's many acts of kindness to the child she had been: his chocolate drops and hugs and stories and words of advice and comfort.

In his lifetime Fosdick received hundreds of thousands of expressions of gratitude, but surely none more moving than this one. The sensitive, gentle young man we see in the letter is not the cocky lad we knew as a Colgate undergraduate. Is it not permissible to conjecture that he gained this new compassion from his own recent journey through hell?

The following fall Harry had a pastoral experience of a different sort as student assistant to George C. Lorimer, minister of the Madison Avenue Baptist Church. His old mentors James C. Colgate and William Newton Clarke had a hand in the appointment. Harry helped in the Sunday services and Wednesday evening prayer meetings. Occasionally he was trusted with a sermon, increasingly so when Dr. Lorimer became ill. At this church Harry learned that even affluent parishioners were burdened with troubles. He learned also that they could be cranky; one of them, when mildly rebuked by Harry, dropped to his knees and prayed that the Lord would bless "our young brother and give him some sense." He further learned that he possessed the power to preach compelling sermons; after a service it was commonly remarked, "Remember that boy's name for he is going to be heard from in the future."

Dr. Lorimer wanted his student assistant to be an ordained minister and after some spirited opposition from the examining council the date was set. On November 18, 1903, Fosdick was ordained in the Madison Avenue Baptist Church. Among the six clerics participating, Professor Clarke came down from Colgate to preach the ordination sermon and President Hall of Union delivered the charge.

VI

As the spring of 1904 came and graduation approached several possible paths opened to Harry. He was invited to become Madison Avenue's associate minister, but declined. His name was put forward for the presidency of Vassar by Dr. Henry M. Saunders, a Baptist minister influential in the councils of the college. The post did not materialize, perhaps, as John D. Rockefeller, Jr., later speculated, because of Harry's lack of demonstrated experience in the field of education and because his "gay, jovial manner . . . gave pause to the more conservative trustees." A third path lay westward to the suburban community of Montclair, New Jersey. Several members of the Montclair First Baptist Church had chanced to hear Fosdick preach, and they were persuaded that he was the young man to fill their vacant pulpit. The call was issued and accepted.

Harry arrived in Montclair in July and the following month he and Florence Whitney were married, returning to Montclair after a Nova Scotia honeymoon. His career was on the wing and his personal life soaring.

Chapter Four

The Montclair Ministry:
Widening Fame
in a Patrician Pastorate

I

The Montclair period is important because in almost every respect it indicated the direction Fosdick's life work was to take. It is also important in its own right. During these eleven years he ministered successfully to a growing church, involved himself deeply in civic concerns, won an advanced degree from Columbia University, received two honorary degrees, joined the Union Theological Seminary faculty, rode the campus and student conference circuit, published articles attracting national attention, and wrote a cluster of little devotional books ultimately read by millions. Further, he and his bride began and completed their family and made strategic professional associations and warm friendships.

II

The novelist Walker Percy, in defense of knocking back a little bourbon, philosophized: "What, after all, is the use of not having cancer, cirrhosis, and such, if a man comes home from work every day at five-thirty to the exurb of Monclair . . . and there is the grass growing and the little family looking not quite at him but just past the side of his head, and there's Cronkite on the tube and the smell of pot roast in the living room, and inside the house and outside in the pretty exurb has settled the noxious particles and the sadness of the old dying Western World, and him thinking: Jesus, is this it? Listening to Cronkite and the grass growing [in Montclair]?" And the novelist Philip Roth could refer to "those pug-nosed Bastards from Montclair." Apparently Montclair to Percy and Roth is a symbol of exurban, upper-middle-class America and the emotional bleakness of such a society.

In Fosdick's era Montclair was a town of 21,550, the purity of this cosseted community being stained by the presence of some 2000 blacks and some 1500 newly arrived, and isolated, Italians. "SERIOUS PROBLEM FOR MONTCLAIR. WHAT IS THE THING TO DO WITH THE ALIEN AND BACKWARD CLASSES LIVING IN IT?" was a question frequently posed by the *Montclair Times*. Despite the presence of straitened classes, it was an affluent town; in 1911, for example, the cost of living in Montclair was the highest in all New Jersey. Its comfortable homes were cared for by servant girls who worked fourteen-hour days, with perhaps only every second Sunday off. This was "the most abominable of all slaveries," one servant protested to the newspaper, "because inflicted by an educated woman upon one of her own sex, who has not had a fair chance in life." Montclair boasted the usual clubs of the well-to-do: golf, cricket, lawn tennis, gun, and hunt. Not a single playground existed, however, for the children of the noncountry-club set. The Protestant churches were competitively numerous, though their fraternal ties were, it was reported, "a beautiful thing." Naturally the "colored" congregations did not share in this churchly fraternity, and even the "Ys" and W.C.T.U. chapters were segregated on the basis of race. Neither the blacks living in Frog Hollow nor the Italians living on Bay Street would have concurred with the community's prideful title, "Montclair the Beautiful." As one sensitive patrician leader bitingly acknowledged: "Anything more sordid and repulsive than the homes of some of the residents of Montclair cannot be imagined. They live in cellars and garrets; they are packed like sardines in a box. They are condemned to an earthly hell."

This, then, impressionistically, was the community in which Fosdick began his active ministry.

III

By every traditional measurement Fosdick's first pastorate was a notable success. At the time of his installation on June 3, 1904, in the small Fullerton Avenue Chapel, the First Baptist Church membership numbered 307. Within only weeks of Fosdick's arrival worshippers packed the chapel and overflowed into the Sunday School room. Within a year plans were laid to purchase property at the corner of Church Street and Trinity Place. On October 17, 1909, when the cornerstone was laid for a $140,000 structure of Norman design, Fosdick declared, "Christianity is founded on a fact, and that fact is the character of Jesus. Christ Himself is the cornerstone." Fosdick declined a $500 gift of gratitude from his people, insisting that the sum be applied to the church's indebtedness; nor did he consider leaving, although opportunities presented themselves, until the church's mortgage and bond obligations were fully paid. At the dedication service in 1911 Fosdick declared, in words anticipating his future career, that the object of the new church "was not the exaltation of the Baptist faith, but the promotion of Christianity on the broadest and best lines." When Fosdick bade farewell in 1915, the church's membership had more than doubled, the budget for general expenses and benevolences had quadrupled, and his salary had increased from $2500 to $5000—and this when the average salary of Baptist pastors in New Jersey was $600.

Fosdick's understanding of the mission of the local church foreclosed the possibility of his church being dark and deserted, tenanted six days a week by mice, silence, and gloom. He guided it into the role of an "institutional" church, open every day, with clubs, societies, activities for young and old, parishioners and townspeople. Two aspects of this busyness merit mentioning. The Men's Bible Class under Fosdick's leadership grew in number until it was obliged to meet in the Y.M.C.A. auditorium. Also, the Wednesday evening prayer service jettisoned its traditional form and became a vital forum—attended by many who were not Baptists—where Fosdick thought through and shared with the group the ideas that became the basis for his first books.

Several features of Fosdick's Montclair years were to be characteristic of his subsequent ministry. For one thing, the pew-rental system was abolished. As the newspaper announcements read: "No pews reserved; all seats free; everybody welcome." Fosdick also extended an open invitation to all Christians to participate in the first Lord's Supper at which he officiated. Although there was some grumbling at this breaking of close communion, soon the worship-service bulletin was to read: "At the close of the morning's sermon we shall gather at the Lord's Table. All Christian brethren, disciples of the Master, are welcome to remain and partake with us." There logically followed a further extension of the inclusive principle. Members of non-Baptist evangelical churches were invited to "work and worship with our congregation" by placing evidence of church membership in the hands of the Church, to be returned on leaving. This was a sort of associate membership (though the term was not used), which anticipated the interdenominational character of the later Riverside Church fellowship.

Long before the Fundamentalist/Modernist controversy of the 1920s,

Fosdick had taken his stand against sectarianism, ranging himself on the side of a religion of experience that took interdenominational and non-denominational forms. In a 1911 sermon he confidently observed, in words reminiscent of those spoken by Albert Barnes almost a century earlier: "Even now there dawns upon our dim vision the dream of some more glorious day when one by one of the sects shall come back with its gift of special vision to add to the Church's fuller thought of God,—the Episcopalian with his dignity of worship, the Congregationalist with his freedom of thought, the Methodist with his fervor of evangelical zeal, the Presbyterian with his brave attempt to rationalize his faith, and the Baptist with his emphasis on spiritual liberty." At the dedication of a Presbyterian chapel he declared, with George Whitefield over a century earlier: "There are no Presbyterians, Congregationalists, Episcopalians, Methodists, or Baptists—only Christians." At an ecumenical gathering he expressed joy to be in the vanguard of the millennium; pleasure in the growing comity among the churches, resulting in the breaking of denominational lines; and hearty approval of the movement that brought men closer to each other in the hastening of the advent of the Kingdom of God. Speaking before the New Jersey Baptist Convention in 1911, he advised that no Baptist church be planted where the religious needs of the community were being met by another evangelical denomination. He continued: "But where religion is interpreted to mean the soul's subjection to a priest, salvation is presented as mediated through a sacrament and the fruits of the Spirit are understood to be ritual not character, there the Baptist Church has a mission. Are you willing to shed money as your fathers were to shed blood to save men from the slavery of priestcraft and the degradation of a magical ritual?" Evidently for Fosdick at this stage of his life, the Christian brotherhood was pretty inclusive, but not to the extent of encompassing Roman Catholicism. In this he was neither more nor less purblind than American Protestantism, not excluding liberal Protestantism, at large.

If Fosdick was, to his credit, emerging in these years as one of Protestantism's leading liberals he was also capable of being a modernist in the pejorative sense of attempting to be up-to-date. One example only. In 1911 he delivered a series of evening lectures dubiously entitled, "Christ Weak? Look at the Men He Has Mastered," including the segment, "How Christ Mastered Sir Oliver Lodge." Lodge, a distinguished British scientist and president of the Society for Psychical Research, believed that the living might have visits from departed spirits and intelligent converse with them. At the conclusion of the address the audience dramatically united in repeating the creed of Sir Oliver. Commented Fosdick to a reporter, in a rather oxymoronic way it may be argued, "Who would have thought it possible twenty-five years ago that a congregation of Christians meeting in an Evangelical Church, should take upon their lips as an adequate expression of faith the creed of the foremost scientist of the generation." There are allusive hints in the record that Fosdick retained a lifelong interest in psychical research, as did a number of prominent Protestant churchmen.

In *The Living of These Days* Fosdick left a moving account of how in Montclair he gradually, painfully, experimentally achieved a new understanding of preaching. "Every sermon," reads a linchpin sentence, "should have for its main business the head-on constructive meeting of some problem which was puzzling the minds, burdening consciences, distracting lives, and no sermon which so met a real human difficulty, with light to throw on it and help to win a victory over it, could possibly be futile." To prepare such sermons he began a practice to which he adhered throughout his life. He rented a phoneless room in a downtown bank and here he secluded himself in study for four hours every morning five days a week. "Only once in many years," he reported, "did anything important enough happen to cause my wife to come down and disturb me." On another instance he confessed that even the Angel Gabriel would have had a hard time getting a morning appointment.

In this practice Fosdick was wise. If the preacher is given grace, if his vision is on rare occasions transcendent, soaring on the wings of inspiration, it is nevertheless to his intellect that he must finally return. Without the discipline of hard study, preaching becomes raving. Without the wisdom that comes from sustained reflection, it becomes banal. And without abrasive encounter with science and scholarship, it becomes irrelevant. That is why Fosdick concurred in J. H. Jowett's oft-quoted warning, "If the study is a lounge, the pulpit is an impertinence."

Once outside the study Fosdick did not wear the scholar's scowl. Old-timers confirm the accuracy of contemporary descriptions of his "gloom-dispelling nature," "genial spirit," "charm of temperament," "stalwart, dynamic, commanding appearance." He was described at the time and remembered in retrospect as "a good fellow" who was "beloved of the young people" and "most affectionately admired and esteemed" by the adults. One parishioner recalled that at the final congregational meeting where sadness at the parting prevailed, Fosdick went from individual to individual crying, "O, I love you all, I love you all!" His successor, Arthur C. Baldwin, reminisced honestly that Fosdick's winning personality had conquered many hearts. "He loved people, they told me. My manners were an unhappy contrast. When he stood at the church door to shake hands as the people went out there was never a sign of weariness, no wavering of the eye to the one who followed. 'He talked to you as though you were the only one.' "

IV

Fosdick's energies and concerns combined to thrust him into Montclair's civic problems. And why not, believing as he then did that the "future belongs not to the city but to the suburb." The populations of large cities, he argued, are almost hopelessly split by differences of race, creed, speech, and interest. The churches have a hard time to make their influence felt in New York or Chicago. "But there is no excuse for this failure in the suburbs," he continued. "The population there is generally homogeneous; each community achieves its own kind of folk; social distinctions are easily bridged; racial divisions are generally negligible; and a large proportion of the people have a background of religious tradition. What an incomparable opportunity to show what Christianity can do when practically applied to the civic, social, and philanthropic life of a community!" On moving to New York, he naturally whistled a different tune. And his generalizations about easily bridged social distinctions and generally negligible racial divisions were, of course, not strictly true even of Montclair.

In 1940 *Current Biography* carried this description of Fosdick's Montclair activities: "One night he might be leading their women's clubs in a fight against the threat of Sunday movies, another week, campaigning against gambling over the bridge table. Once he joined four other ministers in a gymnasium class, and the New York papers published a picture with the heading: 'Five Muscular Christians.' For the most part, he tried to be that." Fosdick shot a testy corrective note to the publishers, denying the antimovie, antibridge crusades. "My ministry in Montclair would be more factually treated if you said . . . 'He did lead a campaign against the town's saloon, but in general his ministry was quiet. A new building was erected for the church, and the membership was trebled.' " What does the record reveal? Nothing one way or another about the bridge question, but quite a bit about the movie and saloon issues.

Initially, in 1911, Fosdick stood firm against the "photo-play invasion," urging the Town Council to reject the license applications for opening a moving picture theatre. He then saw the wisdom of "properly regulated exhibitions" that "would obviate the necessity of young people going to Newark, where temptation assails them," The *Montclair Times* supported the innovation, noting that Montclair was about the only town in the nation without a theatre and the crying need for "a ripple of diversion from the dead level of its life here at home." On April 8, 1911, the *Montclair Times* carried a long letter from Fosdick setting forth "Conditions On Which Moving Picture Shows Should Be Licensed." The conditions are both stern and amusing, including: no garish exterior signs; the interiors so well lighted that it would be possible to read with comfort or recognize the faces of one's friends across the hall; no trashy vaudeville and to be safe no vaudeville at all; no exhibit during school hours; and a citizens' censorship committee because Montclair "might well stand for a finer sieving of the picture than is possible to a board that censors reels for the entire country." Subsequently Fosdick argued that the license be granted to a company, the chief officers of which were nationally prominent clergymen, W. D. P. Bliss and Josiah Strong, whose assurances to him that they would present only uplifting features he shared with the Town Council and the newspaper readers!

Three years earlier New York City's Mayor George B. McClellan had revoked 550 movie licenses until the owners agreed to similar conditions. McClellan's action was in response to the call of every Protestant denomination in the city, all fearful that the movie houses and nickelodeons were corrupting minds and subverting Anglo-Saxon moral and cultural values. One has the uneasy feeling that Fosdick took a "progressive" position, but one so cautious as not to disturb the nice-nelly standards of the good matrons of Montclair; and that in fact he shared their fears that films were alien inspired. Only reluctantly could he bring himself to permit movies in his community and only then under severe regulation by the "better elements." The "lower elements" responded: "Do not uplift me when I go to the moving picture show." At that time, it is worth remembering, the price of an opera ticket in New York was $5; for the legitimate theatre, $1; for the movies, a nickel or dime. Little wonder that the silent films drew the non-English-speaking immigrants and the working classes.*

The saloon question was of far greater intensity to Fosdick personally and Montclair's citizenry generally. The factual situation is reasonably clear. Midway in Fosdick's ministry Montclair had eight licensed saloons, two grocery stores licensed to sell liquor by the bottle, and one wholesale bottling establishment. The saloons were almost all in working-class neighborhoods; there was none in the First Ward—the silk-stocking ward—the farthest from the saloon areas. Yet it was from the First Ward fortress that the prohibitionists sallied to force the unconditioned

---

* The problem with this regnant socioeconomic interpretation is that it ignores the ban on moviegoing then and today by all Pentecostal and Holiness sects whose members are certainly not from the patrician classes.

surrender of their Wet foes. The Episcopal and Roman Catholic churches did not join the crusade, although locally and nationally, individual lay-persons and priests, especially among the Irish Catholics, were ardently opposed to ardent spirits. The black preachers with their women parishioners as allies did join the crusade and locally and nationally so did some black men, including Booker T. Washington. The antisaloon forces would not immediately touch High Society's private clubs, where liquor was openly dispensed or kept in lockers, but the crusaders were not hypocrites and certainly they planned in time to advance on the privileged as well.

Fosdick's position is unequivocal: he sought a Montclair as dry as a powder flask. He and the revered Congregational minister, Dr. Amory Bradford, led the fight so that when "the existing liquor licenses expire, no renewal and no licenses of any kind should be issued within the town limits." Until that grateful expiration day, Fosdick and Bradford petitioned the Town Council to command that the saloon doors be closed at ten o'clock every night except Saturday when the hour would be seven (the beginning of the Sabbath), and entirely on the Sabbath and on holidays. Fosdick's exertions were vigorous and varied. The Anti-Saloon League and the W.C.T.U. held rallies in his church; his parishioners signed petitions; he delivered prohibition screeds; he penned statements to the newspaper; and he appeared before the Town Council advocating in a "resolute, rattling, go ahead fashion."

Fosdick shared the widespread and growing conviction of the early twentieth century, held by liberal and conservative church people alike and by secular progressives as well, that the personal and civic consequences of alcoholic consumption were beyond tragedy. Therefore, the manufacturing, sale, and consumption of all forms of alcohol must be placed under the ban of law. The question of personal liberty was no more relevant than in the arguments conservatives advanced against pure food and drug laws or child labor restrictions or safety and sanitary codes. Paraphrasing Reinhold Niebuhr's famous aphorism, Fosdick held man's capacity for virtue made prohibition possible, but his inclination to excess made it necessary. Fosdick was no sour-visaged killjoy haunted by the fear, as in Mencken's jibe, that someone, somewhere might be happy. Rather, he agreed with the Northern Methodist bishops when they declared that they opposed liquor not because drinking made men happy, but because it made them unhappy.

All very well, and possibly even good. What does not go down smoothly is the class-based nature of the antisaloon movement in Montclair and the nation. It was a reform by which all Americans of whatever varying ethnic strains and diverse cultural backgrounds would be regenerated in the bourgeois mold—which meant, inevitably, that German-Americans would be expected to give up their beer and beer gardens and Italian-Americans their wine and trattorias and Greek-Americans their ouzo and tavernas and Mexican-Americans their tequila and cantinas and Irish-Americans their whiskey and pubs. Observed one student of the prohibition movement: "The saloon and the drinker increasingly appeared to the Protestant middle class, both urban and rural, as a symbol of a culture alien to the ascetic character of American values. What was important was not so much that people drank but that they upheld the validity and the rightness of liquor and beer within the accepted way of life." Fosdick's "disinterested benevolence" assumed a blessed self-giving elite and benighted lessers waiting to be uplifted. In this relationship there is sacrifice and service on the part of the elite, but no mutuality. The intended result of the antisaloon crusade was to make all Montclair citizens sober, but not to establish a community of equal brothers respecting each others' diversity.

Naturally, Fosdick's community involvement was not confined to the issues of movies and saloons. He was chaplain of the chapter of the Sons of the American Revolution, chairman of a religious survey committee, active in the Men and Religion Forward Movement, and leading member of the prewar Community Peace Committee. He urged the Civic Association to provide at least one decent playground for children and supported a Bible School Athletic League that "would aid in solving the 'boy problem.' " He was repeatedly sent to the annual meetings of the New Jersey Baptist Convention, in 1911 serving as a moderator. He was much in demand as a toastmaster and public speaker, "thrilling" audiences with his "earnestness." On two occasions he gave the high school commencement address, in 1906 admonishing the graduates: "Consecrate yourself to the service of your fellow man. There are enough of shriveled souls in our moral morgues who have perished between selfishness and service." Midway in his 1915 commencement address he referred to an individual as being "as black as the ace of spades," and then turned to the principal seated on the platform and inquired solemnly, "A spade *is* black, isn't it?" Inasmuch as there were cards in Fosdick's boyhood home, the question may have been motivated by his relentless determination to preserve his image.*

A project close to Fosdick's heart was a neighborhood house in the Fourth District supported by the Sons of the American Revolution and

---

* Or was it? A wise and charitable individual on reading these lines suggested that was an example of Fosdick's wit. Maybe so, but the person who related the story was in the graduation audience and she assumed at the time that Fosdick was being serious, not humorous.

the Daughters of the American Revolution. The two women social workers for the project were augmented by twenty volunteer workers from
the two groups. "With the American influence of these workers coming
into contact with the Italian and Negro population of that district," Fosdick reported, "beneficial results must eventually follow." Among the
many activities were illustrated lectures, at least half in Italian, "with the
object of educating our foreign population in the duties of citizenship
and character of American institutions." Moreover, there were civic and
cooking classes; singing, dance, and military clubs; and a lending library.
At that time a newspaper happily reported on the ministry of Father
Paul Lisa to the Italian population "because if he succeeds in making
Italians good Christians, it follows naturally they will make good citizens." Avoiding the extremes of naiveté and cynicism, one may honor
the compassion and idealism fueling Fosdick's concern for Montclair's
lower classes and still discern the strain of fear and assumption of cultural superiority in his neighborhood-house activities.

V

If Fosdick's heritage gave a flavor of noblesse oblige to some of his community views, the absence of economic privilege in his background allowed him to have an attitude toward Montclair's working classes that
was sensitive to their needs and rights.

His interest in labor questions is attested by his winning the M.A.
degree under the Faculty of Political Science from Columbia University
in 1908. Commuting to New York on a three-year program, he carried
courses in Communistic and Socialistic Theories, Theories of Social Reform, Principles of Sociology, Social Evolution, Fiscal and Industrial
History of the United States, and Railroad Problems. His professors
were among the most distinguished social scientists in the nation: John
Bates Clark, Franklin H. Giddings, and Edwin R. A. Seligman. His thesis,
"The Trades-Unionism of a Suburban Town," is a field study of the labor movement in Montclair. There was only one small factory, and
Montclair's roughly one thousand union members were overwhelmingly
organized around the building trades. There was also a typographical
union. Fosdick's plea for the end of strife between management and labor
and the necessity of the two groups to recognize the "larger community
of interest" and join in cooperation is unexceptional. But at least the
study is not prejudiced by a bourgeois bias against unions. Moreover,
the research, largely consisting of interviews, brought him into association with union leaders. One spin-off from these personal contacts was

Fosdick's role in launching a social club for the union men of the town. It of course folded. As Fosdick plaintively, yet correctly, observed: "Even 'progressive euchre!' has failed to get the men out, and the lounging rooms are little frequented. The reason is unanimously ascribed to the diversity of elements making social sympathy incomplete. The newly arrived immigrant from Italy and the son of an old New England family may have the same economic interest, but that does not mean they make good club fellows." A second possible unvoiced reason is that the workers felt more at ease in their neighborhood saloons than in a social club "in a prominent place on Montclair Centre." Still, the thesis broadened Fosdick's horizons, and when run serially in the *Montclair Times*, it must have been of educative value to the citizenry.

Several other things suggest the sincerity of Fosdick's concern. The dedication services for the new church included an evening program "held in recognition of the men who labored on the building and their companions among the ranks of working men," and the affair included an address by a union organizer. On another instance a walking delegate was quoted by the newspaper as remarking that "the best presentation of the laboring man's point of view he ever heard was by Mr. Fosdick in the pulpit of the First Baptist Church." Such, however, was the class orientation of Protestant congregations, Fosdick made no gains in bringing union men into the church's fellowship, save in the case of the head of the carpenters' union.

Consider also this instance of Fosdick's courageous concern. In 1910 the *Los Angeles Times* building was sabotaged by a blast of dynamite. Twenty-one persons were killed; property damage was huge. Among those arrested for the deed were J. B. McNamara and his brother. At the start of the trial in October 1911, Fosdick said publicly in conservative Montclair that even supposing McNamara was guilty, at least he freely risked his own life to serve a cause in which he sacrificially believed. "This also should be kept in mind," he added, "that McNamara could have used his dynamite bombs for a century and not done such widespread or subtle harm, nor have been responsible for so many suicides, or caused so much financial loss, as a man like Jay Gould was guilty of in a single week." Fosdick then charged men of "high finance" with the crimes of bribery, corruption, ruthlessness, chicanery. He continued: "Men are in rebellion and the men who rebel are always first of all the men who are down. Oftentimes ignorant and brutal men, they reach out for the first weapons they can find. Those weapons may be dynamite bombs, but if they are the only things in reach those dynamite bombs will be used. The multi-millionaires can bribe, the McNamaras can only blow up factories. Each side uses its own weapons, and typhoid fever is not less dangerous than a bludgeon. Now in this situation the preaching of the Gospel by word of mouth only, by hymns and anthems, is, for a large percentage of the people, futile." These words might have been spoken by Walter Rauschenbusch, the great Baptist prophet whose books then appearing helped sharpen Fosdick's social sensitivity and to whom Fosdick was later to pay handsome tributes in Benson Landis's *A Rauschenbusch Reader* and Dores Sharpe's *Walter Rauschenbusch*.

In 1912 Fosdick again faced conservative disapproval when at a mass meeting he supported the candidacy of Theodore Roosevelt running on the Progressive party ticket; T.R. had bolted the Republican party convention, roared that he felt like a Bull Moose, sang with his followers (including George Perkins of the House of Morgan) "Onward Christian Soldiers," and stood at Armageddon to do battle for the Lord. As a Republican, Fosdick could not bring himself to support the Democratic candidate, although he knew Woodrow Wilson personally. But neither could he swallow the less progressive Republican candidate, William Howard Taft.

In that election year a textile strike broke out in Lawrence, Massachusetts, lasting ten weeks and involving twenty-five thousand foreign-born and unskilled workers—men, women, and children—who were unorganized until the Industrial Workers of the World led by "Big Bill" Haywood arrived to provide militant, disciplined, wise, and courageous leadership. It was one of the most dramatic strikes in the annals of American labor, a magnificent tribute to the fortitude of oppressed toilers and a brilliant victory for Wobbly tactics. "It is the first strike I ever saw which sang," reported Ray Stannard Baker. "Lawrence was not an ordinary strike. It was a social revolution *in parvo*," judged one historian of syndicalism. However ephemeral the workers' gains, the struggle gave birth to the enduring lines: "Hearts starve as well as bodies / Give us bread, but give us roses."

Fosdick was commissioned by *Outlook* to cover the aftermath of the strike, which he did in an article appearing in the June 15 issue. It is remarkably sympathetic to the workers and the Wobbly leaders. To be sure, Fosdick pays the mill owners more than their just due, and he fails vividly to depict the desperate mill and living conditions of the workers. These points aside, however, he aligns with the laborers. Their grievances were real. They were treated like "dumb cattle." The issue for them was "hunger and food, life and death." After an initial, spontaneous surge of violence, reported Fosdick, the strikers, under great provocation, exercised praiseworthy restraint. Concurrently, they were the victims of outrageous extralegal action at the hands of the authorities. The jailed Wobbly leaders were patently railroaded. Bourgeois opinion in Massachusetts was obtuse: "The nobility of France before the Revolution could not have been more blind to the situation than some of the Bostonese." The I.W.W., however, "stepped to the front, assumed the leadership of the disorganized mob, and in one of the most skillfully engineered labor campaigns in our industrial history held together twenty-thousand-odd strikers, speaking some forty different languages and dialects, and won a campaign that raised wages of nearly four hundred thousand textile operatives all over New England." The article closes: "More than anything else . . . the problem of industrial democracy is here, irrepressible in its demand that the tool-users shall not be forever in one class and the tool-owners in another." He left Lawrence, he later recalled, "boiling with indignation at the gross betrayal of all that democracy stands for which the factories in Lawrence illustrated."

Fosdick refers to the article in his autobiography. In this summary he states of the I.W.W. that "we should call them communists now" and charges the jailed leader, Joe Ettor, with "proclaiming what we now think of as Russian communism." This is of course inaccurate. The free-spirited syndicalism of the Wobblies may not remotely be equated with the "Russian Communism" of Lenin and Stalin.

VI

An important chapter in the American religious story, one almost forgotten now, is that of the student conferences that blanketed the land early in the century and attracted tens of thousands of the nation's reverent young people. Assemblies at such camps as Northfield (Massachusetts) and Silver Bay (New York), they studied, played, and listened in hushed excitement to the intense evangelical, missionary, and ethical appeals of John R. Mott, Robert E. Speer, Sherwood Eddy, and a legion of other lay and ministerial speakers. Fosdick was with increasing frequency invited to be a study leader and speaker, at first in the northeast and then at conferences across the country. Sixty years later there were individuals who still remembered studying the life of Jesus with Fosdick at Silver Bay and thrilling to "The Second Mile," given at Northfield in 1907. The associations he made at these conferences with leaders of the stature of Mott, Speer, and Eddy were extremely important to the advancement of his career. At this time also he first met the later great socialist and pacifist leader, Norman Thomas, and preached at Thomas's East Harlem church.

Fosdick also received invitations to preach on college campuses, about as stern a challenge imaginable—"a modern form of being thrown to the lions" to borrow the analogy of the dean of the Harvard Chapel. It was not long before Fosdick was almost annually appearing in the chapels of Cornell, Brown, Harvard, Yale, Chicago, even west to Stanford and south to the Southern Baptist institution, Wake Forest. There is a certain irony in the fact that Wake Forest awarded Fosdick his first honorary doctor of divinity degree in 1912 (two years before Colgate did so) in light of the fact that later many Southern Baptist clergy would dare to listen only clandestinely to the "heretic's" radio sermons.

VII

During the Montclair years Fosdick's voice brought him a modest measure of national recognition, but it was his pen that brought him fame. The first article accepted for publication, "Heckling the Church," appeared in the *Atlantic Monthly*, December 1911. There followed others in such magazines as the *North American Review*.

However, it was not the articles, but six books, that firmly established his name on both sides of the Atlantic: *The Second Mile, The Assurance of Immortality, The Manhood of the Master, The Meaning of Prayer, The Meaning of Faith,* and *The Meaning of Service.* In 1953 Reinhold Niebuhr, assessing Fosdick's significance in American religious thought, judged that these little books "probably exercised more influence in their generation than any other religious volumes. Their sale ran into millions; and for all I know it still continues, for several of them at least are not 'dated' in any way."

One evening in the spring of 1907 Fosdick spoke on "The Glory of the Second Mile" and again on that same topic at a conference that summer. Frederick Harris of the Association Press encouraged him to expand the talk for publication and in 1908 *The Second Mile*, a 52-page volume, appeared. It remained in circulation for over a half-century and enjoyed at least twenty-five reprintings. As late as 1944 *Reader's Digest* carried a condensation. Its message is that it is a vice in our goodness not to do more than is requested in every area of life. "Love is not love until it has forgotten rules. The Christian's 'royal law' fulfills all lesser laws like the Atlantic flowing into the Bay of Fundy when the sky calls to the tide." This beautifully written essay remains to this day inspiring.

The Assurance of Immortality, published by Macmillan in 1913, marks Fosdick's emergence as a Christian apologist. It, too, had its origin in a series of Sunday evening sermons, and it, too, enjoyed much continuing success and many reprintings. Fosdick's view of immortality will be examined later in the context of his theology, so it is perhaps sufficient to note here that *Assurance* consists of three lengthy chapters in which Fosdick insists on the importance of the subject to Christian belief, demonstrates the inconclusive nature of the arguments commonly urged against a future life, and presents the positive reasons for a modern man's assurance that death does not end all. The concluding sentences read: "Death is a great advanture, but none need go unconvinced that there is an issue to it. The man of faith may face it as Columbus faced his first voyage from the shores of Spain. What lies across the sea, he cannot tell; his special expectations all may be mistaken; but his insight into the clear meanings of present facts may persuade him beyond doubt that the sea has another shore. Such confident faith, so founded upon reasonable grounds, shall be turned to sight, when, for all the dismay of the unbelieving, the hope of the seers is rewarded by the vision of a new continent."

The Manhood of the Master grew out of a series of lectures and discussions in the Men's Bible Class and was published by the Association Press in 1913. In its pages the various facets of the Master's character are examined: His joy, magnanimity, indignation, loyalty, endurance, sincerity, self-restraint, fearlessness, affection, scale of values, spirit, concluding with "the measure of the stature of the fulness of Christ." It is devotional in intent, combining daily readings from the Gospels with daily comments and a more extended "Comment for the Week." This design permitted its use by both individuals keeping Morning Watch and Bible study groups. The character of Jesus is set forth as the ideal by which we measure our own character. It is an inspirational little volume, though some of Fosdick's Panglossian commentaries could only have been written before the guns of August 1914. Still, thousands of paperback copies were distributed to soldiers in the American and British services who in their peril found courage and comfort in the book. The later famed English preacher Leslie Weatherhead, campaigning in Mesopotamia, carried a copy with him and was profoundly grateful. Mahatma Gandhi, experiencing the different ordeal of imprisonment, was also sustained by it. Ultimately, it was translated into many languages, including Coptic, Arabic, and Tamil, and it went through many editions, including more than twenty in Britain alone, giving point to the repeated statement that Fosdick's "many books have a wider circulation on our side of the Atlantic than those of any other American divine."

The Meaning of Prayer came out during the last year of Fosdick's Montclair ministry. It would be followed by companion works in 1917 and 1920, *The Meaning of Faith* and *The Meaning of Service*. This trilogy was later brought together under the titles *The Three Meanings* and *The Meaning of Being a Christian*. Read by millions, translated into some fifty languages, these may soberly be argued to be true classics, the most enduring of all Fosdick's volumes. Fosdick was flooded with letters on the occasions of his seventy-fifth and ninetieth birthdays; the well-wishers seem to express their gratitude for the three *Meanings* more frequently than for any of Fosdick's other works. Among the correspondents were those who read them on their first appearing and those encountering them for the first time in the 1950s. Missionaries acknowledged the helpfulness of the little volumes to them in their labors. Liberals who had made the transition from fundamentalism stated the books had saved their Christianity. Even unbowed conservatives had words of praise, especially for *The Meaning of Prayer*, the work Fosdick himself termed "my most influential book." Union Seminary's Professor John Knox said of the trilogy, "No finer books on the meaning of Christian devotion have been written in the last several generations."

When Fosdick announced to his Montclair parishioners a series of six sermons on prayer he did not dream of a book as a consequence. The eagerness of the response, however, led to a series of midweek discussions at which his people spoke of their experiences, difficulties, doubts, and victories. He began to see why the disciples said to Jesus, "Lord, teach us to pray." So, on the Maine coast one summer holiday he set down what really seemed true to him about prayer, not so much for the public as for himself. He tested out the results on his Union students and finally in 1915 the book appeared, with an introduction by John R. Mott. Future Union president Roger Shinn spoke for multitudes when he recalled that from this book "I learned to pray with Augustine, Anselm, Thomas Aquinas, Martin Luther, Christina Rossetti, Walter Rauschenbusch, and Fosdick."

The book devotes a week of study to each of ten subjects: the naturalness of prayer, prayer as communion with God, God's care for the individual, prayer and the goodness of God, hindrances and difficulties, prayer and the reign of law, unanswered prayer, prayer as dominant desire, prayer as a battlefield, unselfishness in prayer. For each of seven days there is printed a Bible passage preceded by some words of introduction and followed by an explication of the relation of the passage to the subject of the week. Then a prayer selected for its special bearing on the passage is quoted. At the end of each week there is an essay called "Comment for the Week" that deals as fully as possible with all aspects of the week's subject. Last of all, the points that have arisen during the week are brought together in a number of questions as "suggestions for thought and discussion." It is a format admirably suited for both personal devotions and group study. Fosdick is concerned to show the reasonableness of prayer—and more, the inevitability of prayer. The bibliography shows that Fosdick studied the question deeply as well as drawing on his own experiences with prayer, especially, perhaps, during his breakdown, when the assurance came to him: "If God is, he cares; if he cares, he cares for personality." "Prayer is the soul of religion" and "failure in prayer is the loss of religion itself." Men complain, Fosdick observed, that because God is not real to them, they do not pray, whereas it would be truer to say that because men do not pray, God is not real.

The Meaning of Faith reveals Fosdick's continuing concern with apologetics, the endeavor to present a reasonable, credible, defensible interpretation of the Christian gospel. "It came boiling up out of the stir of my own spirit," he reported. "It was as easily readable a statement as I knew how to make concerning some of the questions about faith's meaning that bothered me and that I was sure must bother others." Although impersonal in form, it is, he said, "autobiographical in fact." The format is similar to *The Meaning of Prayer*: daily readings, commentaries, and prayers, each of the twelve chapters concluding with a "Comment for the Week." Fosdick again assumes the inevitability of faith ("There are certain basic elements in man which make it impossible to live without faith") before demonstrating the reasonableness of the Christian faith. There are the Fosdickian epigrams: "A God who does not care does not count." And the Fosdickian bite: "Of all the sentiments . . . by which a worthy faith is made impossible, none is so common, in these recent years, as the ascription to God of a weak and flaccid affectionateness." And also the Fosdickian optative mood: "To call our time an 'Age of Doubt' because of its free spirit of critical inquiry, is seriously to misunderstand its major drift. Bunyan's Pilgrim found Doubting Castle kept by Giant Despair and his wife Diffidence and in any Doubting Castle these two always dwell. But who, considering our generation's life as a whole, would call it diffident or desperate? It is rather robust and confident; its social faiths, at least, are unprecedented in their sweep and certainty. Even the Great War is the occasion of such organized faith in a federated and fraternal world as mankind has never entertained before." And finally the Fosdickian inspirational message: "The Master's call 'you can' is answered by the human cry 'I will,' and the man moves out into new possibilities, new powers, and increasing liberty."

Quite unlike the volume on prayer, *Faith* drew the sharp criticism of conservatives who widely employed the term "Unitarian" to define Fosdick's position. Unfazed, he responded vigorously to one Presbyterian reviewer: "I am well aware of the deep aversion with which you regard my interpretation of Christianity but I assure you it does not in the least surpass the profound aversion with which I regard your interpretation of Christianity." Meanwhile, sales surged at home and abroad, G. Bromley Oxnam in India sending a copy to his sister with the note, "It is the best putting of the whole case of religion I have ever read, Sis, and put by one of the sanest and widest read men on this side of the [liberal] fence." In 1960 a missionary recalled digging away at the Chinese translation years before and how helpful the volume had been to him and to some of the younger Chinese, adding: "People may talk as if time has made a great deal of ancient good uncouth, and probably it has. But that . . . little book could be read and pondered to their great benefit, I am sure, by a lot of people who like to look down their noses at anything in the realm of religious literature which antedates Karl Barth or Reinhold Niebuhr or Paul Tillich. . . . I am sure *The Meaning of Faith* still speaks to our human condition." Indeed it does, despite the dated allusions, inspirational tone, and exultant mood. Donald Lee put the case fairly when *Faith* was reprinted: "In an age when it is so easy to believe that there is little that can be done, either about man and his sin, or about the plight of the world, Fosdick still speaks to our disenchantment, encouraging us to an 'optimism of grace' which, though we think we perceive more of tragedy in our 'troubles' than he did, leads us once more to expect great things from God."

The Meaning of Service completed the trilogy. Similar in format to the preceding works, it "is a study in the practical overflow of Christian life in useful ministry." Though the practical and ethical had never been absent from Fosdick's concern, and the theological and apologetic would never be totally or permanently abandoned, *Service* does represent a shift of emphasis away from devotional themes and toward the application of the Christian faith to social problems. Because a discussion of these problems belongs more properly to later chapters, we shall only note here that *Service* in its *specifics* seems more dated than either *Prayer* or *Faith;* yet the larger issue of religion's relationship to the social order remains to challenge Christians today.

VIII

The more thoughtful members of the First Baptist Church had long known that their minister could not be contained indefinitely in Montclair, yet when in April 1915 Fosdick suddenly announced his resignation, to take effect the last Sunday in June, with the exception of a few insiders, the congregation was stunned. His words of affection for his flock were sincere; their resolution of appreciation and love equally so. In his "Farewell" sermon Fosdick compared his position to that of Paul, exactly as he was to do under far more dramatic circumstances ten years later in New York. If the short notice—only two months—occasioned any bitterness, it is not found in the written records or memories of the living. To the contrary, the surviving evidence is unambigious: Fosdick was loyal to the church and the flock remained loyal to their former shepherd. Tellingly, in 1947 Fosdick returned to fill without compensation the Montclair pulpit when the church was temporarily between ministers.

IX

Fosdick was in a position to resign from his Montclair pulpit because Union Theological Seminary had promoted him from associate professor of Homiletics to the newly established Morris K. Jesup professorship of Practical Theology to provide for the teaching of the English Bible. (He had first joined the Union faculty as a lecturer in 1908, followed by promotion to instructor in 1911.) Fosdick's powerful inaugural address is entitled, "A Modern Preacher's Problem in His Use of the Scriptures." The address pounds home the points: "The glory of the Scriptures in the Church has always been their preachableness"; "By nature and by habitual use this book belongs to the preacher"; the Bible must "be preached, and repreached, and preached again as long as the world stands"; "May God help us all to make this school of the prophets a fountain of such preaching in the Church!"

Chapter Five

"The Challenge of the Present Crisis": The Great Crusade, 1917–1918

I

"I say God damn the wars—all wars: God damn every war: God damn 'em! God damn 'em!" Fosdick quotes Walt Whitman's litany at the conclusion of this unflinching passage depicting the horrors of the Great War:

> War is not the gay color, the rhythmic movement, the thrilling music of the military parade. War is not even killing gallantly as knights once did, matched evenly in armor and in steed and fighting by the rules of chivalry. War is now dropping bombs from aeroplanes and killing women and children in their beds; it is shooting by telephonic orders, at an unseen place miles away and slaughtering invisible men; it is murdering innocent travelers on merchant ships with torpedoes from unknown submarines, it is launching clouds of poisoned gas and slaying men with their own breath. War means lying days and nights wounded and alone in No-Man's Land; it means men with jaws gone, eyes gone, limbs gone, minds gone; it means countless bodies of boys tossed into the incinerators that follow in the train of every battle; it means prison camps vicious with the inevitable results of enforced idleness; it means untended wounds and gangrene and the long time it takes to die; it means mothers who look for letters they will never see and wives who wait for voices they will never hear and children who listen for footsteps that will never come. That is war—'Its heroisms are but the glancing sunlight on a sea of blood and tears'—and a man who calls it glorious is mad.

A few pages on Fosdick pictures Marshal Joffre reading aloud "with unsteady voice" a well-worn letter written by a French mother to her son in Canada:

MY DEAR BOY: You will be grieved to learn that your two brothers have been killed. Their country needed them and they gave everything that they had to save her. Your country needs you, and while I am not going to suggest that you return to fight for France, if you do not return at once, *never* come.

Fosdick, oblivous to the cruel, bloodthirsty, and self-congratulatory in the letter, follows it with the volume's final passage:

Multitudes are living in that spirit today. He must have a callous soul who can pass through times like these and not hear a voice, whose call a man must answer, or else lose his soul. Your country needs *you.* The Kingdom of God on earth needs *you.* The Cause of Christ is hard bestead and righteousness is having a heavy battle in the earth—they need *you.*

These quotations are from *The Challenge of the Present Crisis*, a little volume written shortly after America's intervention, which was intended to uplift the morale of the people and to justify, if only in his own mind, Fosdick's early and ardent espousal of a great crusade to succor the Allies and crush Imperial Germany. Fosdick, with Whitman, damns war. His description of the Western Front is Goyaesque. Yet ultimately he wills for the American people both the endurance and the further infliction of this suffering. How can this be? What forces, interior and exterior, compelled him first to advocate and then to extol America's involvement in the new century's first holocaust? By attending closely to Fosdick's words and deeds we hope in this chapter to resolve this question and, in so doing, come to a more intimate understanding of the man and his ideals and illusions.

II

When the guns of Europe erupted in August 1914, Mrs. Asquith, the wife of the British prime minister, remembered that at that moment "I got up and leaned my head against his, and we could not speak for tears." All humanity had cause to weep as the finest young men of a generation went out to "wrestle with cinders." The survivors, some of them, would come to see the war as beyond tragedy, employing such ironic metaphors for the Western Front as lunatic asylum, manic music hall, or theatre of the absurd. In April 1917, after thirty-two months of attempted neutrality, President Wilson appealed to Congress to declare war: "We have no selfish ends to serve. We desire no conquest, no dominion. We seek no indemnities for ourselves, no material compensations for the sacrifices we shall freely make. We are but one of the champions of the rights of mankind." Europe's agony was now also America's agony.

The anguish this decision cost Wilson was not shared by Fosdick, for, unlike the President, since the beginning of hostilities Fosdick had advocated America's entry. From New Jersey to California he preached sermons on "Things Worth Fighting For." He excoriated Wilson for being "too proud to fight," scolded the Republican presidential candidate in 1916, Charles Evans Hughes, for not definitely promising to take America in, and joined a band of clergy in a public statement protesting "any attempt to promote a premature peace in Europe," holding that the "memory of all the saints and martyrs cries out against such backsliding of mankind. Sad is our lot if we have forgotten how to die for a holy cause."

The prewar American peace movement cherished the illusion that peace would be perpetual, war being plainly an irrational tribal anachronism in the law-governed, scientifically enlightened, morally quickened twentieth century. Into this world of progress, peace, and human amelioration, recalled Lewis Mumford, Sarajevo "came like a baleful meteor from outer space." The British foreign minister, Sir Edward Grey, at that agonizing moment stared into the gathering London dusk and murmured, "The lamps are going out all over Europe; we shall not see them lit again in our lifetime." Still, in 1914 and probably as late as early 1917, the great majority of the American people believed it was the duty of the United States to remain at peace, tending the lamps of civilization so that at the last the Old World might rekindle her lamps from those that remained burning in the New. Fosdick's early advocacy of intervention cannot be explained as simply part of a larger tendency within American liberal Protestantism. To the contrary, few liberal preachers were found in the forefront of the preparedness campaign and in this context Fosdick's posture is idiosyncratic. How then are we to understand his interventionism?

For one thing, he was an Anglophile. It is not simply that his ancestors like those of his wife had come from England. Nor is it that the Anglo-American rapprochement antedating 1914 seemingly served America's realistic self-interests. More important is Fosdick's deep absorption in, and total devotion to, British high culture and institutions. When the land of Shakespeare, Bunyan, Tennyson, Milton, Cromwell, and Gladstone became imperiled, his alarm was reflexive.

A second consideration is to recall that Fosdick was not in 1914 a pacifist, nor were many Americans other than members of the historic peace sects, the Quakers, Mennonites, and Brethren. Such organizations as the Carnegie Endowment for International Peace, the Church Peace Union, the American School Peace League, and the older, reviving American Peace Society placed their hopes in human reason, working through arbitration and international law, and in the capacity of moral men animated by pure love to convert wicked men to righteousness, rather than in absolute obedience to the New Testament command that evil should not be returned with evil. Inevitably the conditional, prudential, and fuzzy foundations of their peace convictions melted away in the furnace of the Great War. These peacemakers were, moreover, solid nationalists; for them America's virtues were unique and her interests paramount. If the nation should go to war, they believed, its democratic politics and humanitarian traditions would guarantee that its cause must be just and necessary.

Fosdick saw no tension between true patriotism and New Testament Christianity; both demanded service to one's fellow man, self-sacrifice, loyalty to high ideals, manly courage. His little volume *The Second Mile* explicitly elaborated this theme and implicitly justified wars conducted with forgiveness and fought for noble ends. His little volume *The Assurance of Immortality* played a note he was to sound again and again: the essence of a person is his deathless soul, not his mortal body, and this essence is inviolate, even on the battlefield. "Personal character is an eternal matter, the one means by which the universe can preserve its moral gains. The infinite value of personality which immortality asserts, makes any fight for social justice worthwhile." By extension, for an American boy in a just war to take the physical life of a German boy was made palatable by "the assurance of immortality." His little volume *The Manhood of the Master* depicted a virile Jesus who, though overflowing with goodwill, took scourge in hand over the evils of his day. A year before America's entry, Fosdick instructed a New York congregation of the challenge facing America, the challenge of an "unfinished task" (not to be prematurely terminated by a negotiated peace) "which should be met with courage rather than despair." Surely Fosdick's religious beliefs meshed with Wilson's idealism when the president asked, "Why is it that all nations turn to us with the instinctive feeling that if anything touches humanity it touches us?" He answered, "Because it knows that ever since we were born as a Nation we have undertaken to be the champions of humanity and the rights of men." And when Wilson finally drew the sword Fosdick raised the prayer:

We have grown weary, to the sickness of our souls, sitting comfortably here, while others pour their blood like water forth for those things alone which can make this earth a decent place for men to live upon. . . . And now we lay our hand upon the sword. Since we must draw it, O God, help us to play the man and to do our part in teaching ruthlessness once for all what it means to wake the sleeping lion of humanity's conscience.

For a fourth consideration, we can take as our text a passage from an untitled sermon preached by Fosdick on November 28, 1918:

We never were so excited about anything in our whole lives as we have been about this war, we never felt the deeps within us, the passion for sacrifice, as during this war. It has touched chords in our hearts that nothing but fight has fingers strong enough to get music from. Do you know one thing, that in abolishing war you cannot abolish pugnacity in man and still have left a humanity worth trying to save. Combativeness is an essential element in a Christlike character. Aye, and combativeness is an essential necessity of this world. Sin is still stalking through the world. Now it threatens to engulf the world. Nothing is sacred from it,— womanhood, childhood, home life,—nothing is safe from it. There are some things in this world that are intolerable, and the man who will not say so, and fight, cannot save his soul. Sin is to be crushed by militant righteousness. There are some people who do not like those hymns we have come to sing—

> "Soldiers of Christ arise,
> Gird your armour on"—

or that other one,

> "The Son of God goes forth to war"

A person who is so delicate that he cannot feel a thrill of pride and love for militant righteousness is too delicate for this world.

It was not in Fosdick's nature to walk away from a fight. Nor was it in his character to remain an uncommitted spectator above the raging of great events. At the time Randolph Bourne suggested that American intellectuals followed Wilson unhesitatingly into war out of an "unanalyzable feeling" that this was a war in which they *had* to participate. In retrospect a historian speculated of these intellectuals: "Logic may have dictated nonintervention, but something deeper than logic dictated war. The thirst for action, the craving for involvement, the longing to commit themselves to the onward march of events—these things dictated war." The historian added in words pertinent to Fosdick, they "feared isolation not only for America but for themselves." As Fosdick feared isolation for his nation and church from the titanic actions convulsing Europe, so he feared missing the personal experience of being in on the "great challenge" of his generation; and so to the motivations of patriotism and Christian idealism and muscular Protestantism was added a strong dash of existential romanticism.

A final point. Fosdick, like almost everyone of his age and class, brought to his understanding of the war a set of apparently coherent and complete religious and moral precepts that would finally prove inadequate. His perception of reality was coherent, ordered, purposeful, intelligible, moral. He knew, as did almost everyone, what Glory was, and what Honor meant. This vision may accommodate a tragic sense of life; it may permit an awareness of sin and guilt; it may allow realistic descriptions of death and mutilation in the trenches. But it is not compatible with that dominant form of understanding that originated, arguably, in the application of mind and memory to the events of the Great War— it is not compatible with irony. Absent from Fosdick's perception are the absurd, the ridiculous, the outrageous, the opaque, the paranoid. Hemingway could declare in *A Farewell to Arms* that "abstract words such as glory, honor, courage, or hallow were obscene beside the concrete names of villages, the numbers of roads, the names of rivers, the numbers of regiments and the dates." "In the summer of 1914," Paul Fussell notes, "no one would have understood what on earth he was talking about." Certainly, Fosdick would not have. Nor would Fosdick have understood Eric Leed's concept of "liminality" and the "liminal men" in the trenches, men who were in Laurence Housman's description of British Tommies "infinitely small, running—affrighted rabbits from the upheaval of the shells, nerve-wracked, deafened; clinging to earth, hiding eyes, whispering, 'oh God!' " It's no doubt unfair to expect Fosdick to sound like Sassoon, Graves, Waugh, Mailer, Pynchon, Heller; still, one rather desperately misses even the thinnest vein of irony in Fosdick's war commentaries.

III

In April 1917 the war came to America. Fosdick ruefully relates in his autobiography how exhilarating it was to whip up enthusiasm for the war, playing upon the patriotic sentiments of a Harvard Chapel audience, bringing down the house in his old home town of Buffalo, stumping New York State with a team of speakers that included a British warrior back from the front. "No army in the history of the world ever went out under such a company of Christian gentlemen as ours," he assured parents in a reference to General Pershing and associates. Initially, he found the spirit of the people "limp and apathetic" and, so, he sat down to write the little volume, *The Challenge of the Present Crisis*. It was an immediate success. Over two hundred thousand copies were distributed in America and Britain. The proceeds Fosdick unselfishly turned over to the public cause.

In retrospect he termed it the only book he wished he had not written; he ordered it withdrawn from circulation, explaining, "I was never more sincere in my life than when I wrote it, but I was wrong. What I was mainly driving at in the book was not the business of a Christian minister to be saying." He may be too harsh on himself in condemning the book. Actually, it is a thoughtful, persuasive statement of the case for intervention. Fosdick is aware that the issue is not one of moral white and black. "[War] is the last word in idiocy and infamy as a way of settling international difficulties in the twentieth century." But had America earned the right to draw in her skirts from the crisis, arrogating to herself the special privilege not to choose on a question where our fellows as a whole were compelled to choose? His critique of absolute nonviolence, his distinction between the priorities of peace and justice, his realization of the limits of moral suasion, his comprehension that force could be an instrument of love—these positions sound Niebuhrian and are in truth very close to the case against pacifism as argued by Reinhold Niebuhr in both 1917 and 1941. Fosdick maintained that simply to cite the New Testament will not wash: "The fact is that Jesus did not directly face our modern questions about war; they were not his problems, and to press a legalistic interpretation of special texts, as though they were, is a misuse of the gospels." German *schrecklichkeit* (deliberate terror) in Belgium and France, on the eastern front and on the high seas, "have overpassed the power of reason and gentleness immediately to handle. We must use force. The wolf has come and we must be shepherds and not hirelings."

IV

In February 1918 the *Atlantic Monthly* carried an article by a fire-eating evangelist chastising the passivity of the churches entitled, "Peter Sat by the Fire Warming Himself." The charge is nonsensical. Protestant preachers and Catholic priests with few exceptions marched smartly to the beat of Wilson's drum, supporting the American Expeditionary Force as though it were a Second Children's Crusade (an analogy also drawn, though sardonically, by the French). More specifically, the charge misses Fosdick, for by that month he had crossed the Atlantic on a troopship to begin a half-year tour of duty under the auspices of the Y.M.C.A. and the British Ministry of Information. He spoke and preached in churches,

"Y" huts, open fields, barn lofts. He visited soldiers in trenches, hospitals, training and rest camps, and he met with sailors aboard ships—preaching perhaps or counseling or simply distributing coffee, chocolate, and cigarettes. He came to know fighting men and civilians, American, English, Scottish, Australian, French. And because his name was recognized, he was welcomed at the tables of diplomats, statesmen, and high-ranking military and naval officers. Like the Scarlet Pimpernel, he was here, he was there, he was everywhere.

Fosdick devotes ten pages of his autobiography to his wartime adventures in England, Scotland, and France. The autobiography, articles and sermons written at the time and later, letters he later received, interviews, and above all the 183 pages of "Diary Notes" he kept almost daily permit us to compare his public utterances with his private thoughts.

Fosdick was conscientious, untiring, faithful, capable, uncomplaining, manly, considerate, eloquent. He never gave less than his best in his entire life, and at no moment in his life was his commitment more total. Raymond Fosdick, chairman of the War Department and Navy Department Commission on Training Camp Activities, wrote to his family from France: "I have seen a good deal of Harry and we have had a great time together"; "I hear everywhere of Harry's work. He has made a great impression with the Army. He lived three days in a dug-out in a town that was all blown to pieces"; "Harry is in the thick of everything. I heard him preach in the upper part of a cow barn just back of the lines, in a town that the Germans had filled with gas the night before, so that we had to wear our masks at the alert. You had to climb up by a shaky ladder and the smell of the kine was almost overpowering. He is making a great record and doing a magnificent service which is genuinely appreciated by officers and men. I tell you this because I know you will never hear it from Harry." A lad who made the Atlantic crossing with Fosdick later recalled: "You spoke to us daily on that trip—and never have I been so impressed as I was by you and what you said to us on board the St. Louis. Everyone hearing you were so inspired by what you said that they would have eagerly tore into the Enemy bare handed had they been able to come in contact with them." Other correspondents also recalled the inspiration of Fosdick's presence, one of them telling of a poignant incident when Fosdick, returning to his billet in exhaustion, spread out photographs of his wife and children saying, "O God, they're my prayers!" A British newspaper reported that Fosdick, "a strong and soldierly figure," took a meeting "literally by storm," his "oratorical gifts" so captivating his hearers "they would hardly permit him to close." "Cheers, loud and unanimous, welcomed many of his sayings, and especially his assurance that 'even if Germany knocks our armies off the land we shall fight with you in sea warfare for twenty years, if necessary.' The speech was a soldier's rallying cry, not a professional lecture." Swept by zeal, Fosdick once fired up rear-echelon troops with the tale of an American black soldier armed only with a razor cleaning out a trench of Boche.*

It is to Fosdick's credit that, unlike many American parsons, he did not repeat the more lurid atrocity stories emanating from the Allies' propaganda machine—the bayoneted babies, children with their hands sawed off, women raped and mutilated, crucified Canadians and priests, and all the other "crimes" of the "Predatory Potsdam Gang." Still, he did inform American audiences of some incidents that he knew—or should have known—probably never happened. One example from an exuberant article, "Then Our Boys Came!", in *American Magazine* of December 1918:

> I was with one of our fighting divisions at the front when they were new to the game. A group of Germans came across No Man's Land one day, hands in the air crying 'Kamerad.' Boys from Alabama in the lines were waiting to welcome them. Can you shoot men who cry for quarter and ask the privilege of surrender? Then, suddenly, our machine gun spoke. A keener-eyed American let loose a withering blast of lead that laid the Germans low. What else could he do? He had seen what the others had not—a *grenade* in each uplifted hand. For the first time in centuries war knows no flag of truce. It is impossible to trust a German surrender. The policy of using lies, as one uses guns, to serve chosen ends, has worked down from Wilhelmstrasse to the ranks. The wonder is not that our men take so few prisoners. After their experience, the wonder is that they take any.

The story is at best implausible. At worst it is a plain rationalization for the shooting of surrendering enemy troops. A grenade (potato-masher-type perhaps) in each uplifted hand!† A second example from an untitled sermon preached November 28, 1918:

> Autocracy can reduce men to such abject docility that during the German advance whole ranks of the enemy came forward with their hands across

* This tale may have had a factual basis in the deed of Henry Johnson, a former New York Central redcap, who repulsed a German raiding party, using his rifle as a club after he emptied it point-blank and then going after and killing one German with a bolo.

† Readers of this story told by Fosdick insist that the incident might have happened. I continue to believe to the contrary. Of course, surrendering troops or troops pretending to surrender are capable of deception. My point is that a group of German soldiers were not so dumb as to think they could conceal hand grenades in their uplifted hands.

their eyes,—not fighting,—absorbing bullets until the machine guns of
the British grew too hot to fire.

Not only is this story untrue and unfair to the Germans, it diminishes
the bravery of the British Tommies who had to face a determined, skil-
ful foe. Fosdick might truthfully have said that some German boys were
nerved by alcohol, but that would have required the admission that some
British and French troops were steadied by government rations of rum
and brandy, something he deplored.

When Fosdick related these stories to American audiences, the consequence simply must have been an intensification of the anti-German
hysteria sweeping the land: the proscription of the German language in
the schools, the blacklisting of German composers and authors, the suppression of the German-language press, the surveillance of German-
American citizens. The denouement to all this was ludicrous: pretzels
banned from saloon counters, German fried potatoes deleted from hotel
menus, sauerkraut renamed liberty cabbage, frankfurters remained hot
dogs, and dachshunds renamed liberty pups; luckily it was discovered
just in time that Limburger cheese really was introduced to humankind
by Belgium.

Fosdick was on firmer factual ground when he posed this question of
the Germans:

How could they, calling upon God, do the cruel, bestial things that they
have done . . . ? The official cruelties, the U-boat war, the sack of Belgium, the deportations, the slave systems, the wholesale murders in
Northern France, the massacres of the Armenians—how could the Germans, bone of our bone, and blood of our blood, calling upon God, per-
petrate cruelties like that?

The deliberate destruction of magnificent historical treasures, the systematic laying waste of villages and fields, the official policies of shooting civilian hostages in reprisal, the brutal dragooning of workers are a
matter of historic record, and in this case it cannot fairly be said that
Fosdick was a dupe of Allied propaganda.

Fosdick naturally had much to say about the American doughboys.
Despite the literature of postwar disillusionment—Hemingway, Dos Passos, E. E. Cummings—it would be wrong to suppose that American boys
went off to France in the embittered mood of many shipped to Vietnam
or the grim mood of the Korean War and World War fighting men. To
the contrary, many young American lions viewed the Great War as a
rare opportunity for adventure, glory, sacrifice. In New World innocence
and with fresh, Adamic zeal they set forth with the lines of "In Flanders

Fields" and "I Have a Rendezvous with Death" in mind and the words of "Over There," "Tipperary," and "Good morning, Mr. Zip, Zip, Zip" on their lips. "Cheerful," "plucky," "staunch," "playing the game," "doing one's bit," "the Big Show," "extreme sacrifice," "Going West," "Blighty," "gay courage"—as melodramatic as these words sound to modern ears, it will not do to scoff. Many doughboys themselves apprehended their experiences romantically, not ironically, and their letters home are filled with expressions of exhilaration, wonder, and glory. But not all. Lt. Edward F. Graham (killed August 21, 1918) wrote to his mother in Buffalo's neighboring city, Rochester: "This is a cowering war—pigmy man huddles in little holes and caves praying to escape the blows of the giant who pounds the earth with blind hammers."

In the article, "Then Our Boys Came!", Fosdick begins by describing the Somme battlefields, "a vast area in comparison with whose desolation Dante's Hell must seem desirable," and the sapped and gutted armies of Britain and France. "Then our men came. Young, eager, vigorous, they arrived like strapping Samsons, aflame for a fight." The Marines at Château-Thierry put "every man a red poppy in his helmet, . . . swung up the hill into the battle, where they whipped the Prussian Guard, singing at the top of their voices: 'Hail! Hail! The gang's all here!' " "[They] were knights engaged in a crusade." As to the lads' morals, Fosdick reported seeing only one drunken soldier, and he was in a guardhouse. "I would trust a son to the American Expeditionary Forces as soon as I would to an average American college, if not sooner." "Our boys," he concluded, "are bearing themselves, in combat and personal behavior, with overflowing credit to the folks at home."

Another article, "A 'Y' Canteen Next to No Man's Land," appeared in the *Independent*, November 9, 1918. He describes a canteen with the "Yankee Division." "They are splendid fellows!", he notes. "I wouldn't have missed dishing out that tea last night for anything. My! how good it tastes to them! And going or coming they can get it freely at any hour of the night." He then visited a frontline trench ("as close to the enemy as I am likely to get"), returning to the village where "We blew ourselves—gave away tobacco, chocolate, cookies, to the whole town." The picture he paints seems a little too cozy: "cheerfulness is certainly the prevailing atmosphere here"; "the most happy place in which to live, while war is on, is a dugout on the second line trench"; "all is quiet, and war could not be conducted much less dangerously to the combatants." For him the experience was "very interesting," "*great* sport," a "good time." The article must have been reassuring to the folks at home.

A third article, "The Mothers of Men at the Front," appeared in *Association Men*, September 1918, the tenor of which may be gauged by the editors' preface: "It is the spirit at home which, like a great tide, lifts the heart of the man abroad and maintains his will to fight, is the message Dr. Harry E. Fosdick brings back from a sweep of France and the Front lines, where he has seen our men splendidly Carry On."

There is no need to pile quotation on quotation to make the point that when writing for the home audience Fosdick tended to idealize the doughboys' experiences. The "Diary Notes" indicate that to some extent he shaded the truth in his public statements. His private admiration matches his public admiration for the British. The wounded Tommies he found "Quiet, cheery—tho haggard, pale, sickly, cruelly hurt." Speaking on "How Much Are You Worth?" in an English V.D. hospital he was pleased to bring tears to the eyes of the "poor fellows." But not, alas, to the eyes of an Australian detachment on another occasion, "men obviously *hardened* by war. A cynical atmosphere in the audience—fed up, blasé, embittered, coarsened against appeal. Very difficult to handle, and not at all responsive. Must prepare to meet this!" Fosdick was obviously unsettled by this chilling experience; perhaps he recalled the traumatic Bowery ordeal of 1901.

The diary is silent on the qualities of the French soldiers. Although he finds areas of France beautiful, he is disgusted by the "indescribable filth" of French villages and the "utter primitiveness of latrine arrangements." Do French people ever bathe? Are the children ever washed?

Concerning the Americans, some diary entries correspond with the public expressions: "One feels unworthy to wipe the shoes of these doughboys, rough as sin but loyal as the saints. . . . There is nothing yellow in them. And one damns the white-tied, lily-livered sons of Beliah back home who spread tales of slander about these men." Again: "What a fine, good spirited bunch of young rough-necks and daredevils these fellows are!" But there are also darker observations, which he masked from the public, for example, this entry from late May at the peak of the last powerful German offensive:

Conversation with Lt. _____. War utterly degrading; not 10% of men or officers keeping clean; no redeeming features in war at all. Suffered a good deal of depression here at Haussimot. The war is going very badly; French have no reserves for an offensive; what the Germans gain they will keep; only the Americans can make possible effective counter attack; everything hinges on them—& we are not ready! It looks like a long war and a decisive military victory seems doubtful even then. . . . The war pretty much in Germany's hands, a desperate battle with our backs to the wall our only recourse, America hardly counting at all as yet, our armies untrained, our boys not sobered down to the real meaning of the desperate business, and our 'heroes' a very human, lonely bunch, a majority of them taking such self-indulgence by the way as they can find, and being badly coarsened by the whole experience. Will America's juvenile spirit stand the shock of the facts?

The subject of sex crops up again and again in the diary. At Issoudun he observes the "dark shadows on the moral life of some of the men," one house of prostitution with ten women serving two hundred men "one Sunday p.m." At Blois, informed by a private "that not more than 15 men out of his contingent of 300 had kept straight," Fosdick meditates: "The American boy, utterly unaccustomed to this flagrant, matter-of-fact parading of free sexual opportunity—what can he do? The way Y.M.C.A. sec'ys even go to pieces, C.E. [Christian Endeavor] type of good boys, ministers even." In Paris he notes the "disgraceful conduct of men and officers (the latter particularly)," but he adds the humane thought that some French women solicited not for money, "but for real desire on the woman's part—her husband, it may be, killed in the war." Despite this notice of the "darker side," Fosdick concludes with praise for Pershing and his staff, "high minded men, with right ideas, feeling keenly moral responsibility for men and taking advanced ground."*

The low veneral rate of the Yankees has been documented objectively. Subjectively, it perhaps does not seem incredible that in that ancient age a lot of the American lads would remain virginal or, if married, faithful, though one doughboy aching with longing warned his wife in a letter, "Take a long look at the floor, Martha, because when I get home you aren't going to see anything but the ceiling for a long, long time." Nevertheless, one comes away from a reading of wartime sermons, church press editorials, committee reports, and conference resolutions and addresses bewildered by the repeated insistence that "our boys" must remain clean and pure, unstained by liquor and illicit sex, that they might more efficiently kill Huns. "Men who are clean of life and of good moral character make the best fighters," observed the Superintendent of Army Work of Southern Methodism in Texas. Bishop James Cannon, Jr., wired

---

* When Clemenceau advocated for the American troops the establishment of licensed houses of prostitution, the letter was transmitted by Raymond Fosdick to Secretary of War Newton Baker who read it through twice, and then said with half a smile, "For God's sake, Raymond, don't show this to the President or he'll stop the war." One of Raymond's responsibilities in the United States had been to close red-light districts near training camps and to persuade "charity girls" to take up another form of philanthropy. Kirby Page, soon to emerge as a pacifist leader, served in France with the "Y." Like Fosdick, he was shocked by the sexual adventuring of the doughboys, but unlike Fosdick he got into trouble for making public what he observed. "There is a common saying in Paris," he reported: "The British are drunkards, the French are whoremongers, the Americans are both!"

President Wilson: "The mothers and fathers of our country . . . insist that while their sons are in the army, the navy, or the training camp, they be protected from the liquor and vice traffic. *They fear the possibility of moral and physical evil in the army, navy and camp life more than they fear physical wounding and death by German bullets*" (emphasis added). It is dispiriting to find Christian ministers so unaware of the terrible irony involved in their twin injunctions to the soldiers: remain "morally" unstained while about the bloody duty of killing well. The slogan "Make love, not war," is morally dubious, but surely no more so than "Shoot straight and live straight."

Another aspect of the war that does not come through forcefully in Fosdick's articles (though it does in his postwar sermons) is the condition of the wounded as recorded in the diary. Of the gassed he notes: "Poor fellows—blinded, raw throats and lungs, blistered with mustard—what a dastardly thing that gas is! My most unChristian delight is knowing that we are giving 3 to 1."

In mid-July Fosdick sailed for America with Raymond as cabin mate and Otto Kahn and two naval captains as mess mates. Altogether, it was a rather pleasant way to end the Great Adventure.

Fosdick's service to his country and to his country's fighting men and to his country's allies was admirable. To be separated from his beloved family for six months represented a real sacrifice. And if he ran no real physical danger (through no fault of his own because his courage is unquestioned), he did experience physical hardship and exhaustion. It must be added, however, that in the wartime diary the starring role of the self is notable. "One of my most impressive services," he notes of a farewell talk to boys headed for the front. "Two curtain calls!", he says of another talk. "*A great day*" and a "Great experience" are the recordings following two hospital visits. A corollary is a mild case of name dropping; indeed, the opening six pages consist of a listing of the names of one hundred individuals he has met. Then there are the rodomontade entries, for example: "The trouble with some invertebrate and flaccid pacifists is that they never have been *men*. They are trying the hopeless experiment of being Christian without first having been men. Now a *man* can be converted into a Christian, but a jelly-fish cannot. And when a jelly-fish tries to be a Christian, what he principally succeeds in doing is to misrepresent Christianity." Finally, there are these strange passages: "One comes back from Europe, not so much impressed by the enormity of human sin, as by the cruel effect of human ignorance." And: "This is the meaning of the Y.M.C.A. activity in the present war. Not piety, but scientific management to get moral results."

V

Shortly after returning from Europe Fosdick accepted an invitation from New York's First Presbyterian Church to become its Preaching Minister, about which much more later. For at least eight months, beginning in November, every sermon made reference to the war. It was a major theme of his addresses and articles as well.

In Fosdick's postwar public utterances a franker acknowledgment of the war's ghastliness is immediately apparent; he even quotes with agreement the surreal words of a British Tommy, "Europe is something between an insane asylum and a butcher's stall." He proclaimed in a sermon of May 11, 1919:

> War glorious? These multitudes of women, gathered to make shells to blow to pieces the bodies of men that other women bore; this prodigious outpouring of human energy that, rightly used, would make a heaven on earth, all coming to this, that men who were sound of limb are blown to bits, and men who were sound of mind were driven mad. These endless miles of broken homes, with ruined women and butchered children,—the demoralization of family life over a whole continent,—the most splendid powers of our noblest men harnessed to a task whose end is the bloody soak of a finished battlefield. War glorious? Nine million dead men are its natural fruit. Mothers broken hearted. Widows desolate. Girls who will never be loved. Children who will never be born. These are its memorials. A man who calls that glorious is morally unsound. A man who calls that glorious, preeminently necessary, has consigned the race to hell. And mark it, this military doctrine is no such unique specialty of Germany.

Elsewhere he reminds his comfortable parishioners not only of "men blown all to bits," but of the others behind closed doors, "so hideously ruined that human eyes must never look on them again." Fosdick's wartime descriptions, not without their realism, tended to inspire; his post-Armistice descriptions might have inspired, in sensitive individuals, terror.

Discernible also in Fosdick's utterances after 1918 is a new, or at least stronger, note of man's sinfulness and civilization's contingency. As he informed the delegates to the 1919 Northern Baptist Convention, the war broke upon a fool's paradise, shattering the superficial optimism of humanity's inevitable progress. Men now know that the world is monstrously wrong and can no longer tolerate hearing some Pippa singing "God's in his heaven all's right with the world." As he challenged the First Presbyterian congregation:

I for one will not live any longer in a fool's paradise, reading sweet nothings about "everything coming out well." I cannot nourish my soul any longer on these elaborate war mottoes about "Build a little hedge of trust around today." I make indignant protest against the easy going optimism of prosperous people. I hear a great voice ringing out of an ancient time,—"Woe unto you," "Woe unto you, Chorazin, woe unto you Bethesda, more tolerable for Tyre and Sidon in the day of judgment than for you." Why, here is some one who dares not look with easy optimism upon human nature. "Woe unto you, Scribes, Pharisees, hypocrites, who rob widows' houses and for a pretense make long prayers." Why, here is Some One who does not blind His eyes to the deep seated malignity of human life. "My God,"—my God,—why has Thou forsaken me"?

For Fosdick, the behavior of civilized Germany cast suspicion on all human nature. Can it be that barbarism lies so close beneath our thin veneer, he wondered? "Can it be that our religion is so thin a barricade between ourselves and bestial passion? Iscariot's betrayal always makes men wonder whether they have such diabolical possibilities within themselves." Christmas of 1919 found him surveying "the bitterest spiritual world that ever on a Christmas Eve tried to sing the angels' song and felt it stick in its throat." He continued: "With what glowing phrases did we cover the horrors of the World War while we were in the thick of it. 'War to end all war.' 'War to make the world safe for democracy.' Well, the big guns have done their deadly work, and the main strength of fighting men armed to the teeth with armature of violence has spent itself. Does it look as though this war, or any other war were likely to end wars. Does the world look very safe for democracy?" Science has made man's estate even more perilous, Fosdick noted in *The Meaning of Service.* "There is enough atomic force . . . in a mass of matter no larger than a man's fist to lift the German fleet from the bottom of the sea and put it on the hill behind Manchester." "God forbid . . . that science now should cast its harness over the atomic forces! We are not fit to handle them. Put such prodigious power into our possession in our present state and with it we would damn the race." Fosdick's measured postwar conclusion, stated in the Cole Lectures at Vanderbilt University in 1922 and published under the title *Christianity and Progress,* is: "All the progress this world will know waits upon the conquest of sin. Strange as it may sound to the ears of this modern age, long tickled by the amiable idiocies of evolution popularly misinterpreted, this generation's deepest need is not these dithyrambic songs about inevitable progress, but a fresh sense of personal and social sin."

Still, it would be an error to suppose that Fosdick's experiences in France made him an instant pacifist or that he immediately donned the sackcloth and ashes of repentance or that he quickly questioned the wisdom of Wilson's intervention. To the contrary, his postwar utterances continued to proclaim the justice of the Great Crusade and to laud the unselfish, sacrificial spirit compelling America to take up arms. "I have no use for a man who has not, for four years now, been angry underneath. Anger is one of the sinews of the soul, and he who lacks it has a maimed mind," he cried in May 1919. A year later he condemned Tolstoy's "extreme idealism," arguing that "so long as there are men or nations that are not immediately amenable to moral suasion, there force should be used, and will be!" At Colgate in 1919 he delivered a deeply reverential memorial address to the fallen in France. "For months and years nothing had made any difference to us, except to do something for somebody—not to be altogether useless in a sacrificial generation. We came to understand exactly what Huxley meant when he said, 'The sense of uselessness is the severest shock that any organ can sustain.'" The magnificent sacrifice made by the American boys, he continued, shows "what pugnacity is waiting in the heart of peaceful man for some good cause to arouse it into being against an evil cause." The war has shown the glory of taking sides. "A shambling tolerance that tries to stand on two sides of a great question has shown us that there are things in this world that are intolerably wrong, and that a man cannot save his soul unless he wants to and fights. It would be a great memorial of those men gone if their spirits should descend like the mantle of Elijah, dedicating combativeness for God's sake and the truth against the evil of this world." Let us so labor, he concluded, to make this a "Christian world in which young men will never have again to go down into the hell they visited."

VI

Loathing the spirit of Prussianism as he did, Fosdick consistently demanded that the Hohenzollern dynasty be brought down "abjectly, completely, in humiliating disgrace and ruin." But he tempered this position by noting the temptations to Prussianism in the Allies and America, by distinguishing between the depraved German rulers and the potentially decent German people, by espousing not a Carthaginian peace but rather the goal of "a decent and safe Germany with whom to live. Safety for the world,—not vengeance on a foe, must be our motive now."

Fosdick viewed the harsh Treaty of Versailles as a betrayal of the Fourteen Points and containing the seeds of future wars, a peace that did indeed pass all understanding. But he held as imperative American membership in the League of Nations, the League promising to provide an "ultimate corrective" (in Wilson's words) for the temporary injustices of the Versailles settlement. "I know what I am going to say, every chance I have to say it," Fosdick informed the First Church congregation in early 1919. "The endeavor for a League of Nations is the greatest forward step that humanity has dared to take since the abolition of the slave trade." And so he made a rare direct political appeal to the First Church congregation to support politicians favoring American entry, the congregation for the first time in the history of the church rising in applause. Even after the Senate thrice rejected American membership, he continued to press the question, wisely observing that the member states would go more than half way in meeting us in "finding a formula that gives more [of] an American look to the present organization"; and he publicly rebuked the new U.S. Ambassador to Britain, Colonel George M. Harvey, for announcing that America would have nothing to do with the League.

In a private letter Fosdick gave his full and revealing assessment of President Wilson. He stated he never voted for Wilson, continuing:

When, however, we did get into the war, I think that Mr. Wilson stamped himself indelibly upon human history by the expression which he gave to the necessity for international association to prevent war. I think that his name is safe so far as history is concerned and he will always be regarded as one of the great spokesmen of internationalism and that when in time, as will inevitably occur, most of his major ideas are accepted and worked out, he will be regarded as a very great man. In saying this I do not mean that I regard the League of Nations as a perfect document. I never thought it should be accepted without amendment. But I do think that in the general trend of his policies Mr. Wilson was right and that the attitude which the Senate took is one of the most disgraceful episodes in the history of the nation. I ought also to add that I think Mr. Wilson is chiefly to blame for the defeat of his own policies. Had it not been for his colossal egotism, which seems to me quite insufferable, he could just as well as not have had the thing he wanted. It is this lack of greatness in character which will prevent, I think, his being ranked among the very foremost men of our nation's history. Nevertheless, I do believe that until the general ideals of internationalism for which Mr. Wilson has stood are wrought out, the world is headed straight for a repetition of the chaos through which we have just lived.

VII

Immediately following the war Fosdick's fame mounted rapidly, thanks to such explosive articles as "The Trenches and the Church at Home," the distribution of the sermons preached from the pulpit of New York's First Presbyterian Church, the publication of *The Meaning of Service*, and his joint authorship of the Federal Council's major statement, *The Church's Message to the Nation*. The expanding bubble of reputation is an unimportant side effect, however, compared to what the war did to his mind. Before many years he could say with Whitman, "God damn every war"—and mean it. Among the few ornaments in his stark study at Union Seminary was a cheap and smoke-blackened crucifix he had found in the ruins of a tiny church in war-torn France. Surely it was in 1918 that the question first hit him hard, Jesus' question that he later made the title of a powerful pacifist sermon, "Can Satan Cast Out Satan?"

Chapter Six

"Once It Was Beecher and Brooks, Now It Is Fosdick": A Baptist Preacher in a New York City Presbyterian Pulpit

I

In 1918 three of New York City's historic Presbyterian churches consolidated their memberships and resources. The united church took the name and location of the oldest of the three, the First Presbyterian Church on Fifth Avenue between Eleventh and Twelfth Streets. The Madison Square Presbyterian Church brought to the union wealth, prestige, a liberal theological tradition, and, thanks to its retiring minister, Dr. Charles Parkhurst, stalker of the Tammany Tiger, a reputation for social concern. The University Place Church contributed its vital and socially varied congregation. First Presbyterian's inestimable asset was the frontage of an entire block on Fifth Avenue, comparable to Saint Patrick's Cathedral, in a neighborhood not yet engulfed by commerce, and a beautiful Gothic sanctuary in a parklike setting. Its aging minister, Dr. Howard Duffield, helped guide the union, rejoicing that "the Mother Church of Presbytery is anchored to its historic site." The valuable properties of Madison Square and University Place churches were sold and a handsome endowment fund created for "the establishment of a strong and permanent downtown Presbyterian Centre in the City of New York." The three ministers involved—Parkhurst, Duffield, and Dr. George Alexander—gallantly resigned their pastorates to smooth the union.

While the search for a new pastor of the consolidated church was underway in the late fall, Union Professor Hugh Black and Fosdick were invited to occupy the pulpit, and both men did so, Fosdick on four occasions. When John Timothy Stone, the great Chicago Presbyterian preacher, declined a call, the search committee approved on December 20 the following: "RESOLVED, That this committee recommend that Dr. George Alexander be called to the pastorate of the First Presbyterian Church and that Dr. Harry Emerson Fosdick be engaged as a member of the clerical staff, and his chief duty to be to preach at the services of the church." This resolution was unanimously approved by the Trustees and Session and congregation.

In view of the stormy events that would conclude this relationship, it is important to make clear its origins. In 1918 the General Assembly of the Presbyterian Church, U.S.A., had endorsed the principle of the organic union of all American evangelical churches. For the pulpit of Old First to be occupied by a Baptist seemed in keeping with the spirit of this principle. When initially approached by Arthur Curtiss James and William Morgan Kingsley, key leaders of the search committee, with the offer of a permanent pastorship, Fosdick (as he reported to his brother) "peremptorily refused on two grounds—that I did not believe their theology and would not subscribe to the Westminster Confession and that I was too old and independent to subject myself to the superintendency of a Presbytery." Moreover, he added, his teaching duties at Union were too heavy to permit assuming the multiple roles of preacher, pastor, and ministerial executive. It is important to stress that the church leadership did not pressure Fosdick to sever his Baptist ties. Fosdick never gave the slightest intimation that he would consider doing so. As he assured his brother, "You need have no fear of my falling away from those holy faiths of our Baptist forefathers, concerning which you express such earnest and hilarious solicitude." It was not his intent, as fundamentalists would later falsely charge, to be a deliberate disturber of the Presbyterian peace, though he was sufficiently prescient to write to Jesse Forbes, Stated Clerk of New York Presbytery, "I confess that with some timidity I consented to the present arrangement at the First Presbyterian Church because I feared lest, with all possible good intentions on my part, I might become in some way a source of discord and difficulty to you and yours."

Only when the seventy-five-year-old Dr. Alexander, whom Fosdick greatly respected, had agreed to return from retirement to be pastor (bringing with him presently as an associate the young, handsome Thomas Guthrie Speers) would Fosdick accept the post of Associate Minister or Preaching Minister. At his insistence, the salary was to be $5000—less, appropriately, than that of Alexander. The installation service took place on January 29. There was every reason but one to believe that with this bold collegiate ministry the success of the wise 1918 union was assured—and that single adverse consideration was the reservations of conservatives about a liberal Baptist preaching from a Presbyterian pulpit.

Just as it is important to remember that the church acted openly, so it is salient to the later controversy to remember that it acted legally. On January 13 the Presbytery of New York unanimously adopted a resolution congratulating the church and tending to Fosdick "our best wishes for the success of his labors in the proclamation of the Gospel in the pulpit of this historic church." Upon motion Fosdick was then invited "to sit with Presbytery as a corresponding member whenever it may be convenient." Such was the ebullient mood of the meeting that Dr. Forbes expressed the hope that before long Fosdick would become a Presbyterian. "All he needs, brethren, is to be willing to get along with a little less water." Neither Fosdick nor the fundamentalists would have affirmed the accuracy of that observation. Henry Sloane Coffin, leader of New York's liberal Presbyterians, first suggested that Fosdick become a corresponding member, observing to Forbes: "It is all-important that we keep him in touch in order to have his backing for Presbyterial matters." Clearly Coffin sensed the impending fight. The *Minutes* of the Presbytery reveal that Fosdick attended meetings only rarely; nevertheless, his Baptist affiliation did not bar him from invitations to preach at Presbyterian installation services. The Synod of New York reviewed and did not disallow Presbytery action, thus giving further legal sanction to the arrangement.

II

New York City may be "the graveyard of preachers," as tradition has it, but observing Old First during Fosdick's preaching ministry one could not have guessed this to be so. Sunday morning after Sunday morning for seven years, throngs of expectant worshippers assembled on Fifth Avenue well before the 11:05 service hour, their lines extending several blocks in either direction of the doors. Those especially prompt and lucky were admitted to the unreserved sections of the sanctuary. The others were required to wait until 11:00 in order that members of the congregation might take their reserved places. Exactly on the hour all unoccupied places were opened to the pressing visitors. A young business woman described the scene to her parents:

> To stand in line at church as for the theater strikes the newcomer very near amidships—until he understands. It is a source of amusement to me to be in the midst of the throng for perhaps an hour, so crowded that I can see pores in the fat, pink neck of a pudgy banker who comes in his "topper"

all on a Sabbath morn. I hear, willing or unwilling, the comments of the waiting ones. Some are stoical, patient, uncommunicative. Some are provoked and restless. A few threaten to leave if they don't get a seat pretty soon and I heard one man mutter, "What's the idea?" They conclude that one must have a fat pocket book or a pull. Sometimes a "duchess" will sweep in with assurance through the center door, which is only for pew holders, and be damaged in her dignity by the kind but efficient usher who explains. It is no uncommon thing for the heavy cord that is looped across the entrance to be strained by the waiting, earnest people. Some old timer, always a friend, will whisper data about the church, Dr. Fosdick, the criticism of him, the cause, etc. There is never any real subway "hogging," but there is more pushing than you might suppose. Now and then some one will yield a preference to an older person, but not often.

A young man, new to New York, confided to his diary: "Already the huge auditorium was practically filled and long lines were waiting at the doors. . . . But get in I finally did, and persevered though the usher declared there was not a single seat left. Finally a group of us were placed on cushions on the very altar stairs. Niches, galleries, chapel,—all were filled and lines of people were standing wherever permitted. Dr. Fosdick preached magnificently." Another entry reads: "The usual crowd was present . . . , but I was so early as to be almost in the front line. The head usher came back and asked for volunteers who 'wouldn't get nervous prostration', to sit on the platform with Dr. Fosdick. Two men in front of me volunteered and I made the third and last." He might have added that when Fosdick entered the pulpit the seat that he had just vacated was normally occupied by a standee!

William Morgan Kingsley, head usher, whose corps wore the standard frock coats, once wrote Fosdick a memorandum: "We had a hectic time yesterday in the ushering business. One lady fainted. Two ladies crawled under the ropes on the plea of wanting to go away & then beat down the center aisle. Mr. Lawton held them up. The crowd in the south gallery was dense & passing the plate was difficult and lengthy, as every one wanted to chip in—bless their hearts. This explains why the other chap and I had to sprint down the aisles to catch up with the procession." On another occasion Kingsley reported that a contingent of forty West Pointers arrived saying that they had been promised seats by their chaplain, eliciting Fosdick's sympathetic reply: "I do not know what we are going to do in cases like this, especially when chaplains of military academies begin to lie like rogues in order to get into the sanctuary. Praise be that there is wit, wisdom and grace enough in the Board of Ushers apparently to surmount all obstacles." In unseemly eagerness, some "sermon tasters" entered the north gallery by going up the fire escape. Others who were turned away wrote Fosdick that they were "awfully sore for having been treated so shamefully." "I would expect better treatment from even a theatre," closed one disgruntled correspondent. In reply Fosdick pointed out the problem: How to accommodate several thousand would-be worshippers in a church that normally seats about eleven hundred? "The real issue involved seems to me plain," Fosdick explained. "If we do not keep assigned seats for our church family we would soon have no church family at all. . . . What would happen if we tried to make the church free, in the sense of having no assigned pews, would be that every Sunday it would be completely filled up by 10:30 with casual strangers. That would mean that we would have no church constituency on the basis of whose support and service we could carry on our widely extended practical enterprise in the poorer sections of the city."

At this point it is scarcely needful to note that some who flocked to hear Fosdick preach did so only because it was modish, much like going to Carnegie Hall or the Belasco Theatre or Yankee Stadium. It was an event to relate to folks back home, as one would tell of hearing Caruso (Fosdick was dubbed the "Caruso of preaching") or seeing Barrymore or cheering Babe Ruth.

But curiosity was certainly not the compelling motivation of all. A woman wrote a letter of appreciation to Dr. Alexander, saying: "For the sake of other young people who come to the city as I did, and who need 'food' as I needed it—I rejoice that there is a spiritual table in New York to which every hungry soul is invited regardless of denomination or creed. Otherwise, I should have been barred, because I am not a Presbyterian. Why did we young women stand in line Sunday after Sunday—we who represented many or several denominations?" Because, she explained, "We have to go where there is food if we would be fed—That's why we stood in the 'Bread Line'—to get bread, and we got it. And the best part of it is, that we have eaten it, and no one can take it from us. The First Presbyterian Church may not have known that we returned thanks for the food we received, but we did, and we always shall. And we all say, God bless Dr. Fosdick and the First Presbyterian Church, and we know He does."

A man recalled that in his youth he found himself every Sunday morning in the balcony of the sanctuary. "Dr. Fosdick always made me feel as though he had prepared that particular sermon especially for me. Never before, and never since, have I heard sermons that 'got to me' the way Dr. Fosdick's sermons did. I honestly think I could paraphrase the Apostle Paul and say that in those 1920's 'nothing could have separated me' from Dr. Fosdick and his sermons." Another wrote home, "I have never before heard such clear and true, and at the same time, so eloquent messages. Dr. Fosdick never utters a word of self or of the sensational. No word is ill-chosen, and all his words seem blessed of God."

In the sanctuary on Sunday morning men and women gathered to adore, praise, and give thanks, confess their sins and seek forgiveness, affirm their faith, and dedicate their lives. The beautiful chaste setting, the music, the reading of the scriptures, the prayers, the reading of the long prayer "by dear old Dr. Alexander," the benediction followed by seven soft tones on the carillon and then the amens of the organ—all these elements of the service, and not the sermon alone, led worshippers to meet the Lord where he said he would be present: in the midst of the believing community. As for the presence of multitudes of visitors, one of them made the perspicuous observation: "It is easier to worship among strangers. There is less to distract, less conjecture and small thinking."

Fosdick was not unmindful of the awful challenge of preaching weekly to massed and expectant worshippers. On a brief retreat he wrote to his father: "The crowds continue at the church and I suppose that the anticipation of facing such a mob every Sunday makes the preaching not only exciting but a bit anxious. I do my best not to let the burden of it get through to my nerves but at times I find it difficult to relieve my thoughts, even in hours of relaxation, from the responsibility that the congregation entails." Thomas Guthrie Speers, the young associate minister, felt his own responsibility for the Sunday evening service heavily, too, observing, "If you think there is no difference in the quality of preaching, then you have never heard Dr. Fosdick in the morning and Guthrie Speers in the evening. It is like water after wine."

III

The popular cry of a later generation, "The Church Is Mission," would not have been news to the Old First congregation in the 1920s. In addition to a full parish and community program in the church house they sustained a cluster of "outposts" (as they were called) in lower Manhattan. This was only appropriate, they stated, to "our character as a Missionary Society, which is our real function as a church." Fosdick shared this conviction, vowing that "we will not be a self-absorbed church, a religious club, interested in our own prestige."

One outpost was the Emmanuel Presbyterian Church on the lower East Side; in a neighborhood ninety-seven percent Jewish, the services were conducted in English and Russian and the club rooms and gym were heavily in demand. Bethlehem Chapel and Church of the Gospel on Bleecker Street was another. Here an Italian pastor and staff ministered to the spiritual and physical needs of Italian immigrants. Among the services offered were a day nursery that provided in some cases "the only hot adequate meal of the day," health care, industrial classes for the men and stenography and typing classes for the women, a gym, and religious services in English and Italian. A third was the Madison Square Church House, also situated in an area heavily Italian, where a clinic staffed by nurses performed one of many functions. The Madison Square Boys' Club was close to Fosdick's heart. Started in 1884, its back was to the financial wall in 1920. Fosdick raised the necessary funds to provide a new home for the club, and to it over the years came thousands of Protestant, Catholic, and Jewish boys. These enterprises by no means exhaust the record of Old First's outreach to the city, nation, and world, but it must suffice to note that the congregation gave seventy percent more to benevolence than it spent on self-support, and that at the end of Fosdick's tenure benevolent contributions were more than four times the combined amount contributed by the three constituent churches prior to the merger. The leadership roles of the venerable Alexander and the vigorous Speers must not be minimized, but it may be assumed that Fosdick's preaching was not unrelated to the general vitality of the church.

Of course the church's outposts were supported in part because of a toplofty and not altogether lovely spirit of noblesse oblige. Still, the hand held out by First Church was a hand of assistance and not a clinched fist, and some of the strangers in the land of lower Manhattan were grateful to be succored rather than vexed. The First Presbyterian Church was true to Emil Brunner's vision, "The Church exists by missions as fire exists by burning."

IV

When the time came for Fosdick to depart, the congregation presented him with a letter of appreciation, emphasizing the fact that during his years many younger people of modest means had joined the fellowship. The letter underscored their determination "to be a community church as far as it is possible for a Presbyterian church to be such." Nevertheless, if the general congregation became more socially diverse, the reins of leadership remained in the hands of some of the city's most respected, powerful, and affluent citizens: Arthur Curtiss James, possessor of one of the nation's largest and least-publicized fortunes; William Morgan Kingsley, board chairman of the United States Trust Company and pres-

ident of the board of Union Seminary; Robert W. De Forest, president
of the Russell Sage Foundation and president of the Metropolitan Museum of Art; John H. Finley, *New York Times* editor and one-time
president of Knox College, C.C.N.Y., and the State University of New
York; Charles S. Whitman, former governor of New York—and Henry
F. Whitney, Herbert L. Bodman, George A. Plimpton, Francis L. Slade,
Roger H. Williams, Arthur W. Courtney, William de la Montagnie,
among others.

The triumphs at Old First were not quite complete, as conservatives
delighted in noting. Although the worship services were heavily attended
and although membership did increase, the net gain was not really dramatic; and of the new members, fewer than two hundred were received
on confession of faith. Fosdick once preached every night for a week at
evangelistic services, but feared "that the people who come are very
largely Christian folk from other churches, who take advantage of a
midweek opportunity to attend a service in our edifice." In 1925, immediately after Fosdick's departure, Speers reported that although "ours
is, in many respects, a young people's church," it "is not in any sense a
family church. Very seldom does one see parents and their children
coming in together to worship." Speers found two reasons for this. First,
the church was located in a neighborhood where the old family brown-
stones were giving way to apartment houses and children were increasingly scarce in the area. Second, Speers explained, "while Dr. Fosdick
was preaching, the throngs were so great that it was not pleasant or perhaps even safe for [children]. They were crowded out."

Nevertheless, as Dr. Alexander maintained, any fair evaluation must
take into consideration that Old First expended its spiritual and material
forces in five different centers, the mother church and the outposts. "The
fruits that are gathered at four of them do not appear as attached to the
First Presbyterian Church."

V

Fosdick's preaching in the overflowing sanctuary seemed to many observers reminiscent of Henry Ward Beecher and Phillips Brooks in their
days of glory; and it is not too much to say that by the early 1920s his
fame approached that of those earlier "princes of the pulpit"—to appropriate that abhorrent title. "Once it was Beecher and Brooks, now it is
Fosdick," opined copydesk editors. This mounting fame owed much to
his nationwide platform and pulpit appearances, and with the passage
of each year the speaking invitations increased geometrically. "Never

has my tongue wagged so continuously or disturbed the air in the vicinity of so many people's ears as during these last four days," Fosdick informed his father in 1924. "Just to take the last 48 hours, on Wednesday I spoke to 10,000 people at the Madison Square Garden at the Memorial Service for Woodrow Wilson, and then in the evening spoke at a dinner of 1200 at the Hotel Astor. Yesterday I had two classes here at the seminary and then went down to Philadelphia where we had a great meeting last night with over 3000 in attendance, and from there I returned in the wee small hours in the morning. This afternoon I have been down at the Town Hall speaking at a meeting of the Indian Defense Association, but praise be, I do not have to speak tonight." Truth to tell, there were many such packed speaking periods in these years.

And packed houses as well. When he spoke before the Chicago Sunday Evening Club in 1924 (an annual engagement he filled for thirty-seven years) a reporter described the scene under the heading "Crowds Smash Door: Near Riot to Hear Fosdick":

> One of the front doors of Orchestra Hall was smashed in and an usher was slightly hurt during the rush. For a time it was believed a call for extra police would have to be made. Michigan Avenue was crowded beyond the curb at 6:15 o'clock and within five minutes of the opening of the doors every one of the seats, numbering nearly 3,000 was taken. The "All Seats Taken" sign was hung up, but the crowd would not leave and milled around for an hour, vainly hoping for an opening.

A reporter for the *Epworth Herald,* a Methodist young people's publication, termed the sermon memorable:

> Its illustrations were nearly all biblical. Its ideas were as definitely and unmistakably Christian as could be desired. Its closing argument was a plea for men to seek that thorough and supernatural sort of conversion which to-day is sometimes too lightly stressed even in Methodist circles. If the listener had not known who the preacher was, he would have thought him some great evangelist, or some unusually evangelistic Methodist preacher with a wonderful gift for gospel preaching. The only thing more which the most old-fashioned Methodist could have asked would have been a call for those under conviction to come forward for prayer.

Reactions such as this, which were numerous, led to the judgment that this protean man may be accurately termed an evangelist.

When in the 1920s a student paper carried the plea, "Please don't rattle the funnies during chapel, someone else might be sleeping," it was but one expression of a widespread campus scorn for formal religion. Alfred North Whitehead recalled that when he lectured to college audiences in the 1920s he saw his listeners lean back in ignorance whenever he used a Biblical quotation and in disgust whenever he spoke of religion. And Joseph Wood Krutch, lecturing at Caltech, was told beforehand that he would be well received "if, one, you stop by twelve-fifty so that they can get their lunches and, two, are very careful not to say anything in favor of either religion or morality." All the more surprising, then, considering this milieu, is Fosdick's popularity on college campuses across the land. A veteran Baptist minister said of him: "He has become the foremost preacher in colleges and universities in the country. No man since the days of Henry Drummond has saved and established the Christian faith of professors, students and young people as well as he has."

Fosdick's Cole Lectures delivered at Vanderbilt University, two a day for five days in 1922, became the basis for his important volume, *Christianity and Progress*. They were enthusiastically received; the audiences, Fosdick reported, piling "out in young mobs night after night and even on the last evening, when it rained cats and dogs, kits and puppies, and I expected to have a handful there, the same old crowd of six or seven hundred people tramped up through the rain to the university hall." This scene, which took place in what is patronizingly called the Bible Belt, was repeated on campuses in every section of the country. Columbia University students regularly trooped to his Union Seminary classes as auditors in such numbers as to necessitate tickets examined by guards posted at the classroom door. Hundreds of students were turned away from Harvard's Appleton Chapel and Paine Concert Hall; those admitted on one instance rising to a man in tribute and on another forcing Fosdick to acknowledge repeatedly sustained applause. Editorialized the *Harvard Crimson:* "No one in recent years has appealed to Harvard quite so much as Dr. Fosdick. His powerful and open treatment of subjects which have too long been obscured by superstition, ceremonialism, and sheer mummery, appeal to the critically-minded undergraduate. There is a feeling about Fosdick's work that he preaches nothing that he does not believe." Fosdick himself said of the Harvard men, "They give me great audiences and in spite of their reputation to the contrary are about the warmest and most demonstrative friends that I have ever to speak before."

Here by way of illustration is his stripped down schedule for a single two-week period (the fees received ranged from $75 to $600):

Sunday, 31 May: Bryn Mawr College—baccalaureate sermon
Tuesday, 2 June: Crozer Theological Seminary—commencement address

Wednesday, 3 June: Morning meeting with Justice Louis D.
                        Brandeis;* evening, George Washington
                        University—commencement address
Thursday, 4 June: Ohio Wesleyan University—lecture
Friday, 5 June: Ohio Wesleyan University—morning
                        prayers, evening lecture
Sunday, 7 June: Ohio University—baccalaureate sermon
Tuesday, 9 June: Ohio University—commencement address
Wednesday, 10 June: Walnut Hill School—commencement
                        address
Friday, 12 June: Smith College—invocation
Saturday, 13 June: Smith College—trustees' meeting
Sunday, 14 June: Harvard University—morning sermon;
                        Radcliffe College—afternoon baccalaureate
                        sermon
Monday, 15 June: University of Rochester—commencement
                        address

Naturally, these crowded days offered few leisure moments, save possibly for the hours on the train, and it may be that the innumerable luncheons and formal dinners were as innervating as the actual speaking. Once returning from a Chicago trip to confront his New York responsibilities, he thought it doubtful that he would "get to bed on the hither side of midnight on any night this week." So, although he tried to watch his step, walking daily and golfing, if possible, on Mondays, the speaking strain took its toll. Five addresses in two days at Harvard in December 1923, he reported, took "the pith out of me and I needed a day or two to sleep up." Exactly a year earlier he had been forced to cancel a Harvard engagement and several others because of "an attack of nervous dyspepsia," but after three solid days of rest at Atlantic City, he returned, he informed his father, "feeling exceedingly well and have been hitting the line hard ever since with great content."

All of this is not to assert that Fosdick swept college campuses lighting fires of belief in faith-parched forests of students. Of course, he did not. It does, however, suggest that in the Roaring Twenties some of the "beautiful and the damned" of the Lost Generation of college youth hungered for something more satisfying than that found in the bottom of a flask or in the arms of a flapper or football hero. There was in truth "another part of the twenties"—and Fosdick is part of that "another part."

* As we shall see in Chapter Ten, it is certain that Brandeis and Fosdick talked about the Zionist question.

VI

During these very years, 1918–1925, when Fosdick's voice was bringing him fame and in conservative quarters, notoriety, his pen continued to spread his name. Four major books were published: *The Meaning of Service* (1920), *Christianity and Progress* (1922), *Twelve Tests of Character* (1923), and *The Modern Use of the Bible* (1924). He also wrote extensively for magazines. *Harper's* carried his material regularly; for one series of twelve articles under the general heading "Religion and Life" the magazine banked to his account $500 monthly. The *Ladies' Home Journal* was another favorite outlet for his busy pen, over a score of articles appearing in the decade, for which he received $1000 to $1200 each. The chapters of *Twelve Tests of Character* first appeared serially in the *Journal*. Edward Weeks, editor of the *Atlantic Monthly*, also continued to call on him. And in 1923 the first of ultimately over sixty of Fosdick's writings showed up in *Reader's Digest*, making him that journal's favorite contributor. Fosdick never apologized for writing for these and other middle-brow and upper-middle-brow publications, despite his awareness that in so doing he opened himself to the charge of popularizer. His motivation was clearly not primarily financial. He turned down far more invitations to contribute than he accepted. Rather, he believed that what he had to say was of interest and could be of benefit to the American general public. He once defended writing an article for *Physical Culture* with the explanation, "I must try to reach people where they are."

VII

Further evidence of Fosdick's mounting reputation during this brief span is found in the honorary degrees that increasingly came his way: the doctor of divinity degree from New York University (1919), Brown University (1920), Yale University (1923), and Glasgow University (1924); the doctor of law degree from the University of Michigan (1923) and the University of Rochester (1925); the doctor of sacred theology degree from Ohio University (1925).* The tributes uttered on these occasions were naturally very flattering.

* Subsequently, Fosdick was the recipient, in chronological order, of degrees from Princeton, Union College, Boston University, Harvard, Williams, Columbia, Dickinson College, Colby College, Jewish Theological Seminary, Hebrew Union, and the University of Buffalo. For his part he served higher education by being for many years a faithful trustee of Colgate, Smith, and Barnard, all three schools having a special place in his life. He turned down petitions to become a trustee from Brown and other institutions.

It is also important to note that he was repeatedly approached about pulpits and teaching posts elsewhere, perhaps the most flattering teaching offers coming from the University of Chicago Divinity School and Harvard University. Fosdick's reply to President A. Lawrence Lowell of Harvard reflects the loyalty that is one of his most admirable traits:

> If it were merely a question of coming to Harvard I should delight to do so, but it is also a question of leaving Union, and that I am not yet ready to face. This is a seminary where I was trained, where I was called as an instructor a few years after my graduation, and where I have worked for many years as full professor with constantly increasing interest and joy. There is no reason at this time why I should not continue to the end of my life the deepening enjoyment of these well established relationships. Under the circumstances I am confident that you will understand my desire to remain here.

Incidentally, when in 1922 the University of Chicago hoped to appoint Raymond to its presidency, the Fosdick brothers chuckled when the newspaper confused him with Harry. "You may be sure that Raymond, who is the one really wanted there," Harry wrote to their father, "has not the faintest idea of accepting the presidency, and certainly I wouldn't take it if a nigger boy brought it to me on a silver platter."*

VIII

In the spring of 1921 Fosdick received an invitation to address missionary groups in Japan and China. Thunder was then rolling out of the mission fields. Fundamentalists fearful of liberalism's emasculation of the Gospel message in foreign lands attacked the Christian fidelity of "tainted" missionaries, organizing such counterinsurgency movements as the Bible Union of China, formed in August 1920. Then the Stewart Evangelistic Fund—whose capital had been furnished by Milton Stewart, millionaire principal stockholder in the Union Oil Company and brother of Lyman Stewart, who was the originator and financial backer of *The Fundamentals*, a series of twelve booklets published between 1910 and 1915 that set forth the conservative position—underwrote the tour of an investigative squad to China, whose reports of missionary apostasy further roiled the waters. Concurrently, a conservative layman offered a gift of 100,000 shares of International Petroleum to the American Baptist Home Mission Society for general missionary purposes, contingent on the missionaries subscribing to a fundamentalist creed. Asked to give his

---

* Fosdick's racial attitudes will be examined in Chapter Twenty-Four.

judgment, Fosdick thundered that the "proposition involves nothing more nor less . . . than the buying of the Baptist Churches' subscription to a creed. . . . If I were speaking directly [to the gentlemen of the missionary board] I should certainly ask them what their lowest figure is for another set of creedal subscriptions."

Fosdick was fully aware of the increasingly embittered division and of the contingency of his own mission to the Orient. As he wrote to a former Union student and future dean of Peking University's Theological School, Timothy T. Lew, "Of course, I know all about the Bible Union Movement in China and we have had many conferences about it here. I am sincerely hoping that with the passage of time it may turn out that the bark of this animal is worse than its bite. I confess that it is with some trepidation that I undertake the task of speaking to representatives of both theological camps at Kuling this summer. You can readily see that it is going to be a difficult task and if you have any light that you can throw upon this matter I shall be delighted to receive it." Prior to sailing he informed John D. Rockefeller, Jr.:

As doubtless you know, the situation in the missionary movement in China and Japan is rather serious at present. There is quite a decided break between the reactionary and progressive forces and the reactionary faction have become self-conscious in their desire to suppress all liberalism. I suppose that nothing that any one person can do will solve the problem. Fortunately, however, I am sufficiently in the confidence of both parties so that they both have joined in inviting me to speak to the missionary bodies this coming summer. This offers an opportunity for me to present a common platform on which the two sections may perhaps unite. At least, I hope that the tragedy of an open break may be avoided, for in the course of a few years the kindly ministry of death will have removed many of those who are proving most violently and bitterly obstructive just now.

This communication reveals two important facts. First, as late as the spring of 1921 Fosdick was not yet considered by all fundamentalists to be their foe. The Conference Committee of Kuling, including both the executive heads of the Bible Union and the leaders of the liberal faction, was unanimous in its call to him. He hoped to negotiate a truce and obviously at least some conservatives were willing to accept his mediation. Second, by this date the Rockefeller-Fosdick friendship was close, their association antedating Fosdick's election to the Board of the Rockefeller Foundation in 1916, a position he held until succeeded by his brother in 1921. For the Orient trip, Dr. Simon Flexner of the Rockefeller Foundation fixed Fosdick "for immunity from all the bugs in the Orient," and on Fosdick's request Rockefeller wrote letters of introduction to the general managers of the Standard Oil Company in Japan and North China. Moreover, Rockefeller furnished travel funds to make possible the acceptance of the invitations (other sponsors were the Y.M.C.A. and the Federal Council of Churches), explaining, "I must tell you that my action in the matter was instigated far more by the desire to secure for the missionaries of these distant lands the opportunity to hear you discuss in your clear, forceful and convincing way, the great vital principles of the Christian religion. I believe you can render most important service just at this time, and I count it a privilege to be a partner with you in the enterprise, although a silent and insignificant one." The following year, on Fosdick's urgent pleading, Rockefeller gave, without public announcement, $50,000 toward the creation of a new theological school at Peking University, and Fosdick's millionaire friend Edward S. Harkness gave an equal amount. If sectarianism was baneful at home, both men believed, it was worse in mission fields. "Think of seeing an American Dutch Reformed Chinese!", Fosdick quoted a missionary as exclaiming. Apparently both conservative and liberal Protestant laymen heeded the Biblical injunction, "Go, sell thy oil," to underwrite respectively fundamentalist and liberal causes. Fosdick's argument for at least one first-rate theological school in China for the training of a Chinese leadership was predicated on the conviction that the "glad day shall come when missionaries from abroad will be no longer needed and native churches [will] stand upon their own feet."

Sailing from Vancouver on the *Empress of China*, Harry and Florence arrived at Yokohama on the Fourth of July, proceeding to Osaka, Nara, Kyoto, and Kobe and thence to China by way of Nagasaki. After participating in a series of conferences and visiting Peking and Tientsin, they returned to Japan, finally departing for home on September 10.

In Japan the Fosdicks were grape-juiced and dined by missionaries, Japanese churchmen, and public leaders in private meetings and large assemblies. On one occasion seventy-five Japanese leaders assembled in Tokyo's Imperial Hotel to hear Fosdick's address on "The Christian Interpretation of Life." He also addressed various American and Japanese gatherings of Sunday School workers, ministers, missionaries, teachers, and students. It was at Karuizawa that his impact was greatest. Addressing seven hundred missionaries and Japanese churchmen twice a day for five days, he warmed the liberal listeners and won at least some of the conservatives. "I stood up in Karuizawa," he related, "while the whole company shouted the creed and never opened my lips, such being my habit." Much to his surprise, however, the "wild beasts at Ephesus did not eat me up. There certainly are many varieties of the wild beasts over there but the Spirit of the Lord tamed them and they treated me as well as the lions treated Daniel." A Nagasaki pastor, Toichi Murata, after hearing Fosdick, pledged himself to love those whom he had given up on, to love those whom others had given up, and to love those whom nobody else loved. Recalled a missionary, Fosdick "made a profound impression on all who heard him."

In China Fosdick gave one talk before six hundred at Pei ta Ho and five talks before four hundred at Mokansham. However, it was in the hills of Kuling, where missionaries regularly vacationed to escape the summer heat, that there occurred the most significant encounter of the entire trip. Twice daily for eight straight days he spoke to an assemblage of fundamentalists and moderates and liberals numbering one thousand. It was as "strained and difficult" a challenge as he had ever faced, he reported at the time; and in his autobiography he recalled: "It was like walking a tightrope. . . . The tension was terrific."

Fosdick's purpose, as he wrote to liberal missionary leader, Edwin C. Lobenstine, was to win for the liberals "peace with honor." The last sentences of his Kuling address were surely spoken in a spirit of reconciliation: "The task to which we are called is enormously difficult. God help us so to fulfill it and to preach the Master to the life of our generation in the terms of our generation, as he ought to be preached—Lord of our life and God of our salvation."

Was he successful in his purpose? Yes and no. One missionary judged: "Fosdick practically killed the Bible Union Movement and I don't believe there is another man living who could have done that. His wonderful spirit and message won liberals and fundamentalists alike." Fosdick himself was not quite so sure the Union was slain. Still, "If it should turn out to be true that I have been the means of driving a tent pick into its brow like Jael, I should be extraordinarily pleased with myself for all the rest of my life."

At the time and even decades later Fosdick received letters from those who heard him in the Orient (and not only from liberals) expressing gratitude for his help in "charting our way through the 'fundamentalist' controversy" and returning them to their mission stations "with renewed zeal and courage" and "inspiration and joy." Continuing messages from the Orient, however, made it clear that the war was far from over. "I heard Dick Wilson speak out here," wrote Henry Kingman from Shanghai in 1923, referring to Princeton Seminary's conservative scholar. And "if he isn't a hinderance to the coming of God's kingdom then he isn't the unmitigated ass that I think him to be. Probably it isn't especially forbearing or charitable to call him an ass, and to wish that he might be 'shot at sunrise' but when in work with the students I see the havoc that is created by men of his ilk I find it hard to keep the lid on." Kingman closed: "To men like Wilson I give the credit of being sincere. . . . Unfortunately an ass can be both zealous and sincere and still be an ass." Although Fosdick never regretted the trip, he swore that never again would he willingly be placed in the strained position of having to accommodate his thought to a divided audience of conservative and liberals.

IX

When in 1924 The British Council for the Interchange of Preachers and Speakers Between the Churches of Great Britain and America invited Fosdick to come to Bitain on a two-month preaching and speaking tour, the hosts were stretching English understatement to the limit when they observed, "The programme seems rather formidable as you look at it on paper, but when you analyse it it is really a very easy sort of jaunt." Fosdick's reply that the schedule would "prove disastrous to a dray horse" was closer to the truth, and in mock lament wrote to his father, "I am inclined to think the only place on this planet where a poor sinner like myself is likely to find any rest is either on a ship or an island in the midst of the sea." Save for a few days walking the Scottish Highlands and cycling Shakespeare's country, he averaged two sermons or lectures daily before packed audiences. "I never spoke to so many people in the same length of time in my life," he ebulliently reported to George Alexander.

Fosdick sailed from New York with Florence and their two daughters, and on the morning of May 14 the party hurried from the Southampton docks to London. That very afternoon Fosdick addressed a "vast concourse" of people, chiefly clergy of all denominations, in City Temple, London's oldest and most famous Congregational church. In all its history the Temple was never fuller, a leading churchman reported, "and it could easily have been filled over again by the crowds who wanted to hear him. Never since the visits of Henry Ward Beecher has an American preacher aroused such eager interest." There followed a large reception, Fosdick proving "himself a prince of courtesy in the social intercourse of this hour," exchanging "a few kindly words with several hundred people." For the evening service, despite heavy rains, a queue of several hundreds again waited patiently outside the doors of City Temple for two hours to hear Fosdick, now joined by two other speakers. Asserted one observer, "Surely, never in its fifty years, has the City Temple seen such a day as that on which Dr. Fosdick made his debut at the commencement of his long and successful preaching and speaking tour of the British Isles."

The two-month tour was indeed a triumph, including the bestowal by Glasgow University of the honorary degree of doctor of divinity. (Prime Minister J. Ramsay MacDonald was also present to receive an honorary degree, and perhaps because of this the students were singularly frisky, Fosdick comparing their "freak chorus" to the noise of a "man with a wooden leg having a fit in a tin roof," this riposte further "bringing down the house.") Of the tour as a whole, Dean Lynn Harold Hough observed that "it would be no exaggeration . . . to say that no American preacher since Henry Ward Beecher has had such a reception in England. Dr. Fosdick is the sort of person the British instinctively like." His liberal theological beliefs seemed to the British unexceptional. Stated the *Manchester Guardian:* "The American Modernist simply stands where nearly all Protestant theologians stand in England. He is not in the least advanced according to English ideas." As a famous Scotch Presbyterian Moderator remarked after hearing Fosdick preach, "If this is the type of heretic being produced in America, please produce some more and send them to Scotland." Indeed, "evangelist" was the tag not infrequently attached to the visiting Yankee.

The British liked Fosdick in part because he joshed them, as when he quoted the Irishman who defined an Englishman as a man with all the characteristics of a poker without its warmth and when he quoted the American traveler who observed that the Thames River would not make a gurgle in the mouth of the Mississippi.

The British liked Fosdick also because he patently pandered to England's fading imperial glory. For example, in an address, "England and America," he cried, "Sooner or later, I feel confident that we will be compelled to emerge from any attempted isolation to stand beside you to endeavor to work out in a just and Christian way the white man's great responsibility for the security and peace of the world." Again: "We white folk have, oftentimes without intention, blundered into a perfectly stupendous responsibility for the peace and security of the world, and we must play the game for the safety and brotherhood of mankind." And again: "If Great Britain and America ever do agree about any great thing on this planet it will be done." "England and America united could save the world, and there were no other countries in the world that could save it," is how one newspaper reported a speech and the ensuing "applause" and "hear, hear." Of course, in all this Fosdick made a great thing of his own English ancestry, much to the delight of the audiences.

In fielding questions about the United States Fosdick engaged in a little artful dodging. Prohibition, he replied to one inquiry, would never be repealed because it was a great success. What was the true state of race relations? He responded that all was harmonious in the North and that "they were making rapid progress in the Southern States in the same direction." To an inquiry about immigration, he drew laughter with the unfortunate comment (considering the racial and ethnic bias written into the 1924 immigration law), "Your sons go out to the ends of the world. We are concerned because the ends of the world come to us."

X

The four Fosdicks sailed from Southampton on July 15 with memories of a smashingly jolly time—as their hosts might have phrased it. It is good that Harry should have such memories, for he was returning to the most ferocious fight of his life.

Chapter Seven

The War Within:
The Presbyterian
Fundamentalists Drive
Fosdick from Their Fold

I

No major denomination was more desperately riven by controversy in the 1920s than the Presbyterian Church, U.S.A. Boasting almost two million communicants, ten thousand ministers, and ten thousand churches, these adherents of the Westminister Confession of Faith had social prestige, political power, economic affluence, and a rich intellectual tradition. The liberal wing was strong and growing as the twentieth century opened and deepened, but conservative strength was also formidable and aggressive under the leadership of such champions as the revered layman William Jennings Bryan; the respected Princeton theologian, J. Gresham Machen; the popular revivalist William A. (Billy) Sunday; the wealthy, pious merchant John Wanamaker; and a galaxy of pulpit giants from Clarence Edward Macartney in Philadelphia to Mark A. Matthews in Seattle. In late 1918 Fosdick had stepped into the pulpit of New York's historic First Presbyterian Church as preaching minister in a deliberate ecumenical experiment. Inevitably, the Baptist guest preacher became implicated in the Presbyterian storm, and in 1922 events thrust him into the very eye of the tempest. Three years later the conservatives left him no alternative, as he believed, but to say "Farewell" to Old First. Even as the conservatives congratulated themselves, the liberal lines held. By the end of the decade the conservatives would be on the defensive and, ironically, in the 1930s it would be the conservatives who believed that the triumphant liberals left them no choice but to withdraw from the church of their fathers.

II

The post–Civil War reunion of Old School and New School Presbyterians had not brought theological peace to the denomination. In the 1870s, as millenarian and scriptural inerrancy movements grew, liberal ministers in Chicago and Cincinnati were formally tried on charges of heresy. The drive to root out unorthodoxy stepped up in the 1890s. The distinguished scholars Charles A. Briggs, Henry Preserved Smith, and Arthur Cushman McGiffert were driven from the Presbyterian ministry, the great divorce of the church and New York's Union Seminary occurred, the revision of the Westminister Confession of Faith was fiercely debated, and the General Assembly began to set forth certain doctrines, including inerrancy, as essential to the faith.

The conservative tide did not recede in the opening years of the twentieth century. Five hundred ministers and elders signed a fighting manifesto, "Back to the Fundamentals." Wealthy laymen stepped up their support of bible institutes. The powerful journals, *The Presbyterian* and the *Herald and Presbyter*, launched conservative crusades. Counting Scottish contributors, more than a quarter of the articles in *The Fundamentals* were of Presbyterian authorship, and this major testimony to the true faith was widely distributed by the wealthy Stewart brothers of California. The General Assembly declared that Union Seminary was in no sense Presbyterian and charges were brought to deny its graduates ordination by the liberal (and highly suspect) Presbytery of New York. Above all, the 1910 General Assembly adopted a Five-Point doctrinal deliverance (repeated in 1916) declaring that the inerrancy of scripture, Christ's virgin birth, his substitutionary atonement, his bodily resurrection, and his showing of his power and love by working miracles were each "an essential doctrine of the Word of God"—though the deliverance murkily concluded, "Others are equally so." In a word, conservatives sought officially to brand as heretical any deviation from the restrictive Princeton Theology.

The outbreak of the Great War demolished the liberal dream of inevitable progress. One of many eschatological "signs," it heightened the sense of urgency of the dispensational premillennialists and permitted them to identify modernism with the materialistic *Kultur* of the "swinish Hun." At first glance the initial alliance between the premillennialists and the Princeton scholastics suggests a cynical *mariage de convenance*. On reflection, however, as George Marsden discerned, "the most natural allies of the revivalist fundamentalists were the Princeton theologians who for generations had been firing heavy artillery at every idea that moved and who were almost indecently astute at distinguishing Biblical and Reformed truth from all error." What bonded the two groups was a common concern for Biblical authority, inspiration, literalism, and inerrancy. The dispensationalists required just such a reading of Holy Writ and the Princeton professors' hermeneutics nicely complemented the requirement. It is important to underscore that neither element in this union represented classical Protestant theology. Though naturally the premillennialist-Princeton alliance claimed to possess the faith "once for all delivered to the saints," actually both strains evolved from nineteenth-century evangelicalism, as did the new rival, modernism.

In the war's immediate aftermath conservative Presbyterians threw themselves into new fundamentalist organizations, launched investigations of "tainted" missionaries, lampooned such grandiose liberal enterprises as the Interchurch World Movement, and blocked the liberal-backed Plan of Union with other denominations. Robert Hastings Nichols, liberal Union professor, wrote of the conservative crusade: "In its implacable hostility to any religious teaching but its own, in propagandist zeal, and in its sweeping campaign of proscription and repression, this program resembles that of the Roman Catholic Counter-Reformation; and the strength of fundamentalism is such that the comparison is not idle."

III

Conservative Presbyterian doubts about Fosdick's orthodoxy antedated his 1922 challenge, "Shall the Fundamentalists Win?" In fact they antedated his call to Old First. Throughout his ministry at the Montclair First Baptist Church, in word and practice he aligned with the liberals. His 1915 Union Seminary inaugural address elicited caustic conservative comment. In a letter in 1916, the Princeton scholastic J. Gresham Machen mentioned hearing Fosdick preach: "And he is dreadful! Just the pitiful modern stuff about an undogmatic Christianity." The conservatives fully comprehend Fosdick's successes in reaching multitudes through universally popular early devotional books. The only trouble was—and it was everything—he was reaching them with something that was not Christianity at all. As Machen himself phrased it, "The question is not whether Dr. Fosdick is winning men, but whether the thing to which he is winning them is Christianity." Hard upon the heels of the Old First appointment Fosdick's exacerbating article "The Trenches and the Church at Home" appeared and then there was sermon after well-publicized sermon, none drawing heavier return fire than "Progressive Christianity" preached May 8, 1921.

Early in 1922, the *New York Times* carried an article, "God and Evolution," by William Jennings Bryan, in which the Great Commoner characterized the "guess" of evolution as unscientific and irreligious. On the *Times'* invitation, Fosdick's rebuttal appeared March 12. Deemed by liberals a demolition job, the statement was widely reprinted in periodicals and distributed in pamphlet form. The closing sentences were less than conciliatory: Mr. Bryan proposes "that his special form of medievalism shall be made authoritative by the State, promulgated as the only teaching allowed in the schools. Surely, we can promise him a long, long road to travel before he plunges the education system of this country into such incredible folly, and if he does succeed in arousing a real battle over the issue we can promise him also that just as earnestly as the scientists will fight against him in the name of scientific freedom of investigation, so will multitudes of Christians fight against him in the name of their religion and their God." Only two months were to pass before Fosdick entered a tangled thicket from which there was no scratchless escape.

IV

The issue was joined on Sunday morning, May 21, when Fosdick stood in the pulpit of First Church to preach the most far-reaching sermon of his career, "Shall the Fundamentalists Win?", taking as his unannounced text Acts 5:38–39: "Refrain from these men, and let them alone: for if this counsel or this work be of men, it will come to naught: But if it be of God, ye cannot overthrow it; lest haply ye be found even to fight against God." About this famous sermon, central to the controversy and to Fosdick's career, a few things should be said.

First, one is reminded of the old historiographical question, "Did Lincoln deliberately maneuver the South into firing the first shot at Ft. Sumter?" As the nation was already divided in 1861, so American Protestantism was already splintered in 1922. As Southern states had already taken action, so fundamentalists had already organized. As Lincoln ordered the resupplying of Sumter as a symbolic gesture of his determination to preserve the Union, so Fosdick preached the sermon to alert the fundamentalists that they could not "drive out from the Christian churches all the consecrated souls who do not agree with their theory of inspiration. What immeasurable folly!" It is true that neither Lincoln nor Fosdick wanted war. It is further true that both men thought time to be on their side. And it is finally true that as Southern fire-eaters welcomed the Sumter incident, so fundamentalists welcomed the sermon, forcing the moderates to take sides, as had happened to the states in the Upper South. Clarence Macartney, the respected minister of Philadelphia's Arch Street Presbyterian Church, was deluding himself when he said that "It was the thrusting of the outrageous sermon upon the church at large which has made this incident precipitate a conflict." The sermon was not a stone dropped into denominational waters that would otherwise have remained calm.

On the other hand, Fosdick was kidding himself when he characterized the sermon as a "plea for good will" and kidding others when he wrote (as he did in numerous letters at the time): "It still seems to me a frank, kindly, irenic plea for tolerance, not likely to be misunderstood except by people who persist in misunderstanding it." To be sure, some passages are irenic and the closing prayer is conciliatory: "Hear us this morning as with eager prayer we lift up our hearts and seek from Thee the grace of magnanimity, the ability to differ and yet to love, the beauty of tolerance and of a large heart." Yet what were conservative Presbyterians to think when this Baptist declared from a Presbyterian pulpit belief in the virgin birth nonessential, the inerrancy of the Scriptures incredible, the second coming of Christ from the skies an outmoded phrasing of hope? What were they to think when they heard or read the charge that "just now the Fundamentalists are giving us one of the worst exhibitions of bitter intolerance that the churches of this country have ever seen"? Although the newspapers repeatedly intoned, "Dr. Fosdick Is Not a Fighter," a more accurate description, as discerning observers noted, would have been, "Dr. Fosdick Is Not a Fool." In a word, he carefully calculated the timing and the wording of the sermon and surely knew that it would not be received as oil poured on troubled waters. Fosdick never indulged in homiletical "plunging" and as his admirer and future associate at Park Avenue Baptist Church Cornelius Woelfkin cautioned at the time, "We should not underestimate the qualities of Dr. Fosdick for defensive and aggressive strategy."

A second point. Both Fosdick and Ivy Lee—the nation's most artful public relations man, who claimed the Rockefellers among many personal and corporate clients (and, not incidentally, a genuinely dedicated Christian liberal)—stated that Lee alone was responsible for distributing the sermon to every ordained Protestant clergyman in the country (about 130,000), slightly abridged by Lee and with an introduction prepared by Lee and under a different title. This is the truth, but not the whole truth. Fosdick did not suggest or request the distribution or make the minor revisions. It does not follow, however, that Fosdick wanted this particular homilectic light to be hidden under a bushel. For one thing, he approved its distribution and he approved its reprinting by such liberal journals as the *Christian Century, Christian Work,* and *The Baptist.* For another, he wrote to his father on May 24: "Last Sunday I took up the problem of the Fundamentalists and the sermon will be printed. I shall see that one gets into your hands as soon as it comes from the press. The reaction to it has been encouraging and I am hoping it may do some good." Fosdick knew in advance that at the very least the sermon would be printed and distributed on a smaller scale by Old First. Moreover, he was privy to John D. Rockefeller, Jr.'s activity. It was Rockefeller who paid for the distribution by Lee, a fact suspected but rarely stated at the time, and it was Rockefeller who suggested the revised and less inflammatory title, "The New Knowledge and the Christian Faith," with the recommendation that Lee's subtitle, "Shall the Fundamentalists Drive Liberals from the Church of Christ?", be deleted. As Rockefeller wisely pointed out, "The object in circulating this sermon is to get the views therein expressed widely read and not to stir up discord. The title which I suggest is clear and accurately descriptive,—at the same time it does not breathe of controversy. . . . This is merely a suggestion; whatever Raymond Fosdick thinks wise, and perhaps he will care to take the matter up with his brother, will be satisfactory to me." Raymond took the matter up with his older brother and the title change was made.

Not once in his private or public correspondence at the time or later did Fosdick express regret for preaching the sermon. As he wrote to a Presbyterian leader, "I am profoundly sorry that the sermon has been misinterpreted; I am profoundly sorry that it has caused a disturbance; but I cannot honestly be sorry at all that I preached the sermon. When I get to heaven I expect it to be one of the stars in my crown."*

V

Presbyterian conservatives immediately and passionately expressed their doubts as to whether Fosdick would ever reach that celestial destination

---

* Dr. John B. Macnab, now senior minister of the First Presbyterian Church, put this question to Fosdick in retirement: "If you had to do it all over again, would you do so in the same fashion as you did in the sermon?" Fosdick replied, "I don't think so." This is the only evidence I have uncovered that Fosdick ever had any doubts. Incidentally, Dr. Macnab holds the sermon was clearly provocative, as Fosdick should have discerned, and believes that Dr. George Alexander, Old First senior minister, tried to persuade Fosdick to change the title, though not to scrap the entire sermon.

where the inhabitants wore crowns of stars. Philadelphia's Dr. Macartney, termed by Fosdick "personally fair-minded and courteous"—and who in fact disliked being called a "fundamentalist," preferring the designation "conservative, evangelical Christian"—volleyed a reply: "Shall Unbelief Win?", a sermon carried in *The Presbyterian*, under the editorship of David S. Kennedy, the most militant of all the denominational organs. Macartney wrote to Fosdick to be sure he was not misquoting him, and two of the letters in the subsequent exchange found their way into the press. Contrary to a general misconception, Macartney informed Fosdick, "I have no objection to your being a Baptist in a Presbyterian pulpit. I am ready to have preach in my pulpit . . . any man who preaches the Christ of the New Testament, be that man Baptist, Presbyterian, Episcopalian, or Roman Catholic. But if I believe him to preach any other Christ than the Christ of the New Testament, I feel it to be my duty to cry out against him." He contrasted the "grand particularities" of historic Christianity with Fosdick's subjectivism, rationalism, naturalism, and then concluded, "The Christ whom you preach is not the Christ whom I preach and in whom I put my trust for this life and for that which is to come." As he informed another correspondent, "We have Jesus Christ in the New Testament, and outside of that, silence and darkness." Though even his mother implored, "Can't you leave poor Fosdick alone?", Macartney pressed the attack.

The publication of Fosdick's Vanderbilt Lectures under the title, *Christianity and Progress*, did not soothe matters. Fosdick was called by extremists a "Unitarian Cuckoo" who stigmatized Jesus as "a bastard and His blessed mother a harlot." Much was made of the "consecrated lawlessness" of a creedless Baptist (Fosdick openly boasted of never having repeated the Apostles' Creed in his life) occupying the pulpit of a creedal church. Even the editor of a secular paper observed, "It is not exactly ethical for a vegetarian to accept employment from a meat packer and urge a diet of spinach upon all who come asking for meat."

On October 2 the Presbytery of Philadelphia met in the home of John Wanamaker to discuss the Old First scandal, with the merchant's pastor, Dr. A. Gordon MacLennan and Dr. Macartney taking the lead. At the next meeting, October 16, the presbytery by a vote of seventy-two to twenty-one took the grave step of adopting an overture to the General Assembly. The overture began with the general charge that in the First Church of New York "there had been a public proclamation of the Word which appears to be in open denial of the essential doctrine of the Presbyterian Church in the U.S.A. and subversive of the truth of Christianity as received, confessed, held and defended by the Christian Church in all ages" and, after quoting Fosdick on the virgin birth, concluded, "The

Presbytery of Philadelphia hereby respectfully overtures the General Assembly to direct the Presbytery of New York to take such action as will require the preaching and teaching in the First Presbyterian Church of New York City to conform to the system of doctrine taught in the Confession of Faith."

What had been a hot controversy now became white hot. Sermons were preached, broadsides published, articles and editorials written, letters exchanged, conferences held, and Fosdick was told by one critic, "If I were keeping the doors of heaven I should close them to you." William Jennings Bryan increasingly transferred his energies from secular politics to church politics. His *In His Image: An Answer to Darwinism* (1922) was read by millions, and his argument that "the evolutionary hypothesis is the only thing that has seriously menaced religion since the birth of Christ" was accepted by millions. Believing Fosdick to be the "most altitudinous higher critic" and believing Fosdick's theistic evolution to be an "anesthetic" intended to deaden the "pain while the Christian religion is being removed," on January 8, 1923, he mentioned Fosdick by name in his proposal "to drive out into the open those who oppose the Bible, so that they will fight face forward and in the open." The following month Professor Machen's manifesto, *Christianity and Liberalism*, appeared. In it the brilliant Princeton scholar explained that Fosdick's brand of liberalism was "a religion which is so entirely different from Christianity as to belong in a distinct category." As repetitious as Ravel's *Bolero*, Machen beat upon the theme of Fosdick's "utter agnosticism," "empty sentimentality," "meretricious rhetoric," "pragmatic skepticism"—he was "an opponent of the Christian faith" "ethically far inferior" to the old agnostics "since they did not try to combat, by false pretense, the faith of a creedal Church from within." As the General Assembly approached, other presbyteries (including New York) received memorials to investigate the orthodoxy of the Old First pulpit and ultimately six sent up overtures similar to that from Philadelphia; concurrently, liberals circulated petitions condemning Philadelphia's action.

Fosdick's posture during this stormy period was composed. He honored the advice of his friend Henry Sloane Coffin, pastor of Madison Avenue Church and soon to be president of Union, not to "add any fuel to the flames" by making a fighting statement, for, Coffin believed, "Most of the reactionaries will grow weary unless we feed them with material for controversy." So, Fosdick made no gratuitous statement and he vetoed suggestions to send his sermons to the nation's ministry again, as Ivy Lee requested. On the other hand, when friends sought to defend him by muting his liberalism, he sternly admonished them: "I am a liberal, progressive Christian, holding the new theology root and branch, and I do not want to be defended as though I were not." Again: "Some of these cautious Presbyterians are endeavoring to win my case by representing me as not so much of a heretic as I am sometimes pictured. There may be some truth in it, but it is likely to give the whole case away, for I want to win it as I am sure to win it, not as a member of the orthodox tribe, but as a liberal." He played fair with Dr. Alexander, writing to his senior colleague, "My one concern is that I should not be the occasion of doing harm to the great church with which I have been working and to whose interests I am sincerely devoted. It seems to me . . . that unless the storm immediately subsides . . . I ought at least to put my resignation in the hands of the Session to do with as they see fit."

Of course, he received letters of appreciation as well as vilification, one correspondent jokingly praising his prudence in buying an island off the coast of Maine (Mouse Island), likening the surrounding icy water to a protective moat. His father saw him as another Daniel, but Fosdick dismissed the fundamentalist lions as "rather old, hoarse, toothless, and . . . stuffed." As for the newspaper predictions that he was to be tried for heresy at the next General Assembly: "Of course, that is all nonsense. Not being amenable to Presbyterian jurisdiction I cannot be brought before a Presbyterian court. . . . If only my enemies will keep on judiciously attacking me . . . , I see no reason why this year at the church should not be a great success. The only thing that gives me concern is what on earth I am going to do when they stop attacking me. I fear that life then will be dull, tame, and insipid." Meanwhile, worshippers poured into Old First until "we were taking in water over the gunwale." In January 1923 Fosdick made this prediction to his father:

> I am extraordinarily fortunate in this, that while there has been an immense amount of theological furor against me, there has been none of it within my own congregation. . . . I am therefore enjoying all the reputation that comes to a martyr without any of the pains . . . and am having the time of my young life trying to measure up to the opportunity that it gives me to say some things that need to be said. I really think we are going in the end to get the two things that we want most to get: namely, a real victory for liberalism, while at the same time we are holding together the Presbyterian Church without a split.

Tension was the order of the day when in mid-May almost a thousand commissioners, roughly half laymen and half ministers, assembled in Indianapolis for the 1923 General Assembly. The first business was the election of a moderator. William Jennings Bryan, a far from toothless lion, more vivid than color and louder than sound, was on hand to claim the office for the conservatives. On the fourth ballot he was defeated by

Dr. Charles F. Wishart, president of Wooster College, who, hoping for unity and inclusivism, softly announced, "I look upon my election as a victory for tolerance rather than for liberalism." Later a wiser and sadder Wishart would write to Fosdick, "I am convinced that most of the harm in our denomination has been made possible through one man, Mr. Bryan."

Wishart's judgment invites a few words about the Great Commoner. Bryan did in fact seek to inflict much harm on liberal Presbyterians and more generally on all liberal Protestants, including Fosdick. Recent scholarship has been fairly kind to him and we should be grateful that the older caricature has been challenged. No one denies his generous impulses, authentic progressive concerns, his essential humanity. He was not a narrow sectarian or a foe of social Christianity or a dispensationalist. But he came to Indianapolis determined to save Presbyterianism from heretical modernism. To that end, he actively campaigned for the moderatorship well in advance of the assembly, though he coyly waited until the night before the election to consent definitely to the presentation of his name. And he took his defeat with little grace, stating to the newspapers that the assembly was controlled by the "liberal machine" and informing his followers that the opposition votes came from "All of the politicians of the church," "the college men," "practically all the evolutionists and those who were on the Fosdick side of the case," and "nearly all of the colored delegates."

Defeat had never dismayed Bryan, nor did it now. He proceeded to introduce a successful resolution requiring that all Presbyterian preachers, officials, and teachers in church schools be total abstainers. Other minor resolutions followed. Then came the blockbuster: "Resolved— That no part of the educational fund of the Presbyterian Church in the U.S.A. shall be paid to any school, college, university or theological seminary that teaches or permits to be taught as a proved fact, either Darwinism or any other evolutionary hypothesis that links man in blood relationship with any other form of life." Bryan spoke to his motion for thirty minutes at the beginning of the debate and for fifteen at the close. He plead his case (as his most scholarly biographer records) with fire, wit, and passion, drawing his auditors to their feet, inciting the shaking of fists in both camps, and eliciting a call for decorum from the chair. Liberal observers granted the "clever satire, shrewd pleading, rhetorical brilliance," but they also judged the performance an "undignified, unintelligent," and "regrettable exhibition of unrestrained fanaticism," noting that it was the same speech Bryan had been delivering on Chautauqua platforms for years. With every sentence he lost votes and ultimately the delegates rejected the resolution by a two-to-one margin in favor of a substitute that merely warned against a "materialistic evolutionary philosophy of life." As the substitute resolution was adopted Bryan, appearing unwell, sank into his chair.

The following day his recovery was hastened when the conservatives won a victory that, he reported, "pleased me much more than I would have been pleased by election to the Moderatorship a dozen times." This victory was over Fosdick's defenders and grew out of the Philadelphia Presbytery overture of October, which had been referred to the Committee on Bills and Overtures for consideration and report. The committee's majority report, signed by 22 of its 23 members, recommended that inasmuch as the New York Presbytery at the request of one of its own churches had already appointed a committee to inquire into Fosdick's preaching, the Philadelphia overture should be deemed "needless, if not unfairly intrusive." A single member of the committee refused to sign that report, Dr. A. Gordon MacLennan, pastor of Bethany Church, Philadelphia. He submitted a minority-of-one dissent that expressed sorrow that doctrines contrary to Presbyterian standards had been preached in First Church and ordered the Presbytery of New York "to take such action as will require the preaching and teaching . . . to conform to the system of doctrine taught in the Confession of Faith." MacLennan's dissent further, and importantly, reaffirmed the five articles of faith declared essential by the 1910 assembly. A wearied and depleted assembly with 138 commissioners absent and the liberals perhaps rendered overconfident by Bryan's two earlier defeats, then debated the majority and minority reports for five dramatic hours, MacLennan and Bryan speaking forcefully, as did Macartney who termed the majority report "a pusillanimous document—a whitewash." He noted bitingly the contrast between the assembly's orthodox singing and praying and its unorthodox voting. On Bryan's motion the vote was taken by roll call and the minority report carried, 439 to 359. "It was a sight to make angels weep and devils laugh," lamented George A. Buttrick. Led by William P. Merrill, 85 assembly liberals immediately signed a protest.

For the conservatives, as Bryan exclaimed, "It was a great victory." Not only would Fosdick be "within reach of our stick," but more significantly the assembly had affirmed again as "essential" five doctrines dear to the fundamentalist faith. This "master stroke," wrote one conservative, "will give heart to Christians of all denominations who are fighting this battle for true Evangelical faith." As for the moderates, perhaps the sainted George Alexander spoke for them when he opened the devotional service of the assembly on the morning after the vote with the old, magnificent words, "Though I speak with the tongues of men and of angels, and have not charity. . . ."

VI

The twelve-month period between the adjournment of the Indianapolis General Assembly and the May 1924 assembly was not uneventful. Fosdick found himself the focus of an intensive investigation, as mandated by the General Assembly. This investigation served a central symbolic purpose for Presbyterian liberals and conservatives alike in their desperate denominational struggle.

In keeping with his character, Fosdick's response was to submit a letter of resignation on May 24 to the Session of Old First because, he said, "I am strongly bound by ties of warm affection to the ministers, officers, and members of the Church. . . . My sole reason in presenting this resignation is the welfare of the Church." Unanimously the session declined to accept the resignation and so informed Fosdick on June 3 in a letter in which his services to the church were cited and handsomely praised. Fosdick acknowledged the "beautiful" epistle and assured the session of his strong desire to continue in the service of the church and "always to hold myself at the disposal of the Session to be of use in any possible way." In declining the resignation, as it subsequently explained, the session had no intention of disobeying the General Assembly; it sought merely "to preserve the status quo" pending the presbytery's investigation.

The General Assembly's order to investigate Fosdick's orthodoxy triggered a national response that transcended denominational boundries. The independent religious journals, *Christian Century* and *Christian Work*, came to his defense. Petitions of praise signed by hundreds of faculty and students came to him from Cornell, Mount Holyoke, Columbia, and Southern Methodist, as did hundreds of individual letters of support. All essentially affirmed that his preaching had deepened their Christian faith.

Within the Presbyterian church individual after individual came forward to take up Fosdick's cause in sermons, articles, and press statements, not entirely or even primarily because of personal respect and affection for him, but because they believed that the doctrinal deliverances of the General Assembly were unconstitutional and a threat to historic Presbyterian liberties. Such was the public position taken by Henry Sloane Coffin, William P. Merrill, George A. Buttrick, Robert Hastings Nichols, John A. MacCallum, Murray Shipley Howland, Canada's Richard Roberts, and Scotland's John Kelman, among others. To these men, "Fundamentalism is a monstrous assertion of eccesiastical authority" (Nichols). "It is a sort of theological Prussianism that wants to impress its own 'rubber stamp' on every man's religion" (Roberts). At issue are "those great principles of freedom of thinking and of the dominance of the Spirit, which are the heritage of Presbyterianism and of Protestantism, because they are the essence of Christianity" (Merrill). Regarding Fosdick, "If his attitude towards the Christian gospel precludes him from a Presbyterian pulpit, then scores of us should likewise be precluded" (Buttrick). On Fosdick again, "I feel that I owe it to my own congregation and to the Presbytery to state plainly that if any action is taken which removes Dr. Fosdick from the pulpit of First Church on account of his interpretation of the Christian Gospel, I cannot honestly be allowed to remain in the pulpit of the Madison Avenue Church, for I share fully his point of view." (Coffin). If the General Assembly's Five-Point doctrine had been binding, "I could not have accepted a call to any church in America" (Kelman).

Fosdick's support was widespread. *The Continent* and the *Presbyterian Advance* (edited by Nolan Best and James Clarke, respectively) were both with him. The president of Princeton University, John Grier Hibben, praised him as a "great teacher and prophet of righteousness." Dr. Henry van Dyke, professor, diplomat, and venerable Presbyterian leader, dismissed the famous Five Points as invalid definitions of the Christian faith, surrendered his pew in a Princeton church in protest against Machen's preaching there, and wrote sternly to Macartney: "Rumour says that an attack upon Dr. George Alexander, that venerable saint of God and true servant of Christ, and upon his younger brethren, is to be launched. I discredit that rumour. But if it is true, let this be understood, only over my (ecclesiastically) dead body shall such an attack be consummated." To crowd Fosdick from the Old First pulpit would be "so stupid as to be almost wicked" was an editorial judgment of the *New York Times* shared by much of the secular press. In sum, liberal Presbyterianism echoed Coffin's plea to Fosdick: ". . . for God's sake do not withdraw. You have every provocation, but you would leave the rest of us in a terrible fix. . . . The Fundamentalists can have me, if they like. Here's hoping that the Presbytery will keep its back-bone, and that we may fight this through to a clean finish!"

Far and away the most significant development of this crucial year for the Presbyterian Church was the formulation of the Auburn Affirmation. Fosdick played no direct role in its drafting and circulation, so we shall only mention it, despite its salient and sympathetic reference to the Old First situation. Within two weeks of the adjournment of the General Assembly a small group of ministers began the organizational effort that resulted in the drafting and ultimate publication in January 1924 of a statement with the full title, *An Affirmation designed to safeguard the unity and liberty of the Presbyterian Church in the United States of America.* In time 1294 Presbyterian ministers placed their signatures to this document and it instantly became the foundation upon which Presbyterian inclusivists built their defense against the assaults of the exclusivists. The terms inclusivists and exclusivists are more appropriate here than liberals and conservatives, or modernists and fundamentalists. The statement was less a liberal negative critique of fundamentalist doctrine than a positive constitutional affirmation of historic Presbyterian liberties. Even theological moderates and conservatives could join Coffin, Merrill, Howland, Nichols, Buttrick, and the other prime movers of the manifesto in declaring: "We do not desire liberty to go beyond the teachings of evangelical Christianity. But we maintain that it is our constitutional right and our Christian duty within these limits to exercise liberty of thought and teaching, that we may more effectively preach the gospel of Jesus Christ, the Saviour of the world." Even moderates and conservatives could see the force of the argument that the General Assembly's deliverances of 1910, 1916, and 1923 (the Five Points) were unconstitutional; for the assembly to declare authoritatively that certain doctrines in the Westminister Confession are "essential" is in effect to amend the Confession. This, however, could be done constitutionally only by the joint action of the assembly and two thirds of the presbyteries, not by the assembly alone.

As Fosdick's Presbyterian defenders were active, his detractors were no less so. With increasing frequency he was termed "The Stranger (or Foreigner) Within Our Gates." Protests were made against the advertising of his books in Presbyterian periodicals and the boycott of such periodicals urged. A not untypical accusation appeared in *The Presbyterian*: "Dr. Fosdick is not among us with credentials for deposit. He is camping in a discredited seminary, throwing his students on the rolls of our ministry through the action of the New York Presbytery. He has invaded our mission fields . . . , assails the peace and quiet of the church. . . . It is the boldest exhibition of widespread and fundamental daring that the Presbyterian Church in America ever witnessed."

The Auburn Affirmation was denounced as "bolshevistic and destructive" and its signers branded as "nullifiers" and "disloyal," and they were invited, or rather commanded, to debark from the Presbyterian Ark. As Dr. MacLennan declaimed: "I cry shame, thrice shame, on the Presbyterians of the twentieth century. We owe it to the present generation to keep from being dragged into the slime of Modernism, and we should hand on our historic faith loyally to the next generation." Everywhere the warning was raised, "The church is in danger!" The epithets "materialist," "pantheist," "infidel," "rationalist," and, perhaps most damning of all, "Unitarian," were freely cast about. Conservatives formed committees of correspondence reminiscent of 1776 and mass meetings "in the interest of Historic Presbyterianism" were held in strategic cities, notably New York, Philadelphia, and Pittsburgh. At one such meeting, Dr. Macartney, a Civil War buff, spoke on "The Irrepressible Conflict," saying, "Away with all false prophets who cry to the people of Christ, Peace, when there is no peace." Pittsburgh's Maitland Alexander, Seattle's Mark Matthews, Princeton's Machen, and the redoubtable Samuel G. Craig all announced there could be no peace without victory. Closing the great October 30 New York meeting in prayer, Dr. John McNeill informed the Almighty, "This is but the vanguard of the seven thousand who have not bowed the knee to Baal."

The New York Presbytery continued to be a special target, and there was much talk of its excision. Five members of the presbytery protested because two young candidates for licensure, Henry Pitney Van Dusen and Cedric D. Layman, failed "to affirm their belief in the Virgin Birth of our Lord Jesus Christ." Dr. John Robertson, whom Fosdick termed a "crazy Scotchman," moved that the Session of Old First "be summoned to the Bar of Presbytery for the offense of filling the pulpit by a Baptist minister that subverts by his heretical preaching our Constitutional Westminister Confession of Faith." (Robertson subsequently resigned from the presbytery, explaining, "I have applied for Holy Orders in the Episcopal Church.") Still another member, Dr. Albert Dale Gantz, called for the immediate end of the Old First/Fosdick relationship.

Meanwhile, Bryan was receiving a cluster of letters thanking him for his good work at Indianapolis and seconding the consoling point made by Mark Matthews, "The Tall Pine of the Sierras": "But it was much better for you not to be Moderator. You are in position to lead the church, and if you arouse the laymen and show them what rationalism is costing them both in money and morals, you will be able to bring the church back to orthodoxy." These letters not only looked back to Indianapolis, they looked forward to the next General Assembly. Bryan agreed to nominate Macartney for moderator. "It would be well for our forces to get together at Grand Rapids as early as possible before the election takes place," suggested MacLennan. And it was the ubiquitous young MacLennan who prepared an overture for adoption by the Philadelphia Presbytery mandating "that all who represent the church on the Boards, General Council, theological seminaries and every other agency of the church be required to affirm or reaffirm their faith in the Standards of the church, together with the historic interpretations as contained in the doctrinal deliverances of the General Assembly, notably that of

1910." Of course, the intent was to bar from positions of denominational authority the 1294 signers of the Auburn Affirmation.

It was not a happy time for Presbyterian moderates. The new moderator, Dr. Charles F. Wishart, repeatedly issued pleas for tolerance, patience, forbearance. Dr. Lewis S. Mudge, who held the key post of Stated Clerk, which placed him in close contact with preachers and elders everywhere, quickly came to the conclusion that denominational peace would come only when Fosdick departed from Old First. As he explained, not without sadness, to James E. Clarke, "It seems to me that in the last analysis, the whole question runs back to the homely truth that what we will permit a member of the family to say in the family circle with impunity, we will not allow a visitor or boarder to utter without protest." Especially was it not a happy time at Princeton Seminary for President J. Ross Stevenson and Professor Charles R. Erdman, neither of whom was even remotely a modernist. In fact, Erdman, who termed himself a "conservative of conservatives," had contributed to *The Fundamentals* as authors and editor. In fact, President Stevenson was a critic of the Auburn Affirmation. Nevertheless, neither escaped the public wrath of the extreme conservatives. Machen went further in his private letters, referring to both men as "the enemy"; though he charge Stevenson with "leading the attack against the Christian witness-bearing of our Church," by 1924 he could inform his mother, "I believe I dislike Erdman even more than Stevenson." It was Machen's dread that the seminary was becoming a "cheap, Christian Endeavor" kind of school, and it was his conviction that he was the victim of persecution by the seminary leadership. Ironically, at the very moment Machen was reviling Stevenson, Stevenson was writing Bryan: "We are all exceedingly grateful to you for the courageous fight you are making in the defense of the faith."

Official notice of the General Assembly action mandating an investigation of the preaching and teaching in First Church did not reach the New York Presbytery until June 5. There already existed a committee appointed to investigate Fosdick in response to a memorial from the Harlem-New York Presbyterian Church of Mount Morris Park West, and that committee's membership was retained for the new inquiry. The five individuals were Charles L. Thompson and A. Edwin Keigwin, ministers, George B. Agnew and Alfred E. Marling, laymen, and Edgar Whitaker Work, pastor of the Fourth Presbyterian Church, chairman. When informed of the developments by Presbytery Moderator Harlan G. Mendenhall, Old First's Dr. Alexander replied that the General Assembly charges made "Mighty interestin' readin'—though it is somewhat disconcerting after fifty four [sic] years in the ministry of the Presbyterian church to find myself and the Church which I serve for the first time arraigned as malefactors."

Nevertheless, on September 27 the First Church Session assured Work of its willingness to cooperate in his "delicate task." Having met only twice during the summer, the Work's Committee now began to proceed in earnest. On November 13 the committee met with the Session; present also were Dr. Alexander and Guthrie Speers, the associate minister, and Dr. Duffield, new presbytery moderator. The minutes of the meeting, which were taken by a public stenographer, make fascinating reading. When pressed to state whether they regretted Fosdick's sermon, "Shall the Fundamentalists Win?", the church representatives replied: "I regret it for me" and "I regret some parts of it" and "I regret the way in which it was taken by the people, because of their misunderstanding." Dr. Alexander added only, "[Ivy] Lee was an unfortunate man." At the close it was agreed that the Session would prepare a formal statement for Work's Committee and in the next Session meetings a report was hammered out. Meanwhile, Fosdick met with Work and agreed to submit a statement of his own, soliciting in the task the counsel of Coffin.

In late November the Session transmitted its report only to have it returned by Work; another, fuller statement, dated December 11, was substituted. The Session opened its defense by expressing deep grievance "that a Church, conservative in its traditions and temper, should have become, largely through misunderstanding, subject to suspicion regarding its loyalty and soundness in the faith." The history of the Fosdick relationship was then traced and praised. There followed an admission that the title of the famous sermon was "ill-chosen and provocative," though any disputatious intent was denied. In any event, Fosdick's preaching is ordinarily uncontroversial, being rather "searching, inspiring, and full of the spirit of the Gospel." The document closed with a pledge of further cooperation, the Session confident of convincing Work that First Church "would not knowingly tolerate in its pulpit teachings unevangelical or subversive to the historic faith of the Presbyterian Church."

Concurrently, Fosdick was struggling with his own response to Work. As he relates in his autobiography, the members of Work's Committee were his "staunch friends." They wanted him to remain at Old First, but they desperately needed a conciliatory message to incorporate in their report to the next General Assembly to win the moderates, that linchpin majority in Presbyterianism at large. This Fosdick (after an unacceptable first try) attempted to supply in a letter dated December 28 and designed for public broadcast. In it Fosdick denied maintaining a controversial posture: "Any gentleman dislikes to be a cause of disturbance in a neighbor's household, and as an ordained minister of another denomination preaching in a Presbyterian pulpit I am profoundly sorry that contention has arisen because of me." He defined himself as an evangelical Christain having "no patience with an emasculated Christianity that denudes the Gospel of its superhuman [sic] elements, its redeeming power and its eternal hopes." Fosdick continued:

> I believe in the personal God revealed in Christ, in his omnipresent activity and endless resources to achieve his purposes for us and all men; I believe in Christ, his deity, his sacrifical saviorhood, his resurrected and triumphant life, his rightful Lordship, and the indispensableness of his message to mankind. In the indwelling Spirit I believe the forgiveness of sins, the redeemed and victorious life, the triumph of righteousness on earth, and the life everlasting. This faith I find in the Scriptures and the objective of my ministry is to lead men to the Scriptures as the standard and norm of religious experience—the progressive self-revelation of God in the history of a unique people, culminating in Christ.

In a five-page covering letter of the same date Fosdick attempted to explain his difficult position to Work. He quite understood that Work imagined the statement being read by conservative Presbyterians. But try to see it from my perspective, he pleaded. "I think of it being read by thousands of young men and women who have looked at me in some measure for spiritual leadership, to whom the freer interpretation of Christianity is a matter of spiritual life and death, upon which hangs all the possibility of their remaining allied with the Christian Church. They will read it to see whether I have stood by my colors, have been frank, candid, and true, or have trimmed, hedged, and compromised. That is why my letter must not contain any note of concession that by any possibility could be translated into compromise." After several additional pages, Fosdick then bluntly declared: "No one who knows me personally, hears me preach, lecture, or reads my books, can for a moment suppose that I take an apologetic and deprecatory attitude toward the Gospel which I preach. Upon the contrary, I am proud of it; I believe in it; I stand by it. With all its inevitable limitations and mistakes I am sure that it has in it the seeds of hope for the future generations. I do not apologize for it; I proclaim it: and everybody knows it."

On January 14, 1924, the New York Presbytery met to receive the report of Dr. Work's Committee. Attendance was unprecedented; the church galleries were packed with visitors, mostly ministers from neighboring presbyteries. Dr. Duffield, moderator of the presbytery and pastor-emeritus of First Church, presided. Work's introductory remarks were poignant: "I woud be loath to read a report on this difficult and delicate subject, if I did not believe that the unities of the faith are greater and more triumphant than the diversities, and that there are many of God's people who are united in prayer today that that church may be drawn together, not driven apart." The lengthy document may be summarized: the loyalty, orthodoxy, and constitutionality of First Church were upheld; the charges of heresy alleged and insinuated against Fosdick refuted. The one critical passage concerned the sermon, "Shall the Fundamentalists Win?"; its title was judged objectionable and contentious, its content "open to painful misconstruction and just objection." Still, that sermon was treated as an incident aside because it was only an incident—a default at worst in judgment and not a defection from loyalty to the true Christ. A vote on the report was postponed until February 4 in order that it might be printed and distributed for study by presbytery members.

Fosdick made this assessment to his father: "The criticism of one sermon . . . is largely a matter of judicial process in order to make the general body of the Presbyterian Church, deeply disturbed, feel that the report is not a whitewash. Knowing in advance what was coming I have not been disturbed at all by the minor criticism involved in the document, but Raymond was very mad about it this morning and evidently wanted to rip somebody's scalp off. As a matter of fact, I am inclined to think that the total effect of the report will be to allay the theological storm, and the general expectation here is that the General Assembly in May will accept it."

On February 4 the presbytery did adopt the report overwhelmingly, 111 to 28, but the storm was not allayed. Dr. Walter D. Buchanan, pastor of Broadway Presbyterian Church, immediately announced his intent to forward a complaint (ultimately signed by 22 conservatives) to the General Assembly protesting that the presbytery action did not carry out the mandate of the 1923 assembly: Fosdick's preaching did *not* conform to Presbyterian standards and the Work vindication was therefore invalid and dishonest. When asked if he was surprised by the vindication, Philadelphia's MacLennan replied: "What would you expect the German Cabinet to report on the character of the German Kaiser in 1916?" In mid-February *The Presbyterian* assessed the pre-General Assembly situation in this fashion: "It should be distinctly understood here that Dr. Fosdick is not on trial before the Assembly, for he is not under its jurisdiction. But the Presbytery of New York is on trial. . . . This presbytery has long been the cause of controversy and disturbance, and some decided action may be necessary to save the body." Therefore, let Fosdick resign. "If he fails to do this, he must expect the condemnation of all good and reasonable men, and be accountable to a just God. The gravity of this case makes a loud call upon all presbyteries and presyters to send up to the coming Assembly none but loyal Presbyterians as commissioners."

In May the commissioners met in Grand Rapids at the very moment Fosdick was touring Britain on his triumphant preaching mission. Both the conservative and liberal camps anticipated a "show down" and both arrived well organized. The secular press likened the assembly to a gladiatorial contest from which it would be possible for only one of the combatants to emerge alive, quite forgetting the great number of commissioners of moderate persuasion. Incidentally, every piece of evidence points to the fact the elders were more conservative than the ministers, and the clerical conservatives counted heavily on their lay allies.

The initial victory went to the extreme conservatives when Macartney, nominated as promised by Bryan, narrowly defeated Erdman for the post of moderator. The courageous, conservative Erdman, reported Coffin in admiration, "was sacrificed on the liberal altar." It is testimony both to the conservatives' strength and the liberals' statesmanship that the liberals did not attempt to advance one of their own, wisely putting forward instead a man who was conservative but not an exclusivist. (Robert E. Speer, Presbyterianism's most beloved and respected layman, declined to permit the liberals to advance his moderately conservative name.) Macartney then, as was his right, appointed Bryan to the honorary post of vice moderator and conservatives secured the chairmanship of important committees. Understandably, liberals were plunged into deep gloom. Later in the assembly the conservatives won a second victory when William P. Merrill was dropped from membership on the Board of Foreign Missions, a position he had held for twelve years. Dear old George Alexander then offered to resign from the board, after forty years service to the day, to make room for Merrill.

But these wins were more than canceled out by conservative defeats. No action was taken on, therefore, no action was taken against, the Auburn Affirmation, as conservatives had memorialized. Critically, moreover, the Philadelphia overture to fasten the Five Points upon "all representatives of the Church" was judged unconstitutional by the Permanent Judicial Commission, and this ruling was confirmed by the Assembly.

That left for consideration the Buchanan complaint against the New York Presbytery for its exoneration of Fosdick's preaching. The complaint was closely reviewed by the Permanent Judicial Commission. Fosdick's works and the investigative records were studied. Hearings were held, a young Presbyterian lawyer named John Foster Dulles acting "admirably" (Coffin reported) as the presbytery's legal counsel. The commission faced the task of determining a question of law and arriving at a decision that would pass the assembly and, it was hoped, bring peace to a troubled church. Its recommendation, which was adopted by the assembly, 504 to 311, said that Fosdick's occupancy of the First Church pulpit for over five years as a "guest" was an "anomaly." The recommendation continued:

> In saying so, we do not mean that the First Presbyterian Church of New York must of necessity be deprived of the services of Dr. Fosdick, which they so much desire. We do think, however, that if he desires to occupy a Presbyterian pulpit for an extended time he should enter our Church through the regular method and become subject to the jurisdiction and authority of the Church. If this be done, much of the cause of irritation would be removed. If he can accept the doctrinal standards of our Church, as contained in the Confession of Faith, there should be no difficulty in receiving him. If he cannot, he ought not to continue to occupy a Presbyterian pulpit.

The commission concluded with the suggestion that Fosdick be asked "whether it is his pleasure to enter the Presbyterian Church." At no point in the lengthy report did the commission pronounce Fosdick's preaching heretical.

Seattle's Mark Matthews then unsuccessfully moved the immediate ouster of Fosdick. In the discussion, a fundamentalist demanded that Fosdick be summoned before the assembly for interrogation. A kindly old gentleman then arose, took out his watch and said, "I don't think you can now find Dr. Fosdick in New York. He is at this time addressing the United Free Church of Scotland." "That took down the Assembly!", remembered one commissioner.

Although Bryan announced, regarding the assembly, "We have won every point," not all conservatives agreed. And, save for Merrill's unhappy fate, the liberals were not unhappy—Coffin returning home "singing the long meter Doxology." As he later explained to Fosdick, "The Fundamentalist group in the Assembly, whom I thought in the majority, did not care a jot whether or not you were Baptist or Presbyterian. They consort with Baptists and indeed get leadership from them in many sections of the country." They sought your immediate dismissal from First Church and failed. They sought to have your preaching branded as heretical and failed. In all, Coffin believed the outcome "marvelous—a direct interposition of Providence."

Cablegrams from Coffin and Alexander relating the assembly's "friendly" action were read with skepticism by Fosdick. As he told his secretary, "I hesitate to accept that dictum at its face value—there must be some 'nigger in the fence'—and I shall await the real news before beginning to think about it." Days later, again to his secretary, he doubted if the assembly offered him "an honorably decent chance of staying at the 'Old First.' "

VII

Subsequent to the cablegrams but prior even to his return to New York on July 21, Fosdick was made aware of the conflicting desires of the myriad parties interested in his future at the church. For one, there was the Presbyterian fundamentalist party determined to drive him out, or if he foolishly accepted the invitation to become a Presbyterian, to beat him into conformity with the Westminster Confession stick. For another, there was the Presbyterian liberal party who viewed the assembly's invitation as a marvelous resolution to be gratefully accepted. For a third, there were the liberals inside and outside Presbyterianism by whom acceptance would be interpreted as supine surrender. Then there were First Church members who were willing to bolt from the denomination to be able to keep Fosdick and still there were others, almost equally devoted to him, who were, nevertheless, unwilling to become an "outlaw" congregation. Finally, there were the New York Presbytery and its "Committee on the First Church," again chaired by Dr. Work, committed equally to First Church's weal and the assembly's lawful action. It was a tense time for Fosdick, crammed with conferences and choked with correspondence. At no period in his long life was his judgment and in truth his character put to a more severe test.

George Alexander followed his cablegram with a letter describing the assembly's invitation an "unprecendented distinction." "You know my heart," the letter closed, "and I need say no more." When Alexander presented the assembly's action to the First Church fellowship, however, much of the audience was skeptical, and one parishioner smelled a frame-up to entice Fosdick into the Presbyterian fold simply to be able to kick him out. Pastor Alexander, with tears in his eyes, insisted that the invitation was sincere. Concurrently, Coffin was making this crucial point in a long letter, a point that weighed heavily on Fosdick's conscience because it was repeated by so many Presbyterian liberals:

Now, my dear freind [sic], there have been a lot of men all over the Church who have hazarded their ecleastical [sic] lives in this contest. It has been an easy thing for us in New York but it has been anything but an easy thing for men in Texas and Pennsylvania and Ohio and Kentucky. These men have been here [in Grand Rapids], they have held together nobly and without them we could not possibly have won this result. They keep saying to me if Fosdick does not come in, now that we have staked everything for him, he leaves us in the lurch and robs this victory of most of its significance. Leader after leader, men like Wishart and Hayes and Stone and Swearingen, who have stood nobly by us in this conflict and especially men like Charles Erdman of Princeton . . . have said to me that they sincerely hoped that you would not fail them in view of the fact that they have risked so much for you. . . . You have been the occasion of the conflict and I think there is an almost unanimous feeling among your friends that you owe a pretty large debt to the Church.

Raymond Fosdick, who was in close contact with the First Church leadership, wrote his brother three letters challenging the arguments of Alexander and Coffin. If Harry were to join the Presbyterian Church, it would come "as a tremendous shock to thousands for whom you are the acknowledged leader." The cause you champion, Ray continued, the cause of religious liberalism, is larger than this ugly Presbyterian quarrel, and they are attempting to use you in clear violation of the understanding reached with First Church in 1918. Ray sympathized with Alexander, an old man who had never been a fighting liberal, but Coffin's position was beyond his comprehension. "I had not realized that his predilection for Presbyterianism was so strong." Ray's understanding, and perhaps his brother's, too, would have gained by the awareness that Presbyterianism was in Coffin's blood, it was not a mere predilection.

From London Fosdick wrote a thirty-seven page reply to Alexander (reduced to nine typed pages for transmission). The invitation to become a Presbyterian is unacceptable. For one thing, it is an "ultimatum and I object to the element of duress." For another, "a kind of creedal subscription is required to which I have an unconquerable aversion." For a third, "The same men who have been attacking me will attack me still. Hosts of Presbyterians do not want me to be Presbyterian; they want me out. From the day I come up for ordination and Dr. Buchanan and others begin asking my views on the Virgin Birth and like matters, the trouble would begin." The decision should be closed immediately and not hang fire until the fall. "The Presbytery ought not to be put in the humiliating position of extending me a gracious invitation (I know they would make it *very* gracious) which I must decline."

Such was Fosdick's hold on the hearts of the Old First fellowship, they would not—could not—bring themselves to follow his recommendation of a quick, surgical separation. On July 17 the leadership met informally to hear a reading of Fosdick's reply to Alexander. It was agreed unanimously to send Fosdick a wireless message pleading with him to continue his services and forego his resignation at least until the summer-scattered congregation could come together in the fall. On the following day Coffin, intimately informed of First Church affairs, again pressed the argument for Fosdick's acceptance, ending with the perhaps cruel clincher: "Think also of that saint of God, George Alexander. To see him stand in that Assembly, as he did, and declare himself your yokefellow, and your devoted comrade, was superb. He could not have been more outspoken, more affectionate, more devoted. I trembled for his health daily, but he was unfaltering. Don't break the dear man's heart." In his response, however, Fosdick observed that, aside from some liberal Presbyterians like Coffin himself, "I can find nobody who really thinks that I will consent to the Assembly's proposal or that I ought to." (A Union colleague told him, anyone who had read his Yale Beecher Lectures, *The Modern Use of the Bible,* and learned of his assent to the Westminster Confession "would call you an unmitigated liar and would be perfectly justified in so doing.") A key paragraph followed:

> I would rather be hung in irons than to do this thing I propose. The attacks of my enemies never got under my skin; but the thought of disappointing friends like you is an inward agony. I . . . [said] to Mrs. Fosdick that I had ahead of me the hardest thing I ever have had to go through with in my life. My comfort, if I can find any, in the sacrifice which my withdrawal will cost my friends is to be discovered only in my feeling that I am also sacrificing myself. . . . You may be sure that I would not face up to all that is involved in my withdrawal if I were not driven to it by what seem to me the demands of conscience.

The liner carrying the Fosdick family home from Britain docked on July 21. That very evening Fosdick dined with Dr. Alexander. Two days later he met with the seven most powerful First Church lay leaders, men of large affairs in New York's financial, social, and cultural world. Fosdick informed them that he must either become a Presbyterian or resign—and he chose resignation. "Unanimous and forceful dissent to this decision was made by everyone of those present." The memorandum of the meeting continues: "It was indicated to him as strongly as it was possible to state it that the officers of the First Church there present, and in their belief practically the entire membership, would support the Church in declining to accept his resignation and urging him to continue to preach there, *even to the extent of involving a disagreement with the General Assembly, which everyone realized might eventually lead to a split in the denomination*" (emphasis added). Fosdick then said he had no intention of encouraging a separatist movement. After two hours a plan was formulated. Fosdick would postpone his resignation until a formal invitation to become a Presbyterian was received from the presbytery in the fall. He, of course, would decline, and then submit his resignation, which the church would in turn decline. "This would give us a breathing space of another year . . . ," the memorandum closed. Alexander was to be informed of the proposal and that good man was to be further torn between concern for his parish and loyalty to the larger Church.

Meanwhile Dr. Work, chairman of the presbytery committee on First Church affairs, was in informal communication with Fosdick, Alexander, and members of the presbytery. Fosdick's reply had an "air of finality about it," he noted, but at First Church he still heard talk of a "via media." Puzzled, Work closed one letter, "I suppose the Lord knows all about what his servants are doing. It is well that he is patient."

Toward the end of August, First Church's associate pastor, Speers, informed Fosdick that a welcome-home party would be thrown by our "notorious church" at one of the city's "most fashionable hostelries" as a demonstration of affection and loyalty. "Great guns! man," Fosdick shot back, "is it not enough that my enemies torment me that my friends should put me to the rack as well?" In view of the certainty of his resignation and the unlikelihood of circumventing the assembly mandate, Fosdick absolutely vetoed a "jollification" in the midst of the "agonizing process of breaking up our present regime at the First Church."

As parishioners returned from their vacations the mood at the church became increasingly mutinous. For three days a small group met at Coffin's summer home in St. Hubert's to work out a solution. Coffin was now convinced that Fosdick would never assent to becoming a Presbyterian. "We love you even in your perversity," he wrote, "and while we think your brain and conscience out of gear, we know your heart is Christian through and through." "No, Henry," Fosdick volleyed, "you have that quite wrong. The fact is that my heart is desperately wicked but that my brain and conscience never were more luminously clear. Indeed, despite all the warping that your long association with Presbyterianism has wrought on your otherwise admirable intellect, I am still amazed that you should have thought it credible that after the experience of the last two years I would step meekly up and sign on the dotted line when the General Assembly snapped its fingers. It seems to me ridiculously unthinkable, and aside from a small group of Presbyterian liberals, I can find nobody to whom the proposal is not either a joke or a tragedy if I should go into it."

The New York Presbytery had received in June its order from the General Assembly to extend an invitation to Fosdick. Finally (very tardily in the opinion of conservatives) on September 1 Dr. Work wrote the formal letter. A salient passage reads: "An unusual honor in fact has been paid you, albeit the acceptance of the honor has explicit conditions attached to it. Presbyterian annals, so far as we are aware, contain no record of any previous action of this character. The Assembly could not have gone further in the direction of according you a welcome. At the same time the Assembly could not have done less toward maintaining the order and procedure of our church." Fosdick's response of September 5 was firm and unequivocal, but he honored his pledge to Alexander and Coffin not to make his declination the occasion for a theological attack on Presbyterian doctrine. Fosdick then submitted a warm letter of resignation to Henry N. Tifft, Clerk of Session, First Church, closing with the thought that his service was available until new arrangements could be made, "but I am sure it should not continue long enough to be a source of contention and discord in the Church at large."

Dr. Work hoped the issue was now closed, but knowing the mutinous mood at Old First, he remained concerned, finding it prudent to alert Alexander, "I assume that the Session will realize the futility of any action that could be interpreted as defiance of the Assembly." Alexander, too, was concerned to avoid "revolt and schism," and when Fosdick informed him that his decision was irrevocable and mentioned the possibility of a sabbatical year abroad, the exhausted eighty-one-year-old Alexander sighed, "Mine will perhaps come where 'sabbaths have no end.' "

The fears of Work and Alexander were not groundless. At a joint meeting of the Board of Trustees and Session, September 16, the leadership laid Fosdick's resignation on the table. "We still cherish the hope," Fosdick was informed, "that when the Church at large has learned as we have learned the spirit and aim of your ministry, a way will be found for the renewal in some form, not inconsistent with Presbyterian law and usage, of that comradeship of christian service which has been attended with such signal tokens of Divine favor." The unfolding plan to be presented at a congregational meeting, called for October 22, was "leaked" to Fosdick. "The thing is so simple and daring that it is almost funny," he penned his father. The church would accept his formal resignation and then turn around and invite him to make it his custom to preach on Sunday mornings, precisely as he had been doing for five years, the only difference being that he would have no official standing in the church whatever. "Goodness only knows what will result from my acceptance of this proposal, undoubtedly the heathen will rage, but just what they can do is difficult to say." Anyhow, when he wrote to his father on September 22, he was inclined to accept the arrangement. "Raymond strongly agrees with this attitude and so does Florence. It means a year of strife, I presume, but I guess that I have no right to assume responsibility for declining the desire of the church to see the thing through." Fosdick would not long remain so sanguine about the scheme.

On October 6 the New York Presbytery received the report of Dr. Work's Committee with Fosdick's letter of resignation of September 5. Having carried out its instructions from the assembly, the presbytery now requested First Church to make a final report in November. And that would be that, Work hoped.

It was not an easy time for the First Church fellowship. In the days preceding the October 22 congregational meeting, the church leaders repeatedly caucused and exchanged ideas in letters that were increasingly laced with emotion. Alexander remained eager to retain Fosdick's services. "I will not, however, be pastor of an outlaw Church," he warned powerful lay leader, Robert W. De Forest. "My resignation has long been in the hands of the Session and will be pressed at the first meeting of Presbytery following any defiant action by the Church. In this lawless age it is very easy to proclaim independence, but a decent respect for the opinions of mankind requires a statement of reasons for revolution other than inability to get lawfully just what we want and to get it just now. . . . It is impossible for me to take a parochial view of our present situation. I am deeply concerned for the First Church, but more deeply concerned for the Presbyterian Church, U.S.A., whose heart is right and whose mind will get right if we can be wise and patient." The strain felt by the oak-hearted old man is reflected in a note he wrote to Fosdick: "I am trying to get out of the city for a day or so to check a slight tendency to seek solution for our problems in the watches of the night." Mr. De Forest, for his part, protested any intent of subterfuge. First Church, he argued, had every moral and constitutional right to invite a Baptist to occupy the church's pulpit after Fosdick's official connection had been terminated. As he informed Alexander, "The issue to me is not Dr. Fosdick, nor even the First Church, nor even the Presbyterian denomination, it is the cause of Christian fellowship and church unity."

Meanwhile Fosdick's position hardened. His resignation *must* be accepted. "I will not consent to any continuance of relationships with the First Church involving rebellion in letter or in spirit against the decision of the General Assembly." And he assured Alexander that he would stand with him in opposition to any action leading to schism. To that end, after the congregational meeting he expected that his name would be removed from the front of the church, from the church bulletin, the *Church Tower*, and all advertisements and that he would cease holding office hours. He feared that the congregational meeting might "blow the hinges off the doors." Still he would insist that his services terminate no later than March. "From that time on I shall have nothing to do with First Church." As for the hope of his faithful followers that the next General Assembly could be persuaded to permit him to remain without becoming a Presbyterian, "Personally, I think they have a job on their hands in comparison with which Hercules' cleansing of the Augean stables was an infant's job."

Fosdick never encouraged a secession movement resulting in the formation of an independent congregation. On that count even his severest critic must return a verdict of "not guilty." Yet during that tense time he preached sermons at Old First that must have fueled the anger of his people. Item: "I say to you, my dear people, with whom for years my heart has been, that whatever may happen this week to those relationships that have been so congenial to us, do you in the situation you may be in and let me in the situation I may be in, not talk of surrendering. God hates a quitter." Item: "Just now, in this church situation as a whole, how many of you are there who would like to tell the church what you think of it? How naturally indignant you are at the blindness of the ecclesiastical establishment. What things you say about the church. Many of you think sectarian lines are not simply un-Christian, but anti-Christian, and one of the chief obstacles to the progress of Christianity. Oftentimes you will find the spirit of Satan in the Church and the spirit of Jesus outside." Such statements as these call to mind Justice Holmes's "clear and present danger" example of crying "fire" in a crowded theatre. Small wonder that the newspapers reached such interpretations as: "Fosdick Hints Certain Members Considering Leaving Church."

On Wednesday evening, October 22, in the silence of deep emotion, twelve hundred members of the First Church congregation rose to their feet to accept Fosdick's resignation. Dr. John H. Finley immediately presented a resolution for the ministers, elders, and trustees, praising Fosdick and justifying the actions of the church. It contained this fateful passage: "Therefore, after your resignation . . . takes effect, we invite you to make it your custom when not otherwise engaged to preach in our pulpit on Sunday mornings. We cannot believe that this is in opposition to the mind of the Presbyterian Church." In seconding the motion, William Morgan Kingsley said, "And so here we stand, we stand upon our right to invite Dr. Fosdick to preach to us; it is the right of every Evangelical Church, to invite any Evangelical minister of another denomination to occupy its pulpit; it is a right which never before has been challenged, and on that right we stand. It is not an end, it is but a step forward in a great venture, in an endeavor to persuade our friends that the tie which binds Dr. Fosdick to us should not be severed. Without him we must contract to smaller things; with him we may expand to greater usefulness."

Despite Mr. Kingsley's brave prophecy, it *was* the end—or the beginning of the end. Almost at once Fosdick wrote to the Clerk of the Session naming March as the termination date for his preaching and he wrote Alexander suggesting early November as the termination date of his formal relationship with the church; and on November 9 the session formally accepted the resignation "to take effect at a time to be fixed by Dr. Fosdick and Dr. Alexander after consultation with the Presbytery of New York."

The presbytery assembled on November 17 and voted that a period be placed to the association on March 1, "and there shall be no other date." An ardent minority led (again) by Dr. Buchanan moved unsuccessfully (63 to 18) that the termination take effect "at once." A complaint against the presbytery was then hurried to the General Assembly. Explained Buchanan: "There is room enough elsewhere for Rationalists, Higher Critics, and naturalists. They are at liberty to go where they will and preach what they elect to preach. But God in His mercy close the doors of our Historic Church against those that would trample upon our sacred traditions and our scriptural creed!" Alexander defended before the presbytery Fosdick's "unquestionably Christian" bearing in the entire matter. "He had two ways open to him last summer,—an easy way and a hard way. The easy way was to do what at first it was his impulse to do, that is, to break away in mid-summer from all religion of the Presbyterian Church and accept the invitation to take another pulpit in the City of New York." Instead, he took the hard way and for this "he has my admiration, my confidence, and my respect." A still uncomprehending Coffin received a final explanation from Fosdick as to why he had not become a Presbyterian. To have done so would have left him feeling like "a lying rogue." "I never could look at myself in a mirror again—no great loss, you well may say, but nevertheless a great inconvenience. The thing is for my conscience an absolute moral impossibility. My wife would disown me if I did it; I would disown myself; and as for preaching a sermon thereafter on love of the truth—'out of me!' "

It would require a small volume to set forth all the commentaries on the "Fosdick case." It almost seems as though every churchman and every church paper and every secular editorial writer had and expressed an opinion. S. Parkes Cadman spoke for non-Presbyterian liberals when he stated, "It is not Dr. Fosdick, but the Presbyterian Church which is on trial." Some liberal Presbyterians all along had urged him to stand fast, neither assenting to the assembly mandate nor resigning. To assent, they argued, would deal a fatal blow to the constitutional rights of individual presbyteries and congregations, but to resign would embolden the fundamentalists. A Presbyterian preacher in a small midwestern town who advanced this position closed his letter: "I really feel that I should apologize for this seeming imprudence, but, Dr. Fosdick, I was driven to the point of collapse in a St. Louis church, my first pastorate out of seminary, by the so-called 'orthodox' and I speak with fear and trembling as to the un-Christian extent to which they will go 'in the name of Christ, our dear Lord'! Besides, many of us younger men in the ministry of today look to you as our inspiration."

Considering the massive support he had received nationally, it is not surprising that following the announcement of his resignation a score or more pastoral calls were tendered from churches as distant as England and Hawaii and as close as Brooklyn's historic Plymouth Church—and even closer, Park Avenue Baptist. With wry humor his friend Robert Russell Wicks wrote: "Personally I have the deepest sympathy for a man with a family thus suddenly thrown out of work. We have a position in our church which combines the duties of an assistant minister and janitor. I want to offer you this place in your crucial position. Unfortunately, you would have little preaching to do and the pay would be small."

Some observers acknowledged the "right" of the denomination to say that only a Presbyterian may occupy a Presbyterian pulpit, but wondered as did the *Christian Century*, "Does the Presbyterian church have any Christian right *to be that sort of a church?* The issue does not strike at the church's 'right' but at the church's character."

Then there were the Presbyterian liberals who shared Coffin and Merrill's belief that the assembly's invitation was gracious and acceptable. Even the sympathetic and liberal editor of *The Presbyterian Advance*, James E. Clarke, took this position. Tertius van Dyke echoed Coffin when he reminded Fosdick, "At the General Assembly . . . a number of us risked our ecclesiastical lives on issues which your 'enemies' centered about you." Therefore, to decline the invitation would be to desert your friends. No one put the case for acceptance more persuasively than Charles Wishart. He followed one plea, however, with the moving apology: "One point in my former letter to you I now deeply regret. I should never have mentioned any risk or loss to any of us who have been in this fight. That is of no consequence whatever, and I pray you forget it. If we cannot play a man's part and take a man's risk in such matters, then there is little hope ahead for anybody."

Finally there was the fundamentalist/conservative group. One element, including Machen, Macartney, and Matthews, believed the assembly's invitation to Fosdick should never have been extended. Machen interpreted it as a "great defeat," warning Maitland Alexander, "I think if we represent it as a victory, or if we give the impression that we regard the battle as over, we are traitors to our cause." *The Presbyterian* held that if Fosdick accepted and the New York Presbytery received him (as that traitorous body certainly would), "the end of the matter would be far worse than the beginning." Indeed "The suggestion that the difficulties involved in the situation would be straightened out if Dr. Fosdick would become a Presbyterian seems to us nothing short of monstrous." Machen was relentless. His review of *The Modern Use of the Bible* shredded Fosdick's Yale Beecher Lectures. "I was almost ashamed of devoting so much space in *The Princeton Theological Review* to such cheap, meretricious stuff," he apologized to an admirer. "It was very different when one was dealing with a man like McGiffert." Machen naturally took the affirmative side in a debate in the pages of *Christian Work* on the topic, "Is the Teaching of Dr. Harry Emerson Fosdick Opposed to the Christian Religion?" "Seldom have I done anything that came harder," wrote this bachelor to his adoring mother. In public response to Fosdick's resignation, Machen stated that there was no ecclesiastical irregularity involved in having a Baptist in a Presbyterian pulpit. The trouble lay in the fact that Fosdick "was attacking the very foundations of the Christian faith"; now that he was on his way out, the Church must move against the Presbytery of New York for receiving ministers "who are just as hostile to the Christian faith as is Dr. Fosdick himself." Machen was deeply concerned that, unless the conservatives organized, the 1925 General Assembly might make it possible for First Church somehow to retain Fosdick's services. Incidentally, one of the angriest letters Fosdick ever penned concerned Machen's "miserable representation of what I said, murdering the king's English in a way that I never was guilty of, and substituting the stenographer's phrases for my own. . . . Never in all my ministry have I been treated like this before and there is no excuse whatever for such a thing's happening."

If the assembly erred initially in extending the invitation, all would not be lost if Fosdick accepted, for he must then stand the usual examinations and the whole question of his theology would be "fully aired in presbytery, synod and General Assembly." "We will not have any preacher in our church who is not within reach of our stick," boasted Bryan. "We have the old Presbyterian Church by the tail, and we intend to twist it until every heretic is squeezed out," boasted Matthews to Macartney. Millionaire First Church layman Arthur Curtiss James interviewed Bryan and reported to Dr. Alexander:

I would never have believed that it was possible for a person since the days of the Inquisition to think and talk as he did this morning. He claims that ninety-nine percent of the denomination hold his views and he has "consecrated his life" to split the church and drive out the one percent whose "religion is centered around a bastard." He actually said, referring to Fosdick, "This man does not believe in Jonah and the whale"— and went on at length covering all the doctrinal points at issue and ending his oration by saying "that it is much easier for me to believe that Jonah went in and out of the whale daily than it is for me to believe any part of the doctrine of evolution." If it were not so tragically sad it might almost have been amusing, but it was all said by the Vice Moderator of the General Assembly.

In reply Alexander could only say, and not unfairly, that Bryan was "the strangest compound of conscience, piety and unreason that I have ever encountered."

Whatever the wisdom of the assembly's initial action, all fundamentalists agreed that once Fosdick refused to become a Presbyterian his First Church association should terminate immediately, not March 1. *The Presbyterian*, as always, could be counted on to state the case with directness: "This means that although Dr. Fosdick refuses to qualify as a lawful physician, he is authorized to pour poison into the Presbyterian body for the next three months."

The events surrounding Fosdick's resignation scarcely resolved the Fundamentalist/Modernist controversy within the Presbyterian Church, U.S.A. Plainly put, the liberals were not far wrong in fearing that with Fosdick taken care of, the conservatives planned to move on a broad front: purge the Presbyterian press (witness the fate of Nolan Best, editor of *The Continent*); cleanse Princeton Seminary (witness the momentary fate of Erdman, deposed as student advisor); exscind the New York Presbytery, appropriate its property and form a new presbytery (witness the Chester Presbytery overture and the Buchanan complaint); and even (as Guthrie Speers was informed) censure First Church, dissolve its session, and seize its property. The story of their failure to win denominational control, however, belongs more properly to the history of Presbyterianism and may not be traced here.

VIII

Nevertheless, a final word remains to be said about Fosdick's association with Presbyterianism. In the minds of many his resignation and its acceptance did not absolutely close and bolt the door, whatever the certainty in Fosdick's own mind. Indeed, the events of the spring of 1925 were almost as tumultuous as those of the fall of 1924. The plain fact is that the First Church fellowship was not yet willing to accept the unacceptable, to endure the unendurable. His loyal supporters, comprising virtually the entire membership, persuaded themselves that a way could be found to repossess his presence on the conclusion of his sabbatical. Conservative suspicions on this score were well founded. Fosdick, out of deference to his people, agreed not to pledge his services definitely to another church until after the General Assembly met in May. He assessed the situation in mid-January to his father: The congregation is indignant and resentful. If he were to step at once into some rival pulpit, the dissolution of First Church might follow. The church "is planning to send out propaganda through the Presbyterian fold and commit such assault and battery upon the General Assembly as seems strategic and wise. Personally, however, I think that no General Assembly between now and the crack of doom will eat enough crow to welcome me back to the pulpit of the First Church." The session proceeded to issue a public statement and distribute thirty thousand copies of a sixty-one page booklet, "The First Presbyterian Church of New York and Dr. Fosdick," explaining and defending the relationship. An editorial in the parish paper reflected the stubborn mood: "And another reason why goodbye cannot be said is that goodbye to Dr. Fosdick can never be made actual. Whatever happens this church for decades to come will be 'the church where Dr. Fosdick. . . .' For ourselves we can finish that sentence in only one way: 'The church where Dr. Fosdick preaches.' " Still, again and again Fosdick said, "After the first of March my hands will be off the work of the First Presbyterian Church of New York, but my heart will not be out of it."

On Sunday morning March 1, not long after dawn, the first hopeful worshippers began to assemble outside Old First in a cold drizzle turning to snow. At 10:30 visitors crashed the middle doors, almost tearing them from their hinges, to join the church members, swelling the congregation to eighteen hundred. Such was the density, a standee could not reach his billfold in his hip pocket, finding instead a silver half-dollar in a vest pocket for the collection. The *New York Times* headlined the story of the final service:

DR. FOSDICK MOVES HEARERS TO TEARS IN FAREWELL SERMON. Tells Them He Does Not Expect to Return to First Presbyterian Church. Recalls Paul's Leaving. Calls the Apostle "a Determined Heretic" and Says He's One Himself. Thanks His Congregation. Says Strife That Resulted in His Leaving Was All Outside First Church.

Portions of the *Times's* long account, which capture the intensity of the occasion, may be found in Fosdick's autobiography. Forty years later for a television show, Fosdick, very old but still firm of voice, mounted the pulpit and with fire repeated the words that had stirred his people to tears of sorrow and rage: "They call me a heretic. I am proud of it. I wouldn't live in a generation like this and be anything but a heretic. But I carry some of you on my heart in ways that heretics are not popularly supposed to do. I want you to be Christians. I want your lives for Christ. I want you for Christ now." Though he frankly stated that he did not share the worshippers' expectation of his return, at the sermon's conclusion they rose to sing, "God Be with You 'Till We Meet Again." Women wept and men struggled to control their emotions. "Never before, probably," judged the *Times's* reporter, "had any congregation anywhere sung a hymn with more intimate personal realization of its significance."

The sermon was widely quoted, thanks in part to Ivy Lee's distribution efforts, reminding us, incidentally, that throughout the entire controversy both sides made heroic use of public relations. Conservatives observed sardonically, "Dr. Fosdick Departs with Noise," noting his "arrogance" in taking as his text Paul's farewell to the Corinthian church. His friends countered, "Dr. Fosdick did *not* 'depart with noise,' but amid a hush of heart, that only comes from the conscious presence of God."

Monday evening a testimonial banquet was attended by seven hundred at the Hotel Astor. Those invited included, revealingly, not only the First Church leadership, but also key members of the New York Presbytery and the entire faculty and Board of Trustees of Union Seminary—and John Foster Dulles and Ivy Lee. Mrs. Fosdick's personal guest list included Mr. and Mrs. John D. Rockefeller, Jr., and Mr. and Mrs. James C. Colgate; neither the Rockefellers nor the Colgates attended, either because they were unable to do so or because they deemed it unwise considering the delicate negotiations then underway between the Park Avenue Baptist Church and Fosdick. It says something (not very pleasant) about the concern for public relations that six newspaper reporters were also invited.

Former Governor Charles S. Whitman presided, and it was after midnight before the last glass of "pure Croton" was raised to the Fosdicks. Of the five speeches, none exceeded in warmth that of Mrs. Roger H. Williams. "Men of the First Presbyterian Church!," she warned, "I don't know what your word to Dr. Fosdick is going to be tonight. But I tell you frankly, that—as far as the women are concerned, they are in no mood to make that word 'Good-bye.'" Acknowledging what Kipling said about the "Female of the Species," she continued: "We may even pray for the General Assembly, and hope they will not feel about that, as did little Jane, who had offended her sister Mary. 'Mother,' said Jane, 'make Mary stop praying for me; the things she is telling God about me, are something awful!' " Dr. Alexander then invited Fosdick to preach from the pulpit of First Church the first Sunday of his return from Europe. Patently, First Church was not yet ready to cry, "Uncle!"

Precisely because of this unyielding attitude, Fosdick felt compelled to ask Alexander (granting the doubtful assumption of a narrow technical victory for First Church at the upcoming General Assembly), "Does not your good sense confirm me in saying that I must not and will not return to the First Church under any conditions whatever that leave the door open for a repetition of what we have gone through these last years?" Surely his return would be the cause of more overtures, more uproar and attacks. "You will readily see, therefore, what I fear: that my friends . . . will work hard circularizing the elders and ministers of their communion, and in the end by some chance win a technical victory on a majority vote only to discover that I cannot on such terms return to the pulpit which I have left." Alexander acknowledged the probable accuracy of Fosdick's forecast and for "that reason I am imperilling my influence in the First Church by discouraging some efforts which the more ardent spirits would like to make." Nevertheless, he stood fast on the church's constitutional right to invite an evangelical minister to its pulpit. "The First Church has declared in unmistakable terms not only its desire but its expectation that a way will be found for your return without schism or violation of law. The Session has definitely resolved that during your sabbatical year they will do nothing to dim that expectation or close the door. Do you want to close it?"

Alexander was not unaware of a certain "most extraordinary and alluring" proposal coming Fosdick's way from the Park Avenue Baptist Church. Although Fosdick would not break his pledge to Old First, he did inform Baptists Rockefeller, Jr., and Edward L. Ballard of his absolute conviction that the General Assembly would not make possible his return to Old First. Concurrently, he informed Old First leader William Morgan Kingsley, "*I must never willingly become again a center of disturbance in the Presbyterian Church.*" Therefore, although he would not now accept any call to another pulpit in order not to prejudice the church's case before the assembly, he was sure that he was only postponing a decision that in the end would be made anyway.

On May 6 the session voted to send a memorial to the General Assembly praising Fosdick's services to First Church and defending the legality of its actions and deploring "the attempt on the part of people, remote and ill informed with regard to the actual situation, to break up a relation so happy and fruitful." The memorial closed: "We respectfully ask the General Assembly, by some appropriate action, to vindicate the loyalty and good faith of a church which for more than two centuries has been a mother of churches and a staunch supporter of the principles at the heart of our communion." Informed of this action, the next day Fosdick wrote to Roger H. Williams, now Clerk of Session, insisting that the issue of his return not be raised at the assembly. "I regard the matter as closed and deprecate the continuance of turmoil over it." Both Williams and Alexander replied in sorrow and deep disappointment, though recognizing the cogency of his reasoning.

In January and February Fosdick had fulfilled a number of speaking and preaching engagements, but after his "farewell" sermon his itinerent schedule became incredibly crowded. He addressed students at Haverford, Harvard, Yale, Princeton, George Washington, Ohio University, Wisconsin, Illinois, Rochester, Amherst, Victoria College, University of Toronto, Vassar, Wellesley, Smith, Bryn Mawr, Mount Holyoke, and Radcliffe. He also addressed general audiences in St. Louis, Springfield, Dayton, Philadelphia, Washington, New Haven, Lancaster, Buffalo, Newark, Saratoga Springs, New York, Englewood, Pittsfield, Westfield, and countless others. In mid-April he wrote his father comparing his existence to that of a "highly animated human grasshopper," and which he "hugely enjoyed." "My enemies have certainly set up a great platform for me and wherever I speak it is impossible for people to get in with a shoe horn long before the address begins." The letter closed, "I am in the best of health and spirits and can report the same about the rest of the family. I marvel a little that I can wag my tongue so endlessly without fatiguing what I call my brain, and am beginning to think that probably most of the work is done by the first mentioned." When in the midst of all this croaking he suffered a severe attack of laryngitis and was forced to cancel an engagement sponsored by the Philadelphia Federation of Churches, conservatives naturally rejoiced, and why not, inasmuch as sixty Presbyterian ministers and as many elders in the Philadelphia area had protested the invitation.

In mid-May the General Assembly met in Columbus. Its significance is great in the general history of the church, though we can here allude only briefly to what transpired. In seconding the nomination of Erdman for moderator, the speaker closed, "Our prayer is, 'Give peace in our time, O Lord.' We want peace so that we can act as Christians and shame the devil. Dr. Erdman can give us that peace." Victory went to the Princeton professor, foe of the extreme conservatives. When surrendering the sign of his authority, the outgoing moderator, Macartney, said rather ungraciously, "It is my duty to give you this gavel," and then turned his face away. The Chester overture to exscind the New York Presbytery died in committee and the Buchanan complaint to find that presbytery in "contempt of court" was dismissed. The conservatives, however, did win a victory when the assembly upheld the Judicial Commission's ruling that a candidate for ordination who refused to affirm his belief in the virgin birth ought not to be received into the Presbyterian ministry, an action protested by liberals and one that led to additional years of denominational controversy, which was ultimately settled—to liberal satisfaction—thanks to the healing labors of a Commission of Fifteen suggested by Erdman. As to the memorial from First Church, the Committee on Bills and Overtures voted to pay no attention to it, the committee chairman explaining, "Dr. Fosdick has gone back to the Baptists, the case is closed, and we haven't time to drag it out again."

Machen, noting the disasters suffered by the conservatives, reported that "the church has turned against us in a rather extraordinary way. Last year the whole temper of the Assembly was with us; during most of the time we could have done with it almost anything that we desired. And now what a change! Bitter hostility has taken the place of cordial support; the coalition between Modernists and Indifferentists has proved to be . . . too strong." Still, Fosdick *was* out of a Presbyterian pulpit and that vitcory could not be taken away from the fundamentalists. One observer at Columbus commented astutely: "One hears of men who tremble at the prospects of lost pulpits and baffled careers. A Fosdick can be driven out with entire advantage to his personal fortune, say many younger clergymen, but for the obscure pastor the alternative to a forced submission is dismissal, humiliation and a life of clerical beggary at the doors of other denominations."

By late May there remained only the final farewells and exchanges of letters between Fosdick and Alexander and Speers and the lay leaders of Old First. Only on one point did Alexander question whether Fosdick's actions were divinely guided, and that was Fosdick's acceptance of the Park Avenue Baptist call before going abroad. "If I have said too much forgive me," he closed. That forgiveness was given is beyond doubt when one reads Fosdick's memorial tribute after Alexander's death: "He was an incarnation of that text in the New Testament, 'To be spiritually minded is life and peace.' " The feared dissolution of the First Church congregation following Fosdick's departure did not, of course, materialize. A few individuals, including the church treasurer, did follow Fosdick to Park Avenue, but not many. And those few were mostly new members, not the staunch veterns whose Presbyterianism was in their blood. In 1926 *The Church Tower* finally ceased carrying Fosdick's sermons as a regular feature and at last in 1927 his successor was finally named. "I hope for the best since our people have reluctantly abandoned the hope of duplicating Dr. Fosdick," Alexander wrote. Fosdick returned but once to the Old First pulpit, twenty years later to celebrate a church anniversary. As he wrote his daughter, "Gram and I met scores of our warm personal friends, and it really was a very kindling experience."

IX

Writing to a Presbyterian leader in 1923 at the height of the Fundamentalist/Modernist controversy, Fosdick stated, "I am perfectly willing to admit that I personally am a bent flag pole, but I am unwilling to admit that there is anything the matter with the colors I fly." Indeed, Presbyterian friend and foe alike identified him as a singularly prominent bearer of modernism's colors; he was, to quote a rueful opponent, "modernism's Moses."

Chapter Eight

The War Within:
The Baptist Battle and
Mr. Rockefeller's Resolution

I

Early in 1922 the editor of *Atlantic Monthly*, Ellery Sedgwick, asked Fosdick about the Fundamentalist-Modernist controversy in the Northern Baptist Convention. Fosdick replied:

> The situation in the Baptist denomination is extraordinary. . . . Here in New York the Bapitists do indeed succeed in making fools of themselves but the problem is not at all so urgent and critical as it is in the Middle West. A person like Dean Shailer Mathews of the Divinity School at the University of Chicago could a tale unfold which I think would make a man's hair stand up like quills upon the fretful porcupine. While I am a member technically of a Baptist congregation, I am in fact so far separated from all vital contacts with the Baptists that I have not faced a Baptist audience in a year. . . . Dr. Massee, who has just come to Tremont Temple in Boston, is probably the most egregious ass, or at least one of them, which the Baptist denomination is now presenting for the admiration of men and angels. You might, during this Lenten season, do penance for your sins by going to hear him and see at first hand what it means to be a fundamentalist.

At that moment Jasper Cortenus Massee, ministering to a flock of nearly four thousand Boston Baptists, was emerging as one of the four or five most ardent and powerful fundamentalist leaders among all North American Baptists, and inevitably the forces he marshaled marched against those allied with Fosdick. Yet scarcely four years were to pass before Field Marshal Massee retired from the fundamentalist army, explaining, "I left the fundamentalists to save my own spirit, they became so self-righteous, so critical, so unchristian, so destructive, so incapable of being fair that I had to go elsewhere for spiritual nourishment." The still militant fundamentalist crusaders flung at him the gravamen, "Ichabod—thy glory has departed." That the sincere, intelligent, loyal Baptist Massee should be dubbed an "ass" by Fosdick in 1922 and a "renegade" by archfundamentalists in 1926 suggests the intensity of the conflict within the ranks of Northern Baptists.

At issue were many of the same questions agitating Northern Presbyterians: Scriptural inerrancy, evolution, the virgin birth, and millennialism—the last probably having larger significance among Baptists than Presbyterians, though certainly not all Baptist fundamentalists were premillennialists as Dr. Curtis Lee Laws noted at the time. The Baptist waters were further muddied, however, by the introduction of other controversial matters: baptism by immersion (a rite, not a doctrine), open membership, and the enormous wealth of a single layman, John D. Rockefeller, Jr. Further, the Baptist heritage militated against denominational unity because it contained such diverse elements: on the one hand, a confessional Calvinist tradition stressing correct doctrine; on the other hand, an Arminian emphasis on individual experience and human freedom of choice. Moreover, the Northern Baptist Convention, unlike the Presbyterian General Assembly, lacked centralized authority, owing to the historic Baptist devotion to local church autonomy. As a consequence, both fundamentalists and liberals, as conscience (and strategy) dictated, raised up congregations and leaders unwilling to accept denominational discipline or cooperate for the common denominational weal. The old saw, "Baptists get along best in small groups; preferably of one person each," may be unfair, but at least one scholar reached a comparable conclusion when he observed, "For years the Baptists have been looking at anarchy and seeing democracy."

It is important to remember that, as with the Presbyterians, the majority of Northern Baptists were to be found at neither extreme of doctrine or polity. Chicago's great moderate, James M. Stifler, reasonably informed both fundamentalists and modernists, "If we can stand both of you, we think you should be able to stand each other." This mutual toleration, however, was not to be, if only because the opposing players believed that the deck was stacked by the other side.

II

At this point it is imperative to say a word about the religious concerns of the world's wealthiest Protestant layman, John D. Rockefeller, Jr. For

one thing, his connection with the Baptist faith of his father is central to
the war within the denomination. For another, his relationship with Fosdick is central to the minister's career. However, it would be a mistake to
view that relationship as a variation on the Trilby theme, with Fosdick
cast as Svengali. Conservative Baptists were well aware that the philanthropist's liberalism was not born in a mesmerized state induced by
Fosdick.

Rockefeller, born in 1874, was reared in a pious home surrounded by
devout women and nurtured by a father whose modernist impulses were
not notorious. But neither was the Founding Rockefeller hidebound in
his orthodoxy. He made a gift to Walter Rauschenbusch's New York
Second German Baptist Church and dined in the social prophet's home.
He contributed to the support of Rochester Theological Seminary (where,
in time, Rauschenbusch taught), and although the University of Chicago
did quickly become in fundamentalists' eyes a "hot-bed of heresy," this
accusation did not alter Rockefeller's conviction that the university was
"the best investment I ever made."

Anyhow, the son's religious horizons were broadened at Brown University and then as leader of the Men's Bible Class of the Fifth Avenue
Baptist Church, a class but recently made famous through Charles Evans
Hughes's tutelage. For eight years he devoted three nights a week in
preparation for the class, and despite painful lampooning by the press,*
he was later to recall: "I certainly got a great deal more out of the class
than I gave to it and it was one of the enriching experiences of my life."
In the end he had arrived at a religious position in which the "practical
application of Christian principles" dominated, overshadowing minor issues (he now believed), of doctrine, ritual, sectarian loyalty. It was a
faith at once sincere and sanguine, idealistic and practical, undogmatic
and experiential.

The younger Rockefeller's developing religious position is more than
tangentially related to Fifth Avenue and Park Avenue's liberal ministry,
the congregation moving to the Park Avenue site in 1922. Two especially
influential ministers of these churches were W. H. P. Faunce, whose
scalp was sought by fundamentalists during his later presidency of
Brown, and Cornelius Woelfkin, whose spiritual and intellectual pilgrimage from premillennialism to liberalism was a cause of conservative
consternation. Rockefeller, Jr., rightly termed "Saint Cornelius [a] kind

---

* The lampooning became blistering when in a Brown University YMCA address
in 1902 he drew the unfortunate analogy: "The growth of a large business is merely
a survival of the fittest. . . . The American Beauty rose can be produced in the
splendor and fragrance which bring cheer to its beholder only by sacrificing the
early buds which grow up around it."

of John the Baptist, . . . preparing the way for Fosdick." Sighed one of the more conservative Park Avenue saints at the time of Fosdick's call, "Since I have already taken the plunge under Dr. Woelfkin's liberalism, I might as well swim on across under Dr. Fosdick's leadership."

When the United States entered the Great War, Rockefeller, true to his horror of inefficient competition, played a large role in bringing together in a single campaign the seven organizations servicing the religious and recreational needs of the boys in uniform. In late 1917 he was invited by the Baptist Social Union to present an address on "The Christian Church—What of Its Future?" Subsequently printed in the *Saturday Evening Post*, Rockefeller always believed the address the best expression of his religious views. Not surprisingly, the talk set conservative teeth on edge, dismissing as it did as nonesssential ordinance, ritual (including baptism by immersion), and creeds. It further set aside all denominational concerns, pleading rather cooperation, ecumenicism, interdenominationalism. The church of the future would have as its object the promotion of applied, not "theoretical" religion, and through its involvement in social, moral, civic, educational, industrial, and commercial affairs, there would be realized the establishment of the Kingdom of God on earth.

Religious liberals had first raised the cry of "tainted money" earlier in the century when the senior Rockefeller awarded $100,000 to the American Board of Commissioners for Foreign Missions. By World War I, however, the shouts of alarm over Junior's contributions to religious causes were coming from conservative throats. With a fortune of $500 million, continuously growing, he proceeded on his life's philanthropic work, judiciously distributing, by 1960, $552 million. An important fraction of this total sum involved religious institutions and affairs. Not all of the beneficiaries may be termed "liberal," but the general thrust of Rockefeller's support was in liberal directions. The conservatives' concern is, therefore, eminently understandable, especially when it is remembered that in the years 1919–1933 Rockefeller annually was contributing sums amounting to anywhere from 5.8 percent to 12.6 percent of the Unified Budget of the Northern Baptist Convention. Canadian fundamentalist Thomas T. Shields branded the "Rockefeller Trust" the "most gigantic corruption fund that ever cursed the Christian world," and he observed that "this accursed thing, for it is from Hell, beyond any doubt, had managed to secure a place in the official life of the Denomination."

Rockefeller's vision of "the Christian church of the future" was shared by other successful operants in the modern age of corporate capitalism, particularly by those representing the second generation of secure wealth.

In their rage for order, in their confidence in a professional elite, and in their despair over sectarian rivalry and ruinous denominational competition, they urged a rationalized church, nondenominational and world embracing. There would take place a sort of Taylorization of religion based on the conviction that the organizational principles good for, say, Standard Oil, would be good for the churches. Bureaucratic values and bureaucratic structures were transforming the Protestant churches concurrent with the transformation of American business. Further, religious liberalism appealed to practical men of the world exactly because it tended to substitute good works for rites and rituals, involving Christians in service to society (and no word slipped from business lips more smoothly than "service"). "A technological society gets on with its business when the element of mystery can be reduced if not eliminated," observed a thoughtful commentator, and the rational element in modernism also may have touched a responsive chord in businessmen. Further still, postmillennialism, as Reinhold Niebuhr noted, "is always the hope of comfortable and privileged classes, who imagine themselves too rational to accept the idea of the sudden emergence of the absolute in history. For them the ideal is in history, working its ways to ultimate triumph."*

In assessing John D. Rockefeller, Jr., most historians have emphasized his painful conscientiousness, methodical tenacity, calculating shrewdness, cold reserve, and severe repression of self. Golf bored him, cards he never shuffled, dancing (in private only) was but "a grand form of exercise," and tobacco and alcohol (even wine) were eschewed. He read little fiction and no poetry because his cast of mind was neither imaginative nor playful. Yet he was not uncultured and not without aesthetic appreciation. It was not a yahoo who brought The Cloisters into being or who loved classical music or who appreciated Chinese porcelains or who possessed more than an amateur's understanding of archaeology and architecture or who admired such art forms as stained glass. (He utterly failed to comprehend his wife's absorbing interest in modern art, though that did not deter the spirited Abby Aldrich Rockefeller from helping to found New York's Museum of Modern Art.)

He held himself in tight rein, but not to the point of morbidity. He attended the theatre and in one instance supported (over genteel protests) the performance of Brieux's *Damaged Goods.* Originally a proponent of

---

* However, it must not be forgotten that fundamentalists found generous supporters in the Stewart brothers, J. C. Penney, John Wanamaker, George F. Washburn, and other millionaires, although the French observer André Siegfried was certainly wrong in seeing the whole fundamentalist crusade as a conspiracy by "two hundred of the most bigoted millionaires" to divert criticism of capitalism.

prohibition, he came to acknowledge its failure and publicly favored Repeal. He told and enjoyed listening to stories, even those mildly risqué. On one occasion Raymond Fosdick, seeking to unbutton him a little, sang at the piano a medley of slightly bawdy songs to Rockefeller's initial discomfort and then growing delight. "Teach me the words," he requested. Rockefeller also once asked Harry, who was planning a visit, to bring with him any stories "you may have in your collection that your daughter thinks would not impair my morals." Felled by an attack of gout, he wrote dryly to an associate: "In view of my exemplary behavior throughout life, Mrs. Rockefeller feels that to apply this name to my malady may seem to give the wrong impression. In using it to you, however, I need not fear that result for you well know what a temperate life I have led." Uninterested in group sports, he kept his five-foot-six-inch frame (always conservatively garbed) hard by horseback riding, hiking, wood chopping, and rare games of squash and tennis. Incidentally, it was on Harry's urging that the Rockefeller children were permitted to play tennis on Sundays.

John D. Rockefeller, Jr., was a considerate, generous, self-effacing, kind, loyal, courageous, and above all caring human being—at least as the records reveal regarding his relationships with the Park Avenue Baptist Church and The Riverside Church and Harry Emerson Fosdick.

III

At the first postwar annual convention of Northern Baptists, meeting in Denver in 1919, the simmering denominational controversy was brought into the open. Like their Presbyterian counterparts, Baptist premillennialists had discerned in the Great War an eschatological "sign." "The last days are upon us," warned Amzi C. Dixon. "We who are Christians should look to heaven expecting the Lord's return at any moment." New York's respected Baptist minister and severe Fosdick critic, Dr. Isaac M. Haldeman, had a premillennial vision that demonstrates the contrast with Fosdick's postmillennialism about as sharply as words make possible:

> Christ is coming with the eye of one who is aroused and indignant, in whose being beats the pulse of hot anger. . . . He comes forth as one who no longer seeks either friendship or love. . . . His garments are dipped in blood, the blood of others. He descends that he may shed the blood of men. . . . He will enunciate his claim by terror and might. He will write it in the blood of his foes. He comes like the treader of the winepress, and the grapes are the bodies of men. He will tread and trample in his fury till the blood of men shall fill the earth. . . . He will

tread and trample them beneath his accusing feet, till their upspurting blood shall make them crimson. He comes to his glory, not as the Saviour meek and lowly, not through the suffrage of willing hearts and the plaudits of a welcoming world, but as a king, an autocrat, a despot, through the gushing blood of a trampled world.

Certain that the holocaust in Europe was indisputable vindication of their dire predictions about the inevitable decline of the age, premillennialists in 1918 held prophetic conferences of unprecedented size in Philadelphia and New York, and in May–June 1919 there was organized the World's Christian Fundamentals Association, "an event of more historical moment," declared the Baptist fundamentalist William Bell Riley (mentor of Billy Graham), "than the nailing up, at Wittenberg, of Martin Luther's ninety-five theses." Shortly, Dr. Curtis Lee Laws, the able editor of the respected and responsible conservative Baptist paper, *Watchman-Examiner*, coined the term "fundamentalist"—an affirmative term, of course, as he employed it.

Although conservative strength was mounting rapidly, the well-organized liberals carried the convention in Denver on three points, all seen by conservatives as an attempt at centralization on a liberal basis. It was voted to enter the Interchurch World Movement*; to form a General Board of Promotion with authority to prepare a Unified Budget; and to embark upon a five-year plan, the ambitious "New World Movement." Further, an established journal was purchased by the denomination and renamed *The Baptist*, to the consternation of the editors of independent Baptist papers. Fosdick was invited to preach the convention sermon— part of the larger liberal plot, charged the fundamentalists. He proceeded to capture the delegates of all persuasions with "The Unshaken Christ." Editor Laws praised the sermon and Judge F. W. Freeman, leader of Denver's fundamentalists, did the handsome thing and invited Fosdick to assume the pastorate of Denver's First Baptist Church.

* The I.W.M. was an effort to unite the Protestant churches of America in a unified program of Christian world service. Though not the originator, Rockefeller, Jr., was the principal financial promoter of this colossal, climactic expression of liberal American Protestantism's crusading idealism, centralizing thrust, rationalized efficiency, and rage to Christianize the world through the instrumentality of Yankee dollars. Explained Rockefeller, "The principles of the Interchurch World Movement would appeal to every businessman because it aims to develop the maximum of efficiency in doing the Lord's business." Baptist fundamentalists, such as Haldeman, John Roach Straton, and Cortland Myers, hurled testy criticisms at it, as did Presbyterian conservatives and even moderates, such as the towering layman, Robert E. Speer. The closer one looks at the I.W.M. the more one is persuaded that it was doomed to fail and deserved to fail. However, its investigation of the steel strike of 1919 and conditions in the mills remains to this day the finest, most searching and devastating inquiry into a labor situation ever conducted by a religious organization.

The actions taken at the convention stung conservatives to counter-attack. A call for a General Conference on Fundamentals went forth and just prior to the 1920 annual convention there crowded into Buffalo's Civic Auditorium three thousand concerned conservatives intent on re-affirming, restating, and reemphasizing the historic faith of Baptists. Out of these sessions emerged the National Federation of Fundamentalists, a coalition of respected, responsible, nonseparatist individuals led by Massee, Laws, and Frank Goodchild. Ominously, also on hand were such radical fundamentalists, primarily premillennialists, as Minneapolis's Riley and New York's Straton, whose intemperate addresses on "The Menace of Modernism" foreshadowed the ultimate rupture of the Baptist Right. At the convention itself a resolution to demand an investigation of unorthodoxy in Baptist schools created the wildest disorder: "A sober, reverential body of men and women was transformed into a shouting, hissing, applauding bedlam." The investigation was authorized and the conservatives were on the march.

In 1921 a second preconvention meeting was held in Des Moines at which a statement of faith was adopted. Though moderately phrased by Goodchild, it was designed to isolate and expose modernists. For strategic reasons this doctrinal statement, later known as the Des Moines Confession, was not pressed on the convention. However, on motion of Judge Freeman a gift of oil stock worth $1,750,000 with creedal conditions attached was accepted. Fosdick, it will be recalled, bitterly protested this bald purchase of "the Baptist Churches' subscription to a creed for one hundred thousand shares of International Petroleum."

Feeling the pressure, prior to the 1922 convention liberal Baptists organized The Roger Williams Fellowship, claiming to stand for historic Baptist liberties and true evangelism. At the covention when militant fundamentalists urged the adoption of the New Hampshire Confession (more rigorous than the Des Moines Confession of the moderate fundamentalists), Cornelius Woelfkin shrewdly offered the substitute motion: "The Northern Baptist Convention affirms that the New Testament is the all-sufficient ground of our faith and practise, and we need no other statement." After three hours of spirited debate, the substitute carried, 1264 to 634. Obviously the liberals were joined by many moderates and perhaps even some conservatives who opposed the abandonment of the historic Baptist position of freedom. James C. Colgate reported elatedly to Fosdick that fundamentalist propaganda had not fooled the rank-and-file Baptists. "To your tents, O Israel!" became the fundamentalist cry. Laws admitted to having lost this battle, but not the war, and to Bryan (who as guest convention speaker "mightly illuminated the folks and mightily confounded the enemy") Massee expressed confidence that "we gained a great strength from the defeat." Fosdick had then just preached "Shall the Fundamentalists Win?" and that sermon's ghostly presence haunted the convention as he had intended.

Immediately before the 1923 convention, ultrafundamentalists, dissatisfied with the "pusillanimous" posture of the National Federation of Fundamentalists and the "temporizing" leadership of Massee, Laws, and Goodchild, formed the Baptist Bible Union. Led by the Texan J. Frank Norris, the Canadian T. T. Shields, the Minnesotan W. B. Riley, New York's Straton, and Michigan's Van Osdel, it was North American in scope, fractious in spirit, abusive in action (one thinks of Straton standing on a table at the 1923 convention to denounce the presence of the president of Brown University), and persistent (as a moderate wrote) "in putting in 'plenary verbal inspiration' and 'Pre-Millennial Second Coming,' and other extreme articles in their Confession of Faith." Fosdick faced many foes, but none more implacable than the "Bible Union crowd."

Fosdick had last attended a convention in 1919, but his name was often on Baptist fundamentalists' lips. The scholarly Dr. Goodchild reviewed both *Christianity and Progress* and *The Modern Use of the Bible.* He found Fosdick's reduction of God to "the Creative Reality" in the former volume rather less appealing than Mary Baker Eddy's "the Divine Mind." The latter volume was "specious," leaving the faithful a "mutilated Bible." Straton replied to Fosdick's controversial sermon with one of his own entitled, "Shall the Funnymonkeyists Win?" When forty-seven New York Baptist ministers adopted a resolution of tribute to Fosdick, Straton would have them remember that Fosdick was a Baptist bootlegger, a Presbyterian outlaw, the Jesse James of the theological world. Straton courteously invited Fosdick to a series of public debates in Carnegie Hall (all profits to go to the suffering Armenians) and kindly offered Fosdick (should he lose his Old First job) the use of the Calvary Baptist Auditorium, providing only that Fosdick "return to the faith of his fathers." The Texan "Two-Gun" Frank Norris (who was acquitted of fatally shooting an unarmed man in his study), not to be upstaged by Straton, invited Fosdick to public debates "in a half-dozen leading Cities of America."

The responsible Dr. Laws, initially believing Fosdick to be "the very embodiment of fine fraternity and genial friendliness," found the sermon "Shall the Fundamentalists Win?" to be a "bitter arraignment of good and true men; a gross and unpardonable ignorance of facts; a remarkable illustration of the intolerance of liberalism." When Dr. Laws heard a rumor that Fosdick was to be nominated for the presidency of the Northern Baptist Convention in 1925, Fosdick reassured him, "Man of peace that I am, if I were nominated I would not run and if I were elected I would not serve."

Some Baptist criticisms of Fosdick were informed and sincere, whereas others were vicious. To the editor of the Southern Baptist *Western Recorder*, Fosdick was "floriferous," "foxy," and "spiritually unfumigated," much concerned with "Presbyterian cash" and not at all with "Baptist doctrines." Some private epistles went further, one correspondent calling Fosdick an "indescribable Thing-in-human form . . . spewed up by Satan from the slimy depths of Hell. . . . If you do not like my Christmas felicitations you can go to hell . . . you syphilitic louse." Little wonder that when golfing, Fosdick and his companions would tee up the ball, growl "That's Straton's head," and wallop the shot. Little wonder, too, that when a Philadelphia minister defamed Fosdick, a worshipper informed him that if he did it again, "I shall rise from my seat and denounce you and your contemptible unchristian blackguardism." Little wonder, finally, that by the winter of 1923 such was the intensity of the controversy that New York's Episcopal Bishop William Thomas Manning publicly pleaded for a Christmas season armistice: "A little time of silence and thought and prayer will be of help to all of us."

IV

When in May 1925 the newspapers announced Fosdick's acceptance of the call to the Park Avenue Baptist Church, few knew that Rockefeller (and one or two other key leaders, notably James C. Colgate) had for years been stalking Fosdick with all the cunning generally ascribed to the senior Rockefeller's business tactics. As early as 1912 both Rockefeller and Colgate had favored Fosdick as their pastor. As we know, the Fifth Avenue congregation moved in 1922 to a new building on Park Avenue, a lovely Gothic structure eliciting the observation of Ralph Adams Cram, "Very good. Might have done it myself!" At that time a few church officers, led by Rockefeller, began quietly to look for a successor to the aging Cornelius Woelfkin who desired to retire. An informal conference was held with Fosdick. He made it clear that he was not prepared to leave the First Presbyterian Church.

Still, the Park Avenue leaders maintained intermittent contact with him. Early in 1923 Colgate wondered if Fosdick would care to preach Sunday evenings in the new church. Fosdick declined, pleading "no margin of strength," and doubting the wisdom of occupying two pulpits simultaneously. From time to time in that year Rockefeller dropped flattering notes to Fosdick and notes about him to church officers. In

March of 1924 Colgate again made an approach: "Our feeling is that the Park Avenue Church and you have enough in common to make it almost a duty to compare notes and see whether we can get together in a way helpful to both." Raymond Fosdick pressed the Park Avenue suit for his employer, Rockefeller.

By the early fall Rockefeller's mind was set. Fosdick would be offered the Park Avenue pulpit and if he declined, Rockefeller personally would purchase a site and build a church on Morningside Heights for Fosdick. "Had that proposition gone through," he later ruminated, "the entire expense of housing the enterprise would have been upon me, and the tremendously heavy burden of organizing and getting into shape a new church group would have been upon Dr. Fosdick." In October Harry Edmonds, director of International House (a Rockefeller creation for foreign students studying on Morningside Heights) presented Fosdick with a proposition: the erection of a great "*inter* or *un*denominational" cathedral on Riverside Drive seating five thousand "for the liberal minded people of the community." Fosdick replied: "Whether or not something of that sort will ever be wise, or possible, I cannot now with clear vision foresee. I must acknowledge, however, that a good many people besides yourself have thought of it, and I have tucked it away in the files of my mind for further reference." Another International House individual presented a similar plan to Rockefeller, wondering if he would subscribe one-half the estimated cost of $3,000,000 minimum." "The big thing to decide," the letter closed, "is whether there is enough in the idea to outlast the ministry of even a man like Fosdick." Concurrently, Ivy Lee was thinking bigger: a $10,000,000 church for Fosdick in the vicinity of Columbia University open to all who believe in "Jesus Christ as guide and master." The necessity of Rockefeller monies to consummate the vision was assumed.

In October the Harry Fosdicks and the Raymond Fosdicks motored with John D., Jr., to the family estate near Tarrytown to visit the senior Rockefeller. In December another conference was held. By the end of 1924 the pressure on Fosdick to be aligned with Rockefeller, either as Park Avenue pastor or in a new Rockefeller-financed church on Morningside Heights, was enormous. But Fosdick was as toughly independent as Rockefeller was tenacious, and on January 11, 1925, in a long conversation with Colgate he definitely turned down a point-blank invitation to become pastor of The Park Avenue Baptist Church. Remember, at that time Fosdick had pledged to First Presbyterian Church not to commit himself to a new post until after the Presbyterian General Assembly met in May. The day following the conversation Colgate dropped Fosdick a fatherly word of advice: "I do hope . . . you will make no mistake in deciding what you will do after you have had your year of rest and travel. . . . The most dangerous time in a man's career,—whether it be business or otherwise,—is when he is on the crest of a wave." Colgate continued, "Do not permit yourself to be overwhelmed by the crowds attempting to hear you preach and lecture. Probably one of the greatest sermons ever preached . . . was preached to a congregation consisting of one Samaritan woman who did not move in the highest circle of society." Fosdick acknowledged the "good advice." "You are absolutely right in everything that you say and of course I have mulled over the matter a good many times. I fear greatly the danger in which I stand of being pushed out of connection with the historic Christian organizations and forced to start an independent movement without traditional backing. It may be that will be necessary, but I hope that it will not and I have been a great deal concerned about the very peril in the situation to which you so wisely refer."

Meanwhile, Rockefeller continued silently to negotiate for prospective church sites on Morningside Heights. In early March he described four possible tracts to Fosdick, requesting that Fosdick rank them "in the order of their desirability." Concurrently, a new plan was evolving in the minds of the Park Avenue leadership: Fosdick would be called to Park Avenue and then the entire congregation would move to a yet to be constructed edifice on Morningside Heights. This plan, to sell the present church and remove to the "Columbia University district under the leadership of Dr. Fosdick," was presented to a joint meeting of the Board of Trustees and Deacons on March 24. Assembling in Rockefeller's home, the dinner seating was so arranged (as Rockefeller later revealed) "that a number of men known to favor Dr. Fosdick would speak before the one or two doubtful members' turns came." The joint boards unanimously voted to lay the proposal before the entire congregation on May 22. A committee chaired by Rockefeller was authorized to carry on the negotiations regarding Fosdick and the new site, strict confidentiality being enjoined on all present.

April saw Fosdick and the Baptists draw closer with many conferences and exchanges of telegrams and letters. Increasingly certain that the General Assembly would not make it possible for him to remain at Old First, Fosdick, nevertheless, did not want a formal offer until he was ready to accept. In mid-April Rockefeller resigned as chairman of the search committee (he remained as a member), pleading that he was "rather overworked this winter," but in reality believing it wise to play a less conspicuous hunter's role in the bagging of the Fosdick lion. In one meeting between the philanthropist and the preacher, Rockefeller topped Fosdick's protest that he did not wish to be known as the pastor of the richest man in the country with the widely reported counterthrust, "Do you think that more people will criticize you on account of my wealth, than will criticize me on account of your theology?"

On April 17 Fosdick wrote to Edward L. Ballard, chairman of the Park Avenue Board of Trustees, reviewing and confirming the conditions under which he would consider a call—conditions discussed in earlier conversations. The letter is important because Fosdick makes clear, in concrete detail, what he expects of the Park Avenue Baptist Church and what the church may expect of him. "You will bear me witness," the letter reads, "that I have not sought nor encouraged this proposal, that I have been cautious and critical about it, that I have thought of all the objections I could find, and naturally have shrunk from the heavy burdens which it would impose on me as well as on the church." Nevertheless, Fosdick found the adventure exciting and put forth these conditions:

1. A larger church be built in the vicinity of Columbia University.
2. A free opening of membership to all disciples of Jesus Christ. "This would mean that any one who accepts Christ as the revelation of God and the ideal of man may come into full and equal membership in letter from any church, and that any one joining with us on confession of faith for the first time might be immersed, sprinkled, or (if Quaker scruples are present) welcomed on verbal confession, as each individually might choose."
3. Ministers chosen to serve with him should be selected on the basis of their Christian character and efficiency, and their sympathy with his ideals, rather than on the basis of their denominational ordination.
4. No partisan name suggestive of exclusiveness, as denominational names are, should interfere with the public understanding of "what we are trying to do"; therefore the new church could be called "The Morningside Church" or some similar name of non-partisan color.
5. The ministry should be collegiate in nature; that is, the other ministers would not be "assistants" in the ordinary sense, but coordinate pastors carefully departmented with differentiated responsibilities.

Fosdick warned: "That there would be an uproar against us from certain quarters is obvious. That the Baptist Association to which the church now belongs might excide us is at least possible, although I personally hope that may not occur. If the adventure is undertaken, we should be prepared to meet such opposition without surprise or disturbance." Fosdick was later to add a final stipulation: his salary must not exceed $5000.

On May 4 the joint boards met, assenting to every condition save only that the word "Baptist" *might* appear in the subtitle of the new corporate name. Three days later Fosdick was invited to appear before the boards for the sake of gaining a complete understanding of his position, "all of which questions Dr. Fosdick answered fully and frankly, and to the complete satisfaction of all present." On motion a call was unanimously approved. On May 15 the congregation was informed of the recommendation, subject to its ratification. On May 22, after a two-hour discussion, congregational approval was given. The formal call was extended May 25; the formal acceptance given May 26. "Life is rather hectic but I am alive and kicking," Fosdick informed his father, "and so far as I can see coming out on top of the world."

Memorial Day Sunday the pastor-elect preached his first sermon. A great throng overflowed the sanctuary of the Park Avenue Baptist Church. Outside, in a line three deep, hundreds of others sought vainly to catch a word that might drift out. The sermon was a plea for a church inclusive enough that Lincoln might feel free to join. It was also an evangelical proclamation that the vitality of Christianity from the start was in the "individual soul's immediate, firsthand, personal experience of the grace of God in Christ." But surely the most moving words were spoken by the saintly Woelfkin:* "He that cometh after me is preferred before me; you must increase, I must decrease. He that hath the bride is the bridegroom; but the friend of the bridegroom who standeth and heareth him rejoiceth greatly because of the bridegroom's voice. This my joy therefore is made full. Accept then this pulpit from one who loves you sincerely; who gives you his benediction and bids you Godspeed in the Master's name." On the church steps following the service the parchment-faced senior Rockefeller smilingly bestowed shiny dimes on children while his son declined to comment, saying only to the reporters, "But the occasion speaks for itself, doesn't it?"

V

The occasion did not quite speak for itself, or if it did, what was "said" was subject to different interpretations. For one thing, a small band of Park Avenue Church parishioners, an estimated fifteen percent of the

---

* Said W. H. P. Faunce of Woelfkin: "He was the only man I have known to whom the ancient title 'saint' seems not inappropriate."

total membership of seven hundred, objected to the seemingly remorse-less course of events. These individuals felt that a coterie of church lead-ers had railroaded the thing through; that to move to the strange new site with its transient population would mean the end of the Park Ave-nue Baptist Church as such, the breaking up of home ties, the abandon-ment of a lovely sanctuary only three years old; that Fosdick's condi-tions meant the abandonment of cherished Baptist ways; that the church was staking its future on one mortal man; and that in any case it was "selling out to build and exploit a preaching auditorium for Dr. Fosdick." Prior to the congregational meeting John B. Trevor, associated with Rockefeller, wrote him a reasoned, forceful protest, closing: "In express-ing these views, you, of course, understand that I fully appreciate that the Board of Trustees . . . have acted fully within their rights in taking the action which they have done, and they have, in their own opinion, acted AD MAJOREM GLORIA DEI, as our Jesuit friends profess, but to be perfectly frank, I believe that this action, aside from all questions of the wisdom which I challenge, involves in fact a moral breach of trust." At the congregational meeting Mrs. Marshall Clarke rose to speak for the old church and rites, with the Rockefellers and two of their sons sitting in "tense silence." Suddenly, Mrs. Clarke placed her hand to her tear-filled eyes, uttered a choked cry, and fell fainting. An-other dissenter denied any intent of splitting the congregation, modestly saying that her course was not of the slightest interest to anyone, but that when the time comes "it is possible if not probable that some few will prefer to unite with another Baptist Church instead of going to one which drops the name as well as the tenets of the Baptists." Ultimately, of those present, only seventeen voted against the proposals and of these, only seven refused a motion to make the actions unanimous. A writer in the *Western Recorder,* in an article entitled "Shall the Baptists Acknowledge the Standard Oil Church?," said of the Park Avenue minority: "I would like to organize that little group into a New Testa-ment church, and place it in the heart of New York. They are of the stuff of which martyrs are made, and if I were pastor of a church like that I would take as my text for the introductory sermon, 'Fear not, little flock, it is your Father's good pleasure to give you the kingdom.' "

This was not how Fosdick and Woelfkin viewed the dissenters, both men expressing private delight at their departure. As Woelfkin wrote Fosdick: "I am glad that the irreconcilables have all withdrawn, some two dozen in all. They were Haldemanites, Moorites, Stratonites, Hi-vites, Jebusites, Perrezites, Moabites, Ammonites and other ITES. But the old guard—Armitageites, Fauncites, Johnsonites and the Woelf-kinites will stick by the stuff."

Beyond the confines of the congregation the news of Park Avenue Baptists' action sparked much criticism. Considering the source of the Rockefeller wealth and the "oiliness" of Fosdick's sermons, Straton suggested that the new church resulting from the "oily proposition" bear instead of a cross an enormous electric sign carrying the legend "SOCONY"—the Standard Oil Church of New York. A cross, in any case, he said, "would be inappropriate to the message of modernism which has rejected the cross." Straton also observed that "Mr. Rockefeller has recently tightened his grip on our denomination here in the Northland by paying the debts of our Women's Missionary Societies and making other large gifts to our missionary work." (He did in fact meet the deficit "in the name of my mother.") Straton then proceeded to present to the New York Baptist Ministers' Conference a resolution of censure, which was not passed.

Straton was, of course, not alone in his criticism. Haldeman howled, Fountain fumed, Norris termed Fosdick a greater peril than Clarence Darrow, Shields wondered "Can Fundamentalists Get Money from God as Modernists Do from Rockefeller?," and Riley warned, "When one man [Rockefeller] can control the financial world, the educational world, and practically the religious world, it looks as though the day of the Anti-Christ is not distant." The Baptist Bible Union saw the call to Fosdick as "obviously part of a plan to extend to the whole Baptist denominational life the influence of the Rockefeller Foundation, which already has succeeded in converting nearly all of our educational institutions into hotbeds of modernism." Smitten hip and thigh, Fosdick wryly wrote Coffin: "You Presbyterians certainly have handed me a job. When I think of what I have shouldered, thanks to the exigency of being ousted from the First Presbyterian pulpit, my stomach sinks to my boots and my head turns to water within me."

VI

Matters were not at all helped by a brochure entitled, "Call of Doctor Fosdick to Park Avenue Baptist Church," published by the church and nationally circulated by Ivy Lee. Among other materials the brochure carried a plain statement that the church intended to practice open membership and also not require of members baptism by immersion. It appeared to conservative eyes to be the opening shot of an aggressive propaganda campaign to convert the churches of the Northern Baptist Convention to the Rockefeller/Fosdick position. Surely it was provocative for Fosdick to say in a sermon that was widely quoted by horrified

Baptists: "When I stop to think of it, I was brought up in a church where in arguing about the quantity of water necessary to make a proper baptism enough energy has been expended almost to save the world. One wonders jealously what might have happened if all that consecrated thoughtfulness had been expended on something that really mattered." This is certainly not a fair statement of Baptist understanding of the rite; even such a liberal as Shailer Mathews would term it a misrepresentation. In light of later developments, let Park Avenue's intent be clearly and succinctly stated by an excerpt from a letter by Fosdick dated June 18, 1925:

> In the new church which is proposed we shall insist upon no ritualistic requirements for admission to church membership. We will immerse those who wish to be immersed, sprinkle those who wish to be sprinkled, and receive on verbal confession of faith in Christ, a Quaker, for example, who may have conscientious scruples against all ritualistic observances. The sole requirement for membership is a loyal discipleship to Jesus, and no non-ritual requirements are insisted on, that being left altogether to the conscience of the individual.

The gauntlet thrown, conservatives picked it up at the Northern Baptist Convention meeting in Seattle in June. As Charles H. Sears, superintendent and executive secretary of the New York City Baptist Mission Society, reported back to Fosdick, "the fight was on and . . . Park Avenue was at the center of it." At the onset a sharp skirmish took place when conservatives sought to unseat the four Park Avenue church delegates, Dr. and Mrs. Woelfkin and Dr. and Mrs. Eugene C. Carder (Carder was associate minister), on the grounds that with the call to Fosdick the church had ceased to be Baptist. The conservative move was turned back by a three-to-one vote, the majority accepting the position that since Fosdick's pastorate was not to begin until his return from Europe and since *at the moment* the church had complied with all requirements for membership in the convention, there was no legal reason for disqualification of the delegates. Prior to the three-hour debate and vote, Woelfkin moaned with a smile, "The next time they put a noose around my neck I want them to drop the handkerchief and go on with the business." Even after being seated, Woelfkin told Rockefeller, "It seemed that we were sitting upon tacks with the business end up, for constantly there were opportunities sought to open the issue again on some other grounds."

Later in the convention extreme conservatives protested Woelfkin's nomination for reelection to the Ministers' and Missionaries' Benefit Board. Shaken, ashen-faced Woelfkin advanced to the platform to withdraw his name, liberals near him pleading, "Don't speak, leave yourself in the hands of your friends. You are safe." His magnanimous words to the conservatives left half the audience in tears: "Had you decided that I could no longer walk side by side with you, I should still believe that though my path would verge away from that which those who had excluded me must follow, I might yet enter the New Jerusalem, whose twelve gates open upon every horizon. Even though I might come in by a gate opposite to that which they should enter, I cherish the belief that we shall know each other better when the mists have rolled away." Ultimately his name was returned to the list by an overwhelming vote, with even conservatives in support; indeed it was a conservative who made the motion.

Denver's Judge Freeman, however, then pressed a resolution expressly aimed at the Park Avenue Baptist Church, the salient passage of rebuke reading: "That we do hereby express our keen regret and emphatic disapproval of the course announced by said church, which has given and will continue to give much pain and disquietude to large numbers . . . , and we hereby express to said church our keen and fraternal hope that it will not pursue the course it has announced." The resolution passed unanimously, liberal delegates sitting on their hands.

It is absolutely crucial to an understanding of convention developments to recognize that the explosive issue was not Park Avenue's intent to practice open membership (though this, too, exercised Bible Union fundamentalists), but the church's announcement that it would practice, if desired, baptism by sprinkling or even not at all. At the convention the liberals deemed it prudent not to go to the mat on the baptism matter in order, as Woelfkin reasoned, "that a good many of the conservative but not fundamentalist ministers of the West might be able to go home and face their constituents and not be driven into the arms of the Bible Union propagandists." This was precisely the assessment of the convention mood Fosdick received from Charles Sears. Moderates might reluctantly accept the principle of open membership, but on sprinkling they would align themselves with the fundamentalists. On the last day, official notice was given by Judge Freeman that at the *next* convention an amendment to the bylaws would be introduced, defining a Baptist church as "one accepting the New Testament as its guide and composed only of baptized believers, baptism being by immersion." In view of the fact that the Bible Unionists were largely turned back (with the defeat of the Hinson motion) in their inquisitorial efforts regarding missionaries, it is reasonable to conclude that Seattle was not a victory for either fundamentalists or modernists and that in the year ahead moderates would be the swing-group.

At least one Park Avenue leader reacted angrily to Freeman's adopted resolution. James C. Colgate, past treasurer of the Northern Baptist Convention, fired off a letter to the Denver judge with an unveiled threat to curb the "credit of the Convention with its banks here in the city." He asked bluntly what the fundamentalists really wanted of the Park Avenue Church: "I feel sure that if the Church is not wanted in the Convention it will make no attempt to remain. As representative of the Fundamentalists and the mover (probably author) of the resolution adopted, what are your views and the views of your group in the matter? Do you want us out or in; to co*operate [*sic*] or not?" On receiving a copy of the letter, Fosdick concurred in Colgate's question, personally believing "that the most dignified thing for us to do is to send no delegates to the Northern Baptist Convention until they are anxious to have us do so." He added the thought, "I suppose that we must be particularly careful not to put ourselves in the position of using financial pressure to get our way."

As the summer days of 1925 melted away, however, the Park Avenue lay leadership increasingly trimmed on their original intent to baptize by other than immersion those who so desired. Their hedging is fully understandable. They received information from liberal and moderate leaders across the nation that if Park Avenue showed restraint on that point only, a denominational rupture could be avoided. Every other progressive reform contemplated by the church could be supported by the progressive wing of the convention, but it was demanding too much of that embattled wing to do suicidal battle over sprinkling. Fosdick, too, received similar intelligence, and before sailing for Europe on August 29 he and Charles W. Gilkey, friend, former student, and soon to be dean of the University of Chicago Chapel, thrashed the matter out on Fosdick's Maine island, Gilkey having been in close contact with other liberal leaders.

Concurrently, Fosdick was in communication with Colgate, Ballard, Carder, and Rockefeller, all of whom expressed the hope that Fosdick might agree not to insist on the *immediate* institution of baptism by sprinkling, making possible a public announcement to that effect. If Park Avenue gave way on that issue, argued Ballard, it could then send a delegation composed of Colgate, Rockefeller, and Secretary of State Charles Evans Hughes to commit "assault and battery upon the next Northern Baptist Convention" (the phrasing is Fosdick's, not Ballard's, but that was Ballard's meaning). Initially Fosdick demurred: "Having taken our position . . . it would be ruinous to retreat now and I hope that my spikes are driven in deeply enough so that no one will even try." By late August he was relenting a little. He still thought a public recanting strategically unwise. "We are going to surrender a big advantage," he wrote Ballard, "if we nervously fidget and bargain and play politics to stay in the Convention and forget that the Convention is more nervous than we are about the matter." Why make a voluntary statement now, surrendering a bargaining point with no similar concession from the fundamentalists? "I do not like to give up something that I want and then whistle for the results." Nevertheless, Fosdick now agreed, there was not the slightest reason why Park Avenue should practice sprinkling during his year in Europe or even immediately upon his return. He added: "I can afford to bide my time on that issue. I say frankly that if there were the slightest likelihood that the church would try to surrender any other item in our program—welcoming into full membership members from other Christian churches and also folk coming for the first time without any insistence on immersion—I should have to leave at once, no matter how much I wanted to stay."

And so Park Avenue and Fosdick played a waiting, unaggressive game. The irrepressible Ivy Lee was leashed, Fosdick feeling "certain that it will be better for us to restrict anything that might look like propaganda to the narrowest possible limits." The Southern New York Association received from Park Avenue a letter assuring "all of its sister churches of its unchanging friendship and devotion to the cause of our Master." Rockefeller advised that should the subject of sprinkling come up, the church leaders answer that the question is not before us "and will not be before us, if ever, for a considerable time yet." Only Dr. Woelfkin counseled against a policy of appeasement, jacking up Fosdick in Geneva with the old Scottish war cry, "Having flung the heart of Bruce let us come up to it." Reasoned Woelfkin: "Even if we were to affirm a purpose of falling into line with all the old conservative practices, I am sure they would keep up the fight on us, if not on the ground of church polity then upon the ground of progressive theology. I therefore agree that nothing would be gained by retracing a single step at this time, and certainly much would be lost by giving broadminded Christians, with whom we hope to do our larger work, the idea that we are either playing fast or loose with our convictions or lack a genuine sincerity in our movement." Within months Woelfkin would declare to Fosdick, "Egad, I am for dropping the very name Baptist and all its impedimenta. 'I'll set my foot with him who goes farthest.'"

By early 1926 Fosdick had come to see the wisdom of the Park Avenue Church issuing a public statement explaining its position. He wrote to Ballard, somewhat disingenuously, "I can only attribute to misunderstanding or to extraneous reasons for antagonism that have nothing to do with the case the strife that our stand has occasioned." On February

25 Gilkey wrote Fosdick a long letter detailing the conferences being held by liberals and moderates in anticipation of the next meeting of the convention in Washington. The fight can be won "provided we avoid a showdown on the 'bloody angle' of the form of baptism." Otherwise, "on the immersion question nearly all the middle-of-the-road men and the entire organization force will go against us, where always previously they have carried us to victory." For God's sake, Gilkey pleaded:

> If you could see your way clear to say to Park Avenue or to any of us, your friends, that while you hold your private convictions [as to the option of sprinkling] without change, you have no desire to press them on your church to the extent of affecting their denominational relationships, and if you can authorize either them or us to use such a statement in private conference previous to Washington, and if necessary publicly, I believe that with such assurance from you we can win open membership clear at this time and avoid a fight at the Convention. Failing such assurance, I fear we are in for a defeat whose consequences to the liberal cause among Baptists I dread to contemplate.

On March 20 Fosdick flashed the green light in a cablegram to Gilkey:

> Church has adopted English custom open membership. No form of baptism except immersion contemplated by church's action. This arrangement has had my consent. Have no desire by pressing personal opinion further to endanger church's denominational relations which I value highly. Use this privately. Letter follows.

In a covering letter to Gilkey and in one to Ballard, Fosdick confirmed his permission to the Park Avenue Church to announce now publicly that it was not the church's intent to baptize in any form other than immersion, adding, "It will be a matter of poignant regret to me if the Northern Baptist Convention feels it necessary to take action which will make such cooperation impossible." Fosdick, Gilkey, Ballard, and Baptist liberals generally were satisfied that the fundamentalists had been deprived utterly of their case, and they would not have time to work up another one before the convention met. In a handwritten note to his secretary, Fosdick was a little more candid. He termed the compromise a "makeshift" and the compromise definition of a Baptist church to be proposed to the Washington Convention "disgraceful." In two years the Park Avenue congregation would move up to Riverside Drive and alternative forms of baptism or no baptism at all could be effected, he suspected, without agitation. "Anyway, if they are firing us out of the denomination at Washington on 'open membership' we can take it and win out; if we were fired out on the matter of alternative modes [of baptism] we should go with the maledictions of liberals as well as fundamentalists, and that would make it very difficult to serve the general cause of progress."

On May 17 the Park Avenue Church sent a public statement to the Northern Baptist Convention protesting the 1925 Judge Freeman censure, announcing that no delegates would be sent to the Washington meeting in order to avoid "dissension and strife," and declaring that "the Park Avenue Church has no intention of practicing sprinkling as a form of baptism and that our pastor-elect has no intention, whatever his personal views may be, of asking the church to do so." The last statement is of course an untruth. Park Avenue's plans regarding baptism were momentarily masked for strategic reasons, but quite shortly, on October 27, 1926, to be exact, the church blithely went ahead with its original program no longer to require baptism by immersion and in time sprinkling was accorded to those so desiring that mode.

Meanwhile, what of the larger picture between the 1925 Seattle and the 1926 Washington meetings? Briefly, the fundamentalists, especially the Bible Unionists, continued their cannonading. The liberals, with Gilkey emerging as field general, joined forces with the moderates led by J. W. Brougher to seek peace without capitulation. Dr. Brougher was drafted by the Board of Promotion to lead a six-month nationwide "Play Ball" crusade of reconciliation and in a Chicago conference with liberals it was agreed to recommend to the Washington Convention the compromise "Brougher resolution." This resolution, though bitterly challenged by the Bible Union fellowship, was adopted. It declared that immersion was the only Scriptural baptism, but left the local churches free to practice as they wished. The only requirement explicitly stated was that official delegates to the convention must have been immersed. For his healing role Dr. Brougher was elected convention president. Massee supported Brougher's reconciliation efforts with an impassioned plea for denominational peace so that the Lord's business of evangelism might be pressed. Straton left the convention in disgust, after again denouncing Rockefeller. Riley rebuked Brougher and Massee with the reminder, "This is not a battle. It is a war from which there is no discharge." But it did seem, at least for the moment, that the Fundamentalist/Modernist controversy in the Northern Baptist Convention was almost over.

Gilkey expressed satisfaction that "out of the whole unhappy controversy open membership has been won, clean and clear," and thanked Fosdick for making this possible by bending on the immersion question.

"So far as the Park Avenue Church is concerned," Fosdick wrote of the Convention's actions, "all that I can discover is that the leaders are very well satisfied and we all of us feel that we have gangway sufficient to start on, at any rate."

VII

In his 1956 autobiography Fosdick termed the Fundamentalist/Modernist controversy of the 1920s an "ephemeral affair" involving "belated issues" and assumed that "the slow but inevitable processes of education" would doom the "outdated thinking" of the fundamentalists. The surge of conservative piety in the era of Dwight D. Eisenhower and Billy Graham made Fosdick's prediction instantly dubious; developments in subsequent decades made it radically untenable. By the 1980s one third of adult Americans claimed, with their presidents, the experience of being born again. Charismatic Christians, perhaps as many as 6 million, were found in both Pentecostal and mainline churches, Protestant and Catholic, and in their charismatic communities. Additional faithful were cured of illnesses by the touch of a revivalist's hand accompanied by the words, "Jesus, heal!" An apocalyptic fever raged, prompting *Newsweek* to record "The Boom in Doom," and if the alliteration seems too clever by half to be applied to the awful scenario predicted by premillenarian prophets, it is perhaps not unjust to such popular tractarians as Hal Lindsey, author of *The Late Great Planet Earth*, a work that sold 12 million copies. The airwaves were filled with heavenly messages and as choirs sang "Amazing Grace" and evangelists commanded, "Pray with me!," the audiences (150 million at their radio sets, additional millions at their television sets), responded "Thank you, Jesus" and "Praise the Lord." Bumper stickers proclaimed "Honk If You Love Jesus!" and "I've Found it!"; tabernacles saw scenes of religious ecstasy, the faithful writhing and speaking in tongues. On college campuses students crusaded confidently and T-shirts announced the salvation of the wearers. Even subtracting the most primitive ranters, chanters, rollers, and glossologists and forgetting for the moment the converts to Eastern mysticism, there remained millions of Americans testifying to a quickening of the spirit. While many are termed, and call themselves, "new evangelicals," there are additional millions shading to the right who may be properly characterized as "fundamentalists." Even the antievolution crusade of the 1920s has seen a rebirth as zealous creationists took up the old cry, "Every day is a lovely day for an auto-da-fé."

Therefore, when in *The Living of These Days* Fosdick claimed, "We won our battle," he was correct only in the limited sense that the liberals were not driven from the churches. It may very well be that for tens of millions in every era Fosdick's liberalism could never adequately answer the terrors of human existence. Nevertheless, when he added, "it was one of the most necessary theological battles ever fought," he was right on the money, for other millions found in his evangelical liberalism the only religious answer possible for them.

Chapter Nine

Further Cannonading
in the Turbulent Twenties

I

Because Fosdick's port was raked in the 1920s by Presbyterian and Baptist and other fundamentalists, it does not follow that religious radicals and secularists sportingly held their fire on his starboard. It is to this and other cannonading that we now briefly turn.

II

Albert C. Dieffenbach was editor of the influential journal, the *Christian Register*, and he and his paper represented the theological radical wing of American Unitarianism. Dieffenbach believed evangelical Christianity and true liberalism to be mutually exclusive, and he expected Fosdick, as modernism's putative leader, to shake the dust of the evangelical denominations, leaving those fossiled relics to the fundamentalists, and to swing free to the Unitarian position. When Fosdick did not succumb to his importuning, Dieffenbach judged modernism defeated in its battle with fundamentalism, sighing that although Fosdick "made a noise like a major prophet," he really preferred to be a popular preacher rather than another Luther. "He is a lost leader," the Unitarian editor finally concluded in 1927.

But Dieffenbach spoke only for the left wing of Unitarianism. In both America and England Unitarians (and Universalists as well) endlessly stated that Fosdick's theology would do no violence to the Unitarian position. Comparisons between Fosdick and William Ellery Channing (and

Theodore Parker) were drawn. "Sectarian pride may be flattered by the discovery that America's most popular preacher is teaching principles that Unitarianism was maintaining a hundred years ago," declared the respected John Clarence Petrie. A British Unitarian, admitting a "subtle, indescribable 'something' about Dr. Fosdick's preaching which defies analysis," concluded: "Though Dr. Fosdick cannot be classified by our present methods, it seems fair to say that the atmosphere of his preaching is such that many Unitarians—perhaps most Unitarians—would feel thoroughly at home in it."

Fosdick was in friendly correspondence with such Unitarian leaders as Francis Peabody and Isaac Sprague, and in 1922 he was invited by S. Adolphus Knopf to occupy the pulpit of All Souls Church, New York's oldest and wealthiest Unitarian church. Fosdick believed the exclusion of Unitarians and Universalists from the Federal Council of Churches "nonsensical" and "deplorable," and it aroused his "indignation." "I hate this whole narrow, bigoted spirit of sectarianism, as I hate the devil." When asked about the Riverside fellowship, he replied: "Our definition of a Christian . . . is very broad and we should certainly count the Unitarian and Universalist churches Christian churches, and welcome people from these churches just as freely as we would people from Methodist and Baptist congregations."

Here is another illustration of the difficulty of pinning an unambiguous label on Fosdick. Fundamentalists charged that he was a Unitarian. Dieffenbach definitely denied him the accolade. Other Unitarians were not quite so certain, but nevertheless maintained that his "disposition is essentially Unitarian" and that "he is manifestly fighting the same battle as we are in behalf of religious liberty and a better world."

III

There was one group at the opposite pole from Unitarianism, a group not usually classified as fundamentalists, who were certain of Fosdick's position—and they did not like it. They were the High Episcopalians or Anglo-Catholics. Fosdick returned the compliment, writing to liberal Episcopalian editor Guy Shipler, "I pride myself a little on my ability to put myself in other folks' places and see things through their eyes. But I must confess that the capacity of mine breaks down absolutely when I come to deal with the Anglo-Catholic." Shipler's *The Churchman* editorially defended Fosdick, and Fosdick counted among his New York friends such liberal Episcopal rectors as Melish, Guthrie, Reiland, Grant, Parks, Bowie, and Stires. But it is worth noting that Ivy Lee could report that judging by his mail (in response to the distribution of Fosdick's sermons) and next only to the Presbyterians, "the people who are most intolerant of your attitude ecclesiastically . . . are Episcopalians." Bishop William Thomas Manning was vocally critical; matters were not helped when Dr. Karl Reiland, rector of Saint George's Church, invited Fosdick to assist in the wedding of his daughter, only to have Fosdick's participation vetoed by Bishop Herbert Shipman. Nor were they helped when *The Living Church* sided editorially with conservative Presbyterians in the First Presbyterian Church cause célèbre. Fosdick was further piqued because on occasion Episcopal rectors would not provide a letter of transfer to a parishioner planning to leave to join Fosdick's church.

A cranky snobbery is not the primary explanation for High Church criticism. Substantive disagreements on matters of ecclesiology, liturgical forms, and a sacerdotal clergy were involved. Natural exception was taken to Fosdick's rather arch reference to "the tactual unction of a Bishop's fingers" and to his declaration that "the two denominations whose characteristic attitudes are most hostile to the achievement of church union are, I think, the Episcopalians and the Baptists." Natural bewilderment followed his definition of the church of the future: "The united . . . Church must be comprehensive enough to welcome high church Episcopalians and Quakers, without asking either of them to forego or compromise their freedom of thought and action." Natural anger was the reaction to his assertion that only "human stupidity" stood in the way of pan-Protestant unity because denominational differences "have no pertinence to any important question in modern life." Ministers and laypersons in the new church, Fosdick maintained, would be permitted "to think out their theology, ecclesiology, and ritual preferences, as they please." What Fosdick does not comprehend, observed the Episcopal *American Church Monthly*, is "the unhappy fact that there are some people who are peculiar enough to have convictions" and their "convictions do stand in the way of any such hazy, vague, anarchic agreement to disagree as he has in mind." The Riverside Church embodied Fosdick's vision of the church of the future, but it was not, and could not, be the Living Church of the Anglo-Catholics.

IV

When Fosdick maintained, as he did throughout his life, "The only important conflict in theology is the conflict between humanism and theism, between a religion without God and a religion with God," Raymond Fosdick, whose religious faith had now disappeared, became so exasperated that he petitioned Walter Lippmann to set his nutty brother straight, saying, "Harry and I have fought, bled and died on many a field of argument and when I saw this article of his [against humanism], I realized that it would require a cleverer pen than mine to show it up. And for the sake of the cause it ought to be shown up." In *A Preface to Morals* (1929), Lippmann, then America's most distinguished public philosopher, sought to steel his fellow citizens to the hard truth: "Until and unless a man feels the vast indifference of the universe to his own fate, and has placed himself in the perspective of cold and illimitable space, he has not looked maturely at the heavens." A mature philosophy of scientific "disinterestedness" must replace the consolations of theism. The "loss of certainty" is the fate of modern man. In explicating his argument Lippmann invidiously contrasted the majestic absolutes of past faiths with meretricious modernism, adding the stinging rebuke, "No painter who ever lived could make a picture which expressed the religion of the Rev. Harry Emerson Fosdick." In reviewing the volume in the *New York Evening Post* Fosdick charged Lippmann with holding an essentially fundamentalistic definition of Christianity, not at all comprehending what liberal Christians believed. Lippmann was locked into a "naive and medieval" notion of theism. Fosdick closed the review with the suggestion that Lippmann "some time try to secure an enterprising artist who will paint a picture of 'disinterestedness.'"

A year earlier in *American Inquisitors* Lippmann had chided Fosdick and his followers with the imaginary dialogue over a question of dogma:

Modernist: We can at least discuss it like gentlemen, without heat, without rancor.

Fundamentalist: Has it ever occurred to you that this advice is easier for you to follow than for me?

Modernist: How so?

Fundamentalist: Because for me an eternal plan of salvation is at stake. For you there is nothing at stake but a few tentative opinions none of which means anything to your happiness. Your request that I should be tolerant and amiable is, therefore, that I submit the foundations of my life to the destructive effects of your skepticism, your indifference, and your good nature. You ask me to smile and commit suicide.

Thus it was that in the 1920s Fosdick fought on many fronts, and although the fundamentalists, the Dieffenbachs, and the High Episcopalians came at him from the varied points of the religious compass, he was never permitted to forget the even deadlier critique of the nontheistic humanists and scientific naturalists. Few books hit thoughtful Americans with greater force than *A Preface to Morals*, except perhaps one published in the same year, *The Modern Temper*, in which Joseph Wood Krutch directly challenged Fosdick's vision with the stern words: "The universe revealed by science . . . is one in which the human spirit cannot find a comfortable home. There is no reason to suppose that a man's life has any more meaning than the life of the humblest insect that crawls from one annihilation to another." When one adds to the names of Lippmann and Krutch those of other towering agnostics/atheists on both sides of the Atlantic in the physical and social sciences and in arts and letters as well, one is better able to comprehend Fosdick's conviction that the ultimate conflict in the twenties was between "a religion without God and a religion with God." At the end of the decade in his first conversation with Reinhold Niebuhr, Fosdick confided his belief that each generation had only one battle in its system and would have to trust to the next generation to fight other subsequent battles. Fosdick and his generation fought to sustain belief both in abiding stars (against the denial of the naturalists) and in changing astronomies (against the constancy of the orthodox).

Chapter Ten

"A Pilgrimage to Palestine" and the Abrasive Aftermath with American Zionists

I

Fosdick's ten months' sabbatical abroad was "altogether exhilarating and rewarding," he reported, "free even from so minor a mishap as missing a train or losing a suitcase." He preached in Geneva before the League of Nations Assembly, traveled the Nile, toured Greece, visited Rome, trekked the Sinai Peninsula by camel, spent two unforgettable months in the Holy Land, returned to Europe by way of Syria and Turkey, and thence to Vienna, Berlin, Nuremberg, Dresden, and finally Paris and the battlefields of the Great War. The lands of the Bible especially fired his imagination. "I never enjoyed any journey so much," he thanked a friend in Jerusalem, "and never expect to enjoy any journey so much again until it is my privilege to come back to the Holy Land." How he had been able for years to deal with the Book "without the illumination of the land" he could not imagine. He recorded "A Pilgrimage to Palestine" in twelve installments for the readers of the *Ladies' Home Journal*. The following year the articles were brought together in a book of the same title. When republished in the 1970s by the Arno Press, it was hailed as "outstanding among its kind in its lucidity and its illuminating movement from ancient to modern periods in dealing with locations sacred to three historical religions." Unfortunately, Fosdick's intense interest in that area brought him into a sad but probably inevitable controversy with American Zionists who detected in him a pro-Arab bias.

II

The four Fosdicks sailed from New York on August 29, 1925. The girls, ages fourteen and twelve, were to be placed in a Swiss boarding school, La Marjolaine. Their father had selected the school with care, exchanging many letters with the directress, informing her in one epistle, "Far be it from a father to undertake the estimate of his own children, but I am sure that you will find our little ladies amiable and responsible girls who will give you no trouble. So far as their studies are concerned, they have maintained a high rank always."

On September 13 in connection with the opening of the League of Nations Assembly he preached in the Geneva Cathedral of Saint Pierre, from the pulpit once occupied by John Calvin. The invitation to do so, "a matter of some diplomatic delicacy," his brother reported, had first been extended and declined in 1924. The sermon itself was a plea to end war, with the League, World Court, and "an international mind, backed by a Christian conscience" as the instruments of peace. At Harry's request, Raymond and Ivy Lee arranged to have it widely quoted in the newspapers and twenty-five thousand copies were distributed in pamphlet form. In writing about the publicity arrangements, Fosdick added, "Having a *glorious* time! Never want to work again! Find I am a natural-born loafer! Meeting everybody, seeing everything—that's my style—low thinking and high living—I revel in it!"

Presently Harry and Florence crossed the Mediterranean to view the archaeological treasures of Egypt, going up the Nile by steamer to the First Cataract. James Henry Breasted, the distinguished University of Chicago Egyptologist, happily was on the scene to be their guide. In his pocket was a pledge of $10 million from Rockefeller toward the construction of a new Cairo Museum, a project ultimately vetoed by the Egyptian government. "Our trip to Egypt was a glorious success and we have every reason to be thankful for all the circumstances which conspired to make it so beautiful an experience and so happy a memory," Fosdick wrote Raymond. Once again the Rockefeller connection had smoothed the path.

Departing Egypt, the Fosdicks made their way to Greece where Mr. and Mrs. Henry Morgenthau, Sr., were their hosts. Morgenthau, a wealthy, prominent member of New York's old German-Jewish community, was a former ambassador to Turkey. His ardent anti-Zionist attitude* may have influenced Fosdick's thinking on the subject. As Christ-

* Morgenthau terminated his membership in Rabbi Stephen S. Wise's Free Synagogue because of Wise's Zionist activities. Morgenthau described Zionism as the

mas approached Harry and Florence returned to Geneva to pick up the girls in order that the family might spend the Holy Season together in Rome.

In late January Fosdick briefly returned to New York to consult with church leaders about architectural plans for the projected Morningside Heights church. In early March Harry and Florence approached the Holy Land by way of the Riviera and Sicily, the girls remaining in their Geneva school.

III

The following weeks were a time of joy, excitement, fascination. Never perhaps was Fosdick's whole being so caught up in an experience, as his letters, "Holy Land Diary,"† autobiography,‡ and *A Pilgrimage to Palestine* reveal. The first installment of the account appeared in the December 1926 issue of the *Ladies' Home Journal*, accompanied by the drawings of Henry J. Soulen. "I never in my life enjoyed writing so much," Fosdick said of these seventy thousand words that poured from his pen the instant of his return.

To traverse for the first time the lands of the Bible was a deeply moving experience. Words like "thrilling," "glorious," "incredible," "moving," "majestic," "amazing," "awesome" abound. "Jerusalem," one diary entry reads, "is still to one who stays there long enough to see and understand it 'the glory of the whole earth,' and Palestine a land of such thrilling interest as no other country in the world can possibly supply." Of the Mount of Olives seen in the distance at sunset, "If Turner had painted it no one would believe it." On reaching the crest of Mount Sinai he recorded, "One of the most impressive days of my life." And the view of Masada, "one of the most tragic spots in the world," is described as "one of magnificent desolation, extraordinarily impressive." In both the diary and the articles he qualifies his enthusiasm with the observation that "nothing in Palestine under a roof is much worth seeing and nothing in Palestine out of doors is not worth seeing." The reason

---

"blackest error . . . the most stupendous fallacy in Jewish history." Zionism was "wrong in principle and impossible of realization . . . unsound in its economics, fantastical in its politics and sterile in its spiritual ideals." His granddaughter, the historian Barbara Tuchman, has written a thoughtful explanation of Morgenthau's position and the reasons for it, entitled "The Assimilationist Dilemma."

† A 188-page pocket-size notebook in Riverside Archives, the first entry dated March 10, the final dated May 15, kept in longhand.

‡ The autobiography errs in placing the Sinai caravan at the beginning rather than in the middle of the Holy Land adventure.

being, with a few exceptions, that "Almost everything that men have put under a roof they have spoiled for the intelligent visitor." A passage from Fosdick's autobiography captures the essence of the pilgrimage:

> Well, not only is Palestine talked about in the Bible, it illumines and explains the Bible, until one visualizes its personalities and its events as though one were seeing them afresh. To spend a moonlit night on Mount Tabor, to walk with memories of the Master over the hills of Nazareth or beside the Sea of Galilee, to stand on Neby Samwil and see Bethlehem and Calvary only five miles apart, to see the amazing acres of wild flowers, which Jesus saw, fairer than Solomon in all his glory, to rest beside the very well where Jesus talked with the woman of Samaria, to sit under the olive trees on the hill where he made his decision in Gethesmane—such experiences left an indelible impression on my thought and life.

The *Ladies' Home Journal* artist who accompanied Fosdick reported that despite hardships and even possible perils, "If Dr. Fosdick decided we were going to a certain spot we went, and we always managed to get back." The *National Geographic* staff representative and photographer, Maynard Owen Williams, who joined the Sinai Peninsula camel caravan traversing in reverse the probable route of Moses, noted that Fosdick's "enthusiasm was always betraying him into enviable ecstasy." He was, Williams continued, "a constant inspiration and delightful friend. His lady, gracious companion of our wanderings, proved to be the best fellow of all." In the evenings, over cups of hot tea, Fosdick would read from the Bible to the little band and then they would sing songs of home accompanied by Soulen's one-octave harmonica. From both the public statements of Williams and Soulen and their personal letters to Fosdick there can be no doubt that they came to stand in awe of his courage, indomitability, consideration, and high spirits, to say nothing of his intelligence and erudition.

In reviewing the book, *A Pilgrimage to Palestine*, New York's great liberal minister John Haynes Holmes observed that the interpretive comments "show Dr. Fosdick's essentially modern mind at its best." Of course, what Holmes found praiseworthy conservative reviewers thought lamentable. One conservative saw the volume as a denial of the trustworthiness of the earlier Hebrew records and a reduction of the supernatural to the natural. Another charged Fosdick with using the trip as an excuse to propagate the doctrines of liberalism; Fosdick found only what he wanted to find, saw only what he wanted to see, and the book was, therefore, a perversion of the truth. A more accurate title, another reviewer suggested, would be "The pilgrimage of a theological liberal to Palestine."

In truth the work is laced with typically Fosdickian statements. "You cannot explain Christ by his environment; his secret runs far back into the abysmal depths of personality," he writes on one page. On another in reference to Amos: "I stood there thinking of all the superstitions of Islam and the mummeries of degenerate Christianity that curse Palestine today, and of our popular religion in the West with its cheap and credulous substitutes for goodness—its ritualism, creedalism, ecclesiasticism—and I wondered afresh at that astonishing man who on this spot twenty-seven centuries ago thundered the truth as though God himself were speaking: 'I hate, I despise your feasts, and I will take no delight in your solemn assemblies.' "

It is understandable that Fosdick should view the Holy Land through liberal lenses, but these lenses made it impossible for him to find anything commendable in the Christianity of the Eastern peoples. A diary entry describing five Christian services—Greek Orthodox, Roman Catholic, Armenian, Jacobite Syrian, Coptic—going on at once in the Church of the Holy Sepulcher employs such adjectives as "bedlam," "garish," "gawdy," "hideous," "ear-splitting," "distressing," "disgusting." "Here is superstition," he comments, "imposture, pretension, and ugly paganism masquerading under the disguise of the Cross. Whatever else he [Jesus] might have allowed, he would not have allowed this. This is the kind of unreality he came to dislodge. Was it not enough that he was crucified? Must the reputed site of his crucifixion thus be made a profane and pagan place?" Fosdick asserts the religious life of the Eastern churches "largely has degenerated here into outward form with small ethical result." A visit to a Greek Orthodox monastery reveals the monks to be "ignorant, lazy, stupid, frowsy, a mongrel breed." The chicanery and ignorance of the Christian churches in Jerusalem are appalling. The Eastern churches' and the Roman Church's three chief exhibitions in the Master's land are monasticism, militarism, and mummery. He notes that guards are posted "not to keep Eastern Christians from fighting, but to keep Western Christians from stealing! Nothing safe from them—they even bring hammers to chip away the rock from the Holy Sepulcher. The Eastern Christians may have exhibited at times very bad tempers, but it remains for American and British Christians to require a guard to keep them from deliberate malicious pillage and vandalism. As between the two, there is reason for preferring the hotness of the one to the callousness of the other." Despite this, the conclusion must stand that Fosdick displayed almost no sympathy for, and little understanding of, the Christianity he found in the Holy Land. It is one thing to view matters from a liberal perspective; it is another to wear cultural Western blinders.

Conservative Christian critics and Jewish spokesmen as well questioned Fosdick's invidious comparisons between the Old and New Testaments. After Sinai he meditates, "I was thankful when I came away that religiously we stand no longer at the mountain of the law." And again, "There a great soul [Moses] struck bravely out on a venture whose consequences he could not see. Yet glorious as it was, it was a primitive beginning. Belief in a mountain-god whose back can be seen by human eyes, a god of war who sends his chosen tribesmen on ruthless raids to slaughter even children without mercy, is a long way behind us—or at least it ought to be." He concludes, "Amid the memories of Sinai's thunderous deity I heard the voice at Sychar: 'God is a Spirit: and they that worship him must worship in spirit and truth.' " Later Fosdick ends a discussion of the cruel Hebrew conquest of Palestine with the thought: "As for the religion of it, I do not see how any one who on the ground thinks the matter through can be tempted to identify the god who was supposed to order, superintend, and bless all this with the God revealed in the greatest of the Hebrew prophets and, above all, Christ. They are not of one spirit. The Hebrews, with their tribal god who stood for them against all others and backed them up in any assault and battery upon other folk, shared the current theology of all ancient nations."

Not surprisingly, these passages and others were found offensive. Rabbi Samuel Schulman, Temple Beth-El, New York, publicly rebuked Fosdick, adding this sharp advice in a private letter to him: "We know . . . , as Jews, that we have in the Old Testament the highest reaches that the human spirit made in getting at God. And we feel that we have a sufficient Revelation from God in the Old Testament. . . . I do not hesitate to say, we think that there are some parts of the Old Testament which are superior to New Testament literature. I have always admired you, and I therefore speak freely to you. It will help religion more and more if the method of contrast be dropped entirely and we go on doing the work of to-day and getting our inspirations from our respective faiths and Bibles." Fosdick replied: "As you will see, my contrast was not between the Old Testament God and the New Testament God . . . , but between the conception of God as a warlike, tribal deity in the earliest manuscripts of the Old Testament, and, on the other hand, the God of the great Hebrew prophets and of Jesus. I cannot imagine any intelligent rabbi who would not make this same distinction. Certainly, it involves nothing but appreciation of the great prophets of your faith, who are the great prophets of my faith, too."

Most controversial of all was the final chapter, "Palestine Tomorrow," in which Fosdick discusses the future of Arabs and Jews in the Holy Land, a subject of deep concern to him to the day of his death. Before examining this subject it is necessary to say a word about the American

Colony hostel where the Fosdicks stayed while in Jerusalem, described by Fosdick as "a Christian brotherhood which tests religion by its fruits."

In 1947 Dr. William Foxwell Albright, distinguished Professor of Semitic Languages, The Johns Hopkins University, wrote, "There is one Protestant organization in Palestine—the so-called American Colony—which has been consistently anti-Zionist and which has lost no opportunity to create a spirit of antagonism toward Jewish activity." Dr. Albright continued, "Owing to the vast number of tourists with whom it has come into contact, the anti-Zionist point of view of the American Colony in Jerusalem has been diffused far and wide through English-speaking and Scandinavian countries. In some cases, especially selected guides have been chosen in order to influence important visitors. The violent anti-Zionism of some prominent Americans can be traced to a few days spent at the American Colony." Then in a footnote Dr. Albright added, "It is probable that the anti-Zionism of Dr. Harry Emerson Fosdick is due to this influence."

Nineteen years earlier Rabbi Stephen S. Wise, New York's great Free Synagogue leader, champion of reform, and ardent Zionist, had pronounced the same judgment on the American Colony. "I do not trust the American Colony," he wrote a fellow American Zionist after Fosdick had publicly urged in 1928 that travelers to Jerusalem stay there. "They have the mind and attitude of [*New York Times* editor John] Finley and [former Ambassador Henry] Morgenthau [Sr.]—nominally pro-British, in fact bitterly anti-Zionistic; tremendously strong in their sympathy with Chalukah Judaism [charitable dole from abroad for Orthodox Jews in Palestine] but hostile to the nth degree to Chalutzim Jews [pioneering Jewish settlers]." Rabbi Wise wondered if the World Zionist Organization should either pressure the American Colony into using Jewish guides or broadcast Fosdick's recommendation of it with the warning, "if people want to have no understanding of 'the new Palestine' from the Jewish point of view, they should go to the American Colony, etc., etc." He closed with the thought, "It would be a savage thing to do, but heaven knows they deserve it." As it happens, Rabbi Wise had written Fosdick an extremely cordial letter just prior to the pilgrimage supplying him with a list of individuals to look up who "can help you to see the things that have come to pass in Palestine as a result of the incoming of Jews in the last fifty years, and particularly, the past ten years." The individuals mentioned could be counted on to present the case for Zionism. Rabbi Wise then invited Fosdick to address the Jewish Institute of Religion on his return, closing delightfully: "P.S. You owe it to me to come. I am having a devil of a time [on] account of Christianity. I preached a perfectly good and harmless Christmas sermon last Sunday, giving a

Jew's view of Jesus, based on [Joseph] Klausner's book, 'The Life of Jesus' which Canon [Herbert] Danby has done into English, and all my good and gentle and 'Christian' brothers, beginning with the orthodox and culminating in [Rabbi Samuel] Schulman, are treating me as if I were a grand heretic worthy of execution, instead of being a poor, mild-mannered, utterly harmless person, feebly echoing the things which you bravely utter."

What may be said of the assertions and fears of Dr. Albright and Rabbi Wise? Fosdick openly acknowledged his gratitude to the anti-Zionist Morgenthau, his host in Athens, and his friendship with the pro-Arab John Finley, First Presbyterian Church lay leader; for three decades, publicly and privately, he made no apologies for his relationship with, and admiration for, the American Colony in Jerusalem. Founded in 1881 by Horatio Spafford and his wife, devout Presbyterian lay people, its work was carried on by their daughter, Bertha Spafford Vester. One historian described the American Colony's activities as "akin to those of an American settlement house" and in her memoirs, *Our Jerusalem* (with an introduction by Lowell Thomas), Mrs. Vester flatly denies any pro-Arab, anti-Jewish bias. "For almost seventy years the American Colony has served Jerusalem," she asserted. "It has kept its doors open to all who come; housed the homeless, fed the hungry, cared for the ill. It has never taken sides in political or religious issues. From the beginning it has been the meeting place and refuge of Christian, Moslem, and Jew."

This is essentially how Fosdick saw the American Colony. He stayed at its hostel, and he came to know and admire Mrs. Vester. Her adopted half-brother, Jacob Spafford, a Sephardic Jew converted to Christianity, served as Fosdick's guide and interpreter in the Sinai wilderness. In 1927 Fosdick became chairman of the American Colony Aid Society and later honorary president. In 1948 Lowell Thomas and Fosdick exchanged letters about a projected lecture tour by Mrs. Vester, Fosdick saying, "I don't know that I have ever met quite her equal in her drive and courage in the face of all sorts of obstacles." In the 1950s Fosdick helped to secure funds for Mrs. Vester's work from the Ford Foundation and from the Riverside Church. He also became president of the American Colony Charities Association, which supported a children's hospital and welfare center and an outpatient clinic. In 1955 Fosdick gave Mrs. Vester permission to use this quotation: "The work which the American Colony Aid Association is doing in Arab Jerusalem and the surrounding country is indispensable. The need is pathetic and desperate and Americans should be grateful for the opportunity which the American Colony Aid Association affords to help alleviate at least a little the suffering there. All of us who know Mrs. Vester and her associates are enthusiastic about the service which they are rendering." In a touching letter of appreciation, Mrs. Vester recalled visiting the Fosdicks' in America, asked about the daughters and Mrs. Fosdick, and concluded: "P.S. I can say 'dear Florence,' but I haven't got the courage to say 'dear Harry.' "

IV

Having established Fosdick's association with the American Colony, in itself sufficient (Dr. Albright believed) to find him guilty of "violent anti-Zionism," we shall now examine further his open opposition to "political Zionism" and his active compassion for the Palestinian Arabs both before and after the creation of the State of Israel in 1948.

"I was not aware that I was really anti-Zionist, much less am I violently anti-Zionist," Fosdick replied to a correspondent who had called Albright's allegation to his attention. In any case, he continued, "the American Colony ought not to be blamed for any views I have," for, he explained, while in Palestine he had sought the counsel of Jews and Arabs alike. His diary and articles demonstrate the truth of this statement. He visited Zionist colonies, finding them "very impressive." He ate the Passover supper with a Jerusalem family and was "impressed all over again with the passionate love of this people for the Holy Land." He met with the great Zionist leader Dr. Chaim Weizmann and also with the head of the Palestine Zionist Executive, Colonel F. H. Kisch. He talked with the leading British jurist in Palestine, a Zionist, as he had earlier sat in the chambers of Supreme Court Justice Louis D. Brandeis to hear the Zionist case presented. Dr. Judah L. Magnes, founder and first chancellor of Hebrew University, was his mentor in Jerusalem and guide on a trip to Tel Aviv, a city Fosdick found modern, progressive, and prosperous. And if Fosdick followed up on the names supplied by Rabbi Wise, he conversed with other Jewish leaders as well. Therefore, the charge that he was blinded by the alleged pro-Arab bias of Mrs. Vester and her American Colony guides or that he refused to hear the Zionist argument simply will not stick.

In a score of instances Fosdick declared himself to be a "disciple" of Dr. Magnes. This is the heart of the matter. Rabbi, scholar, seer, moral teacher, pacifist, civil libertarian, creator of the Kehillah of New York, Magnes left America in 1920 to found the Hebrew University of Jerusalem as an intellectual and spiritual bond and the hearth of a Hebrew renaissance. He was, in the words of his biographer, "the conscience of Zionism"; but by the time the Israeli state was born in violence "he was a solitary figure in Palestine" and among American Jews the "object of passionate obloquy," for his had been a different Zionist vision. Magnes, "the only important Zionist leader to transfer his home to the land of his beliefs," according to Barbara Tuchman, held the conviction that in the Holy Land Jews and Arabs should form one commonwealth, that Palestine should not be partioned between them, and that it was both right and possible to bring into being a binational state. In this dream there need have been no dispossession, no terrorism against the British, no assassination of Count Bernadotte, no massacre at Deir Yassin, no bombings and terrorist raids by the Arabs, no decades of Israeli-Arab wars, no deaths of American marines. This generous dream, rooted in a prophetic conviction of the universal brotherhood of all men, was not to be. Very probably it could not have been after the Holocaust understandably fueled Zionist zeal and in light of Arab fears and pride. Still, Magnes's watchword *Ihud* (Union) gripped such saints as Martin Buber and such scholars as Hannah Arendt; and for Fosdick, Magnes was the wisest counselor on "Palestine Tomorrow."

It is difficult to summarize this final article in the *Ladies' Home Journal* series (and final chapter in the book) and do justice to Fosdick's position, especially when it is remembered that the words were written in 1926. He understands the depth and warmth of Jewish loyalty to Zion. The long-cherished dream of restoration to their ancient lands has become the more alluring in the twentieth century as Jews continued to suffer prejudice, confinement, and pogroms. With courage and energy, he writes, the Jews are "making Palestine once more to blossom like the rose." Still the economic problems are severe, the land cannot sustain the expected two and one-half million Jews to be settled there, and the success of Zionism will depend on the willingness of American Jews to pour out millions of dollars annually for at least a quarter of a century.

Most dangerous, Fosdick believed, is the myth that Palestine is a land without people waiting for a people without land. To the contrary, "no one understands the situation who does not see that over half a million Moslem Arabs, who easily constitute seventy-three per cent of the population, naturally regard with suspicion, if not with rage, the deliberate endeavor to make a 'national home for the Jewish people' in their country." The Arabs know that they do not have the faintest chance in competition with the incoming Jews, and if the Jews do keep coming in the poor Arab will either resort to violence or else be submerged. This knowledge "makes the Arab afraid and angry and the Jew confident and aggressive." Fosdick based his statements on conversations with Bedouins, Jerusalem Arabs, and the Grand Mufti. When a Zionist leader pronounced there can be only "one National Home in Palestine, and that a Jewish one, and no equality in the partnership between Jews and

Arabs, but a Jewish predominance as soon as the numbers of that race are sufficiently increased," an angry Arab responded to this statement by informing Fosdick that "all Islam around them, in Syria, Arabia, Egypt, like a sea around the enisled Zionism of Palestine, would rise in fury." The situation, Fosdick judged, was loaded with dynamite. However, "If the generous ideals of moderate Zionism become dominant, coupling Arab and Jew alike in the plans for a rejuvenated Palestine, then there will be hope." He concluded, "While tragedy is obviously possible, I personally hope that Zionism may succeed."

He expressed essentially the same thoughts in a talk before the Union Theological Seminary alumni on May 24, 1927. Zionists in New York were quick to respond in public statements, Rabbi Wise saying Fosdick's misgivings were largely unjustified and that there was no danger of Zionism "drifting into the control of nationalistic extremists." Subsequently, Wise received an angry letter from Colonel Kisch saying that the Palestine Zionist Executive was "exceedingly put out" by Fosdick's remarks. The communication closed: "I believe Dr. Fosdick is generally regarded in America as a friend of the Jews, if so—when this mischief is explained to him, I trust he may be induced to modify his statement with at least as much publicity as he originally gave it." Wise passed the letter along to Fosdick "With affectionate greeting, as always, my dear Harry."

Fifteen years later in early May 1942 Wise gaveled a conference to order in New York's Biltmore Hotel. In attendance were 586 American and 67 foreign Jewish leaders called together by the Emergency Committee for Zionist Affairs. The delegates listened in somber silence to reports on the fate of European Jewry. In an impassioned final session the fateful Biltmore Declaration was unanimously adopted. There could be only one response to Hitler's monstrous "final solution": the establishment of a Jewish state in Palestine. From this moment on, America's Jews became overwhelmingly committed to this course.

A tiny dissenting band of Reform rabbis met the next month to formulate a "non-Zionist" program and soon there was born the American Council for Judaism, the single organized, continuing effort of a remnant of American Jews to decry the wisdom of establishing a "National Jewish State in Palestine or anywhere else." The few thousand adherents it attracted were in the anti-Zionist tradition of Classical Reform, of German rather than of East European background, and generally of upper or upper-middle-class status, including Lessing Rosenwald (chairman of the board, Sears, Roebuck) and Arthur Hays Sulzberger (publisher of the *New York Times*). Not surprisingly, the American Council for Judaism received Fosdick's sympathy, as he agreed with its position that "Judaism is a religion of universal values—not a nationality" and its affirmation "that nationality and religion are separate and distinct; that no Jew or group of Jews can speak for all American Jews; that Israel is the 'homeland' of its citizens only, and not of all Jews."

The council came immediately under ferocious, orchestrated attack. It was "a dastardly stab in the back" and "treasonable to every high Jewish interest." Its members were "Jewish escapists," "self-hating," and "assimilationists." The assault continued over the years. One historian charged the council with seeking "to sow seeds of distrust" and of "pro-Arab policies" and another historian characterized its opposition to Zionism as "vicious" and "most useful to Christian and Arab anti-Zionists"— "its propaganda constituted Jewry's own contributions to the Arab cause."

As the years passed, and the State of Israel became a reality, the council's small membership dwindled. Especially did the rabbis depart, save for such stiff-kneed individuals as Rabbi Elmer Berger, who as late as the 1970s, organized with other council members a new group, American Jewish Alternatives to Zionism, Inc. In 1960 Fosdick was petitioned by the council to make a statement, and he authorized the following:

> The American council for Judaism is standing for truths very important to all Americans. Sympathetic, as we are, with the State of Israel and hopeful, as we are, that it may flourish and may succeed in contributing to the peace, stability and prosperity of the Middle East, we resent the Zionist endeavor to make the State of Israel the center of patriotism for American Jews. The Jewish people here are Americans like all the rest of us, and Judaism is not a nationalistic cult, but is one of the great universal faiths. As a Christian whose religion is rooted in the prophets of Judaism, I share with multitudes of Americans a sense of gratitude and a heart full of good wishes for the American Council for Judaism.

When pressed by critics to explain his "anti-Israel" position and support of the "perfidious" council, Fosdick invariably placed himself with Magnes. "I lived through the tragic days when the leadership of men like Judah Magnes was rejected," he wrote to one critic, "and the political extremists came in on the Jewish side, and were met by similar extremists on the Arab side. I do not blame one side alone; both sides are at fault. But I am sure there is one thing America cannot do, and that is treat Israel as though Israel were America's baby to be taken care of. Our function is to be impartial in the conflict, where I am sure at least 50% of the blame is on Israel's side. Judah Magnes died of a broken heart because of the failure of his policy, and I see little hope until his policies are put back into full force again. Meanwhile, I pray for Israel, as you do, and for the Arabs too." Fosdick also raised the question of "divided loyalty," an imputation deeply embittering to most American Jews. "The idea that American Zionists as individuals are not loyal patriots is ridiculous . . . ," Fosdick wrote to a critical rabbi. Nevertheless, "What is giving deep concern to increasing numbers of Americans, both Jews and Gentiles, is the public-pressure aspect of Zionist strategy in this country. The idea of a 'Jewish bloc vote,' used in the interests of a foreign state, is dangerous and represents, from the standpoint of the Jewish people themselves, an unwise policy that is awakening grave concern."

In the eyes of American Zionists Fosdick's sins were compounded by his membership in a new group, American Middle East Relief, Inc., which was formed in early 1948 "for the purpose of raising and expending funds to be used exclusively for charitable, educational and benevolent causes" and also to help "the advancement of the people of the Arab East in their economic and cultural renaissance." Among its leaders were Yale's Professor Millar Burrows and Princeton's Professor Philip K. Hitti and Douglas Horton, dean of the Harvard School, all distinguished scholars. Originally elected vice president of the corporation, Fosdick declined the post because of his age (he was over seventy), but he did serve actively on the board of directors and use his influence with the Rockefeller Brothers Fund to secure monies to aid the "over one million fear-ridden and helpless Palestinian Arab refugees." One historian noted that in the effort to raise funds "its meetings invariably whipped up anti-Israel sentiment." Perhaps. It is relevant to note that Fosdick's sister, Edith, was then teaching in Beirut and kept him informed of the "desperate conditions" of the refugees; nor is it irrelevant that Fosdick's older daughter, Dr. Elinor Fosdick Downs, in the early 1960s did nutritional work in Lebanon among Arab refugee children.

In 1949 Fosdick joined the Executive Committee of the Holy Land Emergency Liaison Program, Inc., Henry Sloane Coffin, chairman, William Ernest Hocking, honorary chairman, Alfred M. Lilienthal, secretary. "Ostensibly," writes historian Hertzel Fishman, "its purpose was to coordinate American volunteer interests for the Arab refugee problem, but in fact it tried to serve as a public relations agency for the Arab cause with respect to Palestine." Such statements must be approached with caution. Much writing on Zionism in America seems to interpret any expression of sympathy for the Arabs as hostility to the Jews.

On one particular point many historians are simply off base, and that is when they make an intimate connection between anti-Zionism and liberal Protestant pacifists on the one hand and between World War II interventionists and pro-Zionism on the other hand. The connecting lines are too tangled for this hypothesis to be sustained. To be sure,

Fosdick and the editors of the *Christian Century* had both opposed American intervention in World War II and both were supposedly anti-Zionist. To be sure, both Reinhold Niebuhr and Paul Tillich had been critical of liberal pacifism and both were leaders of the pro-Zionist American Christian Palestine Committee. "This merely is another illustration of the principle," charged Dr. Albright, himself a member of the American Christian Palestine Committee, "which has led prominent Christian pacifists to share the same platform with fascist and anti-Semitic America First propagandists." This is not only unfair, it is untrue. For example, among the American Protestants most sympathetic to a Jewish homeland in Palestine were John Haynes Holmes and Ralph Sockman, both members of the American Christian Palestine Committee, yet both liberal pacifists who opposed intervention in 1941. On the other hand, among the American Protestants most notoriously anti-Zionist (and indeed anti-Jewish according to their critics) were Henry Sloane Coffin, president emeritus of Union Seminary, and Henry Pitney Van Dusen, president of Union, both ardent interventionists and critics of pacifism. There are too many prominent exceptions for either a pacifist/anti-Zionist connection or an interventionist/pro-Zionist alliance to be credible.

In 1948 Virginia Gildersleeve, dean of Barnard College, formed the Committee for Justice and Peace in the Holy Land. It is unfortunate that Fosdick lent his name to this group for, as Gildersleeve's autobiography makes clear, her sympathies were indeed overwhelmingly with the Arabs. Two years later Fosdick again lent his name, this time to American Friends of the Middle East, Inc., a group, formed by Dorothy Thompson, whose major role—even Thompson's sympathetic biographer notes—"soon became criticism of America's pro-Israel policy and defense of the Arab position" and whose budget received funding from Arabian oil and C.I.A. sources. It is possible that Thompson took her position because the *New York Post* had dropped her column in 1947 under pressure from the American Jewish community, an act, she said, of "character assassination." Although she had been an early enemy of Hitler and befriender of European Jewry, Thompson's coolness to the establishment of a Jewish state in Palestine forfeited her the friendship of the once-admiring American Jews, and they slew her professionally. Observed her biographer, "For Dorothy, the bitterest blow was the discovery that Zionists equated criticism of their policies with anti-Semitism."

Few individuals were judged more traitorous by American Zionists than Rabbi Morris S. Lazaron. In 1959 he wrote *Bridges Not Walls: A Challenge to All Faiths*, a volume pleading for religious cooperation, emphasizing the universalism of Judaism and its common ground with

Christianity, but arraigning political Zionism. He wished the preservation of the State of Israel, "built with so much energy, idealism and sacrifice," but its preservation as a Middle Eastern state for the Israelis, not Israel as a national nucleus for all the Jews of the world. Inasmuch as Fosdick wrote the praiseful preface, it is not surprising to find his personal copy inscribed by Lazaron, "To Harry Emerson Fosdick. Comrade and friend with deep appreciation." "The author has been very merciful in dealing with us Christians," Fosdick had written, "but he presents a challenge which should lead us to sterner judgments on ourselves."

It has already been noted that the major Protestant group supporting the establishment of a Zionist state was the American Christian Palestine Committee. Its secretary, Carl Hermann Voss, a graduate of Union and an intimate of Rabbi Wise, contacted Fosdick in 1955, requesting that his old Union teacher meet with the committee in the hopes of persuading Fosdick to join them. Fosdick vetoed a group meeting, but invited Voss to lunch in order that he might get "a lot of valuable information from your well-stocked mind." A meeting of minds was impossible; still, Fosdick could say several days later: "While it is true that our interpretations of Zionism's history and meaning differ, and our evaluations of the present situation are not at all points the same, yet in our desire for a constructive solution of the Arab-Zionist problem on the basis of Israel's continuance we are at one. In wish I could be more hopeful than I am about the possibility of finding that solution, before the rising tension causes the tragedy of open war. Certainly a humane settlement of the cruel refugee problem is basic." Voss remained one of the outstanding Christian champions of Israel, whereas Fosdick remained true to his compassion for the Arabs as well as for Jews. Yet such was Fosdick's hold on the hearts of men, a year before his death he received an admonition from Voss: "Stay well, dear friend, and know that we think of you more often than you realize—and all that time with gratitude and affection."

V

An American Zionist might be appalled by Fosdick's record regarding Palestine, he might at the very least find Fosdick's statements naively remote from the cruel realities of the Jewish experience and excessively tender in its humanitarian concern for the Arabs. Judah Magnes's noble dream melted in the ovens of Belsen and Auschwitz; after the Holocaust the longing of the surviving Jewish people for some part of this earth's surface exclusively their own became overpowering—and that spot now *had* to be the peculiar land of Israel. But do Fosdick's views on Palestine mark him as an anti-Semite?

It is frequently charged that Fosdick's pacifism had no answer to Hitler's "final solution." To that assertion two answers may be given. First, few Christian Americans anguished more than Fosdick over the fate of European Jewry, denounced more sternly the hideous Nazi persecutions, or labored more valiantly to permit the victims of Hitler's wrath to find asylum in America.

Second, it is now certain that Britain and France did not go to war with Germany in 1939 to save Germany's Jews from persecution; it is equally certain that in the conduct of the war the salvation of Europe's Jews from extermination was low among Allied priorities. In ascending order of despicability, the record of the U.S. government is disgraceful, the record of the British government is shameful, the record of the Vichy French government is vile. Prior to 1939 Germany's Jews were not so much locked inside the Third Reich as they were locked out of other lands, including the United States, by official policy administered by indifferent and even anti-Semitic officials. Indeed a 1938 Roper poll disclosed that 67.4 percent of Americans believed their government should not admit greater numbers of refugees and as late as 1943 eight out of ten citizens were opposed to increasing quotas for refugees from Nazi-ruled countries. Not only did immigration quotas remain rigid, but the State Department bureaucracy blocked the admission of over 1 million Jews who could have legally entered the nation. After the outbreak of hostilities, military considerations—the defeat of the Axis with a minimum of Allied casualties—dominated the thinking in London and Washington. Planes could not be spared to bomb the rail lines leading to the death camps or the gas chambers and crematoria themselves. The idea of sending food packages to certain camps and ghettos was opposed because it flouted the blockade on which British strategy traditionally placed high hopes. The sacrosanctity of the blockade, however, did not prevent the Allies from supplying the entire food needs of the population of Axis-occupied Greece from 1942 until the end of the war. Up to thirty-five thousand tons of foodstuffs per month were permitted to be sent to Greece. In contrast, the International Red Cross was allowed to send no more than a total of forty-five hundred tons for the use of inmates of concentration camps between 1943 and 1945. Germany's proposal to exchange 1 million Jews for trucks and food may have been unthinkable in the midst of a war for Allied survival, but surely it was odious to decline the Rumanian government's offer to release seventy thousand Jews via the Black Sea against payment of a per capita departure tax. The first shots fired by British combatants in the war were not aimed at German soldiers but at Jewish "illegals" trying to enter Palestine. At the Bermuda Conference in the spring of 1943 the United States gave its negotiators secret orders *not* to offer to accept any more Jews in America or pledge funds for rescue operations or provide naval escorts for ships carrying refugees or offer refugees space on empty ships.

If anything gave World War II a moral basis, it was Germany's monstrous "final solution," yet 6 million Jews were not saved by England and America,* and it is shamefully clear that neither nation was willing to jeopardize military victory by ransoming the victims in Hitler's slaughterhouses. They left undone things that ought to have been done, and there was no health in their policies regarding European Jewry. In reviewing the oft-excoriated record of Fosdick and his fellow pacifists, it must be remembered that few Christian Britishers or Americans come into this particular court cleanhanded. The Office of War Information in the United States, for example, eager to use atrocities to inflame public opinion against Germany, deliberately avoided the most horrifying atrocity of all, the extermination of the Jews, on the ground that the story would be "confusing and misleading if it appears to be simply affecting the Jewish people." As one historian bitterly observed, "Truth has to be suppressed if it sounds like propaganda." Even Rabbi Wise collaborated with the U.S. government in concealing the whole truth because he feared that a strong advocacy of the Jewish cause might bring the loyalty of American Jews into question and create an anti-Semitic backlash.

Shortly after Hitler came to power Rabbi Wise returned from Germany and met with a group of Christian ministers in Fosdick's home to alert them to the imminent destruction of Germany's Jews. At that time, also, Fosdick responded to a call from Franz Boas, the great German-Jewish Columbia University anthropologist, "to meet entirely privately" with a few others to explore what might be done about the Nazi pogroms. Moreover, it was Fosdick who drafted a two-page statement, ultimately signed by twelve hundred Protestant clergymen and made public by the National Council of Jews and Christians, protesting "the present ruthless persecution of the Jews under Herr Hitler's regime." Wrote Fosdick: "It is our considered judgment that the endeavor of the German Nazis to humiliate a whole section of the human family threatens the civilized world with the return of medieval barbarism." To a correspondent who rationalized Hitler's policies, Fosdick tartly shot back:

---

* The government of Vichy France actively, even ardently, collaborated in hunting down French Jews and sending them to their deaths. The record of French intellectuals is, generally, one of shame.

these policies are "one of the cruelest things in the history of Western civilization." Unlike many Americans, including later ardent interventionists, Fosdick's condemnation of Nazism was instant, vocal, and forceful. In an address of October 26, 1933, before the Federal Council of Churches he declared Nazi Germany a "pagan state" and decried its persecution of Jews. He joined others in urging the boycott of the 1936 Berlin Olympic Games, holding that it "would make clear to the Nazi government that its cruel treatment of 'non-Aryans' is repugnant to the conscience of the world." In that year the Pro-Palestine Federation convened an American Christian Conference on the Jewish Problem, which Fosdick attended. The conference declared that if Christian people were unable to stop the horrors in Europe, then civilized communities should help "the victims of barbarism" to "reach a land where their lives and inalienable rights may be reasonably secure. Their natural place of refuge is Palestine." Whether Fosdick's presence signified assent with the final clause is moot, but we do know that he was a member of a large cluster of committees and organizations designed to provide assistance to Jews hoping to escape Hitler's maw. On repeated occasions he accepted invitations from the American Jewish Congress to be a sponsor of anti-Nazi rallies. In 1937 he was a sponsor of an event staged by the National Council of Young Israel and on at least three instances he helped raise funds for the Israel Orphan Asylum. "The appalling persecution of the Jews in Germany is an outrage to the conscience of the civilized world," he informed the readers of the *New York Times* in 1938. "It is a tragedy if nothing can be done to prevent this cold-blooded, brutal pogrom." One thing the civilized world could do was to provide a haven for the oppressed, he argued. "I wish that the United States would open its doors by a special act of Congress to hundreds of thousands, if need be, of these dispossessed persons, especially our Jewish brethren," he wrote to a Jewish refugee in 1946. One of his last public efforts was to join Eleanor Roosevelt in securing funds for schools for Jewish and Arab children in Israel.

The hammer of Hitler's wrath did not fall on Jews alone, some 4 million other unfortunates also dying in his death camps. On October 6, 1936, Fosdick invited to Riverside Church a group of Christian leaders for the purpose of succoring the thousands of Christian refugees from Germany, many of whom were of Jewish ancestry. Among those who addressed the concerned group were Paul Tillich and Erika Mann, the exiled daughter of Thomas Mann. Out of the conference there emerged the American Christian Committee for Refugees from Germany (Aryan and non-Aryan Christians). To raise funds for their purpose, the committee produced a film entitled, *Modern Christian Martyrs*, which was

Amie Weaver and Frank Sheldon Fosdick: A wedding portrait

Harry (left) with his twin siblings Raymond and Edith

Fosdick's great mentor,
theologian William Newton Clarke

A Colgate University scene

A. J. Evans, 1901   E, L. Elliott, 1901, Bus. Mgr.   J. A. Williams, 1901   R. W. Burroughs, 1900
H. E. Fosdick, 1900   H. S. Foster, Editor-in-Chief   W. M. Parke, 1900

MADISONENSIS BOARD

Editor Fosdick and friends

On the eve of departing for New York's Union Seminary

Courting in the good old days—
Florence Allen Whitney
with Harry at her summer home

An outing with daughters Elinor and Dorothy in Maine

premiered before two thousand in Riverside Church on April 12, 1937. John G. McDonald, former high commissioner of the League of Nations Commission for Refugees from Germany, gave a brief introduction. Fosdick narrated, saying that "in Germany under the surface is going on the most cruel persecution a supposedly civilized country has been guilty of since the barbarous days of the Middle Ages, not against Jews only, but against all with whose opinions the Nazi government disagrees." He closed, "Help these refugees from Germany, I beg you, and then help to keep this accursed thing, Fascism or Naziism, out of America." The film was denounced by the German press as a "disgusting, lying film" and a "scandalous hate film."

Fosdick was not blind to anti-Semitism in his own nation. He supported Jewish philanthropies, helped sponsor the National Conference of Jews and Christians, and flayed anti-Semitism in sermons and public statements:

Everybody knows that anti-Semitic prejudice is present in this country. Probably every man in public life receives letters, often anonymous, always ignorant, brutal, vindictive, often obscene and revealing a pathological state of mind, reviling the Jews. When from this underworld of America's mental slums one comes to more refined and sophisticated racial discrimination, the presence of a potential anti-Semitic crusade is still evident. All Americans who care for the fine traditions of our democratic heritage should take this to heart. Every Jew, like every man of every other race, has a right to stand on his own feet and be treated in terms of his own personality unhampered by group suspicion and prejudice about his race. His race happens to be one of the most distinguished and creative on earth. The contribution of Jews to this country has been and is incalculable. Where anti-Semitism leads to is now so terribly illustrated in Germany that even the first flames of such a conflagration should be stamped out here.

At age eighty-two Fosdick, then living in retirement in Bronxville, New York, wrote a letter to the local paper, one of his last public statements. The letter protested that a Jew, a distinguished musician, had been unable to purchase a home in Bronxville. Our discrimination is quiet, Fosdick reminded his neighbors: "Nevertheless it is deplorable. It is un-American, undemocratic, un-Christian."

Many years after Fosdick's death the Zionist question continued to rage. Despite his credentials as a Jew, a socialist, and a long and ardent champion of a Jewish homeland in Palestine, I. F. Stone felt compelled to pen the *Confessions of a Jewish Dissident.* "I find myself—like many fellow American intellectuals, Jewish and non-Jewish, ostracized whenever I try to speak up on the Middle East," he wrote. "Finding an American publishing house willing to publish a book which departs from the standard Israeli line is about as easy as selling a thoughtful exposition of atheism to the Osservatore Romano in Vatican City." Fosdick would have understood the point.

VI

Fosdick knew the enduring friendship and admiration of some Jews. One such was Rabbi Stephen S. Wise. Fosdick repeatedly praised Wise and participated in celebrations honoring him. In return Wise said publicly: "Fosdick—the least hated and best loved heretic that ever lived"; and at the Baptist's death a delegation from the Free Synagogue attended the memorial service. Wise had been founder-president of a new rabbinical seminary, the pro-Zion Jewish Institute of Religion, and in 1957 Hebrew Union College*/Jewish Institute of Religion bestowed on Fosdick the honorary degree of doctor of humane letters.

A second friend was Rabbi Louis Finklestein, chancellor of Jewish Theological Seminary, center of Conservative Judaism, located only yards from Union Seminary and Riverside Church. Finklestein was a scholar, pacifist, and "virtually the only Conservative rabbi to resist Zionist demands in the mid-forties." Neighbors, he and Fosdick were both great walkers, and for years the two men passed without speaking, the rabbi hesitating to introduce himself to the famous preacher, the Baptist fearing to force himself upon the bearded Jewish scholar. One day the ice was broken and a warm friendship begun. "My admiration for Dr. Fosdick was total," Finklestein stated. Never once did Fosdick deny the chancellor a request—to conduct a preaching workshop at the seminary, to write a jacket blurb for a book, to discuss how refugees might be succored. Finklestein always believed that Fosdick felt a special obligation to the Jewish community and would never say "no" to him, and so Finklestein was careful that his requests were not trivial. He may have been right, for when the Jewish Theological Seminary desired to confer on Fosdick the honorary degree of doctor of letters in 1955, Fosdick reluctantly interrupted a vacation in Maine, explaining to another: "I could not as a Christian say no to them, for it might easily be misunderstood. I warmly appreciate their gesture of goodwill, and so I have to run down for a few hours in order to accept . . . and to say thank you." Finklestein remembered Fosdick's birthdays with warm letters,

* Reform's rabbinical seminary, originally opposed to Zionism, by that date had swung to pro-Zionism.

one closing, "It is a great joy to think of the years we were neighbors and when we met so often. We are greatly indebted to you here at the Seminary, but you have made the debt easy to bear." Like Fosdick a pacifist, the rabbi knew what it was to be torn apart, as he knew also what it was to feel the fury of coreligionists. However, Fosdick was never able to understand his friend's scrupulous honoring of every jot and title of Hebrew law and ritual. "In heaven's name," the Baptist once asked the chancellor, "why must ten *men* (not women) be present at a service?" It is nice to note that Fosdick's glowing blurb for Finklestein's *The Jews: Their History, Culture and Religion* pays special tribute to "Professor Albright's excellent essay" in it, considering Albright's earlier accusation of Fosdick's "violent anti-Zionism." He also praised Rabbi Joshua Liebman's *Peace of Mind*.

Other Jewish Theological Seminary scholars sent Fosdick their manuscripts for him to read or inscribed copies of their published work. He heard from not a few rabbis thanking him for this or that, one saying, "Without ever having taken your course at Union in Homiletics, you have given me much guidance *in absentia* as if in a 'correspondence course,' through your books and writings." From time to time he counseled Jews on religious questions. One woman who had left the faith of her fathers wondered if Riverside might not be her new church home. After five conversations, Fosdick wisely advised, "Hazel, Riverside Church is not for you." The woman idolized Fosdick, and they continued to work together in various social agencies.

During the construction of Riverside, Fosdick's congregation worshipped in Temple Beth-El on invitation of the trustees. Rabbi Nathan Krass welcomed the Baptists saying, "I am a friend and admirer of your eloquent, inspired and commanding figure, Dr. Fosdick." Later, rabbis were invited to preach from the Riverside pulpit. Later, also, during the war Jewish midshipmen at Columbia worshipped in the Riverside chapel.

Just possibly Fosdick did about all a pacifist could do to atone for the Christian crime—and the pagan crime—of anti-Semitism.

Chapter Eleven

A Church Is Raised
on "The Hill"

I

Returning from his glorious sabbatical, Fosdick devoted the remainder
of the summer of 1926 to writing *A Pilgrimage to Palestine* at his Maine
retreat. In the fall, physically refreshed and mentally "high," he assumed his duties as minister of the Park Avenue Baptist Church. The
church flourished. The Fundamentalist/Modernist controversy gradually
abated. Plans for a new edifice on Morningside Heights proceeded with
as much dispatch as possible for a building that was to rival a cathedral
in proportions. In 1931 the Riverside Church was dedicated. It was a
good period in Fosdick's life.

II

On Sunday morning, October 3, 1926, expectant worshippers four abreast
formed a line a block long, from the doors of the Park Avenue Baptist
Church to Lexington Avenue. The occasion was Fosdick's first sermon as
minister of the church. The congregation numbered fourteen hundred,
assembled in the nave and gallery and in the men's auditorium, which
had been equipped with amplifiers. Some of the hundreds who were
turned away scurried to their radios to catch the service broadcast by
WJZ. In the sermon Fosdick alerted his people:

> I adjure you, do not be easy on me as your minister. Hold me up to high
> standards. Here in America, so prosperous and self-complacent, it is going

to be easy this generation to preach respectability, but to preach real Christianity, that searches personal life and social relationships, will be hard. Hold me to it. And as I ask you not to be easy on me, I ask you also not to expect me to be easy on you. I shall proclaim no diluted Christianity harmonious with popular prejudices, but just as piercing and penetrating a gospel as I can compass, which I hope will disturb your consciences, as it disturbs mine, about the quality of life which we live in business, in society, in the Nation and in private character.

Fosdick's pastorate began with a service of prayer on Friday evening in preparation for the Lord's Supper, and on Sunday afternoon a communion service was observed and thirty new members welcomed, some with the rite of baptism, some simply with the extension of the "Hand of Fellowship." Among those welcomed were the Fosdicks and their two daughters. Dr. Woelfkin preached at the evening service. In all, the inauguration was "an overflow of joy and thanksgiving at the coming of Dr. Fosdick"; Fosdick himself recorded that he "returned from the Sunday's work and worship somewhat wearied but very happy."

III

"I have finished the happiest year of my life and am looking forward to a restful holiday," Fosdick reported in June 1927. "Everything is going, at the Park Avenue Church, far better than I could have expected and the future looks very bright and promising." Indeed, things were to continue to go well at the church. The granite structure itself, of French Gothic design, might be called a beautiful chapel, cruciform in shape, seating only some seven hundred in nave and gallery. (On Fosdick's arrival additional worshippers occupied other areas). Wood carvings and stained glass, comunion table and French cross, richly appointed chancel and a baptistry actually looking like an altar—all contributed to an atmosphere of worship. John D. Rockefeller, Jr., provided a magnificent tower and carillon, one of the earliest in America, in memory of his mother.

During Fosdick's first year 158 new members joined the Park Avenue fellowship, of whom half were Baptists and one-fifth Presbyterians, and the growth continued solidly, if not dramatically. Naturally it was necessary to augment the staff, particularly the addition of an able business manager, George Heidt, who remained during the vaster Riverside years. Fortunately for Fosdick and the congregation, Dr. Eugene Carder was persuaded to stay as ministerial associate, for few individuals served the church with greater devotion and effectiveness. Dr. Harold Vincent

Mulligan also remained as organist and director of two salaried choirs. The church support budget in 1929 totaled $143,000 and the benevolence budget $143,000. The pew rental system survived until the congregation moved to Morningside Heights.

Fosdick's Sundays were full: an address, perhaps, before the Men's Class at 9:45; morning worship service at 11:00; Communion Service at 4:00; evening worship service at 8:00, though frequently in the evening there would be a guest speaker, such as Sidney Hillman, labor leader; Owen Young, industrialist; Robert Speer, missionary leader; Walter Damrosch, conductor; Henry Canby, critic; Commander Richard Byrd, explorer. Because of the press of visitors a ticket system for seating was adopted and regularly fourteen hundred individuals crowded into the church, the usher corps performing valiantly. The morning service was conducted with majesty and solemnity, more liturgical in form and sacramental in spirit than in many Baptist churches. God was worshipped in the beauty of architectural setting and in the beauty of ritual as well as in the beauty of holiness. All the more disquieting, then, were those rare instances when a man stood and shouted, "Dr. Fosdick! That is not so!" or a woman arose to cry, "That will do for you, you blasphemer, we've heard all we want of you!"

The official church records, the file of *The Church Monthly*, and Fosdick's pastoral letters make abundantly clear the church's concern to serve both its own members and the city, nation, and world. On Sunday morning, June 30, 1929, the last service of the congregation was held in the edifice that had been its home for seven years, Fosdick appropriately preaching on "The Meaning and Use of Change."

IV

Meanwhile construction of the new structure on Morningside Heights was underway. As we have seen, even as Park Avenue negotiated in the spring of 1925 for Fosdick's services, agents for Rockefeller were scouring Morningside Heights for possible sites, at least four locations receiving serious consideration. On May 1, 1925, an entire block on Morningside Drive was purchased in the name of the Empire Mortgage Company, a real estate holding company of the Rockefellers. Columbia University's President Nicholas Murray Butler protested, asserting that the university had been counting on acquiring the property and suggesting to Rockefeller an alternate site for the church. Nobody's fool, Rockefeller knew the alternate property belonged to a wealthy widow who already had rejected offers from Columbia, Barnard, and Union, as he reminded Butler pointedly.* Nevertheless, the Morningside Drive block was highly improved with modern apartment houses and to construct a church on it would require razing the buildings and evicting the tenants, Columbia professors. Consequently, an exchange was made with the John B. Pierce Foundation, Inc., for a plot at the corner of Riverside Drive and 122nd Street, Rockefeller presently conveying the property to the church free of incombrances. The market value on the date of the gift was $1,257,440. In later years Rockefeller gave additional gifts of land to make possible Riverside's physical expansion.

The site was splendid, for it meant the church would stand upon a high rocky bluff overlooking Riverside Park and the Hudson River, assuring a tower view that would sweep in all directions: north beyond George Washington Bridge; west to the nearby green and dun ramparts of the Palisades and on a clear day beyond to the Orange Mountains; east, past a cluster of academic institutions to Long Island; and south to the serried towers of Manhattan.

Columbia's President Butler, somewhat given to hyperbole, termed Morningside Heights the American Acropolis and the American Mont Sainte Geneviève; for once his extravagant language was appropriate. Grouped within this area slightly more than a half-mile long, from 110th Street to 122nd Street, and slightly less than a half-mile wide, from Morningside Avenue to Riverside Drive, were Columbia University and its affiliated institutions Teachers College and Barnard College, Union Theological Seminary, Jewish Theological Seminary, International House, Horace Mann School, Lincoln School, Juilliard School of Music, Saint Luke's Hospital, Cathedral of Saint John the Divine—and Grant's Tomb, "the final horror of the Civil War." Immediately to the north of the privileged hill lay the festering valley of Manhattanville, beyond lay Harlem, City College, and the mountainous pile of the Columbia-Presbyterian Medical Center. On "The Hill" itself there existed only one Protestant parish church, a small fundamentalist church, said Fosdick, "doing more harm than good." The move to Morningside Heights cannot be set down as another effort to keep ahead of the slums or the encroachments of business. As a matter of fact, the congregation left Park Avenue at the very time that street was turning into New York's symbol of wealth. The move was not away from but toward the city's crowds. At the peak of the Heights, overlooking the Hudson and the city, the church took its stand. And there it stands today with no thought of running.

* On the death of the widow and after complicated negotiations, Rockefeller ultimately did acquire the property, which became, as his gift, the future site of The Interchurch Center.

Before construction could begin, indeed, before even architectural plans could be drawn, it was necessary to reach a decision between two fundamental and radically different concepts. One idea was for Rockefeller personally to build and personally own a huge skyscraper combination church and commercial structure, renting the ecclesiastical part to the congregation and the other area to commercial tenants.* The alternate idea was to erect a church edifice only, financed in part by Rockefeller money, but also by the sale of the Park Avenue Church and by contributions from other parishioners, ownership being vested in the congregation. The latter idea was wisely adopted. To be sure, legal and tax considerations figured in the decision, but vastly more important was the conviction of the unwisdom of a Rockefeller-owned combination church and commercial building—a conviction shared by the church leadership, rank-and-file membership, Fosdick, and Rockefeller himself. Key leaders Colgate, Ballard, and William R. Conklin pointed out the anomaly of merging a consecrated building with a business structure and predicted that Baptists of all persuasions would resent Rockefeller being permanent landlord. Fosdick made his position plain, voting "clearly and unqualifiedly" against the first plan. Rockefeller, too, understood that the plan would place both him and the church "in a very vulnerable position," and he was relieved when the trustees and deacons on August 6, 1925, unanimously scotched it.

Happily, the lovely Park Avenue Church was purchased by the Central Presbyterian Church for $1.5 million, occupancy to take place after June 30, 1929. This sum could now be applied to the new construction, and it was satisfying to the conscience of the congregation that the Park Avenue building would continue to be a place of Christian worship.

There remained the selection of a name for the projected new edifice. Ultimately, after many suggestions and a poll of the membership, the name adopted was "The Riverside Church in the City of New York." John B. Trevor, an independent soul, protested that "Riverside Church" lacked dignity, sounding like "Riverside Apartments, Riverside Hotel, Riverside Garage, Riverside Tennis Courts, etc.," and suggested instead, "Christ Church by the Riverside" or "Christ Church" alone. Rockefeller agreed that the name was "colorless and insipid," but that Trevor's suggestions "would seem to link the church so closely with Christian Science churches as to cause misunderstanding and confusion." Trevor was finally mollified when it was pointed out to him that "we have followed the precedent which our church has followed in naming all

---

* Knowledgeable readers will remember that the practice of combining religious and commercial ventures under one great roof then enjoyed quit a vogue across the nation.

of the church edifices which it has occupied, from Suffolk Street to Fifth Avenue, then to Park Avenue and now to Riverside Drive."

V

With their Park Avenue home sold and Riverside uncompleted, it was necessary for the congregation to find a place to worship from October 1929 to June 1930. In late December 1928 Trustee Conklin phoned Benjamin Mordecai, chairman of the Congregation Emanu-El building committee, to inquire if the Baptists might worship in Temple Beth-El, at Fifth Avenue and 76th Street, recently vacated in favor of a new temple some blocks south. Mr. Mordecai presented the appeal to the trustees, Louis Marshall presiding. "My own opinion," said Mordecai, "is that . . . it would be a very graceful thing to do and would be highly appreciated not only by the Fosdick Church but by the whole Christian Community." Permission was enthusiastically given. The trustees declined to accept any rental payments and the only expense to Park Avenue were incidental ones of gas, electricity, and heat. A Baptist leader meeting a member of Congregation Emanu-El exclaimed, "That was a very generous thing you did"; and then forgetting himself, he added, "That was a Christian thing to do." "Christian!" said the friend, "What do you mean—'Christian?' That was a Jewish thing to do!"

And so for nine months, beginning October 6, 1929, a congregation still Baptist worshipped in a splendid synagogue seating nearly two thousand. The Sunday service was linked by telephone to the completed Assembly Hall on Morningside Heights where a second congregation of perhaps five hundred gathered, mostly older church-school classes and Columbia students. It was, incidentally, a vigorous time for the new minister of religious education, C. Ivar Hellstrom, whose duties required him to climb the steps to the nineteenth floor of the Riverside tower, as the elevators were not yet working. When the Baptists attempted to press on their Jewish hosts a gift of appreciation in the form of either a memorial in Temple Emanu-El or a $20,000 check toward Jewish philanthropies in New York, the Temple trustees resolved their "unwillingness to accept any fund for any purpose in appreciation of its acts." Irving Lehman then informed Ballard, "We feel that for what we gave without cost or sacrifice we can accept no material return in any form." He concluded, "We shall always cherish the friendship existing between the congregations, happy in the knowledge of its inherent strength." It is well that a congregation composed of Rockefellers, Trevors, Aldriches, Hugheses, Cranes, Colgates, Conklins, and Ballards met fraternally a

congregation composed of Marshalls, Lehmans, Altheimers, Guggen-
heims, Schiffs, Ochses, and Strauses.

VI

In the five years following Fosdick's acceptance of Park Avenue's call
and as the congregation worshipped first in the Park Avenue sanctuary
and then in Temple Beth-El, plans were drawn for the new Morningside
Heights edifice, construction begun, and a modern Gothic-inspired "cathedral" completed. Unquestionably, Rockefeller, chairman of the Building Committee, was the church leader most central to the enterprise,
though Eugene C. Carder, ministerial associate, gave close, daily, informed attention. In the summer of 1925, before Gothic had definitely
been decided on, Rockefeller requested (and paid) leading architects to
draft preliminary plans: Ralph Adams Cram; McKim, Mead & White;
and York and Sawyer. Ultimately, the associated architects chosen were
Henry C. Pelton of New York and Charles Collens of Boston; the
builder, Marc Eidlitz & Son, Inc., of New York. Pelton and Collens had
been the architects of the Park Avenue Church as Eidlitz had been the
builder. Presently, contracts were let with outstanding designers, artists,
and craftsmen in the United States, England, and France.

Initially, the Building Committee did not believe a Gothic style could
be adapted to the requirements of a church auditorium with proper
audition and sight lines for twenty-five hundred worshipers. However,
Collens and Pelton traveled to France and Spain to study famed cathedrals and churches for inspiration, believing "he who designs a great
church in anything but Gothic has lost a divine spark in the structure
itself which only that great art can supply." At Bordeaux they found a
precedent for placing the main entrance at the side of the church rather
than at the axis of the nave; in Gerona and Barcelona they were impressed with the low, wide vault of the nave, which contrasted with the
high, narrow echo-filled vaults of the northern Gothic cathedrals; and
in the fortress Church of Saint Nazaire at Carcassonne they found their
inspiration for an eleventh-century Romanesque chapel to join the narthex of the church proper, a mixture inspired by the proximity of the
old and new cathedrals at Salamanca. Nevertheless, for their guiding
architectural principle they turned to Chartres Cathedral, though (as
they insisted) it must not be assumed that Chartres "has in any sense
been copied." Here was a bold type of Gothic design that would fit the
practical needs of the church. The Riverside tower was going to support

twenty-two floors of office space as well as a seventy-four-bell carillon totaling in weight over one hundred tons, including the great twenty-ton Bourdon, the largest and heaviest tuned carillon bell ever cast. The older of Chartres's two towers offered a sturdy precedent. Thirteenth-century form was to be the servant of twentieth-century function.

Both Rockefeller and Fosdick have recorded that early on Rockefeller approached the preacher—a bit apprehensively—saying, "I suppose that the only thing you are interested in is a large auditorium primarily fitted for preaching." Fosdick denied the assumption:

> I do want two things in the new building very much—beauty, harmony, worshipfulness so that all who come in will be subdued and quieted by the "rightness" of the rooms, and then warmth, intimacy, homelikeness involving good acoustics and the massing of the people as near the pulpit and each other as possible. They are not easy to combine. The second can be had always cheaply by sacrificing the first; the first can be gotten by any good architect, but often with frigidity, oppressive stateliness that would freeze any congregation and take the heart out of any sermon. I do want a warm church to preach in.

Time and again Fosdick pressed the case for a sanctuary fitted for worship where not the pulpit but the high altar would be central and where beauty of proportion and perspective, of symbolism and color would speak to the soul even when the voice of man was silent. A chancel, he patiently explained to his Protestant people, was not aristocratic and haughty, but democratic. "It is open, with a few steps leading the people up to the altar. It is a high platform that shuts the people off. A chancel puts the minister at the side, where he belongs, mostly out of sight except when he must be actively in operation, and leaves the eye free for the cross and the altar that represent God." What a "slaughter of beauty" Protestants have been guilty of, constructing churches of "architectural degeneracy and hideousness." Fosdick warned his people that it would be a poor bargain to exchange the Park Avenue home for the Riverside house, however beautiful that new house might be; and he anxiously wondered aloud to his colleague Carder, "What if the Riverside adventure should be a flop?" "That lamentable exchange of a home for a house we do not propose to make," he commanded. "We must carry the home into the new house, domesticate the larger edifice, flood it with spiritual atmosphere and make it the habitat of a happy and fruitful fellowship."

Several years later when the Roman Catholic Corpus Christi Church, which is modeled after early American architecture, was under construction nearby, Fosdick remarked to his friend Father George Barry Ford, "It's odd that I have built a Roman Catholic structure, and you are building a New England meeting house." "Well, Harry," Father Ford answered, "someone has to keep Protestantism alive on Morningside side Heights." Incidentally, when Father Ford was being given a tour of the uncompleted Riverside, his Roman collar was spotted by a stone polisher, who was working on his knees. With a twinkle in his Irish eyes the man said, "Father, God forgive me for being on my knees in this heathen place, but I'm getting fifteen dollars a day."

On November 20, 1927, the cornerstone was laid with a flourish, the ceremonies beginning at Union Seminary and ending at the site, the church leaders attired in top hats and Prince Albert coats. Thirteen months later, with construction proceeding apace, the Fosdicks were having dinner with friends Dr. and Mrs. Philip Stimson, and other medical people. When the phone rang and one of the doctors was called away, Fosdick remarked, "I'm certainly glad I'm not a medical man, for I would hate to miss this delicious soup." Moments later the phone rang again, and when Fosdick took the receiver he heard his younger daughter cry, "Father, the church is blazing!" Rushing to the scene only blocks away, Fosdick witnessed masses of flame being driven by a stiff wind from the north to the south end of the structure, where the partly enclosed tower acted as a flue. As the fire gained headway the flames were driven through the five great aisle windows on the east side of the church and directed like a blowtorch against the two adjoining apartment houses on Claremont Avenue. With tears rushing down his cheeks, Fosdick ran into the apartments to help the fleeing inhabitants with their furniture and clothing. Five alarms brought firemen from distant parts of the city. The police department estimated that one hundred thousand spectators watched the blaze, some from the New Jersey Palisades. Water was pumped into the building until late the following afternoon. What had been a colossal furnace became an ice-covered shell strewn with water-soaked wreckage. The official figure of the loss covered by insurance was set at $1,766,338.66. New York State promptly passed a new law making wooden scaffolding illegal.

"We go on from here!," Fosdick exclaimed to his colleague Carder, and to Rockefeller he wrote: "I sympathize with you more than with anyone else, unless it is Mr. [Robert] Eidlitz, whose grief last night was too deep for expression. You have loved this new building into existence detail by detail and I am sorry beyond measure. . . . Nevertheless, nothing is destroyed that cannot be put back; nothing has been done that cannot be done again. I live in the thought of this inevitable recov-

ery of our lost beauty. In the meantime, I want you to know how absolutely you can depend on the 'gameness' of the ministers and the
church staff. We will not only make the best of this situation but we
will make the most of it." He advised Ballard to guard against arson:
"I have no idea that the last fire was of incendiary origin but I am sure
the next fire is likely to be."

Despite the inevitable delays occasioned by the fire, the church rose
rapidly, and on October 5, 1930, Fosdick conducted a majestic opening
service. As the great tones of the sixth largest church organ in the world
swelled out, the congregation of almost four thousand sat in quiet anticipation. (An equal number were turned away.) The chancel glowed with
the white of the elaborately carved Caen stone chancel screen and the
burnished cross and the twelve candelabra of the altar. Above shone the
deep-hued colors of the clerestory windows of the apse. The great vault
of the nave was lighted by thirty-four stained glass windows, the glass
not the heavy opalescent that darkens but the singing, transparent pig-
ments of the Middle Ages. The congregation rose as the choir of fifty
vested in blue and white began the processional hymn. Presently the
call to worship, sanctus and invocation, the reading of the scriptures,
prayer, offertory, sermon, recessional, and the distant intoned "Amen"
after the benediction. "Although I wanted all this beauty," said Fosdick,
"I am sobered by it."

In the afternoon a communion service was held and the "Hand
of Fellowship" extended to sixty-three new members. Fosdick radio-
grammed his joy to Rockefeller, who had consciously absented himself
in order not to monopolize the reporters and detract from the solemnity
of the occasion.

Sunday, February 8, 1931, marked the beginning of a week of dedication services involving many distinguished church leaders and also
a reception honoring the Protestant, Catholic, and Jewish laborers (and
their families) whose skills had brought Riverside into being. The morning service opened with the singing of a processional hymn composed
by Fosdick and closed with a prayer Dr. Woelfkin had written as he lay
on his deathbed. Fosdick described the hymn as "a very personal prayer
on my part" that the new adventure not suffer the calamity of failure.
Protestants in America ranging from Episcopalians to Southern Baptists
and Christians worshipping in many languages across the globe know
that the opening lines are:

> God of grace and God of glory,
>   On thy people pour thy power;

Crown thine ancient Church's story;
Bring her bud to glorious flower.
Grant us wisdom, grant us courage,
For the facing of this hour.*

VII

Sculpted from a trio of three-ton blocks of Indiana limestone, the pulpit
of the Riverside Church is carved with figures of twenty major and
minor prophets. It is so placed as to be seen from every seat in the
broad nave. The wooden canopy over the pulpit displays the architectural motif of a medieval cathedral. Preaching on the subject of peace,
Fosdick once threw the challenge, "Can you imagine Jesus in khaki?"
After the sermon an unpersuaded worshipper returned the challenge:
"Can you, Dr. Fosdick, imagine Jesus preaching from the ornate pulpit
of this lavish church?" This individual was not the only critic of the
architecture of Riverside.

Some hold that great cathedrals make a mockery of the Man from
Nazareth, agreeing with Auden's judgment, "Cathedrals, Luxury liners
laden with souls." The Riverside Church would not please them. Some
living in the twentieth century share Sir Henry Wotton's seventeenth-
century opinion of Gothic: "This form, both for the natural imbecility
of the sharp angle itself, and likewise for its very Uncomeliness, ought
to be exiled from judicious eyes, and left to its first inventors, the Gothes
or Lombards, amongst other Reliques of that barbarous age." The Riverside Church would not please them. And some saw Riverside as "a
violation and betrayal of both Gothic tradition and steel construction,"
to cite the verdict of Walter A. Taylor, A.I.A., lecturer in the History of
Architecture at Columbia University.

In response, Charles Crane, authorized to speak for the architects,
attempted to justify combining Gothic precedent with a modern steel
structure. "Here were some humans," Crane imagined some future historian judging, "still practicing a two-thousand-year-old religion, who
built a church in a style of acknowledged beauty and in full harmony
with their traditions, yet they took full advantage of the modern development of science, engineering skill and materials to create a building

---

* Fosdick composed three other hymns, all well received but none as beloved as
"God of grace and God of glory," although he told a Southern Baptist minister that
" 'O God in restless living' " in his judgment "in many ways goes deeper." Incidentally, more requests were received by the hymnal committee for "God of grace
and God of glory" to be included in the new Pilgrim Hymnal than for any other
twentieth-century hymn.

of endurance exceeding the average of their time, completely equipped and adapted to the requirements of their period of civilization." Fosdick himself explained: "We have had a long time to outgrow Gothic but when it comes to a kind of architecture that will make people want to pray, we have not outgrown Gothic. That is the plain fact of the matter."

When today one worships in the Riverside sanctuary, prays in the chapels, ascends the four-hundred-foot Laura Spelman Rockefeller Memorial Tower, and tours the rooms designed for education and recreation, one is hard pressed to imagine a Christian church raised in the first third of the twentieth century better fitted to endure into the twenty-first century.

VIII

"This competition in the newspapers as to whether we are a 'Rockefeller' or a 'Fosdick' church is likely to wax fast and furious," the minister wrote the millionaire in 1926. "I wonder which will win! I judge that at present we are, as you say, breaking about even, and that you are tarred with my stick about as much as I am with yours. I am bearing up wonderfully myself; I do hope that it is not going to be too much for you." Of course, The Riverside Church transcended the lives of both individuals, as both prayed that it would. It did not and does not officially bear the name of Fosdick or Rockefeller. Asserted the *Christian Century* in 1951:

> Riverside Church is more than the projection of a few remarkable personalities. It is, to be sure, the sounding board for a great preacher like Dr. Fosdick, and his successor, Robert J. McCracken. It is a testimony to the faithful stewardship of a great layman like Mr. Rockefeller. But it is more than that, much more. It is a *church*. It is a church with a history, a tradition, a congregational entity, a sense of mission, an ongoing vitality which in its totality is more than the sum of the contribution of individuals.

Of course, many laypersons other than Rockefeller also gave of their time, talents, and fortunes to make possible the new church—James C. Colgate, William M. Crane, Edward L. Ballard, Albert L. Scott, Winthrop W. Aldrich, to mention only a leading few. Nevertheless, it was John D. Rockefeller, Jr., more than anyone else, whose vision, energy, and dollars brought Riverside into being. His initial contribution totaled $10,573,542, a figure masked from the public and indeed from most parishioners and far higher than the contemporary widely estimated *total* cost of the church, $4 million. Rockefeller's financial support continued for three decades and continues through endowments to this day. As Christmas of 1959 approached, the old man sat by the window in the winter sun reviewing his life. His meticulous nature led him to request a final accounting of his contributions to The Riverside Church. $32,462,187 came the reply, with the notation: "All of the above gifts are completed gifts and you do not retain any interest in or control over them. The situation then is as you hoped it would be."

Perhaps the dying Rockefeller permitted himself a smile of satisfaction, for The Riverside Church, the Fifth Avenue Baptist, and the Park Avenue Baptist had commanded, beyond dollars, his hours, many thousands in all, and not once did he express regret for giving so freely of himself and his fortune to this church. Fosdick correctly said that Rockefeller loved the new edifice into existence. He might have added that Rockefeller also sweated it into existence. The Rockefeller Family Archives contain hundreds of letters concerning every detail of its construction. At its completion in 1930, he personally wrote letters of appreciation to a score of individuals—architects, designers, builders, craftsmen. These letters are models of thoughtfulness and they are his own, not those of a ghost writer. The replies (not at all fawning) brim with admiration for him. Rockefeller's intuitive sense of what is meet and proper commands respect. When asked permission to place his father among the church's six hundred figures of great men of history, he demurred, saying, "I cannot tell you how deeply I appreciate the suggestion which the Iconography Committee has made and which I know Father will be much touched by. The one thing which he would have in mind in considering this gracious suggestion would be what is best for the enterprise. I feel sure you will agree with me that it would be unwise to put any living man, particularly a capitalist, in the chancel screen. Therefore . . . my judgment is clear that some other personage should be selected." Twenty-five years later in 1955, when his contribution of $15 million made possible a major new addition to the church, South Wing, he again forbade the suggested employment of the names Rockefeller Chapel and Abby Aldrich Rockefeller Room. Incidentally, the only living person among those honored in stone or glass was Albert Einstein. When the great scientist visited New York in 1930, he expressed a desire to see "that oddity," and when shown his sculptured figure over the West Portal he exclaimed, "I will have to be very careful for the rest of my life as to what I do and what I say." Rockefeller's wisdom (or prudence) as chairman of the Building Committee is further illustrated by the fact that the Women's Group was granted permission to select their own architect and decorator of the Women's Floor. As he dryly noted, the women's victory was "doubtless due to the pull which my wife has with the Chairman of the Building Committee."

Two days before the dedication of the church, the Deacons and Trustees tendered Rockefeller a dinner in grateful recognition of his leadership. At the ceremony Fosdick recalled how his father had returned the house key to him as he was leaving home for Colgate. "With real feeling, therefore," Fosdick continued, "I hand this [golden master] key to you, Mr. Rockefeller, in the name of your friends here, saying that it is a symbol that your Father's house is open to you day and night." Presently Rockefeller wrote Fosdick a note: "May God give you strength and health and power to do His will and may your hands be upheld by all those who surround you to the end that this house of worship, reared by the hands of men, may ever point the way to the true and living God and guide men into a natural, trustful, helpful relation with Him. Please know, dear friend, of the deep love which I have for you and of my constant gratitude to God for the way in which He is using you."

Chapter Twelve

"You Are the United Church in Local Guise": The Riverside Church Fellowship

I

There are in this church many members of many denominations and many faiths. In welcoming you into our membership, we do not ask you to give up any belief or form that is dear to you but rather to bring it to us that we may be enriched thereby. We invite you not to our table or the table of any denomination but to the Lord's table.

In these words Fosdick welcomed Riverside Church members, old and new, to the sacrament of the Lord's Supper. Riverside was the realization of his long-cherished dream of an inclusive interdenominational fellowship open to all who "believeth in the Lord Jesus Christ." In 1927 when the Riverside dream was taking shape, Fosdick predicted: "This movement toward inclusive churches is on, and nothing can stop it. It will gain momentum as it proceeds. In view of the futility of overstocked towns with poverty-stricken, struggling churches disgraced, to start with, by the pettiness of the reasons behind their separation, it seems likely that practical support will increasingly drift to comprehensive communions and that belated forms of denominational organization will gradually be starved out." The following half-century did not see this prediction fulfilled, but neither did Fosdick's retirement in 1946 see the Riverside adventure collapse as various Cassandras had foretold. If Fosdick and the original Riverside fellowship during sixteen years of economic depression and then war had not labored valiantly in building a solid foundation, the church might today be only a lovely museum.

Instead, under Fosdick's immediate successor, Robert James McCracken, the church flourished as the entire nation bathed in a torrential postwar surge of piety. Under *his* successor, Ernest T. Campbell, the church gallantly endured as the national religiosity momentarily receded and Morningside Heights witnessed troubling, challenging, demographic changes. As the 1970s closed the church continued with high morale to meet intensified challenges under the new ministry of William Sloane Coffin, Jr. In times good and bad Riverside has steadily gone about the business of enfolding infants, nurturing the young, sustaining the mature, comforting the afflicted, proclaiming the Word, celebrating the Risen Lord, burying the dead, serving the neighborhood's needy, succoring the broken world. Fosdick's successes and those of the original fellowship were not unbroken, but they did bequeath to future generations an enduring physical, financial, and spiritual legacy.

II

At the onset a sympathetic fellow-liberal minister said plantively, "Harry Fosdick is very inspiring as a preacher, but I doubt if you could take him as a guide in practical church affairs. He hasn't what you call the church sense." Other observers also miss any strong doctrine of the church in Fosdick's thought. They charge that the divine dimension, the church as the body of Christ, is subordinated by Fosdick to the human dimension, the church as a voluntary community of followers of Christ bound together through loyalty to him and his teachings. They note that of the six key ideas in the Scriptures developed by Fosdick in *A Guide to Understanding the Bible*, none deal with the church. Fosdick was not unaware of his neglect of ecclesiology, once apologizing to his people, "I blame myself in this regard, that, in the three books of sermons supposed to represent my message, there is not a single one devoted to the church."

Still he had a point when he gave this explanation to a young scholar: "I have been too busy working in the church to ever construct a doctrine of it." He served the church, defended it, built it, and loved it. He believed that the church should be "the point of incandescence where, regardless of denominationalism or theology, the Christian life of the community bursts into flame."

Ultimately, however, he did not give his final loyalty to the church, "which is a human organization that has committed every sin in the calender, as well as conserving some of the most beautiful spiritual realities handed down by our fathers. My primary consecration is to the spirit of Jesus Christ. Whenever I see the church being true to this, I am for the church, and whenever I think the church is false to this I am for reforming the church." He understood how ecclesiology could become corrupted to ecclesiolatry by those Christians who worshipped the church instead of the Lord of the church.

III

"You are the united church in local guise," Fosdick informed the Riverside fellowship. The spirit of open arms—whosoever will may come—swept into that fellowship individuals from Roman Catholic and Greek Catholic and Jewish backgrounds as well as those from two-score different Protestant denominational antecedents and also some from the land of unfaith. Fosdick once reported:

> All sorts of people come within our range—downright pagans who have seldom been near a church, children of mixed marriages who have learned little or nothing religiously one way or the other, lost Protestants who have been in the City for years doing nothing about either their Christianity or their church affiliation, rolling stones who have roved all over the world gathering no religious moss, and rebels, brought up in a type of faith they have discarded, who at Riverside begin to wonder whether, after all, an intelligent faith may not be possible.

At the time of his retirement only about one third of the membership had Baptist backgrounds, both the president of the Board of Trustees and the chairman of the Board of Deacons were Methodists, and one of the three ministers was a Congregationalist. The Riverside communion of saints was not, to employ Fosdick's imagery, a chain gang at lockstep with one long whip cracking down the line to prevent any individual's deviation.

Nevertheless, Fosdick comprehended the dangers in the Riverside experiment. Interdenominationalism must be more than a brusque dismissal of inherited ritual. It must welcome differences rather than merely tolerate them, demonstrate its avowed conviction that "liberty of the individual is based not on the idea that what one believes is unimportant, but on the idea that it is too important to be arbitrarily regimented and controlled by external authority." Fosdick had no inerest in Riverside being a community church. "Twigs that snap out of the camp-fire lose their flame and fall, charred sticks; but put them back and they will burn again, for fire springs from fellowship." Thus, it was incorporated as a Baptist church under the Religious Corporation Law of the State of New York. It maintained working ties with the Northern (later Amercan) Baptist Convention, and after Fosdick's retirement (but with his blessing), it affiliated also with the Congregational Christian Churches, that body then merging with the Evangelical and Reformed Church to form the United Church of Christ. Today, therefore, Riverside is affiliated with both the American Baptist Churches in the U.S.A. and the United Church of Christ.*

The nucleus of the fellowship were the 846 members of the Park Avenue Baptist Church congregation who transferred to Riverside's rolls. In the church year 1931–1932, 346 new members were received. No subsequent year during Fosdick's pastorate enjoyed such a growth. Indeed, by the time of his retirement membership was at a "relatively stationary level" and growth "practically static." Measured by membership statistics alone Riverside was less than a spectacular success story.

Still during Fosdick's pastorate membership grew fourfold to reach thirty-five hundred in May 1946. Moreover, this growth occurred in a decade of economic depression when mainline Protestant church membership cascaded like the Great Bull Market itself, and also in the dislocating war years that followed the Great Depression. Riverside's modest membership triumphs were won in what was for American Protestantism in general a time of trouble and in spite of the fact that Riverside did not proselytize.

A close study of new admissions reveals approximately 60 percent were by "Letter of Transfer," 20 percent by "Confession of Faith," and 20 percent by "Reaffirmation of Faith" or "Experience." If desired, and only if desired, admission might be preceded by baptism either by immersion or sprinkling. As in many churches, Riverside had several categories of membership: regular, affiliated, and contributing. Fosdick agreed with Henry Sloane Coffin that in their concern for sheer size too many ministers had ceased to be shepherds and become ranchers instead. Therefore, when a member moved away Fosdick urged the individual not to request a nonresident membership in Riverside, but rather to join a church in his or her new community, explaining that "it has seemed to us unwise and unfraternal to build up an absentee membership across the country. We feel sure that from the standpoint of the general welfare of the Kingdom of God it is better to encourage people to find in their own communities churches where they can worship and give."

---

* In the 1960s and 1970s unsuccessful conversations looking toward additional affiliations were carried on with Methodist and Presbyterian spokesmen.

IV

In terms of the varying religious backgrounds of the membership, Fosdick's dream of an inclusive church was largely realized, but may the
same success be claimed for inclusiveness of social class?* Responding
to an inquiry on this point, Fosdick explained:

> As a matter of fact, if you could live with us here you would soon find out
> what very ordinary people we are. I could count on the fingers of one
> hand all the people in the church that could be called wealthy. We have
> 5,000 people in our various organizations now,† and they are the most
> ordinary, garden variety run of people, many of them economically almost
> as much up against it as those you find in the southwest. Nevertheless,
> there are certain types of economic problems that I do not face here, and
> know all too little about. We are for the most part a group of professional
> people, especially teachers, lawyers, doctors, and students, and while we
> may be as poor as Job's turkey, as many of us are, we most of us have
> had the privileges of education. The selective influence in a church like
> this is not primarily economic, but intellectual, and that can be just as
> dangerous as the economic privileges ever were to an understanding of
> what the rest of the world is up against.

Four years following his retirement he elaborated:

> I tried to do the best I could to make the Riverside Church inclusive. We
> have succeeded very well in making it an interracial, international, inter-
> denominational church, but it still remains, in spite of everything, a fairly
> class church; that is, a middle class church of white collar people, largely
> professionals, students, teachers, doctors, lawyers, social workers, small
> businessmen, and so forth. There are undoubtedly members of labor
> unions in the church, but they are members of professional labor unions.
> There aren't any miners anywhere around us, nor carpenters, nor plumb-
> ers, nor such, so far as I know that are members of the church. It isn't
> because we have the spirit of the *haberim* and have wanted to keep them
> out. I recall the Chairman of our Board of Trustees lamenting that we
> were not representative in better fashion of the labor unions. It's a tough
> problem, and Protestantism has got to face it one way or another.

These statements agree with other analyses of the Riverside membership. The Park Avenue nucleus appears to have been largely of British
stock, permitting Fosdick in his early sermons to refer to "your ances-

---

* In Chapter Twenty-Four attention will be paid to the racial composition of the
membership.
† Not all who belonged to Riverside's organizations were church members.

tors and mine" in the British Isles and to spoof the congregation by saying, "Some of you mid-Victorians here, the last frazzled remnants of a once mighty race." Moreover, the Park Avenue nucleus did contain more than a few individuals of affluence, and scrutiny of the individuals in the photographs in the *Church Monthly* reveals many apparent patricians. But as the years passed the fellowship became more inclusive. The proportion of the very wealthy declined. Professional people, middle echelon businessmen and women, social workers, municipal employees, a fair sprinkling of those connected with the arts, students in professional schools, housewives—these contituted the essential elements in the fellowship. Riverside remained a "class" church—as Fosdick acknowledged regretfully—but measureably less so than in the Park Avenue days; and if it drew to its doors few blue-collar workers, it is difficult to see how it might have been otherwise.

At the time of his retirement, Fosdick greeted his successor, McCracken: "Forget as soon as possible that you are preaching to New Yorkers. Most of us aren't; we come from the 'sticks.' If ever you faced plain, ordinary human beings, who needed the Christian gospel to help them live, you'll face them here." The places of birth of Riverside's members is not recorded, though we do know that in 1938 there were 1782 *regular* members who *lived* in Manhattan and the Bronx and 1031 members who commuted from Long Island, Welfare Island, Brooklyn, Staten Island, New Jersey, Westchester County, and Connecticut. We shall have to take Fosdick on faith as to his people's origins in the "sticks." But we don't have to have his authority to realize that, like their less fortunate brethren, people of education, intelligence, and relative material comfort have need of the sort of fellowship they found at Riverside.

V

Fosdick agreed with the old adage that the Christian ministry is the greatest of all callings and the worst of all trades, adding: "For myself, if I had a thousand lives I should like in this generation to go into the ministry with every one of them." He had little understanding of, and no sympathy with, the concept of an ordained sacramental priesthood, fearing such a priestly class obscured what the New Testament called the priesthood of all believers. He deplored in an evangelical church the identification of the church with its minister, as though the church were to be thought of in terms of the preacher's name, as a play on Broadway is associated with its star performer.

Historically the call to be a Protestant clergyman had been primarily a call to preach, but Fosdick comprehended that modern, large metropolitan churches such as Riverside imposed manifold and heavy responsibilities on the minister in addition to preaching. All about him he saw ministers being "swept off their feet by the demands of their own organizations, falling under the spell of bigness, and rushing from one committee to another to put over some new scheme to enlarge the work or save the world." He believed that no man, if he is by interest, training, and temperament a preacher, can be the executive head of a metropolitan institutional church, with direct responsibility for all its varied activities, without neglecting either his preaching or his organizational responsibilities or breaking down. "At this point," he argued, "the analogy of a business organization, when applied to a church like Riverside, is utterly inappropriate. The chief executive of a business is a businessman; he does not have, once a week or more, to make a speech on which depend the central meaning and purpose of his vocation; he does not face, as an equally essential part of his lifework, the interviewing of all the customers who come to him with personal, spiritual problems; he is not called on to enter day by day into the joy of their weddings and the grief of their funerals, nor is he responsible for the visitation of sick customers and the personal welcoming of customers' children into participation in the business. Any minister who, in a church like Riverside, tries to be at once *the* minister and *the* chief executive is, in my judgment, up against an impossible proposition."

Fosdick's solution was the formation of a collegiate ministry, initially a staff of three ministers with separate functions but equal status. "It takes the grace of God," he acknowledged, "and a high type of unselfish spirit and character for men to work together as colleagues, equal in status as ministers of Christ, with mutual loyalty supporting one another and harmoniously agreeing on common policies." The men* who joined him in the Collegium were not in the least "assistants." They were mature, experienced individuals who did not view Riverside as a way station on their journeys to pastorates of their own. They had defined, important responsibilities and real authority. Broadly speaking, one minister served as executive officer and one as chief educational and recreational director, whereas the worship services were Fosdick's major concern. Most important, all three ministers were in the chancel every Sunday and participated in the worship service; none lost their priestly vocation however deep their involvement in administrative matters.

Fosdick once stated, "I am a genius as an organizer. My genius con-

---

* The first woman joined Riverside's ministerial staff in 1959, the Reverend Phyllis Taylor.

sists of disliking the details or organization and getting someone else to take care of them." His associates had real freedom, too much, in the judgment of friendly critics. To this he replied, "Stressing equality of status, the collegiate set-up can be interpreted to mean that all the ministers must be in on everything—which is precisely what it was intended to prevent. If all three ministers must confer on all decisions, it means that the burden of carrying the whole parish on his mind which, under the older set-up, rested on the minister-in-chief, now rests on each of the colleagues, which is no gain at all."

However sincerely Fosdick believed in the Collegium ideal, one suspects that in the eyes of the congregation and in the eyes of the public at large he was seen as *primus inter pares*. After Fosdick's retirement a veteran layman wrote Rockefeller: "Dr. Fosdick's modesty which is so marked in him and so infrequently an element of leadership in our time, obstructs to a degree his views of his methods of operation of the church. . . . We who worked closely with the three ministers until his retirement from active responsibility in organizational problems never doubted who was the human head of that church. Like all good executives he gave free rein to Drs. Carder and Hellstrom within the areas of their responsibility but when a decision involving policy was required it was based finally upon Dr. Fosdick's wisdom." Clearly this was Rockefeller's own understanding. When in 1933 Fosdick wrote him about his salary and those of his colleagues, unselfishly requesting there remain "comparative equality in salary," Rockefeller replied:

The position you have always taken, namely that your colleagues were joint leaders with you in this great enterprise, is a fine one and has been an inspiration to them. That that position has involved anything like a parity of salary or anything even remotely approaching it, had never occurred to me. I think it would be almost impossible for you to convince any one of the trustees that there should be such a comparison in salaries, and that so far as your colleagues are concerned, they would turn a deaf ear to any such attempt. While the president of any corporation might want to have his vice presidents receive the same salary as himself, or salaries approaching his, that there should be such a relation in salaries is a situation that is almost unprecedented in the business world. I cannot, therefore, bring myself to agree with you in this matter.

Fosdick declined to accept Rockefeller's analogy to the business world and the salary he received remained close to those of his ministerial colleagues, Eugene C. Carder, Norris L. Tibbetts, and C. Ivar Hellstrom.

Born in Canada and built like a lumberjack, Carder was called to the Fifth Avenue Baptist Church in 1919 as an assistant minister. After much soul searching he agreed to join in the Riverside adventure, saying to Fosdick, "In so much as in me is I am ready." Fosdick never tired of singing Carder's praises—to Rockefeller and all with ears to hear, including the universities contemplating awarding Carder honorary degrees—and when finally his associate retired in 1943, Fosdick quoted Saint Paul, "I thank my God upon every remembrance of you."

On Carder's departure the major organizational and pastoral responsibilities were assumed by Norris L. Tibbetts. For Tibbetts, then in Chicago, it was a call to "come home," for he had been Fosdick's student at Union and an assistant at the Fifth Avenue Baptist Church. Fosdick's admiration for Tibbetts was total.

The third colleague was C. Ivar Hellstrom, appointed in 1929 as new Director of Religious Education. "I thank God for the ministry I was permitted to share with Ivar Hellstrom," declared Fosdick, and he backed the words by supporting Brown University's decision to award Hellstrom an honorary doctorate and urging (without Hellstrom's knowledge) Columbia University to do the same.

VI

"One of the most hopeful factors in our enterprise . . . ," judged Fosdick, "is that Riverside is so largely a layman's church, with so many laymen and laywomen engaged in its direction and its work, or enlisted because of its influence in serviceable enterprises in the City in which the church is interested." Riverside had no formal constitution, but the principle was firm that the membership at all times is the ultimate authority with respect to every phase of the church's activities; and in truth the church's lifeblood was the freely given time, talents, and dollars of dedicated laypeople. Fosdick would have had it no other way for, he said, a "church's bigness means nothing unless it bears fruit in transformed and dedicated individuals." Elsewhere he said, "Ministers are like leaves; they fall off in October; but the main stem and continuous growth of the church inheres in the great mass of laymen who stand by and carry on and increase, and see it through. The church, therefore, cannot live and grow just because ministers are called of God. It is the church's laymen who constitute the abiding continuum of the fellowship."

In the Fosdick era the Board of Trustees was far more powerful than the Board of Deacons, and the continuity of trustee leadership was remarkable and belies any claim that the Riverside fellowship achieved a sort of Christian communism—a utopian classless society where status had withered away. Seven members of the twelve-man Board in 1931 (excluding William M. Crane, honorary vice-president) were still members in 1945. They were John D. Rockefeller, Jr., John D. Rockefeller, 3rd, Albert L. Scott, Winthrop W. Aldrich, A. LeRoy Chipman, William R. Conklin, and William H. West. Most of those missing in 1945 had been cut down by death, notably James C. Colgate and Edward L. Ballard, the latter a towering figure in the church's affairs who served as president of the board from 1913 to 1932. The same names were invariably put before the congregation by the nominating committee, and invariably the corporate gathering saw the nominees accepted without significant dissenting vote. In most instances the trustees were linked to Rockefeller by paternity, marriage, or business and philanthropic connections; the monthly meetings of the board were held in Rockefeller's offices. It would be unfair to the memory of such staunch independent-minded and independently successful men as Ballard, Colgate, and Scott, to mention only three, to suggest that they were Rockefeller puppets. He may have been *primus inter pares,* but the emphasis should be placed on *pares.** The trustees were bound by a common commitment to Riverside's weal, a common involvement in New York's religious and philanthropic life, and a common devotion to liberal Christianity's purposes in the nation and the world. (Ballard and Scott were leaders in the famous and controversial Rockefeller-financed Laymen's Foreign Missions Inquiry.) It must be added that success in New York's business and financial world was a requisite qualification for Riverside's Board of Trustees. Trustee Frederic A. Cole put it plainly in a letter of resignation to Ballard:

> The affairs of the Riverside Church have grown, as you know, to such proportions that they require the most careful supervision and critical oversight. In some respects they have become almost commercial in character, requiring an expert business manager with a large corps of paid assistants. As Jim Pratt [another trustee] said the other day, our meetings are becoming almost more important than Bank Directors Meetings. Membership in the Board of Trustees carries great responsibility and should be held by such men only as are willing and able to assume responsibilities both executive and financial. The committee assignments are no sinecures; the work of all the committees being most important and exacting.

* By the time of Fosdick's retirement there were emerging as key trustees such individuals as Columbia Professor Noel T. Dowling and William T. Gossett, son-in-law of Charles Evans Hughes and soon-to-be vice-president and general counsel of the Ford Motor Company.

In the Fosdick era the Board of Deacons exercised relatively little independent power compared to the trustees, tending to defer to the ministers' wishes, which led at least one deacon to declare the church "priest ridden" in Fosdick's day. Even before Fosdick's retirement, however, and not over his opposition, the deacons were moving in the direction of the exercise of greater authority and independence. As in the case of the trustees those nominated to the Board of Deacons almost invariably received congregational approval. The board knew a measure of stability in the continuing presence of such individuals as Harry Fish, Arthur Bestor, Elmer Sanborn, Philip Stimson, Rollin Tanner, and Marshall Clarke. In the mid-1930s several men, notably Francis Harmon and Frank Miley, strengthened the deacons' ranks, and by 1946 James Hodge, Robert Walmsley, and Clifford Petitt were emerging as leaders. Much more than the trustees, and understandably so, the deacons represented such fields of endeavor as teaching, medicine, and religion.

Like the trustees, however, the deacons were all men. In 1940 for the first time the congregation was canvassed to ascertain its wishes on the question of female deacons. The matter was still being debated in 1945, but when the elected and appointed leaders of the church were polled, of the fifty-seven who responded, only twenty-four favored the reform, so, a motion "was made, seconded and carried that further consideration of the matter of women on the Board be discontinued for the present."* Fosdick gave guarded endorsement to the idea, saying, "Personally I have always felt that it was somewhat of an anomaly that a progressive church like our congregation here at Riverside should not have women on its official Board. I welcome the work of this committee in canvassing the general situation, and recommending to the Board of Deacons their findings."

VII

It is not necessary to subscribe to Parkinson's iron law to accept as inevitable the creation of a large staff as an accompaniment to Riverside's membership growth and multiplying activities. Apart from the three ministers, a permanent staff of approximately seventy was required to maintain the building and the church's programs. This permanent staff was supplemented by a part-time staff of 150, including the choir, the teachers in the church school, and others. For all the good will and high hopes that launched the Riverside experiment, it might well have

* In the late 1940s the reform was accomplished and today women serve on the Board of Trustees as well.

been fouled with organizational barnacles had not a careful watch been kept. Indeed, the important Mark Jones (he was a consulting economist) survey of 1939 reported: "Regardless of how the problem is stated, the situation is an impossible one. The Church is trying to do too much." At that time Fosdick himself reported the "ministers here are terribly driven" and the professional staff "strained to the utmost." And so structural and staffing reforms were naturally made during Fosdick's ministry and later.

VIII

In 1979 Riverside's new minister William Sloane Coffin, Jr., reported the church was blessed with an endowment then valued at $40 million, adding, "Thanks to the generosity of John D. Rockefeller, Jr., it is now possible for poor people to run the church—and many do." The endowment maintained and operated the physical plant, making it necessary for the congregation to raise only its program costs, a sum less than half the total budget. This situation would not have been displeasing to the original Riverside fellowship and indeed was the intention from the beginning.

In 1943 Fosdick summarized for the congregation the church's financial arrangements:

> In your giving to this budget you are not giving a penny for any deficit. We cut our garment according to our cloth last year, and there is no deficit. You are not giving a penny to any debt. This church has no debt. You are not giving a penny to any physical repairs on this building. That is all cared for by invested funds. You are not giving a penny, even, toward 90% of the running of this building, week in and week out. Your gifts cover only 10% of that; 90% is cared for by invested funds. You are not giving a penny to anything that in these days might be thought a dispensable luxury, such as the carillon, for example. That is cared for by invested funds. This is the reason why with a church support budget of about $275,000 we ask of you in gifts for that budget only about $96,000. But, my friends, that $96,000 covers the vital program that goes on in this church! That vital program depends absolutely on the voluntary gifts of the congregation. We want that budget raised. Come taxes, high cost of living, what you will, this program of service must be maintained.

The Riverside pledge motto read: "From each according to his ability; to each the utmost in spiritual nourishment which Riverside could supply." Even acknowledging that the great majority of the membership enjoyed only modest incomes and that the Depression reduced many to marginal straits, it is still difficult to credit the membership with sacrificial giving. "Church membership," concluded Mark Jones's survey, "seems to be without any positive relationship to financial participation in the Church's work." Here are a few supporting facts drawn from Mark Jones's survey and from a 1939 study of church giving conducted by John D. Rockefeller, 3rd, and from more general church records:

Item: Between 25 to 35 percent of the Riverside membership pledged nothing at all, and their financial support, if any, was by way of plate collections.*

Item: In 1939 there were 5 pledges (representing 6 people) that accounted for 42 percent of the money raised; 209 pledges (representing 305 people, or 8.7 percent of the total church constituency) accounted for 74 percent of the total money raised.

Item: In 1946 after the booming war economy had reversed cascading incomes, the amount of the average pledge was only $62; in other words, hundreds of members pledged under $25 annually.

Item: It was not until the fall of 1946, after Fosdick's retirement, that Riverside's leadership agreed that the time had come for a full-fledged Every Member Canvass for the 1947 budget. It was a notable success, suggesting that during Fosdick's ministry the majority of members had depended excessively on the largess of the wealthy few and also that the majority had not been approached in an effective manner.

In 1937 Fosdick reported "that for certain types of work in this building the church is paying less than any other non-profit institution on this hill, with one exception. Now, that won't do. How can I on Sunday preach Christ in this pulpit when I know that is going on in this church." Clearly he had a point. A 1941 study disclosed that Riverside's wages were about in the median of the wages paid at Columbia, Barnard, Union, and Juilliard, with resultant "loss of good men through competition with regular industry, and also an increased turnover in personnel, especially among porters." Concretely, nine church employees received over $3000; seven between $2000 and $3000; thirty between $1200 and $2000; twenty-six $1200 or less.

A final word about the financing of the Riverside enterprise. Rockefeller made personal gifts to the church ranging from famous paintings to a reconditioned upright piano. He wrote a fair number of people

---

* The percentages varied, though not dramatically, from year to year.

seeking their dollars for the church. He sometimes paid the traveling expenses of visiting preachers, and when General Eisenhower became president of Columbia, he offered to pick up the Eisenhowers on Sunday mornings should they wish to attend Riverside with him. He paid the entire salary of Kamiel Lefévere, perhaps the world's greatest living carillonneur. He presented Fosdick (and Fosdick's successor, McCracken) with generous gifts, some of which Fosdick accepted and some he declined. He augmented the salaries of the ministers Carder, Tibbetts, and Hellstrom. For example, over a period of twenty-six years Rockefeller gave Carder sums totaling $42,800, not counting Christmas checks and checks to help out with heavy medical expenses.

IX

Only a Dr. Pangloss could review the Riverside record and see a communion of literal saints. In fact Fosdick once said, "Mark this strange fact that the church is the only organization in the world that advertises itself as a company of sinners." Still, acknowledging the "spotted actuality," toward the end of his life Fosdick correctly saluted the Riverside fellowship: "They carried Christ where I was never able to go; they displayed the Christian spirit in relationships I never had a chance at; and they put their intelligence and skill at the disposal of the Church with results that I never dreamed were possible."

Chapter Thirteen

"We Have Maintained the Adoration of God and the Proclamation of the Gospel": Worship in the Riverside Church

I

Reviewing his Riverside ministry with its myriad facets, Fosdick emphasized that "at the center of the church's life we have maintained the adoration of God and the proclamation of the Gospel." Man's nature is such that he needs particular times and places for communion with the divine if all his living is liturgically to show forth the divine. It is out of the context of concrete acts of religious observance that religious conviction emerges on the human plane. In providing the times and places for the encounter between God and man through Jesus Christ in Christian worship, Riverside's being and mission were supremely set forth. If a church most truly knows herself in corporate worship then liturgy must be thought of both theologically and ecclesiologically. Riverside's gathered congregation worshipped in varied forms bespeaking the diverse religious backgrounds of the members and reflective of their and their ministers' noncreedal theology. As a "free" church not bound to any ecclesiastically required form of worship, Riverside was able to house under its roof, Fosdick boasted, many "types of worship commonly housed under separate sectarian roofs," ranging from the simple Quaker meeting to the congregational preaching service of the kind familiar in most mainline Protestant churches, to the liturgical service without sermon composed of music and litany, to worship through drama, and to worship through instruction and discussion. Of course, in so doing Riverside ran the danger of embracing what has been called "a kind of liturgical Esperanto" at the expense of the integrity of worship. With as many as sixty-five hundred men, women, and children worshipping on a given Sunday—morning, afternoon, and evening—and additional hundreds on days other than the Lord's Day, manifestly how these Christians practiced their most bounden duty and solemn obligation and richest privilege is central to the life of the minister, Fosdick, who conceived, planned, and conducted worship with them.

II

It already has been remarked that one misses any strong doctrine of the church in Fosdick's thought, just so does one search in vain for any full, sustained articulation of his understanding of corporate worship. He explained his neglect of ecclesiology on the grounds that he had been too busy working in, and for, the church to ever construct a doctrine of it, and perhaps his failure to elaborate a theology of worship can be similarly explained. Therefore, we must be content to glance at his few scattered statements on the subject and note the variety of worship services held in Riverside during his ministry.

One major statement was made in a pastoral letter written on the eve of Riverside's completion:

That this is to be a significant year in the church's life goes without saying. It takes much more than a house to make a home, and the completion of our new building is not so much the end as the beginning of our real task. To be sure, the new building itself should be an inestimable help to us in our spiritual ministry to the city. Beauty is a roadway to God. Our characteristic Protestant tradition has too much neglected that fact and has relied too exclusively on talking. It has often reduced worship to a few exercises of devotion appended to a sermon. Such starvation diet will not serve rightly the needs of the spiritual life and we should rejoice that we are to have a structure made for worship, conducive to worship, in which worship can be made beautiful and effective.

Let me, therefore . . . , lay it on your consciences that you use the church for worship. Too commonly our Protestant congregations come to church, as they go to a lecture, to have somebody talk to them. They do not come to do something themselves—to worship and so be carried out of themselves by something greater than themselves to which they give themselves. They come in the passive voice instead of the active. Worship, however, is not a function which the minister can perform for the congregation—it is a cooperative act in which all the congregation should partake. Anyone can *feel* the difference between a lecture-hall audience and a worshipping church. The minister's attitude can help create the spirit of the latter but it is the people themselves who really produce it.

Especially in our case, where so many casual visitors are present in our services, we need to lay this matter to heart. We want everyone who enters our church to be hushed and inspired by the spirit which pervades our worship. Let us not be afraid—as so many Protestants are—of outward expression of devotion, kneeling in prayer if we feel like it, and certainly joining actively and heartily in the services.

Moreover, while it is true as Matthew Arnold said that "we philosophize best alone and worship best together," let us not forget that long Christian tradition in favor of using the churches for private devotion. Our church and chapel will be open every day for prayer and meditation. Not once a week but all the week by day and night we wish the new building used—and not least by those who find it a refuge from the city's confusion, where private prayer is natural and the fever of the world is stilled.

Several themes in this statement surface again and again in Fosdick's admonitions to his fellow Protestants. He abjured "sermon-ridden Sunday mornings" in "glorified lecture halls" in which worship is only "opening exercises." Why is it, he mused, that Protestants "must have someone forever talking to them." This uninterrupted garrulity of Protestant worship corrupts the integrity of worship and instead of a dialogue between the people and God, worship is debased to a one-way speech by the preacher to the congregation involving only the auditory sense of the worshipers rather than all their faculties. Fosdick further discerned that in contrast to the Roman Catholic mass, the sermon is selective, appealing to a certain intellectual stratum and excluding other types of mind. "This is one reason why Protestant churches in America, centering their worship in a sermon, have so largely become class organizations— religious clubs appealing to a narrowly selected group of ideas and traditions. So long as patriotism is expressed by saluting the flag, everybody can indulge in that symbolic act, and each can find in it his own meaning. If, however, patriotism's expression should be thought of as listening to discourses on the Constitution, that would eliminate wide ranges of the nation's population, whoever was engaged as the expositor."

Fosdick was further concerned that the American disease of spectatoritis was infecting Protestant worship. "In one realm after another we are only spectators. So in church we watch the ministers and the choir indulge in prayer and praise. Thus to go to church is an external act . . . ," not genuine worship. Fosdick understood the actional character of worship and deplored the passivity of the congregation in respectable mainline Protestantism. Spectatoritis was one consequence of the undisciplined devotional life. Having made no preparation in prayer, meditation, fasting, confession, scriptural study, family devotions, Protestants fail to fulfil the serious conditions for receiving anything in public worship. "They saunter in, saunter through, saunter out. Great things, however, are greatly arrived at." Fosdick begged his people to recall those methods of Christian nurture their forefathers used to call the "means of grace," observing that Protestants had sloughed off one observance after another and the "more liberal we have grown the more we have emptied our lives of all methods of spiritual nurture." He spoke hard words about one aspect of discipline: the necessity of punctuality at the worship services. "I do not want to preach to people who come struggling in just before the sermon. Such folk ruin the whole spirit of the service and deserve to be shut out. . . . It might have a wholesome effect for our church to say that people who do not care enough for worship to come on time must not come at all."

Fosdick sought to recover the lost accent of beauty in Protestant corporate worship and under his guidance Riverside moved in the direction of more formal services with increased emphases on order, historicity, uniformity. Protestantism at its best had worshipped God in goodness and truth, but beauty had no such place, with a resulant aesthetic starvation. Yet, said Fosdick, for multitudes beauty is the major highway to fellowship with God. Recognizing man's imperious love of beauty, he strove to heighten his congregation's sense of wonder, reverence, adoration, and so to make worship "an affair of joy and festival as well as of goodness and truth."

"Worship—being carried out of one's self by something higher than one's self to which one gives one's self—is a necessary function of the human soul." Such was Fosdick's definition. Elsewhere he wrote, "The word itself means worship, the recognition and appreciation of real worth." In worship, he explained, one is made to remember values too easily forgotten. Worship enables a person to reorient himself, to regain his sense of direction. Worship helps a person to withstand the evil in his life. Worship is an experience in which one rededicates one's life. Fosdick's understanding of worship is perhaps excessively subjective and experiential. To be sure liturgy is for man, not man for liturgy, but Paul Hoon's theological critique of the category of "worship" is relevant here. "Actually," Professor Hoon pointed out, "worship defined as the ascription of supreme worth to God can apply to the dance of the sun worshipper or the prayer wheel of the Oriental, to the rites of a mystery cult or the thought of the philosopher, as well as to the prayer of the Christian." Hoon continued: "To the exent that scholars, pastors, and congregations have so uncritically absorbed ways of thinking bound up with worship understood as 'worthship,' much Protestant worship has become flabby rather than holy, folksy rather than numinous, hortatory rather than adoring, feminine more than masculine, and one is not surprised that it often appeals to infantile elements in human personality."

There is in New England a humanistic church in which, according to the irreverent, the last time the name of God was heard was when the sexton spilt some hot lead on his hand. One may find Fosdick's theology of worship thin and too much focused on man. Still, it is well to remember that Fosdick's pastoral prayers typically began:

Eternal God, so high above us that we cannot comprehend thee and yet so deep within us that we cannot escape thee, make thyself real to us today!

Eternal God, who art before all, in all, and beyond all, we worship thee.

Eternal God, our Father, we draw near once more in awe and reverence to worship thee.

Almighty God, whose heights are higher than our thoughts can climb, whose depths are deeper than our plummets sound, we worship thee.

O God, who wast, and art, and art to come, before whose face the generations rise and pass away, we worship thee.

Spirit of the living God, discover us today. Come through the tangled pathways, grown with weed and thicket, that have kept us from Thee. We cannot reach to Thee; reach Thou to us, that some soul who came here barren of Thy grace may go out singing, O God, Thou art my God!

Eternal God, who art the hope of the ends of the earth, we worship thee. Thou art very great. The heaven of heavens cannot contain thee, much less these temples which our hands have builded. As high as the heaven is above the earth, so are thy thoughts higher than our thoughts and thy ways than our ways. May we not belittle thee by our worship, but do thou enlarge us.

III

The eleven o'clock Sunday morning preaching service quite naturally drew the largest numbers of worshippers. The fact that the congregation arrived early and eager, the fact that latecomers could not nonchalantly assume to find an empty seat waiting for them, generated an electric atmosphere that sparked the morale of clergy and laity alike. To be sure unlike the First Presbyterian Church and Park Avenue Church days, rarely were crowds turned away, save perhaps on Easter when not even the opening of the chapel, assembly room, gymnasium, and ninth-floor meeting room could accommodate more than the absolute capacity of 4050. But if "Standing Room Only" was not the rule, nevertheless, for the sixteen years of Fosdick's ministry, Sunday morning attendance averaged 2300 persons, only slightly short of the main sanctuary's 2480 capacity. Especially gratifying was the fact that the summer months saw only a slight falling off. Fosdick's concern for Columbia University summer students led him to preach five or six sermons during July and early August.

Several studies conducted by the church suggest that on any given Sunday probably not more than a thousand of the worshippers were Riverside members; that is, perhaps 60 percent were visitors.* Members were issued admission cards and front sections of the nave were reserved for them. Visitors were either seated immediately in the galleries and rear of the nave or were asked to wait in the chapel until just prior to the service when any unoccupied pews on the main floor were opened to them. A member who perchance arrived late was expected to go up to a gallery, which was exactly what Rockefeller quietly did on occasion. Naturally some visitors were irritated by this seating arrangement. On being asked by an usher to show his ticket, one visitor, Millar Burrows, reported: "I was so stunned that I couldn't recover anything like the spirit of worship through the whole first part of the service. Then Fosdick began to preach, and O man!—nuff sed." Another wryly wrote Fosdick: "I *heard* you preach just once at Riverside. The usher placed me behind a pillar so I could not see you. I planned to expend a bit of my wrath on that usher after the service but he was so tall and muscular." Fosdick defended the card system, for if all reservations for the members were disregarded, long before the service began they would be "either pushed to the side-lines or crowded out altogether, much to their displeasure," as sometimes happened in the summer when the system was suspended.

Painstaking care was given to every mechanical and aesthetic aspect of the service. Experts attended to the microphones, earphones, amplifiers, and loudspeakers. Others attended to ventilation and heating. A doctor was invariably on hand. The Board of Ushers, one hundred strong, termed by Fosdick his Guard of Honor—whose duties included a protective one, for there was always the fear of his being attacked by a demented soul—wore the uniform of respectable Protestantism: cutaway, striped gray trousers, wing collars, black-and-white ties, gray gloves, spats, and carnation in lapel. The choir and ministers were of course gowned, Fosdick believing: " I am sure a gown is the most modest of all ways in which a man can appear in the pulpit. The real purpose of a

* The "visitors"—that is, nonmembers—in many cases might have been regular worshippers, not simply one-time sermon tasters.

gown is not decorative, but to hide the man in his functions." Fosdick's
Baptist forebears might well have discerned a hint of liturgical vanity in
all this fastidious attention to detail. A service of formal beauty, Fosdick
would have replied, heightened the drama of man's encounter with God;
it was not a matter of pretty dramatics.

As all ministers must be, Fosdick was intensely concerned with the
place of music in the morning worship service. After the carillon prelude
by Kamiel Lefévere, this element of the liturgy became the responsibility
of the organist and choir director, Harold Vincent Milligan, and then in
1940 his successor, Frederick Kinsley. On the twentieth anniversary of
Milligan's association with the Park Avenue/Riverside fellowship (a
celebration involving the choirs of eight churches and a handsome tribute
by Walter Damrosch), Fosdick observed that "adoration" found little
place in Protestant worship. "And the people need it. There is that
within us which looks not down nor out but up, which craves the beautiful expression of reverence and admiration and worship and adulation,
and in this church Dr. Milligan has helped us all to adore the living
God." And he did so, Fosdick continued, without ever using "music
ostentatiously, as though it were something in itself to be shown off—
always as a ministry to worship." Fosdick and Milligan (and then Kinsley) labored together to integrate music into the worship mood of confession and contrition, affirmation and adoration, Fosdick not infrequently
seating himself quietly in the rear of the sanctuary to enjoy the choir's
Saturday afternoon rehearsals. The choir, fifty strong, garbed in cas-
socks, cottas, and caps, included artists of national reputation and also
each year a certain number of selected Juilliard students.

Milligan enjoyed international recognition as musician, composer, and
scholar. Fosdick was the author of four hymns. Riverside's nave and
chapel organs, erected under Milligan's supervision, were costly. The
church's acoustics were splendid. The choir was large, skilled, and its
soloists outstanding. The congregational voices—the true choir—numbered several thousand. Many are the tributes to the musical dimension
of Riverside's morning worship service. And it may be true that as Fosdick moved toward a more liturgical service, the music became increasingly majestic, antisentimental, objective, and "universal." Still, questions
arise. Why did the most frequently sung hymns continue to be the
familiar "How Firm a Foundation," "Faith of Our Fathers," and "God of
Our Fathers"? Why was such an uninspired hymnal as H. Augustine
Smith's *Hymns for the Living Age* employed? Why did the *New York
Times* report that Fosdick's favorite anthems were "Hark my Soul!
Angelic Songs Are Swelling" and "Ho, E'vry One that Thirstest, Come
ye to the Waters"? Why did "A British Pilgrim" report in an American

Episcopalian magazine that he found Riverside's standard of hymn and anthem low: ". . . the high-water mark was Stainer—but it was water. The general congregational musical atmosphere was what one might describe as sol-fa and Rolls-Royce."*

However tentative the judgment must be on the service's element of hymn and anthem, no such ambiguity surrounds the high moment when came the call, "Let us pray." Worshippers in Riverside remembered Fosdick's prayers with an intensity of gratitude exceeding perhaps even that felt for his sermons. When finally in 1959 he published for the first time a book containing fifty-six general prayers offered in behalf of the congregation, eighteen prayers that center on special occasions or particular days in the Christian year, and thirteen litanies of praise and petition, his successor, McCracken, stated that "A great part of the secret that drew worshippers in throngs to The Riverside Church year after year is here uncovered." Fosdick considered the pastoral prayer the weakest place in Protestant church worship, too often the prayers being casual, vague, narrowly self-centered, jumbled, and banal. "No wonder that prayer time is often put to somnolent use!" When the nonliturgical churches decided to dispense with officially recognized forms of public prayer and to trust the individual ministers with the responsibility of formulating their own prayers, they took a fateful step. This sacred, soul-searching task called for "deep and sympathetic insight into human need, for sensitive awareness of both individual and social problems, and for faith in God's grace and mercy; and it demands dedicated and careful preparation as much as does the preaching of a sermon." Fosdick gave consent to the publication of these prayers only with "hesitation and misgiving," explaining that his long resistance stemmed from the knowledge of the perils that beset the public prayer and the pitfalls so often trapping his own feet.

Despite the pitfalls, Fosdick's feet were in fact not often trapped. His public prayers, averaging from five hundred and six hundred words, are marked by intensity, well-ordered structure, and clarity and dignity of language. They are also characterized by concreteness, eschewing the vague and confused generalities that are the death of the public prayer. They riveted the attention of the worshippers; further, although they have the communal quality that prayers offered on behalf of a congregation must have, the individual in the particular pew is always present in them. The prayers deal with needs that are both personal and social. The individual's struggles of the soul are remembered—one's fears, one's anxieties, one's doubts, one's prejudices, one's trivialities, one's baser

* The visitor went on to praise Fosdick's prayer and sermon, the sermon being "quite the most memorable sermon I have ever listened to."

nature, one's prospect of death—at the same time the prayers lift up to God the associated needs of the world—its need of peace, of justice, of brotherhood. Consistent with his theology, Fosdick's prayers are suffused with the sense of divine resources and, therefore, of human possibilities:

> Eternal God, Thou Light that dost not fail, we worship Thee. We seek Thee not because by our seeking we can find Thee, but because long since Thou hast sought us. We do not seek the sun but open ourselves to its light and warmth when it arises. We do not seek the fresh air of heaven, but open our windows and, lo, it blows through. So may our hearts be responsive to Thy coming and receptive of Thy presence.

Sunday after Sunday Fosdick carried up to God the prayers of the Riverside worshippers, but he also commended to them the practice of daily prayer, for each person must pray for himself, "Spirit of God, descend upon my heart," and "there can be no proxies." *The Meaning of Prayer*, published in 1915 and termed by Fosdick his most influential book, remained his fullest statement on the subject. In this little volume he begins by observing that prayer is the most universal of all experiences. Such is its naturalness, men always have prayed and always will pray. In some form or other, it is found everywhere, in all ages and among all peoples. But if prayer be merely a tendency and, therefore, spasmodic, occasional, undisciplined, it becomes simply a selfish fitful demand to be extricated from a tight situation.

Fosdick then gives his understanding of prayer as communion with God. The great gift that comes in prayer is God himself—other things are incidental. Prayer is a privilege and the man who misses the deep meanings of prayer has not so much refused an obligation; he has robbed himself of life's supreme privilege—friendship with God. This understanding solves the false dilemma created when prayer is viewed either as a childish begging things from God or as spiritual gymnastics—what Horace Bushnell called "mere dumb-bell exercise!"

Fosdick continues by expounding the conviction that God cares for individuals: "A God who does not care, does not count." How can this be in light of the vast immensity of the universe? Admittedly the imagination staggers. But the Gospel affirms that the soul of each forced laborer on the Amazon is of more value than all the mines of Johannesburg, all the diamonds of Kimberley, all the millions of all the magnates of America. It affirms that in God's sight all the suns and stars that people infinite space are of inferior worth to one human soul, dwelling, it may be, in the degraded body of some victim of drink or lust. Prayer seen in light of this Christian truth becomes at once the claiming of our sonship, the appropriation of our heritage.

Chapter 4 of The Meaning of Prayer argues that prayer is not a way of getting God to do our will, but rather the means to opening our lives to God so that God can do what He wants to do. Therefore true prayer consists not chiefly of our talking but of our listening.*

Fosdick is fully cognizant of the difficulties and costs of prayer and these he discusses in Chapter 5. In "Prayer and the Reign of Law," Chapter 6, Fosdick's position is that although there are no good prayers that God *cannot* answer, there are many prayers God *must not* answer. The problem of unanswered prayer on reflection is really a problem of misunderstanding. All true prayer receives some kind of answer. The answer may be "No," because we ask in ignorance. The answer may be "Wait," because we are not ready to receive the good we ask. God may deny the form of the petition in order that He may grant its substance, as when we pray for a *thing* and God gives us a *chance*. Finally, even when God cannot answer affirmatively the man's petition, He can answer the man. If the circumstances cannot be changed—the cup not passed—God always stands ready to supply the needed faith, wisdom, courage.

Fosdick continues with the thought that prayer is life's hunger and thirst; it comes out of our deep needs and it cries for the things we want. Our prayers are often unreal because they do not represent what in our inward hearts we sincerely crave. Insincerity is one of the most notable causes of failure in praying. For example, we entreat God to save us from sin in general, but we do not want the answer enough to burn the bridges across which specific sins continually come. If real, our prayers are often dangerous because the heart's dominant desire may be bad, as when the prodigal in Jesus' parable said, "Father, give me the portion of thy substance that falleth to me." And just because no man can escape the prayer of dominant desire, the inevitable measurement of his life are the heights or depths of his prayers.

The penultimate chapter discusses prayer as an inner battlefield: "Prayer is a fight for the power to see and the courage to do the will of God. No man's life can altogether lack that struggle, if he is to achieve dependable integrity that cannot be bought or scared. The best guaranty of a character that is not for sale is this battlefield of prayer, where day by day the issue is settled that we shall live 'not as pleasing men, but God who proveth our hearts.' "

The volume's final concern is unselfishness in prayer, and here Fosdick makes two central points. First, a man can pray unselfishly for himself,

---

* As he wrote elsewhere: "Without prayer there are some things God cannot say to us, for prayer is the listening ear. Without prayer, there are some things God cannot give to us, for prayer is the hospitable heart. Without prayer, there are some things God cannot do through us, for prayer is the cooperative will."

for no man yet bore all the consequences of his own sin; a man may rightly pray to be released from the bondage of sin for the sake of the commonwealth and the Kingdom. Second, praying for others follows naturally from God's love for all men and from the need of all men to live in relation with others. Because God's purposes include all men, intercessory prayer becomes the means of casting one's lot with God's eternal and righteous purposes.

From time to time Fosdick had further words to say concerning prayer. In none of these places, however, does he go much beyond the thoughts expressed in the earlier volume. Taken collectively his writings on prayer express a passionate belief in both the necessity and power of prayer. Man's dependence on a merciful God is beautifully affirmed. As in all his apologetic thinking, Fosdick's controlling concern is the experiential, empirical consequences of the prayer experience: "prayer as power"; "prayer as interior relaxation and serenity"; "prayer as spiritual companionship"; "prayer as dominant desire"; "prayer as an interior battlefield in which character is forged." Muted, though not entirely absent, is the understanding of prayer as repentance, confession, contrition. Fosdick's doctrine of man made impossible any emphasis on the profound humility of man's moral estate; his doctrine of God insists on the continuity between God and man everywhere.

Furthermore, Fosdick subscribed to a concept of natural law operating in an evolutionary framework that made it, virtually, impossible for God to intervene directly in His World. His distinction between what God *cannot* do and *must not* do is unconvincing. Such a limitation of God's freedom does not square with the Living God of the Scriptures: "Behold, the Lord's hand is not shortened, that it cannot save; neither his ear heavy that he cannot hear" (Isaiah 59:1). A single illustration of Fosdick's rejection of all supernaturalism, which concurrently reveals a certain nonchalance concerning the desperation of men in intense travail, is found in a widely quoted statement made in 1930, though in fact the same view was expressed earlier and later. "The crude, obsolete supernaturalism which prays for rain," he charged, "is a standing reproach to our religion . . . disastrous to true religion." Such prayers are "ignorant travesties" of true prayer. Well, why should not Christians pray to God to bring moisture to a parched land? Why must God not break through to answer the anguished prayer? One bitter correspondent described the conditions endured by hundreds of thousands of poor drought-sufferers and then asked, "How could even a seven-year, Egyptian famine affect a high-salaried minister in a six-million-dollar skyscraper cathedral in opulent New York, with the Rockefeller fortune back of it? It has made little difference to Dr. Harry Emerson Fosdick whether it rained or not. . . . Suppose you were younger, Doctor—say by about fifteen years, when your daughters were small—living in the Shenandoah Valley on a little farm, your apple crop a failure, brooks bone-dry, credit gone, and your girls hungry; and even suppose you entertained the same theories you do now—don't you think physical distress might cause you to forget your sophistication, and that almost unconsciously, oppressed by your childrens' wants, you might drift into the country church and find yourself joining silently with others in prayer for a little rain? 'Ignorant travesty!' " Even as Fosdick was writing his disquisitions on prayer, a rural Southern preacher was offering up the authentic petition:

> Lord, send us rain. The ground is dry and hot and burns the bare feet walking over it. The tobacco leaves next to it are curling up. The cotton plants are wilting in the sun. The corn stalks are already stunted in their growth, the fodder leaves are withering, there won't be anything but nubbins, and Lord thou knowest I hate worse than hell to shuck nubbins. So, Lord, send us rain. Don't send us any flimsy drizzle drazzle. Send us a gully washer and a trash mover.

IV

There are those who hold that the full liturgy of communion and sermon should be the normative liturgy of the Church, Karl Barth once criticizing worship with only the sermon and no Eucharist as "torso liturgy." Such Christians would not have been satisfied with worship in Riverside. Midway in his ministry, when plans for the new church were just unfolding, Fosdick made this vastly revealing reply to a private inquiry:

> With regard to your conception of the sacraments, I fear that I am an alien and outlaw. Baptism is a beautiful ceremony of dedication. The Lord's Supper is a memorial meal kept in remembrance of his matchless sacrifice. But as for me, I am too much of a Quaker at heart to feel any of the high sacramental significance which often seems to me dangerously close to magic that I find among my more Episcopalian brethren. If I had my way, however, I would have a church where all the methods of approaching God should be used by those who find them useful. I would have every form of worship from the sacrament of the Eucharist to a Quaker meeting. All that I can say is that as for me personally, the Quaker meeting would probably mean more than the sacrament of the Eucharist.

Such an incomplete understanding of Holy Communion could only lead to its diminution in Riverside's life of worship, though certainly not to its absolute demise. Its celebration followed an irregular pattern over the years. Some years the communion service was made part of the morning worship service, usually the first Sunday in each month, beginning in October and going through June. During July and August there might be a special service at 8:30 A.M. Other years normally the service was united with the Sunday afternoon service of music and only quarterly at the 11:00 A.M. service, though Fosdick noted that in doing so, it made the "Communion Service . . . even less representative than it usually is of our church membership, and that is poor enough." On Easter Sunday the celebration was in the afternoon. Mark Jones's survey tabulated that nine communion services in the church year 1937–1938 saw an average attendance of only 503. Fosdick's colleague, Norris Tibbits, acknowledged the "small attendance" at the afternoon services. Of course when the Lord's Supper was celebrated as part of the regular morning worship service, the numbers were much greater, 1723, for example, on January 2, 1944.

It is only fair to add that individuals whose memories run back to Fosdick's ministry report that the afternoon communion services, especially, were intensely compelling. Fosdick did not preach; rather, he would stand with hands folded and without Bible or notes recall from memory passages from the Scriptures. These meditations, reported one parishioner, "were out of this world, never showy, always on target and moving, and always appropriate in voice and gesture." Fosdick employed a combination of different records of the institution of the Lord's Supper and "A Litany of the Cross" of his own composition. Prayer was offered before the bread and after the wine,* the worshippers partaking of the elements individually in the pews when they had been passed from Fosdick to the other ministers and in turn to the ushers. At the close the choir sang the "Agnus Dei," followed by the recessional congregational hymn and then the benediction from the ambulatory. No offering whatever was taken. Perhaps it is fair to say that the service of Holy Communion as celebrated in Riverside was superior to Fosdick's memorial theory about it.

On Sunday afternoons when communion was not celebrated, the worship service consisted entirely of music, no spoken word being uttered except the benediction. At this service, Fosdick explained, "We do not talk about religion; we sing about it." The people of Riverside clearly found these afternoons of worship compelling. The service drew between 16,275 and 38,535 individuals annually. Of course, the Ministry of Music included many other aspects. Special programs were presented

---

* Of course, the element was actually grape juice.

during the Christmas season and Holy Week involving such guests as opera singers, Grace Moore and Lawrence Tibbett, and violinist Albert Spalding. The choir sang several great choral works each year. The Riverside Church Symphony Orchestra performed. Organists of international renown gave concerts on the magnificent Aeolian-Skinner organ.

V

As the construction of Riverside drew to completion, a group of Quakers, with no church home of their own on Morningside Heights, wondered if it might be possible for them to hold an hour of worship in Riverside each First-Day to be conducted after the manner of Friends. Fosdick naturally urged the Board of Deacons to extend an invitation to do so, making clear that Riverside "would have no organizational relationship or official association directly or indirectly with the Society of Friends as such." The deed was done and a growing group of Friends met in silence on the fifteenth floor of the tower to engage in what they revealingly call "the work of worship." Sixteen years passed and on the eve of Fosdick's retirement he responded to a letter of appreciation with the words: "You know with what cordial regard I think of the Friends' Meeting at The Riverside Church, and how definitely I feel myself aligned with the sort of principles for which the Friends stand."

VI

Wednesday evenings were set aside for "serious study," as Fosdick phrased it, for the people of Riverside and the community, and these occasions were an extraordinary element in the church's ministry of worship.* Large numbers gathered to hear speakers, such as Reinhold Niebuhr, Rufus Jones, Norman Thomas, Michael Pupin. "A more keenly alive and responsive congregation I seldom, if ever, have seen," Fosdick said in importuning a guest speaker. However, it was Fosdick's presence that drew crowds numbering twelve hundred, overflowing the Assembly Hall, filling the chapel and areas of the nave. Regularly, in the fall and again in the spring Fosdick would give a series of lectures, ranging from five to nine in number, on a particular subject. It was common knowledge that when he was working on a book, the lectures in a series would

---

* One Wednesday evening a month, however, was a distinctly devotional meeting in preparation for the Lord's Supper the following Sunday.

develop chapter themes he had blocked out. After a lecture he would field questions from the congregation; they were valued clues for his exposition in the book to come. Testimony is unanimous, coming from Union professors and students and Columbia professors and students as well as from less technically informed individuals, that Fosdick's performance both as speaker and respondent to questions was enormously impressive.

VII

These larger elements of the Ministry of Worship did not end the matter for the people of Riverside. Drama was regularly used as a medium of worship and an important volume on the subject emanated from the Riverside leaders. The Riverside Guild, a group of young people, four hundred strong, faithfully included worship services in their activities. As did the various grades of the Church School. And also the Men's Class and the Women's Society and the Women's Bible Class. Even Fosdick's Sunday afternoon radio sermons brought together in the chapel a devoted following unable to attend the morning service.

Under Fosdick's shepherding at least some of the large Riverside flock experienced—or were given the occasion and setting to experience—the "holy anxiety" of worship.

Chapter Fourteen

"The God That Answereth by Christian Education, by Friendly Fellowship, by Community Service, by Money Given to Good Causes, Here and Around the World, Let Him Be God": The Riverside Church Enterprise

I

Among Peter De Vries's most memorable creations is the Reverend Mackerel of the People's Liberal Church: "the first split-level church in America," with an auditorium, gymnasium, kitchen, psychiatric clinic, and "a small worship area at one end." As an urban institutional church Riverside possessed all of the activities rooms of the People's Liberal Church and many more as well, but as we have seen Fosdick could say, as the Reverend Mackerel could not, "at the center of the church's life we have maintained the adoration of God and the proclamation of the Gospel." Among John Updike's most memorable creations is the Reverend Tom Marshfield whose weekday visits to deserted churches bore for him "the same relation to God that billboards did to Coca-Cola: they promoted thirst without quenching it." Had the Reverend Marshfield visited The Riverside Church and witnessed daily perhaps two thousand adults and children eating together, playing together, studying together, discussing together, laboring together for humanity's weal as well as worshiping together, he might have found that the Lord was present too. The weekday activity taking place in Riverside was an extension of the action of worship in which Christ was exalted and then met among his people.

II

Large as Riverside's membership was, it was Fosdick's determination that it be "an intimate companionship with friends" where "the personal fel-

lowship of a country congregation is made possible in a city church."
He explained, "The more numbers come to us, the more important it is
to keep individual persons central in our thought." A "church's bigness
means nothing unless it bears fruit in transformed and dedicated individuals." At the onset of the experiment the people of Riverside declared
their intent "to preserve an intimacy of fellowship in a large institution,
so that none need feel the loneliness of a crowd." For Fosdick, the "communion of saints" meant not only the historical and mystical fellowship,
but something vital and human, a fellowship in which people knew each
other and helped each other in matters both spiritual and temporal. Fosdick called on his people so to demonstrate their care and concern for one
another that it might again be said as it was said in the first century, "Behold how these Christians love one another."

Appropriate to Riverside's character, the church school from the onset
was experimental, bold, and controversial. It attracted the admiring attention of religious educators across the country, although a few critics
charged that the religious "education" gained by the children was dangerously drained of normative content, with John Dewey edging out
John the Baptist. The anticipated enrollment of a couple of hundred
swelled to almost eight hundred, thanks in part to the fact that the Religious Education Center of Palisades, New Jersey, and the Union Seminary School of Religion, probably the outstanding experimental and
demonstration center in the field of religious education, melded their
enterprises with Riverside's.

Innovative and "free" in the sense that no standardized curriculum
was slavishly followed, the school was in no sense a casual operation,
the supervisors and teachers, respectively, putting in twenty-five and
eight hours weekly, on the average. C. Ivar Hellstrom worked carefully
with such supervisors as the famed progressive educator Sophia Lyon
Fahs and a corps of paid teachers who either were, or had been, school
teachers and a band of volunteer assistants drawn from individuals
working in education at Union and Teachers College. A vital element
was the Parents' Fellowship, especially as many of the parents were not
Riverside worshippers, although in time many became church members
precisely because of their children. The Parents' Fellowship involved the
parents far more frequently and closely than the traditional annual or
semiannual parent-teacher meetings; indeed Hellstrom and his associates
provided wise family counseling in matters emotional and physical as
well as religious. Such was the enthusiasm among the teenagers, they
insisted that their classes meet on Friday evenings as well as Sunday
mornings. Summing up on his retirement, Fosdick said:

Certainly, I am strongly impressed with the work our Church School is doing—with the extraordinary quality of the worship services the children themselves conduct; with the vital relationships maintained between the School and the children's families through the Parents' classes; with the stimulating result of the School's influence on the boys and girls as it appears in the Communicants' Classes in which it has been my privilege each year to share; with the loyalty to the church which the School's graduates show, returning from college year after year to the alumni gathering at Christmas time; with the seriousness of such boys and girls from the School as sometimes consult me about their life vocations, some choosing the Christian ministry.

A youngster raised in Riverside worshipped, studied, served. He also played. In the church his body was exercised, mind quickened, morale lifted—his hunger for sheer fun fulfilled. If artistically talented, a youth was afforded the opportunity to compose, sing in a choir, play in an orchestra, or write, direct, or act in a play. For the athletes, there were a range of facilities and teams. Riverside broke with evangelical Protestantism's dreary legalism by permitting dancing. Fosdick once sharply replied to a cleric critical of Riverside's relaxation of the old prohibitions: "What troubles me is that Christian churches should waste their time on such trivialities as trying to keep people from dances, movies, card playing and Sunday sports as though they were the great sins of the world. It is this sickening and ridiculous triviality of Christian churches that is one of the greatest barricades to the progress of a serious Christianity in the world. Such matters are not even matters of morals primarily, but of good sense, of keeping a balance in one's schedule. To be sure, all of them—dancing, Sunday sports, movies, and card playing—can degenerate into real and dangerous evils in a community, but the cure of that is not to try to eliminate them, but to elevate them, and put them back into normal and healthy use." Fosdick understood that for youngsters to drink cokes and dance in the parish house was in modern America about the only alternative to their drinking from flasks in a parked and darkened car. He was aware of New York's allures and, therefore, permitted on New Year's Eve dancing to continue, after the Watch Night Service, until 2 A.M.*

---

* Riverside was not a Gothic-style country club. On New Year's Eve 1945, five hundred young people remained in the church to dance, but only after having joined with over one thousand other individuals in the worship service. Fosdick gave two reasons why card playing was not permitted in the parish house: "First, that card playing can be done in the home, and we need our church facilities for those things that require space and cannot so easily be taken care of in the home. Moreover, the long experience of institutional churches has been that card playing

The Riverside Guild, also under the mentorship of Dr. Hellstrom, was a fellowship of college and postcollege-age youths. From a nucleus of ninety young people coming from the Park Avenue congregation, the group quickly soared to over five hundred. It was a benediction to the young unmarried adults of the community, many coming from the "sticks" and from foreign lands and finding New York as cold and lonely as the far side of the moon. Precisely because the guild was open to non-members of Riverside, it became for many an avenue to church affiliation. The group sponsored some thirty-six activities, happily blending high jinks with high purpose, for although some of the activities were social and avocational, others served New York's orphans and aged, derelicts and immigrants. And as Fosdick desired, a service of worship was at the center of the regular Sunday evening gatherings.

Younger married couples found companionship in the Epicures—a group getting together one Saturday night a month, on occasional Friday evenings for such activities as bowling, and in the summer, outings to the beach and mountains that included the children. Of course, the venerable organizations, the Women's Bible Class, the Women's Society, the Men's Class, continued to be the backbone of Riverside's fellowship structure and the fellowship home of the maturer members.

Hellstrom and Carder (and Carder's successor Tibbetts) officiated at their share of marriages, but in his long lifetime Fosdick performed thousands; indeed such was his hold on the young people in Riverside that numbers of them, particularly the women, would not consider being married by anyone other than him, and more than one wedding date was set in consultation with his crowded schedule. The form Fosdick followed combined elements from the Episcopalian and Congregational services together with his own contributions. If the bride and groom desired an exchange of rings or no ring at all or other modifications, he honored their wishes. Fosdick's form did not require the bride to promise "to obey." As he explained, "Everybody knows you would not keep the promise, if you made it, so why make it?" The form included the prayer:

O Eternal God, Creator and Preserver of all mankind, Giver of all spiritual grace, the Author of everlasting life, send Thy blessing upon these Thy servants, this man and this woman, whom we bless in Thy name, that they, living faithfully together, may surely perform and keep the vow and covenant betwixt them made, and may ever remain in perfect love and

is not a good social fellowship recreation. There is more quarreling over card playing than any other one thing. It segregates people and does not mix them up. In a word, it does not do the thing that we want to do, which is to encourage fellowship instead of cliques."

peace together, and live according to Thy laws through Jesus Christ our Lord. Amen.

Fosdick did have one inflexible rule: he would not marry young people he did not know or whom he had not counseled. Characteristically, the marriage fee was returned to the couple as his wedding gift.

When death came to a member of the Riverside flock, Fosdick's response was akin to Goldsmith's portrait of a shepherd: "But in his duty prompt at every call, / He watched and wept and prayed and felt for all." The thousands of services he conducted were simple yet stately; the spirit one of thanksgiving and triumph, revealing of his faith in the Risen Lord. The committal at the grave was a drastically simplified form of that found in the *Book of Common Prayer* (for which he expressed "profound distaste"):

> Forasmuch as it hath pleased Almighty God to take unto himself the soul of the departed (or our friend, or this child), we therefore commit his body to the ground, earth to earth, ashes to ashes, dust to dust, and his soul to God who gave it, in the assurance of faith believing that which is written: "Blessed are the dead that die in the Lord."

To keep the ministers informed of illnesses and deaths, births and divorces, promotions and firings, everything of that sort, the Riverside membership was divided into geographic zones under zone leaders—in many cases husband and wife. Not many individuals in need of pastoral help were lost in the crowd. For its part, the church kept the parishioners alerted to its varied activities by the sustained mailing of printed matter. "If you don't find anything else in your mailbox," said a student, "you can count on something from Riverside. And it's always attractive."

III

Although The Riverside Church was in truth for many an island of worship and social companionship in the sea of humanity of New York's Upper West Side, it was for many also a springboard into that sea for Christian service. On a thousand instances Fosdick voiced the conviction that the life of Riverside should not be divorced from the life of the community, that the church not become an exclusive religious club bent on its own selfish enjoyment. The Christian congregation, like the individual follower of Christ, is under a commission to serve others, and for a church to seek purity in isolation from a corrupt and corrupting society would be to pay the high price of irrelevance. "Our building," he commanded, "must be used to the utmost; it is wicked to have it otherwise." In one of his last sermons he reminded the Riverside flock:

> Once a week we preach here, but seven days and nights a week we are at work here, in practical service. Recall that ringing slogan of Charles Spurgeon's: "The God that answereth by orphanages, let him be God!" We have tried here to illustrate that. The God that answereth by boys' clubs and girls' clubs, by playgrounds for children, by day nurseries and consultation on family problems—let him be God! The God that answereth by practical help to folk in trouble, by finding jobs for the unemployed, by psychiatric assistance for those inwardly distraught—let him be God! The God that answereth by Christian education, by friendly fellowship, by community service, by money given causes, here and around the world, let him be God.

At the beginning of their adventure the people of Riverside declared that no human service that lies within the church's power to render the community is alien to it. At the conclusion of his ministry Fosdick gave his measured judgment: "Riverside Church . . . is what it is, both in fact and in reputation, in no small measure because it renders so much service with no regard to any return. In our appraisal of our program, it is important, even from the standpoint of our own long-range self-interest, that we use as our criterion the value of our various activities in terms of their vital Christian usefulness to all sorts and conditions of men, women, and children."

Riverside did not so much impose a prearranged program on the community as ask the community what it wanted from it. One area of the program after another came into being not because it was planned with foresight, but because the community, organizing itself under the church's roof, created it. A weekday nursery and kindergarten was a godsend to working mothers and student mothers who were not necessarily Riverside members. A vacation school happily filled the summer hours of youngsters locked in the city. An Arts and Crafts Department originally designed for Riverside children, was extended during the stress of the Depression to adults, and came to offer twenty-one courses, ranging alphabetically from bookbinding to weaving. Business and professional women banded together to form a club and Riverside soon housed a flourishing society numbering over four hundred members. The Riverside Symphony Orchestra was self-created by people in the church and community under the uncompensated conductorship of a Columbia music professor. The Uptown Y.M.C.A., lacking adequate facilities, was cordially given permission to use the church's gym, and so poor youngsters were enabled to play basketball in wretched weather. An organization for foreign students came into existence. A Department of Social Service, funded in 1932 and headed by a professional, succored hundreds of needy families and found jobs for several thousand unemployed, eliciting from Frances Perkins, then Commissioner of Labor of New York, the praise, "From my point of view it is a really significant experiment, and as far as I know, a unique one." Further, over the years scores of community groups utilized, at no cost to themselves, the church's meeting facilities, including perhaps one of its ten kitchens. Clearly Fosdick was convinced that the place for the local church to *start* ministering to others was the local community. Riverside's benevolences included such proximate organizations as the Manhattanville Day Nursery and Saint Luke's Hospital as well as many others, ranging from Harlem to the Bowery.

IV

Although fully ministering to New York City, the members of Riverside recalled that their Lord commanded that they be His witnesses not just in the city of the Temple, Jerusalem, but in all Judea and in Samaria and unto the uttermost parts of the earth. Consequently, the church's benevolence dollars helped sustain such distant domestic causes as an Indian college in Oklahoma and a migrant workers' program in the South.

Regarding foreign missions, Fosdick found the good and the evil, the wise and the unwise, so intermingled that it was exceedingly difficult to sort them out. Nevertheless, he drew a distinction between missions as proselytism and missions as service. "Concerning the first," he judged, "I have grave doubts and misgivings. To share our best ideas of life with others is natural and right; but proselytism, as the missionaries have too often conceived it, starting with dogmatic assurance that we alone are custodians of truth and that the only hope for the victim of our propaganda is to agree with us and be converted to our point of view, is in theory and practice, I think, false and dangerous. Missions, as service, however, I am enthusiastic about—whether in New York, Tokyo or Bombay, and in educational institutions such as the Near East Colleges and medical institutions such as I have seen in China I am deeply interested." He argued for better rather than more missionaries and for the raising up of home-church leaders.

When Fosdick first teamed up with the Park Avenue Baptist Church, as much was given to benevolences as to church support; but on moving to Riverside, this was no longer possible, for as he explained, "much of our local budget is in itself benevolence." And so the ratio between benevolences and church support became about 30 percent to 70 percent.

Initially, also, missionary giving was channeled through the boards of
the Northern Baptist Convention, but in 1934 Riverside discontinued this
historic practice. In the future the church would support causes and types
of work individually investigated and vouched for by a Riverside committee, the controlling criterion of choice being "the quality of its contribution to the Kingdom of God on earth, rather than its denominational
affiliation."* The result was an imaginative annual selection of causes
around the world.

* At this time John D. Rockefeller, Jr., acting on his own convictions but with
Fosdick's advice and support, terminated his personal annual gift to the Unified
Budget of the Northern Baptist Convention.

Chapter Fifteen

"On Being a Real Person": A Protestant Preacher as Confessor and Counselor

I

"I am commonly thought of as a preacher, but I should not put preaching central in my ministry. Personal counseling has been central." Fosdick gave this surprising assessment in his autobiography and also on many other occasions. A pastoral letter informed his congregation that in times of special need his study door was open to them for personal consultation. "I would rather help individuals than preach sermons," he assured the flock. "Were I not a minister," he once reported, "I should probably be a psychiatrist." Summarizing his Riverside years, he placed counseling "at the center of my ministry" and judged that activity of "vital importance."

Repeatedly Fosdick asserted, "My preaching at its best has itself been personal counseling on a group scale." Counseling and preaching are "mutually indispensable to each other," he believed, and the preacher "approaches the pulpit as though one were beginning a personal consultation." Later we shall examine Fosdick's theory of preaching more closely, to see whether counseling and preaching are in fact "mutually indispensable" rather than discrete situations and discrete functions inevitably imposing on the minister a kind of schizophrenic condition. We must ask whether Fosdick and others were accurate in assigning to counseling a more central position than preaching in his career. Primary or not, Fosdick's involvement in pastoral counseling and its ancillary concerns was deep, and to these matters we now turn.

Fosdick's interest in pastoral counseling emerged with force only in the 1920s. Here is yet another illustration of his genius for addressing the dominant need of the times. Prior to the Great War his major writings were devotional in character. Then came the emphasis on the reconciliation of science and scholarship and religion as demonstrated in such works as *The Modern Use of the Bible*. As the 1920s gave way to the 1930s and 1940s, the emphasis once again shifted, this time to the counseling of psychologically troubled persons and the writing of such articles as "How to Keep Out of the Psychiatrists' Hands" and such books as *On Being a Real Person*. Not serendipitously these were the years when pastoral counseling by confident, self-conscious, clinically trained individuals seemed about to become the main function of the ministry, eclipsing its other historic tasks. These progressive concerns are not absolutely a matter of chronology and they definitely do not characterize him as a chameleon crossing a patch quilt, but they do again demonstrate the essential correctness of Albert C. Outler's observation that the story of Fosdick's life is the biopsy of an epoch.

II

Early in 1927 Fosdick gave an address before one thousand churchmen gathered for the annual meeting of the Greater New York Federation of Churches in which he observed that Protestantism needed a parallel to the Roman Catholic confessional, saying:

> We modern Protestants fail in some things. Our Roman Catholic brethren in keeping the confessional have pretty nearly wiped us off the stage in one feature of human service. . . . For six years I have conducted—Baptist though I am—what I call a confessional. . . . I have an office where people who know they are spiritually sick and mentally disturbed can come with their problems. Why shouldn't I minister to them? Never again will I be without such a place where people can meet me alone. Week after week I meet nearly as many people as a priest. They are mentally unbalanced—sick souls who need ministration.

Fosdick recalled the "howl" of protest and the "unexpected storm" touched off by the address and the ensuing accusations of his "going over to popery." The *Christian Century* blazed, "Dr. Fosdick Drops a Bomb," and it is certainly true that the religious and secular press featured the story and scores of ministers commented. There is a certain disingenuousness about his remembrance of the event. In 1927 he was much in the public eye, thanks not the least to the astucity of Ivy Lee, and virtually everything he said was given a "play." A less celebrated clergyman might have expressed honest surprise at raising an "unexpected storm," but one suspects that Fosdick anticipated differently, especially in light of his conscious employment of the term "confessional." Why borrow from Roman Catholicism a term freighted for Protestants with emotion when he believed (as he privately wrote) "the whole theory and theology behind the Roman Catholic confessional is as impossible to me as it is to you"? Nor does it appear from scores of commentaries that the charges of "popery" were widespread; therefore, Fosdick's martyred tone is uncalled for.

The great majority of the criticisms focused on two points. First, Fosdick was charged with using the term "confessional" in a popular, loose sense and not as defined and understood in the Catholic sacrament where the penitent surrenders the secrets of his heart to the priest as to an agent of God and in turn is granted absolution for sins. Protestant churches have no such power to require periodic confessions from their members and Protestant ministers have no comparable powers of bestowing satisfaction.* Fosdick was well aware of the differences between pastoral counseling and the Catholic sacrament and by employing the term "confessional" he confused rather than illuminated the point he sought to make, namely, the therapeutic value of confessing one's faults and unburdening one's troubles to another individual, sympathetic and skilled, in the presence of God together.

Second, with equal frequency critics observed that "Dr. Fosdick, as usual, is about five centuries behind the times." Exclaimed one Presbyterian, "I have never heard of any active pastor in a Protestant church doing otherwise than seeking to minister unto sin-sick, sorrow-stricken souls. I am confident that there is not a real pastor anywhere in America who is not daily open for consultation with troubled souls, whether in sin or sorrow or any other problem." Said a Baptist, "Dr. Fosdick hasn't advanced anything new. I think every preacher in the land has heard confessions from his earliest advent into the ministry." Said a Unitarian: "No one who has been pastor of downtown city churches such was mine . . . , but knows the number of people who come to him for various excuses, but really to unburden their minds and souls. . . . I have talked with many ministers of all denominations and I find the quiet hours that I have given to burdened souls have been duplicated by them. . . . Where all this time has Mr. Fosdick been, that he should at this late hour of his ministerial experience call for something which we all know we have already in Protestant as well as Catholic churches?" Fosdick's call for a Protestant confessional may have been "a bomb," as the *Christian Century* stated at the time and Fosdick later remembered,

* However, the injunction to engage in auricular confession was still found in the Protestant Episcopal *Book of Common Prayer* and in most forms of Lutheranism.

but it was a curious one, "as old as the hills," "hoary with age," and "another instance of much ado about nothing," to cite contemporary clerical comments.*

Fosdick's critics, however, were only half correct in characterizing his advice "hoary with age." The Christian ministry of the care of souls is indeed as old as the catacombs. "To view pastoral care in historical perspective," wrote two historians, "is to survey a vast endeavor, to appreciate a noble profession, and to receive a grand tradition." Nevertheless, the thirty or so years preceeding Fosdick's address had seen a movement profoundly reshaping the nature of pastoral counseling, and it was to this genuinely new movement that he sought to alert his audience. The aim remained to heal sometimes, to remedy often, to comfort always those who lived in not-so-quiet desperation, but the methods were being dramatically altered. The counseling process was no longer to be a casual conversation while visiting folks with, perchance, some words of comfort, reassurance, warning, exhortation, or if-I-were-you type of advice. It was not to be confused with the sustained, supportive, and emotionally nourishing relationship a parishioner might have with his parson. As Seward Hiltner not uncharitably observed, the earlier pastors proceeded by art and assiduity, but "even when they did well, they knew not what they did."

The new counseling was characterized by system and structure, that is, conducted within specific time limits and at a discreet and private place; and it was further characterized by inductive analysis and scientific evaluation by clergymen who had completed a program of professional training known as clinical pastoral education. Because of this professional competence the counselor was consciously accepted by the counselee *as* counselor, possessing specific skills as well a more general sympathy.

This emerging pastoral counseling drew on the new body of knowledge going under the various names of psychology, dynamic psychiatry, psychotherapy, psychotherapeutic service, psychoanalysis. Its tutors were the medical and psychiatric systems. In an age of galloping professional-

---

* James C. Colgate, Fosdick's oldest and closest mentor, reported finding this limerick posted at his club:

> When Fosdick starts confessional, it
>   ought to entertain the cuss
> If Jim each week confesses, all the
>   stories he tells us.

Colgate passed this along to Fosdick in the hope that "It will also help you to understand the non-spiritual atmosphere in which I have to live, and make you a little more lenient when I do actually confess."

ization, it was deemed imperative that ministers augment the "art" of sympathetic understanding with the information, procedures, and training of the increasingly prestigious professions.

The new pastoral counseling emerging in the early twentieth century was an integral part of the broader search for efficiency, rationality, and specialization, but it was also clearly grounded in the moral fervor, social gospelism, and social consciousness of the progressive era. Concern for the unfortunate who are broken physically by poverty and prejudice and are found in slums, sweatshops, and prisons was logically extended to the unfortunate who are broken mentally and are found rotting in asylums or living emotionally darkened existences outside of institutional walls. "The crusading psychiatrists were as much Progressives as they were doctors," said one historian of these early pioneers. More astringently, another historian said of them: "The Progressives were consciously motivated by altruism. Direction was to come from the Man of Good Will who had transcended his own interests; he governed by the right of his moral superiority."

To this amalgam of professionalization and altruism in the new pastoral counseling there was added a growing interest in the psychology of religion. Fosdick read the studies by William James, George Albert Coe, Edwin Starbuck, James Pratt, and others and came himself to believe that "religion is increasingly dealt with today not in ecclesiastical or theological but in psychological terms. Increasing numbers of people mean by religion, not first of all a true church or orthodox system of theology, but a psychological experience."

A final element contributing to the new understanding of counseling was a long-standing clerical sense of insecurity about the other professions and the conviction that the ministry must modernize if it was not to ride like Vercingetorix behind Caesar's chariot. The psychology of religion movement, noted E. Brooks Holifield, had itself developed such a functional interpretation of religious experience that therapeutic application seemed to be the next logical step. When it was endlessly repeated that the important consideration of any religious experience was the result it achieved, then it became natural for the psychology of religion to shade into the therapeutic.

So, in the context of much larger movements in psychotherapy and mental health, there developed a new pastoral counseling whose origins went back at least as far as 1906 and the formation by two Boston Episcopal priests, Elwood Worcester and Samuel McComb, of the Emmanuel Mission to make moral and spiritual counseling more "scientific." Two years before Fosdick's 1927 plea, one of his former Union students, Anton T. Boisen, began training a handful of divinity students at the Worcester State Hospital where, supported by Rockefeller funds, he had been studying schizophrenia; in 1926 he published an article entitled "The Challenge to Our Seminaries" with the salient thesis that "in mental disorders we are dealing with a problem which is essentially spiritual" and its plea for the clinical training of pastors. Boisen's subsequent work and writings, especially the epochal *The Exploration of the Inner World: A Study of Mental Disorder and Religious Experience* (1936), entitle him to be regarded as the father of clinical pastoral education. Revealingly, in 1924 Boisen and Fosdick had a talk during which, Boisen recalled, "you graciously told me of your personal acquaintance with the little-known country between mental disorder and religious experience which I have been trying to explore."

By 1930 the clinical movement had gained sufficient momentum to warrant the formation of The Council for the Clinical Training of Theological Students and there followed, in part owing to a split between Boston and New York groups, the birth of such organizations as The Institute for Pastoral Care, The Association for Clinical Pastoral Education, and the Academy of Religion and Mental Health. By 1943 thirteen seminaries had clinical training programs and in less than a decade the number grew to forty-three. Concurrently, there appeared a number of classic texts by Dr. Richard Cabot, Russell Dicks, Carroll Wise, Seward Hiltner, Wayne Oates, and David Roberts—to say nothing of the influence of such individuals as Paul Tillich and Martin Buber. Concurrently, also, there came into existence such journals as *Pastoral Psychology, Journal of Pastoral Care*, and *Journal of Clinical Pastoral Work.*

Quite naturally pastoral counseling was informed by the ideas of individuals (setting aside for the moment such giants as Freud and Jung) outside the ranks of the ministry, such as Rollo May and Carl Rogers.* Rogers's *Counseling and Psychotherapy* (1942) became the Magna Carta of nonmedical psychotherapy, bringing the psychological profession into the business of therapy, thereby breaking the monopoly that medicine and its psychiatric speciality long held. Rogerian therapy was nondirective, client centered, inspirational and pragmatic, and eminently congruent with a dominant mood of American Protestantism; consequently, it "became intensely influential on pastoral counseling" and indeed "exerted an almost normative influence upon pastoral counseling in American Protestant circles."

The emergence of this new pastoral counseling, not surprisingly, found pastors hard-pressed to seek something special that clearly demarcated their office and functions from those of other caretakers, healers, guides, and teachers. How to avoid the total secularization of the pastoral task

---

* Though neither would enter the ministry, it is interesting that both were seminarians at Union during Fosdick's era.

was a real issue. Clergymen wondered whether this new corpus of knowledge could be merely borrowed and applied to the minister's activities in much the same way that a traveling salesman might apply "psychology" to the selling of his wares. Numerous were the warnings to ministers to avoid the temptation to think of themselves as amateur psychiatrists, their church as an observation clinic, and their flock as "queer fish" ripe for diagnosis.

The sought for demarcation between pastoral counseling and secular therapy had both a practical and theological basis. On the practical side, the work of pastoral care cannot absorb the average pastor's waking hours to the total neglect of his liturgical, homiletical, educational, institutional, evangelistic, and community responsibilities. A minister cannot afford to devote himself simply to the few persons in most acute need. Moreover, as the leader of a religious community he sees individuals who would for the most part be considered "normal" by psychopathologists and the issues with which he deals are more varied than those of the average psychiatrist or psychologist.

On the theological side, the pastor, unlike the secular therapist, is a representative Christian person bearing the wisdom, resources, and authority of the Christian faith. Christian counseling, unlike secular therapy, involves the atmosphere of communion that is established between two people who come into the presence of God together. God becomes the third person in the relationship. Not simply a dialogue, but a *tri-alogue* comes into being. Pastoral counseling, in Tillich's definition, "is a helping encounter in the dimension of ultimate concern, using traditional terminology in the religious dimension." He continued: "The power of the New Being of the divine Spirit, which alone makes successful pastoral care possible, transcends the personal existence of the counselor. He does not have to be a great personality or a great theologian or a great minister in order to be successful in his work. For he does not have to mediate himself to the counselee, but to something which is above both of them." No secular therapist would say with Tillich, "saving the person is healing him." No secular therapist would say that his authority comes from the stamp of Christ's character. No secular therapist would say that the client is not really helped until he is reconciled with God or that the client's only hope are the Word and Spirit of God. Christian counseling is concerned with the re-creating of a new life, not just in bringing antithetical drives into harmony or reinstating the "normal."

Of course, these professed aims of Christian counseling strike secular analysts as utopian and dangerous. "I would regard any therapy," asserted one psychiatrist, "that tries to heal by putting us in touch with a transcendent dimension of experience, or some form of universal principle, as more a biotherapy than a psychotherapy." Such longings, he continued in words with which Freud would have concurred, "stem from our earliest narcissistic wishes for perfection via the union with an all-powerful parent."

Fosdick's place in the new pastoral counseling movement is a curious one. He made no major theoretical contributions to it. He neither considered himself, nor was considered by others, to be an expert in the field. Seward Hiltner, who indeed was a leading authority, said of him: "He never did detailed analysis of instances of pastoral relationship with people out of which we have come to feel develop the new and corrective insights of the field. Such work was, he felt, the task of others, and he has dealt with generosity and appreciation with those who have attempted it. We continue to believe that he could have done this, had he set his mind and attention to it. But in that event, he would probably have had to divert himself from those areas in which he remains without peer, the interpretation to the layman of the faith in terms that connect with the realities of experience including the new insights of psychology." This assessment seems accurate. When asked in 1957 by the editor of *Pastoral Psychology* to contribute an article, Fosdick replied he could "neither discover nor by will power create any interest in writing an article on the subject you suggest," adding that "everything that I care to say about it I have just recently said in my autobiography." (Nevertheless, the February 1960 issue of this journal did carry an article by Fosdick entitled, "The Minister and Psychotherapy.") Even his best-selling *On Being a Real Person*, as the introduction openly acknowledges, was "not at all a treatise about personal counseling. I have said little or nothing concerning the techniques of that difficult, delicate art. My thought has been centered not on the counselor but on the people who consult him."

If Fosdick's theoretical contribution to the science of counseling was minimal, at least it can be said that he realized three essential things. First, he understood that respectable people in respectable churches were not immune from the terrors of human existence. "I never yet knew a man who on intimate acquaintance did not turn out to be dealing with handicaps," he observed. And he once informed the affluent Park Avenue Church parishioners that the church's name should be changed to the "Park Avenue Mission Hall." They were among the multitudes whose sobs each evening followed the sunset around the world.* Second, he

---

* Of course, Fosdick was mistaken when he asserted: "Would any physician, psychiatrist, or minister expect to find on Park Avenue or Fifth, on the average, fewer hectic, nervous, unstable lives than on poorer streets? Upon the contrary, nervous prostration is rather a speciality of the prosperous and statistics indicate

comprehended that however many social activities his churches sponsored, the coffee-and-cake-and-smiles routine could not mask interior
hells, and that perhaps this routine, so pleasant on the surface, actually
contributed to the further isolation of persons in despair. Third, he knew
that it was his business to be the shepherd of his flock, even though they
possessed, in many cases, fat pocketbooks and paunches and boasted
Wall Street business addresses and handsome brownstone home addresses. Would denying these coupon-clippers pastoral care, containing
as such care did both the message of grace and the message of judgment,
further the Kingdom of God in, say, Harlem or the South Bronx?

III

While minister of the First Baptist Church, Montclair, Fosdick was a
good shepherd, comforting the sick and dying, consoling the bereaved,
and visiting his flock in their homes where surely on occasion they must
have unburdened their troubled hearts to him. Concerning this early
counseling little is known, though there are hints from his own pen that
he tended to be judgmental, moralistic, and rigid. On coming to the First
Presbyterian Church in New York he announced he would hold formal
consultation hours in his church office, and there began his engagement
in the new pastoral counseling. The first day he found fourteen people
waiting in the anteroom and he had to deal initially, according to his
autobiography, with a "case of homosexuality."* (Rather incredibly,
even for that era, he elsewhere reported that until that day "never
knowingly had I met a homosexual." And this after almost two decades
in the ministry!)

In inviting personal consultation Fosdick immediately found that he
had undertaken more than bargained for, being utterly without formal
training. He possessed more than ordinary good sense, some experience
garnered from his Montclair days, and insights not fully understood
from his own breakdown, but that was about it. Confronted with a case
far beyond his power to diagnose or to treat, in his bewilderment he
turned to Dr. Thomas W. Salmon, then professor of psychiatry at Co-

---

that suicide occurs most frequently among the well-to-do." There has yet to be an
epidemiological survey that does not demonstrate an inverse relationship between
socioeconomic class and mental illness. All studies show that the poor tend to have
more psychopathology. In fairness to Fosdick, it must be added that when he made
this statement the belief was still widely held in the medical profession that
neurasthenia was limited almost exclusively to the wealthy and refined.

* Elsewhere he reported finding fifteen people waiting, the first a "suicidal case."
Once again we are reminded that Fosdick never spoiled a story in the telling of it.

lumbia University and medical director of the National Committee for
Mental Hygiene. The two men had known each other for years, possibly
because Salmon had been in the employ of the Rockefeller Foundation
since 1913 and possibly because Salmon had been associated with Raymond Fosdick during the war where Salmon had served brilliantly as
chief of the Division of Psychiatry of the A.E.F. Salmon was a leading
pioneer in the field of mental health and this gallant, vulnerable, sickly
yet athletic, often impatient but always compassionate man carefully
guided Fosdick, working with him in case after case, explaining diag-
noses and therapies. "I have learned to love him as I have loved and admired few men I have known," said a grateful Fosdick after Salmon's
death in a sailing accident in 1927; and Fosdick in gratitude served as
one of the vice chairmen, together with General Pershing and others, of
the Thomas W. Salmon Memorial Lectures given annually in New
York's Academy of Medicine. Dr. Salmon's untimely death prevented
the fruition of an arrangement to establish a clinic at Riverside Church
where he and Fosdick planned to unite the resources of medical science
and Christian ministry in the care of troubled souls.*

Salmon's ideas about counseling clearly shaped the thinking about
counseling of the technically innocent Fosdick. "He was the family doctor in psychiatry—the general practitioner," judged Salmon's biographer. "He was ingenious and resourceful and shrewd; he was 'common
sense in action.' He liked the use of parables and the telling of stories."
He was undoctrinaire, open-minded, and not tied to any one school of
psychoanalytic thought. Much the same observations could be made of
Fosdick's counseling and one suspects that this common angle of vision
brought the two men together in the first instance.

Certainly Fosdick never considered a partnership with an unreconstructed Freudian; one might as easily imagine a mongoose lying down
with a cobra. In a dozen or so places Fosdick made passing reference,
usually critical and usually uninformed, to Freud and his epigones.
There is no evidence that he read the Viennese giant's works. His library does contain Ernest Jones's biography, but only the first volume is
marked and that but slightly. Fosdick's animus is almost unqualified, unlike that of some Protestant thinkers, David Roberts, Reinhold Niebuhr,
and Paul Tillich for example. In one book Fosdick chided Freud for being "haunted by anxiety about death and the meaninglessness of life," as
if this was all to be said about the great, brave moralist without a moral-

---

* At that time many pastors formed alliances with neurologists, psychologists,
and psychitarists, no alliance being more famous than that between Norman Vincent Peale and Dr. Smiley Blanton and their psychiatric outpatient clinic at Peale's
Marble Collegiate Church in New York.

izing message. In a letter he predicted that "Freud in general and psychoanalysis in particular are on their way out," with psychoanalysis doomed soon to be classed with phrenology. In a volume on psychology he marked one passage, "Insane Freudianism!" In a sermon and the little apologetic book, *Dear Mr. Brown*, he reported this dubious event:

> Some time since a patient came to me in tears after consultation with a Freudian psychiatrist. I know that patient. Like all of the rest of us he has native animal urges, but he also has a fine spiritual life, involving deep reverence for personality in himself and others, and a high faith in God. And that psychiatrist had told him that unless he threw God away, stopped bothering about morals and his spiritual life, and exploded his animal instincts, he could not be happy. One wonders why even a Freudian cannot see that it is dangerous to repress one's best in order to give explosive vent to one's worst.

Perhaps this particular miscreant psychiatrist did give such advice, but if so he would have been disowned by Freud, Fosdick's intimation to the contrary. In a word, Fosdick's mistrust and misunderstanding of Freud was comparable to Freud's own implacable hostility to monotheism (which doubtless in turn shaped Fosdick's judgment of Freud); therefore, it is not surprising that Fosdick could report to a troubled soul: "I have been very careful in my own personal counseling to keep contact with non-Freudian psychiatrists who had a constructive and basically religious approach. The Freudians, it seems to me, are all the time taking people apart, and finding it utterly impossible to put them back together again." In another letter he stated: "Personally, I have always steered away from psychoanalysis, regarding it as undesirable; save as a desperate last resource." In only a "minimal number of instances" did he turn to this last resource. Even his most charitable statements are hedged, as when he observed: "The sane use of psycho-analysis has been of proved value, when not carried to extremes, but there is still a wide field of research to be covered before it is possible to reach down to the roots of human nature and give the preventive treatment which is best and most effective, after all." Although the phrases "sane use" and "not carried to extremes" remain unclarified, some psychiatrists in Fosdick's judgment met these caveats, for he did refer troubled individuals to them and they did undergo psychoanalysis.* And Fosdick himself when asked by his

---

* Frances Eaton, a professional Red Cross worker and then social service worker, found herself troubled by upsetting physical symptoms. She called her cousin, Florence Fosdick, who presently said, "This is something for Harry,'" and immediately an appointment was made. Fosdick then referred Miss Eaton to Dr. Charles Lambert of Columbia-Presbyterian Hospital. She entered into extended and ultimately enormously helpful psychoanalysis. At the conclusion Dr. Lambert refused to present a bill, saying, "I am doing this for Dr. Fosdick."

wife's cousin, "Harry, have you ever considered undergoing psycho-analysis?", gave the surprisingly moderate reply, "Yes, I might have done so but I could never find the time."

And so Fosdick did collaborate with "non-Freudian"* psychiatrists, finding their services "invaluable." On many occasions, however, he counseled individuals to seek further help not from a psychiatrist but from a "wise" neurologist, such as Dr. Edwin G. Zabriskie, head of the Neurological Institute at Columbia-Presbyterian, because, Fosdick explained, "psychiatrists all too frequently do more harm than good in dealing with 'nervous breakdowns.' " Aside from his hostility to Freudian analysis, apparently Fosdick was eclectic in his sanction of therapies, at one time or another giving his approval to such adjuncts of psychotherapy (or such were their original intent) as insulin shock therapy, electroconvulsive treatment, hypnotherapy, and tranquilizing drugs.

Believing as he did about Freudianism in particular and psychoanalysis in general, Fosdick was baffled to find himself the target of Dr. O. Hobart Mowrer's magnum-calibre blasts. Mowrer, a research professor of psychology at the University of Illinois and one-time president of the Amerian Psychological Association, in the late 1940s in a series of papers, articles, and books launched a sweeping attack on psychoanalysis and on the "Babylonian captivity" of pastoral counseling to Freudian and Rogerian methods. To Mowrer the sham of psychoanalysis and the shame of Protestantism's capitulation to it was total—and he said so in vigorous, crusading language:

> We have tried to believe that personality disorder is basically an *illness—mental* illness; but we are now increasingly persuaded that the problem is fundamentally *moral*, that the guilt which is so obviously central in psychopathology is *real* rather than false, and that only a moral attack upon this problem can be successful. We had hoped that an easy solution might be found for personal evil; and we have tried both the doctrine of "cheap grace" (in religion) and the strategy of denying the reality of sin and guilt altogether (in psychoanalysis), but neither has worked. And so today there is a growing readiness to accept the verdict that "therapy," or "salvation," is possible only at a great cost; the cost of self-revelation, deep contrition, and a radically changed way of life.

In pressing his assualt Mowrer identified Fosdick as one of the leading clerical capitulators. "Today," he wrote, "there are literally thousands of ministers who are under the spell of Tillich, Fosdick, and the other

---

* Inasmuch as Freudian insights were inescapable, probably the term "neo-Freudians" is more appropriate, for no theory or practice of analysis could be totally "non-Freudian."

Freudian apologists." Tillich and Fosdick were guilty of trying to "legiti-mize" Freud. Fosdick's *On Being a Real Person* was "one of the earliest and most transparent indications of this victory of the Freudian view." Mowrer repeatedly referred to the "Freud-Fosdick position" and shredded George Anderson's *Man's Right to Be Human*, a volume by the director of the Academy of Religion and Mental Health for which Fosdick wrote a laudatory preface.

At first glance it all seems quite strange. Mowrer denigrated and mis-interpreted Freud, but so did Fosdick. Mowrer believed psychoanalysis to be "not only nontherapeutic but actually pernicious," but, with rare exceptions, so did Fosdick. Mowrer predicted "it will take its place along with phrenology and mesmerism," the identical analogy employed by Fosdick. Mowrer highly praised Alcoholics Anonymous, a group strongly supported by Fosdick. What, then, was it that divided the two men? The answer is found in an exchange of letters in 1959, Mowrer's being espe-cially argumentative and lengthy, one running to eleven closely typed pages. In that year Mowrer sent Fosdick the draft of an article to appear in the *Christian Century*, requesting a critique. "Your opening paragraph seems to me shocking," Fosdick replied, and Mowrer added a second moderating paragraph. The article, though written on the invitation of the magazine editors, "was formally accepted and then mysteriously re-jected" (Mowrer later reported), and it finally appeared in *Foundations*. Perhaps the psychologist held the minister responsible for the rejection, though there is nothing in the record to suggest that Fosdick attempted to block publication. The heart of Fosdick's replies may be found in three statements:

> You disdainfully condemn what seems to me, will all its faults and fail-ures, one of the most important movements in my generation. This dif-ference in evaluation is caused, I think, by the difference in our angles of approach. In my seminary days I never heard a word about personal counseling as a part of a minister's function. I came in contact with the new dynamic psychology and its techniques the hard way, and it has en-riched my usefulness as a minister beyond measure. The teaming up of the minister and the psychiatrist has been an invaluable help to the parish pastor in dealing with all sorts of problems—not psychotic and neurotic alone, but often throwing light on very humdrum, practical perplexities. To this inexpressibly valuable service, which the new alliance has ren-dered, you seem blind. . . .

> Of course there are dangers in this new teaming up of religion and psy-chotherapy. Especially if a minister makes a professional speciality of psychotherapy—in a mental hospital, for example—he can easily be tempted to substitute some therapeutic technique for the redeeming truths

of the gospel and the possibility of being "strengthened with might by God's spirit in the inner man."

Your experience, accepting Freud and then rejecting him, must have been critically influential on all your thinking. You seem to have Freud on your mind all the time. You even say: "Take away psychoanalysis and what do you have left?" I should answer that we have everything left that is most worthwhile in the psycho-therapeutic field. The phrase "dynamic psychiatry" for you is apparently indentical with psychoanalysis. With me it never involved insights, won for us in the psychosomatic field in the last decades, that have nothing to do with psychoanalysis.

Mowrer remained quite unpersuaded, continuing to hold that "you vacillate hopelessly between the Judeo-Christian view that we sicken from sin (aggrieved conscience) and the Freudian view that 'conscience is a prattler' (Michalson's phrase)." Unruffled as was generally his wont, Fosdick calmly reported to Anton T. Boisen that he was having "a friendly controversial correspondence" of great interest with Dr. Mowrer. Although Boisen recently had been publicly critical of Fosdick's doctrine of sin and guilt (in an article in the *Chicago Seminary Register*), Fosdick cordially and characteristically said to him, "You have made an incalculable contribution to the growing cooperation between religion and psychotherapy, and we are all indebted to you beyond the possibility of payment."

Who were those who came to see Fosdick for counseling? Apparently he saw both parishioners and strangers, the mighty and the meek, blacks and whites, "all sorts of people," he reported, "from murderers, crooks, and courtesans up."* Such was his fame that individuals came from off the streets of New York and also from thousands of miles away. One thinks of Ruby Bates, whose perjured testimony of being raped brought the spectre of the death penalty to nine black boys in the infamous Scottsboro case. Miss Bates while in New York, troubled in conscience, visited Fosdick in his study one evening in March 1933, and he urged her to return to Alabama and tell the truth, arranging for her to contact a minister in Birmingham and providing the funds for a warm coat.

Where and when did Fosdick see troubled people? Generally he gave afternoon hours three days a week to counseling in his church study. These sessions were tightly scheduled and appointments were made weeks, even months, in advance. But many individuals, including his

---

* He did not engage in group counseling, now so popular, but he did see couples together, sometimes after an initial session with only one of the spouses, recognizing that the other spouse was part of the problem and, therefore, part of the solution.

daughters and the counselees themselves, report that he also saw people in his apartment in the evening and on a moment's notice if the situation seemed desperate. With close parishioners, he sometimes suggested the problem be discussed over lunch.

How long were the counseling sessions and on how many occasions did Fosdick see the same individual? In the absence of appointment books and case history files,* the answer must be impressionistic. According to some sources, the appointments were limited to fifteen minutes, a woefully inadequate period in the universal judgment of counseling experts. Yet Fosdick reported, "We talked for two hours" in regard to one person; "In two hours he went out a new creature" in regard to another; a "few hours later" in regard to a third; and "he spent two hours with me that day" in regard to a fourth. One individual wrote him recalling "that day in 1932 when I stumbled into your office somewhat of a wreck and came out an hour or so later with the horizons lifted and with a sense of a power available to see me through." Another testified: "The two hours I spent with him were two of the most memorable hours in my life. He was one of the major factors in rescuing me from the depths of depression and I shall never cease to be grateful to him." A third expressed gratitude for the hour Fosdick spent with a family member. And a fourth reminisced: "On both occasions he was open, available, and took as much time as needed." In sum, appointments may have been scheduled to run fifteen minutes, but it is manifest that some sessions ran considerably longer.

As to the number of interviews with a given person, the evidence does not permit a firm answer. Although Fosdick reported helping a young man win his battle with alcoholism after many months, surely such extended counseling was extremely rare. Indeed, one's impression is that one or two or three sessions were normal. Again experts would find this troubling, holding that the pastor does not have a real counseling relationship in a one-interview situation and that two or three interviews would be sufficient only in short-term crisis or situational counseling. At this point, however, it must be remembered that Fosdick had a corps of professionals to whom he could and did refer his people for more extended care.

What actually transpired in the counseling sessions is also conjectural and any description must be stitched together from fragmentary sources. It does appear that Fosdick's counseling, which was, of course, informed by psychology, was just as definitely not clinical. It was characterized by intensity, directness, affirmation, and authority. To be sure, as counselees

---

* If these records once existed, they apparently have been destroyed.

have testified, Fosdick was not harshly judgmental nor was he unsympa-
thetic; individuals did feel what the psychotherapists call "acceptance."
It goes without saying that Fosdick's counseling did not remotely resemble classical psychoanalysis. Neither does it much resemble Rogerian
therapy, with its nondirective, nonconfrontational, passive emphasis. As
Fosdick preached for a decision, so he counseled for a decision. In both
activities the goal was the transformation of human lives; and in both
the Holy Spirit was assumed operative. Quite obviously in his counseling
there was a lot of listening, but also considerable "preaching."

One imagines this scene in the small, simple yet beautifully appointed
study in the Riverside tower: Fosdick, immaculately attired, is poised
erectly in his chair, radiating assurance and authority. The visitor speaks,
Fosdick listens, and then come his words, "It is all right. . . . Yes, that
is so, but let us look at it this way." Finally, perhaps Fosdick kneels in
prayer: "If we confess our sins, he is faithful and just to forgive our sins,
and to cleanse us from all unrighteousness." This scene is not entirely
fanciful. One individual, in thanking Fosdick for the greatest experience
in his entire life, remembered: "When you knelt in a posture that reminded me of the crucifix itself and prayed for me in your office, I was
stricken with conviction as same as Saul of Tarsus when he looked upon
the Christ-like Stephen being showered with stones." Recalled another
individual: "So puissant is Dr. Fosdick's personality, that even fifteen
minutes with him may leave one weak—as if one had been fighting a
hypnotic spell."

Individual after individual has spoken of the intensity of Fosdick's
concentration in and out of counseling situations. "I thought his gaze
would burn a hole through me," was the experience of more than one
person. His skilled, sensitive probing found individuals revealing their
innermost thoughts and releasing their most tightly reined emotions.
Some believed his powers of opening up another to be almost eerie. His
counseling manner might be compared to that of a circling sharp-eyed
hawk looking for a disturbance in the underbrush. His confidence that
burdens can be laid down was a kind of emanation of his being, rubbing
off on even the most despairing. And when he spoke there was a power
behind his words that made them resonate inside the client, giving them
a weight and significance that actually changed the way the individual
thought and felt. "It is a truism *en route* to platitude," observed one
scholar of counseling, "that the effectiveness (however defined) of a
therapy is inadequate evidence of the independent validity of the theory
that rationalizes the therapy, since charisma . . . or some other inter-
personal dynamism may have operated." That Fosdick possessed charisma

by virtue of his ministerial office, his national reputation, and his puissant personality cannot be disputed.

Fosdick's counseling was not permissive in that sinful conduct was condoned. When asked if his sympathetic understanding made for ethical relativity, he responded: "Absolutely not. I held Christian ideals very high for those who came to me for help." Therefore, Fosdick's counseling tended to be specific and direct: "Go and do thou likewise." When asked if he truly believed that men could be made new, he responded: "The fact of conversion, the possibility for complete transformation in a man's life, is very real to me. The divine potential in man *can* come out on top and take charge of a life." Troubled souls can be nerved with great affirmatives. Judgment and grace are two sides of the same coin; the purpose of judgment is grace, the healing of the hurt and disruption of dis-grace. "You are a fine, clean, high-minded spirit. Stop identifying yourself with your worst self," he once commanded a young man "confessing a gross sin." "What do you take me for? A fool? Do you think that you can talk as you have about lost faith in God without revealing that emotionally you are all messed up? Now you have had a love affair," he once interrupted a young woman who had "talked for about three minutes on how her theology had gone all to pieces." But Fosdick also remembered that the message of judgment comes first of all to the messenger of judgment.

Fosdick's own suicidal breakdown, he repeatedly claimed, gave him "clairvoyance" into the troubles of others, and doubtless this is true regarding people gripped by depression. By the 1920s when he began systematic counseling he was in his forties and had seen a lot, including the Western Front, and doubtless these decades of living seasoned his counseling. And Dr. Salmon's tutoring opened to him the world of clinical psychology. Nevertheless, he was also capable of saying things that seem not particularly profound and advising things not necessarily wise.

After Freud, for example, was it really possible to continue to believe that children inhabited "a fairyland of lighthearted innocence" or a "blessed Garden of Eden, not yet wholly banished from the earth," a notion itself unknown before the Enlightenment. Questions also arise concerning the profundity of Fosdick's understanding of human sexuality. He did not remain prudishly silent on this subject; indeed he once faulted a volume dealing with marriage because of the "complete absence of any reference to the physical problems of the sexual relationship in marriage." And his own *On Being a Real Person* contains some specific incidents of wise counseling of married couples whose sexual relations were "imperfect and unsatisfying" owing to the wife's frigidity. At no time did Fosdick intimate that the act of love between man and wife was a base (but probably inevitable) surrender to the coarser instincts; nor did he prohibit marital intercourse when conception was not the purpose. He always held that sex is a gift of God, a good and natural impulse when fulfilled within the context of marriage. Nevertheless, Fosdick's posture was hardly latitudinarian, and he would not have framed the issue as do many Christian ministers today: "What sexual relationship is appropriate to and expressive of the human relationship involved?" Patently, he believed homosexuality "abnormal" and his counseling must have reflected this conviction. Couples living together out of wedlock were violating moral law. In one specific case he advised and arranged an immediate marriage. In another case membership in Riverside was denied, Fosdick explaining, "The Riverside Church like any Christian church stands for the Christian family. You have adopted a mode of life, which, if it should prevail, would make the Christian family impossible."

Of course, infidelity was not countenanced, although one questions his counseling in his description of the following case:

> Why is it that when the lower passions get control we cannot give them vent and be at peace like the beasts? They are not ashamed. They do not do as we do—go around for years with dark chambers in their hearts at the thought of which they cringe and yet to which continually with fascinated reminiscence the footsteps of their mind are drawn. Here is a man who had committed a fearful crime against his family. They never could have found it out and yet he brought the family to me and in their presence made full confession of his guilt.*

Of course, premarital sexual activity was also not countenanced. His advice to one young gallant was so strong that the lad recalled that only his grandmother in Edinburgh had ever talked to him like that. A young woman was told that "heavy petting" was "wrong and dangerous." A shy, nervous lad was informed, "As for your sex life, I congratulate you on being a virgin at twenty-six. There are not many young men who achieve that." Boys and girls were warned not to lose the power to be ashamed of themselves: ". . . when you have been bad secretly and others have not found it out yet, you know that sense of being wrong that rises in you, that inner voice that says, Shame on you! until you

---

* In fairness to Fosdick it should be noted that by the time he wrote *On Being a Real Person* he had come to this wiser position: "Some wrong, let us say, in the realm of marital infidelity has been secretly committed, and for the good of the family it should be kept secret. . . . The one who did the wrong should carry it, should burn his—or her—own smoke, and not becloud the skies of his home with confession. Let him settle the matter with his own soul, with some trusted counselor, with God!"

can't be comfortable until you have tried to make things right again."
Surely at least some of the listening youngsters took this as an allusion
to their practice of the "solitary vice."

It is pretty apparent that Fosdick's counsel to troubled individuals engaged in illicit sexual activity was to cease and desist and that "illicit"
meant all activity outside the bonds of holy matrimony. Fosdick's "hot
certainties" stand in sublime contrast to the "fun morality" ("consumer
mentality" might be the more appropriate phrase) of *Playboy* magazine,
but one wonders how well they conformed to the realities of American
society even in a pre-Hefner era.

Questions continue to arise. "I wouldn't take anything for some of the
miracles I've seen happen," Fosdick said, "and I'd go to prison before I'd
tell a court anything that was told me by a person who came to me for
help." He may be believed, for his courage is unquestioned. Nevertheless,
his sermons and writings are studded with case histories drawn from his
counseling, and although names are never mentioned, too often individuals
would certainly recognize themselves and also be recognized by their
loved ones and associates.

Reservations aside, countless individuals believed they were helped—
even saved—by his care, "kind and compassionate" they recorded. And
they loved him. Said one person to Fosdick's secretary after a rekindling
counseling session, "He has put the stars back into my sky." If the actual counseling sessions were perhaps too brief and too few, Fosdick's
support, financial* as well as spiritual, had no termination. For example,
a woman widowed when her husband was killed in an accident was comforted immediately. When the delayed depressive reaction struck, she
was counseled. When physical illness then assailed, and Fosdick was informed, he said, "I'll send my friend Dr. Philip Stimson right over."
When her children came of college age, Fosdick arranged for them to receive financial aid at Colgate and William and Mary. Small wonder the
woman's cup of gratitude overflowed. Her experience of sustained support was not unique. That is why Fosdick's picture was found, almost as
an icon, in the studies and bedrooms of numbers of his pastoral counseling flock.

IV

Despite Fosdick's intense concern, his manifold other responsibilities obviously limited the number of hours he could spend in personal consulta-

---

* For thirty-five years Fosdick received considerable funds annually from the
Davella Mills Foundation to be used by him in assisting needy people. Fosdick
terminated the arrangement shortly after his retirement.

tion; and although the number of people who came to him over the decades totaled in the hundreds, it is clear that he touched far more lives by letter. This ministry of consultation and consolation through the post is one of the truly great, though little recognized, chapters in Fosdick's life. Thanks to his national stature, not the least owing to the "National Vespers" radio hour, he received weekly several thousand letters. The National Council of Churches took care of requests for copies of his radio sermons. Letters that could be answered with a form reply were handled so. But that still left many requiring a personal reply, and these were handled so, with two exceptions: "obviously crazy letters and obviously discourteous letters." Most of the personal responses were dictated, then typed, and signed(!) by "National Vespers" secretaries.* An astonishing additional number, however, were written by his firm hand.

Some of the messages Fosdick received were heart-wrenching. "I fear you are ill!," wrote a lonely New Jersey soul. "Last night . . . I read one of your sermons for comfort. I want so much to drop in for a call on you, to hold your dear hands, kiss you, and tell you that *no one* has ever taken your place to me and *no one* ever will." Some of the messages were gallant. "I could never count the number of disagreeable tasks I have faced," confessed another woman, "(and sometimes it was as uncomplicated but as difficult as *not* committing suicide for one more day), reminding myself with a grin,—'Well, for this cause Titus, left I thee in Crete,' taken from 'Handling Life's Second Bests' [a famous Fosdick sermon]." On occasion Fosdick would reply that the problem "calls for a face-to-face talk" and an appointment would be set up. The Riverside congregation was definitely not excluded from Fosdick's correspondence, and they could count on receiving notes in some hour of bereavement, anxiety, illness, special joy. There was nothing repetitious about these notes. Each was adapted as if by some spiritual alchemy to the exact need of the recipient. For example:

> Of course you have "quandaries" and unanswered questions. The older I grow, I think the more I have. If we could wholly understand this universe and our life within it, it would have to be a very little pint-size place. It is too big, too deep, for our minds to encompass and fathom. Even Jesus cried, "My God! my God! Why? . . ." But I am sure of

---

* A "National Vespers" executive reminded Fosdick in 1946 that "Ethel has signed your name at least thousands of times, during the past seventeen years, on letters you have dictated." That Fosdick received "crazy" and "discourteous" letters is beyond question. One poor soul, a spinster in her thirties, wrote him hundreds of letters sharing a revelation in which she was to bear a new Messiah fathered by Fosdick. At the other extreme, "an escaped inmate of a whole series of insane asylums," as Fosdick described the individual, threatened him with death.

Mind behind the universe, Purpose running through it, Meaning in it, Destiny ahead of it. And I am sure of an available Power, in whose fellowship we can find strength to do what we ought to do and to stand what we must endure.

I am quite heartbroken over the sad news that just has come to me. How impossible it is to explain an event like this so as to make any sense out of it at all. All my heart goes out to you for I have carried enough grief vicariously, in intimate friendship with many people, to know well enough what this kind of thing means. Of course, you will be patient with yourself . . . , but, in the meantime, it is a desperately difficult thing for anybody to stand up against. After all, if we have any sound spiritual stuff in us, we can pay our last tribute to those we have loved best by carrying our grief for them in a noble fashion. Not being embittered by it, but rather sweetened and elevated, and making of the whole experience, birth, growth, love, joy, and death, a total whole that we are glad to have had as a whole, and out of which we make an interior sanctuary that hallows life. I am praying for you that you may have wide margins of reserve around your need, and deep wells to draw your comfort from. Blessings on you always.

It is utterly unreasonable for you to think of God as causing the death of your lovely child because he disapproved of a decision that your husband made concerning remaining in the ministry. Surely, you have only to state the matter objectively to see how foolish it is for you to entertain such an idea of God. Do you suppose he goes around killing lovely babies because he disapproves of something their parents do? You know in all your logical and Christian moods that that is not only ridiculous in itself, but is really blasphemy against the character of God. Mrs. Fosdick and I did not leave the ministry. We decided to stay in because the doors continued to open on enlarging service. Nevertheless, we lost a lovely little baby. What kind of God is it that would kill some babies because their parents stayed in the ministry, and kill other babies because their parents didn't? We believe that God is a Christlike God. Just picture Jesus doing what you are accusing God of doing, and you will how ridiculous it is.

I am writing you because I have you on my heart. I know from long experience that while the shock of a loved one's death may be terrific when it first comes, often it is months afterward before the worst results of the blow are felt. If you are finding the endurance of your grief very hard to bear—perhaps hardest of all—at about this time, it would not be unusual, so I am writing now. You and your husband had a long and beautiful marriage, and all your friends have rejoiced in your mutual happiness. I trust that you are living in the light of those happy years, and are doing honor to them by your courage and constancy. I wish I could see you and talk with you, for I remember you and your husband with sincere respect and affection. I can think of no finer counsel to give you than to live during your final years as he would wish you to live—not crushed by his going, but uplifted by his memory, and keeping a brave, serene and steadfast heart. That is what he would want. It would hurt him deeply if you surrendered to grief and caved in. You will not do that I am sure. . . . You are not alone! You can be strengthened with might by God's spirit in the inner man. And your husband can be your present companion too in the secret places of your heart. Forgive me for writing so intimately. I am nearly seventy-five years old, and you belong to my generation. These last years are important. We can make them strong and beautiful. May God give us both grace to win the victory!

Fosdick's humanity is best documented by his continuing compassionate concern for a young Union student who in 1920 broke mentally and was doomed to live out her life in mental institutions. In 1973 at age seventy-six, "near death," "in great physical agony" ("tonight is hell"), this person described Fosdick's blessed ministry to her. She was a woman who likened her "suicidal insanity" to "Satanic Possession" carrying the punishment of "Eternal Damnation." Fosdick sustained her with "about 30 beautiful letters." His framed picture in her room brought comfort. He called her "Saint Helen"* and assured her, "Saint Helen, remember that the character of God is merciful." He countered the fear of "Eternal Damnation" by writing, "I shall probably get to the Heavenly Places before you do, my dear—but I will be there to meet you when the saints come marching in." He reached her heart with the pledge that she had his appreciation, admiration, and affection. He closed his letters, "Warm heartedly I lift a prayer for you." The Catholic chaplain at the Menninger Foundation Hospital informed Fosdick that his letters, which the woman shared with the chaplain, "were a great help to her and sustained her faith through very difficult periods." Dr. Gardner Murphy, famous in the field of mental health and also at the Menninger Foundation, wrote Fosdick about the woman "who owes so much to your wisdom and generosity," adding his own gratitude for Fosdick's "enormous inspiration" ever since Murphy had studied at Union.

Equally as moving is the case of a man whose wife and son both committed suicide. He entered a mental hospital—for life, he believed. Two years of living death followed during which period he refused to speak, to reply to the simplest question, and when letters came they fell from his lap unread. One day while sorting books in the hospital library, he reported, "I spied a volume that bore a name familiar to me in bygone years. I can see the faded gilt letters now—'by Harry Emerson Fosdick.'" As if by evocation he stood again at the dock at Boothbay Harbor where

---

* The name has been changed. Several years after our correspondence, death brought release to this dear, tortured soul.

sputtering to the little Juniper Point wharf came a rickety old motorboat, at the wheel of which stood "a fuzz-haired, sun-baked pilot—Harry Fosdick!" He read the book, *The Power to See It Through*, and it saved him. On the man's release Fosdick wrote him: "You know how intimately I entered in the troubles that faced you and your family, and how burdened I was at the load you all had to carry. All the more I appreciate the triumph that you have won, and the inner strength that must have been necessary to win it." Surely the Good Samaritan lived anew in the twentieth century in the comforting letters of Harry Emerson Fosdick.

V

The man saved by reading *The Power to See It Through* had long known Fosdick and perhaps this personal relationship gave Fosdick's printed words a saliency they otherwise might not have possessed. Even so, the pellucid fact is that his writings brought counsel and comfort and, yes, a sense of God's grace to multitudes who had never felt Fosdick's physical presence. A woman stricken with inoperable cancer became (in her words) a prime candidate for the "Mrs. Sorry-for-herself" award of the year until she discovered Fosdick's books and "as some people take to liquor or dope—I have taken to Dr. Fosdick!" Fosdick's words gave her the power to face her terrible fate. Precisely because Fosdick reached far more through his published works than through his correspondence (much less his personal counseling), a glance at those works most germane is required.

The first thing to note is that in a very real sense much of his writings are "germane." Witness even the titles of the compilations of sermons: *The Secret of Victorious Living, The Power to See It Through, Successful Christian Living, Living Under Tension, A Great Time to Be Alive, On Being Fit to Live With,* and so on, all bearing testimony to his conviction that preaching is counseling on a group scale. Keeping this in mind, we may home in on the nonsermonic writings designed to give guidance down the paths of mental and moral and spiritual health. Fosdick once expressed his personal affection for Dr. Norman Vincent Peale, author of such best sellers as *A Guide to Confident Living* and *The Power of Positive Thinking,* adding however that "his harp has only one string." Fosdick's harp had many strings, but he, too, struck the notes of positive thinking in such articles as "What Do You Say to Yourself?" and "How to Keep Out of the Psychiatrists' Hands" and a cluster of books. Although Fosdick did not beguile his readers with roseate pictures of the Kingdom of Good Adjustment as did the more puerile preachers of positive thinking, he does not stand entirely outside their company. Scholars recognize this when they include him in their studies of the American quest for health and happiness. Ann Landers recognizes this when she cites his definition of success: "To laugh often and much; to win respect of intelligent people and the affection of children; to earn the appreciation of honest critics and endure the betrayal of false friends; to appreciate beauty; to find the best in others; to leave the world a bit better, whether by a healthy child, a garden patch or a redeemed social condition; to know even one life has breathed easier because you lived."

In 1923 *Twelve Tests of Character* appeared, a dozen essays first presented in the pages of the *Ladies' Home Journal*, marking Fosdick's debut as a guide to "right living." "The papers are an endeavor to stress some fundamental tests of character which our new generation is tempted to forget," he explained. "With many overhead schemes for the world's salvation, everything rests back on integrity and driving power in personal character. 'You cannot carve rotten wood,' says a Chinese proverb. Nor can you carve decrepit and decayed character into any economic system or scheme of government that will work happiness for men. It is an old emphasis, but it is indispensable, and just now we may well get back to it." The volume was an instant success, the initial printing of twelve thousand selling out in two weeks. Sales apart, it was not one of Fosdick's better books. The tone is inspirational and exhortative, with constant references to heroic overcomers: Livingstone and Judson, Milton and Beethoven, Nightingale and Keller, Brooks and Moody—and Jesus. The quotations and allusions are familiar, the warnings conventional, the affirmations unexceptional. The prose. as always, is smooth and flowing and occasionally an epigrammatic spark is struck and obviously the book had its many admirers. Nevertheless, many readers today would find themselves initially bored and ultimately exasperated by its high anodyne tone.

Three years later there appeared *Adventurous Religion*, a collection of essays first presented in the pages of the *Ladies' Home Journal*, *Harper's Magazine*, and *Atlantic Monthly*. Although the focus is the state of religion rather than mental hygiene directly, the theme of the "intimate relationship between healthy religion and wholesome living" is never far offstage. "Religion's central and unique property is power to release faith and courage for living," the reader is informed, "to produce spiritual vitality and fruitfulness and by that it ultimately stands or fails." Thus is religion reduced to a pragmatic test! Reinhold Niebuhr (then still in Detroit) raised the tart question, "How Adventurous Is Dr. Fosdick?," in a review in the *Christian Century*, which he later apologetically described (after having come to know Fosdick) as "written in my brashest and most sophomoric manner." Actually, Niebuhr's assessment of the volume strikes one as sober and mature: "There is adventure in the religion which he [Fosdick] delineates, but it is adventure like that of the knights of chivalry. It develops within the limits of the age and does not challenge the age itself."

When historian Donald B. Meyer surveyed *The Positive Thinkers,* he found it appropriate to entitle the chapter dealing with Fosdick's book, "The Empty Adventure." Wrote Meyer: "Fosdick was perhaps the first of the great liberal preachers to be confronted in its full by the fact that for millions of persons it seemed reasonable to expect a comfortable world, that for millions a comfortable religion and healthy-mindedness seemed the most plausible reflection of reality." Fosdick never in this volume or elsewhere embraced a comfortable churchianity; to the contrary he exhorted his readers to live victoriously. Nevertheless, Meyer was not far off the money when he concluded: "Fosdick's message seems to come to rest simply in the assurance that sick people could get well by a technique and that religious faith would climax their cure." In the end, getting well was the great adventure.

These sincere, rather simple writings in a therapeutic vein in the Prosperity Decade were followed by others in the Depression Decade, but all of them merely adumbrated Fosdick's most popular book, *On Being a Real Person,* published in the war year 1943. As was so often the case, the chapters had first undergone a dry run in the Riverside Church Wednesday night lecture series. The most unequivocal thing to be said is that the volume was an immediate and continuing success. The editors of the *Reader's Digest* were sufficiently impressed with advance proofs to issue a condensation of the book even before Harper & Brothers brought it out. For weeks it alternated with Wendell Willkie's *One World* at top place on the nonfiction best-seller list. It was made a Book-of-the-Month selection. It ended the year ranking fourth on the nonfiction sales list. Sales of the clothbound edition alone exceeded three hundred thousand by the time of Fosdick's death.

Who were these readers? Fosdick modestly declared in the introduction that it was not intended for professionals in the field of personal counseling. Nevertheless, some professionals, including Karen Horney, did read it, recommended it to their patients, and thanked Fosdick for his help. Confessed in admiration Gordon W. Allport, "We psychologists must learn from you how to make our thought accessible to John and Jane Citizen." Fosdick did intend it to be read by fellow ministers and others similarly situated, such as teachers, whose vocation is inseparable from the avocation of counseling individuals. This readership was substantial. Ultimately, however, the volume was designed for the sorts of individuals who had come to him for counseling, those who pass for normal or near normal: "Ordinary people—some mildly disturbed, others distracted, unhappy, fissured personalities, up against circumstances they feel inwardly inadequate to handle, or moods and feelings they do not understand and cannot bear to live with." The jacket statement claimed "this book will help any intelligent person," not Everyman. Seward Hiltner termed the book excellent, "but apparently not suitable for those below the college level." The writing reveals a distinct class orientation. For example, the book tells us we are "polite today, morose and uncivil tomorrow; obliging and well-bred in business, crabbed, churlish, and sulky at home; affable with one's so-called 'equals,' gruff and snobbish with one's servants; a good sportsman on the golf links, an ill-natured jostler on the subway; kindly at church, snarling and peevish at the office." Certainly, Fosdick has in mind in this passage a businessman who works in an urban office, possesses servants, plays golf, and attends church. Indeed, everything about the book attests its middle- and upper-middle-class orientation. The individuals cited from history and contemporary life for purposes of illustration (and inspiration) would be familiar names to most readers of this class. The quotations from the field of literature would be recognized in middle-brow cultural circles. The psychological authorities most frequently tapped are J. A. Hadfield (15 times), William James (12), Ernest Hocking (10), Gordon Allport (10), Carl Jung (9), Ralph Waldo Emerson (8), William Sadler (8)—a "safe and sane" list for a minister to incorporate. When disbelievers are mentioned, Freud and Krutch for example, it is generally for the purposes of refutation. Among theologians, Calvin, Barth, Brunner, Niebuhr go unmentioned, and clearly the Old Testament (only 3 references) provides little guidance to successful living.

These faint damns are intended as praise for the book's accessibility. It is beautifully designed to meet the concerns of a very broad class of Americans. And it is, emphatically, superior to most of the thousand guides to health, wealth, and personal power then (and now) being purveyed.

"The central business of every human being is to be a real person," the volume opens. Fosdick acknowledges that every life begins its struggles with the possibilities and the limitations of heredity and environment, but in good Jamesian fashion he comes down on the side of freedom and responsibility. "We . . . accept responsibility when we succeed; we may not slough it off when we fail. We cannot have our cake and eat it too. Indeed, in the face of difficult situations, when life is limited in endowment and threatened by circumstances, we most need to accept our responsibility to be real persons." Setting aside the fact that nonthesists—Freud, Sartre, Lippman, Bertrand Russell for example—would agree, this stern counsel is admirable. (One might wish, however, that the supporting example of the lame Sir Walter Scott and the lame Lord Byron—Scott overcoming his handicap and living a "radiant life" and Byron permitting his lameness to make him "sceptical, cynical, and savage"—had been omitted.)

A "real person," we are told in Chapter 2, is an integrated person, one who has brought order into the "blooming, buzzing confusion" of his life.* Modern man desperately needs to be saved from *Zerrissenheit* (torn-to-pieces-ness), and it is an illusion to suppose that social reforms will eliminate anxiety, what Kierkegaard called the "dizziness of freedom." A real person is *integrated*, capable of moving forward along his chosen road with clarity of vision and purpose; his life becomes "coherent, steady, one-directional." Fosdick wisely warns that he is not describing a placid life. The cud-chewing cow is not the most integrated of creatures. Integration alone does not insure a high and worthy life for it "ambiguously makes great saints and powerful sinners." Napoleon was a *strong* person but not a *good* person. Hence, integration itself needs a criterion. And this brings Fosdick to the quite correct position that integration is "hierarchical" in character. "It involves a scale of values, with some supreme value, or complex of associated values, so organizing life that one gladly foregoes lesser aims, and resists contradictory enticements, rather than sacrifice life's chief aim and highest worth." The chapter concludes with the admonition that for these values around which our lives are organized we must turn "to the insights of the great religious seers" for one becomes a real person by a process that is "inward and spiritual." This is not quite identical with the older proclamation: "Man's chief end is to glorify God, and to enjoy him forever."

Chapter 3 compassionately expounds on "The Principle of Self-Acceptance" and shrewdly notes the methods individuals use to escape a haunting sense of inferiority: the "smoke-screen" method, the "sour grapes" technique, fantasy, retreating into illness. Not surprisingly, the last sentences argue the case for "religion."

Not unaware of the perils of preoccupation with one's self, Fosdick now turns to "Getting Oneself Off One's Hands." The advice advanced is sensible, practical (vigorous physical exercise is the enemy of morbid subjectivity), and laudable (living in the service of high ideals and other individuals), though somewhat short of the sovereign demand to sell all; take up the cross; to offer up an only, a beloved, Isaac. The chapter

---

* However, the British novelist Graham Greene once observed, "To find an 'integrated' persons one would have to look in a lunatic asylum."

"Dealing with Fear and Anxiety" analyzes first what these demonic forces do to us and then presents the resources and tactics that deprive these monsters of their power. Fosdick with much perspicacity says of fear: "Like fire, it is a great and necessary servant but a ruinous master." He recognizes the objective basis for much anxiety: "Life can be cruel and terrible, and anyone who expects to escape that fact is asking for a life at sea without storms." Get out into the open the object of our dread and frankly face it. Substitute for brooding imagination direct action. If wrong conduct, as opposed to an unbased morbidity, is the source of our dread, religion provides the resources to right that conduct. "Jesus went to the heart of the matter when he set a mustard seed, the smallest thing he knew, over against Mount Hermon, towering 9,000 feet above the sea, and said that faith like a seed could move obstacles like a mountain."

"Handling Our Mischievous Consciences" is the chapter on which Dr. O. Hobart Mowrer based his charge that Fosdick accepted "the Freudian notion that man sickens, not from sin but from excessive conscientiousness." Actually, much of the chapter deals with how individuals deny, excuse, rationalize their sinful behavior. But Fosdick does make this compassionate and liberating point: "When conscience has fulfilled its function it ought naturally to stop, but commonly it persists, torturing its victim long after the torture had lost all value. These people who cannot forgive themselves suffer the more cruelly because they suffer from too much of a good thing—like a jammed automobile horn, which, having fulfilled its rightful function of warning, now keeps up an unintermittent blare. Moreover, this trouble is the more serious because, while a jammed horn is recognized as abnormal, a jammed conscience is often regarded as the voice of God. Upon the contrary, one of the main therapeutic functions of religion is the dissipation of such remorse through the gospel of God's forgiveness. The ancient cry of the Psalmist, 'Blessed is he whose transgression is forgiven, Whose sin is covered,' has never ceased in the church, and today the farther we go into the intricate labyrinth of conscience, the more the need of it becomes clear." (Elsewhere Fosdick had observed, "Sometimes the personal counselor does not know which is worse, the moral ignobility of the irresponsible or the personal disintegration of the over-responsible.") This chapter illustrates Fosdick's humane counseling in the realm of sexuality—a boy's masturbatory guilt, two wives unable to find joy in intercourse with their not inconsiderate husbands. Dr. Mowrer to the contrary, Fosdick is not condoning sin but illustrating the mortmainlike grip of unmerited shame.

The chapter "Using All There Is in Us" has some sane things to say about accepting the drives native to our constitution—pugnacity, will to power, sexual desire, for example—and how to elevate and redirect them in the service of society and personal harmony and wholeness.

Fosdick's suggestions for "Mastering Depression" are of real moment and profundity, not the least being: *"Take depression for granted.* One who expects completely to escape low moods is asking the impossible. Not only is there plenty in life to be depressed about, but by its very nature emotional tone has an up-and-down gamut."

The sense of inner inadequacy to meet life's demands is one of the commonest causes of personal disintegration. Nothing crumbles one up more quickly than the feeling of helplessness. In "The Principle of Released Power" Fosdick acutely observes of such individuals: "One cannot blow on one's hands, put one's back into it, and *will* peace of mind, purity of heart, freedom from bitterness under abuse or from despondency under misfortune. Dealing with stormy emotions by will alone is like hammering on water—it does not still the waves." Therefore, another technique altogether is needed. "Power is primarily a matter not of self-generation but of appropriation. Not strenuous activity but hospitable receptivity is the ultimate source of energy. The Psalmist is right about the blessed man being 'like a tree planted by the rivers of water.' " And it is religion that brings a transforming access of power. As Paul said, "In Him who strengthens me, I am able for anything." The volume closes with an explication of this thought in a chapter revealingly entitled, "The Practical Use of Faith." The final sentence reads: "A constructive faith is thus the supreme organizer of life, and, lacking it, like Humpty Dumpty we fall and break into pieces, and the wonder is whether all the king's horses and all the king's men can ever put us together again."

A reviewer, thinking to praise Fosdick, termed him "the neurotics' Dale Carnegie." The comparison is unfair. *On Being a Real Person* is far more searching, gritty, and wise than anything Carnegie ever wrote. It is an earnest, sensible, informed book of indubitable help to many of its readers. The criticism of it, for the most part, came not from psychologists questioning Fosdick's technical expertise, but from religious reviewers questioning his theology. Another reviewer, also thinking to praise the volume, unwittingly revealed the basis for most of the theological criticism when he said: "It also is a sincere tho not at all obtrusive plea for religion—not Protestantism, not Catholicism, nor Judaism, nor Christian Science, nor Buddhism, nor Mohammedanism, nor any special brand of religion, but for some fundamental religious faith to be the 'everlasting arms' which are man's surest refuge and comfort in despair." Exactly! In these pages there is a maximum of self and also a lot about Jesus' "insights" into human nature, but a minimum of the God who most fully revealed Himself in the Incarnation and the Christ who redeems man. Fosdick's test of "religion" is as empirical and his definition as spacious as that of Dwight Eisenhower when the president said, "Our government makes no sense unless it is founded on a deeply felt religious faith—and I don't care what it is." This in essence was the nature of the criticism of mainly Roman Catholic, Anglican, and conservative Protestant reviewers. They had a point. It might further be noted that although the volume is critical of egocentricity, its very popularity suggests a growing unhealthy narcissism. Finally, the volume's perspective on evil is rather attenuated. Fosdick's theology and the whole meliorist thrust of the mental health movement prevented him from recognizing fully the radical diabolism stalking the world.

VI

"If I were not a minister," Fosdick wrote an associate in 1928, "I think that next in order, I should be glad to give my life to the cause of mental hygiene. I thoroughly believe that it is one of the great movements for human welfare and that it warmly deserves intelligent backing and financial support." Believing as he did he supported the movement to the extent that his time and energies permitted.

In 1909 Clifford Beers with the encouragement of Adolf Meyer and William James brought into being the National Committee for Mental Hygiene, soon to receive major support from the Rockefeller Foundation and involve Fosdick's mentor, Dr. Salmon. By the time of Fosdick's death the movement had mushroomed. New organizations were formed, the National Mental Health Act passed, and the National Institute for Mental Health established. Over the years Fosdick wrote scores of endorsements and sponsored financial appeals for these organizations and served on their advisory boards. Dr. George C. Anderson, director of the Academy of Religion and Mental Health, informed Fosdick that "you were probably the most outstanding single force besides myself that helped bring the Academy into being."

As a minister Fosdick saw physical suffering that had passed beyond any possibility of an ennobling effect on character and had become protracted torture—when the only merciful prayer was that the end might come speedily—and he came to support voluntary euthanasia, petitioning the legislature of the state of New York to enact legislation making this possible "under careful safeguards." He once explained his position to a Roman Catholic nun:

> All we are endeavoring to get done is to save some lives from the necessity of long-continued needless suffering, after life has practically come to its end and only pain remains. This is a situation which modern science has created. It is, in a sense, quite new; that is, modern science can now prolong life far beyond the time when, in the older days, one would have fallen peacefully on sleep. Physicians now prolong existence as long as it can be prolonged, despite the fact that the pain is intense, the meaning of life gone, and no hope for recovery remains. This seems to me one of the most intolerably cruel things going on in the world today. It is one of the indirect evil results of modern science, and we have every right to protect the victim of it, as thousands of physicians wish to do, and an increasing number of ministers think it our Christian duty to do.

Suicide was another matter altogether, romantic existentialists to the contrary. "I do not believe that suicide ever can be right," Fosdick wrote a correspondent. "It is not unselfish; it is one of the most selfish things anybody can ever do. The worst torture, I think, that I see in human life comes in households and among friends where one member has committed suicide. There is no heritage so terrible that anybody can leave to the circle of his friends. . . . You cannot say that everybody who feels like committing suicide ought to commit suicide. In that case I would have committed suicide as a young man when I had a nervous breakdown and thought my career was ended. . . . No individual is fit to be trusted with such responsibility, for it is universally true that when anybody feels like committing suicide, he is in a psychiatric condition and needs hospitalization as a sick person."

As a minister Fosdick had to deal with cases of alcoholism. He dreaded that perhaps most frustrating of all counseling experiences, as all ministers acknowledge. What to do with an alcoholic? Therefore, when Bill Wilson in 1939 sent Fosdick a copy of *Alcoholics Anonymous* he grasped it in gratitude and his praiseful review appeared in three religious journals. In 1940 Fosdick represented the world of religion when Rockefeller arranged with Wilson's struggling group a dinner to inform New York's financial and civic leadership of A.A.'s purpose, and though Rockefeller's ultimate financial support was parsimonious, doors were opened, publicity given, and funds raised. There was $5000 deposited in the treasury of the Riverside Church for Wilson's personal use and the Riverside lay leaders Albert Scott and A. LeRoy Chipman gave of their talents. For his part, Fosdick never ceased to praise A.A. He wrote testimonials for the A.A. magazine, the *Grapevine*, contributed to *AA*

Today, and spoke at meetings. "After your talk last night," Wilson wrote Fosdick in 1941, "any number of people remarked how you touched them, how well you had identified yourself as one who has resolved hopelessness by spiritual means. Perhaps the most pungent observation came from old Tom Mulhall, now club caretaker, and one time New York fireman liberated from Rockland Asylum a year ago. Exclaimed he from the kitchen: 'My God what a blast—what a shame that man ain't an alcoholic too!'" In turn Wilson was invited to speak at the Riverside Church. Wilson's gratitude to Fosdick for being the first clergyman to endorse A.A. was exceeded by the minister's thankfulness. "The debt is on the other side," wrote Fosdick. "I am endlessly grateful." Fosdick also served on the advisory board of the National Committee for Education on Alcoholism.

Although a secular organization, A.A. retains an affinity for the religious vocabulary of surrender, conversion, and salvation; and its philosophy affirms the spiritual principle that humans are "Not-God," that they need to give-to and sacrifice-for each other, strengthened through prayer and meditation. "I have listened to many learned arguments about God," judged Fosdick, "but for honest-to-goodness experiential evidence of God, his power personally appropriated and his reality indubitably assured, give me a good meeting of A.A.!" As A.A. is congruent with Fosdick's understanding of the power of faith, so it meshes nicely with the Zeitgeist of the mental hygiene movement.

As a minister, Fosdick received a number of inquiries as to his judgment of Christian Science, New Thought, spiritualism, and psychical research. Regarding Mrs. Eddy's church, he acknowledged that "nothing floats without some good wood in it, and . . . Christian Science has floated because it does have some solid timber." Still, he found its metaphysics "impossible," some of its theories "quite incredible," and its rejection of scientific medicine "a positive danger." He informed one woman, "I . . . never think it worth while to attack Christian Science, but always to endeavor in my own life and teaching those things which make Christian Science valuable, that people will not think they have to go to Mrs. Eddy's church in order to obtain them." Couéism he deplored. Tipping tables, Ouija boards, and palm and tea leaf readings he lampooned. However, psychical research was another matter. He followed with interest Dr. J. B. Rhine's experiments in parapsychology, believing the Duke professor "has found something there which needs careful examination." He found impressive the evidence that "telepathy is a demonstrable fact." He wrote one individual, "I have no doubt at all about Extra-sensory Perception," and he reported to another that on the whole question he was keeping an "open mind." This receptive posture was shared by many leading Protestant churchmen.

VII

In the midst of all of his helping activities—counseling in office and home, writing letters of consolation and advice, penning personally helpful articles and books (to say nothing of sermons), supporting a raft of organizations, all in addition to performing baptism, wedding, and funeral services and visiting the hospitalized—was there the time and energy to continue the old custom of pastoral calling? The answer is "not much." His ministerial associates and lay zone leaders did visit in homes in times of trouble and perhaps not many of the flock were "lost." Still, was Fosdick correct in his insistence that social calling in the home was a waste of time?

Is the pastoral ministry an activity reserved for crises or special moments in the rites of passage from birth to death? A Riverside parishioner who "vastly respected" Fosdick, nonetheless noted that save for a very small inner circle of lay leaders, few in the fellowship spent so much as an hour in their entire lives in his personal company. After his retirement, a maiden lady wrote Fosdick a note from her apartment near the church:

I love my home. Sometime, if you and Mrs. Fosdick are able to come, how I would love to fix you a cup of tea. A minister has never said a prayer in my home. I have an old fashioned notion that a house is never a home until the minister has been there and blessed it. Dr. McCracken with his family problems is far too busy to do this as are all of the ministers at the church. So are you, I know, but maybe sometime you will need a cup of tea badly enough to come. I just want you to know that you would be welcome and that I would be highly honored. If you do come, I hope that you are not afraid of small, timid, lame cats, because I have one. Thank you for being such a wonderful man and for giving people like me a faith to live by.

The logistics of pastoral calling in a large metropolitan church are formidable. But just perhaps having a cup of tea in a parishioner's parlor, with no particular problem to be solved, furthers the Kingdom of God in a way that no formal, clinical counseling session can do. Maybe all the restless activities sponsored by The Riverside Church and all the aid made available did not quite satisfy the hunger of some parishioners for a quiet talk with their pastor about this or that in the intimacy of *their* homes, not the minister's study.

Still, it will not do to close on a downbeat note. On his eighty-ninth birthday Fosdick received a telegram from Helen Roebling, the grand-daughter of the great builder of the Brooklyn Bridge, reminding Fosdick that he and the bridge shared a common birthday and observing that the two "have so much in common." The telegram closed, "I think with gratitude of all the wonderful bridges you have built for thousands of us with love and admiration." How lovely and how apposite!

Chapter Sixteen

"If Gold Rust, What Then Will Iron Do?": A Protestant Preacher as Husband, Father, and Friend

I

Lord Acton's gloomy observation that "great men are almost always bad men" is not without ample biographical confirmation, but there is just enough counter evidence to prevent it from being a universal principle; the life of Harry Emerson Fosdick is precisely just such evidence. Ministers are not made less dizzy than others by man's condition of radical freedom, as even a casual acquaintanceship with clerical biographies reveals. Yet it is their fate that other men think of them in terms of Chaucer's, "If gold rust, what then will iron do?" It is a fair question. On an occasion honoring Fosdick at Union Seminary, Reinhold Niebuhr said: "In assessing Fosdick's religious influence I hope it will not seem irrelevant to observe that it was so potent not only because of his remarkable gifts of mind and heart both in the written word and in the pulpit, but also because he revealed a remarkable degree of Christian grace in his life. One ought to expect a theologian to be a Christian; but one can not take it for granted, as those of us who are theologians well know. At least one can not take for granted that general and yet very unique quality of 'grace': a complete absence of egotism in its various forms of vanity, jealousy and pride. Since Fosdick was the most celebrated preacher of his day, and since pulpit success is a notorious corrupter of character in the ministry, this quality of grace was the more remarkable. I will dare offense by reporting a personal experience to adorn my appreciation of the totally unspoiled character of a great man." Niebuhr cited the instance and then concluded, "Subsequent experiences only reinforced the impression of a man who was singularly devoid of preoccupation with self." However controversial Fosdick's public career, however "wrong" his positions may be judged, in this chapter on his private life we do glimpse that rare phenomenon, the "rose without the thorn."

II

Neither strikingly handsome nor awesomely commanding of visage and figure, nonetheless, there was about Fosdick's physical presence a suggestion of strength, authority, aliveness. He stood five feet, eight inches. The body was muscular, the carriage soldierly, the hands square. A ruddy complexion intensified the blueness of the penetrating eyes, eyes gentle yet shrewd. The chin was round, the lips generous, the nose straight, the forehead high. The head was abloom with frizzy brown hair, a foliage he detested as a youth but joked about as an adult. The metallic rasp to the voice was curiously not unpleasant to the ears of most listeners. At the age of thirty he looked twenty and at the age of forty, thirty. Inevitably this youthful appearance slowly surrendered to the remorseless signs of age. The hair thinned and grayed and then whitened. The eyes required spectacles, first the pince-nez type and then the rimless and steel-rimmed varieties. Wrinkles lined the high brow and crinkles edged the corners of the eyes. The photographs of Fosdick in his early years are less appealing than those of his later years. There is about the face of the younger man a touch of self-importance and priggishness, perhaps in part because of those pince-nez, whereas the face of the older man appeared to others to be "radiantly homely" and like the "perplexed face of a maiden aunt." A friend reported that even when eighty-five Fosdick's "whole being seemed to glow with interest, attention, humor, exuberance, and joy."

However, observers never confused Fosdick's vitality with wildness, the energy with loss of control, the humanity with impetuosity, the warmth with slaphappiness. His movements were precise, deliberate, measured whether in buttoning a coat or unscrewing a pen or wiping spectacles. His speech, too, in conversation was paced, carefully self-conscious as he sought for the right word, the most appropriate phrase, almost as if language was an instrument too precious to be used casually. "I would never think of speaking without ordering my thoughts," Fosdick once observed in regard to his public utterances, but the statement also applies in a more limited way to his conversations. His dress complemented the manner. The suits well tailored, conservative in cut and color; the shirt collar always clean; the subdued tie straight; the fresh hankerchief in the breast pocket neatly folded. He never wore jewelry, not even a wedding ring. Though his being was charged with great vitality, there was nothing frenetic about him. He possessed an air of intense calm, of burning imperturbability.

His conservatism of dress, calculation of conversation, deliberation of movement may have had many causes. Fosdick was after all a clergyman, and a flamboyant style was not a hallmark of his calling in his era. Moreover, he was much in the public eye, his deeds and words closely attended to and reported in the press; a slip of the hand or tongue would not be overlooked. Further, his key benefactors were late Victorians of conservative manner and his parishioners were for the most part of bourgeois background, as indeed was Fosdick himself. Yet one suspects that another factor played a role. Fosdick lived with the memory of the nervous breakdowns of both his parents and of his own youthful crack-up, and he lived in fear of a repetition of that nightmare. He had to keep a tight rein. He had to live a careful, ordered existence. Moderation, control, the husbanding of physical energy, the cooling of passions, the calming of excited nerves were essential to his sanity and survival. In 1949 while in the hands of "a doctor at the Neurological Institute" he wrote to his younger daughter, "It isn't easy to work hard, as you must have to work hard, with the inherited Fosdick disability." He defined that disability in a letter to a friend as being "hypersensitive, highstrung." His wife, children, relatives, and close friends were well aware that this turbulent, passional side to his nature was controlled by conscious act of will.

Fosdick never suffered a second nervous breakdown nor is there any evidence that he ever came dangerously close to doing so; the warning signals always came in time to permit the proper calming measures to be taken. His ruddy complexion, clear blue eyes, sturdy build, and erect bearing did not totally belie his general condition of health during the first half century of his life. Indeed, considering his long working days, the pressures of his manifold responsibilities, and the bruising nature of the battles that engulfed him, it is extraordinary that his health held as long as it did. But when he was in his fifties the toil, stress, and mounting years began to take their toll. His constitution did not suddenly fall apart like the Deacon's One-Horse Shay—after all, he lived to be ninety-one—but health troubles did come with increasing frequency and severity.

The first serious blow came in April 1935 when he underwent an operation for the removal of a benign tumor of the gall bladder. This knocked him out of action for six months, leaving him with "a profound doubt as to whether I ever shall be able to run upstairs and as for having wit enough to write a sermon or energy enough to deliver one, that certainly seems beyond the wildest bounds of credibility." This privately expressed dismay was not evident in the tone of a public letter to the people of Riverside, whom he assured "need have no concern about the ultimate outcome of my escapade with surgeon" save that "whatever else NRA may mean it would be enforced on me as No Running Around." He returned to the pulpit in late September, but after two months of going at it hard, he found it necessary to cancel his December speaking engagements and rest up, explaining, "This doesn't mean that I am ill, but simply that at my extreme old age a major operation does take the stuff out of one." Fosdick was approaching the age of sixty; by the mid-1930s he had lost fifty percent of his hearing in one ear, wore glasses to correct astigmatism, and had had his tonsils removed. He accepted the hearing loss philosophically and took the opportunity of the 1937 tonsilectomy to "hide out" happily in a hospital for six days. He now began to pace himself, cutting back his speaking engagements, including those at Harvard, Chicago, Yale, and Princeton where he had been accustomed to preach annually for thirty years, explaining, "As I grow older, I discover to my amazement that my strength does not expand with my years, and that like other human beings I have to cut my garment according to my cloth."

Troubles of one sort or another continued and by the year of his retirement, 1946, he reported to a daughter: "As you might expect Gram is going strong. How the old gal keeps up the pace she travels, I am sure I do not know. Certainly, I feel about twenty years older than she acts. Nevertheless, I'm putting up a very good bluff, and so far as I can see the general public does not suspect that I am rapidly disintegrating. Perhaps I'm not, but I certainly shall be glad when this year is over, and the last formal doings are wound up, and I can lie down and rest in peace without having to get up the next morning and write a sermon." Again he wrote to his daughter: "Mother, as always, is full of pep and ginger. She keeps going marvelously, and runs the house and everybody in it with the greatest competence and efficiency. I wish she could be as peppy as this for twenty years to come anyway. As for me, I'm not badly off, but if it were not for this church, and my desire to see it through until next May, I'd go up to the hospital tomorrow and have my gall bladder out, like your friend Stettinius. He was a wise boy, and I need to have the same thing done. I do not propose to go on living with this dietary problem, these cramps, etc. any longer than it takes me to have that gall bladder out when I have my first good chance." Only months after this letter he underwent the removal of the gall bladder. He also suffered from carcinoma of the prostate, involving the bladder; blessedly the cancer did not move into the bone but remained localized.

Retirement brought a return of reasonably good health for two years, but in 1948 he was felled by what he called variously "digestive troubles," "a rather disagreeable and persistent siege of nervous indigestion," and "nervous sag," which left him feeling "like running away from the thought of work—which is a brand new experience for me."

One unfortunate April Sunday in 1955, Fosdick returned to Riverside to preach and gave it, he reported, "all I had. I came home, went to bed and passed out. It was a cerebral spasm. Somehow I got up, fell over, taking a lamp with me. The family heard it and came running. So I decided to quit." This was not all. Before Fosdick's great heart stopped at age ninety-one he was treated for high blood pressure and placed on a salt-free diet; for congestive heart failure resulting in shortened breath and moisture-filled lungs; for arteriolosclerosis; for kidney failure; for continued prostate problems; and for crippling rheumatoid arthritis.

In reviewing Fosdick's medical record two points are important. Despite an inherited delicateness of constitution, until almost sixty his general health was good; the robust appearance was not deceiving. Second, when the body began to wear out, he faced the conditions squarely. On the one hand, he was not a hypochondriac; on the other, he did not deny the reality of his ailments. No one ever heard him whimper about the injustice of the unwelcome visitations. There was not a milligram of self-pity in his makeup. Even in the last years when arthritis imposed its cruel confinement, his serenity filled his nurses with adoration. "When I go to the hospital to be operated on," he said to a friend, "I roll off all my responsibility and leave it to the surgeon." He also once wrote: "I have just heard with great regret that you are in for a session with the surgeon. . . . My heart goes warmly out to you, and I sincerely hope that the first few days may pass without too much trouble. After that you will be so magnificently taken care of that the experience is likely to be memorable, rather than merely unpleasant. I have been through the surgeon's hands enough to have had that experience happen to me anyway, and I used to get so fascinated watching the technical, scientific perfection with which they took care of me that I forgot to be bothered by the unpleasantness of the occasion." Likewise, he said to his successor at Riverside that when the time came for him to die the problem would not be his, but God's: "I completely trust Him. I know whom I have believed and am persuaded that He is able to keep that which I have committed unto Him against that day." Unafraid of death, Fosdick never turned his back on life. Toward the end he dryly remarked to his personal physician, "I'm ready to go, but I notice that every time I feel bad I call you, Dr. Jones."

Without being at all a hypochondriac, Fosdick nurtured his dicey health carefully. He indulged in an occasional cigar or pipe of tobacco, usually after dinner, but never in cigarettes. On rare occasions he sipped a beer, but not a highball, although in his last years on doctor's orders he was given a brandy ration: "I like this stuff!" Father George Ford recalled hearing Fosdick once exclaim. His "trick" stomach prevented his being either a glutton or gourmet (on the unlikely assumption that he might have been tempted in those directions), and individuals who dined with him remember that he "ate like a bird." However, his letters mention with relish Maine lobster, boiled in pots of seawater and seaweed, and steaming shore dinners, and it seems that when his stomach permitted he enjoyed food well enough; certainly his stocky build does not suggest ascetic fasting. (He loathed dining in restaurants, but this was a matter of temperament, not cooking.)

Exercise was essential. Golf supplied one form, though less and less as time passed. Usually the weekly game was on Monday morning, though not invariably: "I did get a little tired last week," he wrote to his father in 1923, "and after spending a night or so of broken sleep I ran over to Montclair on Friday noon, played eighteen holes of golf with Raymond, another eighteen holes on Saturday, and came back as fresh as a daisy for my work on Sunday morning." He also played squash and tennis occasionally and had a tennis court built on his Maine island. He chopped much wood there and loved the sweat and good physical tiredness that came with it. Above all, he hiked when on vacation—in New England, the West, Scotland, Switzerland, Germany, anywhere he might be—and he walked when in New York. He walked if possible every day either before lunch or in the late afternoon and always on Saturday afternoon, rain or shine. Dressed informally and shod in Maine moccasins he would strike out down Riverside Park to 72nd Street and stride back—about five miles. He walked briskly and preferably alone. On Saturdays his thoughts were on the morrow's sermon and as he rehearsed the words sometimes became audible, to the excruciating embarrassment of his young daughters, when they joined him.

Fosdick burned the midnight oil when a tight schedule absolutely demanded it, but was not one of those blessed souls who regularly managed on four or five hours of sleep. A concert or play downtown might keep him up until midnight, but it was widely understood by hostesses that the Fosdicks would depart from dinner parties at nine sharp, perhaps long before the other guests, to meet his fairly early retiring hour. He sought sleep by saying to God at day's end, "Now you must take over and carry the load. I have done all I can today." If God failed in

His duty and sleep did not come for several consecutive nights, Fosdick would taper off his pace and perhaps leave town for a short period. In midpassage of his long life he began taking occasional brief naps, and almost always did so on Saturday afternoon. If sleep did not come on a Saturday night he attributed it to a tension entirely normal, not to neurotic anxiety, and he took sedatives to permit the required rest.

In a word, Fosdick neither abused his constitution nor too tenderly pampered it, but he did watch his step prudently; and as a consequence he knew reasonably good health for half a century and not unreasonably bad health for almost half a century.

III

When in *On Being a Real Person* Fosdick described an "integrated person," the model might have been he whom he saw in the shaving mirror each morning. He struck others as being in absolute control of himself and in command of every situation. He radiated strength, mastery, steadiness, purpose, self-acceptance. He won the respect of "big" men quite without conscious effort on his part. He had that quality the Romans called *gravitas,* a quality associated in American history with Washington, Lee, Henry L. Stimson, and George C. Marshall. The familiar barbs often hurled at clergymen miss Fosdick by a sea mile. He was no limp-wristed sissy. Yet neither was he buffoonishly bluff and falsely hearty, affecting tweedy dress, sonorous voice, and Rotarian manner. And he was also free of that unctuous piety, sniveling sanctimoniousness, and Uriah Heep self-deprecation that in some quarters passes for godliness. His former student and part-time chauffeur said that he had the feeling that if the car had broken down, Fosdick could have fixed it or coped with any sort of emergency. A Union colleague recalled that when an intruder entered his home during a Fosdick visit, Fosdick, then in his seventies, resolutely searched in the dark yard for the fleeing man. All who knew him agree that he would have been a good man to have along on a tiger hunt.

The self-mastery extended to the control of his anger. If no one remembers seeing him in a rage, associates and secretaries knew he was fully capable of stubbornly planting his feet and growling, "Well, they may think they can budge me, but I'm not going to do it!" He bore no grudges for perhaps the same reason he did not permit himself outbursts of temper: it was uneconomical, a dissipation of energy.

The associate minister in charge of furnishing Fosdick's study in the Riverside Church made this revealing observation: "He has been working in that study for two years now and insofar as I can see there hasn't been a thing moved an inch from the place where it was put when we first set the room up. He simply moved in on top of the furniture we had placed there and went to work. Mr. Gandhi achieves his reputation for not being dependent upon things by divesting himself of all things. . . . Dr. Fosdick achieves an even more significant independence of things by sitting down in the midst of all kinds of things, of everything he could possibly want, and proving himself to be absolutely independent of them by altogether ignoring them and doing his work, doing his work not because of them but in spite of them. From this point of view, he is the most independent spirit I have ever known."

Fosdick's self-possession freed him from the taint of trying to please everyone, freed him from self-defeating hatreds, and also freed him from being thin-skinned to criticism. As a reporter noted at the height of the Fundamentalist-Modernist controversy, "He reads the most virulent criticism of himself with the detachment of a Buddha meditating upon the eight paths of Nirvana." Of course, this self-assurance, this spirit of determined reasonableness, this display of "limitless, unfailing goodwill toward everyone, friend and foe alike" must have been a source of exasperation to those who proclaimed themselves his enemies. And, of course, this posture prompted some to term him excessively self-confident. Although false, the characterization is understandable, for he was unnervingly serene, even in the heat of battle.

Everyone agreed that Fosdick possessed *gravitas*, yet some found him short on that sunny quality Americans associate with Henry Clay, Al Smith, and FDR. In his old age he remarked wistfully to an associate, "You know, there are not many left who call me 'Harry.'" But this same associate, an editor at Harper's and Riverside lay leader who had known and worked closely with Fosdick for years, invariably called him "Dr. Fosdick," as did almost everyone else. There were, of course, exceptions, especially among those whose relationships went back to the Montclair years, but at Riverside Church he was "Dr. Fosdick" (even to Carder, Hellstrom, Tibbetts, his successor McCracken, and Rockefeller) and at Union Seminary he was "Dr. Fosdick" (save only to a very few, such as Coffin and Buttrick). "You don't have to set the stage for Fosdick," his Riverside colleague Carder once explained, "and you don't have to call him doctor; and largely because that is so you never think of calling him anything else." Even so, there is no record that Fosdick ever said to a long-standing and close associate, "Cut out that 'doctor' business and please call me 'Harry.'" However, some former students in their later years opened their devoted letters, "Dear Father Harry."

The truth is, even Fosdick's most ardent admirers, those who expressed boundless love for him, acknowledged that his manner did not invite a slap on the back or knee. Indeed, to many his reserve was impenetrable. It was not that he struck them as icy, but that he appeared a very private person who would not willingly permit a full revelation of himself. In conversation he stuck to the point, drawing out the other individual. And one did not lightly halt him to engage in idle chatter. His consciousness of the preciousness of time in fact led some to find him brusque. There was much to preoccupy his mind and while in the company of another, perhaps riding in a taxi together, he would fall into a great silence, leaving the other distinctly uncomfortable. Or, absorbed in thought, he might with sightless eyes pass by an acquaintance and fail to return the greeting. Although Fosdick had a near-photographic memory for what he read, curiously he was not good at remembering names or faces, even failing to recall on second meetings some whom he had counseled. Yet he was adept at faking it and was greatly assisted in the dissimulation by his wife, who did have the gift of name-and-face recall. In a receiving line, for example, Florence would turn to Fosdick and say, "Dear, you remember Mary and John Smith from those happy Montclair days," and Fosdick would pick up on the cue and reply with warmth, "Of course I do. How grand to see you again, Mary and John." Naturally the couple rejoiced that even after many years Fosdick recalled their names. In Maine Fosdick called on a woman whom he had not seen for many years and she expressed surprise that he remembered her name. He responded, "There it is posted above the door. I may not be very smart, but I can read."

In sum, testimony is almost universal that Fosdick inspired respect, even reverence, but some found his reserve formidable.

Very few, however, viewed him as pompous or prideful; indeed his modesty was legendary. He repeatedly refused requests from sculptors and painters to sit for them, saying, "Never under any circumstances can I spend time in an affair of this type."* As an adult he came to accept his " 'ayrick 'ead of 'air," and would even stoop down and encourage young children to run their hands through it. Introduced by the bald-headed Henry Sloane Coffin as "the man with the crocheted hair," he responded, "Mr. Toastmaster, I would far rather have hair that is crocheted than hair that is nit!" And he liked to tell the story of the woman from the South who after hearing him preach for the first time announced, "His very hair do proclaim him to be a man of God." In time the hair thinned, leading to an incident revealing of the man's

---

* The portrait by Louis Jambor, hung at Fosdick's order in an "inconspicuous place" in Riverside Church, was done from photographs and without Fosdick's prior knowledge.

humanity. While dining at a ranch, a steak knife slid off the platter being served by a twelve-year-old waitress (the daughter of the ranch owners) and stuck quivering on the one bald spot on Fosdick's head. The wound was very gory. The sobbing child fled to the kitchen certain she must have killed the guest. Fosdick drew out the knife, pressed a napkin to his bleeding head, and joined the girl in the kitchen, saying as he hugged her, "Dearie, don't cry. You know this wound is a long way from my heart."

Story after story might be advanced to illustrate Fosdick's modesty. When his brother congratulated him on a new volume of sermons, there came back the reply: "I suspect that your brotherly affection and good-will got the better of your sober judgment, but I am glad that at any rate you think there is some good stuff in the book. The older I grow the less I think well of my preaching." In one instance he responded to a handsome compliment by saying, "There's no such thing as the greatest preacher in the world. I just did what I could." On another occasion he confessed, "Like every other preacher I had my good days and my bad days. I preached some sermons I don't even want to remember."

Fosdick liked to tell on himself the story of the old Maine fisherman who greeted him with the recognition, "I listen to you every Sunday." And then added, "Yes, I turn the radio on every Sunday morning and keep it on all day." One weekend the Fosdicks joined the Philip Stimsons at their summer home in the country. Returning at a good clip on Sunday morning to deliver Fosdick in time for the eleven o'clock service, Dr. Stimson was stopped by a patrol car at the foot of the George Washington Bridge. The Irish police officer was unimpressed by Dr. Stimson's explanation of the urgency of his mission and the fame of his passenger. Fosdick remained unperturbed and even amused, observing that if detained too long he would simply walk the mile to the church. In his annual reports to the president of Union Seminary Fosdick prefaced his lists of books and articles with the disarming words, "During the year I have been guilty of the following publications."

On receiving a letter of apology from a Princeton Seminary professor who had earlier condemned Fosdick's views, Fosdick replied: "I think it highly probable that if I had heard your criticisms I might have defended them as quite justifiable. Any one who, like myself, has lived this last half-century amid the many theological contentions that have arisen must have said many unwise and unbalanced things." When a doctoral candidate subjected Fosdick's theology to fierce criticism and sent Fosdick a particularly biting chapter, Fosdick replied cordially: "You have a right to your special theological standpoint, and from that standpoint you have described with the most friendly spirit the way my theology looks to you. In some regards it does not look that way to me—my ideas of God do not seem to me 'vague' nor does the theological basis of my ethics seem 'unsteady' nor does my method of Biblical interpretation seem 'fanciful'—but I am entirely willing to let you have your say, and I am grateful that I come off as well as I do. Indeed, my chief reaction to your chapter is amazement that a Southern Baptist could write as appreciative an appraisal of my theology as you have succeeded in doing." At his retirement party Fosdick responded to the fulsome tributes by saying, "I must confess that more than once this evening I have thought about a funeral service where the clergyman delivered so eloquent and laudatory a eulogy over the dead that when he had finished the deceased man's wife got up and looked in the coffin to be sure there had not been a mistake."

As Fosdick was not vain, neither was he dour. He would have agreed with John Wesley that "a sour godliness is the devil's religion." True, some individuals found his reserve impenetrable. Yet others remember his embracing congeniality. On the job he was indeed Mr. Root-of-the-Matter. In other situations, however, when his mind was not preoccupied, he was affability itself. His smile was radiant, his eyes twinkled in amusement, his chuckle was hearty, his handshake was warm. He enjoyed a good story and was himself an adroit teller of tales. He did not dominate conversations. He was known to cheer lustily at local baseball games in Maine. Henry Pitney Van Dusen once alluded to the "Mephistophelean delight which lurks always not far beneath the surface of his mind," and this wit sparkles in Fosdick's letters to his father and brother and to such close friends as William Pierson Merrill. When, for example, Merrill twitted him for using the word "undergirdled" and begged him to "repent and return to the kindly shelter of the English language," Fosdick shot back a long reply that began: "I . . . found your lamentable letter. . . . It quite broke my heart. Not often in my brief lifetime have I received so discouraging a shock. You see, I always had thought of you as a liberal, a man of enterprise, to whom adventure was as the breath of his nostrils. I realized that you were a Presbyterian. I had long noted the almost universal effect of Presbyterianism upon its adherents. I had seen how conventional it makes them, how given to conformity, to quoting from creeds, referring to constitutions and by-laws, and even looking up the dictionary. But whenever I became discouraged by such things I said to myself, 'There's Merrill. He at least is a free spirit. He at least has resisted the pressure of conformity and subservience.' You will imagine, then, how cruel a shock it was to receive your communication which revealed the fact that even you have been looking up the dictionary." He then defended the word "under-girdling" as being "built on regular lines most conventional, and vouched for in Holy Writ. Some day I am really going to work up some new words, some swithering blingers of words, some horriferous tumulumusses of words that will make the literary goose pimples rise all over you. Some day in creative joy I am going to force the lexicographers to write a new dictionary altogether, which, as you will agree, is the very spirit of a liberal. In the meantime, farewell, O fallen idol of my dreams!"

On one occasion at Riverside in 1941, when the great debate over intervention in the war was raging, with Fosdick, of course, supporting the path of peace, the opera singer Lawrence Tibbett (whose family was associated with Riverside) elected to sing as a solo, "Arm, Arm, Ye Brave" from Handel's oratorio "Judas Maccabaeus." "If that solo isn't a lusty call for armament I never heard one," Fosdick confessed to fellow pacifist George A. Buttrick, "and I haven't gotten over laughing at the joke on me."

With family and a few very close friends Fosdick permitted the barriers to drop completely. Albert L. Scott was one such friend. Scott's son once returned to the family apartment to find his father and Fosdick sprawled on separate sofas, each man with a cigar in one hand and a beer in the other, talking desultorily. Once the Philip Stimsons and the Fosdicks were offered the use of a home in the country for a weekend vacation and unexpectedly found an outdoor swimming pool. The two men, not having bathing suits, went skinny-dipping after having secured from their wives a promise not to peek. Philip and Harry splashed and laughed like porpoises and the women, though tempted, honored their promise. These are not snapshots of a man whose repression was so absolute as to be neurotic.

Fosdick was a stiff-kneed man who never kowtowed before the high and mighty. Even more admirably, he never browbeat those in lesser stations of life. He was not a bully. His ministerial colleagues at Old First Presbyterian, Park Avenue, and Riverside without exception loved him. Said McCracken, "Dr. Fosdick is one of the great souls of our time and indeed of all time." His personal secretaries adored him. A Riverside elevator operator wrote Fosdick in retirement: "I have never forgotten your cheerful grin, the warmth of your greeting, your steadfastness of purpose and unswerving faith. I remember you so well as a man whose countenance mirrored the joy of his religion." The caretakers of his Maine retreat found him a fair, generous, honest, congenial employer. The Arizona Elkhorn Ranch owners idolized the Fosdicks: "how we loved them and their sense of humor too." The housekeeper at another vacation lodge reported that their cheerful "good morning" "gave her courage to carry on in a most distressing time." The supervisor of the Bronxville apartment where Fosdick lived in his last years testified that Fosdick was a gentleman with a great sense of humor, uncomplaining even in the face of crippling arthritis. His nurses remembered him with affectionate birthday cards, in part because he was an uncomplaining patient and in part because he generously shared his gifts of flowers and candies with the nurses and other patients. He remembered the "National Vespers" radio staff with Christmas cards and gifts.

Fosdick expected efficiency from his subordinates, but he tempered his requests with warmth. For example, when making a special request of one secretary, he added, "I am sorry you are the sufferer this time. I hope you believe in the church before you are through!" On another occasion this secretary received a request which was prefaced: "I hope you had a grand vacation and returned feeling fit. You will probably think that you need to feel fit when you receive this letter." There is not one shred of evidence that Fosdick treated those under him as objects; even those individuals who found him curt do not charge that he observed a double standard of behavior with equals and inferiors.*

Though unscarred by any serious imperfections of character, Fosdick must bear the charge of being excessively concerned that even minor scratches be hidden from public view; he honored too fully the old ad-

---

* There is a rumor that Dr. Harold Vincent Milligan, organist and choir director of the Park Avenue and Riverside churches for twenty-five years, was driven to a series of nervous breakdowns because of the coldness of an unappreciative Fosdick. The truth is that Dr. Milligan had a very serious drinking problem, although this was described in the church bulletins as a "nervous condition." The truth is also that Fosdick publicly praised Dr. Milligan in the most glowing terms; the church expressed its gratitude in anniversary celebrations of his ministry of music, involving such luminaries as Walter Damrosch; and Fosdick wrote him warmly supportive letters and counseled with his wife when the organist's condition necessitated a "rest." "Please do not let anything at this end of the line weigh upon your mind," Fosdick pleaded with Milligan on one such occasion. "Forget us altogether. . . . Under no circumstances return before you plan, and if you write that you will have to extend your visit in Kerhonkson, we shall all understand that perfectly." When in 1940 Milligan finally resigned, *The Church Monthly* carried a handsome tribute with the closing, gently masked statement: "It had been hoped and expected that a few months' rest would restore our friend and colleague to his place here, but the physicians have advised against his attempting to carry this particular responsibility and he has, to our great regret, resigned his post." It might be added that Fosdick regularly would slip into the sanctuary on Saturday afternoon and quietly listen to the choir rehearse. In a word, the rumor is unfounded.

Milligan's successor, Dr. Frederick Kinsley, was asked to resign after only five years. Again, Fosdick cannot be convicted of acting unfeelingly. Criticism of Kinsley was widespread and persistent. Fosdick successfully used his influence to find Kinsley another position, praising him as "one of the most agreeable and cooperative men it has ever been my privilege to work with," and Kinsley wrote Fosdick a warm letter of appreciation.

age, "What is the use of being gold if you appear to be brass?" It is not that the private man contradicted hypocritically the public image of gold; he was no Tartuffe. But rational calculations of propriety bore too heavily on his conduct. One misses in his life an element of Dionysian joy, a dash of wackiness, a touch of spontaneity, a splash of vulgarity, a hint of casual disarray. One doubts if he ever did anything just for the hell of it.

For example, when Albert Scott's son found his father and Fosdick at ease with their cigars and beers, the son was commanded by his father to vow that he would not relate what he saw until both men were dead. Fosdick himself remarked that should he be seen in a beer garden, "people would talk of me as though a bank had failed." Surely to worry about such a trival "transgression" suggests an excessive sensitivity to public opinion.

In 1938 Dorothy Fosdick wrote to her father: "Just between you and me, I'll keep all the details of 'bedroom littleness' quiet when someone comes to me for information for your biography! That pledge is my chief birthday present to you on your sixtieth—and I hope after knowing my fidelity (!) you will rest quieter o' nights." No breath of scandal ever grazed Fosdick for the good reason that in his life there was no scandalous conduct. Why, then, this obsession that even minor peccadillos be masked from the public?

Fosdick's nobility of character is best summed up in a statement he made to Union students on the occasion of a ceremony at the seminary honoring his fiftieth graduation year: "I have seen it all—from the horse and buggy to the atomic age—but the greatest truth in the Bible to me still remains, 'What if a man gains the whole world and loses his soul.'"

IV

Fosdick consciously limited the experiences he permitted himself, but there was one experience indispensable to his happiness and, arguably, his health and even survival. That was marriage. Some Protestant preachers never feel the need to marry—Phillips Brooks, for example. Fosdick, however, was the sort of man who desperately required the intimate companionship and nurturing care of a wife, the union with another of heart, mind, and body. In Florence Allen Whitney he found the perfect partner. As it is inconceivable to imagine Fosdick as a lifelong bachelor, so it is almost inconceivable to imagine a better-paired couple. One knows experientially, observationally, and statistically that many marriages are disasters and that most marriages perhaps are only marginally and sporadically happy. Yet one knows, too, that a very few marriages must be pronounced "good"—for the Kingdom of God, it was said long ago, is like a man who gives a marriage feast. When Harry Fosdick and Florence Whitney joined in matrimony, the result was a good union of sixty years filled, the husband recalled, with priceless memories of companionship.

Florence was born in Worcester, Massachusetts, on September 4, 1878, her ancestral roots dating back to colonial times. Her father was one of the city's leading merchants and a dedicated Baptist and supporter of Baptist causes. She was graduated from Smith College in 1900. Presently, she visited Colgate where her uncle taught. A party was underway one Friday evening in the president's home. When Florence entered the library, Harry's heart pounded. On Sunday he wrote his mother that he had found an angel whom he intended to marry. He rushed Florence with headlong determination. Other swains presented themselves, but Harry gave them small chance. His preliminary collapse turned into utter rout. "I was my own man no longer," he later recalled, "and never have been since." When Florence returned for a second visit, Harry felt his first clear gleam of hope. That summer on his way to New York and Union Seminary he detoured to Westminister, Massachusetts, where the Whitneys maintained a country home, and one evening he stammered a proposal—and was accepted. Marriage was prudently postponed until August 16, 1904, in order for Fosdick to complete his studies and receive his first call to Montclair.

Florence was an attractive woman: slight, dark haired and with a flawless complexion and a voice like velvet. She possessed vibrancy, good health, abundant energy, and sufficient sturdiness to play golf and tennis and hike and camp. Her enthusiasm was infectious. She radiated friendliness, yet withal was a gentle-woman of dignity. She was intelligent, well read, and her husband's severest literary critic. Music she loved as she did nature; she had an exceptional knowledge of flowers, birds, and trees. She remained involved with Smith College and in 1950 was awarded an honorary degree of doctor of humane letters. For years she was a member of the National Board of the Y.W.C.A., earning this tribute from her colleagues: "It was a joy to work with her, for she brought an infectious enthusiasm and buoyancy to everything she did." She never seemed discouraged by problems, the tribute continued, but rather "she looked upon them as challenges to be met with courage and faith." Indeed "eagerness," "enthusiasm," "cheerfulness," were terms employed by many in their remembrances of her. She pulled her load at Union Seminary and at the nearby Horace Mann School attended by the Fosdicks' daughters. She was instrumental in the formation of a neighborhood center. At Riverside she was long a leader in the Women's Society and fostered the Nursery-Kindergarten Weekday School for the children of working women. (At the time of her death it was asked that in lieu of flowers contributions be made to a permanent fund named after her to support the school.) Clearly the women of Riverside (not excluding the wives of the other ministers) adored her.

Of course, Florence Fosdick was not a superwoman. She feared flying, but then travel by plane did not become commonplace until near the end of her life. She also suffered jimjams before speaking in public, her husband once reporting that "for about twenty-four hours before she speaks she is about the most miserable girl on the face of the planet. I have no doubt, however, that she is making a mighty good speech and I am going to take her to the Philharmonic tonight and let music assuage the turbulence of her savage breast." But testimony is virtually unanimous that Florence Fosdick was a wonderful woman in her own right and her husband a lucky fellow. Perhaps the highest compliment came from a man many years her junior who reported that if he were invited to a dinner party (and if there were no pretty girls his own age present) he hoped he would be fortunate enough to draw Florence as his table partner.

Florence Fosdick was as authentically integrated a person as her husband, but she was not "liberated" as that terms came to be understood by a later generation. That is, she did not place her career, interests, or self-fulfillment above or against those of her husband. She was a fiercely loyal, utterly devoted, unflaggingly protective, unfailingly helpful wife. She shielded Fosdick from those who made excessive demands on his time and energy. She watched his health with hawklike eyes. She spared him all household chores, including the paying of bills. She improved his manuscripts. She smoothed social situations—remembering names, making apologies when Fosdick slipped away from a group ("Harry has another appointment . . ."), picking up the conversation when her husband's mind was preoccupied and checking him occasionally with a "Now Harry!" and entertaining guests in his absence. Even though guests might be at the table, Fosdick always took his Sunday noon meal on a tray in his study, conserving his energy for the afternoon radio broadcast. People felt comfortable with Florence, she made them feel at ease, as they did not always feel in the presence of Dr. Fosdick.

Harry and Florence were friends as well as husband and wife. Observers sensed a feeling of harmony between them. They liked each other and enjoyed each other's company. "I confess that I like this kind of monogamy," said Fosdick on their fifty-third anniversary. For Harry, age could not wither nor custom stale Florence's charm. As happens, a kind of telepathy grew up between them. Repeatedly, they had the experience of one saying something and the other replying, "Why, I was just thinking that." And when suddenly, unexpectedly, Florence died, the aged husband found comfort in his few remaining years communing with her. In thinking about Florence and her husband there comes to mind the farewell words of Juliet to Romeo: "My lord, my love, my friend!"

Because of this harmonious love between Florence and Harry their two children* were nurtured in a family atmosphere of security, serenity, and happiness—or so they recall. Of course, no childhood is *totally* free of conflict, jealousy, anxiety, pain, darkness. We may presume only to insist that insofar as the evidence permits a judgment, the Fosdick girls did know, thanks to both parents, childhoods of rare equanimity. Millions of parents have had their hearts broken by their children and additional millions in their heart of hearts know that sooner or later their children will renounce them. Florence and Harry never knew that fear or that crushing experience. That they did not was a matter of luck, or grace, but it is at least partially attributable to the fact that they were wise and loving parents.

Elinor was born in 1911 and Dorothy in 1913. When the family moved from Englewood, New Jersey, to a faculty apartment at Union, both girls attended the nearby Horace Mann School, Teachers College experimental enterprise. Both were bright as pennies, won medals for scholarship and citizenship, and held student offices. They were aware of their father's fame, but could not understand why people flocked to hear him speak when, after all, they heard him daily.

Crowded as Fosdick's hours were, he found the time—he made the time—to read aloud to the girls, rock them in his arms and whisper comforting words when they had bad dreams, counsel them in their troubles, and play games with them. Both girls were high spirited and chatterers, Fosdick once reporting about them: "They are now back with snuffly colds but with apparently undiminished pep. They make just as much noise as ever, the only difference being that, having colds in their throats, it is a different kind of noise." When naughty, a sharp look of disapproval from their mother more than substituted for a spanking.

To be a parent is to worry, and when the girls were young, Fosdick experienced a stab of concern when late one night he heard Dorothy call in alarm from her bedroom. He rushed in to find a thoroughly embar-

---

* A third child died in infancy.

rassed young man who had climbed through the apartment window thinking it was the Union dorm room of his brother. Fosdick could only exclaim, "Why Paul Penfield, what are you doing here?"

Fosdick once said, "I happen to be a Baptist minister, but it never occurred to me that my obligation to my children was to make Baptists of them." Nevertheless, on Easter Sunday 1925 he personally baptized them into the membership of Montclair's First Baptist Church in a deliberately unpublicized ceremony, and the following year both parents and children were received into the membership of Park Avenue Baptist Church. Ordinarily, family morning prayers were said (though not while vacationing at the Maine summer home), and in the evening the girls were taught the prayer:

> O God, our heavenly Father, hear my prayer tonight. If I have done wrong deeds or thought wrong thoughts today, forgive me, and help me tomorrow to do better. I thank thee with all my heart for home and friends, for food and play, and all the blessings that make life beautiful. Make me more worthy of them all.
>
> Bless Mother, Father, Sister, and all my dear friends and family everywhere, and all the people whom I do not know and need thy care tonight. For Jesus sake! Amen!

One of the girls when little asked her father if God had a skin. Rather shocked, Fosdick exclaimed that, of course, God did not have a skin; whereupon the daughter burst into peals of laughter. And, when Fosdick demanded what she was laughing at, she said: "To think how funny he must look without one!"

When Elinor was thirteen Fosdick wrote to his father:

> The children are riotously well. Elinor begins to look quite like a grown-up girl and my paternal heart goes pit-a-pat once in a while when I look at her. She reminds me again and again of mother. Every once in a while I catch in her eyes a look so distinctly like mother's that it almost startles me. Plainly, I have got to get around to the idea that at least one of my daughters is a young lady before long and you can bet your bottom dollar that I am going to be the best beau she has for several years yet before some young feller cuts me out. We have just finished reading together Herbert Pyle's "Men of Iron" and if Ruth hasn't read it she ought to get it. It is a ripping good story.

Elinor's love for her father is equally transparent. On his fifty-fourth birthday Fosdick received from "Eli Fuz," then at Smith College, a charming letter: "I have been thinking *'special* hard and loving you oh-so-much! You're the best and grandest Dadda-boy that ever was made—and I don't care who knows it." A later birthday letter reads in its entirety:

> Dearest Daddy, *HAPPY BIRTHDAY!!!* How I wish I could be home right now to give you a big bear hug, squeeze, and kiss!! I'm sorry I can't be with you, but I want you to be *sure* and know how *very* much I love and adore you. You are the most wonderful, and understanding, and altogether admirable father in the world, and your eldest and first-born is proud indeed to be a member of your family. Oh—dadda-boy—it's been a long time since we've had a good old pow-wow together, and so much has happened in the last few months—but I'm saving it all up for you, as I don't want you to miss out on anything that happens to me because I need your fatherly support and advice. I've never been happier in my life, and I must say I've led a pretty happy existence so far. It's all your and mumsie's doing, and I want you to know I am speechless with gratitude whenever I think over the course of my life. You may be the "savior of the masses" and the "greatest minister in the world"—and that's quite in line with my thoughts too—but to me you're my Daddy first and foremost, and I love you! Here's to many more Happy Birthdays, and years and years of increasing happiness to the head of the fuzzy-wuzzy clan! Adoringly—Eli Fuz

Upon graduating from Smith College and after consulting with Dr. Simon Flexner of the Rockefeller Institute (thanks to her father's good offices), Elinor entered the Johns Hopkins Medical School. While there she reported to her father: "Helen, the dear old colored mammy cook, also asked about you. She thinks you're just about God himself, and as a consequence I get the corner piece of cake, the biggest piece of pie, and breakfast as late as I like Sunday mornings. It's sorta nice having 'God' in the family. Very bestest love, and no 'April fooling' about it either. Eli Fuz." She received her M.D. in 1937, Fosdick, as it happily happened, delivering the commencement address.

In 1939 Dr. Elinor Fosdick was wedded to Dr. Roger Sherman Downs at the Maine summer home, Fosdick performing the ceremony. Two children were born to them, Patricia and Stephen. Then came Pearl Harbor. Dr. Downs enlisted in the Navy as a medical officer and was assigned to duty in the Mediterranean. Over sixteen months passed before a brief leave permitted him to again take his wife and young children in his arms. The cruel war sent him back to the Mediterranean while Elinor lived in Litchfield, Connecticut. Early in 1945 Lt. Downs was assigned to the Port of New York to study the medical aspects of submariners' lives. The joyous reunification of the family was brief beyond tragedy. On February 5 Lt. Downs, a handsome, engaging young man, returned from a day spent in a bathoscope to the Fosdicks' apartment and went to bed. He and Elinor had just found an apartment of their own in New York and Elinor was at their home in Litchfield arranging for furniture to be shipped. The next day when he did not appear from his bedroom the maid entered to find him dead. He had been cut down by a massive cerebral hemorrhage at age thirty-four. Fosdick drove to Litchfield to break the cruel news. "That was the hardest thing I ever had to do in my life," he confided to a family friend. To another he wrote, "The blow that has fallen on our household is very heavy, but you may be sure that the resources are ample to meet it. Elinor . . . in particular is standing up with fine courage."

Elinor did more than endure; she triumphed. She won for herself a splendid career in medicine: in Geneva, Switzerland, for two years with the World Health Organization; in Lebanon working with malnourished Arab refugee children; in New York City's most prestigious hospitals and medical schools and Columbia University; in charge of all medical services in the Bronxville schools. Equally inspiring, without a husband she raised two splendid children. Patricia, following in the footsteps of both parents, became a medical doctor, and in time was married to a fine man of Jewish heritage. Stephen became a lawyer and in time was married to a charming Dutch girl, a Roman Catholic, and their child, Margot Ann, brought much joy to great-grandfather Fosdick in his final years.

Fosdick retired in 1946, moving to a spacious house in Bronxville. Elinor and the children lived with Harry and Florence until the children went off to college. What might have been a tense and trying housing arrangement proved in fact to be pleasant. For one thing, Elinor and the kids were in Geneva for two years and the Fosdicks were often off on long vacations, providing breathing space for all. For another, Harry and Florence did not interfere with Elinor's authority. Above all, the grandparents adored their grandchildren, and they in turn loved "Gramp" and "Gram." Fosdick once jokingly observed to daughter Dorothy: "We need somebody now who can persuade Steve to stop devising refined masculine methods of teasing Patty, and someone who can persuade Patty to eat a meal inside of an hour and a half. When, therefore, you think that you are having difficulty with Russia, cheer up! It's nothing compared with running 606. In all seriousness, they are darlings, just natural high-spirited youngsters, and we are having a marvelous time with them." Not unlike other grandfathers, Fosdick was generous with presents. One Christmas he gave the kids a small sailboat and an outboard motor to drive their rowboat, which were accompanied by a loving poem. Like other grandfathers, Fosdick enjoyed telling stories about his grandchildren. A particular favorite was one about six-year-old Patty taking the bus to Riverside Church with her grandfather; as the great shapes of the church and Grant's Tomb came into view, Patty cried, "There's Gramp's church and there's Gramp's tomb." Clearly Elinor was the sort of daughter every father dreams of claiming. When young she brought him much joy and when mature much comfort and companionship, and her children were the apple of their grandfather's eye.

Dorothy, too, was the source of much happiness and pride. She too attended Smith College, but unlike her older sister, she concentrated on history, economics, and political science. She then went to Columbia, where she took her doctorate in public law. Invited to join the Smith faculty, she taught and wrote until 1942 when she was called to the State Department's Division of Special Research to make plans for the postwar world. She served with American delegations to the Dumbarton Oaks and San Francisco conferences, which helped frame the United Nations, and to the General Assembly of the United Nations. When the powerfully influential Policy Planning Staff of the State Department was created, Dorothy was the only woman to join this brilliant group of movers and shakers: George F. Kennen, Paul Nitze, Louis Halle, C. B. Marshall, and as advisors, Hans Morgenthau and Reinhold Niebuhr. It was a signal honor, and in recognition of this (and her scholarly writings) she was the recipient of numerous honorary degrees. Subsequently she served as a senior advisor on the staff of Senator Henry M. Jackson, her special expertise being national security matters.

Dorothy had more than a touch of both parents in her. Trim, curly-haired, attractive, intelligent, energetic, enthusiastic, good-natured but capable of directness, and possessing taut nerves, her parents probably found her the more spirited of the two children, and she and her father would argue briskly about public affairs. Her devotion to her father is well expressed in a birthday letter: "I love you from the depths of my heart, am as proud as punch of being *your* offspring, and think that nobody ever in this wide-world or in 100,000 years of history had a pater to compare with mine. So just remember, when the Church makes a fuss over you tonight, that your own daughter knows you're a darn sight better man than even those dear people *imagine!*"

Because Fosdick was an adoring father, he shared Dorothy's pain when her romance with Adlai Stevenson ended. Governor Stevenson and Dorothy first met at the U.N. Conference in San Francisco in 1945. After Stevenson's marriage broke up in 1949, his need and nature were such that he entered into simultaneous romances with several smitten women, including Dorothy Fosdick. Adlai and "Dicky" enjoyed each other's company in Washington and elsewhere, including a visit with the senior Fosdicks in 1951 at their Maine retreat!* It is clear from Stevenson's biography and volumes of published letters that the love-stricken mature woman gave her heart fully to the Democratic leader, whereas he gave his heart only partially to her. That the romance passed, that marriage never materialized, seems more of a commentary on Stevenson than on Dorothy. In any case, their love affair is a testimony to Dorothy's intelligence and attractiveness, for Stevenson would never have suffered a foolish woman gladly.

Dorothy, like Elinor, was a splendid daughter and she sustained her parents with love and comfort to their last days.

Fosdick's five-year-younger brother Raymond was graduated in 1905 from Princeton, where he came under the enduring spell of Woodrow Wilson, then Princeton's president, and the progressivism and idealism imperishably linked with that flawed great leader. Raymond then received a law degree from New York School of Law. His future law partners would ruefully but accurately observe that he practiced law only when there wasn't anything more interesting to do. Raymond quickly became involved in reform investigations in New York City, where he caught the attention of John D. Rockefeller, Jr., and in 1910 began a lifelong association about as intimate as Rockefeller ever permitted. During the Great War Raymond was tapped chairman of the War Department and Navy Department Commission on Training Camp Activities and later saw distinguished service in France as civilian aide to General Pershing. With the coming of peace he was appointed by President Wilson to the position of Under Secretary General in the League of Nations. When the United States failed to enter the League, Raymond returned to close involvement in Rockefeller philanthropies (though to retain his independence he was formally a member of a prestigious New York law firm), and in 1936 he was named president of the Rockefeller Foundation.

Recalled a Foundation associate: "Ray Fosdick had so warm and so friendly a personality that the whole atmosphere within the staff of the Rockefeller Foundation changed when he became president." Testimony is unanimous in supporting this portrait. He was sunny, witty, cultivated, urbane, at once a Wilsonian idealist and a Gotham pragmatist. He rattled off tunes on the piano as readily as telling mildly bawdy jokes. Unlike his brother, he reveled in Manhattan's restaurant and theatre life. Though raised a Baptist and initially not inactive in church administra-

---

* After the visit, Stevenson wrote young Stevie Downs a letter in which he dubbed "that celebrated old explorer and navigator, Dr. Fosdick, the scourge of Boothbay Harbor."

tive affairs, sometime in the early 1920s his piety melted away until he did not have enough faith, he confessed, "to put on the back of a postage stamp."*

Ray and Harry delighted in each other's company and in Ray's presence Harry's measured merriment became less so. Relatives and friends recall that at family dinners the banter between the two brothers was frolicsome. Even when apart, the twitting continued. Once Ray received a letter that he passed along to his brother with the notation, "for your encouragement." The letter read: "I was the first man in the United States to have hookworm. Then I joined the Baptist Church and was saved, and my mind has been blank ever since. Has the Foundation any work for me in gynecology or obstetrics?" When a demented California woman requested that Florence Fosdick and Ray free her from the "unwelcome & degenerated behavior" of Dr. Fosdick (actions, she charged, witnessed by Mr. Rockefeller and made possible through "soul glandular connections"), Ray noted laconically: "Dear Harry: Here is a letter that came to me from one of your girl friends. Of course, I can't keep up with your affairs. . . . I notice that she says she has never met you in any material way. How do you communicate with these women spiritually? I have never been able to do it." At the occasion of Harry's sixtieth birthday party held at Riverside, Ray rose to protest having to toast his brother with a glass of ice water ("I thought it was going to be a party"); mischievously recalled Harry's "preaching" to his stalled boat engine in a vocabulary "significantly theological"; alluded to guiding his brother away from moral pitfalls and writing his sermons; and closed: "Harry, I would put it like this: Forty—no, that's too long—thirty years more of a useful and radiant life with plenty of sermons to preach and plenty of books to write; thirty more birthdays, a peaceful end, and not too much hell afterward."

Ray delighted in being mistaken for his brother and rejoiced in compliments received on "his" published sermons. Once, however, *Time* did a story on Ray's presidency of the Rockefeller Foundation accompanied by a photograph of Harry, eliciting from Harry a letter to the editors: "Sirs: I never was particularly pleased with my face and am quite will-

* Chancellor Louis J. Finklestein of neighboring Jewish Theological Seminary, Harry's friend, wrote a biography of a second-century rabbi, a humanist and pacifist, but who also obeyed the smallest observances of the Law. Fosdick read the book with growing puzzlement and then walked over to Chancellor Finklestein's office, inquiring: "I just don't understand. How could this great rabbi, with all his humanity, with his pacifism, have been such a legalist and ritualist?" Finklestein was tempted to reply: "I just don't understand. How can that great man, your brother Raymond, be so noble, so good, so concerned with mercy and justice, and be a humanist, not a theist?"

ing anyone should claim it that wants to. I am fond of my brother, however, and am sorry to have it wished on him. The picture which appeared in *Time* purporting to represent Raymond Blaine Fosdick unquestionably represents me instead. That is hard on my brother. He really is much better looking than *that*. Harry Emerson Fosdick. P.S. I am, too."

After Hoover's triumph in the presidential election of 1928, Harry tongue-in-cheek wrote Raymond: "Once more I am convinced that justice rules the universe. All during this last miserable political campaign I was plagued by the fact that many people could not distinguish between you and me, so that I had to answer letters from all over the country lambasting me as a renegade and apostate because I was supporting Smith; but now the election is over, the country has been saved, peace, prosperity, and progress shine once again upon us and reviews of your last book are coming in kindly attributing the authorship to me. I am sure that God is in his heaven and that no one can tip the everlasting beam of the infinite righteousness."

The bantering must not be permitted to mask the real bond between the brothers.* Nor should it be permitted to obscure the fundamental seriousness of both men. Their discussions often involved weighty matters of politics (religious and secular), diplomacy, and economic and social problems. Harry once wrote to Raymond in Paris: "Well, I mustn't get started, for I am full to busting on the international situation and shall be mighty glad when you get back in the fall so that I can have somebody to talk to without having to measure my language for purposes of publication. There are certain areas of the international situation where nothing but extreme profanity is adequate and in the situation which unhappily I occupy in the public eye I am not allowed this normal and wholesome method of expression save in the bosom of my family." When the *New York Times* speculated that Harry might be a witness for the defense in the famous Scopes trial, Ray shot him a letter the next day advising against the appearance on four grounds: Harry "would waste a lot of time hanging around the courtroom" waiting to be called; "in the minds of a good many people it might look as if you were hunting publicity"; the motives of the defense lawyers, Dudley Malone and Clarence Darrow, were not to be trusted; and the case was not "really of great importance." Harry heeded his brother's advice.

The love of Harry for Raymond found its fullest authentication following a shattering tragedy in 1932 at Easter. Winifred Finlay Fosdick, Raymond's wife of twenty-two years, fatally shot their two sleeping children and then turned the weapon on herself. An unsuspecting Raymond

* Raymond dedicated his autobiography "To my brother Harry Emerson Fosdick with a lifetime of affection."

awoke to quiet, only then discovering the scene of horror. "Win," as she was affectionately called, had long suffered strange and terrifying moods, and it is clear from letters exchanged among her husband, brother-in-law, and father-in-law that her emotional health was a matter of loving concern to her family. Psychiatrists diagnosed her condition as manic depression and professional help was sought, but no one suspected how desperate her state had become.

After the deed the devastated husband's own sanity hung in the balance. Harry (canceling all traveling engagements) and Florence took him into their home for agonizing weeks as he confronted the reality of his loss. Raymond's perilous condition is documented in letters from Harry to a gravely concerned and magnificently supportive Rockefeller. Gradually Raymond was able to sleep unbrokenly for a few hours and to keep a few bites of food down. Gradually he was able to play several games of tennis, a few holes of golf, concentrate for consecutive minutes on a book. Surviving, barely, the shock, Raymond slowly returned to his ebullient and energetic self, and by 1936 he was ready to accept the presidency of the Rockefeller Foundation and marry a fine woman, his secretary Elizabeth Miner. He later said of the period following the tragedy: "I know from my own experience that a man can make terms with sorrow and learn to live with it. But against loneliness there is no protection; it creeps through the stoutest armor, and it can make life merely a series of gray days."

When the newspaper reported the tragedy, a man suffering a comparable loss wrote Harry wondering if God could forgive a woman who killed her own children, and Fosdick replied: "We ourselves, with all our fallibility, are sensible enough to recognize that insanity does away with all responsibility. My sister-in-law was not more morally responsible for what she did than a tuberculosis patient is for having a rising temperature in the afternoon."

Raymond's religious faith, as we know, faded in the 1920s, but not his essential humanity. Because the Rockefeller Foundation played some role in the development of the atomic bomb, the hideous device rested heavily on his conscience. When his car radio carried the announcement of the dropping of "Little Boy" over Hiroshima, Raymond, guilt-ridden, began to shake uncontrollably and was forced to pull over to the side of the road, where he became physically ill. Days later he wrote an associate: "It seems to me that America has taken her place among the conquerors of history who have won by utter ruthlessness. Nothing that Attila or Genghis Khan ever dreamed of can match our wholesale slaughter of civilians in Hiroshima and Nagaski."

Raymond's twin sister, Edith Wellington Fosdick, also knew Harry's enduring love, although circumstances did not permit sustained companionship, as was the case between the brothers. Miss Fosdick began her career in social work, served in France in World War I with the Y.M.C.A., and then began "teaching her way around the world": California; Kobe College, Japan; Chinling College, Nanking; the American College, Athens; and the Woman's College, Istanbul. She had harrowing experiences in Europe on the eve of World War II and immediately after the outbreak of hostilities, finally reaching the safety of New York via passage around the Cape of Good Hope. (Her brothers had cabled in great urgency that she leave Europe before the storm broke.) She lived in retirement at Columbia's Butler Hall, near the Fosdicks' Union apartment, and summered in Maine, adjacent to the Fosdick's island, and so at least in the last years of her life she was physically close to her brothers. It was good that they were near for at the end she suffered from a progressive arterial disease, necessitating the amputation of a leg. Understandably depression gripped her. Harry described her death to a friend: "There was nothing ahead, so the doctors said, except more and more disastrous limitations, and probably further amputation, so that Edith was praying for the swiftest way out. It came in the form of a cerebral hemorrhage, which brought coma almost immediately, and Edith slept peacefully away. While, therefore, we deeply mourn her loss, we also rejoice in her liberation. There are times, as you know well, when death is a welcome relief, and it was that to my sister."

We know that Harry adored his mother who died in 1904, but it must not be assumed that Harry resented the woman Frank Fosdick took as his second wife in 1907. To the contrary, all evidence suggests that Harry admired and liked Myrtilla Constantine (only three years his senior) and appreciated the care and companionship she gave Frank. From the union a child was born, Ruth Sheldon Fosdick, and again all evidence points to an affectionate relationship between Harry and his half-sister. When Ruth married Rufus Horton Jones, Jr., in 1939, the ceremony took place in the Riverside Chapel, Raymond gave the bride away and Harry officiated. Myrtilla died in 1950 at age seventy-five after a long illness, comforted to the end by letters and visits from her stepsons. Ruth Jones survived Harry by four years and there is no hint of discord between them. Indeed, "Myrtie" and Ruth, Harry and Raymond, and their families (and Edith after 1939) saw a lot of each other in Maine during the summers, anticipating in their letters coming together and in the autumn recalling happy memories.

In addition to immediate family ties, there was a large circle of Fosdick-Whitney relatives, and these clan relationships appear tight and affectionate. Cropping up in Harry's correspondence, showing up at holiday dinners, turning up for visits at the Union apartment or Mouse Island or at the Whitney's home in Worcester, Massachusetts, or country home in Westminster, Massachusetts, or at Raymond's home in Montclair were a whole tribe of "Grandpas" and "Grandmas" and "Aunts" and "Uncles" and nieces and nephews. Harry Emerson Fosdick was surrounded by kin who expressed their love in this fashion: "Dear Harry: Blessings on you, this your ninetieth birthday. Looking back over the years I discover I have known you for more than two-thirds of that time and that it would take almost another ninety years to tell you what 'Uncle Harry' has meant to me. How very much richer my life has been for your contribution to it."

Inevitably life exacted its toll from these people. They were not immune from business failures, accidents, mental crack-ups, ill health, the disabilities of old age. These terrors of existence are compellingly captured in a letter Fosdick wrote his father concerning a relative and his plight:

There is, I regret to say, no heartening news about _____, _____. _____ has had a specialist from New York go up to examine him and he is totally and hopelessly blind. He cannot even lift his lids and he never will be able to see. He is also quite without sense of taste or smell. Next Monday he will appear in court and plead guilty, throwing himself upon the mercy of the court. _____ and _____, I think, are taking it for granted that he will go to prison, and are hoping for a short term. They already are making investigation as to some place where they can have him sent where as a prisoner he will be able to learn Braille. Everything has gone, so far as financial support is concerned. _____ and _____ _____ have nothing whatever left, everything has been carried down with _____'s collapse, except possibly their house, which may yet be saved. _____ and _____ expect to have _____ and _____ with them this winter. _____ says that the people in _____ are seeing nobody. _____ is very weak and is able to sit up only about two hours a day even now. They remain shut up in their house and I think are greatly helped by letters from their friends. At any rate, the expression of gratitude which came to me for a letter which I wrote to _____ would indicate that they grasp at any straws of friendliness in sight. It is all too terrible to think or write about at length, and I have long since reached the place where my nerves are numb and can feel no more than they have felt already.*

* It would be unkind, I think, to identify the individuals in this letter.

V

An old deacon once offered up a prayer at the installation of a young
pastor, "Oh Lord, if Thou wilt only keep him humble, we will keep him
poor." Happily Fosdick did not share the demeaning experience of thousands of parsons in America who were compelled to live, at best, in
shabby gentility, without books, travel, cultural opportunities, leisure
time, reduced in the end to tired and fawning creatures. Fosdick escaped
this fate in part because his official boards were too wise to pinch in his
case, but primarily because he carved out a handsome income independent of his ministerial salary. "I do not have to preach in order to live,"
Fosdick once gratefully told his congregation. He then proceeded to describe the temptation to blunt the Gospel faced by ill-paid preachers with
families to support. Fosdick, definitely, was not unmindful of the hard
words of Jesus concerning the perils to the spirit of acquisitiveness and
his style of living is not illustrative of Veblen's mordant observations
concerning "conspicious consumption." Still, as he reported to Rockefeller, his income placed him among the less than four tenths of one percent of Americans who received over $25,000 annually, and when he
prayed for those whose hearts might be hardened by wealth (he informed Rockefeller) "I think of *myself*" and "I pray with myself in
mind." Indeed, inasmuch as his annual income often considerably exceeded $25,000, he belonged to an even more exclusive company of
affluent Americans.

Fosdick's concluding salary from the First Baptist Church in Montclair
was $5000. This was the sum he next received from the First Presbyter-
ian Church. And this was the modest sum he insisted must accompany
his call to the Park Avenue Baptist Church. As he wrote James C. Colgate, "The maximum salary which I am willing to receive is $5000. You
would know, of course, without my saying so, that my interest in this
adventurous enterprise of which we are thinking is not at all financial,
but I shall be glad to have that fact made unmistakable by the definite
understanding that my salary shall not in any case exceed five thousand
dollars a year." Colgate concurred in order "that no suggestion to the
effect that you had been bought could be made by those outside of our
church who would care to attack our actions." The figure was raised to
$7000 in 1928 and to $10,000 in 1930 to partially compensate for a reduction in his professorial salary owing to a lighter teaching load at
Union, but he refused hikes in the depression, explaining to Rockefeller
that "I have been and still am unwilling, especially in times like these,
that either directly or indirectly any such increase should be made in my

salary." Indeed, on the eve of retirement he received from The Riverside Church only $9,265.36 per year.

What conclusions may be drawn from this salary situation? Clearly Fosdick was not avaricious, for, as he notified Rockefeller, ministers in comparable pulpits in New York, even those much younger than he, were making at least $15,000, and should he pass from the scene through death or retirement Riverside would have to pay his successor about that sum. Equally apparent is Fosdick's concern not to *appear* avaricious, and his call to Park Avenue at only $5000 drew national attention. A possible unhappy consequence is that lay leaders throughout the country mused, "Well, if the great Fosdick receives only $5000 from Rockefeller, surely our minister will be happy with half that amount." In fact, a group of students at Union during the Depression, believing that Fosdick still received $5000, pledged themselves never to accept a salary exceeding $3600—a fair sum relative to that received by their mighty mentor.*

Fosdick's total income was augmented by $3600 received from Union and by the spacious, handsome apartment on the second floor of Knox Hall provided free by the seminary. In 1934, however, he reduced his teaching load and accepted as compensation only the apartment—and even the apartment came not at his insistence, but Union's. Moreover, Fosdick insisted that his retirement allowance be forfeited, informing Union's President Coffin: the allowance "I have no right to whatever and I am sure you agree with me in this obvious judgment."

Patently Fosdick had a comfortable income derived from his twin salaries as minister and professor, but it was money from other sources that lifted him into the ranks of the fairly affluent. He won fees as high as $1000 for a single speaking engagement. He won stipends as high as $1200 for a single article. And over the decades he earned tens of thousands of dollars in book royalties. His voice and pen, both in much demand, therefore, added measurably to his regular salaries, and even after his retirement from Riverside and Union in 1946, he continued to enjoy an annual income of about $50,000. In addition two small trusts were held in Florence's name at the Worcester County Trust Co. and the Chase Manhattan Bank. Moreover, First Presbyterian, Park Avenue Baptist, and Riverside provided funds to defray costs incurred in the conduct of his ministry and he also had access to funds to be used in lending a financial helping hand to individuals in distress. Finally, Rockefeller showered him with gifts. Some Fosdick declined, such as an offer to

---

* Some individuals believe that Fosdick's modest salary must have served as a drag on the salaries received by his associate ministers at Riverside. Perhaps this is true, but it must be remembered that on his insistence (and over Rockefeller's reservations), he received but little more than his associates.

place a chauffered limousine at his beck and call (Fosdick elected to continue to whistle for a taxi on Broadway to make his appointed rounds). Others he accepted: a dictaphone; a fur coat (with close instructions on its care); vacations at Williamsburg with every expense paid down to the morning newspaper; in times of major illness the finest medical care Dr. Simon Flexner and the Rockefeller Institute could supply; and a little "free will" fund totaling $25,000.

Fosdick's circumstances enabled him to turn over to others some of the chores that burden ordinary mortals. In 1924 he reported: "Florence is happy in her household arrangements. She has gotten a lovely southern girl who is studying here to do the upstairs work and stay with the children evenings in return for her room in our house and her breakfast with us. She really is an addition to the family and the children have quite fallen in love with her. Florence also has landed an Irish cook who served us breakfast this morning for the first time and looks as if she might be a promising acquisition for the menage. Lucile, our old colored standby, had the house all cleaned and set up for us so that Florence has not had a hard time after all." In 1928 he reported: "While I am dictating this letter let me report that Mrs. Fosdick and I have been flourishing since Mrs. Wells and you put us wise to French maids, as we never flourished before so far as our household menage is concerned. We have had the same two French maids these two years and they are the best we ever had." Union's Mr. Price cared for the seminary courtyard in which the girls played; Mr. Wesley Barrett and Captain "Chick" Pinkham cared for the Maine island and maids for the "cottage"; a yardman and servants helped maintain the large home in Bronxville into which the Fosdicks moved in 1946; "Nursie" helped look after the grandchildren; and at the end a corps of round-the-clock nurses provided final care. All this may not spell "poshness," but it does spell an "Upstairs, Downstairs" world of servants known to relatively few in Fosdick's era and beyond the reach of all but millionaires today.

Fortunately Fosdick's finances permitted extensive travel, for his health dictated that he escape periodically from the pace and pressure of New York.* In the early years the Fosdicks camped and hiked in the West. Much later they regularly vacationed at the Elkhorn Ranch near Tucson, owned by their friends the Millers, where they became much beloved by the "regulars." The ranch, covering 10,000 acres and drawing never more than twenty-five guests, possessed unpretentious adobe quarters. The Fosdicks did not ride, but after Harry had spent a morning at his desk, they would walk, enjoy the magnificent desert visits, and

* We already have related his travels to Japan and China, speaking tour of the British Isles, and "A Pilgrimage to Palestine."

perhaps picnic. At about age fifty, Fosdick began taking regular two-week winter vacations, soaking up the Florida sunshine at Sebring or New Smyrna Beach. Bermuda beckoned at least once. The Whitney "farm" in Massachusetts was frequently visited and on occasion Rockefeller invited the Fosdicks to Williamsburg. Lake Placid was visited, also. Summers Harry took the girls to a fishing camp "far up in interior Maine" and later, after the death of Elinor's husband, he accompanied her and her children on camping expeditions in the North Woods, convinced that it would be handy to have a man along.

"My wife and I still think of Scotland as a kind of second home," Fosdick claimed, and one summer he and Florence went directly to Scotland and never went south of the border. Europe, too, they loved. They cruised the Mediterranean. They traveled the Rhine by steamer, reporting on their second visit "the beauty of this river-valley seems more alluring than even our memories of it." In 1928 all four Fosdicks hiked the Bavarian and Swiss Alps. In 1930 Harry recorded climbing the Feldberg, "the highest mountain in Germany." On another vacation Fosdick observed from Italy, "Never was weather more beautiful. We have not been interrupted for a single hour—such clear, delightful, sunshiny days week after week as I never saw before." The medieval towns of Germany they found fascinating. From Bayreuth came a letter: "We are having a wonderful time with Wagner—seven operas in one week!" After the war daughter Elinor was visited in Geneva.

Clearly the Fosdicks did a lot of traveling in their long lifetimes and enjoyed doing so. Harry was not a workaholic, uneasy whenever off the job. But neither was he a loafer. He arranged his summer vacations so as to always be in the pulpit during the Columbia University summer school sessions, drawing numbers of student worshippers. He usually wrote during the morning hours, if billeted at a resort or ranch, such as Elkhorn. Those things he saw and experienced while traveling often laced his sermons.

Though called by invitation or beckoned by interest to much of the globe, it was to the Maine coast that Fosdick returned most often, his "first love among all places on earth," his "terrestrial replica of Heaven." In the early years for many summers the clan—Frank and Myrtilla and Ruth, Ray and Winifred and their children, Harry and Florence and the girls—gathered in rented cottages on Juniper Point, Boothbay Harbor, Maine. Then in 1919 the Fosdicks and the G. Ellsworth Huggins, old Montclair friends, purchased Mouse Island, set in a deep ship channel some two thousand feet off the coast; and in 1924 they completed "simple cottages" (Fosdick's description) on it. Green water lapped at the island's rocky, irregular shores. On it were beautiful woods of spruce, birch, pine, and fir and wild rose and raspberry bushes and heather imported from Scotland. Fosdick loved to walk the paths around and through this setting. By mutual agreement, "Gurry" Huggins assumed responsibility for the buildings on the island while Harry watched over all things natural—and watch with care he did, voicing anguish when storms felled favorite trees.

The cost of the Fosdick "cottage," excluding plumbing and electrical outfitting, was $10,250, and in 1924 for this sum Fosdick commanded a spacious stone structure with three porches, living room, dining room, kitchen, toilet, two maid's rooms, upstairs sleeping porch, daughters' room, owner's room, mother's room, study, guest room, two baths. When inviting the Woelfkins to visit, Fosdick was not exaggerating when he said, "We have plenty of room, plenty of help, plenty of food, lots of sea, woods, water, and wind, and no two people could ever possibly be more welcome anywhere than you will be."

Because Fosdick rarely passed a full day even on vacation without reading and writing, he built a study on a point where a good "Sou Easter" blew spray on the windows and there, warmed if required by a fire in the stone fireplace, he knew perfect isolation save for a field telephone connection with the main house. (Later a second study was built for Dorothy.)

Because the children and their friends spent many glorious summer days on the island, Fosdick laid a grass tennis court and renovated two bowling alleys in the boathouse, part of the original hotel on the island, which had burned in 1913. The children tended their lobster pots in the *Flicker* while Fosdick puttered about the bay in the *Vagabond*. Harry's preference for a power launch over a sailboat was the source of much bantering between him and Charles Gilkey. When Gilkey rebuked Harry for heading straight into wind and wave and foolishly receiving a soaking, Fosdick deplied: "Many a time in that old sailboat of his the sun has set, he has lost his wind, and he would have stayed out all night if it had not been for my motor boat."

When finally ordered by his doctor not to go out in his boat alone, Fosdick growled, "All right, then, I am through with this place." When his share of the island was put up for sale, he estimated that he had "invested at least $35,000 in the property."

Though friends kidded him about "The Lion" living on Mouse Island, Harry loved the place and the Maine natives, "real people not yet spoiled by the sophistication of modern civilization." Working in his study mornings, chopping down dead trees or boating afternoons, relishing evening oyster roasts on the beach, reading aloud with Florence or in comfortable silence with visitors for an hour or two at night followed by a solid night's sleep—such a regime restored Fosdick body and soul. Invariably he contrasted glorious Mouse Island to New York, that "miserable," "wicked," "uproarious" city. Such was his Maine addiction, the Fosdicks ventured several Christmas vacations there despite ten degrees below temperatures and ferocious boreal winds. He did not even mind preaching at local churches one or two times a season. Fosdick was not exaggerating when he reported, "As a matter of fact, my little island off the Maine coast has probably kept me alive, and I justify my vacations there on that basis."

Manifestly, in New York Fosdick did not have many leisure hours. He read omniverously, but despite the inevitable newspaper accounts to the contrary, mystery stories were not his dish, nor was other light stuff. He had no real hobbies, though late in life he did take up shooting 16-mm films. Bridge bored him, though he and Florence played an occasional hand of rummy before bedtime or hearts with the girls and Union students. Modern art he did not understand and confessed, "I don't like modern art at all." Movies and plays drew him only infrequently. However, he and Florence regularly attended concerts at Carnegie Hall and he had a real appreciation of classical music. The Century Club was the one club in the city to which he belonged, joining in 1916 under the sponsorship of Andrew D. White. (Later Fosdick in turn was to sponsor Rockefeller's son, David.) The Century Club was founded in 1847 by a group of New Yorkers whose twin objects were "the cultivation of a taste for letters and arts" and the promotion of "social enjoyment" among its members. Membership (its constitution states) "shall be composed of authors, artists, and amateurs of letters and fine arts." To be sure, early in the century the club rejected the distinguished scientist Jacques Loeb because he was a Jew, and apparently the color line was not broken until Ralph Bunche entered as a guest of Edward R. Morrow.* Still by almost every comparative club standard, it was not snobbish and did not kowtow to wealth alone; the membership did have broad cultural interests. Harry (unlike Raymond) was not much caught up in the club's conviviality and welcomed it primarily as a place to have a quiet luncheon conversation.

Essentially, Fosdick was in New York City but not of the city; he could never have said with Walt Whitman of Manhattan: "O an intense life, full to repletion and varied! The life of the theatre, bar-room, huge hotel, for me!"

* As late as 1983 women were excluded from membership, a cause of consternation.

VI

Unlike King Lear, Fosdick grew old knowing honor, love, troops of friends; the names of these friends we have encountered earlier or will meet in later chapters. "Friends are necessary to a happy life," he once observed, and the happy, incontrovertible fact is that he won and held the friendship of not a few of the leading Americans of his era. Not less important, as scores of letters to him reveal, he was blessed with the friendship of many who could lay no claim to national greatness.

In closing this account of Fosdick the man, it is revealing and important to note that the Fosdick/Rockefeller, Jr., relationship never fractured. In 1937 Fosdick conducted the funeral service of the Founding Rockefeller. In 1948 when Rockefeller, Jr., lost the most important person in his life, his lovely, spirited wife, Fosdick comforted the grief-stricken husband by his presence, letters, and memorial words and prayers. When Rockefeller, Jr., died in 1960, it was the aged Fosdick who lifted up prayer and benediction at the memorial service. Fosdick followed the careers of the Rockefeller children with interest, and they in turn appreciated the minister they had known all their lives, as their letters to him reveal. Perhaps the Fosdick/Rockefeller, Jr., mutual fondness is best expressed in a prayer Fosdick picked up from a missionary who reported a Siamese elder petitioning:

> O God, bless John D. Rockefeller,
> his wife and children; and bless
> all his buffalos and elephants and
> may they all prosper.

To which Fosdick added: "In this comprehensive petition Mrs. Fosdick and I cordially join. Blessings on you, your family, and all your buffalos and elephants."

Chapter Seventeen

"Gladly Do We Teach": Thirty-eight Years as Union Seminary Professor

I

Four years after graduating from Union Theological Seminary and while serving his first pastorate, in 1908 Fosdick was invited by the seminary to be lecturer in Baptist Principles and Polity, thus, an association was renewed that continued until his retirement from the faculty in 1946 and, indeed, unofficially until his death. In 1911 he was made instructor in Homiletics, being promoted to associate professor in 1914. The following year he resigned from the Montclair pastorate to become Morris K. Jesup Professor of Practical Theology, a post he held until 1934 when the pressures of the Riverside pastorate forced a reduction in teaching and his title became adjunct professor of Practical Theology.

During Fosdick's long tenure, Union was one of the nation's outstanding seminaries.* Its faculty was internationally renowned, interdenominational in character, and drawn from the British Isles and the Continent as well as the Americas. Fosdick was the first Baptist and third non-Presbyterian to become a professor. In time, adherents of the Roman Catholic and Jewish faiths were added. Its students came from across the land and from over the oceans, averaging in number about 250 regular students and about 150 special students. (Enrollments mushroomed in the immediate postwar era at the very moment of Fosdick's retirement.)

Fosdick believed Union was the greatest seminary in the land, and he was a totally supportive faculty member. A single example illustrates

---

* In 1910 the seminary moved to Morningside Heights to occupy two city blocks. When The Riverside Church was built, a passageway connected the church and the school.

this point. In 1923 Union sought to raise $4 million for additional build-
ings and endowments. The General Education Board, a Rockefeller philanthropy, was approached. Dr. Wallace Buttrick, chairman of the board,
initially rejected the petition. Raymond Fosdick informed his brother of
the bleak news. Harry replied with a six-page exposition of Union's
greatness, uniqueness, and value to the Protestant world, an exposition
notable for its force and persuasiveness. Thanks measureably to Harry's
intervention and Raymond's good offices, Rockefeller, Jr., contributed
$1,083,333. Nor was this all. Edward S. Harkness and Arthur Curtiss
James, both well known to Harry and both his strong admirers, gave
sums of $1,250,000 and $365,000 respectively. Moreover, Harry stumped
the East making talks in support of the successful fund drive. Union's
faculty in the first half of the twentieth century included leaders in the
world of scholarship and theology and titans in the power structure of
the Protestant Establishment, but surely no professor was more loyal
than Fosdick or served the larger interests of the seminary with more
effectiveness.

                                    II

Fosdick regularly offered expository classes devoted to the Epistle to the
Hebrews and to the Book of Jeremiah. In his estimation, no character in
the Old Testament "towers so high as Jeremiah. His was the richest
experience of personal religion . . . known on earth before our Lord."
Such were the popularity of these classes, students petitioned for them
to be offered even more frequently.

Fosdick's major lectures came under the rubric of Practical Theology.
Taking various titles over the years, they tackled what was for him (and
the students) an urgent problem: the interpretation of the Bible in light
of modern scholarship to the end that the ancient truths of Scripture
might continue to speak to the mental categories of the twentieth century. Out of this course came the two major works, *The Modern Use of
the Bible* and *A Guide to Understanding the Bible*. In 1922 he provided
a prospective student with this synopsis of the course:

> The course is divided into three sections. In the first section I trace the
> history of the methods of Biblical interpretation, with a brief treatment
> of those forces which have made classical methods of exegesis impossible
> and require a new approach to the use of the Scriptures. In the second
> section I trace certain apparent contradictions between Biblical methods
> of thinking and our own. In particular, the contrast between Biblical cos-
> mology and modern science, Biblical angelology and demonology and

modern psychology, Biblical apocalyptic expectations and modern social hopes, miracles and law, Jewish-Grecian interpretations of the person of Jesus versus modern categories. In the last section I endeavor to sum up the abiding messages of Scripture in terms of their development through the manuscripts of the Bible chronologically arranged.

For young men and women going out into preaching and teaching, these classes in Practical Theology were a blessing. Room 207, the seminary's largest auditorium, was filled to overflowing. Joining the Union students were students and faculty from Columbia, Teachers College, and Barnard. The crush was such that tickets of admission, collected by a porter at the door, were required for entrance. Some visitors who were turned away sat on steps outside the open door. When Fosdick strode soldierly into the classroom, his robe (a student remembered) floated behind him like a cloud of glory, and the air crackled with anticipation. Regularly at the lecture's end the class rose and burst into applause. Apparently even the curious heathen were captivated. Reported another student to Fosdick: "I recall often the good grace and temper, the twinkling humor with which you met skeptical baiters from Columbia who had come over to your course in the Bible and who as a result of your humble and inquiring spirit must have departed more reverently and more thoughtfully than they came in."

After 1915 and until 1934, Fosdick taught either four or six hours weekly, and when one considers the concurrent demands on his energy, it is understandable that he should admit to a slight weariness, once saying to his father, "I must confess that an hour's lecture before so large a group requires a great deal of output in energy and pep." Even the January break between semesters did not bring total relief. When the Fosdicks went to a country inn for a week in 1923, for example, Harry carried with him several hundred exam papers to grade.

In this large lecture class Fosdick practiced two supposed teaching sins: he sat rather than stood and he read lectures written out in full. He pulled it off because the lectures were characterized by clarity, precision of language, force, and appositeness of illustration and were delivered in Fosdick's riveting manner. John C. Bennett, who entered Union as a student in 1926 and went on to become the seminary's president, judged that this course was one of the most popular in the history of the seminary. Fosdick "did more than anyone else to bring the results of critical study of the Bible to that whole generation. He too was an apologist, partly by argument, but, perhaps more, by fresh exposition concerning the meaning of the Bible. It is hard to exaggerate what a source of emancipation it was for thoughtful people of that period to learn that the Bible was not a book of Fundamentalism."

Fosdick had another seminary duty that he did not take casually: that of regularly preaching, on invitation of the students, the Friday morning chapel message. To be sure, student and faculty daily chapel attendance was strongly encouraged, especially during the presidency of Coffin, but it is further true that Fosdick on Friday drew a packed chapel, including individuals not connected with Union, one of whom described Fosdick's ten-minute meditations as "homiletic jewels with unforgettable impact."

III

Two former Union students, Robert Leonard Tucker and Halford E. Luccock, once fell to reminiscing, and they came to the agreement, "We are what we are by the grace of God and the perseverance of Harry Emerson Fosdick." Union alumni directories and other sources disclose that many of American Protestanism's most luminous figures studied under Fosdick. Additional hundreds went out to become steady, effective, locally beloved but nationally unrecognized laborers in the Lord's vineyard. They did not, many of them, forget their mentor. Samuel McCrea Cavert, who did go on to fame, expressed a widely held sentiment when he wrote Fosdick: "It is fifty-five years since I began to know you as a student at Union seminary. And during all the years between then and now you have never ceased to be an inspiration to me,—more so than any other Christian minister of our generation. And how many others there are who feel this way about you! I don't believe you half-realize *how many* there are." Wrote another, "Your approach to the Faith has held vs. Neo-orthodoxy and Mr. Tillich and his conferees and Hamilton, Van Buren, Altizer, Bishop Robinson, Bishop Pike and his meanderings, and Mr. Barth! Et al!! I've passed 65, and retire this year. Only God knows what an inspiration and anchor to the windward you've been to many of us, all unbeknownst to you. Thank you." And still a third wrote: "I shall always remember with particular gratitude your statement one day, 'Do not strain yourself to believe.' That took the artificial lid off of my world and made my quest for knowledge a joyous adventure. From that time on I have had a grand time disagreeing with St. Paul or Peter or Jeremiah or any of them and appreciating them all the more because of the freedom to do that."

It would be possible to fill a hundred pages with comparable general testimony, but rather than do this let us home in on student recollections of Fosdick's homiletics class, for it was in this intimate, intense setting that Fosdick's personality was felt most powerfully. Not surprisingly, the witnesses report different experiences of the class and differing opinions of the teacher.

A selected group of students, not more than a dozen each term, would meet with Fosdick in James Memorial Chapel. Two weeks prior to the class Fosdick had asked for volunteers, usually two in number and never more than three, to prepare sermons ten to fifteen minutes in length. (Those who exceeded the time limit "got the gong.") Fosdick tossed out an assignment by taking a text, a topic, a life situation, a quotation, a problem, or a chapter from Scripture. From the chapel pulpit the volunteer would preach the prepared sermon (after outlining it on the blackboard), Fosdick listening intently and taking notes in shorthand. At the sermon's conclusion, Fosdick would ask with great deliberation, "Now-what-shall-we-say-to-Mr. Smith?", and then proceed to comment, perhaps also by a few deft touches remodeling the blackboard outline. The other members of the class would presently be invited to join the critique.

Naturally enough, the students found the experience harrowing, one reporting: "I was so scared I started in the middle of my sermon and then went to the beginning and forgot the end." A few managed to conquer their stage fright. When Rollo May, who became a distinguished existential psychiatrist, preached on "Suffering," Fosdick sat silently in awe and then after a long pause said only, "You know all about it!" When Ralph Sockman, the future Methodist pulpit giant, concluded his student sermon, Fosdick dryly allowed how not even a homiletical professor could spoil him.

Although all agree that Fosdick's comments were incisive, most students remember them as being appreciative, positive, supportive, never cutting, sarcastic, or unkind. Future Union president, Roger L. Shinn, recalled: "He listened to our first halting sermons, then criticized them with kindly but penetrating insight." A few, however, found them pretty stiff. On one instance Fosdick said to a student, "Stein, you're as shy as a maiden!" On another, he requested that a poor student drop the course, enroll in the seminary's public speaking course, and then perhaps reenroll in the homiletics class the following year. A third reminded Fosdick of this experience: "One time you criticized me for a much too abrupt beginning, and drew some conclusions from the way I preached as to how I would probably make love. As it happened, I had been studying with a friend just before class, and had suggested that the meetings were worth attending. She was sitting in the shadows at the back of James Chapel when you gave your vivid description!" Still the majority shared another student's assessment of Fosdick: "I cannot recall his ever failing to offer appreciation and constructive help. No matter how poor the sermon was he would invariably find something good in it, something he could praise." And how a student would glow when Fosdick would say of the sermon, as he often did, "You're bowling down my alley." Even the laconic comment, "I think you can learn to preach," was appreciated. Even when a sermon was demolished, in retrospect a student reported, "How much I learned from that and subsequent encounters and how it hurt and helped to get my mental knuckles soundly rapped."

Although Fosdick admonished his homiletics classes to shun flowery language, although he advised them that understatement is always more effective than overstatement, he pressed this point: "You are preaching for a verdict; you always want to get your congregation to do something or believe something." Moreover, "Preach to the class and to me, never to an imaginary congregation. This should be a real, not an artificial preaching situation. I will never give any man an 'A' unless he makes me want to be a better man." Preaching must not be bland or coldly rational. "Risk the purple passage." A future Union professor, the respected Paul Hoon, was asked by Fosdick after a practice sermon, "Hoon, you're a Methodist, aren't you?" "Yes," replied Hoon. "Well, then, where's the *passion?*" A future distinguished biblical scholar, Millar Burrows, was assigned a temperance sermon to see, Fosdick explained, whether he could get fighting mad about something. Not being an ardent prohibitionist, Burrows admitted to falling down badly on the assignment. William A. Spurrier recalled this incident: "There was a black student in this . . . class who had near-perfect diction, a marvelous speaking voice, and was obviously an educated and fairly sophisticated person— just like the rest of us white fellows thought we were. So the black delivers this sermon in a most polished and careful style, modulated and refined, cultivated and clear—beautiful—so we all thought. Fosdick's critique was as follows: Mr. ———, your sermon was excellent in substance reflecting the heart of the Gospel. As for your delivery: it was clear, concise, orderly and exceedingly well-tailored. But where was your passion, man? Don't you believe what you preached? Have you no feelings? Surely, one of the great talents of your people is your history of suffering, hope, despair. You can understand the Gospel better than we because of what we have done to you. So do not imitate our refined clarity; let go with your spiritual passion, man, let go and let us have it.' "

Fosdick's homiletic suggestions became legendary among his former students. A few samples:

"Don't raise more rabbits than you can run down."

"A sermon ends like a spear point, not like a broom."

"Let the skeleton stick out."

"Tell your congregation where you are going. Before you turn a corner, flash a light on the street sign."

"Don't misquote; don't miscredit a quotation; don't guess about any scientific or historical fact or biblical reference; look it up."

"You should be able in one sentence to state the aim of every sermon."

"Play fair with your text; don't wrest it out of context."

"Preaching is sometimes like trying to put drops into someone's eyes out of a ten-story window."

"Take care lest all your sermons seem like just another slice off the same loaf of bread."

"There is a variety of stops on the homiletic organ and diversity in preaching is essential."

"Beware of falling into the habit of 'omnibus' preaching, into which you pile all sorts of stray thoughts one after another."

"After all, problems of delivery are largely problems of structure."

"Preach first of all to yourself; if it hits you it will usually hit somebody else."

"Never let your congregation reach the gate of another thought while you are still sauntering down the lane."

"Avoid seeming to be saying, 'I am Sir Oracle, and when I ope my mouth let no dog bark.' "

"The more strongly you feel the less personal you should be."

"A good story loses the attention of your audience for five minutes."

"The man who thinks he has mastered preaching is a technician, no doubt; the man who feels that preaching has mastered him is an artist. The power is not in you but through you."

"Does preaching ever become easier? No, it never does."

"Any Sunday you are willing to talk about the man in the pew and his problems, he will be willing to listen."

"If your people like you they will listen to what you have to say; if they do not like you, they will not listen to anything you have to say."

"When I am stalled in preparing a sermon, I sit down quietly and ask, 'Fosdick, what does this mean to you in terms of your own experience?' "

Not surprisingly, at least a few students had reservations about Fosdick's homiletics class. For one thing, they report, he concentrated more on form than substance. He did not often say to a student that which Coffin often did say: "Well, that was forcefully delivered, clear and well-organized, even clever—but is it the Gospel?" For another, when Fosdick reported spending one hour in the study for each minute in the pulpit (perhaps thirty-five hours!) or referred to his secretaries who assisted him, some thoughtful students realized that as parish ministers this would never be—could never be—their experience. There is, moreover, a question as to whether Fosdick unintentionally failed fully to honor Nietzsche's clarion call, "Follow not me but yourself." Fosdick's colleague, Professor G. A. Johnston Ross once turned in a class and pointed across Claremont Avenue to where The Riverside Church was rising and said, "Take care, gentlemen, not to develop a sense of inferiority as you measure yourselves with that incomparably brilliant man; see to it that what *you* have to give, you give!" Because Fosdick was a modest man, it is difficult to credit that he consciously sought to groove all of his students in his particular style, but because his personality was so powerful, it was difficult for his students not to emulate him. Maybe a former student put the case most fairly in a letter to Fosdick: "Time was when foolishly we all wanted to be 'Little Harry Fosdicks.' You've had that same power over men that Brooks had when every preacher longed to be a little Brooklet. But now that we have grown to manhood, we are contented if only we can feel we are bringing to our tasks the same sort of joyous, Christ-like self-dedication that we always felt in you."

Union students were divided in their perceptions of Fosdick's personality. Although virtually all respected him, some remember him as reserved and impenetrable, whereas others recalled his approachability and personal kindness. No doubt the students were aware of the ferocious demands on Fosdick's time and energy and were hesitant to knock on his office door to engage him in casual conversation. They did not call him "Uncle Harry" as they did call President Coffin "Uncle Henry" (behind his back) and they did not debate with him in nocturnal "bull sessions" as they did with Reinhold Niebuhr. For his part, Fosdick regretted that his other commitments curtailed his personal contacts with students, and he grasped every little chance he could to talk. "He never turned down a student who wanted a personal conference, even though an appointment might not be available for weeks," judged one student. "Dr. Fosdick would take time for any student who wanted to see him," said another. Fosdick himself reported to President Coffin in 1928 that "I have given a great deal of time" to "personal conferences with students." Although his daily walks along the Hudson were usually solitary, if a student fell in step (and agreed to a brisk pace), he was happy enough to talk, and Robert W. L. Marks recalls doing so "many times," as do other former students. When President A. C. McGiffert created a new faculty committee to "safeguard the mental health of the Seminary students," Fosdick agreed to chair it. Russell L. Dicks, who became a leader in pastoral psychology, reminded Fosdick of a crucial event in his student life: "I still remember quite vividly a morning in your study when you offered to loan me $300 to pay for my hospitalization. . . . It was one of the experiences which helped steady me through the stormy weather which followed." Other students, especially those from foreign lands, received loans or outright gifts of money from him.

The Fosdick apartment was not perpetually open to students, but neither was it inviolably sealed. Florence invited her husband's classes to tea and graduating seniors were invited in small groups to a series of Saturday morning breakfasts. After one such breakfast a senior reported to his wife in amazement, "Do you know what? Mrs. Fosdick calls Dr. Fosdick 'Harry'!" The wives of married students received Florence's special solicitude, and they adored her. When Elinor and Dorothy became of datable age, students called on these attractive young women and perhaps found themselves playing hearts with them—and their father.

The truth is that Fosdick welcomed personal contacts, however curtailed by necessity, and even as he counseled over the years hundreds of individuals in his Riverside office he counseled scores of students in his Union office, and these students have recorded their gratitude in abundance. Nor did the counseling always terminate on graduation. One person deeply troubled by a developing situation in his first pastorate wrote his former teacher for advice and Fosdick immediately set up an appointment. The advice was wise and comforting, Fosdick saying in part: "Darnell, you have a trickier situation to handle than I have. I am floating a barge here at Riverside; I could walk all over it and it would not sink. You are paddling a canoe. And a canoe is easily upset, unless you keep your balance." The Reverend Darnell closed the story: "So I came back and paddled my canoe."

IV

Union's faculty was never large in Fosdick's time, numbering fewer than thirty full time. But because his tenure extended over a period of thirty-five years, he was associated with a number of luminous figures in the world of Christian scholarship, of whom some were his former teachers and some former students. "Union Seminary lives by its brains," President Coffin often proclaimed; in truth it did. William Lyon Phelps wrote in his newspaper column that he would rather be an impresario at the opera or a lion tamer at the circus than the president of Union Seminary; indeed there were a number of fiercely independent lions on the faculty. If clawing went on, however, it seems not to have been savage by comparative faculty standards, and the record does not show Fosdick either mauling or being mauled.* Maybe the Union scene was not an Edward Hicks's peaceable kingdom, but just possibly Professor Cyril Richardson best assessed the collegial situation when he observed: "Our contribution has been to create a common life of Christian dedication, learning and worship despite, and indeed *because* of the wide variety of our several views and the diverse churchly heritage we represent." At Union there was "the genuine harmony of a Christian community." Concluded Richardson, "We have learned to live together, to think together and to worship together with mutual respect and without backbiting, and to a very large measure to accept each other's criticism of us with grace and without rancor."

At Union Fosdick served under four different presidents: Francis Brown, Arthur Cushman McGiffert, Henry Sloane Coffin, and Henry Pitney Van Dusen. When Brown was at the helm, Fosdick was only a junior faculty member; Van Dusen entered office just a year before Fosdick's retirement, so, naturally he was closest to the other two presidents.

Fosdick was elevated to the Jesup professorship during the presidency of McGiffert, his former teacher, and there was a feeling of mutual respect between the two men. When Fosdick accepted the call to the Park Avenue Baptist Church, he wrote President McGiffert from Egypt raising the question as to whether it was in the best interests of the seminary to allow a chair professor "to assume such heavy extra-mural responsibilities." He continued, "You will understand also how eager I shall be in every way to conserve the best interests of the Seminary. I myself wished to raise the issue and not leave it for anyone else to raise." The letter further carried the information, "I turned down Harvard and the University of Chicago this year because my heart has always been at Union and I wanted to stay." McGiffert vastly appreciated Fosdick's selflessness.

When Coffin was elected president in 1926, Fosdick cabled congratulations and followed with a long letter saying, "I have talked with you about the matter before and you know that it is a dream of mine come true that you should be President of the Seminary." At Coffin's inauguration dinner, Fosdick spoke heartfully for the faculty. For his part, Cof-

---

* At one faculty meeting, a candidate for appointment was being discussed and Fosdick spoke in opposition, explaining: "I like Professor _____. He is a gentleman and a scholar and he does his work well, but in all conscience I cannot vote for the man because we already have a man on our faculty who thinks as he does."

fin explained to Fosdick his reason for leaving the Madison Avenue Church pastorate and accepting the presidency: "The decisive factor with me was the plight of the Seminary. This has been the most pathetically impoverished year spiritually in its history since I have known it. We missed you sorely, and [Eugene] Lyman's absence left a big void. We had a poor student body with no outstanding leaders, and the 'educational approach'* captured the men to the exclusion of all prayer and genuine upreach for spiritual reserves. But thank God you and Lyman will both be on deck next winter. Some day I want a good hour or so with you on Seminary problems. I don't suppose there is a chance of our getting Mrs. Fosdick and you here [at our summer home]. That would be ideal; but failing that please keep some free time for a long talk. There are puzzling problems to be faced in organization and personnel." Every shred of evidence supports the judgment that Coffin held Fosdick in "extraordinarily high esteem" (his words), and affection, too; and Fosdick felt exactly the same way about Coffin.†

If Fosdick had any faculty enemies, the evidence has disappeared. On the other hand, the evidence is abundant that he enjoyed the friendship, if not always the intimacy, of not a few. Among the colleagues who gave his manuscripts close readings before publication were James Frame, Julius Bewer, McGiffert, John Knox, Cyril Richardson, and John C. Bennett. Among the colleagues whose scholarship he praised were John Baillie, Ernest Scott, and Eugene Lyman. Others he would term a "warm personal friend" or say of them that "I was very affectionately fond." These feelings were mutual, Mary Ely Lyman, a former student who was appointed professor of Philosophy of Religion, wrote to Fosdick: "Then the next stage—actually becoming your colleague. Incredible! But it happened. And I came to love Florence so dearly when we lived as neighbors under the same roof. My love, dear Harry, goes to you across all the miles. Glory be to God!" It is further worth remarking that a company of brilliant younger scholars, too numerous to name, who perhaps did not come to know Fosdick closely because they joined the faculty as he approached retirement, nonetheless remembered him in admiration on his later birthdays.

* Coffin loathed the influence on ministerial training of John Dewey's educational philosophy, an influence dominant at Teachers College and strong at Union thanks to such professors as George A. Coe and Harrison Elliott.

† This is not to say that the two men invariably agreed, as we know from Chapter Seven and shall see in Chapter Twenty-Six. Moreover, Coffin firmly believed that Union's primary responsibility was to train individuals for the pastoral ministry, and when a student, R. H. Edwin Espy, won a coveted scholarship to study theology in Germany, Coffin sought to dissuade him from accepting for fear that it would deflect him from the pastoral ministry. When asked his advice, Fosdick urged Espy to seize the opportunity—and he did.

Speculation has it that Fosdick and Reinhold Niebuhr were neither friends nor friendly, and logic supports the speculation. Niebuhr's religious realism challenged Fosdick's religious liberalism; Niebuhr's initial Christian Marxism, Fosdick's political liberalism; Niebuhr's support of Roosevelt's interventionist foreign policies, Fosdick's near-pacifism; Niebuhr's cultural sophistication, Fosdick's essential cultural conservatism. But here logic betrays, for the rumor is false.

On Niebuhr's arrival on the Union faculty in 1928, Fosdick invited him both to preach and speak at the Park Avenue Baptist Church and later to occupy the Riverside pulpit. He also recommended that Niebuhr give a series of lectures at the New York School of Social Work in order that his younger colleague might augment his income. And all this despite Niebuhr's recently published critical review of *Adventurous Religion*.

In the heat of the interventionist debate in 1941, Fosdick sided with a fellow pacifist, Harold Bosley, against Niebuhr but, nonetheless, informed Bosley that Niebuhr is "my dear friend" and "I love him and his family most dearly." When invited to contribute a chapter on Niebuhr's preaching to the Library of Living Theology volume devoted to Niebuhr, Fosdick declined explaining that although he had heard him lecture he had not heard him preach, adding, "Reinhold Niebuhr is a warm personal friend of mine, and for him and his family I have deep respect and affection." In other letters and in conversations he reaffirmed this feeling.

The most telling proof of Fosdick's attitude toward Niebuhr is revealed in an exchange of letters with Rockefeller in 1944 in which Rockefeller inquired about the "radicalism" of Niebuhr and the propriety of his teaching at Union. Fosdick's response is unequivocal and merits extensive quotation at least as much for what it tells about Fosdick as for what it says about Niebuhr.

Dr. Niebuhr is . . . definitely anti-communist, a distinguished intellectual leader who last year was given the Doctorate in Divinity by Oxford University, and who is recognized as one of the outstanding figures in theology in our time. I may tell you confidentially that President Conant of Harvard, a year ago, tried every pressure he could bring to bear to persuade Dr. Niebuhr to accept a professorship there. It was an immense relief to President Coffin, and to the entire Seminary when he decided to stay. He is certainly a liberal on economic and social questions. I suppose that to call him a conservative type of socialist would describe him as well as anything, and he is interested in this campaign to help reelect President Roosevelt. If, however, you could know him and his fine family—

Mrs. Niebuhr is a professor at Barnard College—as Mrs. Fosdick and I do, you would never think of his presence on the Union Faculty as anything but an honor to the institution. He is primarily an outstanding leader in this generation's theological thought. He is a vigorous, provocative, stimulating personality, honest and forthright, and in his religious thinking he is so concerned about conserving the values in our Christian tradition that he is often called neo-orthodox. One often disagrees with him in detail, but always loves and admires him.

Niebuhr was a fierce polemicist and it is certainly true that he found Fosdick's sense of sin attenuated and his pacifism "the last product of the old liberalism." Yet his public tribute to Fosdick on an occasion at Union honoring him was about as handsome as any mortal might wish. To private individuals he testified that "Dr. Fosdick is the most accomplished preacher I know" and he is "a great ethical teacher" and "We do not always agree, yet no one will disagree with you more graciously than Fosdick." To Fosdick he offered this bargain: "If you will be a pessimist with me decade by decade, I will be an optimist with you aeon by aeon." And after reading Fosdick's autobiography, Niebuhr typed a note of affection and admiration, closing, "So thanks very much for the book, but even more for your friendship, and even more for the grace of your life."

If this evidence does not serve to dispel the rumor, there is the further testimony of two key individuals. Dorothy Fosdick underscores the friendly feelings between the Fosdick family and the Niebuhr family by pointing out that she is the godmother of the Niebuhrs' daughter and that she and Mrs. Ursula M. Niebuhr are to this day the closest of friends. Mrs. Niebuhr, chairman of Barnard's Religion Department and a person of exceptional intelligence and attractiveness, confirms this and says of the relationship between her husband and Harry: "They were good friends, and what is more, friendly colleagues."

Niebuhr was primarily responsible for bringing another giant to Union in 1933, Paul Tillich. If the documentation is pretty full concerning the Niebuhr/Fosdick association, it is virtually blank concerning the Tillich/Fosdick association. Judging by what Tillich's biographers and his wife Hannah, in her memoirs, have to say about the suffocating stuffiness of Union faculty social life (from the Tillichs' cosmopolitan Continental perspective), it is entirely possible that the Tillichs and Fosdicks saw little of each other socially. But Fosdick helped to secure Rockefeller funds that made it possible for Tillich to have a post at Union and the two men worked together on the American Christian Committee for refugees from Germany. For his part, Tillich could recall: "The cooperation of the fac-

ulty has been perfect. During seventeen years at Union Seminary I have
not had a single disagreeable experience with my American colleagues."*

V

In May 1953 on the occasion of Fosdick's seventy-fifth birthday, a dinner was given in his honor at Union. The primary birthday present was
a gift of $250,000 from John D. Rockefeller, 3rd, to establish the Harry
Emerson Fosdick Professorship. President Van Dusen announced its
terms: "To honor Harry Emerson Fosdick for his distinguished contributions as teacher, preacher, writer and counselor, and to strengthen the
training of the present and oncoming leaders of the Christian church so
as to enable them in their generation, as Dr. Fosdick has in this generation, to interpret the abiding truths and experiences of the Christian
faith in terms relevant and compelling to contemporary life." Fosdick responded in gratitude and then privately wrote Rockefeller, 3rd: "I am
sure that I do not deserve to have this professorship set up in my
name. . . . The Seminary has meant much to me; from my student
days up I am unpayably indebted to it. I find it difficult to imagine a
'Fosdick Professor' there! You are all very kind, most generously kind,
and I am deeply grateful." Possibly few at the banquet knew that Van
Dusen and Rockefeller had urged Fosdick to be the first occupant of the
chair, an invitation he declined in part because of age and in part because he questioned the good taste of accepting an appointment to a
chair founded in his honor, but above all because he believed the chair
should be used to bring in a younger and fresher mind.

VI

What makes a great teacher? To attempt to answer the question is as
vain as the effort to map Valhalla. All one can say—and perhaps all one
need say—is that hundreds of Fosdick's students judged him to be a
great teacher and that he brought to the classroom those same qualities
that characterized the other areas of his life: painstaking preparation,
mastery of subject, clarity and accessibility of thought, forceful expression, enthusiasm, the ability to connect the subject to the students' lives,
concern for each student as an individual, and a puissant personality.

* If anything, even less is known about the Dietrich Bonhoeffer/Fosdick relationship. Bonhoeffer studied at Union in 1930–1931 and took Fosdick's course, Brief
Sermons, but it is not recorded what he thought of it. In 1939 Bonhoeffer returned
to the United States for a brief visit and heard a sermon at Riverside Church. He
did not like it, but it is not known if Fosdick preached that Sunday.

Chapter Eighteen

"And How Shall They Hear Without a Preacher?": The Conceptualization of Preachable Sermons

I

As a Servant of the Word Fosdick was aware of the awfulness of his commission, and never long absent from his consciousness was Paul's anguished cry, "For necessity is laid upon me. Woe to me if I do not preach the Gospel." To be sure, God will always break through to speak to men who listen in faith, but if the pulpit were mute how handicapped would be the encounter. Paul's "And how shall they hear without a preacher?" remained a legitimate query after nineteen centuries—this despite the low estate of Protestant preaching in much of Fosdick's era; the increasingly contemptuous tone in which the word "preacher" was pronounced; the growing insistence that preaching was indeed literally "foolish"; the seeming triumph of pastoral psychology; and a liturgical revival that often (and wrongly) found an inevitable tension between pulpit and altar, sermon and Eucharist, as though preaching was not worship and the true sermon not a sacramental act. Augustine knew better when he described preaching as an "audible sacrament."

Fosdick was not unaware of the perils in Protestantism's historic emphasis on preaching. "Many of our churches have had reality pretty well washed out of them by the constant deluge of hastily prepared talk," he noted on one occasion. And on another he warned, "We have preached too much and not well enough. We need less quantity and more quality. The homiletical currency has been badly inflated and we need a return to the gold standard." As we know, in his autobiography he made personal counseling central, adding, "Indeed, I distrust a preacher to whom sermons seem the crux of his functioning."

Let these statements not mislead however. If Fosdick had "majored" in pastoral counseling and pastoral care more broadly and merely "minored" in preaching, as did growing numbers of ministers, his influence in his own lifetime would have been severely reduced and the memory of his name today much faded. Though he counseled hundreds in his study and thousands in his writings, clearly the majority of his waking hours were devoted to the preparation of sermons, and these sermons when preached from pulpit and radio studio and printed reached millions.

In fact, there is much evidence from Fosdick's own lips to support the judgment that he was first and last a preacher. "The center of Roman worship is the sacrament of the Mass; the center of Protestant worship is the sermon," he said in 1929. "The call to be a Protestant clergyman has always been primarily a call to preach." In his spiritual autobiography he wrote that "the pulpit has been primary in my case." He once lifted up the prayer: "Whoever stands in a pulpit, bless thou his spirit and touch his lips with a coal from off the altar that he may speak thine everlasting Gospel, carrying thy truth far into the hearts and consciences of those who hear." Surely his charge to his successor at Riverside reflects his own ministry:

> Welcome to this church. It is a seven-day-a-week affair with more things going on here than you can possibly keep track of. Don't try to. Most of all we want your message in the pulpit, born out of long hours of study, meditation and prayer. Guard your morning privacy as a sacred trust! We have called you because we believe you are a great Christian with a message for this generation. That you will wisely counsel with us in practical affairs, and be endlessly helpful in personal consultation, we take for granted, but what most of all we want from you is that on Sunday morning you should come into this pulpit here like Moses with the word of God, emerging from his communion on the mountain, who wist not that his face shone.

Boring into Fosdick's life one ultimately becomes convinced that he was in essential agreement with John Killinger: the preacher "would like to be all things to all men, but there are times when he feels the need of saying, 'This one thing I do.' And the one thing claiming precedence over all the others, demanding to stand at the center, because it has been the distinctive, necessary task of the ministry in every age, is the matter of proclamation. Nothing else will substitute for it. Its priority is absolute. It alone is capable of bringing to heel the multitudinous and variegated duties which yip and yap at the minister's coattails like the mutts of hell wherever he goes." A Roman Catholic observer once predicted that "If Protestantism ever dies with a dagger in its back, the dagger will be the Protestant sermon." The transcendent fact of Fosdick's ministry are his labors to prevent that death from that source.

II

To a generation and more of Protestant preachers Fosdick was a lodestar. It would be a work of supererogation to document that fact, and only a few pieces of evidence need be advanced by way of illustration. First, the judgment of the religious world. Liberal Protestantism's leading journal, *Christian Century*, repeatedly asserted that "Fosdick . . . stands alone as the pre-eminent American preacher of our generation" and "It is doubtful if anyone in the American pulpit in this century has had more influence on the art of preaching." A denominational organ, *Christian-Evangelist*, reported, "No segment of the Church in the 1920's and 1930's was unaffected by the preaching and writing of Harry Emerson Fosdick." The Duke Divinity School *Bulletin* termed him "One of the great indigenous figures in American ecclesiastical life, its leading homiletician, in theory and practice." A seminary dean saluted him as "the preeminent voice in American Christianity" and "the preacher *par excellence*." Reinhold Niebuhr called him "the most celebrated preacher of his day." Martin Luther King, Jr., said to him, "If I were called upon to select the greatest preacher of this century, I would choose your name." Ralph Sockman believed him the most influential interpreter of religion in his generation. Henry Pitney Van Dusen averred he was "the most winsome and convincing interpreter of Christian Faith in our time." Halford Luccock informed his homiletics classes at Yale that Fosdick was the best writer of the Gospel known to man, next to Saint Paul. Individual after individual said Fosdick was a "giant" whose preaching was "the best combination of evangelical persuasiveness with intellectual and moral awareness that American preaching has had in this twentieth century." "All over Christendom men have learned to look to him for light and learning."

Second, the judgment of the secular world. Reported *Time*, Fosdick's voice "was the best-known and most influential one in Protestantism during the '20s and '30s." Reported *Newsweek*, "Harry Emerson Fosdick is still down in the books of more than one generation of Americans as the model of the Protestant preacher." From the South came the *Atlanta Constitution*'s assessment that he was "the greatest preacher in America during the past 100 years." From the Midwest came the judgment of the *Chicago Tribune:* "For fifty years Harry Emerson Fosdick has moved across the religious backdrop of our times like a giant." The *New York*

Times's obituary declared that he left "his mark on the style of virtually every American Protestant preacher." In 1976 a major study would show that Billy Graham had replaced Fosdick "as the best-known American preacher."

It is the business of historians to combat amnesia, an affliction endemic among Americans. Robert T. Handy believed that "No history of Christianity in America in the twentieth century will be complete without considerable attention to this man." Elsewhere Handy and his colleagues H. Shelton Smith and Lefferts A. Loetscher recorded that Fosdick's was "the pre-eminent voice of the American pulpit" in his era. Sidney A. Ahlstrom noted the completion of The Riverside Church and added, "During the next fifteen years Fosdick was the nation's most influential Protestant minister." He was, wrote Clifton E. Olmstead, "the star of the American pulpit." He was, wrote Kenneth Cauthen, "the most eminent preacher of his time."

Fosdick's influence crossed the Atlantic. Judged the *Manchester Guardian*: "Probably no preacher in contemporary America has been more read, in Britain and in his own country, than Dr. H. E. Fosdick." And Edgar De Witt Jones opined: "The peoples of other countries think of Dr. Fosdick as first among American preachers, just as they think of Reinhold Niebuhr as first among our theologians." Elsewhere Jones stated, "The most preeminent pulpit of the Christian faith in America, if not in the world, is that of Harry Emerson Fosdick in Riverside Church."

Fosdick once responded to a critical interviewer, "I may be a liberal, but I'm evangelical, too!" He understood that he was, in the words of Paul, called to "do the work of an evangelist"; and perceptive observers place him in that great preaching tradition. The evangelist Charles B. Templeton asserted that "the greatest evangelist of the past century was Harry Emerson Fosdick. . . . It may be that, though anything but typical of his predecessors, he will be seen to have been the outstanding evangelist of his day." The *Christian Century* concurred, saying, "He has stood within the evangelical tradition and preached the great doctrines of God and Christ and grace and regeneration with a consistency and power which no conservative theologian could excel."

In 1961, fifteen years after Fosdick's retirement, Louis Harris & Associates conducted a survey of theological students. When asked the question, "What man or woman who has lived in this century do you most admire?", the leading replies in order were: Albert Schweitzer, "my father," Mahatma Gandhi, Harry Emerson Fosdick, and Reinhold Niebuhr. That is pretty heady company for a preacher.

This public record is substantiated by hundreds of letters in Fosdick's private correspondence files. "You are the one who has doubtless influenced my preaching and ministry more than any other man," wrote one person. "Perhaps I should not tell others lest they blame you for me." Recalling hearing Fosdick preach, a woman added: "I shall never forget that sermon and that is saying a good deal, for I have forgotten more sermons than anybody else on earth." Scores of correspondents confessed, "I can say quite honestly that, under God, I owe more to you in your contribution to my ministry than I do to any other living man."

On occasion Fosdick was introduced to a group of clergymen with the concluding sentence, "I give you Dr. Fosdick, whose sermons you have heard and preached." And more than one minister averred, "In one of my very best sermons Dr. Fosdick says . . ."; Fosdick's friends expressed mock pity for him because he was the only preacher in the nation who could not crib from Dr. Fosdick. Across the land ministers wondered what Fosdick does on Sundays without Fosdick to quote. On Fosdick's retirement a correspondent informed him: "It is rather hard on the other preachers of America, though—they'll have to go back to preaching your old sermons, now that there isn't a new one every week from which they can 'borrow one or two ideas.'" Naturally fundamentalist ministers could not cite Fosdick by name, and so were forced to introduce a quotation with the innocent words, "As someone else has said. . . ."

Across the nation and across the seas his sermons were conned by clergymen seeking to prime their homiletic pumps, England's famed Leslie Weatherhead musing: "I wonder how many of his illustrations have found their way into English sermons! I must have used hundreds." Indeed, many ministers reported deliberately refraining from reading too many Fosdick sermons to avoid the temptation of plagiarism and the consequent danger of becoming only a Fosdickian echo. At the height of his fame individuals went to the foolish lengths of trying (they informed him) "to copy your word inflexions and your voice timbre!"

Of course, some ministers preached as their own entire sermons written by Fosdick. Some confessed and repented. Others were refreshingly shameless. On one occasion in Maine a young minister boldly lifted a classic Fosdick sermon in its entirety. The last person to greet this preacher at the door of his church that Sunday was an elderly man who expressed interest in the sermon and pleasantly inquired as to how long it had taken the preacher to prepare. "Oh, it took me about three hours," replied the youthful person, loftily. "Young man, that sermon took me twenty-one hours to prepare!," declared the summer visitor, in what became immediately apparent as a full-pulpit voice, frequently broadcast over radio. "Well, Dr. Fosdick," replied the parson with charming brass, "You keep writing 'em and I'll keep preaching 'em!"

One likes to think that Fosdick roared with laughter when he read the following letter from a Methodist parson in Alabama:

> I have just finished preparing my morning sermon for tomorrow. It was not very much trouble to prepare, for it was stolen almost bodily from your latest book, "What Is Vital In Religion." This is simply a letter of appreciation for your sermons and for you. I am not a smart man, and added to my lack of intelligence is a monstrous laziness. I told the Lord all that when he called me to preach, but he called me just the same, and I have had not one qualm of conscience about stealing your sermons. This letter is long overdue, for I have been preaching your sermons for almost twenty years. I do have one complaint: some years ago, I used one of your sermons at a morning service, and you happened to use the same one that same afternoon on National Vespers. That night a member of my congregation told me that someone had sure stolen *my* sermon fast. I am sorry to learn from the preface of your book that this will be your last volume of sermons. I had hoped for more. Lest you be too troubled about me, let me say that I have every book of yours published together with a large file of Church Monthlies from Riverside, and I believe with their help I can hold out for another twenty years, if God so wills.

A saying commonly attributed to the fundamentalists went, "That would have been a good sermon if Dr. Fosdick had not written it." On occasion he would receive a plea (which he naturally found delicious) from some individual who, having cribbed a Fosdick sermon, received the praise of rock-ribbed saints who would insist (to the poor preacher's terror) on printing the sermon as fundamentalist propaganda! Read one such petition: "The joke is though, that the rankest Fundamentalists are the most enthusiastic about my paper [a Fosdick sermon], and are insisting that it be published. What shall I do? I want the chance to read some more of your sermons to them, but *I must not mention your name.* The narrow-minded church papers and preachers have warned them, and their prejudice is like a cork in a bottle,—they won't let anything into their minds that will lead them astray. It proves to me that it is the *label* they fear and not the doctrine itself." Characteristically, Fosdick's reply was gentle, granting the individual permission to use his sermons without attributing his authorship. "I am more than willing that this should be done, glad to have my message spread in any way whatsoever."

Maybe McCracken summed it up best when he said at the memorial service for Fosdick: "He was at once the inspiration and despair of countless fellow-preachers, his sermons models of the preaching art, and how often more than models God alone knows."

III

Andrew W. Blackwood, Professor of Homiletics, Princeton Theological Seminary, touched a nerve when he said in his assessment of Fosdick's preaching, "If any young man wishes to learn what to preach, he may look elsewhere; if he would learn how, he should tarry here." Blackwood was not alone in raising hard questions about the content of Fosdick's sermons and the theory behind them. "These sermons," observed a Baptist reviewer of a Fosdick volume, "make a reader think profoundly but there is lacking that urge and hope which could save a dying thief." Across the Atlantic a British conservative expressed a similar view of another volume: "When he writes on faith, which he does most admirably, he speaks rather as a psychologist than as a theologian. When he preaches on God his attitude is that of a thinker rather than as one who proclaims a revelation. His Christ is the Hero rather than the Redeemer." The point was often pressed by conservatives that in adjusting the Gospel to modern culture, Fosdick's preaching went too far, trimming as well as tailoring it to fit the times. In 1968 a student of Baptist preaching concluded sadly that Fosdick seemed dated already because "there is little in the theology of preaching for Fosdick that anchors it in any of the eternals: God, Jesus Christ, the Bible. The definition of preaching he has given could well be the job description of a clinical psychologist." Another writer reached a similar conclusion: "The printed sermons of Fosdick have a way of disintegrating in the memory instead of leaving some vivid essence, as the best sermons do. They are thorough and competent and kindly and intelligent, and they are carried along by well-controlled indignations and steady morals, but there is nothing astonishing or piercing—there are no lasting thoughts."

In 1961 Allan McDiarmid completed an extremely searching Th.D. dissertation entitled, "A Critique of Harry Emerson Fosdick's Concept of Preaching as Counseling on a Group Scale." The author's thesis is that preaching and counseling are discrete functions that cannot be combined and should not be attempted. Counseling is a one-to-one situation; preaching is not. Counseling requires artful listening on the part of the minister; preaching is (in Augustine's phrase) "the ministry of the tongue" wherein the preacher putteth Christ into the worshippers' ears. When Fosdick said that preaching is futile without insight into what is actually going on in the lives of the congregation, McDiarmid replied: "He does not seem to take into account the probability of there being a body of truth that they should have presented to them irrespective of their ever-changing personal patterns and immediate needs."*

To conclude this section of criticism it is appropriate to quote two lengthy passages from the severest scholarly analysis of Fosdick's preaching ever penned, a dissertation by Harry Black Beverly, Jr., entitled, *Harry Emerson Fosdick's Predigtweise, its Significance (for America), its Limits, its Overcoming*, written under the direction of the theological faculty of Basel University. Beverly charges:

> Fosdick is right in wanting to help the people from the pulpit but he has forgotten the commission and central conviction of the Christian preacher that he is being used by God to tell again the decisive encounter of God with man in history in Jesus the Christ, crucified and resurrected for all men. This Kerygma is relevant and must be made relevant; this Event has solved man's problem of Sin; this must be communicated to the congregation "pastorally" in their own language. Fosdick's perspective of "religious' counselor" must be implemented with that of a proclaimer of a Word which shatters even men's best "religion." The perspective of one who is solely concerned to present techniques for integrating the personality is necessarily quite different from the perspective of one who is convinced that he is participating in Christ's revelation in our own day to our own "flock."

> His insight into contemporary man combined with his able ability to speak to his times in an intelligent and intelligible manner should have made Fosdick an able witness to Christ in our century. However, Fosdick's inadequate grasp of the Gospel produces sermons whose message or content is inadequate. His sermons attempt to deal with modern man and his need of help. They obviously communicated but his message proclaimed no Gospel to solve man's problems; no message about the redemptive acts of God in history on man's behalf; no witness to Christ as Lord or Savior in the majority of them. Instead, "positive faiths and inner resources" (what man has and does) have replaced Christus Victor (what God did and does). The mesages thus fail to deal adequately with the contemporary situation of man or to serve the Gospel. A Christian sermon begins, not with a problem, but with a Word which reveals and speaks to man's problem. Fosdick is indeed right in wishing to speak a word to the peculiar

---

* In the essay "Personal Counseling and Preaching" Fosdick himself noted a peril when he warned: "If his [the minister's] field of private counseling is confined pretty much to neurotic disorders, his pulpit may all too easily reflect the fact. Every Sunday he will be telling people how to overcome anxiety and fear and achieve peace of mind. He rides a hobby, attracts an audience of nervous patients, and in the pulpit becomes a homiletical neurologist."

situations of his times but he is wrong in starting with the occasions and situations themselves. Only an expository sermon has a Word to speak to the times; any other type of preaching only offers words of human wisdom which may or may not be wiser than the words they hear outside of the Church of Christ and may never be God's own Word to the situations.

IV

As Fosdick never wrote a book setting forth his theory of pastoral counseling, despite his stature as a counselor, so he never explicated at book length his theory of preaching, despite his preeminence as a homiletician and despite pleas from all quarters to do so. It is a pity that pressures of time (or so he reported) forestalled his writing a book on preaching. However, he did not leave interested individuals entirely in the dark. In 1928 he penned a highly influential article entitled "What Is the Matter with Preaching?", and the substance of this *Harper's* article is found in his autobiography in the chapter entitled "Learning How to Preach." These major revelations are augmented by such essays as "How I Prepare My Sermons," "If I Had Only One Sermon to Preach," "The Christian Ministry," and "Personal Counseling and Preaching." Most students of Fosdick's preaching rely heavily on these sources to the neglect of two other illuminating works. One of these is his inaugural address at Union, "A Modern Preacher's Problem in His Use of the Scriptures." The other is *The Modern Use of the Bible*, for as the preface states, "Upon the basis of the approach to the Bible here set forth I have done my preaching from the beginning of my ministry."

In view of his towering influence on homiletics it is indeed a pity that Fosdick never fully expounded his theory of preaching. It is also unfortunate for another reason. What he set forth in "What Is the Matter with Preaching?", "Learning How to Preach," and "Personal Counseling and Preaching," especially, are not absolutely accurate indications of what he actually preached and do not do full justice to his sermons. The consequence is that students sympathetic with the theory of "life-situation" preaching or "project method" preaching have too exclusively appropriated Fosdick as their champion, whereas, concurrently, defenders of "expository" preaching have too rigidly excluded him from their honorable ranks. Fosdick is not blameless in this for he made statements about preaching incongruent with other statements and with the sermons themselves.

During the early part of his first pastorate, Fosdick recalled, the sermons he prepared in torment left him dreadfully unsatisfied when preached. Although artfully enough delivered, thanks to his training in public speaking, they did not catch fire; there was no kindling response from the congregation. Nothing happened. They could as well have been left unsaid. The explanation, he came to reason, for the emptiness and futility of his efforts lay in the fact that the sermons established no connection with the real interests of the congregation. He weighed adopting either the model of the older expository preaching or the newer topical preaching and decided against both, at least as these models were narrowly conceived. Expository preaching followed a rigid pattern: elucidation of a Scriptural text, its historic occasion, its logical meaning in the context, its setting in the theology and ethic of the ancient writer; and then, at long last, application to the auditors of the truth involved. Such a sermon presupposed that the congregation came to church that morning primarily concerned about the meaning of ancient texts. "Only the preacher," Fosdick somewhat petulantly concluded, "proceeds still upon the idea that folk come to church desperately anxious to discover what happened to the Jebusites."

On reflection the topical model seemed even more dubious. Such preaching turned pulpits into platforms, sermons into lectures, as the minister searched the newspapers for timely topics, straining for "relevance." Fosdick refused to buy stock in this homiletical bubble, correctly seeing that no man is sufficiently omniscient to speak intelligently on such a wide range of specialized topics and that, above all, worshippers do not come to church to hear opinions on themes that editors, columnists, and radio commentators have been dealing with throughout the week.

Finally, Fosdick labored his way to a concept of preaching which he labeled the "project method," an unfortunate pedagogical term, too narrowly defined as "personal counseling on a group scale." Midstream in his ministry he summarized this concept in a sentence: "In general, my gospel is to get hold of live issues that really matter in the life of people, to look at them long enough so that I believe something about them terribly hard, to baptize my conviction in the spirit and truth of the New Testament, and then to put it across to the people as hot as I can." His autobiography carries this elaboration:

> People come to church with every kind of personal difficulty and problem flesh is heir to. A sermon was meant to meet such needs; it should be personal counseling on a group scale. If one had clairvoyance, one would know the sins and shames, the anxieties and doubts, the griefs and disillusionments, that filled the pews, and could by God's grace bring the saving truths of the gospel to bear on them creatively as though he were speaking to a single person. That was the place to start—with the real

problems of the people. That was a sermon's specialty, which made it a sermon, not an essay or a lecture. Every sermon should have for its main business the head-on constructive meeting of some problem which was puzzling minds, burdening consciences, distracting lives, and no sermon which so met a real human difficulty, with light to throw on it and help to win a victory over it, could possibly be futile.

A famous Scotch preacher, Fosdick was fond of relating, was once greeted by an admirer who exclaimed: "That was a wonderful sermon." Retorted the minister: "What did it *do*? What did it do?" Fosdick was convinced that every sermon's central motive should be some definite object to be achieved. An essayist might be content with the discussion of a subject, but a preacher can be content only with the attainment of an object. A sermon should creatively get things done, then and there, in the minds and lives of the congregation; it should be a convincing appeal to a listening jury for decision. The preacher's aim is to "bring some forked lightning in that would hit something." Fosdick repeatedly said he could not get well under way on a sermon until he clearly saw what he proposed to get *done* on Sunday morning. His preaching started where people lived; the sermon, therefore, was a means, never an end. A Riverside clerical colleague judged, "He did not preach for preaching's sake; he preached for people's sake." That is why he believed that one of the best tests of a sermon is the number of people who afterwards wish to see the preacher alone. And that is why he somewhat misleadingly (as we shall see) defined a sermon as "an animated conversation with an audience," elaborating:

> I found my sermons becoming more and more co-operative enterprises between the preacher and the congregation. When a man takes hold of a real difficulty in the life and thought of his people and is trying to meet it, he finds himself not so much dogmatically thinking for them as co-operatively thinking with them. A preacher can easily play "Sir Oracle," assertive, dogmatic, flinging out his dictum as though to say "Take it or leave it," and such preaching has its appeal to credulous and emotionally impressionable minds. It has lost its influence on intelligent folk, however, and the future does not belong to it.

Because champions of project method preaching raise up Fosdick as the premier practitioner of this method and because in his statements he gave them some justification for doing so, champions of expository preaching have denied that he was a true Servant of the Word. But Fosdick maintained that he went beyond the project method—that his preaching was the "project method-plus"—and both friend and foe have often failed to note this. He did in fact proclaim God's act in Christ so that, hearing the Gospel, men might be saved. On four instances spanning three decades he expressed this conviction: ". . . it is a great day in a minister's life when, having seen what miracles can be wrought by Christ's truth and power brought to bear on individual souls, he mounts his pulpit sure that a sermon, too, can be thus a medium of creative and transforming effects. No longer on Sunday is he merely making a speech about religion; he is engaged in an engineering operation, building a bridge by which a chasm is spanned so that spiritual goods on one side— the 'unsearchable riches of Christ'—are actually transported into personal lives on the other." When the preacher "lifts a great truth, he intends, like a pile driver, to drop it on something. He has a subject, of course, but when he chose his subject, he had an object. He proposes that somebody that morning should face his Damascus Road." That "great truth," Fosdick often said, is found in Scripture, sometimes in a single text, sometimes diffused throughout the Bible. He insisted that in his preaching the Bible's importance was not diminished. "Upon the contrary," he maintained, "I had been suckled on the Bible, knew it and loved it, and I could not deal with any crucial problem in thought and life without seeing text after text lift up its hands begging to be used." In fact he went so far as to claim that project method preaching might also be expository: "I do constantly use the expository method in trying to dig into the experience that was behind a great text of Scripture."

At the heart of Fosdick's understanding of preaching was the conviction that "The word of God is not an abstraction to be dealt with apart from the people who are to receive it. I've heard it preached so that it was completely irrelevant to a man's thinking and living." And so he exhorted his Union classes: a sermon's "aim is to send people out of church different from what they were when they came in. As you make the central truths of Scripture live for them, you will be helping them toward a first-hand faith. People desperately need, and must have, a religion that saves them, and it is through Christ they are drawn and won. Show them the constraint of Christ. Don't assume that they understand a certain common something called Christianity; as you urge them to be Christian, tell them what, and how." Unless preaching presses for some kind of human verdict and results in some kind of change, whether in the secret chamber of a person's soul or ethically in his or her worldly life, the Word in its fullness has not been served.

In his autobiography he stated afresh what he had long held:

The preacher's business is not merely to discuss repentance but to persuade people to repent; not merely to debate the meaning and possibility of Christian faith, but to produce Christian faith in the lives of his listeners; not merely to talk about the available power of God to bring victory over trouble and temptation, but to send people out from their worship on Sunday with victory in their possession. A preacher's task is to create in his congregation the thing he is talking about.

And so his sermons closed with "I want some choices made here this morning" or "I want some personal decisions made here concerning that." And so scores of worshippers reported what thousands must have felt: Fosdick was preaching to them directly, personally. He reminded them, perhaps, of the story told about John Wesley addressing a vast outdoor multitude. A man named John Nelson reported the experience: "I thought that he spoke to no one but me, and I durst not look up for I imagined that all the people were looking at me."

All very well and even good. Still, Fosdick himself made some statements that might provide ammunition for those critics who found his theories inadequate to a kerygmatic theology of preaching—preaching as proclamation or heralding of the Gospel. Recalling his experiences in France during the Great War, he rather pridefully reported a sergeant remarking after one of his talks, "I don't know what religion he belongs to, but he has a hell of a lot of sense." Patently that "talk" could not have been the Gospel proclaiming and declaring itself. Clearly that "talk" did not proclaim that at one point in the world's history, in the life and death and resurrection of Jesus of Nazareth, God chose to reveal himself in a way that can be known nowhere else.

On at least a dozen instances Fosdick reported that before entering the pulpit he lifted up the silent prayer: "Somewhere in this congregation is one person who desperately needs what I am going to say; O God, help me to get at him!" This petition is unfortunate—if not, indeed, blasphemous—in its suggestion that it is Fosdick's words, not the Word, by which men are saved; and also in its suggestion that attention focuses on the preacher rather than on God, for in true preaching the preacher takes upon himself so completely the form of a servant that he is forgotten.

Fosdick was not arrogant, but occasionally he let slip what can only be termed a prideful utterance. For example, addressing in 1927 a conference of ministers, he boasted: "A man plays golf and then comes to Church where I am going to preach to take a nap—he cannot do it; a woman gives a big dinner party Saturday night and comes to church where I am going to preach to 'relax'—she can't do it. My sermons excite the congregation too much for any napping or 'relaxing.' " He then observed, infelicitously, that every sermon should be "a thrilling thing" because people are tired of going to church and just being told, "Thus saith the Lord."

Nevertheless, these must not stand as the last words on Fosdick's understanding of the preaching office. He deserves a chance to answer his critics and, indeed, to clarify some of his own muddled statements. To begin with, a look at his concept of preaching as "personal counseling on a group scale" is in order. A few moments ago we noted Allan McDiarmid's critique in which the young scholar argued that preaching and counseling are discrete functions that cannot be combined. When McDiarmid sent Fosdick a summary of his dissertation, Fosdick responded in a long letter. Characteristically it was friendly in tone, civil in language, closing with "Benedictions on you and best wishes to you! Very cordially yours." Fosdick did not, however, concede the validity of McDiarmid's critique. Of course, Fosdick acknowledged the difference in physical setting in counseling and preaching situations and differences in method too. "But," continued the letter, "*psychologically* the two are closely akin with exactly the same aim in view, namely, throwing light on real problems, helping persons to see the truth about themselves and their relationships with their fellows, and their God, and bringing about illumination of life and transformation of character. When the Christian minister preaches or counsels, he is trying to do the same thing: bring the grace and power of God to bear on human needs, to renew, transform, and sustain them." Why does a vital sermon invite personal counsel? Because the personal counseling has already begun in the sermon. The preacher has found out the secret trouble of some life, has shown that he understands the need, has thrown light on some inner difficulty, has opened a door to hope in temptation, has comforted sorrow, has brought faith where doubt prevailed, so that what began as counseling in a group continues in the more intimate conversation of the counseling room. "I still am all in favor of a sermon," he concluded, "that gets inside the listener and in Ezekiel's phrase, 'sits where they sit.' "

Fosdick held that preaching and pastoral counseling were two indispensable offices of one vocational task. He knew that the truths of the Gospel were no truths at all if they did not refer men eventually to the contemporary world. The necessary congruence between religion and life was at the very marrow of his pulpit proclamation. Edmund A. Steimle, who followed Fosdick as a professor of homiletics at Union, seems close to Fosdick's position when he described authentic preaching as "the sensitive interweaving of the biblical story with my story, your story, so that new light is shed on both." The biblical story, Steimle insists, is not just an ancient story, it is contemporary. "The primary purpose of the preacher is to interweave the biblical story with my story (your story) so that we can see a bit more clearly (even if we do not want to see!) who we are, what is expected of us, and what the future may hold for us. And that is precisely what the 'proclamation of the Gospel' is all about." Paul Scherer, renowned as a preacher's preacher, who also followed Fosdick at Union, counseled beginning preachers: "You may begin your career with a doctrinaire interest in theology or in preaching as one of the fine arts. But pray God you may find yourself, little by little, drawn to human lives and human hopes and fears."* This is identical with the advice given by Fosdick to earlier generations of Union students. The point being made is that Fosdick's understanding of preaching, so often criticized as superficial, actually sounds much like the positions of some of the most distinguished students of homiletics of a later era.

A question may be raised concerning the relationship between reason and revelation in Fosdick's preaching. Because he did not, with Luther, see reason as a "whore," he has been characterized by some as a pure rationalist. Because he resisted the kind of authority satisfied with the bowed head and unenlightened mind, he was charged with throwing out revelation. These characterizations and these charges require clarification.†

A sermon, said Fosdick, is "a mediation of the revelation of God in Christ." Preaching "is an opportunity so to mediate a knowledge of God and the saving power of Christ that lives can be transformed." The preacher starts not with reason but with revelation, and in the Bible is found the supreme expression of the Christian revelation. As he flatly put it: "I wouldn't start a sermon with reason—always the primary element is a revelation. What else am I up there for?" Again Fosdick said straightforwardly: "No, I'm not a Thomist. This idea of climbing up to God by my reason. No, no, it won't do. We start—I am more orthodox than people think I am. We start with grace. There is something given to us that we can't explain, can't reason through."

Rationalism has its limits. "I do not believe that God can be discovered at the end of an argument," Fosdick held. "There is many a kingdom of heaven that you do not get into head first!" "Faith always sees more with her eye," he wrote in 1917, "than logic can read with her

---

* Said Philipps Brooks in the nineteenth century to the divinity students at Yale: "Preach doctrine, preach all the doctrine that you know, and learn more and more; but preach it always, not that men may believe, but that men may be saved by believing it."

† Robert M. Shelton, "The Relationship Between Reason and Revelation in the Preaching of Harry Emerson Fosdick," unpublished Th.D. dissertation, Princeton Theological Seminary, 1965, is an enormously valuable work, especially because Shelton in 1963 taped an illuminating interview with Fosdick.

head." Neither in religion nor in any other realm of spiritual reality can we get to the deepest truths or the greatest experiences by means of reasoning alone.

It does not follow, however, that reason is the "enemy" to be slain; that to reason about the Christian faith with perplexed enquirers is to commit high treason against the faith, as some theologians would have it. The preacher must start with revelation, but it isn't a revelation, no matter how true the exposition may be, if the man in the pew does not get it. Revelation is not simply from the God end out toward man, Fosdick argued, it is the receptive capacity of man too. And this is the point where reason performs its duty. Man receives the revelation and then endeavors intelligently to think through what God has done, to fit the revelation into the rest of man's knowledge and experience. If you do not reason about revelation, you are taking it secondhand and consequently it never becomes real in your life. "It takes reasoning even to discern the limits and insufficiencies of reason." Reason, said Fosdick in a memorable phrase, is "the God-given power of clarification, so that we can love the Lord our God with all our mind." The preacher tries to talk about the revelation reasonably, and although faith is not reason, faith is reasonable. "But there will be times," Fosdick comprehended, "when the mystery must be acknowledged." He said elsewhere, "Existence must be content with a fighting certainty."

Ralph Sockman believed Fosdick to be "a magnificent biblical preacher," but a lot of critics charged that his preaching was not Bible centered, and it is now necessary to comment on this troublesome question.

In his 1915 Union inaugural address Fosdick declared that the Bible "belongs to the preacher," the "glory of the scriptures in the Church has always been their preachableness," and that the Bible must "be preached, and repreached, and preached again as long as the world stands." In his 1924 Beecher Lectures he observed that the preacher deprived of his Bible would be as "lost as a judge without the Constitution, thrown back upon the bare ideal of Justice without historical content." In his 1938 *A Guide to Understanding the Bible* he stated the conviction that "the central ideas of Scripture, in whatever changing categories they may be phrased, seem to me the hope of man's individual and social life." In 1960 he informed an inquirer that a serious preacher must preach from a background of deep biblical study, adding, "I surely had my own critical struggles in that realm, and it is with me a matter of fundamental importance."

Fosdick's preaching was, then, Bible centered; and because rooted in Scripture his preaching was timeless as well as timely. Some ministers who were identified with the life-situation method or the project method

or the counseling-on-a-group-scale method largely banished Holy Writ
from their sermons; not so, however, Fosdick. But neither were his sermons exactly "expository," at least as that term is generally understood.
Absolutely central is his conviction that the preacher's function is to re-
produce the abiding experiences of Scripture in the lives of the congregation, above all that supreme experience of the Bible, the response in
contrition and faith of the disciples to Jesus. Unless that ancient experience was reproduced, unless the "unsearchable riches of Christ" were
actually transported into personal lives, the sermon had failed. Elmer
Edwin Burtner, the most searching student of Fosdick's use of biblical
materials, reached this profoundly true conclusion: "He wanted to make
God real to needy men and women—real in his righteous judgment, real
in his fatherly care and helpfulness. He tried to make Christ so real that
the experience of meeting him would happen all over again, so real that
he would appear to modern men as he appeared to the first Christians as
the special enterprise of God undertaken in man's behalf, apart from
man's deserving, and at a cost only Calvary could tell."

As a bridge has to reach both banks of a stream, so a sermon must
reach both the Bible and modern worshippers. In his sermons Fosdick
made that double contact because of his famous theological conviction
of "abiding experiences in changing categories." The experiences revealed
in Scripture must be validated within the experiences of twentieth-century man. Fosdick was acccused of calling for "new faucets" when he
wrote: "Men who threw away the living water of the Gospel because
they disliked the water-buckets in which their boyhood churches presented it, are living spiritually thirsty lives when there is no reasonable
need of their doing so." But if he called for "new faucets," it was because
in them modern man could find the living water of the Gospel as they
could not in outmoded buckets. He sought to get at both the basic experiences of the Bible and those of his people and then he tried to bring the
two together.

In assessing the evidence that Fosdick's sermons suffered from theological malnutrition, it is helpful to remember that he always considered
himself an interpreter, not a systematic theologian. J. V. L. Casserley
made an illuminating point that applies to Fosdick well: "Apologetics is
an ecclesiastical activity that takes place on the frontiers of Christian
Commitment. Its discussions are necessarily of a somewhat elementary
character." To be sure a preacher must not buy comprehensibility with
the coin of unfaithfulness to the Gospel. He would be a popular pulpit
prince perhaps, but certainly not a Servant of the Word. Fosdick was
willing to face the charge of anthropocentrism, however, in order to meet
troubled and puzzled men and women where they lived. He was ready

to risk the epithet "popularizer" in order to present the Gospel in terms and language accessible to those not possessed of doctorates in theology or sacred literature. Seeking to bring into the Church of Christ individuals dogmatists would exclude, he was prepared to be termed latitudinarian and syncretic. If apologetics is to be worthy of its name, it must speak to people, it must speak in understandable concepts and words, and it must not be exclusionary. Fosdick was concerned to make God reasonable to individuals that God might be made real to them.

A God made real resulted in transformed lives. Fosdick was a persuasive Christian apologist, but ultimately he must be seen as an evangelist, a preacher who reached the heart through the intellect. "Religion begins," he wrote in *The Meaning of Faith*, "when the God outwardly argued is inwardly experienced." In that early devotional volume he argued that every man was faced with the choice between religion and irreligion, God and no-God, Christian faith and unbelief: "A man can avoid making up his mind, but he cannot avoid making up his life."

Fosdick's evangelism carried on the pronounced tendency of late nineteenth-century preaching to soften dogmatic structures and mute the note of man as sinner in the hands of an angry God. Henry Ward Beecher cried: "I will *not* worship cruelty. I *will* worship Love—that sacrifices itself for the good of those who err." Said Fosdick: "Our fathers used to preach in order to convict men of sin. If someone here is self-complacent and content, that would be real service. But for the most part I would rather preach not so much to convict men of their sins as to convince men of their possibilities." And: "One of the profoundest laws in the universe is that, wherever there is sin and sorrow, there is only one way out. Someone who does not have to do it, for the sake of those who do not deserve it, must take on himself the burden of their need."

Late in his life Fosdick expressed this thought: "Most of the time I am glad that I have retired, but once in a while I wish I were young again. I think I should be more urgent, more personal, more aware of the critical importance of individual decision than I used to be." He was being too harsh on himself. His preaching *was* magnificently urgent and personal as he fulfilled his own dictum: "The central task and the crowning privilege of the Christian preacher are to present Christ."*

---

* Fosdick's understanding of the preacher as prophet will be examined in later chapters in the context of his heavy involvement in social issues.

Chapter Nineteen

"Sweating Blood": The Preparation and Presentation of Preachable Sermons

I

The empty pew is the preacher's perfect work. Fosdick was determined to be innocent of that arraignment. It has been shown that criticisms of his concept of preaching were not rare; nor were criticisms of the content of his sermons. But no one could dare assert that his preaching emptied the pew. This chapter will comprise an investigation of the reading, writing, and speaking habits of a preacher widely hailed as a "homiletic genius."

II

Because Fosdick took all of life as the province of the pulpit, he did not only draw from the books in his study. The great preachers, with few exceptions, are those who have lived in the world and experienced that which the world both affords and inflicts. Hell may be other people, as Sartre (half-truthfully) claims, but to shelter oneself from human contacts is to attempt to escape from existence; rare is the individual who can preach authentic words without having known authentic human relationships. It may even be the requirement of great preaching that the minister shall have glimpsed hell at least once in his life. To be sure, if the preacher refuses to glean ideas from books he will probably be convicted of solipsism; yet there is an aridity about ideas known only objectively, never existentially.

Fosdick once reported that he got his illustrations "primarily from per-

351

sonal life, from keeping my eyes open and watching things go"; and toward the end of his life he acknowledged how much the preacher "needs the abiding treasures of experience." Like all superior preachers, Fosdick drew from what he saw and heard and endured over a long and full and rich life.

But it was hardly one of reckless abandon, and missing from his sermons, not surprisingly, were those things missing from his life. John Hay's aphorism is applicable here, "Love your neighbor, but be careful of your neighborhood." Fosdick's ministries were in a New Jersey suburb and New York City, but in Gotham his haunts were (aside from the early Bowery mission) Fifth Avenue and Park Avenue and Morningside Heights—and the Century Club, Carnegie Hall, and the Metropolitan Opera House. It seems likely that Yankee Stadium and Ebbets Field, Small's Paradise and the Cotton Club in Harlem, the jazz spots on 52nd Street and the coffeehouses in the Village, the tiny Chinese restaurants on Spring Street and San Gennaro's festival on Mulberry Street, the West Side tenderloin and "Texas" Guinan's speakeasy never knew his presence. He was in the city but not of the city—at least not Al Smith's and Jimmy Walker's and Damon Runyon's and Cab Calloway's city. Fosdick saw much at home and abroad, but much remained outside the periphery of his vision. His sermons are informed by a pastoral and bucolic sensibility, not by an urban one. They smell of the orchards of upper New York, the heather of Scotland, the pines of Maine, the mountain air of Switzerland, the fresh waters of Lake Chautauqua, and the salty ocean surrounding Mouse Island.

Some men are good in the worst sense of the word, leaving to kind men the task of healing the wounds inflicted by their "goodness." Fosdick, however, was a good man in the best sense of the word, surely in part because he knew existentially the tragic dimensions of life: his own youthful breakdown, his mother's early death, the ordeals endured by his brother and sister, the cruel loss suffered by his daughter Elinor, illnesses, the slander of foes. Still by any comparative measurement. Fosdick was blessed. He was nurtured by loving parents. Florence was to him a faithful, adoring wife. The two children were physically and mentally healthy and supportive to the end. Personal violence was a stranger. He loved his work. His star ascended steadily and throughout his life he enjoyed honor, love, obedience, troops of friends and admirers. Even at the end, though fearfully crippled, he did not face death alone and uncared for. Thus, despite the terrible things he encountered in his pastoral counseling sessions, Fosdick could not preach from the personal experience of a beaten or abandoned child; a cuckolded husband; an unfaithful, guilt-burdened husband; a father scorned by indifferent children; a re-

Dr. George Alexander,
venerable senior minister
of "Old First"

First Presbyterian Church

Fosdick at the height of the
Fundamentalist/Modernist
controversy

Park Avenue Baptist Church (now
Central Presbyterian Church)

The Riverside Church

The nave of The Riverside Church

"Gramps" with Stevie and Patty Downs

Fosdick and his Scots successor Robert James McCracken

peated career failure; a debt-ridden breadwinner; a battered loser in battles with booze or drugs; a helpless sufferer disfigured or crippled by physical deformity; a soul for whom God's reality faded and then disappeared. There were depths of existence foreign to his experience and, therefore, perhaps inevitably, unsounded in his sermons.

III

Fosdick partially compensated for the gaps in his experience by voracious reading. Those who heard his sermons and read his books marveled at the apparent range and richness of his reading. "Awe" is the only word to describe their response to the myriad allusions, references, citations, and quotations studding his works. Ralph Sockman estimated that Fosdick spent one hour in sermon preparation for each minute of sermon delivery. Robert James McCracken guessed that sixteen hours, on the average, were poured into each sermon, "to say nothing of long-term preparation." Close students of Fosdick's preaching reached similar figures—sixteen, twenty, thirty hours—although when confronted with such conjectures, he once commented, "I wish that were true!"

Whatever the precise figure, it was impressive. "I read all the time, and read omnivorously," he reported. On another occasion he replied to an inquiry: "First I read all kinds of books if I have reason to suppose that they were good—novels, biographies, etc. Second, I did a great deal of reading concentrated on special fields of research—Biblical, theological, etc." He advised younger ministers always to have a book within reach to take advantage of every spare moment and also to make every vacation a reading spree. Often he had several books going at once, one at home, one at the church, one at his seminary office, and a paperback for the train.

Fosdick was in constant fear of his time being nickeled-and-dimed away, and it has been shown that he kept his morning hours sacrosanct from intrusive invasion. During these guarded hours he read and wrote with intense concentration and great efficiency; few precious moments were frittered away. Also, many evenings were spent reading. He praised the uses of solitude and tried to practice what Emerson called "selective attention." A note to his Riverside successor offered this advice: "I share your concern over uninterrupted mornings for study. Working in my room at home, I insisted on *that* for twenty years. Stick to it! If you have difficulty managing it in your church office—as may be possible—there will be some place in that town where you can find a hide-out and shut yourself off in complete isolation."

There are several ways to fix more precisely on what Fosdick read. One, an examination of the footnotes and bibliographies cited in his published works, other than the undocumented volumes of sermons and magazine articles. Two, an examination of the allusions, illustrations, references, citations, quotations in his published and unpublished works, including sermons and magazine articles. Three, an examination of the works in his personal library. Four, an examination of the works he recommended in his personal correspondence. And five, an examination of the "Notebooks" deposited in the Fosdick Collection at Union. We shall see that no single one of these approaches is entirely satisfactory, but that by combining all five a reasonable fix can be reached.

In resigning from the board of directors of a certain organization, Fosdick explained: "This is not at all that I am in general too busy, for everybody is too busy. It is because, in particular, holding as I do a professorship at the Union Seminary where I teach, and building up this new parish in the Riverside area, I face week after week an interlocking system of definite appointments which makes attendance on Board meetings absolutely impossible." This statement and many similar ones suggest what should be obvious: not all of Fosdick's waking hours could be devoted to reading and writing; there were simply too many other demands on his time. His mornings were inviolate and some evenings were free and his vacations were in part working ones, but surely no more than half of his time was spent in the study. He *was* a voracious reader, but common sense and close examination tell us that his reading was not limitless.

Having made this general, and uncritical, observation, a further word about the five approaches. Almost all of the books written by Fosdick, other than the volumes of sermons, contained footnotes or bibliographies or both. It was a simple task to assemble these citations, and such a compilation does provide an important clue to Fosdick's reading, but not a definitive one, for two clear reasons. He read much not cited in footnote or bibliography; and he cited at least some items he never read (a practice not unheard of even in the historical profession).

A second approach, far, far more arduous, was to assemble lists of all allusions, illustrations, references, citations, quotations in all of Fosdick's writings. Such lists might be fed into a computer and the whole mass quantified. We would then know precisely the number of references to, say, Lincoln; the number of quotations from, say, Milton; the number of citations from, say, the Book of Jeremiah; the number of allusions to, say, the ocean; the number of illustrations from, say, Shakespeare's plays. The computer had to be abandoned when it became evident that Fosdick frequently drew materials from second- and third-hand sources and that, therefore, a computer analysis would seriously distort what he actually read. Nevertheless, these lists are valuable for impressionistic purposes.

A third approach involved a page-by-page examination of the 1400 volumes in Fosdick's personal library given to the Evangelical Seminary of Puerto Rico, described in the "Essay on Sources." Naturally some books were unmarked by Fosdick, some slightly marked, some heavily so. In those marked, the margins contained small checks and such brief notations as "drama," "sermon here," "note," "capital statement," "foolish," "great," "VIP!," "?," "very important," "good," "NB," "!," "intolerable arrogance," "colossal arrogance," "nonsense," "irrationality." Furthermore, on the back inside cover there are page numbers jotted down accompanied by such obrservations as "very important on Jesus' entry into Jerusalem," "excellent on the cleansing of the temple," "excellent on paying the tax to Caesar," "Martha & Mary necessary to give our Lord a perfect hospitality. Sermon: Martha over Mary. Mary over Martha. Jesus both!," "Front of *Bulletin*," "good on capitalism and communism," "an excellent description of the religious climate I was raised in!"

On several instances Fosdick reported, "I bought most of the important books which I read" and "I made a habit to own the significant books which I was reading." Nevertheless, these fourteen hundred volumes clearly do not represent all or even most of the books he read in a lifetime. For one thing, virtually without exception the works are nonfiction, and it is reasonable to assume that Fosdick decided that a seminary library would not be interested in novels. Second, although he had the means to purchase books, surely he relied heavily on library copies and borrowed volumes. This speculation becomes a certainty when one notes that hundreds of titles cited by Fosdick in his writings are absent from his personal library.

A fourth approach was to take notice of works he recommended to inquirers. Not infrequently an individual would write asking him for the titles of the best books on a given subject, and presumably those he endorsed were those he had read. He once prefaced a list with the observation, "When it comes to recommending cooks, psychiatrists, and books I often feel myself baffled and uncertain."

Before turning to the fifth approach, an important, if obvious, point requires remembrance, namely, a substantial amount of Fosdick's reading time was chewed up by newspapers and magazines, including at least sixteen religious and theological journals.

Finally, the fifth approach. In the Fosdick Collection at Union there are twelve soft-leather loose-leaf notebooks. Nine of them are crammed with quotations and anecdotes and clippings arranged alphabetically by author. Three of them are elaborate indexes arranged alphabetically by subject matter with cross listings. For example, the subject "Hell" receives thirty-three cross listings with such guides as:

Hell, appearance of to Christian.   Bunyan, J. 6
Hell, changed into paradise.   St. Catherine. 1
Hell, Dante's beard darkened in.   Dante Ali. 2
Hell hath no fury like non-combatant.   Chesterton, GK. 3
Hell I suffer seems Heaven, to which to.   Milton, John, 2r
Hell, infants span long in.   Calvin, J. 2
Hell, would drink whiskey if it plunged him into.   Carey, S. 1
Hell, quotation from sermon on.   Edward, J. 1
Hell, will change climate of.   Emerson, Ralph W. 18

Examining these notebooks is akin to looking into a magician's bag of tricks after marveling at his act. The statement stands that Fosdick was a voracious reader of serious material. But these notebooks prove also that he borrowed heavily, often from works of no great depth, and when documentation was required, he cited sometimes, but not always, not the secondary but the original source. This is not to level an accusation of plagiarism. He made no secret of his borrowing or of the practice of tracing back to the original source a quotation lifted second- or third- or fourth-hand. His friends in the ministry knew this. He advised his Union students to check scrupulously every quotation and fact encountered against the original document. His editor at Harper's clearly understood and sanctioned the practice. One of his secretaries recalled, and not in condemnation:

As for his conscientiousness, as you know his writings are full of quotations. He was meticulous about exactitude in these and that they be documented. One of my tasks was to locate the original source of every quotation he used whenever it was possible to do so. For example, if in his reading he ran across a quotation from H. G. Wells which someone else had used, he wanted the original source from Wells' writings. The secondary source would not do. Fortunately we had at our disposal for this purpose the use of the libraries at Columbia, U.T.S., the New York Public Library, and on occasion the Jewish Theological Seminary. After submitting to him the Index for *On Being a Real Person,* I received from him this note which reads in part: "I question whether it is fair to leave out names—maybe there are no more—like Carroll Wise whose material I used so freely but whose name appears only in the References. Put him in anyway."

Once when questioned about the custom of borrowing, Fosdick's reply was nonchalant: "A friend of mine was once told that he had used what sounded suspiciously like somebody else's material, and he retorted, 'Well, what do you think I buy books for? For the covers?' "

Let the matter be stated clearly. Often Fosdick *did* credit a quotation to a secondary origin. When he did not, that is, when he cited the original source, he did not attempt to hide the practice from those in the know. Nevertheless, the truth is that individuals listening to his sermons or reading his books were left with a slightly misleading impression of the actual range and depth of his reading.

Fortunately for Fosdick, his secretaries were persistent sleuths, in some cases tracing back an item through several intervening layers to its origins. Sometimes they failed, but not often. For example, Fosdick once picked up a story about Leonardo da Vinci from a potboiler and asked his secretary to verify it. She reported presently, "Search in lives of da Vinci fails to confirm this story." Fortunately for Fosdick, also, one of his veteran secretaries, Margaret Renton, was fluent in French, making it possible for Fosdick to cite in the original a quotation from, say, Voltaire or Flaubert or Vandamme first found (in order) in James Stewart, *The Gates of New Life,* Gamaliel Bradford, *Bare Souls,* and Irwin Edman, *Human Traits and Their Social Significance.*

Because friends and publishers occasionally solicited Fosdick to read as yet unpublished manuscripts, he found materials in this form in the writings of such individuals as Rufus Jones, Ralph Sockman, Willard Sperry, Leslie Weatherhead, and Walter Bowie.

Fosdick's corps of friends inside and outside the ministry not infrequently sent him, unsolicited, illustrations and quotations they thought he might use. Sometimes he wrote these individuals to identify an item. For example, when Charles Gilkey quoted Josiah Royce, "God never sat for his photograph," and Fosdick's secretary was unable to track it down in Royce's writings, Fosdick contacted Gilkey who reported that he personally heard Royce say this in a class in metaphysics in 1902. Similarly, when unable to find a quotation from William James, Margaret Renton wrote Rufus Jones to ask where he had first encountered it. Reminisced Ralph Sockman, "I recall more than one written request from him in later years asking me to cite the authority of some reference which I had made in sermon or book. Like some preachers Fosdick borrows illustrations, but unlike some preachers he makes sure that what he borrows is genuine."

True, but the point being made is that Fosdick masked his Tinker-to-Evers-to-Chance technique. For instance, the poet John Masefield's line, "The harm I done by being me," is quoted in *On Being a Real Person* and the footnote cites John Masefield, "The Everlasting Mercy," *Poems* (New York, 1929), p. 84. But Fosdick first encountered this line when reading the galley proof of Willard Sperry's *What You Owe Your Child* who in turn had lifted it from John Reid's, *Why Be Good?* He once quoted the historian Charles A. Beard, but he picked up the statement from a volume of sermons by Ernest Fremont Tittle, who in turn had found it in a work by Will Durant. He once quoted John Robinson and cited William Bradford's *History of Plymouth Plantation,* but in fact the quote came from a biography of Robinson. He once quoted a Confederate general at Shiloh and cited *Battles and Leaders,* but in truth the quote came from an article in the *New York Herald Tribune.* Hundreds of similar examples might be cited.

Having surveyed five avenues to the discovery of what Fosdick read and noted the limitation to each if employed exclusively, let us now brave some broad generalizations based on pulling these avenues together. This approach may do Fosdick an injustice, but the alternative would be to list hundreds and hundreds of titles.

Fosdick steeped himself in the King James Bible, but other versions he found meritorious and helpful. In 1925 he replied to an inquiry, "With regard to your question about quotations from the Bible, I am accustomed regularly to follow the 'American Standard Version.' " He used this 1901 version primarily in *A Guide to Understanding the Bible, On Being a Real Person,* and (for the Old Testament) *The Man from Nazareth, as His Contemporaries Saw Him.* He also found "competent and excellent" J. M. Powis Smith's 1927 translation of the Old Testament and Edgar J. Goodspeed's 1923 translation of the New Testament, published together in 1931 as *The Bible: An American Translation.* He said of James Moffatt's final revision of the Bible in 1935, "I regard Dr. Moffatt's translation as far and away the most valuable of all modern attempts to put the Bible into more easily understandable English. Alike the accuracy and the vividness of his translation are a continual delight, and I find myself constantly turning to the Moffatt Bible to check other translations." However, when in 1952* the heralded Revised Standard Version of the Bible appeared, Fosdick sang its praises, observing that it "is now in a real sense the authorized translation for our Protestant churches. . . . Every Christian should possess this translation."

In the Introduction to *A Guide to Understanding the Bible* Fosdick wrote: "Only some one with no reputation for original scholarship to maintain, free to avail himself of any scholar's work, professing only a transmissive and interpretive function, and interested not in moot details but in general results, would have the hardihood to undertake this task." In the prologue to *The Man from Nazareth* he said: "I have hoped . . .

---

* The Revised Standard Version of the New Testament came out in 1946 and this is the version Fosdick used in *The Man from Nazareth.*

that a modest volume, such as this, written not by a technical New Testament scholar, might be of use in presenting to the ordinary reader some of the results of recent study." And he once candidly admitted to a former student: "I know well that I have only a third-rate mind. Compared to a scholar like Moffatt I am no scholar at all. Whatever I have been able to accomplish has come through hard work, and if I have any virtue it lies in sticking to my last."

These are fair statements. Fosdick did not possess the time, tools, or *possibly* even the intellect to be a biblical scholar, but he did bravely attempt to keep abreast of biblical scholarship so that he might preach sermons grounded in the interpretation of Scripture and write books transmitting to the "ordinary reader" the fruits of biblical scholarship. The total number of hours devoted to this biblical study cannot be known, but a compilation of all the titles cited in the notes and bibliographies of *The Modern Use of the Bible*, *A Guide to Understanding the Bible*, and *The Man from Nazareth* and all the titles in his personal library makes clear that this reading was a very serious matter. Moreover, even the most critical reviewers (and there were many) of these three major volumes generally acknowledged his command of the scholarly literature even as they take issue with his interpretations.*

Fosdick's library contained all the major aids to the study of the Bible: concordances, Bible dictionaries and encyclopaedias, atlases and commentaries, and more generally the *Encyclopaedia Britannica*. The list of biblical scholars he read and cited impresses. It is long and prestigious. Considering the fact, however, that he presumed to transmit to, and interpret for, the "ordinary reader" the findings of the finest and most recent scholarship, a critical observer might note that absent from his citations and his library are the works of such individuals as W. Albright, O. Baab, R. Bultmann, M. Dibelius, W. Eichrodt, F. Eiselen, O. Eissfeldt, P. Forsyth, R. Grant, H. Gunkel, C. Hoskyns, S. Hooke, F. Hort, R. Kittel, G. Lampe, J. Lightfoot, P. Minear, O. Piper, A. Richardson, J. Riggs, A. Schlatter, E. Sellin, E. Thurneysen, W. Vicher, G. von Rad, T. Vriezen, G. Wright. If it were possible to interview Fosdick he might point out that he did in fact read some or all of these authors, but never found it necessary to cite their works or purchase them for his library. He might observe, too, that he encountered these individuals in articles, essays, and chapters in longer books (as we know was true in the case of W. Albright for example). Perhaps a fair judgment is that

---

* It was Fosdick's fate that his ministry ended and his major writing ceased in the decade of the 1940s at precisely the moment when biblical scholarship was undergoing a mighty revolutionary rebirth leaving largely in ruins the regnant interpretations of the nineteenth and early twentieth centuries.

Fosdick read very heavily in biblical studies, but that he missed a considerable amount as well; especially serious is the lacuna in the German scholarship available before the 1950s and his apparent disregard of much Roman Catholic scholarship.

Moving from biblical studies to the history of Christianity, a reconstruction of Fosdick's reading again impresses, but not quite overwhelmingly so. Shading from religious history to historical theology to theology much the same observation might be made. On the credit side, in 1952 Fosdick compiled and edited a significant volume entitled, *Great Voices of the Reformation, An Anthology,* dealing with the major emphases of Protestant thought from John Wycliffe to John Wesley. Fosdick's introduction and commentaries and suggestions for further readings joined with much other evidence point to the fact that although he was not a formal theologian, he was much concerned with theology, historical and contemporary. His library contained the eight-volume edition of *The Ante-Nicene Fathers* by Roberts and Donaldson. Sixteen pages of the notebooks are devoted to St. Augustine (although only one to Aquinas). He read the edited works of Luther and eighteen pages of the notebooks are devoted to him, and in retirement he wrote a popular biography of the Reformation giant. He also read the edited works of Calvin, though one suspects he studied Calvin the way antiaircraft gunners study enemy planes. Obviously he was steeped in the theological ideas of the Americans W. Clarke, B. Bowne, W. Rauschenbusch, R. Jones, S. Mathews, E. Scott to mention only few of many. Across the Atlantic he admired Canon Streeter, Principal Jacks, John Baillie; and Emil Brunner, with whom, of course, he did not always agree; again to mention only a few of many. Scores of additional names from the world of theology might be cited.

Before Fosdick is awarded the highest palm, however, another observation must be made; and it is made with the awareness that he cannot be faulted for failing to keep abreast of theological currents in his twilight years and with the understanding that he may have read much lost from the record. Fosdick discusses Karl Barth in "Winds of Doctrine," but only Barth's brief *Dogmatics in Outline* is in the library (with critical markings) and the notebooks contain only one quote from Barth, and that is secondhand. The name of Rudolf Bultmann is mentioned in *The Man from Nazareth,* but none of Bultmann's works are in the library and his name is absent from the notebooks. No source points to Fosdick having read anything by Dietrich Bonhoeffer. Not a single work by William Temple or C. S. Lewis is in the library. Gustav Aluén's name is mentioned indirectly in "Winds of Doctrine," but nowhere else; the names of F. Gogarten and A. Nygren not at all. Fosdick refers in passing fashion in two books to Paul Tillich and in a letter expressed "a deep sympathy with him and his way of getting at things"; still, no volume by Tillich is in the library and his name does not appear in the notebooks. Martin Buber's *Eclipse of God* is in the library, but that is the only one by the great Jewish seer. Missing from the record of Fosdick's reading are such American critics of religious liberalism as Douglas Horton, Robert Calhoun, Walter Lowrie, and Edwin Lewis (the last of whom thought Fosdick a "scatterbrain"). It is quite astonishing that H. Richard Niebuhr, both as theologian and as historian, is invisible in the record. As for Reinhold Niebuhr, the library contains only *The Contribution of Religion to Social Work, An Interpretation of Christian Ethics,* and *Pious and Secular America.* Is it possible that Fosdick never dipped into Niebuhr's famed Gifford Lectures, *The Nature and Destiny of Man?* (He did own a volume of essays on Niebuhr edited by Kegley and Bretall.)

Fosdick read measuredly in philosophy. Names such as Plato, Aristotle, Epictetus, Seneca, Aurelius, Pascal, Spinoza, Montaigne, Goethe, Kant, Hegel, Schopenhauer, and Nietzsche dot his writings, but inasmuch as no works by these individuals are found in his library, it is difficult to judge the seriousness of his study, although he did own biographies of some of these philosophers. He did in fact read Bertrand Russell and W. R. Inge firsthand and several works by the great Alfred North Whitehead and the banal Pierre Lecomte duNöuy. On this side of the Atlantic Fosdick's clear favorites were Emerson and James. The library contains Emerson's *Complete Works* (twelve volumes), and an astonishing forty notebook pages are devoted to quotes from or about the transcendentalist. Twenty-one pages are given to James, primarily passages from *The Varieties of Religious Experience* and *The Principles of Psychology* and his edited *Letters.* Josiah Royce, William Ernest Hocking, James Pratt, Irwin Edman, Joseph Wood Krutch, and Elton Trueblood are other writers known to Fosdick firsthand.

In the realms of Christian apologetics and ethics Fosdick read widely indeed, including such favorites as William Orchard, G. K. Chesterton, Henry Drummond, and Walter Rauschenbusch.

Moving now to other areas, as one imagines is true of most preachers, Fosdick surrounded himself with aids with such titles as *Familiar Quotations, Cyclopedia of Classical Quotations, Home Book of Quotations, New Cyclopedia of Practical Quotations, The Oxford Dictionary of English Proverbs, The Public Speaker's Treasure Chest, English Words and Their Background,* and of course dictionaries and thesauri. He used them too.

Looking back over his preaching ministry, Fosdick made the flat statement, "I never got much out of books on homiletics." Still, in his library are three volumes by his friend Halford Luccock on homiletics and others with such titles as *What to Preach, The Art of Illustrating Sermons, The Integrity of Preaching, Lectures on Preaching, How to Preach to People's Needs, The Making of a Sermon,* and *So You Want to Preach.*

On another occasion he said, "I never got any help at all from homiletical advice. My help came altogther from reading the sermons of preachers whom I admired, and watching how they did it, and applying their methods and principles to my special aptitudes." Elsewhere he acknowledged, "As any preacher should do, when I do not have to preach I hear somebody else preach." The notebooks make plain that he found ideas and illustrations in sermons printed in such journals as *The Pulpit, The Christian Century Pulpit,* and *The Christian World* (London). He read volumes of published sermons by a raft of contemporary or near-contemporary preachers. Further, early in his ministry he made a conscious, systematic study of nineteenth-century pulpit giants, especially Robertson of Brighton, Henry Ward Beecher, and Phillips Brooks (he later collaborated with Bishop William Scarlett in selecting and editing Brooks's sermons). It must be added that apparently Fosdick spent some of his study hours reading *Short Sermons for Children, More Two-Minute Sermons, Fifty-Two Story Sermons for Children, Children's Story Sermons, 50 Sermon-Talks for Boys and Girls, 52 Sermon Trails for Boys and Girls,* and *Sermons I Have Preached to Young People.*

In 1924 Fosdick wrote a passionate article entitled, "Blessed Be Biography." In it he asserted that no other reading "is so much worthwhile." Biography is the "most interesting, informing and refreshing sort of book"; to him not a luxury but an "intellectual and spiritual necessity." Early and late he made comparable assertions. He read quite literally hundreds of lives of individuals in every era and in broad areas, and it is apparent that biography represented a major investment of his study time. Revealingly, eighteen notebook pages are devoted to George Washington and twenty-seven to Lincoln, a man Fosdick loved above all other Americans.

Once again, however, a mild caveat is in order. It is perfectly appropriate that he should search for inspirational or cautionary illustrations in such group biographies as Plutarch's *Lives,* Gamaliel Bradford's *Bare Souls* and *American Portraits,* Lytton Strachey's *Eminent Victorians,* Bernard Jaffee's *Men of Science in America,* and John Middleton Murry's *Heroes of Thought.* But one wonders about the profundity of such understanding as was gained from reading Elbert Hubbard's *Little Journeys to the Homes of Good Men and Great,* Sophia Shaler's *The Masters of Fate: The Power of the Will,* Dale Carnegie's *Little Known Facts About Well-Known People,* and the Thomas's *Living Biographies of Great Scientists, Living Biographies of Famous Novelists,* and *Living*

Biographies of Great Philosophers. Fosdick's library and notebooks show that he relied perhaps excessively on jejune vignettes.

"I defy the cynicism of these new biographers. They cannot take my heroes from me," Fosdick once thundered. This is a proper challenge to the debunkers, but Fosdick went to the other extreme in masking the "spotted actuality" in his heroes, say Livingstone or Nightingale or Luther or Twain. At the same time, he drew such dubious "pop" psychology conclusions from tormented lives, as the following:

> A few weeks ago I went into the Sistine Chapel at the Vatican and for the first time saw Michelangelo's painting of the Last Judgment. You remember it, painted with the tremendous sweep of Michelangelo's titanic art—Christ, throned upon the clouds, with a face of terror to set children screaming, is hurling multitudes of the damned into the pit of hell. How came Michelangelo to paint that picture? He was sixty-six years old. He was a disappointed, embittered, disillusioned old man, an outcast and an alien in the corrupt court of Paul III. He hated men. Every year he lived he hated them the more and he put all the accumulated venom of his contempt for humankind into the figures of Christ and the damned. I could not worship in that chapel—not that Christ.

Complementing biographies was a very extensive reading in autobiographies, memoirs, diaries, journals, and letters, including the greatest in these forms by Augustine, Franklin, Pepys, Henry Adams, Boswell, Thoreau, Robert Louis Stevenson, T. E. Lawrence, Wagner, James Gallatin, John Buchan, Albert J. Nock, and almost countless others.

The highly respected Robert T. Handy once did a study of Fosdick's readings in the field of history, praising the range and comprehensiveness of these readings and concluding: "World history, the history of religions, Jewish history, the history of the Christian Church, literary history, American history, biography—especially biography—are all fields he traverses in preaching and teaching the Christian faith to modern man." Handy's assessment is too generous, especially when applied to secular history. Fosdick read but moderately in history because so many of his reading hours were consumed by biography. Consider these statements from the article, "Blessed Be Biography":

> Another reason for reading biography is that it supplies a knowledge of history in most palatable form. Some folks can take history straight—its dates and dynasties, its political intrigues, war and treaties; but to some of us a formal historical treatise is likely to be indigestible pabulum.

> I could not easily be hired to read a treatise on the unification of Italy, but the life of Cavour by Thayer will give most of the story set in terms of vivid and unforgettable experience.

. . . while I will use special historical treatises when I must and *tours de force* of historical compilation, like H. G. Well's Outline, when I can, for the vivid visualizing of the past I will turn to biographies.

These are hardly the statements of an individual held in Clio's thrall—at least to the extent that written history is held to be a form distinct from biography.

Fosdick read moderately in the social sciences—anthropology, economics, political science, sociology—and, not surprisingly, fairly heavily in psychology. About this seemingly impressive reading in psychology a reservation or two are in order. Aside from the works by William James, many of the volumes cited in *On Being a Real Person* are absent from the library, but this may be because he decided against sending them to an evangelical seminary. Undoubtedly Fosdick did read Jung's *Modern Man in Search of a Soul* (although it is not in the library), for the notebooks contain four quotations which appear to be taken directly from it; still, the passage, "About a third of my cases are suffering from no clinically definable neuroses, but from the senselessness and emptiness of their lives," was picked up in A. C. Craig's *University Sermons* and verified by a secretary: "O.K. as on p. 70 of *Modern Man in Search of a Soul*." For a second thing, uncongenial figures were either neglected (e.g., Freud) or totally ignored (e.g., Wilhelm Reich). Contrariwise, congenial figures (Gordon Allport and J. A. Hadfield and William Sadler for instance) are embraced uncritically. For a third thing, Fosdick read entirely too many inspirational tracts with titles like *The Secret of Happiness, The Twelve Principles of Efficiency, What Makes Us Seem So Queer, Outwitting Our Nerves, The Art of Being a Person, Life's High Hurdles,* and *Brave Enough for Life*.

Although it would be an exaggeration to say that Fosdick successfully bridged the gulf between C. P. Snow's famous "two cultures," he had far more than a passing interest in science. It is indicative, for example, that nineteen notebook pages are devoted to Thomas Henry Huxley, "Darwin's bulldog," and thirteen to Louis Pasteur. He was familiar with the nontheists Ernest Hackel and Bertrand Russell, but sought their refutation in the writings of Alexis Carrel, J. Scott Haldane, James Jeans, Edwin Slosson, and Alfred North Whitehead and in E. L. Long's *Religious Beliefs of American Scientists* and Bronislaw Malinowski's *Science and Religion; a Symposium*. Because Fosdick saw sharply the challenge of science to religion and because he believed a reconciliation possible, he made a major effort to "keep up" with scientific developments in the twentieth century.

Imaginative literature—the novel, poetry, and drama—received from

Fosdick selective attention. On the one hand, his youthful love affair with the great men and women of English letters continued in maturity unabated.*

Among the Russians, Fosdick read Dostoevsky and Tolstoy; among the Germans, Thomas Mann; among the French, Victor Hugo. Of course, there were other Continental authors known to him, but not terribly many. His heart lay across the Channel. His sermons and writings brim with references to Thackeray, Samuel Butler, Lamb, Galsworthy, Meredith, the Walpoles, Trelawney, Walter Scott, Barrie, Matthew Arnold. In the notebooks, twenty-eight pages are devoted to quotations from or about Robert Louis Stevenson; twenty-two to George Eliot; ten each to Kipling and H. G. Wells; nine to Dickens. Many of these statements, however, were encountered by Fosdick at second- or thirdhand. Revealingly, the notebooks contain only one secondhand quote from Maugham and two secondhand quotes from D. H. Lawrence and none at all from Joyce or Virginia Woolf and other moderns. Devoted as Fosdick was to British letters, it seems that he found earlier authors more congenial than those of the deepening twentieth century.

A comparable observation might be made with respect to American authors, though Fosdick read much less in American letters generally. He admired Hawthorne and believed *The Scarlet Letter* "the greatest novel that has been written in America yet." He quoted from Melville's *Moby Dick.* Apparently he adored Mark Twain, for fourteen notebook pages are given to him, though a lot of the material is taken from Bigelow's biography, and Fosdick either ignored or disguised Twain's darker and scatological writings. He read at least two of Steinbeck's novels and probably Fitzgerald's *The Beautiful and the Damned,* Sherwood Anderson's *Winesburg, Ohio,* and Cabell's *Something About Eve: A Comedy of Fig Leaves,* although one cannot be positive because of his custom of coming across a quote once or twice removed and then footnoting the original. The notebooks reveal that the one quote from Henry James was lifted from Halford Luccock; the one from Jack London from Harold Bosley; the one from Ellen Glasgow from Ralph Sockman; the three from Dreiser all from secondary sources. Fosdick quotes Edith Wharton, but from an article rather than her novels. One suppose he was familiar with the novels of Sinclair Lewis for he once accepted an invitation to lunch with the author when *Elmer Gantry* was in the gestation stage. He could scarcely have escaped Mencken and five notebook pages are given to the

* As noted earlier, the library is virtually no help in reconstructing Fosdick's fiction reading because less than a half-dozen titles of the fourteen hundred volumes are in this category, setting aside sets of the collected plays of Shakespeare and the collected poems of Robert Browning.

gadfly, including excerpts from *Prejudices*. On the other hand, all seven George Jean Nathan quotations are taken from Henry Leach's *Living Philosophies*. Where are Hemingway, Dos Passos, Faulkner, Thomas Wolfe, James T. Farrell, Richard Wright, and Robert Penn Warren?

"On or about December 1910 human nature changed," observed Virginia Woolf. The inescapable conclusion is that Fosdick's acquaintanceship with twentieth-century authors was too limited to permit him fully to enter the world as perceived and meditated upon by their modern sensibility. How ironic that a man identified with religious modernism should have been so fundamentally unreceptive to cultural modernism.*

A partial explanation was provided by Fosdick in 1955, in answer to a question about his favorite poets: "You must remember also that Tennyson and Browning were my contemporaries; they overlapped my life and I knew them as poets while their poems were still being written. I think the most influential poet was probably Wordsworth, to whom I was introduced in my high school days, and for whom I had an abiding admiration." Once again comes the startling realization that, though Fosdick died during Nixon's presidency, he was born almost a quarter of a century before the end of Queen Victoria's reign.

In the same context Fosdick also said: "I have no theory whatever on the use of poetry in sermons, and such use of poetry as I have made in my sermons has been not by rule but by intuition. It was Donne, wasn't it? who said that poetry is 'the contraction of the immensities.' So often one can find in the great poets a profound matter briefly stated, and the temptation to make use of it is quite irresistible."

Fosdick knew intimately the major British poets, or rather those antedating Yeats. Twenty-four notebook pages are given to the Brownings; seventeen to Tennyson; fourteen to Wordsworth; seven to Keats. He often cited Shelley, Bryon, Coleridge, Burns, and Francis Thompson, believing "The Hound of Heaven" to be the "greatest poem of our generation." Apparently he read neither Yeats nor Auden.

As for Americans, many pages of the notebooks are devoted to Longfellow, Lanier, James Russell Lowell, Whittier, and Whitman. Edwin Arlington Robinson's poems are noted, but one Robinson line is taken from a book by James Gordon Gilkey and another from a book by Halford Luccock. Where is T. S. Eliot?

Regarding drama, there is not much evidence to go on, with the exception, of course, of Shakespeare, thirty-one notebook pages being devoted to the bard. Shaw, too, was known with some familiarity, but otherwise references to plays are scattered: Ibsen's *Peer Gynt*, Marc Connelly's

---

* This point will be developed in Chapter Twenty-Two.

The Green Pastures, Thornton Wilder's *Our Town*. It is worth noting that the only notebook reference to America's greatest playwright, Eugene O'Neill, is lifted from a *Reader's Digest* inspirational article, "Turn Your Sickness into an Asset."

Fosdick knew much about the individual lives of authors because of his reading of biography, and he also studied several meritorious works of literary criticism by V. L. Parrington, Van Wyck Brooks, and Alfred Kazin. He relied heavily—perhaps excessively—on a score of anthologies with such titles as *Quotable Poems, Ruth's Gleanings; An Anthology of Prose and Poetry, Poems of Justice, The World's Great Religious Poetry, The Home Book of Verse, Library of the World's Best Literature, The Golden Book of Faith; An Anthology.* As to the world of music, he owned the authoritative *Grove's Dictionary of Music and Musicians,* but he also tapped for sermonic purposes such crutches as *Songs of the Average Man* and *The Golden Treasury of American Songs and Lyrics.*

Clearly books were to Fosdick meat and drink. He read a staggering amount of first-rate writing in broad areas. Still two major reservations must stand. Fosdick read too lightly in twentieth-century imaginative literature and too frequently he riffled meretricious stuff solely for homiletical purposes.

IV

Students of Fosdick's sermon preparation have given the impression that his filing system was like the common law in Holmes's day—"chaos without an index." Fosdick contributed to this misapprehension when he replied to inquiries in this fashion:

> I had no filing system for assembling and arranging sermonic material. . . . I had a drawer in my desk into which I threw clippings, notes on episodes, conversations, illustrations, etc. and . . . I trusted my memory to recall what I had thrown into the drawer, when I wanted it.

> As for the material itself I never had a filing system. When I ran across something that I wished to jot down I kept an empty drawer into which these notations were loosely thrown. I have a pretty good memory and generally I would recall what I had put in the drawer when I needed it, and once in a while I'd run over what was there to see if anything was relevant to the sermon I had in hand.

> . . . unlike many of my fellow ministers, I never had any system—such as a filing system etc—by which I gathered and kept in any orderly fashion illustrative material for my sermons. . . . I had a drawer in my

desk into which I threw notations of suggestive ideas that casually came
to me from anything I saw or heard.

What, of course, Fosdick fails to mention is that in addition to that
cluttered desk drawer he kept those nine crammed notebooks made accessible by a three-notebook elaborate index.

Fosdick possessed (in his own words) "a very retentive memory." A
ministerial colleague termed the memory "photographic," and he believed that Fosdick "could recall an entire printed page four or six years
later." Whether "photographic" or merely "very retentive," Fosdick's
memory was adequate to the task of recalling, when writing a sermon,
the books he had read, drawing them down from his library shelves,
and checking the notes he had made in them.

Finally, Fosdick kept a notebook in which he jotted down ideas for
possible sermons; sometimes, he reported, "having twenty or thirty, on
which I was gathering material and which Sunday after Sunday would
furnish me with something I would try my hand on." "Then," he observed, "it's like going to an apple tree saying, 'this one is ripe now.'"

Unlike some preachers, Fosdick prepared his sermons week by week;
he did not have a comfortable backlog. (His study on Mouse Island was
the scene of much summer writing, but there he composed books not
sermons for the year.) On Monday morning at nine, or Tuesday morning if he absented himself from New York for a Monday of relaxation,
Fosdick began the preparation of next Sunday's sermon. He worked in
his home study steadily, efficiently, without interruption until noon or
possibly one. The schedule was maintained on succeeding weekdays. Uniformly, he reported, the sermon was completed by one o'clock on Friday.

The preparation began on Monday or Tuesday with a considerable
period of brooding. As he described it:

> I sit down with pen and paper and practice what the psychologists call
> *free association of ideas*. That is, I jot down haphazardly any idea that
> comes into my mind, which directly or indirectly bears upon the matter in
> hand [e.g., the sermon's object and some truth relevant to its accomplish-
> ment]. At this stage I do not consider how the sermon will begin or end
> or what its structure may turn out to be. I give free gangway to my mind
> and let it pick up anything within the scope of the sermon's object and
> subject which it may chance to light upon. If an idea is only a vague in-
> timation with no development or application evident, I do not labor it. If
> an idea branches out into consecutive suggestions, I briefly note them. I
> observe no logical continuity in accepting any suggestions that may come
> but jot them down. This process may go on for hours—*one idea awakening
> another* and all of them an unorganized jumble and potpourri, without

order or logical connection; but, not infrequently, when this stage is finished, I have the basic material, the loose bricks, with which the sermon will be built.

He then would reflect on the illuminating truths found in the Bible and in general literature and gained in counseling and in his own personal experiences. Gradually, there began to emerge a rough charcoal sketch of the sermon. When matters were going well, the structure was not so much deliberately created as it came naturally out of the material as though by spontaneous suggestion. At last he started writing and "after that it was as God willed!"

Without exception, every word of every sermon was handwritten with meticulous care and many corrections. He always thought with his pen in his hand. "I do not see how," he observed, "anyone can keep strength of thought and variety and facility of language and illustration if he does not discipline himself to the severe task of writing everything he says."

He explained the reason for writing the sermon out in full. "Writing forces careful consideration of phraseology, makes the preacher weigh his words, compels him to reread what he has written and criticize it without mercy, constrains him to clear up obscurities in thought and language, begets discontent with repetitious mannerisms, and allows the preacher, before he mounts the pulpit, to listen, as it were, to his own sermon as a whole and judge whether it would hit his nail on the head were he an auditor."

On Saturday morning he sat down to rethink the whole sermon as if the congregation were visibly before his eyes so as to be absolutely sure that he had not allowed any pride of discussion or lure of rhetoric to deflect him from the major purpose of bringing "the grace and power of God to bear on human needs, to renew, transform, and sustain them." The sermon was always ready for the pulpit Saturday noon.

Impatient to meet his congregation face to face, perhaps it was necessary to coax sleep with a sedative. In the morning he "warmed up" his voice with exercises suggested by Walter Young, Enrico Caruso's coach, from whom he took voice lessons for eleven years early in his ministry.

Trusting his powerful memory, Fosdick at first prided himself on not taking any scrap of paper into the pulpit. This method of delivery he abandoned in time, in part because one excruciating Sunday his vaunted memory failed and after making his first point he suddenly forgot what came "secondly," and in part because he found that memorization consumed too much time in additional preparation and imposed too great a strain during presentation. Consequently, he began the practice of taking an outline into the pulpit, having reviewed the written sermon until it was in his mind and heart and his mind and heart were in it. This extemporaneous method he used during the major portion of his ministry. Probably the sermon came out very much as written, but the point is moot, for the handwritten sermon manuscripts were destroyed immediately and the preserved versions are those taken down in shorthand by his secretary during delivery. In his later years, however, he decided to experiment with preaching with a full manuscript before him, in the hope that it would take less out of him. Fosdick dictated the sermon to his secretary to be typed. The experiment was a success. As he explained, "I have found that one can have the full manuscript in front of him and can read it as though he were not reading but talking, with just as much freedom, spontaneity, colloquial directness, and person-to-person impact as though no manuscript were on the pulpit. Just as one can *write* for listeners, so one can *read* for listeners, combining the advantage of a manuscript's careful preparation with the freedom of face-to-face address."

If Lincoln in fact admired the preacher who looked like he was fighting a swarm of bees, he would not have been happy in Fosdick's churches, for there was nothing eccentric about Fosdick's pulpit manner. He mounted the pulpit not slouchingly, but soldierly. His posture in the pulpit was erect, but not awkwardly stiff, the feet separated, the right slightly in advance of the left. The gestures were few and restrained. Sometimes he moved his shoulders slightly from side to side; sometimes he bobbed forward from the waist to emphasize a point. For the most part his strong hands gripped the folds of the robe; seldom the pulpit sides. Never did he point a finger at the hearers, because it suggested scolding. Occasionally, he lifted a single arm to drive home a point of great moment or extended forward an open, upturned hand. His piercing eyes maintained a very direct contact with the audience, and this is one reason why a listener felt that Fosdick was speaking to him or her alone. Because the sermon had become so much a part of him, he once reported that "I forget that I am reading." And rather than turn the pages of the manuscript, he slipped them across one on top of the other to avoid the impression of reading. His facial expressions were restrained, but never mask-like, and they conveyed his emotions perceptibly, especially through his habit of snapping his teeth down on his lower lip. His whole bearing radiated an intense aura of disciplined power.

John Wesley once advised the Methodist clergy, "Scream no more at the peril of your souls," believing "no man can be bullied into heaven, and never was." Fosdick concurred, characterizing the ideal sermon as "an animated conversation with an audience concerning some vital problem of the spiritual life." Elsewhere he described the "essential nature of the sermon as an intimate, conversational message from soul to soul."

Fosdick was too much the evangelist, however, too much concerned to preach for a verdict, to permit his sermons to be merely intimate, conversational messages, and to this extent his statements mislead, although it is true that he did not rant or rage. His voice was not the rotund, deep, rich, or melodious voice of the "orator." Friend and critic alike have described it in such terms as "hoarse," "raspy," "throaty," "metallic," with a kind of "vibrato." Fosdick admitted that he was not graced with an orator's voice and often said that he did the best he could with what he had. At least it was a distinctive voice; people recognized it as belonging to Fosdick. And it was at least a distinct voice; he could be understood because the pronunciation was clear and the articulation exact, and the voice carried well.* And few found it a boring voice, because Fosdick varied its pitch, emphasis, and pace.

Fosdick's sermons ran thirty-five minutes, perhaps a little less as the years passed.† The rate of speaking—about 125 words per minute—was neither rapid fire nor sluggish and might well be described as "with all deliberate speed."‡ Naturally he spoke more rapidly before small groups in an intimate setting than before large congregations in Riverside.

V

Fosdick preached his first sermons in 1903 in those little chapels in the Adirondacks and as student assistant in the Madison Avenue Baptist Church, and he preached his last in 1955 as minister emeritus of The Riverside Church. That is a long, long time for any mortal minister to be confronted with the challenge of preparing preachable sermons. However facile Fosdick's pen, there were periods when he had the syrup and it wouldn't pour and there came a time when the syrup itself dried up. Small wonder that he was more than ready to retire in 1946. His secretary recalled that as retirement approached he was anxious about the fact that his sermon material was dangerously depleted. And small wonder, too, that in 1947 when his successor requested that he permit a sermon to appear in the *Church Monthly,* he responded with the plea:

* Knowing Fosdick's careful nature, the following report from the individual in charge of a Reformation Day Service in St. Louis is not surprising: "I was one of a small group to go with him to the Civic Center where he was to speak. It was the Public Address System that annoyed him. He made us stay with him and literally check out every section of seats, to make certain everybody could hear what he was there to do."

† They were cut to twenty minutes if selected for radio delivery.

‡In private conversation, remember, the emphasis was more on "deliberate" than on "speed."

I want to do anything that you request of me, and I dislike very much disappointing your expectations about that sermon for the Church Monthly. Nevertheless, I must cast myself upon your mercy and beg off. I am putting all the time and energy I have for constructive work into the writing of a book that I very much want to get finished. I am not writing any new sermons at all. I have no idea what I shall preach about on January 25, but it is pretty certain to be something that I have used before, served up in new fashion. Wait till you have preached for twenty years in the Riverside Church and published seven volumes, and you'll know what I'm up against! I have just one sermon that, so far as I know, is band new in material and illustrations, and that has never been published. That to me is more precious than diamonds. I've got to save that from publication so that I can use it at least in the pulpit of my Alma Mater this coming May. You will be merciful and understanding, I know, and will let me off.

When in 1953 *Time* magazine reported that "Fosdick used to preach the same sermon, polished to perfection, again and again to different audiences," and when he was asked about the accuracy of the statement, he responded: ". . . the quotation about my preaching my sermons to different congregations again and again is not correct. I do not believe that in all my ministry I have preached the same sermon over more than three or four times. My practice has been, whenever I thought a sermon was worth preaching again, to repreach it in essentially the same form in which I preached it the first time. While I have done a good deal of itinerant preaching, most of my work has been consecutive week by week production for the same congregation, and repetition of sermons has been only occasional and incidental. I certainly never went on polishing them again and again, as they were repreached."

Fosdick spoke the essential truth. He never preached the same sermon scores or hundreds or even thousands of times as did some ministers, Russell Conwell, for example, with his famous "Acres of Diamonds." Fosdick's first volume of published sermons did not appear until 1933, and at first glance it might seem, as *Time* stated, that he withheld publication to use the sermons over and over again. This is to forget that Fosdick's sermons appeared regularly beginning in 1923 in the First Presbyterian Church's *Church Tower* and then in Riverside's *Church Monthly*. It is to ignore the fact that scores of Fosdick's earlier sermons were widely distributed in pamphlet form or found their way into religious journals. Fosdick's sermons were not kept out of print prior to 1933, and there is no evidence that he wished them to be. Fosdick deviated slightly from the truth, however, in that he preached the same sermon or a slightly altered sermon in more instances than his reply suggests.

VI

The popularity of Fosdick's preaching has been the subject of considerable examination and explanation, notably by Edmund Holt Linn in his published monograph, *Preaching as Counseling: The Unique Method of Harry Emerson Fosdick;* by the contributors to Lionel Crocker's published anthology, *Harry Emerson Fosdick's Art of Preaching: An Anthology;* and also in unpublished theses and dissertations by such authors as Fabaus Landry, Charles Leininger, and Theodor LeVander. It would require a substantial book merely to summarize the findings of these and other students; here only a few broad generalizations may be advanced.

But first, an overarching observation. Professors of rhetoric investigating this acknowledged master of the art of preaching were shocked to learn that Fosdick had read none of the classic texts on oratory (other than those he studied as a college student), knew none of the basic principles of effective public speaking, and consciously formulated no scientific rules of sermon structure. When presented with analyses of his sermons by these rhetoricians, he could only reply, ". . . if I have worked out such a practical technique as you describe, I have rather blundered into it by wanting to get my business done with the congregation as effectively as possible and feeling my way toward that end rather than planning it." And again, "I am reminded of the poet who saw an analysis of his method in writing poetry and was astonished because he had never thought of it before."

One explanation for Fosdick's ability to draw vast audiences is that he spoke to the needs of a large number of individuals, as we have seen, inquiring unbelievers and perplexed believers alike. He well described that audince in opening a 1924 sermon:

> Our sermon this morning is addressed to only one group of the congregation, but one suspects it must be large: those, namely, who want to believe in the Christian God, who wish a sustaining fellowship with him, but who are having poor success in achieving the experience they crave. As the minister's confessional habitually reveals, there are, with reference to their relations with the Christian faith, three sorts of folk.

> There are the utter disbelievers. They will have none of religion. It is to them superstition and credulity, and God as much a myth as the devils of an African witch-doctor. But there are not many such.

There are the great believers, who have grown up into a luminous and convincing life with God like St. Theresa who said that in her heart she had an experience so beautiful that one drop of it, falling on hell, would turn it into a paradise. But there are not many such.

Between these two groups are the mass of men. They are not utter disbelievers and they are not glorious believers. Their faith is hesitant, uncertain, unsatisfying, sporadic, "Lord," they say, "I believe; help thou mine unbelief."

Fosdick was able to reach so many individuals because of his sure sense of where the shoe pinches the modern man. He possessed an almost spooky seismographic sensitivity to what was troubling the minds and burdening the hearts of the citizens of the twentieth century. The Methodist preacher, Lynn Harold Hough, made this thoughtful assessment of Fosdick: "He is as sensitive as a barometer. You are always aware of the intellectual weather as you read after him. He has an uncanny gift for seeing things before other people see them, and for saying things just as other people are dimly groping for the insight he puts into a clear and quickening phrase." If Fosdick was definitely not a reactionary, despite assertions to the contrary, neither was he a rebel. He discerned changes in the temper of the time and generally took a "progressive" position, but he rarely greatly outdistanced his parishioners and rarely beat against the prevailing cultural winds of any given decade.

To the dismay of their congregations, many ministers, probably unconsciously, pursue the same handful of subjects Sunday after Sunday. Fosdick was not guilty of this failing and here is another explanation for his following. He recognized that as one-crop farming exhausts the soil, so one-crop preaching exhausts the audience. He played a variety of stops on the homiletic organ, saving his people from feelings of boredom and ultimate exasperation.

Further, Fosdick struck the affirmative note. "Undiscourageable" may have been his favorite word. As William Sloane Coffin observed, Fosdick never entertained a diminishing thought or emotion, or at least if a few came to visit, he never invited them to dinner. "There was not a person in the room," reported a visiting worshipper after a Fosdick sermon, "that did not feel better as they passed into the sunlight . . . with his words ringing in their ears." He closed one sermon with a reference to the encouragement given him as a boy by his father, adding: "Well, Christian worship ought to do that for us. I want to see you smile, it says. Shoulders back! Chin up! That's better. Now you can go home!" He closed another sermon with the affirmation: "To be Christlike is to be oneself fulfilled. You are not a weed, Christianity says, trying to be an oak tree; you are an oak." Pick up any volume of Fosdick's published sermons and note the sermon titles. He urged his people to learn "How to Stand Up and Take It." He taught them "The High Uses of Trouble." He helped them master the art of "Making the Best of a Bad Mess." In difficult times he encouraged them to be "Christians in Spite of Everything." Doubt properly faced led to faith in "The Importance of Doubting Your Doubts." Fear properly handled became a blessing in "The Constructive Use of Fear." Physical disabilities became steppingstones to greatness in "Handicapped Lives." "Adequate Power Is Available," he promised. "After All, It's Character That Counts," he reminded. "A Clean Life in a Soiled World" is possible and so is "Conquering Fear" and "Mastering Depression" and "Conquering the Sense of Humiliation." Fosdick did not scold but he did admonish "Don't Be Discouraged About Human Nature" and "Don't Let This Grim Generation Get You Down." He assured his flock of the possibility of "Finding God in Unlikely Places." He advised on "The Fine Art of Making Goodness Attractive" and "The Fine Art of Letting Yourself Go." He proclaimed "I Believe in Man" and "No Man Need Stay the Way He Is." "This Is a Great Time to Be Alive," he asserted, and at the end there is the promise of "Life Victorious over Death."

To be sure Fosdick struck the prophetic emphasis in many sermons, as later chapters will demonstrate. He knew that God is not mocked and declared His righteousness. He was aware of the sins of men and the crimes of nations and that both individuals and societies were under divine judgment. His hopefulness walked the sunny side of the street but it never sauntered down Boulevard Pollyanna. Nevertheless, the conclusion stands that Fosdick's preaching was affirmative, intended "not so much to convict men of their sins as to convince men of their possibilities." The Christian "news" is *good* and so Fosdick proclaimed in an era (especially after 1914) when famed figures in literature, philosophy, psychology, and the social and natural sciences were announcing the perennially bad news of the human condition. And before Fosdick is convicted of muting his message to win popularity, it is well to recall that apocalypses sell better than affirmations. It has been remarked that even Dante had a hard time with his *Paradiso*.

Another much admired quality of Fosdick's sermons is their sunlight clarity, the commentators employed such terms as lucid, limpid, simple, direct. One individual, a former Fosdick student and now a famous minister, put it this way: "If after hearing him preach you said, 'Dr. Fosdick, I do not agree with a single thing you said,' he would not be troubled. However, if you said, 'Dr. Fosdick, I did not understand a single thing you said,' he would be deeply troubled and place his arm about your shoulder and say, 'My friend, let us go some place where we can talk this over.' "

The problem is that Fosdick achieved transparency, often, at the expense of accuracy. True, simplification is an inevitable mark of apologetics; the message of a sermon must be made accessible to lay people. True, Fosdick preached for a decision, and this necessitated at least a partial resolving of paradoxes, sanding of contradictions, ignoring of ambiguities. Nevertheless, studying Fosdick's sermons is quite the opposite of adjusting a pair of binoculars. At first glance the focus is sharp and clear, but as one adjusts the binoculars the picture becomes murkier and murkier with each turn of the mechanism. For example: "Once there was no scientific medicine—but then, Pasteur; once there was no nursing for the sick—but then, Florence Nightingale; once there was no religious liberty free from the State's regimentation—but then, Roger Williams." How neat—and how untrue. For example: "Africa in darkness, huge and hopeless and Livingstone seeing that some one was needed there." For example: "Nietzsche, from whom Hitler drew his philosophy." For example: "Schopenhauer's atheism an objective, intellectual conclusion, unaffected by emotion? No! Give him a good father and mother, a devoted wife, some fine children and real friends, and see how long he will go on thinking as he did about life's meaninglessness." And so on and on in sermon after sermon, decade after decade. These are not sharp statements, they are sappy ones. There is a certain irony in the observation that Fosdick's liberal, decent, humane, hope-and-love-filled certitudes were absolute certitudes as uninformed by ambiguity, irony, or paradox as were the certitudes of the most unreconstructed fundamentalists. Nietzsche once observed that if you take away the paradox from the thinker you get the professor; he might have added—or the preacher.

An allied explanation for Fosdick's popularity is that Fosdick expressed, though far more eloquently, vague thoughts his parishioners themselves long had held but could not articulate. This is a tribute to his famed "clairvoyance." Dr. Johnson once wrote, "To great poetry every bosom returns an echo." Fosdick's admirers would say, to his great preaching every soul responds. Still, the question must be asked: if it is acknowledged, to his credit, that Fosdick gave beautiful expression to the thoughts already prowling the minds of his parishioners, what ideas did he advance that were (by bourgeois standards) shocking, dissonant, nonconformist, manic, outrageous. With some exceptions, the thrust of his ideas was like a modern Fourth of July—"safe and sane."

Moreover, in illustrating his ideas, Fosdick, however widely he ranged, rarely entered dangerous or unchartered territory. Surely it was not unpleasing to his audiences to recognize this passage from Shakespeare and that from Browning; this reference to a Beethoven symphony and that to a Mozart opera; this allusion to Lincoln and that to Livingstone; this quotation from Emerson and that from Twain. Fosdick practiced to perfection what Gilbert Highet called "the art of evocative quotation."

To repeat, Fosdick had an uncanny ability to keep abreast of the time, but it is also true that his people were reassured that for their pastor the older Victorian House of Culture still stood in the 1920s, 1930s, 1940s. Indeed many of the same illustrations, quotations, allusions were pressed into service decade after decade. When one encounters in a Fosdick sermon for the first time Tennyson's high command, "Be loyal to the royal in thyself," one thinks, "How marvelous!" But when one encounters its employment for the tenth time, the marvel wears thin. It is possible to wish that his sermons had contained more of "the shock of the new." But, then, if they had, would they have been as popular?

A final explanation for Fosdick's preaching effectiveness is the indisputable fact that he was a consummate craftsman. The sermons are characterized by a perfectly ordered structure. They immediately arrest the attention of the listener, proceed with pace to the elaboration of a clearly stated purpose, and conclude with a ringing affirmation. Vigor, vividness, drama, power, warmth, concreteness, earnestness, beauty are all there. He favored strong, hearty Anglo-Saxon words and disfavored technical ones. Gritty colloquialisms, epigrammatic flashes, gnomic flavoring kept the listener on the alert. Fosdick shunned the bombastic, but not the impassioned. He did in fact "risk the purple passage." Fosdick may describe his style as one of "intimate conversation," but who converses in the splendid diction of the rolling periods he employed? Who in conversation gives voice to these hallmarks of a Fosdick sermon: "O my soul!," "Ah, Jerusalem!," "For see!," "Aye!," "Forsooth," "Ah Christ!," "O knightly youth!"

Yet perhaps "intimate conversation" is not entirely misleading, for other hallmarks of a Fosdick sermon are: "Friend, listen," "But, my friend, that does not account for the facts," "Let us say this to ourselves!," "There may be someone here who . . . ," "Let us get our eye clearly, then, on what we are talking of!," "We are to consider . . . ," "We are to think together today . . . ," "Come further now and see," "I speak to someone like that today as though we two were alone in this church."

Fosdick's people wanted dignity and reason in the sermons of their minister and in that sense they were modernists; but they were also heirs of nineteenth-century evangelism in that they did not want these qualities at the expense of a heartwarming experience. The ultimate court of appeal for every Christian remained: "Whereas once I was blind, now I see." The secret of Fosdick's appeal is that his sermon helped people to open their eyes and their hearts without insisting that they close their minds.

Chapter Twenty

"The Dean of All Ministers of the Air": Radio's "National Vespers Hour" Reaches Millions

I

On May 23, 1938, a banquet was held at the Waldorf-Astoria Hotel to celebrate the fifteenth anniversary of National Religious Radio. On hand were David Sarnoff, President, Radio Corporation of America, Lenox Lohr, President, National Broadcasting Company, and the fifteen preachers then in NBC's radio stable, including such famous pacers as Ralph Sockman, Paul Scherer, Frederick Stamm, Daniel Poling, John Sutherland Bonnell, Walker Van Kirk, Norman Vincent Peale. Each was allotted a two-minute comment. Then the toastmaster introduced Fosdick with the words, "And now we come to the dean of all ministers of the air." Fosdick was permitted ten minutes, and in the course of his remarks observed, "What one says on the air must be universal, catholic, inclusive, profoundly human. Who of us has not grown to be a greater man with a stronger grasp on the fundamentals because he has been talking to a continental congregation where he could not rely on interest in particularism but had to strike the great notes and call attention to the wide horizon?"

On January 2, 1921, station KDKA in Pittsburgh provided a remote broadcast from Calvary Episcopal Church—the first religious broadcast. Within a short time ministers across the nation seized on the new medium and by 1925 licenses had been issued to no fewer than seventy-one local churches or other religious organizations. In 1923 WEAF began carrying Dr. S. Parkes Cadman's afternoon sermons from the Bedford Branch of the Brooklyn Y.M.C.A., and Cadman went on to be the featured preacher of "National Radio Pulpit." Fosdick modestly suggests in

379

his autobiography that Cadman blazed a trail Fosdick followed, and it is true that Cadman rather than Fosdick deserves the title of "Pioneer Radio Preacher." Still, after Cadman's death in 1936, it was legitimate in 1938 to term Fosdick "the dean of all ministers of the air." And it was legitimate in 1946 at the time of his retirement to state: "Dr. Fosdick's ministry undoubtedly is a record in radio broadcasting as no other program, commercial or sustaining, has remained on the airwaves over such an extended period of time." Fosdick's national influence cannot be understood without reference to "National Vespers." Nor can the religious history of the American people since 1921 be fully grasped without reference to Monsignor Sheen's "Catholic Hour" and Billy Graham's "Hour of Decision" and other popular programs. Fosdick was born too soon for television, the medium that boosted the careers of such individuals as Pat Robertson, Oral Roberts, Jerry Falwell, and Jim Bakker. But even when religious television could boast fourteen million viewers, religious radio still held 130 million faithful weekly listeners. Once again it is appropriate to remark how nicely Fosdick's career meshes with the larger currents of American life.

II

"I was still at the First Presbyterian Church," Fosdick recalled in his autobiography, "when I began radio preaching and I had no idea of the possibilities involved. Frankly skeptical of its effect, I undertook it rather listlessly. I used to go down to the studio on Sunday afternoons and sitting at a table, talk into that strange contrivance, the microphone, with no vivid sense of contact with the unseen audience." This is a reference to a special WJZ program, and it may be true. However, on several instances he shaded the truth in regard to the broadcasting of the Sunday morning worship services in the churches he served. "For several years I withstood the broadcasting of my morning service at First Church," he reported in 1926. A year later he said to John Haynes Holmes, "I myself was slow to take this up and through my own negative attitude gave up the opportunity of broadcasting over WJZ while I was at the First Presbyterian Church." Later he claimed, "I was so dubious and luke-warm that the proposal died abornin'. I thought that probably it was a stunt." In a 1939 report on his radio experiences, he asserted: "Let me begin by saying at the start, when broadcasting first came in, I was very conservative about it. I did not at all see its possibilities. It seemed to me likely to be an entertainment technique; and the idea that people would ever take religion seriously over the air seemed dubious. So when, during my ministry at the First Presbyterian Church, I was offered the chance to have the morning sermons broadcast I, quite nonchalantly, discouraged the proposal. If they wanted to hear me preach, let them come to church—was my attitude."

These statements purporting to show Fosdick's initial conservative attitude toward radio do not square with his hunger to broadcast his message far and wide, and in fact they do not jibe with the record. On August 17, 1922, Charles B. Popenoe, RCA executive and station manager of WJZ, New York, approached Fosdick: "We are writing to you with the idea in mind of the broadcasting of religious services from your church known as the First Presbyterian Church of New York, by wireless telephone or radio telephone as it is sometimes called, for the sake of some 350,000 people listening to us every day of the week." Popenoe continued: "We might advise that our main station KDKA at East Pittsburgh is now broadcasting, and has been for the past two years, church services of Presbyterian, Episcopal and Methodist denominations in that city and in every case the most prominent church has been the first to adopt this new science for spreading religion among the people." Fosdick flashed an encouraging reply: "I am interested to discover that already this matter has been broached among the Board of Trustees of the church and has been favorably considered. For my part, it seems to me unquestionable that the church at Sunday services ought to be glad, and will be glad, to take advantage of the broadcasting opportunity which the new radiophone makes possible. You may therefore count in general upon my favorable interest in the proposition which you so kindly presented." Only days earlier Fosdick had been informed of the unanimous support of the trustees to the idea, and he had relayed to the Board his enthusiasm: "I should be glad to claim for our church the prestige and possible service involved in using the Sunday morning broadcasting privileges. . . . So far as I am concerned, therefore, the trustees may count upon my cordial support in this matter." Fosdick then dropped senior minister George Alexander a note stating his affirmative position, explaining, "Certainly every cheap comedian is glad enough to have the opportunity and I shall be glad in every way to accommodate myself to the broadcasting of the message if you and the Trustees of the church think well of it." Alexander's response carried his inimitable trademark: "I know no reason why we should not say, as we have sung, 'Fly abroad, thou mighty Gospel.' " Negotiations dragged and in September Fosdick again wrote Alexander in less enthusiasm, nevertheless, closing, "I did not feel justified in saying 'No' when the initiative started elsewhere, and unless there is some real objection, I presume that we ought to be as cooperative as we can." And in December, the issue still unresolved,

Fosdick informed First Church leader De Forest, "Personally, of course, I should be glad to have the widest possible broadcasting of our services and so informed Mr. Demarest when he wrote me about it in the middle of the summer."

In the end, for reasons the record does not make clear, First Church and Popenoe did not make a deal, but it is evident that Fosdick was dissimulating when he later claimed that his coolness thwarted the consummation. It would not be the first time, of course, that the jilted party in a relationship rationalized the rejection.

Two years later Fosdick and Popenoe did come together in a different arrangement. Fosdick on October 8, 1924, informed Ivy L. Lee, "I spoke to you over the telephone on Sunday with reference to Mr. Popenoe's apparent reluctance to close with me on an arrangement for broadcasting. I am sending this note now simply to say that Mr. Popenoe came across of his own free will very nicely and that according to arrangements I am to begin broadcasting at 3:30 next Sunday afternoon." And so beginning October 12, 1924, Fosdick taxied to plush Aeolian Hall, the "temple of established culture," in the headquarters of RCA to preach over WJZ. He continued to do so until March 22, 1925—fourteen sermons in all. The programs ran from 3:30 to 4:00 P.M. and then beginning February 1 were switched to an evening hour, 8:00 to 8:30 P.M., the change perhaps owing to the fact that Dr. S. Parkes Cadman also was preaching on Sunday afternoon over a rival station, WEAF, then owned by AT & T. Popenoe had earlier warned Fosdick that Cadman "is quite a popular feature [and] you will be having some competition to hold the air audience." On December 21, 1924, Fosdick informed the readers of the *New York Times* that the broadcasting of sermons and religious services was a desideratum.

Fosdick's relationship with Popenoe picked up again in 1926 on Fosdick's return from the Holy Land and assumption of the Park Avenue Baptist pulpit. Beginning October 3 and continuing through the spring of 1927, WJZ regularly broadcast the morning service. Fosdick had snapped at Popenoe's proposition, adding in his reply this revealing thought: "I am particularly pleased that you contemplate strengthening the power of WJZ. I noted in my recent broadcasting that, during the day especially, it was only a comparatively restricted area within which my addresses were clearly heard. If broadcasting is to be done at all, I should be glad to have the reception strong enough to cover the eastern United States at least."

On October 13, 1927, the *Christian World* carried this announcement: "Dr. Fosdick has decided to discontinue the broadcasting of his Sunday morning sermons from Park-avenue Baptist Church, as small churches, especially those in the country, have suffered because their members stayed at home to hear the popular New York preacher on the radio." The paper then went on to describe the new "National Vespers" service. The announcement once again involved a dissimulation to make Fosdick's motives appear nobler than the facts warrant. The truth is as follows: In 1926 the National Broadcasting Company came into being, a wholly owned subsidiary of RCA. The originating station for the NBC Red Network was WEAF, which RCA had purchased from AT & T. The key station for the NBC Blue Network was WJZ. The Red Network was always considered more commercial than the Blue with its "potted-palm aura." The earlier policy of WEAF had been not to compete with the Sunday morning services of local churches, reserving its religious programs for the afternoon. The newly formed NBC decided to follow this practice rather than that of WJZ.* As Fosdick explained, "All that has happened then is that WJZ has taken me off the air Sunday morning and put me on the air over a hook-up from Boston to Chicago on Sunday afternoon at 5:30." He added, "I like that much better," which suggests that he may have been a little troubled by the competition smaller churches faced from the broadcast of the Park Avenue Church 11:00 A.M. service. There was, however, one problem. It was customary for the church to hold a communion service late on Sunday afternoon once a month, and acceptance of the radio invitation would mean missing that service as well as the noncommunion Sunday afternoon services. "However," Fosdick informed a fellow minister, "the opportunity which the radio corporation suggests is too important to be passed up without serious consideration."† The opportunity was seized in October 1927. For the following nineteen years Fosdick was captain of "National Vespers," the flagship of radio Protestant religious broadcasting.

III

Reviewing the letters received from his radio audiences, Fosdick said, "Such messages make clear why radio preaching ceased being for me a performance before a microphone and became a means of vital dealing with the problems of real people." Before looking more closely at "National Vespers," it is appropriate to glance at Fosdick's general philosophy of radio preaching. To begin with radio preaching could not be

---

* However, NBC did sponsor "National Radio Pulpit," first starring Cadman and then Ralph Sockman, from 10:00 to 10:30 A.M. Presumably—perhaps dubiously—this permitted listeners to leave their sets and reach their churches by 11:00 P.M.

† At Riverside the Sunday afternoon communion service was rescheduled so that Fosdick could be present and still meet his radio engagement.

wished away, as he attempted to explain to an angry minister who accused him of pandering to "a growing number of religiously indolent and
socially selfish mortals who morally and financially starve their own
communities and churches who both enjoy and find a sop for conscience
in listening to sermons over the radio.* The broadcasting of church services was here to stay. "Sunday mornings the air will be full of sermons in any case," Fosdick predicted. "The query is only whose sermons
will be on the air. It is needless to name those representing a type of
Christianity which you and I do not believe in. Ought we to leave the
air to their monopoly? I do not believe we should." Fosdick was not
about to permit the fundamentalists to dominate the air waves.

Second, there were multitudes physically unable to attend church—
shut-ins, the temporarily sick, those incarcerated in hospitals, sanato-
riums, prisons, mothers with infants, those required to be on the job.
To such individuals, a religious service on the radio was a blessing.

Third, in the long run the broadcasting of church services tends to
increase rather than decrease church attendance. "This impression,"
Fosdick said, "has been confirmed in me by many conversations with
people who had not been inside a church for ten or twenty years but
who were becoming directly interested . . . because of broadcasting."

Fourth, Fosdick viewed his radio ministry as a supplement to, not as
a substitute for, his pastorate. In 1928 Cadman, then pastor of the Central Presbyterian Church, wrote Fosdick in the strictest confidence: "As
my colleague in Radio work I am asking you, and *only* you among my
colleagues, to tell me plainly what you think about my resigning my
pastorate here." Fosdick's advice *was* plain: "Personally, I should be
afraid of losing the kind of independence that comes to one in his radio
work because he can think of himself as really having a settled habita-
tion in the economy of the Christian church proper, where he belongs,
and from which he draws his native strength. I have felt so strongly
about this matter that not only would I under no circumstances give up
a pulpit for the sake of radio ministry, but I have even stoutly refused all
financial compensation for radio work in order that I might be entirely
independent of any reliance upon the National Broadcasting Company or
a Broadcasting Committee." Not only did Fosdick not receive a penny in
compensation for giving nineteen years to "National Vespers," in all that
time not a single sermon was submitted to NBC for prior review and
possible censorship. Fosdick's freedom was in fact absolute: since there

* Fosdick received many such complaints. The Lynds reported that in *Middletown*
(Muncie, Indiana) many citizens did in fact stay at home on Sunday morning to
hear "Dr. Fosdick." This, of course, was before the afternoon "National Vespers"
came into existence.

was no contract he could be cut off the air by NBC at will and, for his part, he could quit at will.

Every sermon preached in the radio studio had first been preached in a church pulpit. (The only difference was that the radio presentation was condensed to twenty minutes from about thirty-five minutes.) "Often I regretted this and would like to have talked the whole sermon over the radio," he recalled. "At times there were local references that it would have been necessary to elide in any case. So far as the substantial matter and methods of the sermon, however, there is no difference that I can see between a sermon preached in a pulpit and a sermon preached over the radio."

Finally, neither the broadcasting of the morning service or preaching in the afternoon cut into attendance at either Park Avenue or later Riverside. As Fosdick informed Holmes, "A considerable proportion of my Sunday morning congregation is made up of people from out-of-town who have heard me over the radio and wish to see the Indian whom they have listened to."

IV

A further word about "National Vespers." The program was inaugurated by the year-old National Broadcasting Company on October 2, 1927, as a public service. In 1943 NBC put the Blue Network on the block and a new network, the American Broadcasting Company, picked it up, but "National Vespers" was continued. NBC (and then ABC) freely provided several million dollars worth of radio facilities. The first program was broadcast over only sixteen stations, reaching only as far as the Midwest. As the Blue Network rapidly expanded, Fosdick's voice was soon heard on the West Coast and then by shortwave in England, Africa, New Zealand, Australia—seventeen different countries in all. As many as 125 stations carried "National Vespers," although never this number on any given Sunday. Network stations were given the right of taking off local broadcasts when their constituencies demanded; for example, in the autumn of 1941 the Chicago area station elected to carry the Chicago Bears professional football games rather than Fosdick. It is vastly interesting to see how many stations in the South hooked up. "National Vespers" started out as an hour program, cutting to a half-hour in 1931, from October through May. Originally the program began at 5:30 P.M.; over the years the starting time was pushed forward to 2:30 P.M. The *New York Times* in 1946 estimated that Fosdick preached weekly to audiences of from 2.5 to 3 million. A more solid figure is the largest

number of letters received as a result of any one sermon: 8248 following
"A Time to Stress Unity" preached March 12, 1944. Another solid figure
is the largest number of letters received in a given year: 134,827 for the
period October 1944 to May 1945. In 1936 mimeograph copies of Fosdick's sermons were first mailed to listeners on request; in the decade
that followed, over 1 million requests were honored. In addition to "National Vespers," Fosdick regularly participated in a New Year's Watch
Night Service from 11:30 to 12:00 P.M. and irregularly cooperated in
special programs, such as the coverage of President Roosevelt's death.

The sponsoring agency for "National Vespers" was the Federal Council of Churches. Frank C. Goodman, radio officer of the Greater New
York Federation of Churches, was the pioneer coordinator of religious
programming; in 1934 when the Federation relinquished responsibility
for network radio, Goodman became executive secretary of the Federal
Council's Department of National Religious Radio. However, the Federal Council did not financially underwrite the program. Actually, the
expenses were modest, because NBC provided the facilities and Fosdick's
services were free. Virtually the only costs, therefore, were salaries for
the quartet of men singers, secretarial assistance, and the mimeographing
and postage necessary for answering letters and distributing sermons.
James C. Colgate, Fosdick's oldest mentor, was chairman of a "National
Vespers" Committee, and initially this committee hit up a few of Colgate and Fosdick's affluent friends for funds. Later small gifts from appreciative listeners carried the budget. In 1943–1944, for example, the
committee mailed 11,355 letters to contributors and prospects and received as a result $16,882.22—an average of $1.50. On Fosdick's retirement in May 1946, he was succeeded by John Sutherland Bonnell, pastor
of the Fifth Avenue Presbyterian Church.*

V

It is Sunday afternoon. Fosdick has taxied to the studio. "The room itself breathes a spell of peace and quietude, a grandeur which must be
restful to the most tensely strung temperament. The lofty ceiling, the
rich furnishing, the subdued light, the luxurious rug, combine to create
an atmosphere of charm." Fosdick quietly gazes out the window looking
over the apartments and offices of Manhattan. The members of the men's
quartet are going over the music with the organist. The announcer enters
and instantly the atmosphere tenses. Air time shortly comes. Then fol-

* When "National Vespers" went off the air for the summer, it was replaced by
"Sunday Vespers," June to September, Paul Scherer preaching.

lows the organ prelude; the announcement, "Ladies and Gentlemen: NATIONAL VESPERS"; the choral signature; the opening announcement; Fosdick's "Call to Worship"; a hymn; the introduction of Fosdick; the address (so called rather than sermon); prayer; response; benediction; hymn; closing announcement; recessional hymn.

VI

Writing to Fosdick, one woman signed her name, "Grace E. Harbold, Devoted member of your National Vespers parish." That such a "parish" existed is beyond dispute. In *The Living of These Days* Fosdick quotes extracts from the letters of several "National Vespers" listeners. It would be possible to fill many pages with extracts from scores and scores of extant letters from the "parishioners" of "National Vespers." So moving, so convincing are these letters that it is totally correct to say that if Fosdick had done nothing else in his life but preach these radio sermons he would still be entitled to be remembered as a true and faithful Servant of the Lord. Fellow ministers reported that that half-hour might well bear the subtitle of "A Ministry to Ministers." Missionaries reported tuning in at 5:00 A.M. "to hold up during the war years when life was so full of tragic sufferings." One said, "I stayed alive for years" by virtue of the shortwave sermons. Seminarians reported rushing to the common-room radio after dinner to hear "Fosdick from New York." Undergraduates reported vowing, "I must get to New York and study preaching under that man."

The Democratic candidate for the presidency in 1924 said of Fosdick's radio preaching, "Lord, how refreshing to hear a man in the pulpit who has something to say." Inquired a convict in San Quentin, "Did you know that the quietest thirty minutes in this large 'Bay View' hotel is on Sunday evening when your sermon is rebroadcast?" A disabled man lay on his bed with the radio tuned to "National Vespers." When the program concluded he asked himself, "What am I doing lying here?"—and he proceeded to conceive the idea of a "National Employ-the-Physically-Handicapped Week." A fundamentalist confessed to loathing Fosdick's very name, but sitting by the radio "in the gathering twilight I experienced a complete reversal of sentiment and I can't tell you when I have started to work on a Monday morning feeling so much at peace with all the world as I do today. No, I don't think I am a modernist, I am still a fundamentalist, but, Oh! what a load has been lifted from my mind." A retired schoolteacher said of "National Vespers": "It is meat and drink to my soul. I hunger for just such sermons. At 5:30 P.M. I lock my doors,

put out the lights, so that no one may interrupt me, and then listen-in."
Wrote another listener: "I wonder if you can understand what it means
to the dweller in the small town, where the only form of entertainment
is the moving picture, and the choice in those often doubtful, to have
such good things brought to us?" One letter went, "I am a patient in a
Sanitarium in a ward with another man. We have a radio . . . and we
want you to know the joy and happiness we get from listening to you
every Sunday afternoon. . . . We almost always have a crowd of visitors at this time and they, too, get great joy from hearing you. It is fine
to be able to lie abed or sit in a chair listening to you, when we would
not be able to get out to hear the Word in a Church." Said another:
"Please don't think us presumptuous in thus addressing you. You would
not if you could see our family of five, way in the backwood land of
Northern Michigan, on a lonely farm, gathered around our cheap radio,
listening so regularly each Sunday to your magic voice. It sounds to us
as power from God." A Catholic expressed gratitude: "Thanking you
and wishing you many years to teach the old, old story of the brotherhood of man and of God our Creator." Explained a Wisconsin clergyman: "The appeal of your sermon is in the fact that it lives where I
live, it grapples with the thoughts and problems with which I must
grapple, and it doesn't meet my doubts by scolding but by articulating
my dilemma and then showing me 'a more excellent way.' " A wife reported her husband as saying, "Dr. Fosdick's sermon kept me from doing
one thing today and made me do another." Confessed another: "Frankly
it is your teaching that is keeping me and many other young men like
me from entirely forsaking the churches, not to say Christianity."

VII

Fosdick stated the belief that his radio audience was essentially no different in background from the Riverside congregation. This is probably
not quite accurate in terms of social background. The farmers, loggers,
factory hands, waitresses, beauticians, lighthouse keepers and other
agrarian, blue-collar, and clerical working people who were part of the
radio audience were not generally to be found in the Riverside fellowship. Religiously speaking, however, Fosdick was correct. He opened one
radio sermon with the words, "Today we shall not talk to the secularists
about this for they probably are not here, but to ourselves as Christians." That is, he spoke both to Christians secure in their faith and to
perplexed believers groping toward a firmer faith.

Chapter Twenty-one

"The Church Must Go Beyond Modernism": A Faith That Could Not Be Shaken

I

Returning to his pulpit in the fall of 1935 after the illness that had silenced his voice since April, Fosdick preached a sermon entitled "The Church Must Go Beyond Modernism." Theologian William Hordern said of that occasion, "The most decisive moment in the changing course of liberalism occurred one Sunday morning in 1935 when Harry Emerson Fosdick stood up to preach in his beautiful skyscraper church in New York." In that sermon, believed Hordern, "Fosdick dropped an unexpected depth charge into the sea of theology." Headlined the *Christian Century*, "Dr. Fosdick Shifts the Emphasis."

Fosdick began that memorable sermon by insisting that successfully to maintain the thesis that the church must go beyond modernism, we must start by seeing that the church had to go as far as modernism. The achievements of Christian modernism remain not only important, but indispensable. Nevertheless, unless the church can go deeper and reach higher than these real achievements it will fail. Why should this be? In the first place, modernism had been excessively preoccupied with intellectualism. "A man is vastly greater than his logic, and the sweep and ambit of his spiritual experience and need are incalculably wider than his rational processes." Modernism was too exclusively concerned with intellectual adjustment to modern science. But "the world has moved far to a place where mere Christian harmonizers, absorbed with the intellectual attempt to adapt faith to science and accommodate Christ to prevalent culture, seem trivial and out of date. Our modern world, as a whole, cries out not so much for souls intellectually adjusted to it as for souls

morally maladjusted to it, not most of all for accommodators and ad-
justers but for intellectual and ethical challengers."

In the second place, modernism had been dangerously sentimental,
lushly optimistic, and unrealistically romantic, embracing an illusory
belief in inevitable progress but concurrently largely eliminating from
its faith the God of moral judgment. *"Sin is real.* Personal and social sin
is as terribly real as our forefathers said it was, no matter how we
change their way of saying so. And it leads men and nations to damnation as they said it did, no matter how we change their way of pic-
turing it."

In the third place, modernism had watered down and thinned out the
central message and distinctive truth of religion, the reality of God. Confident man, blowing on his hands and seemingly accomplishing miracles
of progress, had relegated "God to an advisory capacity, as a kind of
chairman of the board of sponsors of our highly successful human enterprise." It is necessary to turn again to theology, which means thinking
about the central problem of existence—what is ultimately and eternally
real in this universe. The time has come to quit being apologetic; we must
quit acting as if the highest compliment that could be paid Almighty
God was that a few scientists believed in him. Christianity has its own
standing-ground, the only one that can give hope to man: it proclaims
that the eternally real is spiritual, that the highest in us comes from the
deepest in the universe.

Finally, modernism had too commonly lost its ethical standing-ground
and its power of attack. To adjust Christian faith to the new astronomy,
the new geology, the new biology is absolutely indispensable. "But suppose that this modernizing process, well started, goes on and Christianity
adapts itself to contemporary nationalism, contemporary imperialism,
contemporary capitalism, contemporary racialism—harmonizing itself,
that is, with the prevailing *status quo* and the common moral judgments
of our time—what then has become of religion, so sunk and submerged
in undifferentiated identity with this world?"

As always, Fosdick closed the sermon with a challenge. Let the modernist battle cry be: not to accommodate yourself to the prevailing culture, but stand out from it and challenge it! We cannot harmonize Christ
himself with modern culture. "What Christ does to modern culture is to
challenge it."

At first glance this sermon seems to support the critical charge that
Fosdick was "blown about by every wind of doctrine"—a whimsical play
on the chapter title, "Winds of Doctrine," in his autobiography. Certainly by 1935 the theological weather in the United States had changed
dramatically and with dramatic suddenness. Wintry doctrinal gales had

blown across the Atlantic from the Continent, forcefully hitting American clergymen already shivering in the grip of the nation's worst depression (though the first stirrings of the new realism were felt even before the Crash). In 1928 an American translation of Karl Barth's *Das Wort Gottes und die Theologie* came out and shortly Barth's by now legendary *Der Römerbrief* of 1918 was translated as *The Epistle to the Romans*. Wilhelm Pauck further introduced to American clergymen *Karl Barth: Prophet of a New Christianity?* Emil Brunner's sharp assault on liberalism, *The Theology of Crisis*, appeared in 1929 and three years later H. Richard Niebuhr translated Paul Tillich's *The Religious Situation*. God once again seemed to be speaking German in His search for chronically sinful, incorrigibly faithless, spiritually helpless man.

American churchmen listened in fear and trembling—and hope. Barth and Tillich were the subjects of D. C. Macintosh's 1931 symposium, *Religious Realism*. In 1932 Walter Lowrie in *Our Concern with the Theology of Crisis* not only took up the cudgels for Barth, but took as his mission the spreading of the words of Søren Kierkegaard. In that year Reinhold Niebuhr lanced liberal illusions in *Moral Man and Immoral Society*, unquestionably in America the single most influential critique to that date, a volume Niebuhr later admitted might have been more accurately entitled, *Immoral Man and Even More Immoral Society*. George Richards pled the case for *Beyond Fundamentalism and Modernism: The Gospel of God*. Edwin A. Lewis's *A Christian Manifesto* dismayed his fellow Methodists by its unmeasured indictment of liberalism. In the same year, 1934, Walter Marshall Horton gravitated in the general direction of Barth, in *Realistic Theology*, although Horton's Barthian captivation was never complete. Even Fosdick's younger liberal colleagues at Union, Henry Pitney Van Dusen and John C. Bennett, spoke of "The Sickness of Liberal Religion" and asked "After Liberalism—What?" Bennett opened the latter article with the unadorned assertion, "The most important fact about contemporary American theology is the disintegration of liberalism." In the year that Fosdick preached "The Church Must Go Beyond Modernism," H. Richard Niebuhr, Wilhelm Pauck, and Francis Pickens Miller, in their book *The Church Against the World*, declared, as did Fosdick in his sermon, that "the task of the present generation appears to lie in the liberation of the church from its bondage to a corrupt civilization."

Before subscribing to the cynical "weathervane" interpretation of Fosdick's motivation for his famous sermon, several observations are in order. First, if any one conviction dominated Fosdick's thinking more than others it was that theologies are culturally conditioned. As he argued, "Dealing as they do with eternal verities, theologians are easily tempted to assume that their formulations also are eternal, whereas, if anything on earth is tentative, subject to the push and pull of changing science and philosophy and to shifting popular moods of optimism and despair, it is systems of theologies." In every age the church has expressed its witness in words and deeds as the need of the time required. In 1935 Americans had for six years experienced the hellish reality of economic depression. By that year Japan had conquered Manchuria, Hitler was in power, the Stalinist terror was accelerating with new purges, in East Africa Italian troops were poised to invade helpless Ethiopia, Spain was on the eve of flames, and the signs of the times foretold a new Great War of even more horrifying dimensions than the last one. Even if the Continental "crisis" theologians had never uttered their unfamiliar and terrible words of judgment, historical events would have chastized and chilled American churchmen, whipping them to the task of questioning their cherished roseate beliefs—and it is notable that the greatest American realists came to their neoorthodoxy through liberalism, not through fundamentalism. Why, then, should Fosdick be condemned for "shifting the emphasis"? His autobiographical statement stands as both a confession and a defense:

> Of course I shared the exaggerations of early nineteenth-century liberalism. Of course I preached some sermons then which I could not possibly preach now without radical emendation. A preacher who has lived through the tremendous experience of two world wars without learning anything that has added increased depth and realism to his theology should be ashamed of himself. All of us liberals, whose ideas of God and man were inevitably influenced by the slants and biases of the optimistic era before the wars, have been compelled—unless our liberalism is unteachably rigid and hidebound—to welcome new insights, revise old judgments and acknowledge deplorable omissions in our understanding of the gospel.

For a second thing, note that in this 1956 statement Fosdick speaks of himself as a liberal and then remember (for it is not often remarked) that in the 1935 sermon not once does he employ the term "liberal." The sermon was a warning critique of the inadequacy of modernism and implicitly a call for the deepening of liberalism, but it did not represent a desertion of the liberal cause as the *Christian Century*, for one, feared.

Third, long before 1935 Fosdick had raised warning signals in lectures, sermons, articles, and in his Union classes. The world, he repeatedly cautioned, "is a much wilder, fiercer, profounder place than . . . superficial modernism ever took account of."

Therefore, "The Church Must Go Beyond Modernism" does not in itself convict Fosdick of trimming his sails to run with the prevailing winds.

II

Still, Fosdick himself acknowledged that "My adversaries, and even my friends, have sometimes had difficulty in defining just what my theological position is." We know this to be so in regard to both liberals and conservatives. The point to be made here is that he did not fare uniformly even at the hands of crisis or dialectical or neoorthodox scholars. Many, of course, held his thought "superficial" and "facile." For example, the major Old Testament scholar, Walther Eichrodt, described *A Guide to Understanding the Bible* as "the obituary" of the last century's scholarship.

But this must not be the last word. After reading *The Living of These Days*, Reinhold Niebuhr wrote Fosdick a letter of appreciation for his "creative ministries," continuing: "But I want to write to you particularly because in reading this book I became conscious once more of how much more I agree with you than with Barth, or with Brunner for that matter. This ought not to be surprising because I never had any disagreements with you except on the issue of pacifism, but reading your book made me more than ever conscious of the fact that there are so many values in what is generally called liberal Protestantism which must be preserved, and to which I want to be known to be committed, whether on the battlefront against Barth or against Billy Graham. So thanks very much for the book, but even more for your friendship, and even more for the grace of your life."

After reading *The Living of These Days*, Emil Brunner wrote Fosdick saying: "You will be surprised to get a letter from me. The reason is, that for several weeks I have been in constant conversation with you, reading your wonderful autobiography. I always knew you were a great preacher. Since reading the book, I have become aware that you are also a great man, a great fighter, a great Christian. When I was studying at Union Seminary, I saw nothing of that, being prevented from seeing by Theological blinders. We still do not express our faith in the same words. But I have felt throughout your book, that your heart is beating exactly where mine does. I stand in awful veneration before this great life and work, which God has given. As I am writing now 'The Christian Doctrine of the Church,' the great experiment of your Riverside Church has deeply stirred me." Earlier Brunner had expressed appreciation on receiving a copy of *A Guide to Understanding the Bible*. For his part,

Fosdick termed Brunner a "very loveable and admirable personality" whom he admired and with whom, up to a point—a distant point—he had much in common.

Although there is no direct evidence that Paul Tillich shared Niebuhr's and Brunner's high estimation of Fosdick, it is clear that the two men comprehended that there is no such thing as an acultural religion, independent from its surrounding milieu. Both held that religion and culture are so intertwined that traditional religious teachings must be seen not only as abstract doctrines, but also as expressions of particular cultures. As Fosdick told an inquirer in 1961, "I think you are quite right in saying that while Paul Tillich is a systematic philosopher and theologian, which I am far from being, we have a similar approach to the whole problem of religious thinking. Tillich is intensely interested in the relevance of Christian theology and philosophy to everyday, ordinary, commonplace living. I applaud that, and feel as you suggest a deep sympathy with him and his way of getting at things."

In 1956 Princeton Theological Seminary Professor Emile Cailliet apologized to Fosdick for his earlier criticisms of him, closing the letter with an appeal that Fosdick give "us that book that will provide the philosophical and theological undergirding for the argument so ably made in *The Man from Nazareth*. I confess that it seems strange to ask you to give us what looks like a short Introduction to Christian Doctrine. And yet, how I should love to see you write in your accessible style that little book on Christianity and Sanity we all need so badly!"

Some years ago a cartoon showed one scholar being introduced to another with the words, "This is Professor Schmidt, who dominated German theological circles for a few weeks in February 1968." How apposite this risibility is to the sputtering, erratic course of twentieth-century theology. In his autobiography Fosdick predicted, "Liberalism cannot remain as it was fifty years ago; neo-orthodoxy cannot remain as it is today; there will be a synthesis." Whether a synthesis did in fact emerge is moot, but Fosdick's two other points are certainly correct. As early as 1958 John C. Bennett announced, "It's Time to Go Beyond Neo-Orthodoxy." Barthianism generally did not remain static and Barth himself in *God Here and Now* moved significantly from the "Barthian" position of absolute transcendence toward a more immanental stance. H. Richard Niebuhr and Walter Marshall Horton pled for a retention of the best in liberalism and warned against the worst in Barthianism. A movement "beyond neo-orthodoxy" sought to reconnect with classical Protestant liberalism and urged a new hearing for Schleiermacher, Ritschl, Harnack, F. D. Maurice, William James, and the great social prophet Rauschenbusch, whose voice echoed in the preachments of "The Secular City" theologians. Tellingly, in the Roman Catholic theologians Hans Küng, Karl Rahner, and David Tracy one encounters statements that might have been penned by earlier theological liberals—including Fosdick.*

Fosdick remained an evangelical liberal to the end, his liberalism deepened and chastened, but never disavowed. He had fought a militant fundamentalism and then resisted a fierce neo-orthodoxy, and although it would be untrue to say that he "won" unconditional victories in these theological wars (indeed it would be false to say so), neither can it be concluded that the values of evangelical liberalism were totally repressed by fundamentalism or finally pulverized by Barthianism.

III

Fosdick did not count himself in the succession of Church savants. He steadfastly envisioned his role as interpretive and transmissive rather than creative. Nevertheless: How shall we think of God? How does He reveal Himself? What is His will and Word? What is man's nature? and What is man's destiny?—these were questions much meditated by Fosdick, and the gospel he preached on Sunday morning grew from intensely worked theological soil. Moreover, he did write three important, controversial works of scholarship, *The Modern Use of the Bible*, *A Guide to Understanding the Bible*, and *The Man from Nazareth*, the respected Ernest F. Scott terming the last volume a "work by one of the foremost New Testament scholars." Further, a measure of Fosdick's reputation in Old Testament studies was an invitation from the editorial board of the famed Interpreter's Bible to undertake an exposition of either Deuteronomy or Jeremiah, Walter Russell Bowie pleading, "I cannot think of any greater enrichment for the Interpreter's Bible than to have the message of this great prophet [Jeremiah] put into perspective for the preacher by you." (Fosdick declined because of a commitment to another project.) It is worth remarking here that many of the Church's great theologians historically were pastors as well as scholars, dealing concurrently with the mystery of faith and the practical problems of their flocks, and that is one reason why their words are still helpful today.

And so, although Fosdick never claimed to be a systematic theologian, it is mandatory to review his theological beliefs.

---

* In 1974 Küng reached this judgment: "The wind of scholarship has changed direction in recent years, even though some older warriors would like to remain satisfied with an unsubstantiated 'kerygma' and if necessary perhaps even an irrational *Credo quia absurum* ('I believe just because it seems absurd'). Pure kerygmatic theology has had its day."

IV

How shall we think of religion? How shall we think of theology? Fosdick stood squarely in the tradition of classical liberalism in affirming that faith has its foundations, not on the sands of theological speculation, nor on any external authority, but on the rock of reality, the personal experience of God. "The trouble with many of us," he asserted, "is not that we think God untrue but that we find him unreal." Individuals cannot be argued or coerced into religious belief. But millions can say "on the basis of profound personal experience, There is a living God." These experiences are objectively real. God reveals Himself to man. Man's response to these experiences of God's transforming and sustaining grace is the basis of faith. "A wise theology clarifies them," Fosdick said, "reassures our faith in them, deepens our understanding of them, but, as for me, it is the experience itself in which I find my certainty, while my theological interpretations I must, in all humility, hold with tentative confidence." The disciples acquired their faith, not as a result of their own reflections, but as the result of their experiences. The experiences revealed in Scripture are reproducible today.

Theological systems have their day and then cease to be, for they are but the broken lights of eternal truth. Religion is prior to theology in the same way that flowers are prior to botany. The difference between theology and religion is the difference between the science of aeronautics and actual flight. Said Fosdick, "Theology, like a telescope, is made simply to help people see, and like a telescope it is meant to be looked through and not looked at." He did not, of course, despise theology nor despair of it, but he was "sure that theological concepts are socially and psychologically conditioned, and are tentative, partial, and very faulty presentations of the Divine Reality, which is far beyond our adequate comprehension."

V

How shall we think of God? How shall we think of His revelation? "The fundamental question in religion is what we mean when we say 'God,'" Fosdick asserted in the Garvin Lecture. As an apologist, Fosdick was forced to argue the question of God's existence, but a more fundamental concern appeared when he approvingly quoted his mentor William Newton Clarke, "Not that God is, but what God is, is the first point in the Christian doctrine." Fosdick said in 1952, "The primary problem in Christian apologetics today is not to construct coercive arguments for the existence of God but to achieve a concept of God which will require a minimum of argument, because its intelligibility, reasonableness and relevance to human need carry a self-authenticating authority." Those who throw out God still have the universe on their hands, he frequently observed. To the ancient question, Is the universe friendly to man?, Fosdick's answer was a ringing affirmative: "There is objective reality in this cosmos which persistently implies the presence of objective Intelligence, Will, Purpose."

Fosdick once preached a sermon entitled "The Impossibility of Being Irreligious." There is no escape from faith, from that ineradicable necessity for man to believe in something, to give himself to something, to belong to something. Man is constrained to have a god—"that factor in his life, whatever or whoever it may be, that he does truly worship and serve, belong to and care most about, the unifying loyalty which draws his life together and gives its centrality and singleness of aim." An individual may make a god of science or art, the state or the party, or indeed mammon or Bacchus. It may be one god today and another tomorrow, making of the inner life a veritable pantheon. Or, Ultimate Reality may be the God who gives us the light of knowledge of His glory in the face of Jesus Christ.

For Fosdick Christian faith is precisely what the Epistle to the Hebrews says it is, "the assurance of things hoped for, a conviction of things not seen." Faith cannot be proved before it is accepted. We have to live ourselves into it. How do we know that when Paul says "strengthened with might by his Spirit in the inner man," he is talking about something real? Armored with venturesome faith, we must plunge in, betting our lives that there is a God and that God is love. In a marvelous insight Fosdick noted, "Sometimes we can think ourselves into a better way of acting, but mostly we have to act ourselves into a better way of thinking." Act *now* as though God lived, leap *now* from unfaith to faith, love thy neighbor and serve him *now*, for if you wait for absolute prior proof of God's existence it is *you* who will not have lived. Always Fosdick reserved his most biting language for the uncommitted, the lukewarm committed, the frivolous skeptics, the pert disbelievers, the dispassionate unbelievers— all those pleasantly relaxed in a hammock suspended between triumphant faith and trivial unfaith.

Very late in his life, when the "Death of God" theologians were momentarily riding high, Fosdick was asked why this should be so, and he replied, "Perhaps because there are so many concepts of God that *should* die." The Living God was not a tribal deity, the god of battles, concerned only with the fate of His chosen people. The Living God was not an Apocalyptic Judge waiting in the heavens to do His ultimate vengeance, a God created in the image of kings and tyrants. The Living God was not the Deist's Watchmaker who made His watch (the universe), wound it up and set it a-going and then disappeared. The Living God was not the Efficient Executive portrayed by Bruce Barton or the Kindly Man Upstairs portrayed by the hawkers of peace of mind or a Cosmic Bellhop waiting for men to whistle for His services or a kind of Oblong Blur murkily perceived by the more feckless modernists. Fosdick despised all bogus conceptions of God, ranging from those that bored people to sleep to those that scared people to death. "Surely," he said, "the real God must sympathize with those who hate his caricature." In *Christianity and Progress* he flung these hard words:

> Our anthropomorphism . . . reaches its most dangerous form in our inward imaginations of God's character. How the pot has called the kettle black! Man has read his vanities into God, until he has supposed that singing anthems to God's praise might flatter him as it would flatter us. Man has read his cruelties into God, and what in moments of vindictiveness and wrath we would do to our enemies we have supposed Eternal God would do to his. Man has read his religious partisanship into God; he who holds Orion and the Pleiades in his leash, the Almighty and Everlasting God, before whom in the beginning the morning stars sang together, has been conceived as though he were a Baptist or a Methodist, a Presbyterian or an Anglican. Man has read his racial pride into God; nations have thought themselves his chosen people above all his other children because they seemed so to themselves. The centuries are sick with a god made in man's image, and all the time the real God has been saying, "Thou thoughtest that I was altogether such a one as thyself."

Of course the Creator and Sustainer of the universe can never be fully grasped by mortal man, can never be caught under the butterfly nets of our understanding. Fosdick was fond of quoting the Frenchman who said that "God defined is God finished" and Josiah Royce who put it, "God never sat for his photograph." This being so, when men speak of God they speak in the native language of religion: metaphors, pictures, images. They say that God is like something, expressing what they think is true about God's quality in symbols drawn from their experiences. And what varied symbols have been used to portray the divine!—rock, fortress and high tower, the rose of Sharon, and the bright and morning star, the Ancient of Days and the Hound of Heaven, father, mother, husband, friend, shepherd. They are all inadequate, of course, but, said Fosdick, "it is far truer to think of God in terms of an inadequate symbol than not to think of him at all. The great God is; our partial ideas of him are partly true."

Since when, Fosdick asked, has the Pacific Ocean been poured into a pint cup, that the God of this vast universe should be fully comprehended in human words? Nevertheless, even a pint cupful of the Pacific Ocean reveals its quality. God has a "near end." On several instances he employed this illustration:

> On my island off the coast of Maine I lived with the sea. The whole ocean in its vastness I do not know. I never sailed the tropic ocean where the Orinoco and the Amazon pour out their floods; I never watched the Arctic and Antarctic seas wash their ice packs. Wide areas of the oceans are to me unknown, but I still know the ocean. It has a near end. Its waters surround my island. I can sit beside it, bathe in it, sail over it, watch its storms, and be sung to rest by the music of it.

Believed Fosdick, "Personality is the most adequate symbol we have of the nature of God." Because this is so, "we can commune with him, be inspired by him, depend on him, be responsible to him, and, like our fathers before us, love him so deeply that we will love nothing else too much, and fear him so reverently that we will fear nothing else at all." Of course, Fosdick warned, we must not suppose that in saying this we have lassoed the ontological essence of the universe, supposing God to be *a* person. "But when one takes personality . . . and says that out that high road, immeasurably beyond our present comprehension, lies the truth about the Eternal, he is stating truly the theistic faith. . . . Theism begins with the best we know—mind, purpose, ethical character, love, and starts our thought up that road, assured that in that direction lies the everlasting truth about deity."

"No, I am a Wesleyan," Fosdick once replied to an interviewer. "Calvin's God is my devil." But it does not follow that Fosdick's God was incapable of wrath. Precisely because God *is* love He abominates all that lessens love. He is aroused to anger by sin, to repulsion by evil, to sternness by injustice. Men and nations are under His judgment, and not easily is He mocked. The eternal God is our refuge, but He is not our escape from the consequences of our folly. God created us and gave us freedom, which we abuse, but God loves us too much to let us do evil with impunity. God sets before us life and death; we must choose. "A God who does not care does not count." But we must not sentimentalize God's care into a weak and flaccid affection until one ends up with a "grandmotherly God of coddling love." Fosdick sympathized with worshippers who complained of being "stewed into mush" by saccharine sermons; and he sympathized with preachers when parishioners believed "lovely" to be the highest compliment to be paid a sermon.

Fosdick was fond of quoting Walt Whitman: "Why, who makes much of a miracle? As to me I know of nothing else but miracles." Yet he also held that "supernatural" is "just about the most unredeemable word in the religious vocabulary. It has a bad history, and the picture of God's relationship with the world, which it conjures up in many minds, is one of the chief blockades to intelligent faith in God." How can these positions be reconciled? Are miracles to be understood as supernatural interventions—acts in which God breaches the laws of nature? If so, how could Fosdick, claiming to be a man of the twentieth century, preach sermons with such titles as "This Is a Miraculous World." If not, how could he escape the trap of a thoroughgoing naturalism?

Fosdick was careful not to ridicule the Biblical miracles, but neither did he hold it necessary to accept uncritically all miracle stories as historical facts in order to be a Christian. He maintained, for one thing, that in the Bible "the farther we get away from the first-hand documents the more marvelous the stories become." Contrariwise, the closer we get to the firsthand sources, the fewer and simpler are the miracles. For a second, he contended that all miracle stories should not be placed on the same plane. Some he found "dangerously ridiculous," such as to suppose that God in the ninth century B.C. miraculously sent bears to eat up unruly children or made an axe-head swim. Some he found frankly puzzling: "There is no use pretending that we know more than we do, and about many an ancient miracle-narrative a man may well suspend judgment awaiting light." Some are understandable in terms of modern knowledge, such as the healing miracles seen in the light of psychosomatic medicine. Some were not intended to be taken literally, but are allegories, such as the book of Jonah. Some he could not help believing:

> Wherever a narrative in Scripture describes an experience in terms of miracle so that we recognize that the same kind of experience is open to us or would be open if we were receptive of God's incoming power, that narrative is fundamentally credible and useful. At once, when this approach is made, wide areas of Biblical miracles rise, not only into credence, but, what is more important, into challenge, calling us in our generation to explore the possibilities of divine resource released in marvelous ways through faithful men.

Fosdick was greatly concerned to explain that in the world of the Bible there is no word that can be translated "nature," in the sense in which we constantly use that word, to mean a universal, law-abiding order. Miracles to the people of the Bible did not involve any broken laws, for there were no laws to break; miracles were simply happenings that were unusual, unfamiliar, surprising, rousing awe or admiration. "An axe-head might usually sink in water but there was no reason why God should not make it float if he wished to do an extraordinary thing. It was surprising when he did it, but it presented no intellectual problem whatever. No laws were broken because no laws were known. No Hebrew ever dreamed of such a thing as a mathematical formula of specific gravity in accordance with which an axe-head in water ought invariably to sink."

This strange, ancient world of the Bible gave way with the rise of science. Beginning with the Greeks, cosmic order increasingly became a matter of specific laws, mathematically stated, controlling everything from molecules to stars. In this new world of science there was a natural cause for every effect and an effect for every cause, a world where nothing happens anywhere contrary to law. As one realm after another was taken over by natural law, the sovereignty of the supernatural diminished, and as it did God seemed to dwindle as well. "God was escorted to the frontiers of the universe and bowed out" or, as another put it, "a housing problem arose with regard to God." Miracle, "dearest child of faith" according to Goethe, became the weakest child of faith. Fosdick summarized the effects of the new scientific knowledge of the reign of law on modern minds: "It pushes God away off; it pushes him away back; makes his special help seem impossible; suggests that any providential aid would involve a miracle; and finally makes our immature, childish ideas of him inadequate."

How then, could Fosdick continue to assert: "This is one world. God's world throughout, whose law-abiding regularities, whose amazing artistries, whose evolution of ever higher structures, whose creation of personality, whose endless possibilities of spiritual growth and social progress indicate that it is a spiritual system. God is here, not an occasional invader of the world but its very soul, the basis of its life, its undergirding purpose, its indwelling friend, its eternal goal." The answer can be found in the assertion itself. For one thing, Fosdick did not buy the idea of a bifurcated universe, with nature on one side, run by natural law, and the supernatural on the other, occasionally breaking through the natural order and suspending its laws to perform some marvelous feat. He would not accept a supernaturalism that sees the cosmos as a kind of duplex apartment: "Downstairs the ordinary procedure goes on in its customary way, but ever and again from upstairs something comes down to break up the ordinary procedure on the main floor. So God becomes indeed 'The Man Upstairs.' "

For another thing, warned Fosdick, care should be exercised to avoid excessive obeisance to scientifically stated laws, falsely assuming that they *explain* the universe. After all, these laws are simply our human statements of the way the universe appears to act, and in this live and

marvelously creative universe beyond our power to think, these statements must necessarily be incomplete or mistaken. The concept of "law"
does not exhaust reality, because scientific laws are merely partial plot-
tings of the regularities of nature. The more we know about this universe, the more mysterious and miraculous it is, and all our rules are but
the regulations, *so far noted,* of the way this amazing universe and its
Living God act. Therefore, if a law seems to be broken, then it was not
the real law. A miracle is not a rupture of law; it is the fulfilling of a
larger and higher law than we have yet understood. What looks like a
miracle to man is no miracle to God. Man's limited control of universal
forces may be a counterpart of God's unlimited control. A miracle is
God's use of His law-abiding forces to work out in ways that are surprising to us His will for our lives and for the world.

As a seminarian Fosdick heard Professor McGiffert assert that the
immanence of God was the most characteristic religious doctrine of the
nineteenth century. Recoiling from eighteenth-century deism and influenced by German idealism, the emerging Protestant liberalism embraced
divine immanence. Darwinism made its contribution too. Evolution posited a continuous process of creation instead of creation by fiat, and creation by process demanded the constant presence of the Creator. Because
it is a "growing universe," God is ever at work, the "Eternal Toiler" and
the "Great Adventurer," to employ Fosdick's terms. According to this
understanding, God dwells in the world, works through it, cares what
happens to it, shares its anguish and knows its joys. He reveals Himself
in the beauty and order of Nature, in the evolutionary progression of
history, and in great human souls, Socrates, Buddha, Confucius, and
Gandhi as well as the Christian saints and martrys—indeed in all souls.
"All the best in us is God in us," Fosdick proclaimed. "Whatever spiritual excellence we possess is sunshine from a central sun."

By the end of Fosdick's formal ministry liberalism's divine immanence,
always unacceptable to fundamentalists, was being challenged—and in
many quarters routed—by neo-orthodoxy's divine transcendence. According to neo-orthodoxy, God is radically transcendent, "Wholly Other."
The discontinuity between God and man is absolute. God is the utterly
superior creator and sovereign ruler; man is the creature and utterly dependent servant. Between God and man is an infinite distance and natural
man is utterly helpless to close this distance, unable to know God in any
way or to approach Him the least little bit. The initiative is entirely
God's. Happily for man, God does choose to reveal Himself and man can
accept, with gratitude and thanksgiving. God's coming to man in revelation and redemption is, then, always an act of sheer unmerited grace.

Fosdick sought to walk a path between extreme immanence and radical transcendence, praying: "Eternal God, so high above us that we cannot comprehend thee and yet so deep within us that we cannot escape thee, make thyself real to us today!" He quoted with approval William Newton Clarke: "Transcendence without immanence would give us Deism, cold and barren; immanence without transcendence would give us Pantheism, fatalistic and paralyzing." Nevertheless, although Fosdick may be absolved of the charge of pantheism (of which he was accused), the path he chose came considerably closer to that edge of immanence than to Barth's "Wholly Other" edge of transcendence.

Granting the truth of what the Westminister Confession calls the "so great . . . distance between God and the creature!," Fosdick feared extreme Barthianism made God an absentee monarch, an occasional invader of the world, canceling the meaning of the indwelling and transforming Holy Spirit. Naturally, Fosdick believed he found support in scriptural passages: "If we love one another, God abides in us" and "God is love, and he who abides in love abides in God and God abides in him" and "We are the temple of the living God; as God said, I will live in them."

Fosdick wrestled with the doctrine of the Trinity and believed that more nonsense had been written about it than any other item of the Christian creed. Yet he found profound and vital truth in the experience that lies behind the doctrine. For Fosdick the Trinity could be understood as the one Supreme Being revealing himself in three "personae." Just as an individual actor in ancient Rome could wear several "personae"—several masks—so men experience God's threefold revelation of Himself: as Father-Creator; as historical character, the glorious Christ; and as the Divine Spirit in us, our unseen Friend and abiding Companion. As always Fosdick's concern was apologetic: "I care little whether a man believes a trinitarian dogma,—but I care a lot whether a man has a trinitarian experience: God not simply the Father, not simply the character revealed in Christ, but also the divine spirit that can be within us all."

He who does not perceive that in the Bible God is speaking, believed Fosdick, does not believe earnestly in God at all, for the Bible contains truths without which no man can really live.

For Fosdick, the Bible cannot always be taken literally, but it should always be taken seriously. For Fosdick, the Bible is not a revelation *from* God, but it is a revelation *of* God. He maintained that the Bible *contains* the Word of God, but not that it *is* the Word of God. It is an "invaluable laboratory manual which records all phases of man's life with God and God's dealing with men." It is "a priceless treasury of spiritual truth, and from it have come the basic ideas and ideals on which the best of our democratic culture is founded." It is "an amazing compendium of every kind of situation in human experience with the garnered wisdom

of the ages to help in meeting them." Many critics found these statements appallingly sub-Christian.

In the introduction of his major study, *A Guide to Understanding the
Bible*, Fosdick stated: "Obviously, any idea of inspiration which implies
equal value in the teachings of Scripture, or inerrancy in its statements,
or conclusive infallibility in its ideas, is irreconcilable with such facts as
this book presents." Surely it is unnecessary to note again here that Fosdick did not share the fundamentalist understanding of "verbal inspiration" to mean that each and every word of Scripture is infused with
divine meaning, and must, at least in the original text, be free from all
error of any kind. It is "sheer nonsense," Fosdick stated elsewhere, to
picture God as dictating all the books of the Bible word for word to
various amanuenses across some ten or twelve centuries. Nevertheless,
the Bible is the record of "the creative and directive activity of God"; it
does "involve not only human discovery but divine self-disclosure."

It is clear why fundamentalist scholars found Fosdick's views on inerrancy, infallibility, and verbal inspiration unsatisfactory. But why were
neo-orthodox biblical theologians also disquieted by his statements?
They missed, for one thing, the note of God's radical transcendence pervading the Old and New Testaments alike. They found God's wonder-
working activity downplayed. They charged that Fosdick's emphasis on
reproducible experiences minimized the supreme, shattering, once-for-all
nature of the Bible's record of God's revelation of Himself; in Jesus'
coming there was an absolute end and an absolute beginning. Fosdick's
stress on divine immanence lessened the Book as the unique, decisive,
climactic revelation of God through which alone God can be known.

The most serious flaw in Fosdick's hermeneutical principles, said the
critics, was his inveterate, invincible, evolutionary understanding of revelation, first adumbrated in *The Modern Use of the Bible* and then expanded in *A Guide to Understanding the Bible: The Development of
Ideas Within the Old and New Testaments*. In the latter volume Fosdick
took six strands of developing thought in Scripture and presented them
separately and as far as possible disentangled from their mutual complications: the Idea of God, the Idea of Man, the Idea of Right and
Wrong, the Idea of Suffering, the Idea of Fellowship with God, the Idea
of Immortality. In each case he started with the earliest conceptions to be
found in the Old Testament, showed how they came to be progressively
purified and enlarged and given a deeper ethical and spiritual content,
culminating in the life, teaching, death, and resurrection of Jesus Christ.
He hastened to add that these ideas had not stopped evolving when the
Scriptures stopped. "Every one of the six lines of unfolding thought . . .
has had a long subsequent history of continuing development, and the

end is not yet in sight." On this view, there was not one complete, perfect, and static body of religious truth contained within the Bible. Although Fosdick warned against the chronological fallacy—"the illusion of constant ascent, as though being posterior in time always meant being superior in quality"—nevertheless, in all six ideas he *did* find progressive development from primtive polytheism to the sublime heights of the religion of Jesus, from seed to flower, as it were, or from infancy to maturity.

A number of reviewers found Fosdick's "onward and upward" understanding of the Bible unsatisfactory—not alone because his book seemed to be "an achievement of almost pure humanism" in which "one sees more of human unfolding than of divine revelation" and in which the stress is on "human discovery, not divine self-disclosure." The problem, said the critics, was that Fosdick too faithfully followed the nineteenth-century scholar Julius Wellhausen in assuming that by dating the documents of the Bible the history of its ideas could be reconstructed, as if by tracing the development of *ideas* one was thereby learning to hear God's Word to man. This was rewriting Scripture to suit Hegelian philosophy; it was evolutionary historicism with a vengeance. The date of a particular document in itself tells nothing regarding the origin and value of the revelation contained in it (as Fosdick partially realized). Moreover, the assumption of progression from lower to higher invites invidious selection from the Old Testament to demonstrate its alleged primitiveness, by which the unity of Scripture is destroyed and the earlier portions reduced to mere antiquarian interest. This position seemed increasingly difficult to maintain in the light of the new biblical scholarship emerging even before Fosdick's death.

Despite mounting criticisms, Fosdick held his ground. A developmental approach, he argued early and late, excused the Christian from the impossible task of trying to harmonize the Bible with itself. There was no need to strain to reconcile the unreconcilable; differences were recognized and admitted as particular stages in the progressive development of certain ideas. Second, the developmental approach relieved the Christian from the necessity of apologizing in an allegorical, or any other manner, for the early primitive parts of the Bible. Third, his critics to the contrary, such an approach, he believed, restored to the Bible its essential unity; it is a dynamic book marching from the beginning revelation in Genesis to the climactic revelation in Christ. "Call that expanding outlook on the divine nature," he said in the Garvin Lecture, "either God's progressive self-revelation or man's deepening insight, it comes to the same result."

When the issue was put to him in an interview in 1956, Fosdick began his reply by quoting Jesus: "It was said unto them of old times, but I say unto you." Believed Fosdick, "Now there is a clear statement of the fact that God is a living God. He has never said his last word on any subject; and if you are going to keep up with the living God, you have to keep moving. And the Bible is to me impossible to understand except on the basis of a mighty movement of revelation. Do they mean that Jesus was giving us no more beautiful and profound truth than Moses?" The idea of a static Bible squeezes the life out of it. "Every once in a while there is a flame, and you get a wider horizon. Micah says something, 'What does the Lord require of thee, but to do justly, to love mercy, and to walk humbly with thy God.' You say, by George, we've got something; we've gone ahead. And Isaiah says something and then Jesus comes saying, 'It was said unto them of old times, but I say unto you.' What do they mean, not progressive? Of course it's progressive!"

VI

How shall we think of the Jesus of History? How shall we think of the Christ of Faith? Fosdick's Christology began with the historicity of Jesus. The Man from Nazareth was a real man, not a myth. The historical Jesus was born in the last years of Herod the Great and died during the reign of Tiberius Caesar when Pontius Pilate was Procurator of Judea. He was an itinerant rabbi who ate with sinners and publicans, was regarded by some as a prophet and visionary, aroused the antagonism of influential Jewish leaders, entered Jerusalem during the Passover celebration, was interrogated by the Sanhedrin, tried before a Roman court and crucified as a common criminal. The Scripture's dominant conviction is not an idea but a historical deed: "In Christ," said Fosdick, "God had performed a supremely important act for the world, so climactic that prophecy found there its culmination and so determinative that all man's future was conditioned on it." Paul never said, I know what I have believed. What Paul said went deeper: "I know whom I have believed."

Fosdick was concerned to rebuke those nineteenth-century scholars who argued that the Jesus story was merely a projection of faith, a pure myth, an apotheosis. Far more troubling to Fosdick, however, was the emergence of modern Form Criticism and its more radical exponents, Oscar Cullman, the early Brunner, and above all Rudolph Bultmann who sought to demythologize the Biblical Jesus and his deeds and message. Though these critics did not question that Jesus actually lived and taught in Palestine and died on Calvary, the effect of radical demythologizing was not only to deny the possibility of discovering the historical Jesus in the sense of what is usually meant by "biography" (and here Fosdick would agree), it was further to assert (in Bultmann's words) "that we can know almost nothing concerning the life and personality of Jesus." When Brunner maintained that "The 'historic Jesus' is a corpse" and "How Jesus found God, how he prayed, how he lived is not divine revelation for us," Fosdick was "positively shocked." If this is the new "perfectly faultless theology," he growled, the "neo-orthodox are welcome to it!'

So concerned was Fosdick about the dangers of radical demythologizing, which he believed to be equivalent to the demolition of the historicity of the Gospels, he devoted an entire chapter in a last major work, *The Man from Nazareth*, to a vigorous demonstration of his conviction: "whatever else his contemporaries saw in Jesus, they saw *him*; he was a real man and not a myth." Needless to say, as he reported to Emile Cailliet, this volume came "under some very heavy criticism from the neo-orthodox side of the fence."*

Biblical scholarship today tends to take the position that the Gospels primarily tell us how each evangelist conceived of and presented Jesus to a Christian community in the last third of the first century and that the real Jesus can no more be separated from the theology of the Gospel writers than the real Socrates can be separated from the dialogues of Plato. Nevertheless, the proclamation of the postpaschal community irrevocably connects, as Fosdick held, with the earthly ministry of Jesus, a life in history. Certainly, the Gospels are testimonies of faith, but they could only have emerged and can only be understood in the light of Jesus' life.

For Fosdick the historicity of Jesus meant the humanity of Jesus. "Let us clarify our minds at once," he said in the Beecher Lectures, "by stating plainly that whatever questions there may be about Christ's divinity, there is none about his humanity. Jesus was true man and his divinity must always be asserted and interpreted in such ways as will not cast doubt on that unmistakable fact." Fosdick repeatedly drove home the reminder that the early Church fought its most decisive battles in defense not of the diety of Jesus, but of his humanity, repulsing the heretical Gnostics, Docetists, and Apollinarians.

As fully human, in what sense was Jesus, in Fosdick's understanding, God incarnate in the flesh, "truly God"? "Whenever I say 'God' I think Christ," was a favorite Fosdick expression; as was, "Christ the clearest

---

* It is worth pondering here the judgment of John C. Bennett: "One thing that you can say of Fosdick is that he taught Americans how to demythologize Biblical materials long before we ever heard of Bultmann who used that word. His idea of reproducible experience is exactly that."

revelation of the Divine and the noblest ideal of the human we have."
Fosdick naturally interpreted the experiences of the disciples as progressive. They knew the Jesus of History before they recognizd the Christ of Faith. "At first they may have said, God sent him. After a while that sounded too cold, as though God were the bow, and Jesus the arrow. . . . So I suspect they went on to say, God is with him. That went deeper. Yet, as their experience with him progressed, it was not adequate. God was more than with him. So at last we catch the reverent accents of a new conviction, God came in him." For liberal Protestants of the era, the real question was not whether Jesus is Godlike but whether God is Christlike. Fosdick concurred: "To put the matter simply, in Christian thinking God became Christlike. The divinity of Jesus became not only an assertion about Jesus but about divinity." Everything else is seen awry unless that is clear. The divinity of Jesus is primarily an affirmation about God, Fosdick once confessing, "Sometimes I think I believe in God largely because I cannot help believing in Jesus Christ."

At first glance Fosdick's understanding of the Incarnation at times appears almost creedal:

> How shall men think of God and where shall they find him? how shall God enter into men and redeem them?—these are the profoundest questions of religious life and thought. And men were framing answers to these deepest questions when they said that in Christ the Logos was unveiled, that through him God had crossed the chasm that divides divinity from man, and, taking flesh, dwelt among us, full of grace and truth. God was in Christ reconciling the world unto himself; in his face we see the light of the knowledge of the glory of God; he is the effulgence of God's glory and the very image of his substance; in the beginning was the Word and the Word was with God, and the Word was God—this message is an essential part of the New Testament. He who does not proclaim it is not preaching the New Testament; he has parted company not only with the church's theology but with the experience of God in Christ which belongs at the very center of original Christianity. For, in whatever philosophic terms you may phrase it, the norm of Christian experience in the New Testament was to find in Christ, not simply the ideal life, but the incarnate God of the world where that ideal life must be wrought out.

It is perfectly accurate to say that Fosdick believed in the divinity of Jesus. However, it is also apparent that orthodox and neo-orthodox brethren found his *meaning* of the Incarnation either ambiguous or inadequate. And, after all, Fosdick prided himself on never having repeated the Apostles' Creed or the Nicene Creed, both, of course, containing Incarnational statements unacceptable to him. Fosdick could not believe that Jesus was virgin born. He did not ridicule those who did, but he was adamant that such belief was not essential to acceptance of Christian faith, warning that "no one should tie up in one bundle the virgin birth and the divinity of Christ." Fosdick could not believe in Christ's bodily resurrection. Fosdick doubted whether Jesus ever thought of himself as the Messiah; perhaps he did, but more probably "Jesus' disciples may have read this into his thinking, especially after they were persuaded that he was the Messiah."

Critics said that Fosdick's emphasis was not on God *in* Christ but on God being *like* Christ. They charged that he evaded answering frankly the one great question, "Who do you say I am?" They disliked his rendering of the Fourth Gospel's opening verses: "In the beginning was Mind, and the Mind was with God, and the Mind was God. . . . And the Mind became flesh." They held that in Fosdick's understanding Jesus was scarcely divine in the full metaphysical sense of consubstantiality with the Father, scarcely divine, that is, in the sense of standing in some ultimate, ontological relationship to God the Father that warrants the assertion that he was not merely Godlike but God incarnate.

Above all, critics were distressed when Fosdick said that he believed in the divinity of the Master because goodness, beauty, truth, and love are divine and because this is so there is a divine element in humanity. As God was in Christ, asserted Fosdick, "I think God was in my mother." In the Beecher Lectures he put it in this fashion: "But if Jesus is divine and if divinity hedges us all about, like the vital forces which in winter wait underneath the frozen ground until the spring comes, that is a gospel! Then the incarnation in Christ is the prophecy and hope of God's indwelling in every one of us." On a thousand instances Fosdick pressed home the point: "In the New Testament Christianity is a religion of incarnation and its central affirmation is that God can come into human life." In fact, it is the Master's divinity, not his humanity, that makes it possible for us to emulate him. The same God who entered the human Jesus wants to enter us. That which was divine in Christ was his spiritual quality. Just so are *we* temples of the living God; the Spirit of God dwelleth in us. "You cannot have one God and two kinds of divinity, and while like drops of water we are very small beside his sea, yet it is one of the supreme days in man's spiritual history when the New Testament started men singing that they were 'children of God: and if children, then heirs; heirs of God, and joint-heirs with Christ.'"

This does not mean, however, that Fosdick believed that even the most saintly of men ever equaled God's revelation in Christ. "I feel in relationship to Christ like a land-locked pool beside the sea," he once explained. "The water in the land-locked pool is the same kind of water that is in the sea. You cannot have one sea and two kinds of sea-water. But look at the land-locked pool, little, imprisoned, soiled it may be in quality, and then look at the sea, with deeps and distances and tides and relationships with the world's life the pool can never know."

Midway in his ministry Fosdick informed the Riverside congregation, "I do not know what theory of the atonement you hold, and I might almost say I do not care whether you have any theory at all." And in one of his last books he confessed that "the older I grow, the more I think that I understand the cross best when I stop trying to analyze it and just stand in awe before it." He was not unaware of the historic controversies surrounding the Cross of Christ—about sacrifice, propitiation, substitution, ransom, moral influence. After all he began his career with a B.D. thesis on the significance of Christ's death in Christian thought, preached on the question of what he himself deemed his finest sermons, such as "The Forgiveness of Sins," and devoted a chapter in *Dear Mr. Brown* to "What About the Atonement?" But Fosdick was concerned to cut through obfuscating doctrines to the two central, eternal realities revealed by Calvary: redemption is made possible only by the kind of love that stands behind vicarious sacrifice and, second, that forgiveness is always costly.

Christ's sacrifice manifests this universal law: "Wherever ignorance and sin curse mankind there is only one road to salvation; namely, that someone who does not have to do it for the sake of those who do not deserve it must voluntarily take upon himself the burden of their need and guilt." Christ died as He lived, a savior. Christ's life of saviorhood is to be continued in the vicarious sacrifice of His disciples' lives. We can all share in it. Jesus himself said, "If any man would come after me, let him deny himself and take up his cross and follow me." Perhaps Fosdick most eloquently expressed his understanding of the Cross of Christ as central and determinative, as the moment when sin and grace reached their climactic encounter, in the passage:

> The whole ethic of the New Testament is grace. It is not law; it is not a moral code; it is not external regulation; it is grace. We are to love him because he first loved us; we are to forgive our enemies because we ourselves have been forgiven; we are to lay down our lives for our brethren because he first laid down his life for us; we are to be kind to one another, tender-hearted, forgiving each other, because God for Christ's sake has forgiven us. Freely ye have received, freely give—that is the ethic of the New Testament, and it is the only ethic worthy of a free soul at its best.

Fosdick anticipated Bonhoeffer's scorn of "cheap grace." The cross is the place where "life gets made up one way or the other." Jesus' passion cost God. The cross is the supreme revelation of God's heart—the supreme revelation of His love and of His sorrow. There is no way for God to escape sorrow if He is a God of love. In sorrowfully giving His son the Father revealed to men that He would not fail to give them everything.

The resurrection of Christ may be accepted as fact, believed Fosdick. Apart from it there is no accounting for the Christian Church. Without it, Christianity is an illusion. Referring to the disciples, he once wrote: "Those who lived most intimately with him stood most in awe of him, with mingled love and adoration acknowledged in him a divine authority, felt in him the very presence of their God, gave him the supreme name they knew to express transcendent greatness, Messiah, and after Calvary they were victoriously confirmed in their adoration of him by their faith in his resurrection and their experience of his living presence. That is the astonishing fact with which the Christian church began."

However, as with the Incarnation, many critics found Fosdick's understanding of the Resurrection unbiblical. He rejected the dogma of Christ's physical resurrection, flatly saying, "I believe in the persistence of personality, but I do not believe in the resurrection of the flesh." Patently, major portions of the Apostles' Creed were a stumbling block to Fosdick, as were the Gospel narratives of the empty tomb and those describing the risen Christ as eating, passing through closed doors, and offering His hands and feet to the inquiring touch of Thomas. Fosdick discussed the "tangled" textual evidence in *A Guide to Understanding the Bible* coming down on the side of what might be termed a spiritualized-psychologized interpretation of the physical elements in the Resurrection story. Late in life he summed up his interpretation in a private letter:

> For myself I have come to think with more and more certainty that the appearances of Jesus were of a spiritual sort. . . . Certainly, I cannot make real the idea of an animated body. The contradictions are incredible: on one side a body that can eat fried fish and that is known to the disciples in the breaking of bread, and on the other side a body that appears and disappears and passes through closed doors. That sort of thing seems to me impossible to be believed in by modern minds, although to the ancient Hebrews that was the way in which life after death was conceived.

Himself frequently branded a heretic, on one point of Christology Fosdick returned the compliment. Modern Christians who say that "Jesus is God" may be guilty of the ancient heresy of Sabellianism. Jesus was not, asserted Fosdick, omnipotence, omnipresence masquerading in a human body. The historic phrase "the divinity of Christ" does not signify that the Jesus of History was the God of the universe. "Nobody should ever go to Jesus, to his manger and his Cross, to find the omnipotence which swings Orion and the Pleiades." The Father is not the

Son and the Son is not the Father. It is idolatry to equate the Anointer with the anointed, the One who raised from the dead with the one who was raised, the Sender with the one sent.

Finally, Fosdick was accused of lacking a "high Christology" because he could not say with Karl Barth, "Only the man who knows about Jesus Christ knows anything at all about revelation"; "the confession becomes inevitable that Jesus Christ *alone* is the revelation." In the terminology of theology, Fosdick held that the "special revelation" of the historical Christ-event did not preclude "general revelation" outside the Bible. With what seems to be some heat, Fosdick summarized Barth's dogma: "Except through revelation there is no knowledge of God, and nowhere else before Christ or outside of Christ—not in nature or history, not in the human soul or in any other religious faith—is there any revelation of the true God." This doctrine Fosdick found incredible. God has always and everywhere been seeking man, revealing Himself to man's clouded understanding. The Word of God is a Living Word continuing to speak today to those who listen. The "near end of God" was glimpsed, it may be, by Socrates and Plato, Buddha and Confucius—to consign these to hell, as Fosdick remembered boyhood sermons so consigning them, was to him "stark blasphemy against the character of God." "Has not the Shepherd always been seeking for his sheep?," asked Fosdick. "Has not man's spiritual quest always been an answer to this quest of God? Was Plato merely seeking after God and never finding Him, while Paul was merely found by God without ever seeking Him? Why this extravagant contradistinction, this false antithesis between two indispensables?" All humans, even those who lived before the birth of Jesus and even those outside the Christian Church, are caught up in God's saving grace by the very fact of their existence.

VII

How shall we think of man? How shall we think of man's destiny? Nothing was more characteristic of the liberal theology with which Fosdick was associated than its high opinion of human nature, centered in belief in the worth of each person as a child of God. "Reverence for personality," "dignity of the individual," "sacredness of human life" were phrases worn smooth by repeated handling, and the text, "Of how much more worth is a man than a sheep," was oft cited. This profound conviction, drawn from the belief that man bore in his being the stamp of the eternal, the *imago Dei*, and from the example of Jesus' loving concern for all persons, was at the very marrow of evangelical liberalism. Yet it was on precisely this question of human nature that neoorthodoxy found liberalism most vulnerable and in fact unbiblical. Reinhold Niebuhr asserted that "the real basis for all the errors of liberalism is its erroneous estimate of human nature." The chastened liberal John Bennett observed as early as 1933 that "the best short-cut to an understanding of the present theological situation is to realize that liberalism diverges from orthodoxy and neo-orthodoxy in its various forms in its doctrine of man, and that other differences follow from that." In the judgment of liberalism's detractors, man has entirely too good an opinion of himself. It is pretentious of man to assume he can reason or will himself from sin to unsin; it is utopian of man to assume the Kingdom of God can be consummated in history; it is fatuous of man to assume that history is redemptive. Injustice, violence, catastrophe, cruelty are not simply mistakes, results of ignorance or cultural lag, or the work of peculiarly wicked individuals, but rather are bound into the very existence of the self. Natural man is not innately good and inherently perfectible, waiting for social engineering and scientific planning (and moralist preaching) to work their wonders. So went the critique of liberalism's doctrine of man.

Fosdick's doctrine of man mediated between a one-sided, Pelagian stress on human goodness and autonomy and equally radical Calvinistic and neoorthodox doctrines of man's total depravity, hopelessness as sinner, and absolute helplessness and despair in the presence of the Holy God.

Fosdick understood human nature in terms of the concept of personality. Christianity's great affirmation is that we are made in the image of God. "At our deepest that is what we are." The most characteristic and significant "contribution which Jesus made to human thought was his estimate of human personality, its divine origin, its spiritual nature, its boundless possibilities, its glorious destiny." Preaching on the sacredness of life, Fosdick told his people: " 'The temple of God is holy, which temple ye are.' That is, to Christianity personality is sacred, the most sacred thing in all the universe next to God. In comparison the stars are pagan and the sun and moon profane. For we are the children of the Living God and all our powers the vessels of his service." To Fosdick, personality is the symbol of divine revelation; a revelation of ultimate being. This means "that we have a divine heritage, a divine nature, and a divine possibility." Indeed "the interpretation of the Spiritual World in terms of personality and the interpretation of personality in terms of Christ—that is in brief the summary of Christian theology."

It is important to understand that by "personality" Fosdick meant "soul." Humans possess bodies but personality alone distinguishes what a man is. "My personality," affirmed Fosdick, "is God's most sacred trust to me; it is the thing I am, my soul." In *The Assurance of Immortality* he inquired:

> Are we bodies that have spirits, or are we spirits that have bodies? Which is essentially the man? The Christian affirmation is not that we have souls, but that we are souls; that we substantially are spirit, as invisible as God, since no one ever saw himself or saw another man. The affirmation of the materialist is not that we have bodies, but that we are bodies; that flesh is the essence of us, and that all our intellectual and moral life, like the peal of a bell, is a transient result of physical vibrations, and ceases when the cause is stopped. Between these two affirmations the decision lies: either we are bodies that for a little time possess a spiritual aspect, or else we are spirits using an instrument of flesh.

Fosdick recognized, of course, that forces of nature, constitutional inheritance, and social circumstances condition individuals, limiting their freedom. But man does have a spiritual nature, and it is in his spirit that man is free, and this freedom is God's gift. Man's spiritual nature is immune to the vicissitudes of circumstances. "There are doors in us no man can shut. There are areas of our lives not at the mercy of man and circumstance. All the sources of a man's liberty, independence, spiritual richness, and resources lie in his use of these inner doors that God opened and no man can shut." For Fosdick human nature is not absolutely fixed and human life is never static. Life is an adventure in becoming. "Therefore, the deepst worth of a man is not in what he has, not in what he has done, not in what he is; it is in what he may become."

G. K. Chesterton once chided liberals like Fosdick for dropping the doctrine of original sin, the only doctrine of Christianity that could be empirically verified. Fosdick did in fact repudiate the traditional idea of original sin. Rather, he said, every man is his own Adam. Natural man was not uncorrupted before the fall. Sin is in the nature of man and always has been. It is part of his biological inheritance. Sin is the organization of the self around its lowest motives. It is when we do not love and open ourselves to the highest when we see it. It is the victory of the creatureliness over the spiritual in us. It is not so much for our sins that we are punished as by them. Our sins themselves rise up and slay us.

Accused with other liberals of being a modern Pelagian, Fosdick acknowledged that in his early ministry before World War I he together with much of his generation muted the chord of man's radical diabolism. As the demoniac twentieth century deepened so his understanding of evil deepened. Countless statements from his lips and pen can be adduced to support this:

My friends, when we call men at their worst beastly we insult the beasts. The beasts are brutal but after all they are not so bad. There are depths they cannot sink to. There are evils beyond their reach. They cannot mix beastliness with man's intelligence and science and consummate loyalty and self-sacrifice, and so do and be the abysmal evil man can be guilty of. Alas, no savior saves us who does not save us from sin!

Man is a sinner; there is truth in the old doctrine of original sin, something fundamentally wrong in us from which we desperately need to be saved, and from which science alone cannot save us, nor education alone, nor any automatic evolution, only what the New Testament calls the grace of God, forgiveness, spiritual rebirth, being inwardly transformed by the renewing of our minds.

We are handling the same inescapable experience out of which the old doctrine of original sin first came, we are dealing with the same fundamental fact which Paul was facing when he said, "as in Adam all die": that humanity's sinful nature is not something which you and I alone make up by individual deeds of wrong, but that it is an inherited mortgage and handicap on the whole human family.

Anyone who takes Christ in earnest begins where Simon Peter began, "Lord leave me, I am a sinful man."

Man *is* a sinner. His sinfulness is deep-seated, ingrained—the neoorthodox are right about that. In these days when man's colossal bestiality and wickedness are so frightening, how can anyone fail to see the inherent evil in man, which can turn every seeming good to tragic ill.

It is perfectly true, then, that Fosdick took man's sinfulness seriously. But two additional things need to be said. He never thought that vilification of man enhanced the glory of God. It is permissible to believe in man not because we overestimate him but because we do not underestimate the power of God's saving grace when man opens himself to receive that which God freely gives. And, second, in Fosdick's view sin is a disorder of the self, not a basic corruption of man's nature, his inevitable and universal rebellion against God. To term "sin," as Fosdick once did, as "the one most real and practical problem of mankind" suggests a malleable condition susceptible to resolution.

It must be said, moreover, that to locate sin, as Fosdick tends to do, in man's creaturely inheritance and to identify virtue with spirit is to embrace a Hellenic dualism that is at odds with the Biblical picture of man. Fosdick once replied to an interviewer, "In mind and imagination I am a Greek not a Hebrew." Not surprisingly he seemed to follow a Platonic reading of man as an angel imprisoned in an animal or of man as a soul built in a body like a temple in a scaffolding. This bifurcation sees man not as body-soul, but as soul that has, for a time, a body that is ultimately wholly dispensable. But the war tearing man apart is not between the bestial passions and the highest spiritual nature; rather, the self is divided against the self at all levels. This being so, sin cannot be attributed to our kinship with the brutes and salvation does not come from the triumph of the spirit over the flesh.

VIII

Perhaps no single subject appeared with great frequency in Fosdick's utterances than the persuasion that not even death will separate us from the love of God. The God revealed in Christ Jesus is not a God of "unfinished business." Wherever we go, in life or death, God is there. "To talk about the fatherhood of God, who begets children only to annihilate them, is absurd." Although a man, therefore, may believe in immortality without believing in the goodness of God, he cannot reasonably believe in the goodness of God without believing in immortality.

The God whom Christians worship is a God of goodness and justice. His children, victims of cruelty in this world, must be given the opportunity to taste a life more abundant. Also, those who have sinned and repented must, if God is merciful, be given another chance to become His true sons. And unrepentant sinners, too, must in some way be redeemed. Fosdick reported that the New Testament word for "hell" referred to a place outside of Jerusalem where garbage was burned, continuing, "I do not view hell as being endless punishment. I understand this doctrine in a positive sense—it is a faith that the garbage in this world gets burned up."

Fosdick's understanding of immortality did not mean merely going on and on everlastingly. No, eternal life is not simply postmortem; it is also a present possession. It is a quality of experience, both present and future. Said Fosdick: "To enter here and now into the world of spiritual values so that truth, goodness, beauty and love are one's very being, its substance and its glory—that is the present possession of eternal life. And to have faith that these spiritual values are no casual by-product of a negligent universe, but, rather, the very essence of the real world, and that death has no dominion over them or their possessors—that is faith in immortality." Fosdick's faith in personal permanence was in part derived from the fact that the earth is temporary, sure to be destroyed some day. As it was once uninhabitable, so it would be uninhabitable again. Fosdick stated his position eloquently in his autobiography:

If . . . death is the end of me it is of others too. Then all our ancestors are finally dead, and we and all our children will be finally dead, and with the planet's perishing, the last Robinson Crusoe on this wandering island in the sky will be finally dead, and nothing will be left, no value conserved, no purpose fulfilled from all that was endeavored and done on earth. That inevitably involves a senseless creation which in the end consummates nothing, wastes everything, preserves no values, fulfills no promises, has no meaning. My faith in immortality has been mainly a corollary from my faith that creation cannot be so utterly senseless and irrational.

As for the question of the dimensions of the life to come after the body's death, that is in the hands of God. But Fosdick did write these comforting words to a young woman haunted by the fear of death:

That you fear death indicates that you have had some mistaken and disturbing teaching in your childhood. To fear death is abnormal—death is an inevitable part of life, like sunset, and it can be the beautiful end of a fair day, with sunrise ahead! Your insistence on knowing the details of the future life is foolish, my dear. We are now like unborn babes in a mother's womb. They face not death but birth. Yet they cannot imagine anything true about the new world they are going to be born into. Sunlight and breathing and eating they cannot possibly picture. So are we as we face the unseen world. The truth is going to turn out to be more marvelous than we can imagine. I am sure of that.

Chapter Twenty-two

The Passing of Victorian America:
A Minister's Response to the
Disintegration of the Bourgeois Synthesis

I

Fosdick was born on Queen Victoria's birthday in 1878. In that year the cracks beginning to appear in the Victorian cultural fortress were only visible to discerning eyes. For the large majority of late Victorian Americans—a class, the bourgeoisie, as well as a generation—the great central doctrines of civilization remained unshaken. Among these truths were: the inherent superiority of civility over savagery; the reality and universality of moral law; the certainy of progress; the ascendancy of British-American culture; the sanctity and indissolubility of marriage and consequent exaltation of motherhood and childhood and insistence on sexual continence outside of marriage and sexual "purity" within. High among the custodians of culture designated to protect this imposing Victorian fortress were preachers and professors, and as a member of both professions Fosdick faced formidable challenges. By the time of his death in 1969, implacable forces had reduced to rubble the superstructure of the fortress: absolute moral law gave way to relativized, conditional, situational ethics; the idea of progress became an absurdity; civilized restraint surrendered to unrepressed expression; the cherished classical certitudes structuring art and literature were dissolved in the antinomianism of modernism; and little remained of the older dogmas relating to the proper social roles of men and women and the proper relationships between the sexes before and in marriage.

And yet, if the superstructure was irretrievably lost, it is at least arguable—and indeed was argued by Fosdick—that something eternal remained of the foundations. If this were so, if the foundations remained firm, that is, if it were still possible to be certain with Fosdick of "Mind behind the Universe, Purpose running through it, Meaning in it, Destiny ahead of it," then perhaps not all of eternal worth was lost as the Victorian ramparts fell under relentless battering.

Still, as the decades passed and cultural change accelerated, Fosdick found himself shaking his head and saying with John Marquand's bewildered patrician George Apley, "I wish there weren't quite so many new ideas. Where do they come from?" Maybe Fosdick shared at least in part Apley's further mussings: "I try to think what is in back of them and speculation often disturbs my sleep. Why is everyone trying to break away from what we all know is sane and good? There is only one right way to live; there is only one right way to write and paint." Steeped as he was in the Greek classics, Fosdick was also reminded of Aristophanes' lament, "Whirl is King, having driven out Zeus."

To understand Fosdick's response to modernity, it must again be said that although he must be characterized as a theological liberal, temperamentally he was a conservative. He once illustrated this convervatism with the confession: "My wife says I'd still be shaving with an old fashioned razor if she had not forceably presented me with a 'safety.' And I'm in deadly fear she'll get me an 'electric shaver' and make me change again."

Fully to understand Fosdick's response to modernity, the magnitude of modernism's assault must be comprehended. Dean Inge has Adam remarking to Eve: "You know, my dear, we live in an age of transition." The perception that all generations endure the shock of change, however, should not obscure the further truth that the trauma was uncommonly severe for twentieth-century Americans. The cry of Henry Adams (not Adam) is well known: "My country in 1900 is something totally different from my own country of 1860. I am wholly a stranger in it." But compared to the forty-odd years of Fosdick's active ministry, the changes witnessed by Henry Adams seem merely moderate, and if one brings the comparison up to the year of Fosdick's death, they seem more moderate still.

In this chapter the focus will be on the post-World War I years, especially the 1920s, in part because Fosdick's cultural concerns during his Montclair ministry have been etched already; in part because it was after the war that he first occupied pulpits in America's cultural center, New York City; and in part because of agreement with Gertrude Stein's observation that the twentieth century began not in 1900, but with the Great War. To be sure, the disintegration of the bourgeois synthesis may be dated in Europe as early as the nineteenth century, and at least the beginnings of the "end of American innocence" antedated the Treaty of

Versailles. One thinks for openers of *Fordismus*, Freudianism, feminism, the frustration of spermatozoa, the Armory Show, ragtime, the tango craze, Mabel Dodge's salons, Louis Sullivan, Greenwich Village Bohemians, the *Masses*, Randolph Bourne, *Sister Carrie*, the Road to Reno, and, according to the editors of *Current Opinion* in 1913, the striking of "Sex O'Clock in America." Nevertheless, an even stronger case can be made for the thesis that the twenties marked "the first serious attempt of Americans to make their peace with the twentieth century." For Americans it was in fact only after the Great War, the death agony of the nineteenth century, that "the tension between modern and traditional modes of thought and behavior, was finally played out, and the social changes that had been remaking America for decades finally congealed into a pattern which would shape life in the twentieth century." The passing of Victorian America was not unresisted and indeed was not absolute. It was this tension between the older and newer cultures that made the twenties not only an era of anxiety and anguish, but one of excitement and creativity.

II

Fosdick grew to manhood when bourgeois domesticity was in fullest flower and in a family that was the apotheosis of all that was lovely in the Victorian ideal of domestic life. Unable and in truth unwilling to shake entirely free from the "great expectations" promised and for him found in the prevailing family ideal of his youth, he was sufficiently realistic to acknowledge the flawed reality in that ideal and sufficiently aware to recognize the transformation of marriage in post-Victorian America. One change was the increase in divorce and, as important, the fading of the social stigma attached to divorced persons. Between Fosdick's birth and 1929, the population of the United States grew 300 percent, the number of marriages increased 400 percent, and the divorce rate rose 2000 percent. In 1878 there was one divorce for every twenty-one marriages, but by the end of the twenties the ratio was one in every six—and mounting close to one in three by 1969. Nevertheless, in the opening decades of the new century men and women married in greater percentages and they married younger. Even so, thanks to growing knowledge of contraception, the growing availability of contraceptive measures, and a growing moral sense that conception need not be the intended consequence of all marital intercourse, family size declined. Between 1900 and 1930, moreover, the percentage of married women

living with their husbands who worked for wages outside the home tri-
pled, further contributing to the transformation.

Time and again Fosdick punctured the nostalgic myths surrounding
marriage. He began a 1929 article entitled "What Is Happening to the
American Family?" with the flat statement that a revolt was on against
"old fashioned family life" because aspects of that life were intolerable.
He went on to document the statement by citing a series of old laws
making the wife virtually the husband's chattel. He further noted the
growing millions of wives gainfully employed and winning thereby a
degree of economic independence, and he observed, "What is clear is
that modern women will not stand what their foremothers did, because
they do not have to." The initial section of the article concluded:

> A vehement revolt, therefore, is on against old fashioned family life. We
> may as well make up our minds that it is inevitable. If we are wise we
> shall see that it is desirable. The longer that some of the old legal and
> social taboos are retained, the more disastrous will be the breakage when
> they give way. The eminent churchman who summons the hosts of the
> Lord to "holy indignation" as the chief remedy he has to offer for our
> perilous experimentation with the family is wasting his whistle in the
> teeth of a rising gale.

In this article Fosdick recognized that a couple might wish to marry
without having to face in the early years of their union the responsibility
of children and that it would be hard hearted to insist that they might
not marry until they were prepared to support a family. "To be sure . . .
this modern variation from the historic family depends on methods of
controlling birth; but that it is inevitable, that it is in widespread and
constantly increasing use, that it is often absolutely necessary and generally innocent, most observers would at once agree." Elsewhere he
advised young couples in love and wishing to marry but, because of
circumstances, unable to start a family to "get married as soon as you
sensibly can, even if both of you have to work, and if you cannot afford
to have children those first years do not have them until you can."

Fosdick also acknowledged that there might come a time in a marital
union when divorce became almost certainly the lesser of two evils.
Therefore, he advocated the reformation of the nation's chaotic and
hypocritical divorce laws. Of New York's law as it stood in 1929 he said:
"When two married people hate each other, cannot abide living together,
and, in consequence, have made a hell instead of a home out of their
relationship, they cannot be divorced because they so hate each other
but must go through the legal farce of a mutual agreement by which one

brings charges against the other." Let divorce by mutual consent come, Fosdick argued, although to prevent easy separations for temporary quarrels, a year must elapse between the application for, and the granting of, the divorce.

Fosdick's realism concerning marriage never gave way to cynicism. To the contrary. The finest fulfillment any man and woman ever can find is to love each other so much that they do not want to love anybody else in the same way at all, and so living loyally together and rearing their children in an unbroken home. To be monogamous not because one must but because one may is the expression of a psychological reality. To the "flaming youth" of the Jazz Age he commanded:

> Quit pretending! Own up! In your secret love fancies what do you dream of as the greatest possible good? Any normal person can tell you. You would like sometime to fall in love with some one who will return your love, so that you two may enter into an intimate relationship which neither of you would want anybody else to invade. You would like to have this relationship publicly recognized in marriage, so that all the world may know that you two belong to each other, and that you would like to have children, so that your love life might flow over into other lives that you have brought into the world. As the years pass and you grow older and the sex life naturally retreats into the background, you would like to have affection there to take its place, a great affection that grows up within the sex relationship and stays after the scaffolding has been taken down. And, if life brings you to old age together, you would like to have one die not too long before the other, that there may not be too many years to wait. You would rather have that than anything else in the world.

Believing as he did, it is not surprising that Fosdick rejected Judge Ben Lindsey's famous advocacy of "companionate marriage," a seemingly simple alternative to the confining commitments of ordinary marriage in which the union would be frankly experimental, childless, easily contracted, and easily dissolved. The benefits, Lindsey maintained, would be channeling of youthful sexuality, exploration in mate compatibility, the limitation of children to couples in traditional wedlock, and the elimination of the punitive features of divorce law. In Fosdick's judgment, the so-called "trial marriage" was a pitifully truncated, arrested, balked experience that would prove psychologically harmful to the individuals and socially ruinous to the nation if the practice became widespread.

Fosdick was disturbed not only by Lindsey's specific proposal but as well by aspects of the generally emerging pattern of married life. In 1941 he mused:

> I sometimes wonder whether we are not going to see a movement of reaction on the part of womanhood against some of the major trends of this

last generation that have carried many women far away from home-making, in one of the most significant migrations in all history. I would not surrender a single gain of all the many that have been won this last century of woman's strike for freedom to enter every realm of human endeavor and prove her mettle. But today the deep necessities of our social life, and the profound, inalienable needs and aptitudes of womanhood itself, suggest a compensating movement of balance and counterpoise. One way or another, we must exalt the home—the most indispensable unit in our society. For everybody who ever has learned really to say Our, learned it in the first place as Jesus did in Nazareth, in the holy family.

In 1952 Fosdick approvingly quoted this poem:

> So long as there are homes to which men turn
> At the close of day,
> So long as there are homes where children are—
> Where women stay,
> If love and loyalty and faith be found
> Across these sills,
> A stricken nation can recover from
> Its greatest ills.

Of course, sentiments such as these were fuel for Betty Friedan's famous indictment of the oppressive 1950s, *The Feminine Mystique.*

In countless households in Victorian America the unvoiced thought of both wives and husbands must have been, "The Apostle Paul was wrong: first we marry and then we burn." Sexual frustration was the inevitable consequence of Victorian ideology, an ideology that proclaimed the absence of sexual longing in gently nurtured women, identified wifehood with motherhood, and admonished husbands to restrain and purify their carnal desire. Sensuality was excluded from the company of decency and marriage became nearly a euphemism for institutionalized abstinence, certainly a euphemism for female control of sexuality.* It is important to note that sexual repression had a very real functional basis in a society anxious about preventing conception but without the means adequately to quell that anxiety. The right of a Victorian woman, perhaps already the mother of many children, to say "no" to her husband was a form of freedom as liberating as a modern woman's right to say "yes" to fulfill her own real passional desire. The sexual revolution of the twentieth century was to a significant extent a revolution *within* marriage as contraception made possible the acknowledgment of female desire, separated

---

* I am not unaware that scholars are challenging this interpretation, but at this point their revisionist findings leave me unconvinced.

every act of love from the possibility of conception, and opened to husbands and wives a new mutuality.

It has been shown that in his pastoral counseling Fosdick advised couples living in sexual disharmony, and he apparently did so with some candor. Yet his sermonic references to marital sexuality seem either elusive or antiseptic. On one occasion he spoke of the "dedicated management" of sex as essential to an enduring home. On another he observed, "In marriage, sex is like the green calyx within which grows the flower of an abiding friendship. The calyx is important, but it is not the flower." Repeatedly, he assumed the natural waning of desire, and although he never specified the age at which this could be expected to occur, the subliminal implication is that it is no later than the middle years. Quoting a loving letter from John Winthrop to his wife, Fosdick commented: "That after twenty years! To compare that with those poor bounders, who have exhausted their youth in sexual adventures, are now in their age still trying to be romantic and to get a thrill out of the dying embers, is to compare diamonds with rubbish." It is difficult to know what he meant when he chided "those who make of marriage one sex adventure after another." What can be said with some certainty, however, is that for Fosdick sex in marriage was elevated to a level of mystical euphoria. "Lust" was to be condemned as fiercely as it had been by the Victorians. Coition within wedlock was to be pure and ethereal, devoid of vile "animal" passions. The question to be asked, of course, is whether this "modern" spiritualized understanding of sex might not wreak as much havoc in marriage as the older Victorian view of sex as base and dangerous.

A final point concerning Fosdick's understanding of marriage and the family. In a 1929 sermon he asserted: "Sex is an instinct. That can walk in low places. O my soul, look about this city! But because some of us were reared in Christian families, saw how lovely a Christian home can be at its best and found in the Christian Gospel an interior elevating power, sex with us has not walked in low but in high places and has been very beautiful." In a 1941 sermon entitled "A Clean Life in a Soiled World" he advised a "soiled youth" to remember "a lovely home, where childhood is happy, where marriage is sacred, and the relationships of the sexes are elevated, dignified, and beautiful." In a 1951 letter he described how in his own boyhood home he experienced love incarnate, unselfish, sacrificial, persistent, adding, "How could I deny, or altogether fail to understand, Christ's love when I had experienced the love that my mother gave me? If a boy does not have such a love in his home, I often wonder how he can believe it in his theology." The question to be asked here, of course, is just how comprehensible these descriptions of homes would be to the millions of individuals who were not raised in lovely homes by loving parents—and if incomprehensible, just how helpful.

III

It must have appeared to Fosdick that after the Great War America slipped its Apollonian moorings to launch into a Dionysian sea of unrestrained urges, such were the frequency and sternness of his warnings. But ministers were not the only ones to discern a change in the moral weather, Walter Lippmann remarking the "immense preoccupation with sex" in the twenties and Eugene O'Neill noting that sex had become for Americans the "philosopher's stone." To be sure, there was a part of the twenties that did not "roar." In many communities sheiks and shebas, lounge lizards and flappers, were as rare as a sissy in a Hemingway story or a saint in a Fitzgerald novel. And it cannot be documented that on a special morning between 1919 and 1929 51 percent of the young unmarried women in America awoke to find they were no longer virgins, as Paula Fass has reminded. Nevertheless, if the evidence is ambiguous regarding an increased incidence in premarital intercourse, the older generation was not mistaken about the pervasiveness and casualness of youthful petting and necking and the new sexual orientation, though also sexually restrained, nature of dating. The "flaming youth" were not debauchees, but by prewar standards they were naughty and self-consciously rebellious. Joseph Kett was right on the money when he observed, "The self-consciousness of youth in the 1920s can best be characterized as an aspect of subcultural rather than countercultural behavior." That is, the "revolt of youth" in the twenties was not as angry, as explosive, as revolutionary as "The Movement" in the sixties, but to observers, such as Fosdick, it was disquieting enough.

Not surprisingly then, Fosdick studded his sermons and articles in the twenties with jeremiads directed against "an insane sex obsession so extreme that . . . this may well be called the 'sex decade.'" The warnings continued with references to "exploding animal instincts," "sexual licence with its inevitable remorse, satiety, and self-disgust," shameless sex interest "that would have pleased Nero's fancy to a T," the opening of "floodgates" of filth and nastiness, all amounting to an "explosion in a cesspool." The acerbic tone of Fosdick's strictures against licentiousness must have had many of his fundamentalist theological critics crying, "Amen, brother!"

Amidst all this tut-tutting Fosdick was careful, as in all his preaching, also to strike the affirmative note. The title of one sermon, "Pull Your-self Together," described the message of many, and the title of another, "This Nation Needs a Rebirth of Character," suggests a typical Fos-dickian challenge. "To some youth here, I am trying to say, Will you be independent enough of popular licentiousness to treat sex with honor[?]," he once demanded. After noting the present-day moral loose-ness and observing that in every age some human beings have behaved like beasts, Fosdick added, "And in every generation youth has needed what we needed in my day and you need in yours, that summoning call, Steady, my boy, steady!" He wished for his own daughters that when the time came for them to go off to school "they might become now so habitually familiar with, so habitually in love with all that is fine and high and excellent that when, in new surroundings doors swing open upon evil things, they instinctively will stop upon the threshold and say, Not so, for I never have." Asserting that we cannot wash our linen clean in dirty water, he urged his parishioners to turn away from "sex novels, sex plays, sex films, sex caricatures of psychoanalysis" and re-call anew, "Whatsoever things are pure, whatsoever things are lovely, whatsoever things are of good report; if there be any virtue, and if there be any praise, think on these things." Fosdick continued:

> I wish that for just one young man this morning I might lift again a re-freshed ideal of a high, clean life as the most beautiful gift that a man can give the world! There are two words we use in boyhood that we need for our motto all our life—*honor bright*. To live through young manhood bright; to marry the girl of our love, bringing to her what we expect from her—an uncorrupted character—honor bright; to hand down to our chil-dren after us an inheritance undefiled, honor bright,—what a high and yet what a possible ideal!

Again:

> My young friend, you mistake what some of us are driving at. We want you to be happy just as much as you do. We no more think that sex is taboo and bad than you do. We rejoice in it as a lovely and noble power, so lovely that like every beautiful thing it is easily hurt. When you go away for the summer you can leave your kitchen stove pretty much anyhow; it will be there when you come back. But you would better not leave a violin lying carelessly around. Now, sex is not a kitchen stove. Sex is a violin, with such beautiful possibilities in it that it is worth while keeping it at its best.

One might pile quotation upon quotation, but perhaps the following best captures the lingering high Victorian tone in Fosdick's exhortations:

Let us then, see the truth of self-denial. Young man, would you not some time like to have a Christian home where with honor you could be the husband and the father of it? Have you not come down to this city from some household up the State, some simpler place than the metropolis, but a home you know to be the most beautiful thing next heaven a man can ever hope to have? Well then, you must pay the price. You will not drift into it. If you would have a home like that, there is a kind of life that now you must not live. See! That girl whom you are going to marry; she is alive. You may never have met her; you may not know who she is, but somewhere she is walking a path that, in the providence of God, will some day cross your own. Wherever she walks she is keeping herself high and true for you, and in her mind's imagination you are even now her prince, a man of worth and goodness, whom some day she will gladly marry. Not for all the wealth of the world would she be untrue to you today. Well, how are *you* living? You have no right to take to such a girl a life spotted all over with the smirch of the gutter! You have no right! And, if you do, you will live in secret misery forever, a shame in your eyes whenever you look upon her, a pang in your heart when your clean children clamber up into your arms and look to you as their ideal! To have a home free from that, with memories higher, and beautiful and clean, is worth *anything* that it can cost; and those who have homes like that do not call it self-denial.

Seven years later in a Smith College commencement address Fosdick repeated the lamentation, "Alas for the youth who in the springtime of his days rips from his trees their blossoms to make a transient garland for his hair only to find when autumn comes that there can be no fruit." In this address Fosdick cited Ruskin's proposition that "good taste" is the only morality and Fosdick agreed to set aside for the moment the words "right" and "wrong," substituting the words "beautiful" and "ugly." But he immediately added: "I beg of you, even if you throw over codes and standards, omit the words right and wrong, understand that you have not by any means concluded the matter. Love in your life may be beautiful or ugly. Which will you have it?" Ironically, Episcopal Bishop William Thomas Manning charged Fosdick with scoffing at moral codes and Fosdick's mail carried letters accusing him of advocating "free love." A Smith student, however, who heard the address remembered that the distinction Fosdick drew between the sterile command to "be good" and the call to "live beautifully" guided her throughout her life— and she was grateful that as a young woman she was awakened by Fosdick to this alternative basis of moral conduct.

IV

Regarding male and female differences, perhaps the fairest thing that can be said about Fosdick's position on this treacherous subject is that he saw the sexes as being innately different but ultimately equal. "The two sexes represent two spheres of character," he asserted in *The Manhood of the Master*, "they move in two realms of temperament; the glory of their life together has never been in identity of function but in balanced harmony." Explaining this thought, he continued, "Wherever men live by themselves apart from the civilizing influence of women, their strength runs to roughness, their independent will to rudeness and vulgarity; wherever women live by themselves apart from the tonic, military attitude of man, their idealism runs to sentiment and their powers of loyalty lose their temper. The two need each other for completion." In Jesus we find "combined the idealism, the tenderness, the capacity for loyalty and devotion which make womanhood beautiful, with the heroism, the undiscourageable will, the masterful leadership which are manhood's glory."

In *Twelve Tests of Character* he documented the oppression of women of the past, believing "No revolution in human history is more important than the emancipation of womanhood from such serfdom to her present independence." He gloried in women's successful struggle for legal, educational, occupational, and political freedom. But then he waffled: "Many women of this new generation are not profiting at all by their enlarged privilege; they are simply exhibiting their lack of balance in handling it." Unless we can get out of the new system, he concluded, "motherhood as consecrated, spiritual quality as fine, idealism as exalted, religious faith as cleansing and ennobling as distinguished previous generations, the new system will have failed in its most important object."

In *A Guide to Understanding the Bible* Fosdick gave extended space to the view of women found in the Old and New Testaments, concluding with the judgment that "in Jesus woman found the best friend she ever had in the ancient world. It is no accident that in the movement which he originated it came soon to be understood that the distinction of sex represented no difference of spiritual status; there was 'no male and female.'" In the course of the discussion Fosdick acknowledged that even today millions of women have no status remotely approaching equality with man's, that such a low status is "eminently unfair," and that "When persons are believed to be equal as God sees them, the race must try to make them equal as man treats them."

Some supporters of the feminist movement doubtless will find Fosdick's commitment to the cause unsatisfactory, comparing him to the Laodiceans who blew neither hot nor cold.* Still, several things must be recalled. He was, after all, born a long time ago. Second, his two daughters were raised to acquire professional skills and to be independent. Third, he had occasion to work professionally with numerous women, and there is nothing in the record to suggest that they found him guilty of male chauvinism—or exasperating unconscious condescension.

V

On at least one issue Fosdick cannot possibly be accused of evasion: birth control. As early as 1916, when much of patrician America shared Theodore Roosevelt's fears concerning "the diminution of the birth rate among the highest races" and the guardians of morality, Protestant preachers as well as Roman Catholic prelates, were equating contraception with concupiscence, Fosdick publicly and plainly took a stand, a stand he would hold world without end. He was associated with such agencies as the Birth Control Federation of America, the American Birth Control League, the National Committee for Planned Parenthood, the National Committee on Federal Legislation for Birth Control, and the Planned Parenthood Federation of America, Inc., receiving from the last organization in 1954 the Lasker Award. He addressed various conferences on the subject. His statements appeared in the press and in such journals as *Birth Control Review*. A 1929 article, "Religion and Birth Control," was reprinted in pamphlet form and over ten thousand copies were distributed. He touched on the matter in sermons, although he once replied to a plea, "I question the advisability of setting aside a separate Sunday for a sermon on Planned Parenthood. I do not know just how one would preach a sermon about planned parenthood, thoroughly as I believe in it." He praised Margaret Sanger, the godmother of the birth control movement in America. In his autobiography he noted the hostility of the Roman Catholic Church, believing that someday that church will be compelled to regret its "obscurantist" position. When Sanger's vexatious Birth Control Clinic in New York City was raided by the authorities in 1929, Fosdick publicly suspected the Catholic hierarchy of the instigation and, further, joined with a group of doctors and lawyers and ministers in assuring Sanger of their support.

---

* Regarding woman's suffrage, Fosdick reported in his autobiography that he was initially cool to the movement, but then became a zealous convert to the cause of the Nineteenth Amendment. Aside from this autobiographical statement, the record is totally silent.

In 1953 a tough tussle occurred over whether the Planned Parenthood Federation's Mothers Health Centers should be admitted to the Health and Welfare Council of New York City. Fosdick was chairman of the committee favoring inclusion and this meant tangling with the Catholic hierarchy. After the affray he wrote to a Federation leader: "I share with you great satisfaction in the fact that the fight was made and that we won it. I hope that as you say our affair in New York may be a lesson to communities across the nation, and that our Roman Catholic friends will understand that we do not intend to lie down and be used as a doormat for them to wipe their feet on. I was very sorry to have to enter into a public conflict with the Roman Catholics, but it was absolutely necessary, and I congratulate you on the outcome."

Fosdick's basic position was capsuled in a single 1928 sentence: "You cannot trust God to bring everything off all right if you let the earth's population double every sixty years." And also in a later sentence: "The population problem is the basic problem of the world, and if it is not well handled no other social problem can at all be solved." To the opposition he replied: "The familiar putting of the question . . . , 'Do you believe in birth control?' reflects a serious misapprehension of the issue. Birth control in this regard is much like automobiles. They are not primarily to be believed in or disbelieved in. They are here; they are being used; they will be used. The only real question is, 'How will they be used?'" Fosdick was well aware of the revolutionary nature of the birth control movement, once writing:

> Contraception information, incomplete and uncertain as it may be, gives us mastery over one of the most intimate and vital processes of our lives. We can have children or not have them; we can space children as we will; if our morals allow or are impotent to prevent, we can contact liaisons without some of the old risk of child-bearing; and in general we are handed an instrument of power capable of affecting deeply personal conduct, ethical standards, family life, and problems of population. No wonder folks are disturbed! Undoubtedly something has been let loose which will have a far-reaching and penetrating influence.

Unhappily, the birth control movement existed in uneasy symbiosis with the concurrent eugenics movement. To the dismay of "enlightened" middle-class advocates and practitioners of family planning, such as Fosdick, the lower classes seemed to continue to multiply, ignoring the new scientific techniques of contraception, ignoring the admonitions of the professional experts and their social "betters," stubbornly continuing to bring more childdren into the world than rational planning approved. The eugenics movement in America was born in the Progressive era and was part of the larger cult of efficiency, coming to a full flowering in the "tribal twenties." To be sure it had the support of humanitarian social workers and public health officers who saw daily the tragic consequences of indiscriminate breeding among the poor, the unwed, the mentally and physically defective, but it was also heavily freighted with antidemocratic notions of elitism and even racism, one intrepid eugenicist including among the "unfit" the "dullard, the gawk, the numbskull, the simpleton, the weakling, and the scatterbrain." Even Justice Holmes in 1927 upheld the laws for the sterilization of defectives on the ground that society should have the right to "prevent those who are manifestly unfit from continuing their kind."

Fosdick, sharing the fears fueling the eugenics movement, was caught up in it, although he was never guilty of the viciousness or the dogmatism of its extreme proponents. In a 1929 article entitled "America's Biggest Problem," for instance, he cited once again the misinterpreted studies of the Jukes and Kallikak families and the spurious revelations of the intelligence tests administered by the Army in World War I, which supposedly revealed those "disgenic influences which tend to increase the propagation of the weak and decrease the propagation of the strong." The article pointed to the "peril involved in our crazy unwillingness to use eugenic information to prevent the multiplication of the insane and criminal classes."

Later Fosdick became involved in the voluntary sterilization movement, in 1937 giving his moral support to the Sterilization League of New Jersey and in 1962 endorsing the program conducted in Virginia's Fauquier County, an experiment opposed both by Catholic spokesmen and by Billy Graham. Fosdick said for publication: "I believe very much that there is place for voluntary sterilization programs in our society. Sometimes it's a question of life and death." In 1945 he was approached by the Association for Voluntary Sterilization (at one time known as the Human Betterment Association of America). Though he declined to lend his name, his reply contained the revealing statement: "I feel the profound importance of the population problem and of scientific eugenics as a part of its solution. I have no doubt that sterilization should and will play a part in eliminating the unfit. It involves, however, many problems, technical and legal, with regard to the determination of who the unfit are and many questions of a highly specialized nature concerning methods that lie altogether outside my competent judgment." Subsequently, Fosdick did agree to be a sponsor of the Clergymens' Committee in Support of the Association for Voluntary Sterilization. Amusingly, when an officer of the association came to Fosdick's office to solicit his support, he sat the officer down, ordered his secretary not to interrupt them, and requested the officer to explain in detail the male and female sterilization operations. She recalled that Fosdick was fascinated—"just like a young boy in his first biology class."

VI

In 1934, the year after the Nobel Experiment ended, a spokesman for the Methodist Board of Temperance observed, "We come now face to face with the original problem, which is not Prohibition, but alcohol." This statement might serve as the text for any discussion of Fosdick's attitude toward the Eighteenth Amendment. During his early ministry, as we know, he sought through local legislation to close the saloons of Montclair. For Fosdick, as for millions of Americans, ultimately perhaps for a majority, the personal, familial, and social costs of drinking were so high as to require placing liquor under the ban of law; and if doing so meant a limitation on "personal liberty" good citizens of goodwill stood willing to accept that limitation. It must be said again that we are talking about millions of men and women, most of whom were middle-class living in cities as well as towns and villages, most of whom were progressives on other social issues, and most of whom rooted their humanitarian concern in the Christian imperative. It is true that officially evangelical Protestantism spearheaded the reform, but individual Catholics and Jews also were found in support. It is true that the crusade is associated with old-stock and white Americans, but "recent" Americans and blacks, especially those women of these groups who knew existentially the fury that followed heavy drinking by their menfolk, were not always in opposition. If the Dry forces were elitest in that blue-collar workers were underrepresented in their ranks, it is equally clear that the Social Register blue bloods were also underrepresented; moreover the Drys proclaimed that they were not fighting the working-class drinker but the "System"—the organized and well-financed liquor interests—that robbed the worker of his wages, his job, his health. Finally, the temperance movement was democratic in that it was one of the great social movements open to large numbers of women.

Though an opponent of liquor, Fosdick had not, however, favored the Eighteenth Amendment. While in France during the war, he argued with his fellow "Y" worker and prohibition proponent, Daniel Poling, asserting that the proposed amendment would be a major national catastrophe, for to "make it illegal for a man to have a glass of wine with his dinner would involve us in a reactionary movement, presenting endless difficulty." On his 1924 speaking tour of the British Isles he informed his audiences that the Eighteenth Amendment was enacted because "an overwhelming majority of the American people wanted it," adding: "But speaking personally, I believe that if America had concentrated for ten more years on its Local Option campaign, and its associated policy of education, at the end of that time it would have had the people practically unanimous in favour of Prohibition." He then made a key observation: "The people are against the liquor traffic because it is a bar to progress. The American god is not dollars but efficiency." Fosdick repeatedly urged the economic case, echoing Henry Ford's famous statement, "Booze had to go out when modern industry and the motor car came in." In 1928 he again stated his conviction that prior to the Great War America had been winning the war against liquor at the state and local level and that, therefore, the Eighteenth Amendment had been unwise and unnecessary. In 1957 Fosdick agreed with a correspondent that alcoholism was one of the chief troubles of the nation, continuing:

> I differ with you, however, about solving that terrible problem by an amendment to the federal constitution. That, I am sure, was one of the most grievous mistakes that the nation ever made. I do not see how anyone of mature years, who lived through the Prohibition period can believe that it was a success or ever could have been made a success. That is not the way to handle the problem. Indeed, the very things that you complain about now, the lack of definite, constructive effort to curb the liquor traffic, are due in no small measure to the fact that we were not content to go on with the Local Option procedure that was being really successful, and we spoiled everything by an endeavor to solve this question by an overall federal amendment to the constitution. It never could have worked, and it has done irreparable damage to the cause that both you and I stand for.

On the other hand, one should not suppose because of these statements that Fosdick favored Repeal. On the contrary, he saw nothing to do but back the law of the land and try to make a success of it. He pled for obedience to the law, scolded scofflaws, and argued for the real achievements gained as a result of prohibition, and he did so in sermons, articles, books, commencement addresses, radio talks, speeches at enforcement rallies. His public posture was confident. "It was plainly put in my hearing by Justice Taft of the Supreme Court," Fosdick informed his Park Avenue congregation, "that there is not the least infinitesimal show of a chance that the Eighteenth Amendment and its enacting laws will be repealed, because the overwhelming majority of the people want them there."

The intensity of Fosdick's feeling on the subject is revealed by two incidents. In 1925 Fosdick learned that the Rational American League, an organization working for the return of beer and light wines, had "taken the liberty" of making him an honorary life member. He was outraged: "You will allow me to express alike my amazement and indignation at this unethical proceeding. In the twenty years of my ministry I have never faced anything quite so blatantly outrageous." Still, Fosdick talked much about amending the prohibition laws to make them more acceptable and surely to permit the return of beer and light wines was not an irresponsible proposal. As a reporter at the time said of Fosdick: "With the most beguiling reasonableness, he admits the desirability of of changing the law,—as long as the proposition remains general. But let any one advance a particular change, and he is up in arms." In 1926 Fosdick learned that certain members of the Century Club were forming a committee to seek Repeal. Fosdick viewed the action as "preposterous, not to say outrageous," for it had no pertinence whatever to the purposes of the club founded for the promotion of literature and the arts and was a violation of an unwritten law of club life among gentlemen.

Perhaps Fosdick would have been less confident of the permanency of the Eighteenth Amendment if he had been more familiar—one is tempted to say, at all familiar—with New York's nightlife. Stanley Walker, a reporter who *was* knowledgeable about the city's nocturnal scene, estimated that there were at least nine thousand places where booze could be obtained in Gotham in the twenties. None of these were known to Fosdick, or at least so he stated in 1924: "I have lived for fifteen years in a city, and I have not the faintest idea where I could get a drink if I wanted one." Such a confession, or rather boast, gives point to another observation made by Walker: "Before stepping into a New York pulpit, a minister should have had a year on a metropolitan daily as a cub reporter, assigned to the police blotter and the night courts."*

On October 14, 1928, Fosdick devoted an entire sermon to the Prohibition question. In it he insisted categorically that it was not a political address designed to influence votes for or against Herbert Hoover or Alfred E. Smith or Norman Thomas. "I am speaking without intent to change any man's vote. I abhor partisan politics in the pulpit." One wonders if Fosdick was being totally candid in light of a letter he wrote Edward L. Ballard on November 7, 1928. Ballard and Ivy Lee had recommended that the sermon be printed in pamphlet form and distributed *after* Election Day. "My only comment," read Fosdick's letter, "is that, while I have already given you the privilege of doing this, I wonder a

---

* Incidentally, Walker elsewhere observed of Fosdick's preaching that "there is a strange Rotarian strain running through his sermons which often makes them very unconvincing."

little whether the matter may not be a little pointless by that time." Well, if the point of the sermon was *not* to influence voter opinion, why would delay of publication render the matter a "little pointless"?

Fosdick believed the sermon "the best thing I have done in the pulpit yet on a public question." His brother thought it "terrible." Raymond had this to say of the Hoover crowd: "We have the Anti-Saloon League, the Methodist Church, John Roach Straton, the anti-Catholic bigots, the Ku Klux Klan, the social snobs who think that the Smiths eat with their knives and would not be respectable enough for the White House (shades of Jefferson and Jackson!), the people who delight in whispering small scandal, Wall Street and big buisness, and boosters of prosperity generally—aided and abetted by the Reverend Doctor Harry Emerson Fosdick." In a long letter Harry sought to set Raymond straight, closing with the remark: "What we need more than anything else is a real liberal and progressive party but we have not got it in the Democratic organization of today nor is Al Smith fitted to lead it." Raymond's retort imagined Harry repenting and climbing toward the mourner's bench. "Come, brother come! It is never too late to mend your ways."

Of course Hoover won in 1928* only to lose to Roosevelt in 1932, and in the following year the Eighteenth Amendment was repealed, an action, incidentally, supported by John D. Rockefeller, Jr., who in a public statement confessed that he had come slowly and reluctantly to the conclusion that national prohibition had failed.

VII

In no area of American culture was the clash between the traditional and the new, formalism and modernism, sharper than in the arts; in no area did Fosdick seem so temperamentally unable to shake off the hold of the past and open himself, however gingerly, to the experimental forms of the present; in no area is Fosdick's popularity so revealing of the fact that even after the Great War myriad Americans continued to cherish the standards and expressions of bourgeois nineteenth-century culture. Philistine America was so despised in the twenties precisely because it refused to die quietly.

* Said Reinhold Niebuhr after Smith's defeat: "Never did the racial and economic prejudices of American Protestantism reveal themselves more clearly than in the recent campaign. Here was the Nordic majority rising in arms against the Slavic and Latin immigrants and using as their weapon the political party which expresses the desires and lusts of commercialism without qualification. Of course, the dominant motives were hid under the decent veil of loyalty to a moral ideal—prohibition."

Fosdick did not share the antitheatrical prejudice of Plato, Tertullian, Savonarola, Cromwell, Rousseau, or Anthony Comstock. Indeed Fosdick said, drama originally was a child of the church, and on rare instances he mentioned seeing such plays as "The Merchant of Venice," "Journey's End," and "The Green Pastures" and admiring such actors as Sir Henry Irving, Ellen Terry, and George Arliss. But these few affirmative words are drowned out by bellows of censure of the contemporary stage. Confining his cries to the twenties alone one hears him assert that the American theater is in a "deplorable condition," having largely "fallen into the hands of commercial panders who fed the populace on rottenness." The "present degradation of the stage in New York" is "notorious" and "disgraceful." The authors of "our present-day libidinous drama" are "as despicable a crew of public panders as ever debauched the imagination of a people." The producers "prostitute the drama to ignoble uses" with plays that "appeal to the waist down." "Young man," he sternly said to an imaginary individual in the congregation, "you know . . . that the modern theater in wide areas of its life is rotten and debased, and everything that money can buy and ingenuity suggest and shamelessness dare is done to appeal to passions in young men and women, hard enough, goodness knows, to handle anyway." "Cheap and vulgar drama," "filth in the theater," "unspeakable plays"— such is the Fosdickian litany.

Generally, Fosdick's remedy is to call for a rebirth of "good taste," a restoration of moral standards, the voluntary public boycott of "moral rottenness," and the voluntary public support of "plays that are excellent and of good report." To this end Fosdick agreed to serve on the Board of Directors of the Church and Drama Association (or sometimes League), a group including John W. Davis, S. Parkes Cadman, Otto H. Kahn, Felix Warburg, Dr. Cyrus Adler, Bishop William Thomas Manning, Professor William Lyon Phelps, and four Park Avenue Baptist Church laymen. In this capacity Fosdick spoke at association dinners, sought to interest fellow ministers at a luncheon he hosted at the Century Club, and invited his congregation to join one hundred thousand citizens in sending this message to Broadway: "We will back only decent plays."

Another member of the association was the playwright Channing Pollock. He resigned, he explained, not because the association failed to endorse his 1928 play, *Mr. Moneypenny*, but because of its "persistent futility." He challenged Fosdick, "I defy anyone to show me one play of the least importance endorsed by this association." The irony is that Pollock's intent in writing *Mr. Moneypenny* was "to awaken a distrust of our wasteful ways and slipping moral standards," but the critics dismissed it as a "verbal cartoon in three acts" and it closed after only sixty-one performances.

Such was Fosdick's disgust with Broadway, he hinted that the remedy might extend to official censorship. In 1920 he asked: "Do you know whether . . . the police are in cahoots with evil . . . , whether vile plays that could be stopped are being given and vile resorts are debauching the town's youth?" In 1927 after decrying the immorality of the theater, he continued: "My friends, there is going to be an end to this sometime. The history of the Anglo-Saxon race is clear on that point. We have our faults enough, heaven knows, but at the heart of us we are not utterly decadent. Up to a point we stand moral rottenness and then revolt comes, though it means beheading Charles I and putting a Puritan in his place. There will be an end to this debauch of putridity."

Reviewing Fosdick's position, one thinks of Gilbert Seldes's 1924 observation: "In America, where there is no recognized upper class to please, no official academic requirements to meet, the one tradition of gentility is as lethal as all the conventions of European society, and unlike those of Europe our tradition provides no nourishment for the artist. It is negative all the way through." Seldes must certainly have had preachers such as Fosdick in mind when he lamented that in the Lively Arts vitality and rough play must yield to the refined and genteel "until a sort of Drama League seriousness and church-sociable good form are both satisfied." When Fosdick's archenemy John Roach Straton, the New York Baptist Fundamentalist, denounced the contemporary stage, he was lampooned for not knowing Molière from Minsky, but Fosdick seemed to have escaped such criticism from the press, save for the isolated observation of one reporter that there was a suggestion of something antiseptic about his good humor: "One can imagine him, with no difficulty, talking about 'good clean fun.'"

One cannot fault Fosdick's lamentations on the grounds that bawdiness was absent from the stage; in fact, lewdness and crudeness abounded. George Jean Nathan, hardly a prude, called the 1926–1927 Broadway season "The dirtiest lot of shows . . . ever . . . put on view in the New York legitimate theatres." In that season Mae West's appearance in *Sex* drove the district attorney to close the show as he also did West's 1928 entry, *Pleasure Man*—although it must be added that she could read the line, "Beulah, peel me a grape," and make it sound not like an order to her maid but an invitation to a Roman orgy. What one does question, however, is Fosdick's failure to show any recognition of the fact that the twenties have been all but unanimously hailed as the greatest, if not the only, flowering of the theatre in America, seeing a transformation "from melodramatic piffle to world prominence." It was the time, recalled Walter Kerr, of the American theater's "rush to glory" when a great array of creative people—Eugene O'Neill, Robert Sherwood, Marc Connelly, Sidney Howard, Sherwood Anderson, Philip Barry, Elmer Rice, Sidney Kingsley, S. N. Behrman, Paul Green, Ben Hecht, Charles MacArthur, George S. Kaufman—"together with hordes of ardent playgoers, cared." The brightness, the busyness, the energy, the excitement, the brilliance all seem to have escaped Fosdick. Here is Joseph Wood Krutch's judgment of a time deemed calamitous by Fosdick: "During the immediate postwar years our new plays began for the first time to be widely and successfully produced in the major European countries and for a time, indeed, they all but dominated the European stage. Since 1918 we have had a succession of playwrights who deserve to be called 'serious' in a sense that few of their predecessors do, and we are still part of the tradition which was established then."

Even if not a single "serious" play had been written, the decade would deserve to be remembered as "The Golden Age of the American Musical." What shows! What composers and lyricists!: *Sally, Lady, Be Good!, Shuffle Along, Runnin' Wild, Rosalie, Show Boat, Funny Face, Porgy and Bess, Blossom Time, No! No! Nanette!, The Vagabond King, The Desert Song;* George Gershwin, Moss Hart, Rossetter Cole, Jerome Kern, Cole Porter, Irving Berlin, Richard Rodgers, and Rudolf Friml, Sigmund Romberg, Victor Herbert. We may assume that Fosdick avoided the *Follies* and *Scandals* and *Vanities* shows, but, still, what a pity to have lived in New York then and missed W. C. Fields, Joe Cook, the Marx Brothers, Ed Wynn, Bobby Clark, Bert Lahr, Jimmy Durante, Eddie Cantor, Fanny Brice, Willie Howard.

Considering Fosdick's application of Nice-Nelly standards to the legitimate theatre, it is not surprising to find an aura of bluenosery about his commentaries on the movies. As in the case of the stage he almost never mentioned specific shows or actors. But this lack of specificity did not prevent him from denouncing Hollywood's sex-saturated films, endorsing the newly created Hays Office of film censorship, and serving on the uplifting Motion Picture Research Council of New York. As early as his Montclair ministry Fosdick discerned something not quite respectable about the medium, and he was correct to find mildly naughty such flickering teasers as *What the Bootblack Saw* and *How Bridget Served the Salad Undressed.* Then came Theda Bara, "The Vamp"; Clara Bow, the "It" girl, with her bee-sting lips and dimpled knees, "The Hottest Jazz Baby in Films"; Rudolph Valentino, "The Sheik"; De Mille's boudoir romps and then De Mille's inspired epics placing sex orgies in a biblical setting; the brooding Greta Garbo; the daring Joan

Crawford—films promising in the ads "brilliant men, beautiful jazz babies, champagne baths, midnight revels, petting parties in the purple dawn, all ending in one terrific smashing climax that makes you gasp" and "neckers, petters, white kisses, red kisses, pleasure-mad daughters, sensation-craving mothers, . . . the truth—bold, naked, sensational."

Of course, the hegemony of sex over the screen in the twenties was not total, as witnessed by the popularity of Harold Lloyd, Richard Dix, Tom Mix, Doug Fairbanks, Sr., Mary Pickford, and Katharine Macdonald. But good or bad, dirty or clean, the movies rolled on, until by the end of the decade about 100 million Americans went to them weekly, a number nearly equal to the entire population. Twenty thousand dream palaces offered celluloid refuge, and the new movie houses *were* palaces rivaling the splendors of Versailles and Baghdad. A *New Yorker* cartoon of the period showed a child in a picture-palace lobby asking, "Mama— does God live here?" Small wonder that Fosdick was concerned, for by 1929 it was clear that middle-class America was as addicted to films as the working classes had been earlier; indeed by that date films were *aimed* at middle-class audiences. Fosdick best stated his own position in a private letter: "A lot of movies are cheap, and ought not to be supported. Some movies are among the most beautiful and artistic and uplifting opportunities that we have. The business of a minister in a community is not to keep people from attending movies, but to see to it that the best movies get to town, and then get everybody out to see them." Because the record is virtually silent on this point, the question remains open as to Fosdick's precise definitions of "cheap" and "beautiful and artistic and uplifting."

Exactly the same observation can be made about dancing. Fosdick vigorously defended the supervised dances sponsored by the Riverside Church for young people, finding in these dances no harm whatever. Ministerial assertions to the contrary, in Fosdick's book dancing feet and praying knees did go together. On the other hand, one suspects that the church never witnessed the *"pas de deux uptown"* being legged in neighboring Harlem—the bunny hug, shimmy, black bottom, Lindy hop.

The suspicion deepens when his comments on music are encountered. "Jazz" he seemed to think a four-letter word—and not because of its partial origins in the sporting houses of New Orleans or its early usage as a synonym for sexual intercourse. "We ought to love Beethoven, not jazz," he commanded. "We ought to admire Washington, not our corrupt politicians." "You do not . . . judge music by saxophone jazz; you know there is Beethoven," he noted. He asked, "Why is it that some of us do not like cheap jazz? It is because we have known and loved another kind of music." Again: "But you do not judge music by jazz;

you know there is Mozart. You do not judge architecture by filling stations; you know there is Chartres." Fosdick invariably employed in his frequent condemnations of jazz such vehement terms as "cheap," "coarse," "syncopated barbarity." A typical statement: "If a violin had been made in the first place by Antonio Stradivari himself and if skilled hands had played upon it the compositions of the masters, any cheap endeavor to make it hiccup with syncopated jazz would be resented. The violin would be ashamed." Tell that to Joe Venuti!

Louis "Father Dig" Armstrong was once asked by an admiring socialite to tell her what jazz is, and he replied, "Lady, if you got to ask what it is, you'll never know." It is sad that Fosdick was so culture bound that he was unable to open himself to America's one triumphant contribution to the world of music, and as an unhappy consequence he missed hearing in New York in that glorious era King Oliver and "Fatha" Hines and Count Basie and "Fats" Waller and "Jelly Roll" Morton and Duke Ellington, Cab Calloway, Fletcher Henderson and Bessie Smith, Mamie Smith, Ella Fitzgerald, Billie Holiday.

It already has been observed that twentieth-century literature was for Fosdick an uncongenial country. Suffice to say here that his indictments of "smut" were frequent, and there is absolutely no evidence that he recognized that the literature of the twenties was, in the words of Archibald MacLeish, "the greatest period of literary and artistic innovation since the Renaissance." There is no evidence that Fosdick understood that the postwar decade in America witnessed the most brilliant literary outpouring since the 1840s and 1850s. Wedded as he was to the earlier giants, Fosdick could not understand what Arthur Mizener meant when he asserted of that decade's authors, "If they were lost, they were lost as explorers are, not as the damned are."

Chapter Twenty-three

The Passing of Protestant America:
A Minister's Response to the
Crashing of "A Righteous Empire"

I

During Fosdick's long lifetime the United States witnessed, in the words
of Sidney Mead, "the demise of the Protestant hegemony." In the year
of Fosdick's birth that hegemony appeared indestructible despite the
heavy influx of Catholic immigrants from Ireland and Germany in the
years just preceding the Civil War and despite the fact that on the horizon legions of non-Protestant immigrants from southern and eastern
Europe were poised to "invade." The Statue of Liberty had not yet replaced Plymouth Rock as the symbol of America's promise. As late as
1927 the French author André Siegfried, in a book revealingly entitled
America Comes of Age, observed that Protestantism is America's "only
religion and to ignore that fact is to view the country from a false angle."
The 1920s, however, were merely a kind of Indian Summer for Protestant, Anglo-Saxon, or British-American domination. By the time of Fosdick's retirement and certainly by the year of his death, the older Protestant America had become, in the words of Martin Marty, "as obsolete as
the side-wheel showboat, the cigar-store Indian, or the Fourth of July
oration." The "Righteous Empire" (to borrow again from Marty) had
crumbled. America had changed from a Protestant nation to a "three-
religion country"—Protestant, Catholic, Jew. This new pluralistic society, according to Will Herberg's topology, may be conceived as one
great community divided into three big subcommunities religiously defined, but all now equally "American" in their identification with the
American way of life.*

* To Herberg's three religious communities there should be obviously added a
fourth large group, the unchurched.

Fosdick's credentials as a WASP are of course impeccable.* The purpose of this chapter will be to examine how one Baptist minister of pioneer stock responded to the erosion of that Protestant hegemony that had seemed to secure in his youth and how he reacted to those "new" citizens flooding the country who would (if they could) roughly retire the senior partners from the seats of power or at least force them to share those privileged seats.

II

President Franklin D. Roosevelt once opened an address before the Daughters of the American Revolution, that red-blooded organization of blue bloods who apparently believe that one revolution in American history is quite enough, with the salutation, "Fellow immigrants." And the historian Oscar Handlin opened his study *The Uprooted* with the confession, "Once I thought to write a history of the immigrants in America. Then I discovered that the immigrants *were* American history." With the major exception of those carried by force from their home in Africa and the native Americans who possessed the land before the arrival of the Europeans, all Americans are in truth, whether immediately or distantly, part of a vast stream of immigration. Between the year William McKinley enlisted as a private in the 23rd Ohio Volunteer Infantry in the Civil War and his assassination at the hands of a twenty-eight-year-old Polish-American with the "sinister" name of Czolgosz, 14 million people came to the United States, "new" immigrants from southern and eastern Europe accounting for ever 50 percent of the total by 1900. In the opening fourteen years of the new century the torrent accelerated rather than slackened, an average of 1 million entering annually, and now the "new" immigrants accounted for 72 percent. Among those arriving were 2 million Jews, one third of the entire Jewish population of eastern Europe and Russia, and 2 million Italians, mostly from the poorest regions of the south and Sicily. The tide was temporarily stemmed by the war, but with the coming of peace it was renewed. From June 1920 to June 1921 more than 800,000 individuals entered, and counsels in Europe reported that additional millions were planning to follow them. Then in a series of momentous enactments, Congress dramatically reduced the permitted number of entries from outside the Western Hemisphere to 150,000. Many citizens were now relieved that "their" country

---

* John Higham perceptively noted that by the 1960s WASP had become the only ethnic slur that could be safely used in polite society.

would no longer be "invaded" by those "beaten men of beaten races," those mongrel worshippers of Bacchus or Baal or Marx or the Whore of Rome. Fosdick favored closing the gates more tightly. "I am a restrictionist in immigration because I am not a sentimentalist," he reported. In its early history America could generously cry, "Give me your tired, your poor, your huddled masses yearning to breathe free," but now the situation in the nation and in the world made this open door policy dangerously unrealistic. "How can a man who faces the facts fail to see two things: first, that so far as this country is concerned, we cannot handle the problem physically or morally if, with the population of the globe multiplying itself by two every sixty years, we open our gates freely to the teeming peoples, and, second, that if we should it would not solve any other people's problems." Fosdick's position was directly related to his concerns over the quality of life in the United States and the perils of overpopulation to the world.

Three things must be emphasized here because of the link between immigrant restriction and an ugly nativism buttressed by an insidious pseudoscientific racism. First, save for certain immigrant groups and some social workers and employers hungering for cheap labor, almost all citizens, including the most progressive members of Congress and labor union leaders, favored restriction. The issue was *not* fought along liberal-conservative lines. Second, the total exclusion of Japanese under the act of 1924 (which now meant the total exclusion of all Orientals) was in Fosdick's judgment a "wretched blunder" and "appalling insult." He apologized to a Japanese Christian for "the rude and inexcusable, discourteous bad manners of the Senate." He damned the "abominable journals as the Hearst press" for whipping up national support for this legislative folly in a letter to a missionary in Japan. In a radio sermon he declared: "The Exclusion Act stands as one of the most senseless, needless, intolerable pieces of racial prejudice ever perpetrated by a great nation. If we have any moral indignation to spare on racial prejudice, let us spend a little of it on ourselves!" Third, under the quota system established by the legislation of the twenties, immigrants from the newer sources of southern and eastern Europe were discriminated against in favor of those from the older sources, especially Great Britain. But Fosdick repeatedly warned against buying the "foolish ideas of 'Nordic supremacy' " sweeping the land. Witness this passage from a 1926 sermon:

> Consider . . . the myth about the Nordic race that has gained such popular ascendency among us in recent years. You know how the myth runs. Once upon a time, a long while ago, nature produced some unique germ plasm. There never was, there never will be, in nature's long course, any

germ plasm equalling that. It is the Nordic germ plasm. We have it; we are the superior race and all others are inferior. Now, is there any solid, scientific basis for that Nordic myth? There is not. You know those books by Lothrop Stoddard [*The Rising Tide of Color*] and the rest [*The Passing of the Great Race*], vividly written and widely devoured. But the really scientific books, that are not so popularly written, with one voice deny the fake biology that underlies this unbalanced propaganda.

The fear that the American wheat was being choked by alien tares and that worldwide the great Nordic race was being drowned in a rising tide of color was an important factor in drawing 3 or 4 or 5 million Americans into the hooded ranks of the revived Ku Klux Klan of the twenties. As these anxious men donned their white dream robes, they dreamed that the clock might be stopped and America returned to its fanciful older purity. Inquired Imperial Wizard William Joseph Simmons: "What were the dangers which the white man saw threatening to crush and overwhelm Anglo-Saxon civilization? The dangers were in the tremendous influx of foreign immigration, tutored in alien dogmas and alien creeds, flowing in from all climes and slowly pushing the native-born white American population into the center of the country, there to be ultimately overwhelmed and smothered." Simmons's successor, Hiram Welsey Evans, elaborated: "When the Klan first appeared the nation was in the confusion of sudden awakening from the lovely dream of the melting pot, disorganized and helpless before the invasion of aliens and alien ideas. After ten years of the Klan it arms for defense."

Once again Fosdick alerted his people to "the sin of prejudice" and the perils of the Klan, "that apotheosis of prejudice." "When . . . today you hear a man say, 'I hate Jews, Roman Catholics, Japanese, negroes,' you are dealing with a belated mind. That man may dress like a modern, ride in an automobile, listen over the radio, but his mind is properly dated about a thousand B.C." Precisely because the Klan sought desperately (and successfully in the case of individuals, but not in the case of whole denominations) to be seen by Protestants as an ally, Fosdick took the gloves in a 1922 warning against any such entangling alliance: "The one thing that will never do any good is this utterly un-American thing— this secret order of Protestants making the night its cover and tar and feathers its instruments. To commit the welfare of our institutions to such keeping is to lose them, and the Protestant churches of this country would better say so."

As an old-stock Baptist minister, Fosdick might well have been a Klan Kludd; instead he was importuned to join and accepted membership in a number of organizations formed to battle bigotry.

III

For one year only, 1899, the federal immigration authorities compiled a record of the religious affiliation of immigrants. Protestants numbered 18.5 percent of the total and Roman Catholics 52.1 percent. If this year was typical, it is little wonder that the Roman Catholic Church gained in membership 114.1 percent from 1890 to 1916, and that by the time Fosdick embarked upon his New York ministry there were almost 18 million baptized members, that is, every sixth American and every third church member was a Roman Catholic. Anti-Catholicism had been a persistent theme in the history of American nativism, in fact it was termed the anti-Semitism of nineteenth-century America. Father James Hennessey, S.J., has likened being a Catholic in America in the nineteenth-century and, at least psychologically, until well into the twentieth century to the predicament of a square peg in a round hole. The consequence, historically, to employ the terms of Will Herberg, was a "Catholic claustrophia" matched by a "Protestant paranoia."*

To place Fosdick's attitude toward his Catholic coreligionists in perspective three things need to be observed. First, Fosdick's Baptist heritage made especially sharp his convictions concerning the separation of church and state. Second, during his pastorate in New York, Protestant church membership in the city was equaled by Roman Catholic membership and was not vastly larger than the Jewish population. Put another way, bona fide Protestant membership, white and black, was between only 6 or 8 percent of the total city population. That is, in terms of sheer numbers, in Gotham Fosdick belonged to a minority group. Third, to attribute all Protestant-Catholic tensions to irrational bigotry and to dismiss all religious conflict as sheer intolerance is a secularist fancy, which no devout Protestant, however irenic, would accept, and no loyal Catholic, either, if candid.

In New York's 1922 gubernatorial campaign Fosdick informed his father that he would probably vote for Al Smith's Republican opponent, acknowledged by Fosdick to be "outrageously reactionary." Smith had already served one term as governor honestly, efficiently, and progressively. Was Fosdick influenced by Smith's Catholicism? The letter to the father does not say. We know that Fosdick voted against Smith in the presidential election of 1928. We know that in arguing the decision with his brother he did not mention the religious factor. Further, on the eve

---

* To round things out Herberg also discerned a "Jewish schizophrenia."

of the election, pressed by reporters and responding to the rumor that he was in Smith's camp, he gave this public statement: "In announcing my intention to vote for Mr. Hoover, however, let me say emphatically that the religious question has nothing to do with it and that I abhor the un-American attitude which considers any candidate's ecclesiastical affiliation as a reason either for supporting or not supporting him for office. Let me add also that my preference for Mr. Hoover implies no lack of respect for Mr. Smith as a high-minded and courageous public servant."

Thirty-two years after Smith's defeat the American people were presented for only the second time with an opportunity to elect a Catholic to the Presidency. Fosdick voted for John F. Kennedy and was "proud of it." During the campaign Fosdick publicly praised Kennedy's "forthright and honest statement" before the Greater Houston Ministerial Association, adding, "I deplore with deep contempt the bigotry that is making this anti-Catholic issue such a disgrace in this country."

In 1937, as the Spanish Civil War deepened in cruelty and carnage, the prelates of the Church in Spain issued a pastoral letter in support of the defender of the faith, General Franco, and denounced the anti-Christ Republican forces. Privately Fosdick considered this letter "one of the most vicious bits of propaganda for fascism ever issued in this country," adding, "I am altogether anti-communist, anti-fascist, and pro-democracy." He then joined with 149 Protestant clergy and lay persons in signing a public reply to the Spanish hierarchy.* The famed Monsignor Fulton J. Sheen twice stated publicly that Fosdick admitted to not having read the document and had expressed regret that he had signed it. Fosdick set Sheen straight. He had not "the slightest regret" in signing the statement and he could not "imagine where any valid authority would come" for Sheen's allegations to the contrary. The Monsignor backed off, but only a step. "Do you not think," he asked Fosdick, "that when anti-Christian and anti-God forces are at work religion should join a United Front against their united affront? God must mean more to us than any propaganda masquerading under the name of 'democracy.'" To this Fosdick replied: "I have never felt called upon to take sides in the Spanish conflict, as though I thought all good were on one side and all evil on the other. What troubles me in the present position of the Roman Catholic Hierarchy, as I get its echoes in this country, is that it seems to be forcing a choice between Fascism and Communism; as though influenced by the Italian situation, let us say, if one is anti-communist, he must be pro-

---

* In 1937 also Fosdick joined others in public protest against the bombing by Franco's forces of the Basque city of Guernica, killing eight hundred civilians.

fascist. Personally, I am against both Communism and Fascism and am strong for Democracy." The latter closed: "As you laid your concern on my conscience, so I lay my concern on yours. Nothing would clear up the present difficulty more than to have the Roman Catholic leaders [in the United States] make perfectly plain that they are not trying to drive the American people into a choice between Fascism and Communism. The American people is against both Fascism and Communism and wants neither. It cries, 'A plague on both your houses.' It wants democracy." (A decade later, revealing again that Fosdick was not a good hater, he said for publication in the *Reader's Digest:* "I salute this priest. He is a real servant of the Church, this Monsig. Fulton J. Sheen.")*

In 1949 Sheen's superior, Francis Joseph Cardinal Spellman, found himself compelled to rebuke America's most eminent woman, Eleanor Roosevelt. In her newspaper column, "My Day," Mrs. Roosevelt took a moderate (as she saw it, but the Cardinal did not) position against granting direct public funds to aid parochial schools. Spellman's public letter chastising Mrs. Roosevelt closed, "For, whatever you may say in the future, your record of anti-Catholicism stands for all to see—a record which you yourself wrote on the pages of history which cannot be recalled—documents of discrimination unworthy of an American mother!"

This challenged many Protestant churchmen to come to the defense of Mrs. Roosevelt, including Fosdick's Scotch successor at Riverside, McCracken. Asked by McCracken about the advisability of entering public debate on the vexing question of state aid to parochial schools, Fosdick replied: "By all means speak your mind on it, and on the pretensions of the hierarchy, and the threat of Roman Catholic totalitarian policies. You can do so with genuine respect for the real values in the *religion* of Roman Catholics, so that no one can rightly think of what you say as ill-considered or ill-tempered or merely prejudiced. I am sure that Protestants must stand up and talk straight under present circumstances. I should do that, were I in the ring as once I was."

Fosdick may have been out of the ring, but his Baptist conscience would not permit him to remain silent when his fellow Baptist, President Harry S. Truman, announced on October 20, 1951, the appointment of the first U.S. ambassador to the Vatican, General Mark Clark. In this instance "Give 'Em Hell Harry" Truman was on the receiving end of Fosdick's blistering, unmeasured letter to the President closing, "This deplorable appointment will, I am sure, prove to be as imprudent and ill-advised as it certainly is false to the traditional principles of our Re-

---

* Sheen does not mention Fosdick in his memoirs.

public." Clark withdrew his nomination on January 13, 1952, and Truman announced he would make a new nomination, but never did so.* Protestant fears concerning this issue approached clinically paranoid proportions when the *Christian Century* editorialized in December 1952: "The worst mistake the new [Eisenhower] administration could make, short of plunging the world into atomic war, would be to send an ambassador to the Vatican."†

Fosdick's posture regarding Protestant-Catholic relations is difficult to categorize absolutely. On the one hand, he could be blunt in the extreme. "The absolute autocracy of the Roman Catholic Church," he once declared, "is nothing in the world but a copy of the Roman Empire, and the autocracy of the Pope is only a copy of the absolutism of the Caesars." Fosdick noted the collaboration of the Church with reactionary regimes in Italy, Spain, and Latin America. He thought he discerned an attempt on the part of the hierarchy in the United States to impose its will in matters ranging from birth control to political control. To a Lutheran girl engaged to a Catholic boy and disturbed about having to sign a pledge to raise any children they might have in the Catholic faith, he flashed a warning not to sign the pledge lightly: "No matter what your fiancé may say now, the hour will inevitably strike when you will find yourself separated from your children in the deepest thinking and believing of their lives. I stress this because I have seen so many heartbreaks due to this outrageous condition that the Roman Catholic Church puts upon the marriage of Roman Catholics with Protestants."

On the other hand, over the decades Fosdick said many handsome things, publicly and privately, about the Roman Catholic Church, affirming its positive aspects. He urged the cooperation of Protestantism and Catholicism in common causes: "Let the best in Protestantism do everything possible to cooperate with the best in Roman Catholicism."‡ He shared public platforms with priests in seeking an end to misunderstanding. He numbered priests among his friends, notably George Barry Ford, S.J. And his grandson married a Catholic girl with his blessing.

---

* In December 1939 President Franklin D. Roosevelt had appointed Myron Taylor as his "personal representative" to the Vatican, a deed not requiring confirmation by the Senate.

† In 1984 the "born again" Protestant President Ronald Reagan successfully appointed an ambassador to the Vatican and Protestant opposition to the action was surprisingly muted.

‡ Remember that it was not until after Vatican II, that is, not until the eve of Fosdick's death, that Catholic clergy and laymen were freed from the heavy restrictions placed by the Church on their cooperating with Protestants.

Chapter Twenty-four

Racial Justice:
A Minister's Response
to America's Deepest Sin

I

At 11:05 Sunday morning, May 4, 1969, James Forman, former executive secretary of the Student Nonviolent Coordinating Committee and now spokesman for the newly formed National Black Economic Development Conference, marched down the aisle of the Riverside Church, flanked by six black comrades. He brushed aside two elderly ushers, ascended the six chancel steps, turned around and faced the congregation, leaning on a cane and standing with his legs wide apart. He waited for the choir and congregation to finish the opening hymn, "When Morning Gilds the Skies." Then, as the minister, Ernest T. Campbell, mounted the lectern to speak, Forman began to read the demands of his Black Manifesto. Campbell left the sanctuary, joined by the associate ministers, choir, and many worshippers. Forman proceeded to announce his five demands to the stunned remaining parishioners: classrooms in the church for the use of Harlem residents; rent-free office space for his group, with unrestricted telephone rights; unrestricted use of the church's FM radio station twelve hours a day and weekends and the right to select the station's director and staff; a proportion of the church's assets; and appropriation by his group of sixty percent of the yearly income from all the church's security and real estate investments. Riverside Church had been singled out, Forman explained in a steady voice, because it was a racist institution "in the heart of the Harlem community" and because it was tainted by Rockefeller wealth. The night before, according to Campbell, he and Forman had reached an informal agreement that would have permitted Forman to distribute the manifesto outside the church.

"We are dead serious about our demands, and we are prepared to die for their implementation," asserted the black leader. Forman may be believed. In his autobiography he recalled his feelings that Communion Sunday morning. A hatred beyond anger gave him strength and determination: a hatred of capitalism, racism, the West, and the "so-called Christianity" that "fucked up my young life in terrible ways." Forman recalled the satisfaction of seeing Campbell tremble "at the sight of a black revolutionary standing in his church."*

Fosdick could not have been unaware of the incident. Ninety years old, cruelly crippled by arthritis, only months from death, his mind was still alert. Surely he followed the wide coverage in the New York press and surely his daughters and friends at Riverside supplied him with the details. And he could not have been other than puzzled. Riverside had never drawn the color line and by the late 1960s it enjoyed a very substantial black membership. The Rockefellers generally and John D. Rockefeller, Jr., specifically had contributed millions of dollars to sustain and advance the cause of American blacks living in the South and in Harlem and in such manifold fields as health, housing, education, theological training, recreation facilities, social work, employment programs, unemployment relief, and in the support of such organizations as the National Association for the Advancement of Colored People (N.A.A.C.P.) and the National Urban League.

Moreover, only two years earlier, on April 4, 1967, it was from the pulpit of the Riverside Church that Martin Luther King, Jr., in a famous sermon committed himself to the peace movement and thundered against the unjust war the United States was waging in Vietnam. Indeed King had a standing agreement to preach annually in Riverside, and it was there he preached his last sermon before his assassination. As Fosdick pondered the Forman incident perhaps he recalled the words that King wrote on the flyleaf of the personal copy of *Stride Toward Freedom* the great black leader had presented to him: "If I were called upon to select the greatest preacher of this century, I would choose your name. If I were called upon to select the foremost prophets of our generation, I would choose you to head the list. If I were called upon to select the Christian saints of our day, again I would have to place you on the list. Because of all these things and the inspiration youve [sic] been to me,

---

* Campbell's measured response was set forth in a sermon preached July 13, 1969, entitled "The Case for Reparations." A Riverside Church lay leader, Francis Harmon, was responsible for an injunction to prevent Forman's group from further disrupting Riverside's services, thereby winning from Forman the epithet, "that Rockefeller stooge—the former racist attorney from Mississippi." Some black worshippers at the service scolded Forman as did some Harlem ministers. Ironically, a granddaughter of John D. Rockefeller, Jr., was one of Forman's financial benefactors.

I present you this book." Fosdick, whose endorsement of the book had been used in the advertisements, replied to King in a characteristically modest fashion: "As for that inscription, my dear friend, I never possibly could deserve it. I am a very humble minister of the church and while I have had to fight a good fight several times in my life, I am sure that I never faced the kind of problem that you face with anything like the courage that you have so magnificently displayed."

James Forman hated the "Christian churches for the centuries of exploitation and oppression which they had inflicted on black people around the world." Echoed James Baldwin: "It is not too much to say that whoever wishes to become a truly moral being must first divorce himself from all the prohibitions, crimes and hypocrisies of the Christian Church." Wrote an older crusader for his people, W. E. B. Du Bois, "If the treatment of the Negro by the Christian church is called 'divine,' this is an attack on the conception of God more blasphemous than any which the church has always been so ready and eager to punish." Asserted a black spokesman in 1925, "Of all the groups devoted to social uplift, I have the least hope in the white Christian ministers." Yet Martin Luther King, Jr., was a minister of Christ who commanded: "Jesus still cries out across the centuries: 'Love your enemies.' We must learn to meet hate with love." King, the Southern black Baptist preacher, was murdered for daring to dream of a racism-free America. Fosdick died the following year. In this chapter we shall see how a Northern white Baptist preacher born only shortly after the end of legal slavery in America confronted the sin of racism in society, in the Christian churches, and indeed in his own heart.

II

In his autobiography Fosdick reported that in "my family any kind of racial discrimination was anathema" and his brother in his autobiography expressed the certainty that in the Buffalo of his boyhood "there were no racial prejudices." Both brothers employ the archaic term "colored" and both relate the story of a runaway slave who died of fright while being sheltered in their grandfather's house, a station on the Underground Railway—a story perhaps unconsciously imputing courage to white abolitionists and a contrasting quality to the slaves they wanted to help.

Of course, Fosdick was a child of his time, but it is, nevertheless, necessary to make the hard observation that this crusader for racial justice never quite comprehended the depth and breadth of racism in America and never displayed quite the sensitive understanding of the black experience one might hope from an author of psychological studies. Fosdick very clearly grew in comprehension, contrition, and sensitivity as the decades passed, but it is equally clear that he had considerable growing to do.

A study of Protestant preaching in Fosdick's generation might reveal that much of the "humor" found in these sermons took the form of "funny" stories attributed to "colored folks."* Fosdick was not immune from this particular manifestation of racism—a manifestation all the more telling because innocent of conscious racist intent. References to "as a colored minister remarked . . ." and "Rastus fleeing from a bear . . ." dot Fosdick's sermons in the twenties. And they never totally disappeared. Addressing a gathering of celebrities at the Waldorf-Astoria in 1938, Fosdick reported that in response to a "National Vespers" radio sermon he had received "a letter from a colored CCC Camp which says that the service came in over the air, and, if I remember rightly, stopped two fights, three crap games and all manner of profanity." The audience, it was reported, howled. They might have considered that the Civilian Conservation Corps, one of the justly heralded New Deal measures, had segregated camps for the white and black youth of America. As late as the 1940s Fosdick in a radio sermon told of the "colored minister" who in "an awe-struck voice" offered up the prayer, "O Thou great and unscrupulous God." It almost goes without saying that Fosdick, like almost all white Americans of his generation, employed privately such unfortunate expressions as "I wouldn't take it if a nigger boy brought it to me on a silver platter."

In his early and midministry Fosdick shared in the general assumptions prevailing in the West about "darkest Africa"—a term he used—believing, for example, that when the missionary Mackay arrived in Uganda, he breathed "a new spirit into depraved and barbarous folk." In *The Meaning of Service* Fosdick speaks of "a naked savage nine years old, discovered by a missionary in the jungles of Africa. His father is a worshipper of demons, obsessed by witchcraft; his mother is a native of the forest; his tribe is sunk in the depths of barbarism. He borrows a bit of calico from his mother for a loincloth and leaves his home for a Wesleyan school." Naturally, he is transformed into a civilized Christian of beautiful spirit. And here is a statement from a 1920 sermon:

> Races are not equal. I no more know why than I know why one son of a
> family will be a genius, and another a dunce. Only here is the fact; you

---

* For what it is worth, in the past thirty-five years I have had the occasion to read thousands of sermons preached by white ministers and my strong impression is that the only group to rival blacks as a source of "humor" are the Irish.

put the Anglo-Saxon people almost anywhere on earth, and before very long they will be running the government. The African people after unimpeded tenure of a whole continent for unnumbered ages have never, unaided, been able to establish a settled government. There is no use in blinking our eyes to these plain facts. The solution of the problem does not mean blinking the fact of the problem. The strong and the weak, side by side, in individuals and races; we must somehow live together on this earth.

To be sure, Fosdick tempered his position with disavowals of any biological or innate basis of racial differences, reminding his audience of the barbarism, superstition, and cruelty of the peoples of the British Isles and Europe in earlier times. "For one thing," he cautioned, "if we regard human history in the large it is clear that, *strong and weak alike, we are all coming up together from the same primitive conditions, and that we who in any sense are strong are simply those who are a little way ahead.* Our strength does not belong to us in fee simple to possess and to use as we will. We are custodians of the gains of the whole race for the sake of mankind." Moreover, time and again his sermons carried hard reminders of the crimes committed by the Christian West against other peoples and of the sinful conditions within the dominions of the so-called civilized nations. Yet even when Fosdick's intention was to combat racism his arguments rested on assumptions of white cultural superiority. Consider this answer to a leading racist theorist of the 1920s:

One would like to take Lothrop Stoddard when he was six months old and exchange him for a negro baby in the heart of Africa, of a similar age, and let Lothrop Stoddard grow up in the negro tribe and let the negro child grow up in the finest Anglo-Saxon environment. Would heredity be everything? You know well that Lothrop Stoddard would grow up a cannibal, that he would be afraid of ghosts and believe in witch doctors, that he would marry ten wives if he could possibly gain money enough to buy them, that he would eat meat raw, and be petrified with fright the first time he saw an automobile, if he should ever see one. And you know well that the same night Lothrop Stoddard died of fright [as the runaway slave!] at a witch doctor's curse the negro who had been exchanged for him might very possibly put on evening dress and have a wonderful time listening to Beethoven's Ninth Symphony. Heredity everything? That is nonsense.

Regarding blacks in America, some of Fosdick's statements convey the same sense of white condecension. The "negro problem" was not solved when "we gave him liberty," Fosdick asserted. The "problem" was now the "colored" man's handling of his freedom and must be solved "in the hearts and homes, the schools and churches of the colored races." In a 1925 sermon he maintained that "racial differences are important" and that "Booker T. Washington was right in his great faith: 'We can be as separate as the five fingers, and yet as one as the hand.' "

In light of this endorsement of the Washingtonian position, it is not surprising that in the twenties Fosdick did not believe in the wisdom of interracial marriages. As he preached in 1928, "The fact that all souls are equal before God does not mean that it necessarily is wise to marry across all racial lines. It is hard enough to make a successful marriage when everything is on your side including community of racial inheritance and tradition. Let no man add to the natural difficulties in the way of a successful marriage deep divergencies of racial tradition without thinking a long time." On this question the decades did not bring a change of mind. Answering in 1944 a troubled letter from a young woman, Fosdick affirmed:

> Just because we give [sic] Negroes fundamental justice in the presence of the law, in politics, in economic opportunity, and in educational opportunity, that does not mean we approve of intermarriage. As a matter of fact, I thoroughly disapprove of it, not because one race is superior and the other inferior, but because even under the best of circumstances marriage is not altogether easy to make a success of, and a marriage between two different races, like the Negro and the white man now, interposes colossal obstacles in the way of success. The plain fact is, however, as all students of the problem say, that the blacks no more want to marry the whites than the whites want to marry the blacks. Just because we are fundamentally decent to one another, we do not have to marry Chinese, Japanese, Spanish-American, or Hindoos. All thoughtful students of the problem, therefore, regard the marriage question as an alibi that people use who do not want to face up to the real problem that lies underneath, namely, fundamental justice.

Fourteen years later Fosdick confirmed his earlier stance. Although by 1958 the Riverside Church membership was composed of a number of races, especially Orientals, intermarriage was infrequent, thus, Fosdick noted, Riverside is a "striking argument against the fears of the South that wild intermarriage will result from the mixing of races." And he added, perhaps too readily, that not once in his ministry had he been asked to perform a racially mixed marriage ceremony. Whatever may be said of the pragmatism of Fosdick's posture, surely the Kingdom of God is a kingdom without caste and in such a kingdom racial differences would cease to make any difference whatsoever in even the most intimate of relationships, marriage.

III

It must be frankly acknowledged then that white-skinned Fosdick was unable totally to transcend the cultural conditioning of the white racist society in which he lived. But although this may be the first word to be said, it must not, in fairness, be the last. Fosdick was a faithful servant of the God who is no respecter of persons. Fosdick was loyal to the God who "hath created of one blood all men to dwell on the face of the earth." Fosdick heard the good news that all, bond and free, are one in Christ Jesus. These things being true, Fosdick with increasing clarity proclaimed the judgment on racism of a God who is not mocked.

Racism was "the most evil thing in the world" said H. G. Wells, and Fosdick concurred. Racial prejudice is as ancient as the story of the Tower of Babel and, judged Fosdick, "has in it more concentrate evil, more poison to cause human agony than almost any other cruelty of man." Racial discrimination in the United States embodied the whole Nazi philosophy of race. In a 1939 sermon Fosdick made this telling point when he reported the segregation suffered by Jews in Germany: "Jim Crow cars for Jews—that is an outrage! But Jim Crow cars are not a Nazi invention; they are an American invention. The Nazis, working out their program of racial discrimination, are borrowing some of their techniques from us." In another sermon Fosdick said: "Race prejudice is as thorough a denial of the Christian God as atheism is and it is a much more common form of apostasy. Race prejudice denies the universal fatherhood of God; it denies the New Testament's insistence on the equality of all souls before God; it denies the central affirmation of the gospel, that God so loved the world that he gave his Son, and as for Jesus of Nazareth, who took his hero, the Good Samaritan, from a despised race, anyone who harbors race prejudice parts company with him."

Fosdick supported his scores of general indictments of racism with scores of concrete illustrations of its manifestations in America. In 1919, a year when the land was drenched in the blood of blacks butchered in race riots and lynchings, the parishioners of Old First Church were confronted with this "curse and shame of America," Fosdick concluding the sermon with these severe words: "As one thinks, then, of the abominable sins that we still harbor within the limits of our commonwealth, to our disgrace and the world's amusement, the bestial cruelty, the lawless mobs, the strangling victims, or too often the fagot and the fire, he sees what benediction it would be to us if this old law of Leviticus even, could come to bear upon us, with its sobriety, with its self-restraint, with its lawfulness, with its sense of justice. Eye for an eye! No more!" In another early sermon Fosdick asked the worshippers to consider this situation: "Imagine yourself in Tokyo talking to a prominent liberal Japanese. You have been giving him some Christian admonition about the cruel mistakes of Japan in Korea and when you are all through, with his inimitable Japanese courtesy, he turns and says, 'You are entirely right. We all have our lamentable failures to regret. By the way, I have forgotten just how many people you lynched in your Christian country this last year.' " In a wartime sermon Fosdick beat the same theme: "In the last fifty years five thousand persons have been lynched in this country, a large percentage of them Negroes and many of them under circumstances—tortured, burned alive—that beggar description. That kind of thing is known all over the world, and when some people think of America they think of our treatment of American Negroes, and, contemplating a victory of the white races, they ask, Can any good come out of that?"

Fosdick recognized that de facto segregation in the North was as unchristian as open segregation in the South. "No section of the country is free from blame. Whether it be Jim Crow segregation, the closing of hotels and restaurants to Negroes, the refusal to address them as Mr. or Miss or Mrs., accosting them only by their given names, the denial to them of equality before the law, at the ballot box, and in educational opportunity, or the restriction of their employment to certain narrow fields regardless of their abilities, North and South alike we must rethink our attitudes toward the Negro if we are not to make a farce of democracy. And nowhere is this more true than in our churches where often it is sheer hypocrisy to read from the New Testament, 'There cannot be Greek and Jew, circumcision and uncircumcision, barbarian, Sythian, bondman, freeman; but Christ is all, and in all.' "

Fosdick was particularly incensed by the treatment accorded Negro servicemen in World War II, citing specific instances of black soldiers being beaten by the police for daring to enter a railroad station restaurant and black soldiers transporting German prisoners being forced to eat in station kitchens, whereas their charges dined in station restaurants.

Further, Fosdick asked his white audiences to put themselves in the place of the Negroes and see from the inside how America must appear to them. "We all know the unfair discrimination that makes the Negro people resentful. Of course they are resentful; they ought to be; we would be, too." Of course these prophetic utterances brought from some individuals letters of thanks for freeing them from the bonds of prejudice and from others letters of protest for stirring up Negro unrest.

IV

When Fosdick's granddaughter, Patty Downs, was an exchange student at Tennessee's Fiske University—one of ten whites in a student body of twelve hundred—she took part in a stand-in demonstration to desegregate movie theatres in Nashville, and was thrown in jail. When she telephoned the news to him, he cried spontaneously, "Hurrah! Keep up the good work." Fosdick engaged in no freedom marches. He never stared down the muzzle of a redneck's shotgun or felt the shock of a sheriff's cattle prod or the bite of an attack dog or shared a jail cell with lunch-counter demonstrators. Unlike a sacrificial few, he did not resign his Morningside Heights pastorate to embark on a ministry to Harlem's dwellers. Yet that "Hurrah!" for his granddaughter was heartfelt, for Fosdick had long labored in other ways beside preaching prophetic sermons to rid the nation of the sin of racism.

He appealed to Congress to pass antilynching legislation and sponsored rallies supporting such legislation. In 1935 he signed a "friend of the court" brief for Angelo Herndon, a young black Communist, who was prosecuted and persecuted by the State of Georgia for "attempting to incite insurrection"—that is, for leading a protest march of unemployed blacks and whites. He termed the Scottsboro Case a "miscarriage of justice," was a member of the Sponsoring Committee of the Scottsboro Defense Committee, and earlier (it will be remembered) had persuaded Ruby Bates to recant her perjured story. For years he was a sponsor of the National Committee to Abolish the Poll Tax. When parishioners requested advice as to what to read on race relations in America, he praised Myrdal's *An American Dilemma* as "far and away the most objective, dispassionate, and adequate . . . that has ever been written." He deplored it when Marian Anderson was denied the facilities of Constitution Hall. As one of the electors, he helped choose Booker T. Washington as the first black to be given a place in the American Hall of Fame, and he approved of a statue of the black leader, carved in stone, among the sculptures in Riverside. He congratulated Senator Harry S. Truman for introducing a bill for the acquisition of the birthplace of Dr. George Washington Carver as the first federal memorial to a black. He sent checks to Southern Negro universities, such as Fiske, for the purchase of library books and on retirement, he reported, "I gave away a lot of my books to Southern Negro colleges." He belonged to organizations committed to the end of racial discrimination, such as the Interracial Fellowship of Greater New York and the Interracial Music

Council, Inc., and spoke from Harlem pulpits under the auspices of these organizations.

Fosdick, working with the Citizens' Committee on Harlem, persuaded the Chase Manhattan Bank to break the color line and employ six black tellers. When the bank lunchrooms were closed to the new tellers, he brought this miserable state of affairs to the attention of John D. Rockefeller, Jr., and (hardly surprising!) Chase relented. In 1948 he was chairman of the sponsoring committee seeking to raise funds for Morningside Community Center on the western edge of Harlem. He praised the New York State Fair Employment Practices Commission and publicly urged the passage by Congress of the F.E.P.C. bill before it, a bill calculated, Fosdick informed his readers, "to minimize discrimination solely because of race, creed or color in the employment of persons otherwise fully qualified for specific work opportunities."

In 1958 Fosdick received a letter from Thurgood Marshall, then director and counsel of the Legal Defense and Educational Fund, Inc., informing him that he was being honored for his services as a member of the board of directors of the fund. The award was merited. For years Fosdick had been a member of "The Committee of 100" dedicated to the "Creation of an America of Justice and Equality for Our Negro Fellow Citizens" and one of its activities was to raise monies for the N.A.A.C.P. budget. On June 9, 1953, Fosdick joined Thurgood Marshall and Walter White in sending a telegram to leading citizens soliciting funds for the preparation of the N.A.A.C.P. briefs in the historic 1954 Supreme Court decision of *Brown* v. *Board of Education of Topeka*, the funds to be sent to Allan Knight Chalmers, chairman of "The Committee of 100" and Fosdick's close ministerial friend. The telegram outlined the legal background and closed on a note of urgency:

POSTPONEMENT COMES AFTER THREE YEARS LEGAL ACTIONS UP THROUGH LOWER COURTS, COSTING $58,000 FOR LEGAL EXPENSES, DOCUMENTATION EXPOSING GROSSLY INFERIOR SCHOOL FACILITIES AND EXPENSES FOR EXPERT AUTHORITIES WHO TESTIFIED CHILDREN SEVERELY PENALIZED BY INFERIOR TREATMENT DURING FORMATIVE YEARS. WORK MADE POSSIBLE ONLY THROUGH CONTRIBUTIONS FROM CITIZENS WHO UNDERSTAND SIGNIFICANCE TO NATIONAL LIFE AND IMPACT UPON WORLD STRUGGLE. FUNDS ENTIRELY SPENT. HIGHEST COURT NOW REQUIRES PREPARATION OF ANSWERS WITHIN THREE MONTHS TO MANY BROAD QUESTIONS REQUIRING LEGAL ARGUMENT ON HISTORIC CONSTITUTIONAL FACTORS, SOCIOLOGICAL DATA AND AUTHORITATIVE EDUCATIONAL OPINION. NO MONEY AVAILABLE MEET EMERGENCY. OPPORTUNITY FOR DECENT PUBLIC EDUCATION AFFECTING NEARLY THREE MILLION NEGRO AMERICAN CHILDREN DEPENDS UPON RESOLUTION THIS DILEMMA.

In 1955 Fosdick sent an invitation to concerned citizens to meet with him on November 3.

> Mr. Thurgood Marshall, distinguished chief counsel of the National Association for the Advancement of Colored Peoule, will report on the state-wide reign of terror against men, women and children that led to the unpunished murder of three innocent people in Mississippi within a four month period. Mrs. Ruby Hurley of the N.A.A.C.P. staff will come North from Mississippi to tell us of her experience in uncovering witnesses to Emmett Till's murder. . . . Neither you nor I can help Emmett Till and his widowed mother now. As citizens we must do what we can to rid our nation of a conspiracy that, in 1955, rivals the worst past excesses of the Ku Klux Klan and, in parts of our country, threatens the life of every Negro citizen who dares to exercise his rights as an American. I have asked Mr. Roy Wilkens, Executive Secretary of the N.A.A.C.P., to tell us how we can help.

Fosdick in 1959 on invitation of Bayard Rustin agreed to be one of the chairmen of the Youth March for Integrated Schools. On his ninetieth birthday he received a telegram from the director of the Legal Defense and Educational Fund, Inc., thanking him for his long and faithful service, specifically citing Fosdick's help in securing 222 scholarship grants for young black men and women to study at leading colleges and universities.

When age and infirmity made it impossible for Fosdick to continue to preach he turned to the newspapers to fight the good fight for racial justice. On February 15, 1959, the *New York Times* carried his long and vigorous defense of the N.A.A.C.P.'s struggle to implement the Supreme Court's ruling against segragation in the public schools and an equally unequivocal condemnation of the "massive resistance" movement. In May he sent out a similar letter to a number of papers, the closing sentences of which read: "The people who maintain that these [Supreme Court] decisions should be put into effect are not extremists. They stand for the law. The only real extremists, under our Constitution, are those who advocate defiance of the court's ruling."

Regarding the explosive question of housing, in 1957 Fosdick wrote the foreword to a study conducted by the Committee on Civil Rights in Manhattan, Inc., entitled "Summary of Survey on Country-Wide Instances of Open Housing." In the foreword Fosdick noted that segregation still obtains, explicit in the South, camouflaged but disgracefully real in the North. "This survey . . . provides positive evidence that white and colored people can live together in peace and security. It is my belief that this evidence can be used toward attaining the level of social maturity worthy of a democratic people." In 1960 he supported a bill designed to end discrimination in private housing in New York State. He also corresponded with Governor Nelson Rockefeller regarding the "international disgrace" of the discrimination in finding housing encountered by delegates to the United Nations in New York City. To Fosdick's credit, in that same year he informed the readers of his hometown in the pages of the local newspaper that no black could then buy or rent a house in Bronxville, a situation Fosdick found deplorable, un-American, undemocratic, unchristian.

V

Considering Fosdick's earlier views of "darkest Africa," views both unhistorical and distorted by assumptions of Western cultural superiority, it is a real tribute to his capacity to grow to note that by the end of his ministry the scales were dropping from his eyes. For one thing he planned to will half of his personal library to a seminary in Angola, and although this could not be effected (for complicated reasons not of his making), the wish itself is significant. For another thing, he served on the Advisory Board of the American Council on African Education. He was also on the National Committee of the American Committee on Africa, joining a number of nationally prominent scholars, clergymen, and politicians (including Senators Chavez, Humphrey, Eugene McCarthy, Morse, and Muskie). This nonpartisan organization sought an "American policy toward Africa designed to help the African people achieve national independence, justice and equality." To this end, the committee issued a call for peace in Algeria, signed by Fosdick, which demanded that "The bloodshed in Algeria must end and the right of self-determination must be vindicated." The committee also provided financial aid to Father Trevor Huddleston's churches in South Africa to enable them to defy the racist bans, and it organized a defense fund for the victims of the infamous mass treason trials of 1957. The committee further called together a celebration for Ghana's independence and contributed to a trade union institute in Ghana. Fosdick was most active in seeking to bring to Angola life-saving aid. He addressed appeals for E.R.A. (Emergency Relief to Angola). He distributed an item entitled "I Saw the Horror in Angola" and stated in the accompanying letter, "I cannot strike a pose of neutrality. I too stand with the Africans. And the Africans need our help."

VI

In 1978 the new minister of Riverside Church, William Sloane Coffin, observed in a sermon: Harry Emerson Fosdick "would have been pleased this week to hear Bob Polk, the first black minister of Riverside, say that he thought Riverside Church today was probably the most important interracial voluntary association in the city. But let us thank Dr. Fosdick for preparing the way. Time and again he stated that racial discrimination was the most evil thing in the world." In what sense and to what extent did Fosdick in fact prepare the way?

In 1940 there were approximately 8 million black Protestants in America, a substantial minority of that number, incidentally, worshipping in the large, costly, ornate church of Harlem. About 7.5 million were in separate black denominations. Of the remaining half-million in predominantly white denominations, about ninety-nine percent were in segregated congregations. Thus, about one-tenth of one percent of all black Protestants in the United States—eight thousand souls—actually gathered together with whites for worship. Were any of these few souls to be found in Riverside Church during Fosdick's ministry?

To begin with, black visitors attended worship services and were made to feel warmly welcome, as letters to Fosdick testify in which the authors thanked him for "that graciousness of manner in your reception of a man of another race." Blacks, such as Dr. Mordecai Johnson, President of Howard University, occasionally occupied the Riverside pulpit, though, it seems, usually at the Sunday afternoon rather than the morning service. Blacks utilized the parish house, attended conferences, spoke before various societies, and participated in the church programs. From the beginning of the Riverside adventure, there were a few black members in the choir.

When a white couple protested the presence of blacks in the choir, C. Ivar Hellstrom, Fosdick's associate, replied that he was sorry to lose the couple's membership, but the blacks would stay. When a group of white women protested the use of the powder rooms in the church by black women, Fosdick was coldly furious and gave the objectors a severe tongue lashing.

From the outset, Riverside's members came from all over the world, from all races. Fosdick was being honest when he said that "if we exclude Negroes from our churches and practice segregation in the sense that Negroes can't be members then we might as well be atheists." The *Afro-American* 1945 article, "Riverside Church Doors Open to All," was correct in averring: "It is open to whomsoever will be—black, white, red or brown. You can sit in the front row in Dr. Fosdick's church, in the middle row or in the back row. If you want a seat you get in fifteen minutes before eleven. A dozen or more colored people who attend every Sunday don't find the whites hanging back and refusing to sit beside them."

Still, in the vast Riverside fellowship, a "dozen or more" black worshippers is scarcely eye-blinking. The explanation is not, definitely, that black applicants for church membership were turned away. None were, Fosdick reported, "except in one case and that was not because of his race"; "a white person would have been declined on the same grounds." Rather, the explanation lies elsewhere. First, very few blacks applied, patently preferring membership in the churches of adjacent Harlem. Second, Fosdick was determined not to be a sheep thief. As he once explained:

> In answer to your question as to whether we have made any definite attempt to get the people of Harlem to attend the Riverside Church, the answer is distinctly negative. We should have thought that an invasion of the membership of the colored churches. If we succeeded in winning away their loyal people, it would have been the most well-to-do and the best educated, and the ablest who would have come to us. That would have been a distinct disservice to the cause of Christ in Harlem, where intelligent workers in the colored churches are so desperately needed. I have warm friends, and some of them my former students, who are colored ministers in Harlem. I should not for a moment think of initiating or backing up any campaign that would put me in the position of a sheep-stealer from their flocks. What we have done is to open our membership to colored people whose allegiance naturally belongs to us, especially colored people living at International House or studying at the University. We have very few colored members.

The picture of eleven o'clock on Sunday morning as the most racially segregated hour in America has flashed across the nation and around the world as a symbol of American religion. But this dark picture is lightened by the recognition that the very formation of black congregations and denominations grew out of the hunger of blacks to control their religious associations and thereby to acquire the power that accrues to any organized social group. Black churches historically were central to a rising black consciousness and keys to black culture. Pronounced the black president of the Baptist Ministers Conference of Washington, D.C., "If a church expresses a liberal open policy, but no one of another race joins, I would still consider that church integrated." By this criterion, under Fosdick the Riverside Church was an integrated fellowship.

And maybe William Sloane Coffin was right in stating that Fosdick prepared the way for Riverside's later evolution. In 1960 Riverside signed on the Reverend Robert L. Polk, the first full-time black member of the ministerial staff, and also the Reverend Pablo Cotto to begin a Spanish-speaking ministry. By the 1980s perhaps twenty-five percent of the worshipping congregation of Riverside was black and the percentage of black children in the church school was probably higher.*

Interviewed by a reporter for the *New York Times* on his ninetieth birthday, Fosdick called for improvement in race relations and criticized separatism, saying: " 'Black power' is a dangerous phrase, just like 'white power.' We have to try to work things out together." These words might stand as a reasonable summary of Fosdick's position regarding America's deepest sin. It was certainly an enlightened, advanced position, but not quite that of a "Food-for-Christ." It is a position informed by Christian compassion and reasonableness and good will, but it is an understanding not fully adequate perhaps to the demonic dimensions of America's racism.

---

* These are not official percentages, but are my estimates confirmed by veteran lay leaders. Possibly, the church prefers not to keep officially a racial profile of its membership.

Chapter Twenty-five

Social Justice:
An Evolving Social Gospel
from the Age of Rauschenbusch
to the Age of Niebuhr

I

When the newspapers announced that John D. Rockefeller, Jr., would be the principal financier of the new Riverside Church, the *Daily Worker*, organ of the Communist Party U.S.A., commented: "Fosdick is a 'modernist,' but Rockefeller knows that he can be relied upon to philosophize about the bible and keep the minds of the workers from their troubles with the bosses, and the 'silk stocking' crowd entertained." Of course Marxist dogma proclaims that religion is the opiate of the masses, but it was an old coal miner who probably did not know Karl from Groucho who growled, "The preacher points your eyes to heaven, and then the boss picks your pocket," and it was the indigenous American radicals, the Wobblies, who sang about those long-haired preachers who when asked 'bout something to eat answered with voices so sweet, "You will eat, bye and bye, In that glorious land above the sky; Work and pray, live on hay, You'll get pie in the sky when you die." As a Rockefeller "stooge," the radicals' prediction went, Fosdick of necessity would preach a reactionary gospel from the pulpit of Riverside.

Yet with the enterprise well underway, the liberal *Christian Century* observed, "It must be said to Dr. Fosdick's credit that, not since he became Mr. Rockefeller's pastor has he shown any sign of weakness in proclaiming the social aspect of the Gospel as well as the personal aspect." After Fosdick's retirement New York's famed liberal minister Ralph Sockman judged, "That the Rockefeller millions never muted the prophetic notes of his message is a tribute to the social insights both of Dr. Fosdick and Mr. Rockefeller." And when in 1958 Fosdick's last vol-

ume of published sermons appeared—comprising fifty preached in Riverside—another noted liberal minister, Harold Bosley, in his review underscored the prophetic dimensions of Fosdick's preaching. In this chapter
we shall examine Fosdick's concern with and involvement in economic
and political issues, saving the transcendent issue of war for later examination.

II

Peter Collier and David Horowitz in their formidable volume, *The
Rockefellers: An America Dynasty*, assert that John D. Rockefeller, Jr.,
and Fosdick "often had disagreements," but the authors of this best-
seller (hailed by reviewers as brutally destroying the Rockefeller legend)
cite only one example.* Before proceeding to a more general examination
of Fosdick and social justice, it is mandatory to confront the crucial
question: Precisely how "often" did Rockefeller and Fosdick disagree on
economic and political issues and to what extent did the tycoon attempt
to muzzle the parson? Here is what the record reveals.

On December 19, 1927, Rockefeller wrote Fosdick to say that in his
judgment Fosdick had not been entirely fair in his comments on industry
in a recent sermon dealing with capital and labor. The tone of the letter
is not abusive or threatening, but it is one of self-justification. Fosdick's
reply of December 22 pointed out that the sermon was not intended as
a sweeping condemnation of industry and acknowledged that labor as
well as capital was soiled by greed of gain. Nevertheless, Fosdick re-
stated the "appalling contrast between luxury and poverty" in America,
closing the reply with these unyielding words:

> You say that the business man is sensitive to public criticism. I often
> wonder at his being so sensitive. I say far more critical things about my
> own realm, the ecclesiastical, than I ever dream of saying about the in-
> dustrial realm. My experience is that nobody, not even lawyers, whose
> realm is today being very searchingly criticized, is so sensitive as business
> men. And yet they would surely confess that some of the most serious
> problems of modern life lie in their realm. You speak of the bitterness of
> criticism which you so unjustly suffer, as in the case of the Colorado
> mines. Because of that you are sympathetic and understanding enough, I
> know, to put yourself the more readily into my place. I am very occa-
> sionally and bitterly criticized because, being in a powerful church with

* The three pages devoted to the Rockefeller/Fosdick connection contain a slew
of factual errors and in matters of interpretation demonstrate seemingly invincible
ignorance. For all I know, however, the rest of the book may be sound.

powerful men, I do not (or they think I do not) deal so frankly with the industrial problems as I do with international, ecclesiastical, and theological problems. In any case, you will understand that I, too, have a problem, and must be as balanced, fair, and just as I can manage it.

Rockefeller responded by sending Fosdick three booklets containing addresses he had given on industrial relations, labor relations, and business ethics. Fosdick concluded the exchange by acknowledging receipt of the "interesting" booklets, adding: "Of course, I took it for granted that you were a liberal, and if I had not been sure of your devotion to progressive policies in industry, I never would have dreamed of taking the pastorate of a church in which you were so prominent and powerful a member. Be sure, therefore, that if ever in the pulpit I shoot off a gun on the industrial question I am thinking of you as behind the gun and not in front of it."

It was not unusual for labor leaders, including Sidney Hillman, president of the Amalgamated Clothing Workers of America, to be invited to address interested audiences at first the Park Avenue Baptist Church and then Riverside, and few conservative eyebrows were raised. In 1930, however, a parishioner chanced upon a meeting of the League for Industrial Democracy held in the assembly room of Riverside, a meeting featuring socialists Paul Blanchard and Norman Thomas. The parishioner protested to John D. Rockefeller, 3rd, who passed the letter on to Robert W. Gumbel, his father's Man Friday, who in turn presented it to Fosdick. The minister's response was unequivocal:

I have your letter with the curious enclosure from Mr. Casselberry. If anybody is exceeding his limits I should suppose he was in meddling with something that is not his particular business. The request for the use of our Assembly Hall came through from the League for Industrial Democracy in due course and was taken up by the Committee of Trustees that has the matter in charge. To suppose that everybody in the church believes in the opinions of all the people who from time to time hold meetings in the church is of course nonsense. As for Norman Thomas himself, who made the request after having spoken at one of our own church meetings, I regard him as one of the best citizens of the community, and should always be glad to have him appear on any platform I was associated with. As for Mr. Casselberry's suggestion that there was anything clandestine about this that is of course absurd.

Two years later Fosdick signed a petition "urging the immediate recognition of the Soviet government of Russia by the United States," Fosdick believing that "a frank recognition of the Soviet Union would do more good than harm"—a position, incidentally, widely endorsed by the Protestant leadership of America. Rockefeller was alerted to the minister's deed by a layman but declined to see the correspondence between Fosdick and a church lay leader regarding the matter, saying rather dryly, "The petition was prepared, I think, by men like Mr. Wickersham and Mr. Owen D. Young. Certainly, it was signed by them and was apparently a perfectly innocuous thing."

A decade later Rockefeller raised with Fosdick the question of Reinhold Niebuhr's political views and Fosdick's reply, it will be remembered from Chapter Seventeen, was about as stirring a defense of his colleague as words could muster. Rockefeller also inquired at that time about another Union professor, the Methodist Harry F. Ward, and Fosdick replied in one sentence, "Dr. Ward retired from the Seminary two or three years ago, and we see nothing of him here."

Ward merits further mention. In the 1920s he served as the social conscience of American Methodism, especially in his gadfly role as leader of the unofficial Methodist Federation for Social Service. Few churchmen were more perceptive in discerning or more courageous in exposing the demoniac attributes of capitalism during the Reign of Gold. In 1929 when it was charged that Ward was a revolutionary, Fosdick termed the allegation "sheer nonsense," describing him as "a cultured and high-minded Christian gentleman, a minister of the Methodist Church, with a beautiful family life, and so far from believing in violence is a thoroughgoing pacifist who would not use violence under any circumstances whatsoever. He is a loyal citizen of the republic. . . . A more complete and ridiculous lie could not possibly be told about any man than the National Republic tells about Dr. Ward."

Then came the crash, Ward's travels in Russia, and his return to an America descending, as he believed, into fascism before the final proletarian triumph. Ward repeatedly denied ever being a member of the Communist party; he may be believed. Yet he became a True Believer, blind to the demoniac attributes of Stalin, loyal to the party line, and in Russia he found the final form of the Absolute. "Ward was the burning mystic," wrote Donald B. Meyer, "the pure mystic, in whom the logic of absolute vision burned away all but itself."

By 1935 Fosdick was aware of Ward's journey to the Left, yet he continued to defend his right to teach at Union, saying, "You must . . . understand that here in New York we have both by tradition and by choice set up a theological education upon a basis of university principles, where nearly every conceivable point of view is presented to the students. I don't know anybody else on the Faculty who remotely agrees with Harry Ward. His positions to which you object are objected to in one class room after another, so that the students hear every conceivable point of view from the very conservative to the very radical. There may be such a thing as carrying that principle too far, but certainly I should vote for that rather than for anything that looked like regimented uniformity." This was exactly the position taken by President Coffin in 1940 after Ward's appearance before the House Committee on Un-American Activities and pressure mounted for his dismissal from Union. Ward retired the following year and Fosdick wrote a warm testimonial letter, confined, it must be said, to the happy personal relationships between the Fosdick and Ward families. In later years Fosdick in private correspondence described Ward as "a personal friend," but deemed him a "well-known fellow traveler" who "has been lamentably mistaken in his estimate of communism." For his part, Ward remembered Fosdick's ninetieth birthday with a greeting.*

Rockefeller raised in 1945 a last question concerning Fosdick's economic and political utterances. In the teeth of the depression Fosdick had composed "A Litany of the Nation," repeated at a worship service at least once annually, containing the petition, "From prejudice of race and color, making schism in the commonwealth; *from all inequity that, causing a few to be rich and many poor, begets ill-will and spoils fraternity;* from loss of liberties bequeathed us by our sires and from careless acceptance of our heritage and neglect of its responsibilities." Rockefeller wondered to Fosdick about the fairness of the portion of the petition, in italics, pointing out that some may be rich through no action of their own and "may be using their opportunities as good and faithful stewards in the interests of their fellow men." "Please do not think of replying to this note, which I hope finds you having a wonderful rest in Maine," the self-justifying communication closed. Fosdick, however, elected to reply, documenting the inequality of income in the United States and, as we saw in Chapter Sixteen, including himself among the privileged rich. "When I use the litany I think of *myself*—one of the less than four-tenths of one per cent—over against the share-croppers, for example, and I pray with myself in mind." Although Fosdick closed with words of

---

* Lest this judgment of Ward seem harsh, it should be remembered that the great Methodist preacher-prophet Ernest Fremont Tittle lost all confidence in Ward's judgment and Methodist Bishop G. Bromley Oxnam confided to his diary on May 13, 1941: "I was disappointed beyond expression at Professor Ward. His left-wing drift in recent years has destroyed the scientific outlook. This evening what we really heard was a brief for the Communist Party all under the general theme of Present Attacks Upon Civil Liberties." Oxnam's clear belief that Ward was a fellow traveler is given force by the fact that Oxnam had studied under Ward and earlier had idolized him. Furthermore, Reinhold Niebuhr in his oral reminiscences characterized Ward as a "very naive Christian Marxist" under "Stalinist illusions."

cordiality and gratitude, it is clear that he did not intend to alter the litany.

This then is the record. Whether it substantiates the Collier and Horowitz accusation that the two men "often had disagreements" over economic and political matters is a "judgment call." We do know that in 1921 when certain industrialists were attempting to coerce the churches, Fosdick depicted them as commanding: " 'We will buy you,' they say to the churches and, in particular, to the ministers of the churches—'If you will do as we say, money, if not, no money!' " And to this threat Fosdick replied, "May I be permitted to suggest that these gentlemen have somewhat seriously misapprehended the temper of the Christian ministry of America? I am speaking for multitudes of my brethren when I say, *'Before high God, not for sale!'* " And we do know that the president of the Board of Trustees of Riverside assured Fosdick, "If anybody tries to limit your liberty, he will do it over my dead body."

If it may truthfully be said that Fosdick's oak-hearted parishioners, with only isolated exceptions, stood resolutely for a free pulpit in a free church, this does not mean that he escaped the wrath of others. In the teeth of the depression he preached "The Ghost of a Chance," a hard-hitting sermon on economic injustice and the flaws of capitalism, causing Congressman Hamilton Fish, Jr., chairman of the original House committee investigating "Reds," to classify him with the "pink intellectuals and sobbing socialists."* Shortly thereafter Mrs. Elizabeth Dilling, a sort of antiradical Carrie Nation, sincere and charismatic, won national fame of sorts with the publication of *The Red Network*, subtitled *A 'Who's Who' and Handbook of Radicalism for Patriots*. Among Mrs. Dilling's prized targets were "those present-day Moscow-loving intellectual ministers who rewrite the Bible and teach it in modernistic style so as to leave faith in little besides its covers." The dossier on Fosdick was shorter than those on Jane Addams and Mrs. Eleanor Roosevelt, but contained the warning that his books were "highly recommended by Socialists and other radicals." In some anger, Fosdick commented, "Mrs. Dilling had not the slightest interest in telling the truth about me or anybody else."

In the 1950s, when the apostles of discord were riding high, such patriots as Verne P. Kaulb, organizer of the American Council of Christian Laymen, included Fosdick among those "subversive" churchmen

---

* In contrast, the *Daily Worker* had this comment: "Yes, Dr. Fosdick, capitalism is on trial. And the workers will give the answer. They will not be fooled with the bunk that there can be a cooperative society with the means of production in the hands of a small class of exploiters and profit-seeking parasites who live on the toil of the masses."

"who have aided and abetted God-hating, un-American organizations";
and Louis F. Budenz, a Communist who capitalized on his recantation,
accused Fosdick (and his brother!) of being soft on communism.

III

Considering the pummeling he himself received and considering his lifelong devotion to democracy, it is not surprising to find Fosdick a lifelong
champion of civil liberties.

Post-World War I America, hag-ridden by the spectre of radicalism,
suffered a failure of nerve. The Great Red Scare of 1919–1920 was a
movement of national regeneration dedicated to the removal of the cancer of radicalism, a malignancy allegedly transmitted from Bolshevik
Russia by subversive aliens. The allegedly Communist-inspired strikes
(as charged by the youthful J. Edgar Hoover, head of the Justice Department's newly formed General Intelligence Agency), the bombings (Attorney General A. Mitchell Palmer, John D. Rockefeller, and Justice Oliver
Wendell Holmes were among those targeted to receive the "infernal
machines"), the May Day parades, the formation of the Communist and
Communist Labor parties, all indicated that the "Red" viper (to change
metaphors) had fastened its fangs into Columbia's bosom. What ensued
was not pretty. Swift and sudden raids upon private homes and upon
labor and socialist as well as anarchist and Communist headquarters in
which six thousand suspects were rounded up; imprisonment incommu-
nicado; brutal interrogations; drumhead trials; six hundred deportations.
Ex-baseball player and revivalist Billy Sunday cried, "If I had my way
I'd fill the jails so full of them [Reds] that their feet would stick out the
windows. . . . Let them rule? We'll swim our horses in blood up to the
bridles first." Sunday's final solution was deportation "in ships of stone
with sails of lead, with the wrath of God for a breeze and with hell for
their first port." Alas, much of America shared the revivalist's fears and
concurred in his heroic remedies.

Fosdick demurred. In July 1919 he joined a number of New York
churchmen in issuing a stirring petition for free speech, free discussion,
fair trials, due process of law, and open-mindedness. "A common resolve
to abide by our time-honored principles of free discussion and the regular processes of constitutional government," believed these individuals,
"is the need of the hour. Unhappily, violence, recently employed in the
name of patriotism, has been allowed to go unpunished by the authorities, and has even been praised by leaders in government and in the
press." Six months later Fosdick joined another group of New York

churchmen in publicly protesting the expulsion of five duly elected socialists from the Assembly of the New York State Legislature. Moreover,
in a sermon preached January 18, 1920, he denounced an action that
"will disfranchise a whole minority political party in this State," pointing out that even former Governor Charles Evans Hughes and the New
York Bar Association also lamented the deed. The sermon concluded
with the plea: "And, whatever else this chaotic, confused, perplexing
and tumultuous generation may do to you, let it not do this: let it not
drive you, frightened, back into that most dangerous attitude for the
commonwealth,—an hysterical spirit of reaction!" In another sermon
Fosdick made the telling point that having defeated Imperial Germany,
the United States was in danger of worshiping the gods of the defeated
enemy: censorship, elimination of free speech, autocratic control. "That
old story that runs from Alexander and Amaziah down, repeats itself.
We copy the enemy whom we fought. We, the victors, are transformed
by the vanquished."

The Great Red Scare burned out rapidly in 1920, even conservatives
recognizing the peril to American liberties in the deportations and in the
expulsion of the five New York socialists, but the hysteria bequeathed
many baneful legacies including a revived Ku Klux Klan, a resurgent
anti-Semitism, thirty-two state criminal syndicalism laws, a frightening
teachers' loyalty oath movement, textbook censorship—and the Sacco-
Vanzetti case. Nicola Sacco, a shoe trimmer, and Bartolomeo Vanzetti, a
fish peddler, were aliens, draft dodgers, and philosophic anarchists who
were arrested in 1920, tried, and sentenced to death for the murder of a
paymaster and his guard in South Braintree, Massachusetts. They did
not die unknown and unmarked failures because individuals, convinced
that the men had been convicted because of their opinions and not their
deeds, labored seven long years to secure their retrial. After a final, fatal
review by a commission appointed by the governor of Massachusetts,
consisting of two university presidents and a jurist, the electric chair
claimed its victims on a hushed August night in 1927. The case became
a cause célèbre, dividing American society, John Dos Passos growling,
"All right, then, we are two nations."

Fosdick joined 103 Union Seminary professors and students in petitioning Governor Alvan T. Fuller to conduct a searching investigation
of the fairness of the trial. He later signed an appeal to the Massachu-
sett's governor to commute the death sentences to life imprisonment.
Years later he termed the case a "miscarriage of justice." At the time,
however, he was not certain of the innocence of the men, but he was
certain that he did not believe in capital punishment and that commu-
tation "would have left the case where any new evidence that might in

the future turn up on the case could have some effect, whereas execution puts the matter beyond hope of readjustment, no matter what new light may break."*

A case involving intense feeling and even more extended agitation centered in the trial and imprisonment of Thomas J. Mooney and Warren K. Billings, labor leaders convicted of exploding a bomb that killed a number of people during a San Francisco preparedness parade in 1916, Mooney's sentence being commuted from death to life imprisonment. It was not until 1939 that a governor of California saw fit to pardon the men. Fosdick was a member of the National Church Committee on Mooney and Billings, formed in 1930 and composed of over one hundred clergymen of all faiths. The group urged the governor of California to pardon the prisoners, saying, "It is too late for either mercy or justice to Mooney and Billings. You cannot take fourteen of the best years of a man's life and still do justice. It is not too late to retrieve some shattered remnant of self-respect of the American people." A year earlier Fosdick had joined four other ministers in an identical request of the governor, bluntly asserting that Mooney and Billings are "now serving penitentiary sentences for a crime they did not commit." Fosdick further was a member of the Interreligious Committee for Justice for Thomas J. Mooney, which published a pamphlet entitled *Our American Dreyfus Case: A Challenge to California Justice* and mailed it together with additional documentary material to all the ministers, priests, and rabbis in California. Years later Fosdick pronounced this case, also, a "miscarriage of justice."

More generally, Fosdick belonged to the National Committee for the Defense of Political Prisoners and contributed $250 to its guaranteed bail fund. He also joined in petitioning President Coolidge to restore full rights of citizenship to those fifteen hundred individuals convicted during the war of uttering disloyal statements. When the Daughters of the American Revolution began in the 1920s compiling black lists of sundry radicals (such as Jane Addams,† Dean Roscoe Pound of the Harvard Law School, Rabbi Stephen S. Wise, and President Mary E. Woolley of Mount Holyoke College), Fosdick pursued one such list and said of the

---

* The literature on the case is vast. Almost annually a new study appears purporting to prove the men's innocence or guilt or indeed the innocence of one but not the other. My hunch is that the men may have been guilty, but that even so their trial was grievously flawed. Setting aside such questions as perjured testimony and ballistics confusion, an impartial judge does not refer, as did Webster Thayer, to defendents as "anarchistic bastards" and an unprejudiced jury foreman does not reply to a remark on the innocence of the accused, "Damn them, they ought to hang anyway."

† Dismissed from the D.A.R., Jane Addams remarked wryly that she had thought herself a member for life, but discovered it was only for good behavior.

"Dear Amazon Reactionaries" (as a colleague of the cloth termed the ladies), "If the D.A.R. is going to have a black list, one should pray to be on it; to be on their white list would be a disgrace." When the American Legion, in annual convention in 1929, slandered American Protestantism by the passage of a resolution demanding a Senate investigation of the "radical" Federal Council of Churches, Fosdick's friend, Walter Russell Bowie, rector of the Grace Episcopal Church, New York, declared from the pulpit that the Legion's lobby was a sinister and deadly cancer upon the body of American life. When the Legion threatened a law suit, Fosdick was one of sixty ministers and rabbis who publicly associated themselves with Bowie.

Fosdick's concern for the preservation of civil liberties never waned. In 1935, for example, he reminded President Roosevelt and the members of Congress that the suppression of free speech is the road to fascism. Indeed four years later he protested a proposed New York bill barring Communists from public office; and in 1941 he urged President Roosevelt to grant executive clemency to Earl Browder, general secretary of the Communist party, who was then serving a four-year penitentiary term for passport fraud.

In 1941 Fosdick accepted membership on the National Committee of the American Civil Liberties Union. "I am proud of my association with this organization," he replied to a "shocked and disturbed" correspondent who had discovered his association with the A.C.L.U. For their part, the Board of Directors of the A.C.L.U. in 1959 "by unanimous acclamation expressed . . . its gratitude to Harry Emerson Fosdick . . . , retiring this year after long service on the National Committee." Patrick Murphy Malin, Executive Director, added a personal note of admiration, Malin having studied under Fosdick at Union.

Age forced Fosdick's retirement from the A.C.L.U. in the 1950s, a decade when civil liberties were imperiled as never before in the history of the Republic. Although the era has been given the name of the junior senator from Wisconsin, Joseph McCarthy was in fact more created by, than he was creator of, the Great Fear, which antedated his rise to infamy and persisted after his censure by the Senate in 1954. Indeed, such was the pervasive anxiety of the Cold War age, so widespread was the fear of global Communist expansion and internal Communist subversion, a consternation sincerely held by many and cynically exploited by some, that the nation would have been gripped by McCarthyism even if "Tail Gunner Joe" had never lived. In truth not even Democratic President Truman or Republican President Eisenhower can be excluded from the vast company of America's leaders who fed the public fear.

Protestant clergymen were among those accused of being captured by

Moscow. Earl Browder testified before a congressional committee that the Communist party had considerable success in infiltrating the ministry. Benjamin Gitlow, another Communist party leader, asserted that Communist infiltration of Methodism was highly successful. Herbert Philbrick, F.B.I. undercover agent, spoke of a cell of ministers in Boston. J. Edgar Hoover warned of the party's attempt to invade the churches. One ex-Communist, Joseph Zack Kornfeder, estimated there were six hundred ministers in the United States who were secret party members and "2000 were pretty close to the machine." J. B. Matthews, returning from the Left, testified that more than seven thousand Protestant ministers comprised "the largest single group supporting the Communist apparatus." He claimed to possess a card index containing the names of 8079 Protestant churchmen who had served the Communist cause— whatever that may mean. Daniel Bell, chronicler of American socialism, believed that the proportion of ministers on the "sucker lists" of Communist party fronts was probably higher than any other single group. Congressman Harold Velde of the House Committee on Un-American Activities said that churchmen had committed the "sin" of subversion in criticizing his proposal to investigate the clergy. Another member of the committee, Representative Donald Jackson, charged that Methodist Bishop G. Bromley Oxnam was "to the Communist front what Man O' War was to thoroughbred horse racing" and that Oxnam "served God on Sunday and the Communist front for the balance of the week."*

The clerical lunatic-fringe Right exemplified by Gerald Winrod and Gerald L. K. Smith found Communists under the denominational beds, but so did such respected church leaders as Stanley High and Daniel Poling. The careful historian, Ralph Lord Roy, himself a Methodist minister, gave as his considered judgment that perhaps as few as fifty, perhaps as many as two hundred, Protestant ministers actually joined the Communist party, whereas additional thousands might without exaggeration be termed "fellow travelers." Roy hastened to add that these individuals thought of themselves not as Communists at all, but as loyal followers of Jesus and the prophets, their passion for social justice, their loathing of fascism, their awareness of capitalism's brutalities disposing them to believe the utopian promises of communism and to deny, even to themselves, Stalin's ruthlessness.

The famous Kirby Page poll of 1934 disclosed that out of 20,000 ministers, only 123 favored the establishment of communism in America as defined as that in "Soviet Russia and as represented by the Communist Party in the United States." A poll conducted the following year by the

---

* No patsy, the square-jawed bishop publicly took on the House Committee on Un-American Activities, and the committee partially recanted.

Religion and Labor Foundation found only 36 of 5000 ministers saying they would actively support the Communist party. The number of party members among the clergy was, obviously, at no time more than infinitesimal, and in fact, whatever the figure, the number peaked in the Depression Decade when destitution stalked the land and fascism threatened the world and ebbed even prior to the McCarthy era.

Still, as the public record reveals and private papers confirm, such liberal church leaders as Ernest Fremont Tittle, G. Bromley Oxnam, John Haynes Holmes, Allan Knight Chalmers, and Reinhold Niebuhr were disturbed. Niebuhr, for example, resigned from the American League Against War and Fascism (led by Harry F. Ward) because it became "a very unnatural alliance between religious radicals and Communists." Niebuhr also resigned from the editorial board of the *Protestant Digest* because he informed editor Kenneth Leslie, "you are determined to follow the line of Russia as closely as possible." Similarly, Holmes wrote letter after letter to fellow ministers charging the Communist party of duplicity in seeking the cooperation of the clergy. In 1946, for example, he alerted Niebuhr: "The situation in the Unitarian body as regards the Communists is alarming. At the same time it is so incredible, that Beacon Hill should be taken over by the Reds, that I have to shake myself awake as from a nightmare. The Christian Register, staid old organ of the Unitarians, is now definitely in the hands of the Communists under [Stephen F.] Fritchman's leadership. The young people's organization is being slowly but surely captured. And here you send me proof positive that the Unitarian Service Committee has been taken over and the amazing thing is that most of the ministers and laymen are so innocent that they haven't the slightest idea as to what is going on. I have been bombarding Fred Eliot for months with facts and charges, but seem as yet to have made little impression." Holmes himself confessed in a famous sermon entitled, "Why We Liberals Went Wrong on the Russian Revolution," to having been for years duped by the Communists, saying that "this Russian experience has been the supreme disillusionment of my life. I have been deceived, deluded and disgraced—sold out by those I trusted most; and I am as deeply afflicted as I am utterly disgusted by what has happened." The Berlin-Moscow pact was the final straw in Holmes's disenchantment with Russia. "I am sick over this business as though I saw my father drunk and my daughter on the street. And all the more since I feel that I have deceived myself as well as been deceived." In all of this it is necessary to insist, Lillian Hellman and others to the contrary, that it is hardly Red-baiting to call a Communist a Communist. It is hardly hysterical to assert that the American Stalinists undercut the genuine and serious socialist movement in the United States.

Fosdick's posture in the Cold War era was admirable. In 1949 John T. Flynn, once a New Deal liberal, wrote *The Road Ahead*, in which he alerted 1 million frightened readers to the socialist revolution being promoted by the churches behind a pious facade of religion in a chapter entitled "The Kingdom of God." "I think that chapter is one of the most scandalous things written in my lifetime," judged Fosdick. "It is absolutely unjustified. I know the personalities involved, and John T. Flynn is an unscrupulous liar in what he says about them, and about the work of the Federal Council."

As for Senator McCarthy, here is what Fosdick informed the senators from New York in urging them to censure their colleague: "During a long lifetime I have seen nothing much more abominable in this nation's public life than Senator McCarthy's behavior. It has brought the Senate to an all-time low in the estimation of the free world in general, and of millions of our own citizens. I am convinced that the total effect of his abusive and insulting conduct directed, as it commonly has been, not against communists but against our own army and our Senators, has done the communist cause far more good than harm."

To be sure Fosdick declined to comment on the trial of the Rosenbergs, though only because he felt insufficiently informed on the matter. (Incidentally, Reinhold Niebuhr informed Mrs. Morton Sobell that "the statement is frequently made that the Rosenbergs were subject to a miscarriage of justice, and I know just enough about that situation to believe that there was no miscarriage.") In 1960, however, Fosdick did protest the hounding of Dr. Linus Pauling by the Senate Internal Security Subcommittee because Pauling had called for the cessation of nuclear bomb testing by all countries. Further, Fosdick signed a petition to President Kennedy urging executive clemency for Junius Scales, who was serving the longest sentence ever pronounced on an American Communist.

Beyond debate, Fosdick was as firm in upholding the civil liberties of all citizens as he was in upholding the freedom of the pulpit for himself and his fellow preachers.

IV

In his autobiography Fosdick stated, "I should be ashamed to have preached to such congregations without awakening hostility." Did he in fact afflict the comfortable? Was the Gospel he preached sufficiently prophetic to cause consternation among his parishioners? Did he come to know the meaning of Paul's anguished cry, "For necessity is laid upon me. Woe to me if I do not preach the gospel." Did he comprehend that the full Gospel was a prophetic Gospel? Was he in the mainstream of the Social Gospel movement that came to flower in American Protestantism during his ministry?

The Social Gospel was a movement and a mood drawing from springs as ancient as Amos, "Let judgment run down as waters and righteousness as a mighty stream." Long before Fosdick's ministry Protestants in America had practiced acts of charity, concerned themselves with social issues, and labored to bring about the millennium of a redeemed Christian republic, and it is therefore a mistake to assume that nineteenth-century evangelicals were indifferent to, or above, public questions. Yet the Social Gospel had an identity of its own, however blurred, and it may be roughly fixed in a moment of American history, however venerable its inspiration and pervasive its heritage; it is that particular vintage of social Christianity or prophetic religion associated with American Protestantism in the period between the death of Henry Ward Beecher in 1887 and the publication of Reinhold Niebuhr's *Moral Man and Immoral Society* in 1932. It came of age in the Progressive era, knew a kind of Indian Summer in the 1920s, and then under the impact of economic conditions and neo-orthodox theology, it was deepened and transformed. But though the term itself disappeared in the 1930s, its central imperatives fuel powerful impulses within the churches today that are working for a world of peace and justice.

The movement has been seen as a secularization of religious postmillennialism and it has been intimately identified with the progressive ethos. There is much vadility in this interpretation. It was a late nineteenth- and early twentieth-century response to the challenges of industrialization, finance capitalism, urbanization, and immigration. It was born in fear as well as in hope, in anxiety as well as compassion. Since the first settlements Protestants had prided themselves on being the senior partners in the American enterprise, and in the nineteenth century the American nation and the Protestant denominations had marched to greatness together until the identification between Protestantism and Americanism was almost complete. This identification of Christ and culture resulted in a comfortable "culture-Protestantism" wherein all tension was melted. The churches were more than domesticated, they were virtually emasculated. As the eunuchs of old, they adorned, without seriously disturbing, their master's establishment. Ultimately, the issue was not one of hypocrisy, but of idolatry, not of cultural lag but of conflicting faith. By the end of the century, however, this comfortable marriage was threatened. Industrial capitalism seemed a twin peril, as the new robber barons arrogantly elbowed aside the older patricians and the new proletariat sullenly rejected the prevailing moralistic preaching. It was imperative, therefore, to chastise the hearts of the mighty and scourge the new kings of capitalism who "beat my people to pieces, and grind the face of the poor." It was imperative to regain the lost masses, especially as these masses increasingly were new immigrants huddled in the burgeoning cities. America, once an alleged pastoral Eden peopled by sturdy Protestant yeomen, erect in field or village green, unspotted from the urban world, was being transformed into an urban jungle inhabited by "beaten men of beaten races."

As progressivism itself was not a revolutionary attack on bourgeois society launched by the disinherited, so the Social Gospel's greatest appeal was to Protestants of education and status who worshiped in fairly large and comfortable urban and suburban parishes (mostly in the North), individuals too sensitive to be bamboozled by the Gospel of Wealth yet too secure to be revolutionaries.

"The Social Gospel," said Walter Rauschenbusch, "seeks to bring men under repentance for their collective sins. . . . Sin is not a private transaction between the sinner and God." In modern America, observed sociologist E. A. Ross, we "sin by syndicate," echoing Rauschenbusch's utterance, "We rarely sin against God alone." The Social Gospel, after all, said another, is only the Church aware that it has more than one member. It sought to rescue American Protestantism from the ascendent nineteenth-century individualistic and pietistic ethic by recovering the corporate dimensions of the gospel. It recognized that a man is inextricably entwined in the social fabric, that he is damned by social conditions, that the reform of the structural evils in society enhanced the possibility of his redemption. Like progressivism itself, it embraced social engineering and scientific planning. Like the progressives, the Social Gospelites held an unreservedly optimistic view of the state, and they were as eager to grant the state control over the economic areas of life as over such moral areas as liquor, prostitution, gambling, and lurid literature. The state and the churches were allies in "Christianizing the Social Order" because the Social Gospel mind conceived of the state in a platonic sense, transcending class interests and personal ambitions, a redeemed part of a society itself in the process of conversion. The Social Gospel in its agencies staffed by professionals, fact-finding studies, institutional outreach to the poor, and search for a rational, orderly, efficient solution to society's ills was the religious counterpart to the hard—or scientific— side of progressivism.

The Social Gospel also shared the soft—or moralistic—side of progressivism. Both movements were permeated with moral urgency; both spoke in highly moral language. Unregenerate doers of evil would be toppled from their mighty thrones or lifted up from the sloughs of degeneracy in a great crusade led by an enlightened and righteous elite. With Teddy Roosevelt the Gospelites sang "Onward, Christian Soldiers," and stood at Armageddon to do battle for the Lord. Progressivism relied much on "muckraking" exposures of society's ills, confident that once exposed to public sunlight these ills would be cured. Progressivism relied much on Wilsonian retoric to exhort the people to return to the paths of righteousness. Just so, the Social Gospel prophets were mostly preachers, proclaimers, and educators, strong in the pulpit and on the platform and in the seminaries.

What tends to be forgotten or understated in this interpretation, valid as far as it goes, of the Social Gospel as the secularization of postmillennialism, is its profound belief that Jesus came to save both the individual soul and the human race; it was indeed a *gospel.* As William M. King so forcefully phrased it, "The social gospel was not secularizing the sacred—at least not from its own perspective; it was re-sacralizing the secular." "The service of man," King correctly continued, "was not merely a strategic device or moral imperative; it was also the service of God, an act both of obedience and of worship. And because the historically active, 'personal' God is himself the great reformer of societies and cultures, human service of God must find expression in reform as well."

The wellsprings of the movement lie not solely in the economic conditions of the day and in the ferment of secular reform in America. They lie importantly in the examples of the Christian socialist movements abroad, especially in England and Germany. They lie in a new revelation of the teachings of Jesus, especially relating to the coming Kingdom, for as Rauschenbusch wrote, "To those whose minds live in the social gospel, the Kingdom of God is a dear truth, the marrow of the gospel." They lie in the desperate existential need of individuals (such as Fosdick) to restate the meaning and truth of Christianity in an age of social and cultural change and strain. To these prophets, probably always a minority, even among the adherents of the New Theology, though an extraordinarily significant and sizable minority, reform was a way of being religious. The movement's dynamism stemmed from the belief that reform activity itself embodied a religious experience, an experience of grace.

Reinhold Niebuhr once paid this tribute: "Dr. Fosdick proved in two decades of preaching at the new Riverside Church that no one in our generation could illuminate the ethical issues which modern man faced in our technical society with greater rigor and honest discrimination than he." An old reprobate once growled that it was a mighty poor sermon that did not hit him somewhere, and if we substitute for "reprobate" the Rooseveltian (T.R. and F.D.R.) terms "malefactors of great wealth" or "economic royalists," this statement would hold true of Fosdick's sermons. Fosdick wrote two handsome tributes to Walter Rauschenbusch and counted himself a disciple of the greatest of the Social Gospel prophets.

Yet one must be careful not to identify Fosdick exclusively with the Social Gospel Movement or to think that the terms "crusader" or "reformer" adequately define his ministry. The Fosdickian Social Gospel was always one with a personal foreground and an eternal background. He shared Martin Buber's conviction that "The true meaning of love of one's neighbor is not that it is a command from God which we are to fulfill, but that through it and in it we meet God."

On a thousand instances Fosdick expressed the conviction that "We are here not simply to save people out of the world but to save the world." And: "To talk about the Christian gospel as merely individual and not social is dangerous nonsense. . . . When anyone seriously works for transformation of individual character, he is led not away from social questions but straight to them." And: "It is sheer hypocrisy for the church to say that it cares for personality as sacred and then to do nothing about social conditions that impinge on personality with frightful consequences." And: "Any church that pretends to care for the souls of people but is not interested in the slums that damn them, the economic order that cripples them, and international relationships that, leading to peace or war, determine the spiritual destiny of innumerable souls—that kind of church, I think, would hear again the Master's withering words: 'Scribes and Pharisees, hypocrites!' "

V

Fosdick's New York ministry began on the threshold of the Golden Twenties. It was a time (according to one incomplete but not totally inaccurate scenario) of corpulency and contentment when President Harding "boviated" in the White House for more than two years and President Coolidge napped along the quiet Potomac for almost six; a time of sententious pronouncements that all was well from Secretary of the Treasury Andrew Mellon and Secretary of Commerce Herbert Hoover; from economist Roger Babson and Madison Avenue executive (and Jesus' biographer) Bruce Barton; from the officers of the N.A.M. *and* the A.F.L. For the churches, it was the "Age of the Babbittonian Captivity" when they rendered unto George F. Babbitt the things that were Babbitt's, leaving precious little for God; and when His Son was transmuted into a sort of glorified Rotarian. "Jesus," averred the noted Dr. Frank Crane, "is the great Master Artist in the business of getting along." "Moses," according to a Metropolitan Casualty Insurance Company booklet, "was one of the greatest salesmen and real estate promoters who ever lived." He was a "Successful Personality in one of the most magnificent selling campaigns that history ever placed upon its pages." The churches, admonished by such advice as "Early to bed and early to rise / Preach the gospel and advertise," promoted attendance with such slogans as "Public Worship Increases Your Efficiency" and "A Sermon a Day Keeps the Devil Away" and such sermon titles as "The Irishmen of the Old Testament" and "Two in a Bed"—all leading the "penitent and puzzled parson," Episcopal Bishop Charles Fiske, in 1927 to describe American Protestantism as "The Great Society of the Outstretched Hand."

Happily, this is not the full story and thankfully Harry Emerson Fosdick was a member of that not inconsiderable band of churchmen who kept the prewar flame of prophetic Christianity burning, albeit in Fosdick's case the flame was scarcely burning bush bright.

Specifically, from the pulpit and in public statements he excoriated harsh and unsafe working conditions in mills and mines and, together with official American Protestantism almost without exception, demanded the end of the unconscionable twelve-hour day in the steel industry, until Judge Gary of U.S. Steel finally bowed to public pressure in 1923. He repeatedly lashed out against the "abominations of child labor" and did all in his power (which, of course, proved not enough) to secure the adoption of a Child Labor Amendment to the Constitution. He observed the poverty stalking the land, supporting his critique with facts and figures, and he further noted the physical and moral wreckage resulting from this cruel destitution. He supported the right of laborers to organize, believing they had a right to participate in determining the conditions under which they worked and the wages they received. He drove his point home by noting that "if any group of employers could themselves be put back into such conditions as the laborers faced before the days of labor unions, the first thing those employers would do would be to combine in league for mutual defense," adding that "only a blind man can recommend the endeavor to turn back the clock to the old days before laborers were organized at all."

With other liberal ministers, Fosdick called for the establishment of a cooperative commonwealth and the end of the competitive struggle after profits which only resulted in chicanery and appalling selfishness. "The meanest, most cynical and unscrupulous selfishness that stops at no cruelty and that feels no shame is the fruit of the economic struggle. The New Testament is right: 'The love of money is a root of all kinds of evil.' " He was a member of the committee that drafted the famous report of the Federal Council of Churches, *The Church and Industrial Re-construction*, which demanded that the entire social order be Christian-ized. This far-ranging criticism of laissez-faire capitalism, however, with its call for fellowship and the end of class divisions, was rather vague on just how "the principles of Jesus" might be brought to bear on the con-crete historical situation in 1920.

Above all, in the Golden Twenties what disturbed Fosdick most was the pervasive materialism blanketing the land. America's very prosperity, her very richness, had led to a sickening selfishness and self-contentment. America, he wrote a friend abroad in 1929, "is no place for a man easily to follow the Carpenter of Nazareth. Anybody who is trying to be a Christian in this country at the present time has a serious job on his hands. Nevertheless, some of us are sticking at it, and hope to get some-thing across that will save this country from following in the wake of such notable predecessors as Egypt, Nineveh, Babylon, Rome, and Greece."

VI

In 1928 Fosdick voted for Herbert Hoover, who declared in his trium-phant acceptance address: "We in America today are nearer to the final triumph over poverty than ever before in the history of any land." As it turned out, Hoover was mistaken. Some churchmen attributed the De-pression to the "Providence of God"—to use the wording of the Southern Baptist Convention. "The nations that forget God," the convention con-tinued, "shall not prosper." Poverty was just punishment for a prodigal people. The land was reaping a bitter harvest, the seeds of which were sown in the sinful twenties. If an angry God unleased the Depression, only an appeased God would lift the yoke. Hence economic recovery waited on religious revival. But the revival never materialized. A people shorn of their wealth did not turn to God.

For other churchmen, the Depression was a herald of the last days and men could but wait in trembling expectation; or if their theology was Kierkegaardian or Barthian rather than chiliastic, they remained above the "housekeeping chores" of politics, leaving social reform to "busy-bodies who suffer from a lack of humor" in order to proceed with the main business of the self's confrontation with God.

Some churchmen, such as Gerald L. K. Smith and Gerald Winrod, embraced a crypto-fascism, convinced that America's economic health had been poisoned by a Communist-Jewish virus. Others extoled the

Soviet Union as the world's last, best hope while America staggered like a blinded Samson chained to the millstone of capitalism.

A small but articulate and extremely influential band of churchmen led by Reinhold Niebuhr became in the early 1930s Christian Marxists. Not Communist party members, not innocents duped into following the party line, not uncritical of the repressive aspects of Soviet society or unaware of the utopian elements in the Marxist vision, they sought to do justice to the best insights of historic Christianity and the Marxian dialectic, believing that the "Christian Church should recognize the essential conflict between Christianity and the ethics of capitalistic individualism" and believing also that the "evolutionary optimism of current liberal Christianity is unrealistic."

A much larger element, representing the mainstream of Protestant liberalism, saw in President Franklin D. Roosevelt's New Deal the embodiment of the social justice for which the churches had been laboring since the days of Teddy Roosevelt. As New Deal act after New Deal act was passed it almost seemed as though the president was ticking off for enshrinement into law the "Social Creed of Methodism" and the Federal Council's "Social Ideals of the Churches." Indeed, Dr. Albert W. Beaven, president of the Federal Council, informed the representatives gathered on December 8, 1933, to celebrate the twenty-fifth anniversary of the council's founding: "We rejoice in the many ways in which President Roosevelt's program for recovery embodies Christian social ideals for which the churches have long contended, and call upon our people for the most whole-souled and unselfish support of all those cooperative enterprises of goodwill by which, under the President's inspiring leadership, we hope to achieve the better tomorrow." Among those in the audience who applauded was Franklin D. Roosevelt, who had accepted an invitation to deliver the keynote address.

Still other churchmen remained rooted to a conservative persuasion, viewing "That Man in the White House" a threat to American liberties and the New Deal a betrayal of American individualism. In truth probably a majority of Protestant clergymen continued to find their political home in the Republican party. In 1936, 21,606 ministers replied to the question asked by the *Literary Digest:* Do you *now* approve the acts and policies of the Roosevelt New Deal to date?" Some 70.22 percent, or 15,172, replied no. "For the moment," wrote the perceptive John C. Bennett in 1939, "one of the hardest facts to face is that the success of the most promising political forces in American life [the New Deal] must be in spite of the opposition of the majority of the members of the Protestant churches."

Let us now attempt to place Fosdick on this continuum of Protestant-ism's political response to the challenge of the Depression—a response, as we have seen, ranging from those who were washed in the blood of the Marxian lamb to those who would raise up a man on horseback—a Mussolini or Hitler—to save America through fascism.

Clearly Fosdick did not take a Christian Science attitude toward eco-nomic ills of the country in the Great Depression. With frequency and force he addressed the hellish reality confronting the country. As early as one year after the stock market crash he preached on "Christianity and Unemployment." Driving home the magnitude of the suffering with statistics and quotations from letters he received from desperate unem-ployed, he called for increased government aid and directly asked the businessmen in the congregation why unemployment insurance could not be instituted. Moreover, "Why cannot we stop repeating that insane formula about competition being the life of trade in a new age when obviously competition is the death of trade, and begin drawing the basic industries of our nation together in co-operative planning under wise social control?" He then commented, "If somebody wishes to call that socialism, let him call it socialism! Pretty nearly every decent and co-operative thing we ever have done has been called by somebody social-ism." In another sermon he characterized the economic situation as "chaos," asserted that "nothing except extensive government aid can possibly save us from having stark starvation walk our streets," and maintained that in a mad rush for private profit "We have expended intellectual labor in making money for ourselves out of the capitalistic system instead of expending commensurate intellectual labor on solv-ing the social problems which the capitalistic system has produced." On another instance he noted, "Stalin is not alone in making an economic class his god. A capitalist can do that as thoroughly as a Communist."

In one sermon Fosdick decried the enormity of women in New Jersey factories working for $2 a week, girls in Connecticut sweatshops toiling eighty-five hours a week, children in Pennsylvania sweating for pennies daily—and in the thirties, as in the twenties, he signed petitions favor-ing, and served on a committee seeking, the ratification of a Child Labor Amendment. Also he described the foul tenements of New York into which no direct breath of air or ray of sunshine has ever come, adding, "In New York City are hundreds of thousands of people, honest, self-respecting, industrious, loving their families as I love mine, who, work-ing their hardest at menial and drudgerous tasks, can do no more than support their homes on the bare level of a meager subsistence." In ser-mon after sermon he depicted the joy experienced by a man who found a job, the silent despair of those who searched in vain for employment, saying, "I wonder how many other nations there are on earth where so many common people could suffer what they are suffering here and keep so steady."

Fosdick's usual evenhandedness concerning the class struggle was a bit less evident in the depression. There is a Niebuhrian strain to the observation, "When our class is favored, when it receives support and distinction from the *status quo*, we are almost irresistibly tempted to mass and marshall our thought in support of it. *Most of our thinking about social questions is done, not individually or rationally, but by pressure of class interests.*" Moreover, of the struggles of American laboring men, history would some day declare that they were right, and that the men of privilege had been wrong.

Fosdick gave substance to his words with deeds. He served on the national committee of the A.C.L.U.'s Committee on Labor Injunctions, a group having as its purpose the protection of labor from sweeping and crushing court orders, and he supported a federal anti-injunction bill. He served on a committee of clergymen organized on behalf of striking New York garment workers. He signed a petition urging arbitration in a strike situation. In 1932 he joined twenty other New York ministers in memorializing the Senate to investigate violations of the civil liberties of striking coal miners in southeastern Kentucky. The authorities of Pineville, Kentucky, by means of a telegram to Fosdick, invited the clergymen to come to Kentucky to make a personal investigation of their charges. Fosdick was unable to accept because of pastoral responsibilities, but Reinhold Niebuhr did lead a deputation, returning to cite an old miner who declared, "If you are hungry you are a red and if you tell your neighbor that you are hungry that is criminal syndicalism." The appeal to the Senate was renewed. Closer to home, Fosdick accepted membership on the Emergency Unemployment Relief Committee of New York, and even closer, he worked for more park and recreational areas for children in the Manhattanville-Morningside Heights neighborhood.*

Fosdick, of course, was cognizant that communism was on the march as capitalism lurched and stumbled. "The ultimate decision between communism and capitalism," he declared in a radio sermon, "depends on one point only: Can capitalism so adjust itself to this new world, so move out from its old individualism dominated by the profit motive into a cooperative epoch of social planning and social control that it can become the servant of the welfare of all the people? If it can, it can survive. If it cannot, our children will have some form of communism thrust upon them." (Representative Fiorello LaGuardia, impressed, entered the ser-

---

* Interestingly, he found Robert Moses to be an able Park Commissioner, but "one of the most supersensitive, easily irritated, and pugnacious of men."

mon into the *Congressional Record*.) Fosdick stated as fact that "the communists in Russia are more sacrifically in earnest about what they want than we are about what we ought to want," holding that any American "not shaken out of his complacence by what is going on to-day in Russia is a fool."

On more than one instance Fosdick stated that he was not much worried about the ascendency of communism in America, but he was deeply concerned about fascism. "Have you read Sinclair Lewis's last novel, *It Can't Happen Here?*" he asked the Riverside worshipers in 1936. He spelled out his position in another sermon: "I fear communism, but not as some of my friends do. They fear it as a possible conqueror of America. I think that a needless dread. The totalitarian-state system of communism has little if any chance in this country. Everything in our psychology and tradition is antagonistic to it. Our danger is not so much communism as fascism. I fear the ideas behind communism, not as the conqueror of my country but as the competitor with my Christianity." He continued: "I fear communism because I know that in this country we ought as Christians to be building a more cooperative, more fraternal, more equalitarian and classless society in which we shall be members one of another. That is the goal of both Christianity and democracy. More than others we Christians ought to see that aim and serve it." Fosdick understood that it was a choice between living in a Communist prison or a capitalist jungle, making the point thusly, "one looks at Russia and says with Amos, 'As if a man fled from a lion, and a bear met him.'" In the sermon, "How much Do We Want Liberty?," he observed that the basic strategy of communism is to sacrifice liberty for the sake of equality, whereas the basic strategy of capitalism has been to sacrifice equality for the sake of liberty. "What painful dilemmas life confronts us with!" "Personally," he said elsewhere, "I dread the thought of collectivism which Russia represents as I would dread the devil," and he was appalled at the way in which some liberals were ready to throw away the most priceless rights, liberty of speech and thought and worship and subject themselves to a tyrannically regimented state.

The truth is that Fosdick, by his own acknowledgment, was not a socialist. Even in the Depression decade he had some kind words to say about American business and some words of warning about the dangers of glorifying the proletariat, observing that sin is no respecter of persons, that corrupting power runs through all classes, and that should the meek inherit the earth they would probably be meek no longer. On the political continuum of the 1930s Fosdick might be positioned with Roosevelt's New Deal and this, indeed, is where he seems to place himself in his autobiography.

VII

The war came and with it a measure of general prosperity, though in a relative sense the gulf between the haves and the have nots was not appreciably narrowed. Roosevelt's New Deal was continued under President Truman, and even under Eisenhower's Republican leadership measures once deemed socialistic were accepted matter-of-factly by all save an Old Guard remnant, though massive numbers of citizens remained ill-fed, ill-clad, ill-housed, their poverty masked by a surface glitter of affluence. Fosdick's concern with economic justice continued, but the depression-spurred intensity of the 1930s was somewhat muted. In the wartime sermons preached before his retirement in 1946 he continued to hold before the eyes of his people the vision of a cooperative commonwealth and to open their eyes to the gulf between that vision and the American reality.

Again his sermonic pronouncements were not made in isolation from activity. For instance, at Mayor Robert Wagner's invitation he served on the Mayor's Committee for Better Housing and he informed Jacob Javits of his concern when the House of Representatives cut back the Federal Housing Program, stressing the harmful consequences for New York City. When Mayor Vincent Impellitteri's administration proposed that the city's budget be lightened by eliminating the Day Care Program, Fosdick shot off a letter: "Without this Day Care Program there would be untold hardship to the small children involved. Two-thirds of the mothers are the sole or main support of their family. Without this program they would have to give up their jobs and go on public relief, or if they continued to work the children would have to run the streets. I beg of you, to stand out against this cruel method of cutting the budget."

In 1962 he wrote Governor Rockefeller a "Dear Nelson" letter expressing grave disturbance over the incredibly low wages of hospital workers in New York City and the exclusion of these workers from the collective bargaining provisions of New York State's labor law. He praised the sincerity of the officers of Local 1199, Drug and Hospital Employees, and urged Rockefeller to meet with them, believing that "the right to union representation and collective bargaining is a fundamental one." Also, Fosdick continued to serve on the boards of the Macy Foundation for medical research and the Turrel Fund for underprivileged children, and as will be seen in a later chapter, in retirement he devoted hundreds of hours to recreational and housing projects in the Morningside Heights area.

Concerning communism and the Cold War, Fosdick's posture, never that of a fellow traveler, hardened. Stalin he judged a "tyrant" who was "carved off the same piece of meat as Hitler." The combination of atheism, communism, and Russian totalitarianism he found frightening, "threatening everything we hold most dear." Communism in Russia may have started out with humane and idealistic intent, but the employment of ruthless repression as a temporary means ultimately destroyed that intent. In 1948 in a private letter answering the charge that he was "soft on communism," he termed the charge "a laugh" and asserted that "Communism in general and Russian Communism in particular are public menace #1." And so in 1950 he accepted General Lucius Clay's invitation to serve on the National Council of the Crusade for Freedom, designed to meet, said Clay, "the powerful and determined propaganda attack of the Communists."

We know, on the other hand, that Fosdick was not swept up in the McCarthy hysteria and shortly we shall see that as a pacifist he could not be a Cold War warrior. To the contrary, he saw that in the stiff competition between the two systems that prevailed in Russia and America, the victory "will be decided ultimately by which of the two does the more for the common man." In 1956 he acknowledged that Russia was a prodigious menace to human freedom, despite admirable gains achieved in such fields as literacy. "What troubles me," he continued," is our complacency about ourselves and our failure in seeing that the defeat of the evils in communism can never be achieved by H-bombs. That will take far different policies than we are now relying on."

VIII

How did Fosdick's economic and political convictions receive concrete expression in the polling booth? Only an incomplete answer can be given. Unlike some ministers, except in the instance of Teddy Roosevelt in 1912, he never actively campaigned for a candidate, nor did he from the pulpit endorse a party candidate by name. What follows, therefore, is a mixture of documentation and hunch.

At the presidential level, in 1916 he positively voted for Charles Evans Hughes; in 1920 he positively voted for Warren G. Harding; in 1924 he probably voted for Robert M. La Follette, the Progressive party candidate; in 1928 he positively voted for Herbert Hoover; in 1932 he probably voted again for Hoover; in 1936 he probably voted for Roosevelt; in 1940 he probably voted for Wendell Willkie (because of the war issue); in 1944 he probably voted for Roosevelt again; in 1948 he positively voted for Harry S Truman; in 1952 and 1956 he probably voted for Adlai Stevenson; in 1960 he positively voted for John F. Kennedy; in 1964 he probably voted for Lyndon Johnson; in 1968 he probably voted for Hubert Humphrey. The birthday congratulations that he received from President Eisenhower and President Johnson and from President Kennedy's brother, Robert are a measure of Fosdick's national stature.

At the local level, early and late Fosdick lashed the Tammany Tiger generally and Mayor "Beau James" Walker's regime in particular. Although not a member of the Socialist party, in 1929 Fosdick voted for Norman Thomas in the New York City mayoralty race to the consternation of Fiorello LaGuardia, the Republican-Fusion candidate. "I would give the city a square deal on taxes and assessments," LaGuardia informed the press. "Do you mean that Dr. Fosdick does not want a fair deal?," inquired a reporter. "I mean," answered LaGuardia, "that Dr. Fosdick has no reason to be dissatisfied with Tammany." On that score the "Little Flower" was surely wrong.

IX

In his autobiography Fosdick reminisced: "Many a time as I went into the pulpit I recalled Hugh Latimer's experience that Sunday morning when, headed toward the royal chapel, he heard a voice within him say: 'Latimer, Latimer, be careful what you preach today because you are going to preach before the king of England'; then another voice said: 'Latimer, Latimer, be careful what you preach today since you are going to preach before the King of kings.' " In addressing social issues Fosdick heeded Latimer's warning.

Chapter Twenty-six

"Can Satan Cast Out Satan?": Does Pacifism Have a Place in a World of Hitlers and Stalins?

I

In early May 1934 over eight hundred clergymen and concerned laymen, including Norman Thomas, Reinhold Niebuhr, and Kirby Page, assembled in the Broadway Tabernacle to confront the twin curses of economic injustice and war. Only weeks earlier 12,904 ministers, in response to a poll conducted by the pacifist Page, had vowed not to sanction any future war or participate as an armed combatant, and almost 9000 had pledged their intent not even to serve as official chaplains in wartime. The most dramatic moment in the proceedings came when Fosdick rose to make what the *Christian Century* correspondent termed the greatest address of his life, "My Account with the Unknown Soldier," a sermon first preached in Riverside Church on Armistice Day 1933.

The sermon was an extraordinary confession of things done in the Great Crusade and an unyielding pledge that they would not be done should war break out once again. Fosdick tried to picture the Unknown Soldier, a conscript, no doubt, whom he had met somewhere on the battlefront in 1918. He recalled himself as a minister of Christ speaking to a company of hand grenaders detailed to raid the German trenches, nerving "them for their suicidal and murderous endeavor." Perhaps the Unknown Soldier was in the doomed detachment. "I deceived him. I deceived myself first, unwittingly, and then I deceived him, assuring him that good consequence would come out of the war." "My friends," Fosdick continued in quivering voice, "sometimes I do not want to believe in immortality. Sometimes I hope the Unknown Soldier will never know." For Fosdick, World War I was now symbolized by the image of a pair of hands protruding from the soaked ashen soil like the roots of a tree turned upside down. "I renounce war," came the final cry, "and never again, directly or indirectly, will I sanction or support another! O Unknown Soldier, in penitent reparation I make you that pledge." He added to a *New York Times* reporter, "I'll see you in prison first."

"My Account with the Unknown Soldier" won wide attention in the press and was reprinted in whole or in part in a number of magazines. It was broadcast in pamphlet form and placed in the *Congressional Record*. When Fosdick repreached the sermon at Yale and Chicago universities, the students broke into applause.

Of course, not everyone everywhere applauded. In the column beside the one relating the events in Broadway Tabernacle, the *New York Times* carried an account of a simultaneous meeting at which an Army colonel termed the peace movements on American campuses "un-American" and an Army major charged that the antiwar propagandists were "either too yellow to fight or wanted to grab-off something."

Full war came to Asia in 1937 and to Europe in 1939 and to America on December 7, 1941. "Crack-pot realism" relentlessly prevailed over the "sublime horse sense" of the peacemakers. Yet even Pearl Harbor did not cause Fosdick to repudiate his pledge to the Unknown Soldier. Bishop Paul Jones's aphorism, "A pacifist between wars is like a prohibitionist between drinks," was not coined with Fosdick in mind. On the forty-fourth anniversary of Fosdick's *mea culpa*, after all the butchery in World War II and in Korea and in Vietnam, the fledgling minister of Riverside, William Sloane Coffin, Jr., preached on "Warring Madness." The sermon contained these words: "In the name of Harry Emerson Fosdick, we can all try to change the arms race into a peace race. We, too, must carry on a lover's quarrel with the world, so that when, like Harry Emerson Fosdick, we depart this life, we leave behind a little more truth, a little more justice, a little more peace, a little more beauty, than would have been there had we not cared enough about the human race to quarrel with it, not for what it is but for what it might yet be."

Fosdick more than once quoted Walt Whitman: "God damn every war: God damn 'em? God damn 'em!" About these furious words he would say, "That is not cursing; that is prayer." In this chapter we shall strive to show why the leading historian of the interwar peace movement would write, "The man who more than any other epitomized the acceptance of Christian duty to forsake war was Harry Emerson Fosdick." Fosdick came to believe that nonviolence in international relations was an obligation, not a promise. He could not guarantee that it would work, much less that it would be safe for the United States. He was only sure that it was for him the right understanding of the will of God. Ultimately, there is no way to peace; peace is the way.

II

The history of the organized peace movement in America is a melancholy one. The noble men and women who gave their highest loyalty to the Prince of Peace were never remotely sufficient in strength to maintain unbroken peace in the nineteenth century or deter intervention in the Great War. The very horror of World War I, however, served as a spur to a resurgent peace crusade in the 1920s. By the end of the decade there had been established some twelve hundred organizations for the study of international affairs and perhaps two hundred peace societies. Some of these were richly endowed, handsomely domiciled, and expertly staffed, like the Carnegie Endowment for International Peace, with a Brahmin secular leadership whose legalistic approach to international affairs reflected concern about social convulsion as well as international violence. Others, such as the Fellowship of Reconciliation, the War Resisters League, the Women's International League for Peace and Freedom, and the American Friends Service Committee, were more religiously rooted. Fosdick was more closely identified with such groups, although he always drew just back from the position of absolute pacifism.

The peacemakers (a term perhaps sufficiently imprecise to embrace the amorphous nature of the antiwar movement, or rather, movements) sought international disarmament, curbs on munitions making, repudiation of solely German guilt for World War I, cancellation of scaling down of reparations and war debts, constitutional protection for conscientious objectors and release from prison of those convicted during wartime, arbitration treaties, entrance into the World Court, qualified or unqualified entrance into the League of Nations (not all agreed in this), the outlawry of war, abolition of military training in schools, removal of trade barriers, an end to colonialism and imperialism, the muting of nationalism—in sum, they sought to insure peace by establishing the conditions of peace.

Time was to reveal the conditional, prudential, even conservative nature of the great majority of the peacemakers of the 1920s. But a small minority of absolute pacifists and those (like Fosdick) whose hatred of war was total followed the plumb line straight and true to Pearl Harbor—and beyond. "They were the evangelists of the peace movement. Like Paul on the road to Damascus each had seen a sign and heard a call."

They marched under many banners and their strategies took many names: nonresistance, nonviolence, passive resistance, civil disobedience, nonviolent resistance, Gandhian satyagraha. Whatever the tactics, they shared the common understanding that war is the organized use of physical force to kill wholesale and indiscriminately for national self-interest. They shared the common conviction that international disputes must be settled by nonviolent means, by arbitration, mediation, conciliation, reconciliation—finally, by sacrificial love and commitment to a way of life "that taketh away the occasion of all wars."

Before 1914 pacifism in America had largely been the passion of the historic peace sects—the Brethren, the Mennonites, the Quakers—but after Versailles, American Protestantism was swept by a mighty antiwar fervor and pacifism became almost the "party line" of the ministerial leadership. "Peace is within reach for the first time in history," announced Florence Boeckel, and another peace worker, Dorothy Detzer, recalled that in the 1920s "life seemed to open up a new pathway to peace."

It is revealing that the post-Versailles peace movement in America embraced many of the groups that had supported prewar progressivism and Social Gospelism: clergymen, lay church workers, professors, students, political spokesmen for midwestern agrarianism, and, extraordinarily important, professional women, social workers, feminists. In the United States (unlike France) the Socialist party was too weak to give much muscle to the peace movement, although Norman Thomas was a gallant opponent of war. In the United States (unlike Great Britain) labor unions were both too weak and too conservative to lend much assistance, although a number of individual labor leaders were staunchly antiwar. Nevertheless, in the 1920s a commitment to world peace was almost invariably coupled with a devotion to domestic reform. The peacemakers believed that war grew in the soil of economic and social injustice and that a warless world must also of necessity be a world freed from poverty and exploitation and from class and caste barriers. It was not until the period immediately preceding Pearl Harbor that liberal pacifists found themselves joined by conservative isolationists in common opposition to President Roosevelt's interventionist foreign policies.

It is well known that the Great War bequeathed a legacy of disillusionment and that many Americans sought to retire from the world, like a jilted bride to a convent." Led to believe that American intervention would end war once for all and cherishing the hope of first a peace without victory and then a peace without end, their idealistic expectations were shattered by the hard realities of the Versailles settlement. The failure of the peace meant the failure of the Great Crusade and the failure of the Great Crusade meant the futility of all wars. The folly of intervention could be compensated for only if America firmly resolved never again to be played for a sucker. "About all that America got out of Europe was its army" growled one citizen—"unless it be prohibition and influenza" added another. The historic belief of European wickedness and American innocence gained new currency: in the American Eden all the snakes came from across the seas.

As early as 1920 Germany's sole guilt for causing the war was being challenged, and once the equal guilt of the Allies was "established" by scholars, the moral case for America's intervention broke down. Soon novelists, playwrights, and poets were stripping the war of all glory, journalists were exposing the "truth" about Allied propaganda, and the sinister role of the "merchants of death" was unveiled. Debunking became a common pastime among liberals, reflecting a kind of inverted idealism. Liberal after liberal stepped forward to confess his guilt for baptizing the war, and the pages of such journals as the *New Republic* and the *Nation* became "an historical Wailing Wall where the penitent revisionists lamented their sins and sought forgiveness." Often the result was a sullen and peevish isolationism typified by a remark of one of the Lost Generation's heroes, George Jean Nathan: "If all the Armenians were to be killed tomorrow and if half of Russia were to starve to death the day after, it would not matter to me in the least. . . . For all I care the rest of the world may go to hell at today's sunset."

But just as not all liberals said farewell to reform in the 1920s neither did all liberals say farewell to the world. For many disenchantment *did* take the form of isolationism. But for Fosdick and a host of peacemakers the hope to end war in the world rested on America's greater participation in the affairs of the world. In this decade of peace, pacifism and isolationism were poles apart, for basic to pacifism is the conviction of the essential unity of all mankind overriding barriers of class, nation, and race. Pacifism cultivated an internationalist frame of mind in order to counter nationalism, that breeding ground of chauvinism and militarism and, hence, war. Whether the warring 1930s would see the pacifists and the isolationists pressured into an uneasy alliance was a question for the future.

What many commentators on the twenties fail to realize is that the postwar peace crusade was characterized by hope, not despair. When Fosdick and his fellow peacemakers confessed their repentance for having advocated war in 1917, they did not merely wring their hands; rather, they translated their contrition into action for peace. And it was action informed by a high urgency precisely because the Great War had demonstrated how imperiled civilization was by war. The experiences of

1914–1918 did not "prove" that men will always fight; rather they "proved" that men must either cease to fight or perish. These experiences were universalized and applied to *all* wars. The theological doctrine of a just war seemed a contradiction in terms and the rule of proportionality an absurdity after Tannenberg Forest, Verdun, and Belleau Wood. It was imperative to labor earnestly and tirelessly for peace because of the realization that peace would not come by incantation and that war would not turn its face from men merely because it was frightful.

The pacifism of the 1920s was not simply a modern adaptation of the doctrine of nonresistance of the historic peace sects. For these quietist fellowships, nonresistance was a literal injunction of the New Testament and Jesus' command that evil should not be returned for evil, that the sword should be put away, that one should love and pray for one's enemies, that ultimately one must submit to, but not participate in, the violence of this world. Nonresistance abjures coercion as well as violence, for as the Mennonite Guy Hershberger observed, nonviolent resistance "is simply a form of warfare, since its primary purpose is to bring about the submission of the opposition through compulsion." And Umphrey Lee argued that nonviolent resistance is "still a technique for overcoming a superior force, and has little more relation to the teachings of Jesus than the technique of war." Absolute nonresistance is an assertion of individual conscience in obedience to religious authority, a perfectionist renunciation of the sinful world. Rather than seeking to Christianize the state, which must exercise coercion, its adherents live as patient pilgrims awaiting the reign of peace in another world. When ordered by the state to participate in carnal warfare, the nonresistant will refuse. He will instead obey his Savior and like his Savior submit if necessary to the Cross.

The main body of post-1918 pacifism, however, was not world renouncing but world affirming. It was social rather than individualistic, seeking not simply personal salvation, but the conversion of whole societies. It was not quietist, but active, even aggressive, in pursuing a program of educational, social, and political action. It was not dualistic, holding one standard for the perfectionist Christian community and another for the coercive state, which must live by the sword; it believed the state to be under God's judgment and, thus, sought to Christianize the state. Rather than leaving it to isolated individuals to stand firm in their conscientious refusal to serve in military duty after the outbreak of war, it hoped to create a "will to peace" among the great masses that would make the declaration of war impossible in the first instance. Finally, although refusing absolutely to participate in, or condone, violence, the pacifists of the twenties, unlike the historic peace sects, would resist evil and ultimately overcome evil by means of a superior form of force—moral force or "soul force" as Gandhi called it.

Thus, the new pacifism was a mode of redemptive witness much concerned with the distinction between nonresistance and nonviolent resistance and with the extent to which nonviolent coercion employed in the interests of justice might be ethical. War is invariably unredemptive. The killing of the "enemy" is totally inconsistent with the law of love and the moral order of the universe. But for Fosdick and those other peacemakers committed to seek the establishment of the Kingdom on this wartorn planet, the ideal of nonresistance was inadequate. Those forces in the world that make for war must be resisted and overcome by a nonviolent way of life, program of political change, and technique of social action.

III

As we know from Chapter Five, Fosdick's experience in France did not make an instant pacifist of him and in his immediate postwar utterances he continued to proclaim the justice of President Wilson's crusade and to laud the sacrificial spirit that compelled America to take up arms. Nevertheless, in a famous 1928 article he related "What the War Did to My Mind," and it is clear from this article as well as from sermons preached in late 1918, 1919, and 1920 that in France war was for him stripped of all chivalric romance. Early in 1921 Fosdick preached a powerful sermon, "Shall We End War?," widely broadcast in pamphlet form, designed to build up public support for a naval disarmament conference. In it he drove home the points that there is no longer anything glorious about war; that war is no longer a school for public virtue; that there are no longer any limits to the methods of killing (including future germ warfare); that there are no longer any limits to the cost of war; and that there is no longer any possibility of sheltering civilian populations from death.

In 1922 Kirby Page and John Nevin Sayre, two of the nation's foremost religious pacifists, called together a group of twenty-four prominent churchmen and laymen to discuss the responsibility of churches regarding war. A committee composed of Page, William P. Merrill, and Fosdick penned "The Churches' Plea Against War and the War System."* Signed by 150 religious leaders, it was the first proclamation by representative

* The original typed statement, which is in the Swarthmore College Peace Collection, carried the handwritten notation, "Drawn up by Harry Emerson Fosdick, November, 1922."

Protestants and Catholics that the spirit of war is antithetical to that of the Gospel. Merrill, Fosdick's close friend, was then president of the board of trustees of the Church Peace Union. Although Page and Fosdick were not, according to Fosdick, "intimately close," they did work long and closely together in peace matters, especially as leaders of the Fellowship of Reconciliation, and on Page's death Fosdick acknowledged: "Probably I should have become a pacifist in the end anyway, but Kirby Page helped a lot, and all these years since he had been a challenge and an inspiration."

In 1923 Fosdick made his unqualified commitment to peace, believing "You will get salvation out of hell before you will get redemption for this world out of modern war." He did so in his introduction to Page's major book, *War*, and in sermons, notably "A Christian Crusade Against War" and "What Is Christianity?" In the latter he said:

> For when a man takes Jesus in earnest he must see that war is the most colossal social sin against him of which the world is guilty, that it is absolutely, irrevocably un-christian, that it means everything that Jesus does not mean and means nothing that Jesus does mean, that it is a more blatant denial of every fundamental Christian doctrine about God and man than all the theoretical atheists ever could devise. If a man begins seriously to take Jesus in earnest he must see that all these quarrels between fundamentalists, liberals, high church, broad church, and low church are but tithing mint, anise and cummin if Christians do not really wrestle with this supreme moral issue of our time: Christ against war. And as for myself, the more I consider war, its causes, its nature, and its results, its debasing welter of lies and cruelty, its horror when it is here and its futility when it is gone to achieve any good thing that manhood may dream, I find it increasingly difficult to imagine any circumstances under which I shall again feel justified in sanctioning or participating in another war.

Thereafter not a year passed in which Fosdick failed to make a strong statement against war, in articles, sermons, books, and in his League of Nations' address, "A Christian Conscience About War." He was impassioned:

> I hate war. I hate it because I have seen it. I hate it for what it does to our own men. I have seen them come in freshly gassed from the front line trenches. I have watched the long trains loaded with their mutilated bodies. I have heard the raving of those that were crazed and the cries of those who wanted to die and could not. I hate war for what it forces us to do to our enemies, rejoicing over our coffee cups at the breakfast table about every damnable and devilish evil we have been able to inflict upon

them. I hate war for its results, the lies it lives on and propagates, the undying hatreds that it rouses, the dictatorships that it puts in the place of democracy, and the starvation that stalks after it.*

In 1930 as the world passed from a decade of peace to a decade of war, Fosdick composed the hymn, "The Prince of Peace His Banner Spreads," first sung by the Riverside congregation on Armistice Sunday. The hymn petitioned Christ "His way-ward folk to lead From war's em-bat-tled hates and dreads, Its bul-warked ire and greed."

Fosdick's opposition to war was unyielding in the 1920s, but although he acknowledged the influence of Rufus Jones and was a member of the Wider Quaker Fellowship, his position was not identical with that of the historic nonresistant peace sects. As he once explained, "pacifist" comes from two Latin words, *pax* and *facio*, and it means peacemaker. "It is a positive word, being true to which involves all the strong, intelligent, morally combative faculties we have." Time and again he reported that he could not take "the absolutist pledge of the extreme pacifists." Nevertheless, he added, "I disagree even more with most of my non-pacifist brethren, and since willy-nilly one is called either a pacifist or a nonpacifist, I choose to be called a pacifist. There is, however, no neat solution for the Christian conscience with regard to the problem of war. No matter what position one takes, one is faced with an inner agony of self-contradiction, whether one participates in war or whether one refrains from participation when great issues are at stake." Perhaps Fosdick's position might best be described as the Gandhian one of the resistance of evil with nonviolent means, but, as we shall see, even this oversimplifies because Fosdick believed the United States as a nation would never embrace Gandhian principles in his lifetime.

IV

Essential to the blunting of war was the muting of nationalism through the creation of a countervailing spirit of internationalism. Fosdick once quoted Nurse Edith Cavell, "Patriotism is not enough," and he added that modern nationalism is "the most explicit and thoroughgoing denial of Christianity, its thoughts of God and its love of man there is on earth." The sainted Catholic pacifist, Dorothy Day, used the sardonic term "Holy Mother State" in reference to the modern Caesardom engulf-

---

* It will be remembered that this is not exactly the tone of his reports from France in 1918 to the people of America.

ing the nations, including the United States, and although this phrase was absent from Fosdick's language, his words were equally biting. Nationalism was nothing less than "sheer paganism." For multitudes the supreme object of devotion is the nation, "they know no higher God." Nowhere did Fosdick spell out his indictment more sharply than in the 1928 sermon, "Christianity's Supreme Rival." The gist of the matter, he insisted, "lies in the fact that the dogma of nationalism, as it has developed in the last two centuries, has become a competing religion. I think it is the most dangerous rival of Christian principles on earth." In America hope lay "not in one hundred per centers ready to jump in any direction when the government cracks the whip, but in men of independent consciences, in time of peace or war, willing to defy the nation in the interests of the nation. Every Sunday in the navy the white flag of religion is floated above the stars and stripes. It is the only flag that ever floated above the national emblem. It is the symbol of what ought perpetually to be true about our consciences." Elsewhere he noted that the jingoes had appropriated the motto, "For Home and Fatherland," when in fact it is the peacemakers who truly are for home and fatherland.

The issue of Holy Disobedience versus the claims of a voracious State was brought into sharp focus when in 1931 the Supreme Court by a five to four vote upheld the denial of U.S. citizenship to Douglas Macintosh, a distinguished fifty-four year old theologian, and Marie Bland, a Christian nurse. Neither were absolute pacifists, the theologian declaring his willingness to serve in a just war and the nurse declaring her willingness to serve in her profession in the event of a conflict. But neither would swear their willingness to bear arms in any and every war the nation plunged into. Fosdick informed his congressmen of his profound disturbance and petitioned that legislation be passed permitting the naturalization of conscientious objectors. To the people of Riverside he thundered: "Let this be said plainly and publicly: if Professor Macintosh is not fit to become a citizen, then we are not fit to be citizens, for most certainly we will not support a war that we think is morally unjustified. Since when has any government in Washington become God that it can conscript our consciences to do what we honestly think is wrong? If some hare-brained secretary of state should plunge us into an international conflict that seemed to us to violate all principles of decency and fair-dealing, can the Christian conscience be so feeble as abjectly to fall down before that decision, willing to die for it ourselves and to urge millions of our nation's youth to die for it? Never!"

Even before the existence of thermonuclear weapons Fosdick comprehended that if nobody spoke for mankind, for that faceless, stateless man called "humanity," that if the highest loyalty was given to the peoples of one's own nation-state alone, then what was there to prevent humanity's death?

Fosdick sought to advance internationalism by continuing to urge U.S. membership in the League of Nations, an action that by the mid-1920s was probably opposed by a majority of Americans. Nationalists feared that membership would geld American sovereignty. Isolationists feared that membership would needlessly embroil their country in Europe's quarrels. Some socialists and pacifists saw the League as only a new and greater system of military alliances. (Significantly, the influential *Christian Century* shared this view.) But for Fosdick and most peacemakers in the twenties, the alternative to America's membership seemed to be a weakened League and an increased mood of nationalism and isolationism and irresponsibility. "I believe in the League of Nations," he said in 1928, "not because I think it ideal but because I think it is the most promising nucleus of organized internationalism in the world." So, he supported the Nonpartisan Association for the League of Nations, spoke at pro-League rallies, and dotted his sermons with pro-League references. Still, at the end of the decade he was sufficiently clear-sighted to make this observation: "The real reason why we have stayed out of the League of Nations is that we have been afraid that if we got into it we would be dragged into another European war. I think behind all American attitudes today that must be taken account of. The American people have made up their minds that they will not go into another European war under any circumstances whatsoever and they do not want to join the League of Nations for fear that they be involved in future trouble. There, again, I disagree with them but I see why they think as they do."

Urging membership of the United States in the World Court was almost a mark of enlightenment among the peacemakers, and Fosdick did his part. To a mass meeting in Carnegie Hall in 1923 he declared that failure to join would be an "everlasting disgrace" to the nation, biting out the indictment: "The United States government today will not even touch with its finger tips the single constructive endeavor existing today to end war. The United States Senate will not go into the World Court. There is only one thing that the United States Senate will do with enthusiasm and that is to collect our debts to the last penny." By 1928 his words were calmer although his stance remained affirmative: "I believe in the World Court, not because I think it a glorious finality leaping full statured from the head of the League, but because it is the most helpful beginning we have around with which to build up a codification of international law."

No element in the peacemakers' program now seems so utopian as the

Kellogg-Briand Pact of 1928 in which the contracting parties—sixty-four nations including Germany, Russia, and Japan—renounced war as an instrument of policy and promised to settle all disputes among themselves by peaceful means. There was something (because there was so little of substance) in the pact for almost everyone, except Aristide Briand, the astute French foreign minister, who had initially hoped for a Franco-American bilateral security treaty. The pact permitted the profane Secretary of State, Frank B. Kellogg, to avoid such an entangling alliance. To internationalists, such as Professor James T. Shotwell, it was a way of bringing the United States into closer cooperation with the League of Nations, the first of many steps in building a systematic peace structure. To isolationists, such as Senator William O. Borah, it reenforced the position that the United States would not fight in foreign wars. To idealists, such as Salmon O. Levinson, it seemed the fulfillment of the dream to outlaw war, though in fact the word "outlaw" did not appear in the document. On signing of the pact, the *Christian Century* exulted, "Today international war was banished from civilization," and the Federal Council of Churches sent out a telegram to the churches of America: "Let church bells be rung, songs sung, prayers of thanksgiving be offered." Only a minority of church people expressed doubts about this "international kiss," one of whom was Reinhold Niebuhr who observed, "The general effect of the outlawry programme is to beguile a nation which stands aloof to preserve the advantages of its strength into believing that it stands aloof to preserve the advantages of its virtue."

Fosdick told the one thousand delegates to a 1928 Women's Conference on the Cause and Cure of War that the pact was a turning point in the world's history. "It is hard-headed practicality that used to consecrate itself to war now trying to find a way to peace." It would be a catastrophe of the first order if the Senate should fail to ratify it.* Elsewhere Fosdick stated: "I believe in the outlawry of war, not because I think that all the juridical agreements of all the governments on earth to outlaw war are in themselves sufficient to stop it, but because the outlawing of war is the very gist of what we are after and any approach which does not envisage outlawry as the goal and an important part of the method is in so far paltering with the issue."

Years before the signing of the Kellogg-Briand Pact, Fosdick and much of American Protestantism had advocated the cause of disarma-

---

* Two young radical pacifists heckled Fosdick, hurling "sarcastic flings at the speaker until the room was in tumult." "Why all this hypocrisy and cant, while the next war is preparing right under our very noses?" one of them cried as Mrs. Carrie Chapman Catt futility pounded her gavel and the audience sounded its disapproval of the intruders by hissing and booing.

ment. By voice and pen early in the decade, Fosdick endorsed the idea of a naval disarmament conference, materializing in the important 1921 Washington Conference. He registered his protest to a "Mobilization Day" proposed by the War Department in 1924. He wished well the 1927 Geneva Naval Disarmament Conference and the 1930 London Naval Disarmament Conference; the first was an utter failure and the second a limited success. A proposed cruiser expansion program in 1928 drew his fire. "The big Navy Bill which is now before Congress," he informed the secretary of the Church Peace Union, "is one of the most startling and needless assaults on international hopes of peace that has befallen us since the war, especially as this "outrageous" bill is accompanied by "swaggering and saber-rattling talk." He accepted an invitation from the pacifist editor Oswald Garrison Villard to speak at a meeting in Carnegie Hall to protest this "dangerous," "idiotic," "wild," and "perilous" program.

Villard was treasurer and "angel" to the Committee on Militarism in Education, a group formed in 1925 and dedicated to the elimination of all military training in the high schools and compulsory military training in colleges. Fosdick gave his full support to the committee and in manifold other ways labored to achieve its goals, believing as he did that the greatest hope for a world without war rested with the youth of the world.

Fosdick's peacemaking activities were not conducted without reference to the concrete international situation. For example, he sought the reduction of America's high tariffs and belonged to a committee seeking a scaling down of the war debts owed by European nations to the United States. His trip to the Holy Land, among many other things, led him to a harsh assessment of French rule in Syria, a "disastrous travesty of a mandate from the League of Nations." "It is a sheer piece of dirty greed, and from the public brutality of shelling Damascus to the low morals of forcing public prostitution on the Arabs, there is no mistake on the earth beneath or in hell under the earth that the French have not made." His concern with this area of the globe led him to become a director of a new organization, American Friends of Turkey, designed to support educational, medical, and cultural programs in Turkey.

Fosdick's trip to Japan and China in 1921 sharpened his understanding of the Asian situation, and on his return he wrote a series of articles for the *Christian Work* and also for the *Nation*. "The first impression which needs to be driven home upon those flippant chauvinists who all over America today so light-heartedly chatter about war with Japan," he warned the readers, "is that when it comes it will probably be a thunderstorm in comparison with which this last war will sound like a popping chestnut." He traced the aggressive seizure of the whole world by the white races, all of Asia, save Japan, falling before their rapacity. "This brings us to another truth which the American people need to take to heart," he continued. "Economic imperialism, the desire to exploit the resources of Eastern Asia, is at the root of all the contentions in the Pacific. If war comes it will be a battle of big business in a sense more baldly unrelieved by redeeming motives than any other great war, I suppose, in modern history. There is no real question of national glory to further or national honor to defend; the problem is all about oil wells and coal mines and iron deposits and the price of bean-cake." Regarding Japan: "To be anti-Japanese . . . or pro-Japanese, is nonsense. To be anti-Japanese militarism and pro-Japanese liberalism is the only hopeful policy. . . . And of all the swift, sure ways of killing liberalism in Japan, the most efficient would be to let war talk and war preparations make militarism seem still Japan's one safe alliance. The real alignment today is not America against Japan, but liberal America and liberal Japan together against the jingoes who would bedevil both." At that time Fosdick became a member of the Committee of One Thousand, an off-shoot of the National Committee on American-Japanese Relations, designed to effect better relations between the two nations.

In all this it is needful to say again, that determined as Fosdick was to keep America out of war, he yet judged himself to be an internationalist. In 1925 the National Council for the Prevention of War adopted the slogan, " 'America First'—In the Crusade for a Warless World." Fosdick concurred. Time and again he acknowledged that to avert future wars "it will cost the nations the surrender of some of their national sovereignty." He repeatedly raised the prayer, "Eternal God, Father of all souls: Grant unto us such clear vision of the sin of war that we may earnestly seek that cooperation between nations which alone can make war impossible." Isolationism was, he claimed, anathema to him. He once said that he did not know a single important Christian leader in this country who was in his philosophy of life an isolationist, adding, "To a Christian the world is the subject of redemption; the world is the object of God's care; the world is the Christian's home and the human race his family."

The period between the Washington Conference of 1921 and the Japanese invasion of Manchuria in 1931 was a time in which it was possible to seek greater American participation in the world without having to face the immediate question of whether this desired diminution of isolationism and unilateralism might not heighten the chances of America's being drawn into a foreign war. That is to say, for a brief decade Fosdick and the peacemakers knew the luxury of urging the

United States to accept full membership in a world at peace without reckoning the dues that might be required to keep the peace. Moreover, if America joined the world and if the world stumbled from peace to war, what then? Was it possible and proper to be a member of the international club only in fair times, promptly resigning with the first rumble of thunder?

V

The period between 1931 and 1939 was a time when the world hung suspended between peace and war. For Fosdick and the peacemakers the circle tightened. Was it possible to work collectively to keep war out of the world without committing America to involvement should war break out? And if the United States was unwilling to make such a commitment, how could peace be preserved in the world? Or rather, how could peace be preserved short of the total appeasement of ruthless, predatory nations and the consequent sacrifice of freedom and democracy?

This dilemma sprang inevitably from the objective facts of twentieth century life. The world was contracting. The economic power and consequent potential military power of the United States was expanding. Short of turning back the technological clock and short of America's returning to an agrarian economy, there was no way to halt the globe's shrinking or America's increasing influence. It is obvious, therefore, that every act by the United States relative to Europe and Asia was bound to be consequential. It is further evident that a decision *not* to act might also have fateful consequences. This is not quite to accept the proposition that a great power cannot be insulated against events outside its borders; it rather is to insist that if a great power should succeed in so doing, the results might have just as much impact on world developments as massive intervention.

Factors of foreign trade and investments and domestic prosperity were involved in the equation. Sealed off from the outside world in a determined effort to escape the contagion of war, would America reap the lesser material rewards of a second-class state and perhaps deepen the Depression? Was not economic recovery contingent on the stimulus of preparations for war and the continuance of trade even after the outbreak of war? Also involved were considerations of national honor and prestige. Surely for America to relinquish her traditional rights as a neutral and to surrender responsibility for the fate of Europe and Asia would be to ask her citizens to redefine and scale down the meaning of "national greatness." Further, did not America's very survival depend on checking through collective action aggression across the seas, for if Nazism and Japanese imperialism triumphed in the 1930s would not the United States, standing alone, fall victim in the 1940s? And for millions of citizens there was an additional crucial moral issue: Should the United States take refuge in storm-cellar neutrality, ride out the struggle, and keep her hands unstained by blood? If she followed this course, could white hands cloak a conscience stricken by the fate of conquered peoples pinioned on Japanese bayonets and broken on Nazi swastikas?

"Ninety-nine Americans out of a hundred," estimated the *Christian Century* in 1935, "would today regard as an imbecile anyone who might suggest that, in the event of another European war, the United States should again participate in it." A year later a poll conducted by the American Institute of Public Opinion set the exact figure at 95 percent. Isolationist sentiment reached its zenith in the 1930s. This was not evidence of a new spirit of unilateralism in foreign affairs. The American people had held isolationist convictions since the days of the Founding Fathers. Rather, isolationism reached such a feverish intensity in the thirties exactly because a contracting world and an expanding American power rendered isolationism questionable as a viable national posture even as the fearful nature of modern war was increasingly beyond question. In the nineteenth century isolationism was not much debated. It was a "given"—an unacknowledged gift of "free security" compliments of the British navy. In the 1930s a sequence of events across the oceans made isolationism at once less possible and more desirable. After about 1937, however, increasing numbers of citizens came to question even its desirability, believing it neither moral nor prudent to shirk the task of halting totalitarian aggression. At the same time, the unyielding isolationists, the great majority of whom were not pacifists, found common cause with the opponents of war, whereas the pacifists, the great majority of whom were not isolationists, found common cause with the opponents of interventionism. Starting from different base camps, following different and frequently tortuous paths, the two groups arrived at the same clearing in the woods at the same time and there they joined ranks to face a common foe, the interventionists.

Of the two groups, the isolationists were by far the more numerous. The fine shadings of the term "isolationism" must be left to the Talmudic scholars. It has been explained in terms of geography, occupation, class, religious affiliation, ethnicity, race,* party loyalty, and even personality. Some isolationists were conservatives who feared that involvement in foreign war would spell death to America's free-enterprise system, al-

---

* Historians were late in coming to the realization of the anti-interventionist position of articulate black Americans.

ready threatened by Roosevelt's New Deal. Some isolationists were liberals concerned about the impact of war on American society. War would mean the end of reform and the wreckage of the promise of a cooperative commonwealth; indeed, war would usher in a fascist state at home, totalitarianism entering the back door, ironically, even as the United States fought totalitarianism abroad. Some isolationists were idealists who believed their nation could best serve humanity by remaining an island of sanity in a world gone mad, standing ready to minister to the needs of a shell-shocked postwar globe. Some isolationists were quite prepared to permit the world to hang itself, cherishing the historic belief of American exceptionalism. A few sympathizers of the Soviet Union were pro tem isolationists, following the dictates of the party line, but for these fellow travelers isolationism was a tactical matter to be jettisoned at the will of Moscow. A few rooted their isolationism in admiration for Hitler or Mussolini, but after 1935 this number was infinitesimal. A much larger number, while acknowledging the depravity of Nazism, nonetheless viewed Germany as a shield against Russian westward expansion and Japan as a bulwark against the expansion of communism in Asia. To muddy things further, a considerable group were isolationists with respect to Europe, but hawkish on America's role in Asia.

Perhaps Manfred Jonas's generalization is as close to the mark as any: "Isolationism owed whatever unity it had during the thirties not to geography, nor politics, nor class structure, nor ethnic background, but to faith in unilateralism and fear of war."

Opponents of war were to be found in all ranks of society, but pacifism provided the cutting edge of the antiwar movement and it was from the ranks of the Protestant clergy, more than any other group, that pacifism drew its lifeblood.* The pacifists claimed that they were not isolationists at all, "save only with respect to war." With the breakdown of peace in Asia and Europe, this exception was to be everything.

VI

Japan's seizure of Manchuria in 1931, Mussolini's invasion of Ethiopia, the outbreak of the savage Spanish Civil War, Japan's further conquests

---

* Poll after poll in the 1930s revealed the increasing commitment of the Protestant clergy to pacifism. After reading one such poll the *Pennsylvania Manufacturers' Journal* commented: "It is interesting, if not pleasant to contemplate the number of telegraph poles that would be adorned by white cravats, re-enforced by hempen neckties, should another war be declared—which, may heaven forfend—to test the 'loyalty' of these anti-patriots. . . . The event of a war and the active participation of the clergy against national defense, to which so many have pledged themselves, would give us a brand new national sport: gunning for clergymen."

in China following the Marco Polo Bridge incident, Hitler's devouring of Austria, the Rhineland, Czechoslovakia, and the Berlin-Moscow Pact—these and other events cruelly intensified for Fosdick Jesus' question, "Can Satan cast out Satan?" and sharpened the challenge, "Dare We Break the Vicious Circle of Fighting with Evil?," the title of a 1939 sermon distributed (thanks to Rockefeller, Jr.) to over one-hundred thousand leaders of American life. Further, Senator Richard Byrd had copies of the sermon printed at his own expense and mailed to all the ministers of Virginia, and Representative George Bender of Ohio had it placed in the *Congressional Record*.

On May 2, 1935, in Riverside Church, over two hundred ministers and rabbis, clad in their robes of office, in the spirit of deepest consecration solemnly repeated the pledge: "In loyalty to God I believe that the way of true religion cannot be reconciled with the way of war. In loyalty to my country I support its adoption of the Kellogg-Briand Pact which renounces war. In the spirit of true patriotism and with deep personal conviction, I therefore renounce war and never will I support another." Three years later this Covenant of Peace Group again assembled in Riverside and renewed its pledge to spike a rumor that large numbers of the original convenanters had abandoned their pacifism. Although he was ill in 1935, Fosdick gave his name to the pledge (as he did again in 1938) and opened the doors of Riverside to this group, which was headed by his friend, Allen Knight Chalmers.*

In the fall of 1935 American peacemakers responded to the accelerated disintegration of the post-Versailles peace structure with a great Emergency Peace Campaign (E.P.C.) designed to stave off war, and should war come to the world, to forestall America's entry, the very title of the effort reflecting the peacemakers' sense of urgency. The two-year E.P.C. was the most impressive effort in the history of the American peace movement—at least until the Vietnam War. Never had the peace movement been so united or so clearly in touch with the people, especially farmers, laborers, students, women, and minorities. (Businessmen showed less enthusiasm.) This highly organized, well-financed crusade was not an independent organization but a representative action group, enlisting the participation of many of the societies, both conservative collective security societies and radical absolute pacifist ones, working for peace. Many prominent citizens were involved or at least lent their voices, including Eleanor Roosevelt, Cordell Hull, Admiral Richard E. Byrd, Clark

---

* Interestingly, Dr. Norman Vincent Peale informed Chalmers of his inability to sign the pledge, explaining that although he was prepared to renounce "an aggressive war," if the United States was invaded by a foreign army "I am frank to say that I would meet that with force."

Eichelberger, Charles P. Taft II, and from Britain the pacifists Maude Royden and George Landsbury, former head of the British Labour Party, and member of Parliament Alfred Salter. Clergymen, however, were the head and heart of the campaign. In fact almost every pacifist minister in the land enlisted in this enterprise, almost three thousand of them serving as speakers without pay. Despite the conservative element in it, the E.P.C. was essentially an expression of pacifism, the left wing of the peace movement, the last great effort of the pacifists—as distinct from isolationists, unilateralists, and continentalists—to give leadership to the antiwar passion. The campaign reached its climax on the twentieth anniversary of the American entrance into World War I. On April 6, 1937, its officers launched a mighty No-Foreign-War Crusade. For two intensive months every available resource was committed to the task of so arousing public opinion and so shaping public policy as to make impossible a repetition of 1917.

Because he was still recovering from surgery for the removal of a tumor of the gall bladder, Fosdick was unable to participate in the organizational meetings of the E.P.C., although Ray Newton, Quaker pacifist and codirector of the campaign, believed that Fosdick's support was "essential"; without it, "the loss to the movement will be tremendous." In January 1936 Newton and Kirby Page importuned Fosdick, and, Newton reported, "He was very enthusiastic about what we are trying to do and only regretted that he could not help us more. He will give us more and more time as his health warrants. We could not have asked for a better reception." What Fosdick could immediately do was to issue a personal appeal to one hundred leaders to serve with him as sponsors of a nationwide educational speaking campaign; in the end hundreds of ministers, educators, and peace leaders, in groups of two and three, toured every state but Wyoming. Moreover, Fosdick himself mustered the energy to speak in Madison Square Garden and Secretary of State Cordell Hull, on Fosdick's invitation, participated in the rally. Further, Dorothy Fosdick volunteered to serve on the E.P.C. Council.

Fosdick's participation grew as his strength returned. On January 7, 1937, he and Maude Royden and Sherwood Eddy led a major rally in Philadelphia. Fosdick's address, "Five Sectors of the Peace Movement," was delivered again over the air in February. The address opened by acknowledging the splintered nature of the peace movement, continued with an examination of the five sectors indispensable to the work for peace, and concluded with the plea: "Find the place where you can make your best contribution. For it surely is hypocrisy to call Christ, 'Lord, Lord,' and not take our stand against this accursed thing, this antiChrist."

Two days later the E.P.C. Council elected Fosdick chairman of the campaign and Admiral Richard E. Byrd chairman of the No-Foreign-War Crusade, the climactic Fourth Cycle of the entire campaign, Byrd's selection coming only after much debate, because he had honestly stated that though he was opposed to war, as a sworn naval officer he could not be an absolute pacifist.

On March 4 a mass antiwar meeting was held at Riverside, featuring Fosdick, Royden, and distinguished public servant Charles P. Taft II. Then, on April 6, anniversary of that fateful date in 1917, the No-Foreign-War Crusade was fully launched by a national broadcast of speeches by Fosdick, Admiral Byrd, and Eleanor Roosevelt.* Said Fosdick in conclusion:

> My own stand on the peace movement can be briefly put. First, I want to do everything I can to keep the world out of war and to further all measures of international organization that promise collective security against it. Second, if in spite of that the world goes to war, I want to do everything I can to keep the United States out of war, as at least one place where war's ruinous impact on liberty and democracy shall not be allowed to fall. Third, if the United States goes to war, I being the pacifist I am, expect to stand in uncompromising protest against our government's folly in taking us in. Now, if I can find anybody to stand with me on the first point, I'll stand with him even if he does not believe in the last two points. If I can find anybody to stand with me on the first two points, I'll stand with him even though he does not stand with me on the third. That is to say, I do not want to be a sectarian on the peace question. We who hate war and do not see any reason why our children should be used as cannon fodder in another one belong together, however much we may differ in details. We need to emphasize our common objective rather than our different techniques.

E.P.C. area directors across the land reported receiving thousands of requests for the speech.

Concurrently, Fosdick used his influence to solicit funds for the campaign, sending out appeals by mail and in at least one instance personally visiting Mrs. John D. Rockefeller, Jr., who contributed $5000. As the campaign drew to a close, its work was transferred to the National Peace Conference, in which Fosdick was also involved. Ray Newton wrote to him: "Again let me thank you for all that you have done for the American peace movement. I feel that you more than any other person have been responsible for the fine progress we have already made."

---

* The E.P.C. minutes revealingly read: "It was suggested that Mrs. Roosevelt be given careful guidance with the context of her talk, and that an attack on William Randolph Hearst be made in some part of the broadcast."

Newton was no fool and he knew that talk about "fine progress" could not mask the widening fissures in the American peace movement. Admiral Byrd was not only not a pacifist, he could not be expected to endorse the pacifists' opposition to the government's military and naval armaments program for, he observed, "It is already the policy of the government to arm for defense only." Clark Eichelberger, codirector with Newton of the E.P.C., had long been a leader of the League of Nations Association, and naturally he took issue with the pacifists' support of mandatory neutrality legislation and the pacifists' doubts about the league with its commitment to collective security. Conservative isolationists questioned both the pacifists' universalism and their association with liberal reforms at home. Finally, the pacifists themselves were divided between those of Fosdick's persuasion and the absolutists.

John Nevin Sayre, one of the key leaders of the E.P.C., questioned the appointment of Admiral Byrd to head the No-Foreign-War Crusade; to do so was virtually to "haul down the pacifist flag." At his insistence the E.P.C. Council agreed "that pacifism is to be vigorously set forth as an integral part of the Emergency Peace Campaign." This did not satisfy the towering John Haynes Holmes, prophetic pastor of New York's Community Church and 1917 war resister. In a biting letter of resignation from the E.P.C., he accused it of "compromise, concession, and surrender," fatally undercutting its original religious pacifism. After discussion by the council, a motion was carried that "the resignation be accepted without [sic] regret." Newton told Holmes that the pacifists were not numerous enough or wealthy enough or powerful enough to keep America out of war and that, therefore, the primary purpose of the E.P.C. was "not to promote pacifism but to keep this country out of the next war—which will be a European-Asiatic war."

In two passionate letters, Holmes also personally informed Fosdick of his resignation. "I am so appalled at what is going on in the peace movement today, especially in the Emergency Peace Campaign, that I can hardly contain myself. Good God." The weasel-worded slogan "No-Foreign-War Crusade" represented "treason" to the cause of pacifism and the cooperation with nonpacifists was "pussy footing." One letter closed: "I love you as I rejoice that you love me. But love is not inconsistent with clear-thinking, and uncompromising dedication to the right. The world is in too desperate a plight for any 'mush of concession,' to use Emerson's phrase, in our present fight for peace." Fosdick replied to Holmes in two long letters. One contained the crucial point:

> It is disheartening to have a man like you attack not only this organization, but its ideals. We are well accustomed to the attacks that come from

the militarists. They have been thoroughly frightened of us. In community after community they have organized against us, inspired the newspapers to call us communists and have tried to break down our work. They have reason to be afraid. The militarist elements in this country can handle pacifist organizations as they exist today, but if the pacifists ally themselves with the great mass of the American people who hate war and want peace, then the militarists are in trouble. That's the thing we are trying to do. I think it is the only strategy that has the slightest chance of winning the day in this country.

The other letter closed:

The next time you write suppose we have less heat and a little more light. I should like to be informed. Of course, if you are feeling all broken up because Admiral Byrd wants to come out whole-heartedly for peace, and it may be that he would not agree with you as to the techniques of getting it to the last item of the creed, then I should part company with you on that and think that it displayed on your part a bigotry that you would not wish reduplicated in your attitude toward differences of opinion in the field of religion. Anyway, blessings on you! I still love you dearly.

Holmes's absolutist position freed him from the inescapable internal contradictions of Fosdick's inclusivist posture. This is not to say that Fosdick was mistaken in believing that a tiny band of pacifists could in and by themselves keep America out of war, but only that as the world careened from peace to war the tension between Fosdick's commitment to internationalism and loathing of Hitlerism, on the one hand, and pledge to resist war, on the other, grew greater and greater.

As in the 1920s Fosdick continued to call for a muting of nationalism and the creation of an international frame of mind. American membership in the World Court was desirable, but in 1935 this step was killed by the Senate thanks in part to the opposition of Father Charles Coughlin, Will Rogers, and Hearst. Fosdick shared the anger of the *Christian Leader*: "We have to swallow the galling fact that the foreign policies of the United States are practically dictated by a sensational priest, stuttering comedian and a cynical newspaperman."

The almost magical promise of the League of Nations melted away after Japan's successful aggression in Manchuria, but Fosdick continued to speak of the necessity of "international collective security" and for "international government in the form of international peace." Of course, this is slippery use of language. At no time did he advocate joining America's armed forces with the League's to resist with violence the aggressions of Japan, Italy, or Germany.

He recognized that these three nations "at the cost of desperate public sacrifice are preparing for war, preaching it, glorifying it, dragooning and conscripting even their little children for it." But, he added, "They are doing that, not because they are another kind of human being from ourselves, but because none of these nations has access to or control over enough of the raw materials of this planet to sustain national existence. They honestly think that they face a choice between war and penury and in that dilemma they propose war." He recognized that Great Britain, France, Russia, and the United States sincerely desired peace. "Yet, after all, it is not great credit to them that they want peace, for, having already access to and control over plenty of the raw materials of the earth to guarantee their national existence, why should they want war?" He was in essential agreement with Norman Thomas that if war came it would be between the House of Have and the House of Have Not; between what Kirby Page called the self-righteousness of the surfeited with the self-assertion of the frustrated. Is it, asked the English pacifist Muriel Lester, more evil to covet empire than to cleave to empire? And so Fosdick sought a worldwide economic reconstruction, including the end of colonialism, tariff and monetary policies revision, cooperation between the Have and Have Not nations, and the creation of a sort of world cooperative commonwealth. "We cannot have an economic order overwhelmingly motivated by the acquisitive desire for profits, first for individuals, second for corporate aggregates of individuals, third for nations backing up their corporate aggregates of individuals, and still expect peace."

By the mid-1930s the majority of citizens agreed with the title of Fosdick's address concerning American intervention in the Great War, "We Were Unmercifully Gypped." Intervention had come at the behest of bankers and munitions makers abetted by astute Allied propaganda, the American people now believed.* The two axioms attributed to the "merchants of death" were: "When there are wars, prolong them; when there is peace, disturb it." In the popular mind the Senate Committee Investigating the Munitions Industry, chaired by Senator Gerald P. Nye, had proved the thesis that American intervention was the work of wicked Wall Street bankers and sinister arms barons. We now know that this famous committee originally had the backing of the Roosevelt administration as well as of the pacifists, that it was not antibusiness, that it did not "prove" business was responsible for America's entry, and that actually it had little influence on the formulation of administration policies.

---

* Actually, Fosdick maintained to the end of his life that it was American idealism, sense of mission, and crusading zeal that most fully explains intervention in 1917.

Yet stripping away the more conspiratorial inferences falsely drawn from Nye's investigations, there remained for many citizens the hard conclusion that economic ties had drawn the United States into war on the side of the Allies, her customers, and debtors; and that if intervention were to be averted in a future war, America must remain scrupulously free from economic entanglements with belligerent nations.

Closely attuned to the asumptions of the Nye Committee, but not a direct consequence of the Senate investigations, were the so-called Neutrality Acts of 1935, 1936, and 1937. Just prior to passage of the final 1937 measure, Fosdick stated his position:

> Personally, I should like to see the present session of Congress pass a strigent neutrality measure. It should forbid the shipment to belligerents of all implements and munitions of war; it should forbid all loans and credits; it should modify the old doctrine of freedom of the sea and forbid our neutrals to sail in war areas; it should forbid the shipment to belligerents, or to neutrals for transshipment to belligerents, of all war necessities whatever. It might give to the President some permissive authority to cooperate with other nations against an obvious aggressor, but, with whatever qualifications, Congress ought to pass a strong neutrality measure. Nevertheless, I have small hope that such a law, even if passed, will hold its ground against the terrific pressure of a long-drawn-out war.

Earlier Fosdick had written about a measure before Congress in 1936: "One group in Washington . . . has been trying to get an absolutely effective neutrality law, as though they would build a Chinese Wall about this nation and so automatically insure non-participation in another conflict. I understand they have about given it up. They might as well give it up. We never will get peace by independent nationalism. We will get peace only by interdependent, international, collective action."

The neutrality legislation passed by Congress in the mid-1930s was a victory more for isolationism than for pacifism, though it was endorsed by most pacifists who, indeed, were distressed only by the fact that the legislation gave "such wide discretionary power to the President." The overwhelming majority of diplomatic historians judge the laws a failure. They were predicated on a devil theory of war and designed to exorcise this devil. They were predicated on a false reading of the events of 1914–1917 and false parallels between those years and the 1930s. They flashed a green light to aggressor nations, signaling as they did America's intention to remain neutral. The "cash-and-carry" provision made possible continued war profits, merely placing the risks of the transaction on the belligerent with the money and ships to buy and fetch, and where was the morality in such an arrangement? Although in general Fosdick supported the neutrality acts, he did not cherish utopian hopes concerning their efficacy. What is not clear is where he stood on the question of mandatory versus presidential discretionary invokement. All isolationists and most pacifists favored the former, the advocates of collective security the latter.* When he said of the proposed 1937 law, "It might give to the President some permissive authority to cooperate with other nations against an obvious aggressor," he seemed to stand with the collective security group, but in light of his absolute opposition to the use of America's armed force, this was an exceedingly wobbly stance.

Indeed, if Fosdick's views had prevailed, America's armed might would have remained minimally defensive. Of course, he endorsed the World Disarmament Conference early in the decade, speaking at a mass rally in New York, and also endorsed the later London Naval Disarmament Conference. In 1934 he joined nineteen ministers in protesting to President Roosevelt the Vinson-Trammell Bill, which (they believed) represented an "unprecedented peace time program of naval expansion." The following year he appealed to the president to cancel American naval maneuvers in the northern Pacific† and signed with three hundred other churchmen "An Open Letter to the People of Japan," apologizing for the provocative maneuvers and assuring the Japanese of the friendship of the American people.

In the thirties Fosdick continued to pursue the eradication of militarism from the schools, concurring with Norman Thomas, "If we mean business in our war against war we must dig out the R.O.T.C., root and branch—polo ponies, pretty girl colonels, snappy uniforms and all." Fosdick also signaled his support of the massive antiwar fervor that was sweeping the college campuses of the land. Youth group after youth group resolved against war, demonstrated, and closed campuses with antiwar strikes. Pledging pacifism became au courant among idealistic and socialistic young people. About 81 percent of the 65,000 college students polled by the *Literary Digest* in 1935 indicated that they would not bear arms if American forces invaded another country, and 16.5 percent said they would refuse to fight even if their nation was invaded. Another poll of sixty-five colleges revealed 39 percent of the students holding a position of absolute pacifism. One antiwar strike saw 25,000 students participate, another 60,000, still another 175,000. The Oxford Union Peace Pledge crossed the Atlantic to enjoy a great vogue in America.

* However, in 1937 Reinhold Niebuhr declared himself neutral as between mandatory and discretionary neutral legislation.

† As did Reinhold Niebuhr. In fact in 1938 Niebuhr said that the Roosevelt administration's defense budget "cries to heaven as the worst piece of militarism in modern history" and that its naval program was "the most unjustified piece of military expansion in a world full of such madness."

Three hundred chapters of the Veterans of Future Wars were formed on college campuses, a sardonic society organized by Princeton undergraduates to enable prospective soldiers to collect their bonuses in advance. Vassar girls, unwilling to concede superior imagination to boys, forthwith organized the Gold Star Mothers of Veterans of Future Wars. In 1938 a World Youth Congress met in Poughkeepsie and these representatives of an estimated 40 million young people promised to work against war, though the promise was not a vow of absolute pacifism. Most historians patronize this antiwar movement in the colleges as sophomoric student silliness. It seems less frivolous—in fact it seems deadly serious—when it is remembered that the overwhelming majority of those boys who marched in campus peace demonstrations were in a few years to march off to war without a whimper. And if they survived,* it was to sire sons who perhaps in the 1960s marched in peace demonstrations and then off to their deaths in Vietnam—or to prison or to expatriation in Canada or Sweden. And if they survived Vietnam, it was to return to sire children who today live in the shadow of thermonuclear death.

Early in the fateful year 1939, only months before the outbreak of the Second Great Holocaust, the Fellowship of Reconciliation importuned Fosdick and Allan Knight Chalmers to draft an "Affirmation of Christian Pacifist Faith" and to raise funds to circulate the statement and underwrite a nationwide series of Christian Pacifist Conferences. Ultimately, nineteen hundred ministers gave their signatures to the Affirmation, the key passages of which read:

We believe that God is the Father of all mankind, that his will as revealed in Jesus Christ is universal love, and that Christ's gospel involves the faith that evil can be overcome only with good.

We believe that in the cross is revealed God's way of dealing with wrongdoers, and that to this way all Christians are called.

We believe that war, which attempts to overcome evil with more evil, is a denial of the way of the cross.

We believe that the church is called to the way of the cross.

We believe that when the state in the prosecution of war seeks to compel the denial of the gospel, the church must resist at whatever cost.

We believe that God leads his church into new life through obedience of the individual believer in refusing war for Christ's sake.

---

* And if they survived the Korean War as well, for every veteran of World War II had pals who, staying in the reserves, were called up in 1950 and sent to their deaths in Korea. I speak as a former Marine, 1943–1946.

Therefore we proclaim to a world which is once again madly preparing for war that the gospel of God as revealed in Jesus Christ, which leaves us with no choice but to refuse to sanction or participate in war, contains also its hope of redemption. We affirm our faith that the mission of the church today is to witness with singleness of heart, at whatever cost, to the power of good to overcome evil, of love to conquer hatred, of the cross to shatter the sword.

Harold Fey, executive secretary of the Fellowship, commented on the Affirmation to fellow pacifist John Haynes Holmes: "I wish I could have the privilege of sharing with you the hundreds of letters which . . . I have received on this statement. Nothing I have seen happen in my four years of intimate knowledge of the American Peace Movement has to [so?] strikingly emphasized the depth and sincerity of Christian pacifist conviction as there [these?] letters. And this in the face of the present drive toward war! Ten years ago a man might have put his name to such a document in the hope that it would have a decisive political effect. . . . Now we know it is too late for that, that this may have no effect at all, yet we still speak. By this very fact, incalculable effects may follow. Here we stand!"

From his chairmanship in 1931 of the Fellowship of Reconciliation's nationwide peace meetings through his participation in 1937 in the English-inspired Embassies of Reconciliation to the drafting of the 1939 "Affirmation of Christian Pacifist Faith" Fosdick followed a pertinacious course in the cause of peace.

VII

At three o'clock on Friday morning, September 1, 1939, President Roosevelt was awakened by a phone call from Ambassador William C. Bullitt in Paris informing him that Germany had invaded Poland. At ten-thirty in the morning the president held a special press conference at which he stated his belief that the United States should and could and would remain at peace. He then conferred with Secretary of State Hull and, with Hull's concurrence, decided to call Congress into special session within a short time to revise America's neutrality legislation in order to permit supplies to flow to England and France. The tension thereby established on September 1 between the objectives of keeping the peace and aiding the Allies was to heighten for the next twenty-seven months. During this agonizing period the energies of Fosdick and the peacemakers were expended in five major areas of concern: how to bring an end to the war in

Europe and Asia, how to aid the victims of war, how to keep America out of war, how to prepare for conscientious objectors should America be drawn into war, and how to plan for the postwar world.

Three days after Britain, in response to the Polish invasion, declared war on Germany, Fosdick wrote to a dear friend in England, "How sad I am over this catastrophe that has left in wreckage the things that I cared most for and worked hardest on in public life I shall not try to put into words." Loathing Hitlerism and holding in adoration English culture, he may be believed when he confessed to the Riverside congregation, "Sometimes I live more in Britain than at home, so keen my sympathies, so deep my apprehensions, so desperate my hopes." Yet such was his hatred of war that above all he dreaded its spread and he would recall those months during which America's belligerence became more and more possible as "among the darkest in my life." The darkness was deepened by his conviction, based on memories of World War I, that should war come to America, as he expected, he would be asked to re-sign his Riverside ministry—no war-engulfed people would tolerate a pacifist in their pulpit. His family's reassurances to the contrary were of no avail in easing his mind.

Early in September key leaders of the Fellowship of Reconciliation met with Fosdick, a Christian Pacifist Conference was convened and a Paci-fist Ministers' Fellowship formed, and, ultimately, Fosdick was made chairman of a major new group, the Ministers No War Committee.* This group secured antiwar pledges, sent out noninterventionist literature (with funds partially supplied by the isolationist America First Commis-sion), opposed such Administration measures as Lend-Lease, held rallies in major cities (Fosdick himself spoke in Cleveland and Detroit), and sponsored a Churchmen's Campaign for Peace Through Mediation. "I strongly commend your resolution to promote peace by calling a confer-ence of the American republics to offer the nations now at war the ser-vices of the Western Hemisphere," he wired in May 1941 to Representa-tive Louis Ludlow, author of the earlier defeated national war referendum amendment to the Constitution. "This is the only hopeful and construc-tive way I see out of the present crisis." Niebuhr flayed Fosdick's hopes as utopian, saying that most of the neutral nations in Europe were shiver-ing little mice waiting for the cat to pounce. In the end, the Wilsonian plea, "peace without victory," again fell on ears deafened by the thunder of battle. The idea of a negotiated peace under the sponsorship of neutral

---

* In 1940 Fosdick was also made honorary vice chairman of the National Council for the Prevention of War, a coalition organization formed in 1921 and majoring in political action.

nations may very well have been a hopeless one, but we shall never know with absolute certainty, for beyond a few ceremonial gestures the proposal was never given a chance.

Concurrently, Fosdick continued to preach sermons proclaiming his convictions, saying in his 1939 Armistice Sunday sermon:

> Ah, war! I hate you most of all for this—that you lay your hands upon the loveliest things in human life, that rightly used would make a heaven on earth, and you use them to make a hell on earth instead. You take our courage and far from letting it be a benediction to the world, you use it to bomb cities, and sack cathedrals, and slay men. You take our loyalty by which the earth might be redeemed, and you harness it to an enterprise that inevitably means the rape of women, and the slaughter of children, and the starvation of whole populations. You take our religion, and to help your deadly work you rend our God into pieces, and make of him tribal deities before whom men pray, as old barbarians before our Lord had come, prayed to their idols as the gods of war. You take our science . . . and you make of that an effective implement of hatred. . . . And now, if we let you, you will lay your hands upon one of the finest things in America—our sense of mission, our desire to be of use to the world— and you will employ that to hurl us into the bloody maelstrom of another European war that a generation from now, like the last, will be a record of blasted hopes and futile outcomes. . . . So we are to be Jesus' Good Samaritans, are we? and send another conscript army to Europe to blast cities, bomb families, starve populations, help spread the devastation wider, and add ourselves to the dilapidated wreckage of the nations? That's Jesus' idea of the Good Samaritan, is it? Pardon me if I say, not profanely but with literal exactness, That is a devil of a Good Samaritan!

While the work for a negotiated peace went on, millions were being chewed up in the maw of war, and Fosdick anguished much over their fate. As we know, as early as 1933 Fosdick condemned Hitler's persecution of Germany's Jews and soon plunged into the task of succoring the Jewish and Aryan and non-Ayran Christian victims of Hitler's wrath. Few if any Protestant ministers labored more valiantly than he to find refuge in America for these victims. And few Protestant congregations provided a warmer and more effective welcome than did Riverside's, especially through the generously funded committee, The Riverside Church in Action on Behalf of the Refugees. The charge simply will not wash that because Fosdick and the peacemakers opposed America's intervention in the war against Germany they were blind to Hitler's monstrous "final solution."

On November 10, 1940, a midwestern Methodist minister, Ernest Fremont Tittle, preached a sermon, "Should Europe's Hungry Be Fed?"

Widely broadcast, it came to the attention of the National Committee on Food for the Small Democracies headed by Herbert Hoover, a new organization whose purpose it was to stay mass starvation in Poland, Finland, Belgium, Luxemburg, Holland, Norway, and Greece. Hoover maintained that the carefully controlled conditions under which the food would be shipped, stored, and distributed would prevent its being used to strengthen Germany. Not surprisingly, the plan was killed by the British government and the Roosevelt administration. Fosdick gave his public endorsement to the plan and supported it in sermons, saying, "Mr. Hoover alone is still endeavoring to find some practical way of bringing to a successful issue this desperately needed humanitarian service. I wish to be counted on the side of that endeavor."

Not all churchmen agreed; Fosdick's Union colleagues Coffin and Van Dusen were in vehement opposition, Van Dusen thundering, "Men cry for freedom and are given bread." Meanwhile, the Methodist Tittle was receiving an avalanche of critical letters suggesting that his sermon be sent to Hitler for "of all the persons on earth who might agree with it, it would be that tyrant."

Fosdick was not unmoved by the fate of peoples on the other side of the globe. He was involved in several groups, such as the American Bureau for Medical Aid to China and United China Relief. Further, he was a sponsor of the American Committee for Non-Participation in Japanese Aggression. As he explained to a Presbyterian missionary in Japan, "What everybody in America wants to do . . . is to keep our hands as clear [clean?] as we can from supplying Japan with indispensable munitions of war for its attack on China"—though, he added, such an embargo must not be presented to Japan as an act of judgment on her.

Fosdick and the peacemakers largely failed in their efforts to provide succor for the victims of war just as they totally failed to effect a negotiated peace. As the months after September 1939 passed, it became increasingly evident that they would fail in their purpose of keeping the United States out of war. "What a majority of the American people want," wrote Freda Kirchway in the *Nation*, "is to be as unneutral as possible without getting into war." In the years 1939–1941 America became, in FDR's stirring phrase, "the great arsenal of democracy," and it did so with the concurrence of the majority of citizens as their will was revealed in polls and at the polls, in debate, and in congressional action. The ranks of pacifism and isolationism thinned as the administration's posture toward Japan and Germany hardened, both because fewer and fewer Americans could remain morally neutral toward Japan and China, and Germany and England, and because fewer and fewer continued to believe that the Western Hemisphere would be impregnable from attack should Hitler win control of the Atlantic and Africa and should Japan conquer China, Southeast Asia, and the western Pacific.

At this point it is needful to pause and make a couple of observations about Roosevelt's leadership, other than the transparent one that he bent the Constitution and accelerated the rise of the Imperial Presidency, as associated with Kennedy, Johnson, and Nixon, with the destroyers-for-bases exchange by an executive agreement, the order to American forces to occupy Iceland, the order that American warships should convoy British as well as American vessels in the North Atlantic, and later to "shoot on sight"—and to seek out—German submarines. Perhaps it is true that not until after the famous meeting with Churchill in August 1941 did Roosevelt wish to take the United States actively into the war. If so, he was deceiving himself as well as the American people as he remorselessly followed measures "short of war" that made American intervention not only possible, but probable and in fact virtually certain. In September 1939 he declared, while pressing for repeal of the arms embargo, that no one in a responsible position in national, state, or local government "has ever suggested in any shape, manner or form the remotest possibility" of sending American boys to fight in Europe.* Running for reelection in 1940 and fearful of being seen as a warmonger, he assured the voters, "Your President says this country is not going to war" and "I have said this before, but I shall say it again and again and again: Your boys are not going to be sent into any foreign wars." After his victory he continued to assure the citizenry, "You can . . . nail any talk about sending armies to Europe as deliberate untruth."

Consider Lend-Lease, the transcendent measure committing the United States to aiding the Allies, artfully designated H.R. 1776 and entitled "An Act to Further Promote the Defense of the United States, and for Other Purposes." Fosdick's Ministers No War Committee held that if passed the bill made "probable, if not certain, a swift entry into the war." Isolationist Senator Burton K. Wheeler remarked that Lend-Lease was "the New Deal's triple A foreign policy; it will plow under every fourth American boy." In reply, the president angrily termed Wheeler's remark "the most untruthful . . . dastardly, unpatriotic thing that has ever been said." Yet when queried by a reporter whether the bill would not lead to war, the president replied emphatically, "No, not a bit of it." That really is one of the most disingenuous things said in public life in Roosevelt's generation. The administration's cant in comparing sending munitions to Britain to loaning a neighbor a garden hose was com-

---

* In September 1939, also, Senator Harry S Truman declared, "The role of this great Republic is to save civilization; we must keep out of war."

pounded when the president and the secretaries of War and Navy gave the bald assurance that there was no intention under the bill to convoy merchant ships. Senator Robert Taft held the title of the bill to be a fraud, noted that lending war equipment was like lending chewing gum, and said of the president, "The words of his mouth were smoother than butter, but war was in his heart." As an anti-interventionist Taft might be expected to take this position, but even an ardent backer of Lend-Lease, Herbert Agar, acknowledged: "Our side kept saying in the press and in the Senate it was a bill to keep America out of war. That is bunk." And Secretary of War Stimson clearly saw that to secure Hitler's defeat American belligerency must follow Lend-Lease. The point at issue here is not to challenge one historian's designation of Lend-Lease as "the most unsordid act" but to insist on the dissimulation surrounding its passage.

Three months later Germany invaded Russia and Roosevelt moved to make Stalin eligible to receive Lend-Lease materials, eliciting Senator Taft's dry remark, "Apparently we are to follow Bundles for Britain with Packages for Petrograd." This is a curious business considering that President Roosevelt had announced in 1940: "The Soviet Union, as a matter of practical fact, as everybody knows who has the courage to face the facts, is a dictatorship as absolute as any other dictatorship in the world."* The irony here is that the alleged utopians, such as Fosdick, saw with sharper clarity than the alleged realistic interventionists that with Hitler's defeat and Europe in desolation, Stalin would hope to become (in Fosdick's words spoken at the time) "the residuary legatee of a ruined continent."

This leads to the final point in our pause. Fosdick and the peacemakers saw that to send American boys to be killed by Germans, Italians, and Japanese was to sacrifice them not to save that ineffable "free world" but to secure concrete political entities: the British Empire, the French Empire, the Dutch Empire, Stalin's murderous regime, Chiang Kai-shek's corrupt and brutal regime, and the totalitarian Chinese Communists as well. It is neither Monday morning quarterbacking nor a matter of 20-20 hindsight to say that Fosdick and the peacemakers comprehended that to intervene in 1939–1941 in the wars of Asia and Europe would be to repeat 1917 and continue down an endless road of "perpetual war for

---

* At the time of the invasion, Senator Truman took the position: "If we see that Germany is winning we ought to help Russia and if Russia is winning we ought to help Germany." A year earlier Reinhold Niebuhr had written, "We are not willing to see young Americans die to protect Stalin's type of dictatorship from Hitler's type of dictatorship."

perpetual peace." We now know, as they did not, although some did speculate apocalyptically, that this road might in fact have an end, a thermonuclear doomsday.

The Keep America Out of War Congress was the last stand of the co-operating peace movement before Pearl Harbor. Formed in 1938 with John T. Flynn as national chairman, KAOWC was essentially a pacifist-socialist coalition, Norman Thomas and the Socialist party providing crucial support. Although its members claimed to be "isolationists only with respect to war," it did attract such prominent isolationists as Chester Bowles. As it increasingly drifted into the hands of what pacifist A. J. Muste called "defensists" and as it tended to become a membership organization rather than a collaborating body, such pacifist groups as the Fellowship of Reconciliation and the War Resisters League withdrew from it, although they still cooperated on specific projects. For a season Fosdick gave his support, agreeing to be in 1940 a sponsor of the congress and of a big rally in Washington.

As KAOWC symbolized the noninterventionism of the Left, so the America First Committee represented the noninterventionism of the American Right. Formed in September 1940 to counter the effective propaganda of the Committee to Defend America by Aiding the Allies, America First rapidly boasted 450 chapters and a membership of over eight hundred thousand, approximately two thirds of whom lived within a three-hundred-mile radius of Chicago. General Robert E. Wood, chairman of the board of Sears, Roebuck & Company, was national chairman. R. Douglas Stuart, Jr., the young law student son of the first vice-president of the Quaker Oats Company, was the energetic national director. Although the original policy of barring pacifists from membership was reversed and although one prominent pacifist clergyman, Albert W. Palmer, served briefly on the national committee, pacifists had very little to do with this conservative, isolationist, patriotic, even chauvinistic body.

Fosdick declined an invitation to serve on the national committee of America First because, he explained, it did not share his Quaker peace position or his desire for a world federation. Nevertheless, bound by a shared fear of Roosevelt's foreign policies, Fosdick's Ministers No War Committee accepted funds from America First to permit noninterventionist literature to be mailed to 90,000 ministers and, further, America First distributed a volume, *We Testify*, which contained an article by Fosdick. Also, the Committee underwrote a national "peace poll." To give the survey the aura of academic objectivity, a survey committee was assembled consisting of five university presidents and deans and Fosdick, Fosdick being tapped because he "always got press coverage when he spoke out." Truth to tell, only 5,031 individuals were interviewed and the poll was greeted with little enthusiasm.

In the summer of 1941 John Haynes Holmes formed a Citizen's Peace Petition Committee composed of pacifists, not conservative isolationists, and Fosdick agreed to serve as one of four vice chairmen, although he alerted Holmes two months before Pearl Harbor, "I must confess that I have small hope of the President's acting along the line" of the petition.

A year earlier, immediately following the chilling fall of France to Hitler's legions, the Roosevelt administration began pressing for a selective service measure. As the peril was now clear and present, Congress passed the Burke-Wadsworth Bill by large majorities on September 14. In conscription Fosdick saw another and different peril. As he wrote to Rockefeller, Jr., "My old Baptist heritage about liberty of conscience vs. this whole totalitarian drift is aroused." He had long opposed the drafting of the nation's youth into military service and in 1939 helped start a new publication, *Conscientious Objector*. But it was the proposed Burke-Wadsworth Bill that drew his full fire. On July 30, 1940, he appeared before the Military Affairs committees of the House and Senate to make a ninety-minute statement against passage of the measure and, second, to plead that it be amended to "grant to sincere conscientious objectors on religious grounds either the right to non-combatant service, or to civilian service, or, if the case seemed to justify it, to complete exemption."

Then, on the evening of August 7 he spoke in a nationwide radio broadcast over the Columbia network; Senator Wheeler had requested equal air time to argue the case against conscription. Fosdick pled with the listeners to consider three aspects of the matter. First, "Conscription is the essence of regimented, totalitarian, militaristic autocracy." If conscripting the boys out of their homes is democratic, as the proponents proclaim, why not conscript wealth, industry, factories, labor, educators? Second, voluntary enlistments would be adequate to secure America's defense. Third, "What is this conscript army for? A conscript army is not needed to defend the United States or its contiguous interests. A conscript army is needed only if we are going to send an expeditionary force to conquer, let us say, Europe or Asia. The well-justified suspicion will not down that behind this hectic haste to force conscription on us is the policy of the belligerent interventionists."

The issue hit home in October when eight Union Seminary students refused to register for the draft and were sentenced to a year and a day in prison.* Their public explanation of their refusal was given wide distribution. President Coffin and Reinhold Niebuhr tried to persuade the stu-

---

* Another twelve Union students registered as conscientious objectors.

dents against their course of action, Niebuhr describing them as courters of martyrdom and proponents of anarchism. The faculty "with practical unanimity" passed a resolution declaring: "In this Selective Service Act provision is made for conscientious objectors to participation in military training and an opportunity is afforded for such objectors to state their views. To refuse to register and supply the government with factual information is to refuse what any government has a right to ask of its students." Despite pressure on Coffin to expel "this nest of traitors and lawbreakers," this he did not do. Despite pressure from Coffin, Niebuhr, Van Dusen and other faculty, the obdurate eight refused to register. Fosdick's exact position is not found in the records. He praised young men who declared themselves to be conscientious objectors and said, that if young, this would be his posture also. He helped secure their protection under the law. Therefore, it may be inferred that Fosdick agreed with his Union colleagues that the eight students should have cooperated with the government to the extent of registering. It is worth remarking that some of these young resisters who went to prison in 1940, years later, when gray bearded, again went to prison for obstructing another American war effort—this time in Vietnam.

Events in Asia and Europe made America's march toward intervention seemingly inexorable, and in January, 1941, Fosdick responded to an invitation from the *Christian Century* to participate with ten Christian leaders in a symposium on the subject, "If America Enters the War— What Shall I Do?" "My personal judgment," he made clear, "is that for the United States to become a belligerent in this conflict would be a colossal and futile disaster and, along with millions of others, I should hold that judgment, pacifist or no pacifist." Should war come, and if he were young, he would be a conscientious objector, asking for alternative civilian service, "the harder the better." But, of course, the more precise question for him was: as a minister of Christ in the United States today, if this nation now becomes an active belligerent, will I support the war? And what would I do in case of invasion? "My own answer is clear: resist, whether by violent or non-violent means." He then honored those who would follow the Gandhian path of tireless, courageous, nonviolent resistance, but added that those who rely on America's meeting invasion with a mass movement of nonviolent resistance were "trusting moonshine." He summed up his position: "Honoring the consciences of all who resist aggressive evil whether by violent or non-violent means, trying in the church I serve to minister alike to the needs of the conscientious objector and the conscientious soldier, all the more in such a crisis I should try to keep Christ where he belongs—on his judgment seat, above the strife, standing for a way of life that condemns both aggressor and defender, and offers the only hope of salvation from their joint guilt and their insensate brutality. I will not use my Christian ministry to bless war."

Though hoping to avert intervention, which would be "the greatest tragedy in the history of the Republic," Fosdick increasingly expected his hope to be dashed. Nevertheless, in or out of the war, he understood that there was no way for the United States to escape from the vast problems and disasters that confront mankind. "That seems to me a fool's paradise. Belligerency or no belligerency, we are inextricably part and parcel of the world, and, soon or late, every evil that afflicts it is our evil, every catastrophe that befalls it is our catastrophe." And so in April 1941 he accepted an invitation to serve on the Federal Council of Churches' famous Commission to Study the Bases of a Just and Durable Peace under the chairmanship of John Foster Dulles, for whom he had, at that time, "profound admiration."*

VIII

During the twenty-seven months when America hung suspended between peace and war, Japan continued to apply the flame to China's already blistered flesh, and then pressed aggressively southwestward into Indochina. In Europe the countries of Denmark, Norway, Belgium, the Netherlands, Luxemburg, and France suffered invasion, defeat, and Nazi occupation, while in southern Europe Rumania, Hungary, and Bulgaria became Axis satellites and Yugoslavia and Greece Axis victims. Britain gallantly resisted Göring's Luftwaffe with "Blood, toil, tears, and sweat"— and Spitfires and Hurricanes—but it seemed incredible that England alone could long endure. Then, in June 1941 Hitler turned on Russia, storming apparently victoriously toward Moscow.

In the terrible spring of 1941, Maude Royden, the respected English pacifist who had worked with Fosdick in the E.P.C., found her pacifist faith melted by the flames of Britain's bombed cities, and she sent a stern command to her old comrades, the pacifists safe in America, "Do not preach to us. Pray for us if you can. If you cannot, let us alone. We are doing what we can." And in the United States Reinhold Niebuhr stung the pacifists with the scorpion words: "Will the moralists who think that it would be a simple matter to make peace with Hitler if we only called an economic conference and promised to allocate raw materials, please be quiet while we weep?" Niebuhr growled in unvarnished reference to the

---

* In 1942 the commission published *A Righteous Faith for a Just and Durable Peace*, Fosdick contributing one of fourteen chapters.

pacifism exemplified by Fosdick, "If modern churches were to symbolize their true faith, they would take the crucifix from their altars and substitute the three little monkeys who counsel men 'to speak no evil, hear no evil, see no evil.' "

Royden's conversion from pacifism to armed resistance and Niebuhr's pilgrimage from the wish to keep America out of war to the desire to halt fascist aggression at the risk of war were the consequence of the dangerous developments in Europe and Asia. Discerning the signs of the times, other peacemakers also converted to interventionism, until by late 1941 the ranks of the clerical pacifists were decimated and a commanding army of churchmen stood with Niebuhr. Among them were Episcopal Bishops Henry Knox Sherrill, William T. Manning, Henry Hobson, and William Scarlett; Methodist Bishops James Cannon, Jr., G. Bromley Oxnam, and Francis J. McConnell; the renowned evangelist Sherwood Eddy and Presbyterianism's most prestigious layman, Robert E. Speer, and American Protestantism's greatest statesman, John R. Mott, and Princeton Seminary's president John A. Mackay—and an additional raft of the most powerful churchmen in American Protestantism. The pacifist-interventionist division was especially cruel for Fosdick because many of his Union Seminary colleagues—individuals to whom he was devoted—lined up with Niebuhr: President Coffin (how this wrenched Fosdick's heart!), William Adams Brown, John C. Bennett, Paul Tillich, and most militant of all, Henry Pitney Van Dusen. Further, Fosdick's colleague at Riverside, Norris Tibbetts, was in the interventionist corner, as was his dear Baptist friend, Charles W. Gilkey. The only shining thing in this whole wretched business dividing Fosdick from his ministerial friends is that not in a single instance was a friendship permanently ruptured—still another tribute to Fosdick's character.

Interventionist churchmen sought to influence the editorial policies of denominational journals, the declarations of denominational assemblies, and the positions of denominational agencies—as they had every right to do, for the peacemakers were engaged in identical activities. They placed their signatures to petitions to inform the Roosevelt administration of their support. They testified before Congress. They formed new committees and joined secular groups, such as the Fight for Freedom Committee, Friends of Democracy, Inc., and the Committee to Defend America by Aiding the Allies. They conferred with American and British officials, including Secretary Hull and the British Ambassador, Lord Lothian, and cooperated with the British Information Service. They also endeavored with success to redirect the attitudes of such established peace societies as the Church Peace Union and the World Peace Foundation.

What can be said concerning this great debate between Niebuhr and his fellow interventionists and Fosdick and his fellow pacifistic noninterventionists?

First, war did come to America as Roosevelt's opponents anticipated.

Second, almost all leading diplomatic historians have defended Roosevelt's foreign policies, blasted the "isolationists," and justified this necessary, if cruel, war against the Axis. To be sure, in very recent years several sympathetic studies of pacifism have appeared, and "isolationism" has received less judgmental and Roosevelt's leadership less reverential evaluation. Still, the statement stands that in the historiographical war, the Roosevelt supporters continue to win.

Third, scholars make much of the fact that Fosdick and the pacifists found themselves in the unlovely company of Nazi sympathizers (a pitifully tiny group even among German immigrants), anti-Semites, Anglophobes, economic reactionaries, political right-wingers, isolationist moral eunuchs indifferent to the fate of any human being not a U.S. citizen, hubristic patriots confident of America's moral superiority to other nations, and, for a season (August 1939–June 1941), Communists as well. To this presumably devastating observation, it may be replied that it requires a courageous individual to take the position demanded by his principles when that position associates him with unpopular groups he himself loathes. Moreover, the guilt-by-association tactic cuts with a double edge. If the pacifist case against intervention can be thrown out because nonintervention was also the position of America First and Father Coughlin and the *Chicago Tribune* and the pro-Nazi Bund, then logically the Niebuhrian cause for intervention is tainted by the support given by such frenetic Episcopal Anglophiles as Hobson and Episcopal Tories as Manning; such power-hungry ecclesiastics as Southern Methodist Bishop Cannon; such movie moguls as Goldwyn and such press magnates as Luce; such career-minded men as Dean Acheson, Allen W. Dulles, and Joseph Alsop; and, of course, after the invasion of Russia, all American Communists and all who followed Moscow's marching orders, whether party members or not, such as Fosdick's colleague Harry F. Ward. The point is that Niebuhr, too, found himself in unlovely company, not excluding those who cynically sought war to profit financially and all those neurotic war lovers driven by sadistic or masochistic compulsions.*

* On December 13, 1941, Senator Robert Taft replied to the historian Arthur Schlesinger, Jr.: "Nor is Mr. Schlesinger correct in attributing the position of the majority of Republicans to their conservatism. The most conservative members of the Party—the Wall Street bankers, the society group, nine-tenths of the plutocratic newspapers, and most of the party's financial contributors—are the ones who favor intervention in Europe. Mr. Schlesinger's statement that the business community in general had tended to favor appeasing Hitler is simply untrue. I have received

Fourth, opponents of the Roosevelt administration's foreign policies were subjected to much personal abuse. The debate was understandably bitter because the issue was so fundamental, a life and death matter for the participants involved, perhaps, and for their sons, their nation, the world. To be sure, interventionists were on the receiving end as well. Niebuhr complained to *Christian Century* editor Charles Clayton Morrison about the "self-righteousness of the whole pacifist wing of the church." To another correspondent Niebuhr said of the pacifists, "With the exception of a saint like Richard Roberts, I haven't noticed any large evidence of Christian charity in their attitudes." And to a third he said in gratitude, "Your letter was so mild compared to most of the letters I get from pacifists, that it left me quite unhurt." Fosdick himself acknowledged, "I see letters written by Christian pacifists to their non-pacifist brethren that for bitterness, acrimony, venom and dogmatism pass all decent bounds."

But Fosdick then added, "I see statements made by Christian non-pacifists about their pacifist fellows that for scorn, misrepresentation, rancor and contemptuousness are appalling." The fury of the interventionists is understandable, but the brutish accusations they poured on those who disagreed with them ring discordantly, coming as they do,

---

thousands of letters on both sides of the question, and I should say without question that it is the average man and woman—the farmer, the workman, except for pro-British labor leaders, and the small business man—who are opposed to war. The war party is made up of the business community of the cities, the newspaper and magazine writers, the radio and movie commentators, the Communists, and the university intelligentsia." Taft might have added to the antiwar group blacks who had yet to win their own fight for liberty at home. He might have added, also, Norman Thomas and many socialists. "I left the Socialist Party in 1936," recalled Reinhold Niebuhr, "because of its isolationist attitude toward the struggle against Nazism." This is interesting because only months earlier Niebuhr had declared: "I do not intend to participate in any war in prospect. I take this position not on strictly pacifistic grounds, for I am not an absolutist, but simply because I can see no good coming out of any of the wars confronting us. The position of Russia on the one hand and of Germany on the other hand in any of these wars would not affect my decision." And only months before that statement he had declared: "I will refuse to participate in any international war on pragmatic grounds. Another war will be suicidal to our civilization, and it will be caused by the fact that the Western nations are maintaining a social system which makes the kind of economic reciprocity upon which peace must be based impossible. For this reason I will refuse any kind of participation in the next war." As late as 1938 Niebuhr, when he correctly discerned war on the European horizon, asked, "Will the war . . . be a war which any decent person can sanction? It does not seem so to us." "Therefore," he added, "we find ourselves inclining to abstention not as a matter of absolute pacifist principle but as a matter of immediate policy." Considering Niebuhr's position after 1938 it is perhaps understandable why the pacifist John Haynes Holmes could say confidentially: "Niebuhr has a mind that is controlled by his latest fad and fear, and I don't think that such a mind is great."

from the self-proclaimed champions of the values of Western civilization. Said leading interventionist Herbert Agar of Herbert Hoover, "Hitler has no more stubborn helper in all the world." Secretary of the Interior Harold Ickes included the names of Oswald Garrison Villard and Norman Thomas in his list of "Nazi Fellow Travelers." The *New York Evening Post* printed a cartoon portraying Hitler with his arm around Senator Wheeler with the caption, "You're my boy." The Methodist pacifist Tittle received letters branding him a "Nazi neurotic." The *New Republic* designated the American First Committee "the most powerful single potential Fascist group in the country today—the group that is polarizing every Fascist force among us." Whether the isolationists like it or not, charged Alexander Woollcott, a member of the Eastern literary establishment, "they are working for Hitler." It was said of the owner of the *Chicago Tribune*, "Hitler likes him." One isolationist senator was dubbed a "Twentieth-Century Benedict Arnold"; another was compared to Quisling and Laval. It was kindly acknowledged that General Wood of America First did not take orders from Berlin, "They merely think the same thoughts the same day." "Axis dupe," "Nazi agent," and "appeaser"—ah, that most perfect epithet!—were tossed about as casually as balloons at a circus.

Then came Charles Lindbergh's speech on September 11, 1941, before an America First audience in Des Moines when he asserted: "The three most important groups who have been pressing this country toward war are the British, the Jewish, and the Roosevelt administration." Roosevelt himself angrily retorted that the speech "could not have been better put if it had been written by Goebbels himself." The speech, in the judgment of the interventionists, proved the "Lone Eagle" to be a "barafaced anti-Semite." The Council Against Intolerance in America (actually an organization formed to bring America into the war) sent out by the thousands a letter that opened: "The enemies of freedom have assailed our beloved country! Imitating the Nazis, such men as Mr. Lindbergh and Senator Nye are injecting the poison of racial and religious prejudice into America life. They are seeking to destroy liberty." Fosdick believed (as did almost every leading peacemaker) that Lindbergh's speech was "a lamentable blunder," but the Council's letter he deemed a "most intolerant and unfair attack."

Concurrently, pressure was being placed on individuals to conform to the interventionist line. For example, Villard was squeezed out of the *Nation*'s editorial offices and John T. Flynn from the *New Republic*'s. For example, President Butler of Columbia University delivered an almost undisguised ultimatum that any faculty members who did not agree with Roosevelt's policies might as well resign. For example, a rabbi in

Asheville, North Carolina, reported in torment to John Haynes Holmes receiving an ultimatum from the president of the congregation: "I think it behooves you to realize that when war and protection of our American traditions are on the lips of all the people of this country, that you as the spiritual leader of this community must fall in line with these views and preach them rather than talk against them." The president had issued the ultimatum after receiving this recommendation: "It is the considered opinion of your Worship Committee that in view of the existing critical international situation it is highly inadvisable and indeed detrimental, to expound the theory of pacifism from the pulpit. Your committee, therefore, recommends that our Rabbi be instructed to confine his sermons to religious or non-political subjects." The names of a handful of pacifist rabbis are known to historians. What is unknown is the number who met the fate of Rabbi Robert P. Jacobs, Congregation Beth Ha-Tephila, Asheville.

Fifth, almost all scholars, whether diplomatic historians, political scientists, or theologians, have concluded that Niebuhr completely demolished the case for pacifism. His "realism" became almost the party line of the new breed of intellectuals who came to occupy the seats of prestige and power in the postwar decades. Down what paths did this "realism" lead the country?

Sixth, a central charge of the Niebuhrians was the immorality of the noninterventionists who would purchase America's peace and security with the blood of brave Chinese, British, French, and Russian soldiers. It was this hidden lovelessness of the neutralist position that unfailingly triggered Niebuhr's polemic vehemence. "Proclaiming love, demanding love, anticipating love, the effect of neutralism was to sanction division and isolation," writes Donald B. Meyer in summarizing Niebuhr's critique. "The neutralists could not identify themselves with the other men because of the image they held of themselves and that, concomitantly, was true because they could not find in themselves the needs and the weaknesses of other men." Yet Niebuhr, unlike Van Dusen, never called for outright intervention, nor before Pearl Harbor did the Roosevelt administration request that war be declared on Hitler, Mussolini, or Imperial Japan. Cutting through all the persiflage, it is almost certain that Roosevelt, at least until August 1941, sought to wage a proxy war through Britain and the Soviet Union. It may be argued that "all measures short of war" was the most immoral of all positions. If the "war against tyranny" was in fact "our" war, then the United States should have flung itself into the crusade openly and fully, committing without measure the lives of American boys. As it was, Niebuhr (and the Roosevelt administration) asked only that the American people be the "arsenal of democracy." And just what sacrifice was involved in sending "Bundles to Britain" and a handful of volunteer Flying Tigers to China? Allied soldiers might now be armed with American weapons, but no American blood was to be shed with theirs. No Americans would be expected to kill or be killed. No devastation would come to American cities. The defeat of Hitler could be accomplished, the American public was assured by President Roosevelt, with no greater sacrifice than the lending and leasing of materials. Americans would experience the thrill and delicious pride of having participated in a great moral struggle to defeat tyranny without having suffered or directly inflicting suffering. Indeed arming Britain and Russia and China would boom the American economy. Whatever may be said in defense of the "realism" of this position, surely it has nothing to commend it as a morally superior policy.* To repeat, if the Roosevelt administration believed the fate of civilization hinged on the outcome of the war, then the American people should have been persuaded by the president to give their lives in this great cause. Yet the president (and Niebuhr) repeatedly assured the citizenry that the United States need not be drawn into war.

Furthermore, just who were the utopians and who were the realists from 1939 to 1941? It is ironic that the so-called realists, such as Niebuhr, kept insisting that America's unneutral policies need not lead to war, surely a utopian hope, whereas the so-called utopians, such as Fosdick, realistically assessed the high odds against the gamble of assisting the Allies without being drawn into war.

Seventh, in a sermon before Pearl Harbor Fosdick stated: "Even yet . . . there are lovely ladies who will say sweetly to a man, 'Wouldn't you die for your country?' I know the answer to that, Yes, I'd *die* for my country. But that is not the realistic question about war. The realistic question is: 'Wouldn't you *kill* for your country, screw your bayonet into another man's abdomen, bomb a city and indiscriminately murder mothers and children, let poison gas into a population, and so on and so on?'" In the great debate the Niebuhrians spoke of the sacrifices necessary to be endured, but only rarely—if indeed ever—did they acknowledge what the "defenders of democracy" would be called on to inflict to defeat the enemy.†

---

* Senator Arthur Vandenberg confided to his diary, September 15, 1939: "My quarrel is with this notion that America can be half in and half out of this war, that we can bravely sustain our erstwhile allies and yet retain an insulated security which—if we are really in earnest about this business of 'helping the democracies'—is utterly cowardly as a public policy for a country like ours."

† Niebuhr did imply that the war might require the employment of terrible measures when he said in 1940: "If Hitler is defeated in the end it will be because the crisis has awakened in us the will to preserve a civilization in which justice and

IX

Bitter as was the debate over intervention, divided as was American Protestantism, it is essential to remember that the Body of Christ was not utterly broken. As pacifist John Haynes Holmes wrote to interventionist Henry Smith Leiper: "It has been my prayer that we might all stand together and suffer together, for we shall all need the comfort that every comradely heart can give. But if there are those who cannot be with us pacifists, we shall understand, and will find strength in the thought that they also understand us and give us sympathy if they cannot give support. My heart to you, dear friend. Pardon me if I have said anything that seemed to be unkind—it was not so intended."

---

freedom are realities, and given us the knowledge that ambiguous methods are required for the ambiguities of history. Let those who are revolted by such ambiguities have the decency and consistency to retire to the monastery, where medieval perfectionists found their asylum." Holding this view, quite naturally Niebuhr later defended the dropping of the atomic bomb over Hiroshima and Nagasaki and still later took the position that although the United States could renounce the first use of the hydrogen bomb, the United States could not disavow employing the hydrogen bomb—nor, he insisted, could the United States disavow bombing cities without capitulating to the foe who refused to disavow doing so. It is true that Niebuhr's name was among those who signed the Federal Council of Churches' condemnation of the bombings of Hiroshima and Nagasaki and it is also true that he believed that a warning bomb first should have been dropped over a nonpopulated area of Japan. But he criticized the Federal Council's report because it "does not make sufficiently clear what was the conviction of most of us—that the eventual use of the bomb for the shortening of the war would have been justified. I myself consistently took the position that failing in achieving a Japanese surrender, the bomb would have had to be used to save the lives of thousands of American soldiers who would otherwise have perished on the beaches of Japan." This statement, made in a letter to Harvard President James B. Conant, March 6, 1946, is echoed in a letter to Robert Calhoun, March 13, 1946.

Chapter Twenty-seven

"And the War Came" and the Wars Continued: A Peacemaker in Wars Hot and Cold, 1941–1969

I

The Monday following Pearl Harbor Fosdick entered his church office and said to the secretaries, "Well, I thought you girls would be down in the Navy Yard signing up." For himself, he kept his pledge to the Unknown Soldier never to use his ministry to "sanction or support war"—at least to his own satisfaction as he interpreted the meaning of that pledge. So different was the temper of the country from the virulent intolerance of 1917–1918 that it was not necessary for him to keep that prison tryst he had predicated following his Unknown Soldier pledge. Indeed, the fears he had expressed to his family about being hounded out of the Riverside pulpit should war come to America proved totally unfounded.

The week following Pearl Harbor Fosdick much pondered the question of "The Church of Christ in a Warring World," the title of the sermon preached December 14 and repeated over "National Vespers" December 21. He began by acknowledging: "Our nation is at war, not as a matter of choice but of fact, and this situation confronts us, saying, You, the churches of Christ, hating war, as you ought to, finding in it, as you should, the denial of everything Christ stands for, what positively are you going to do for your generation now? What is your special function in this needy time?" For one thing, the church must not separate itself from its people and nation. Leaven works not by getting out of the meal and standing off, but by staying in, vitally participant in the unleavened mass with which it deals, as the Master taught. "God helping us, we will not reduce ourselves to the condition of the unleavened meal; we will keep a differential and distinctive quality; if grace be given us, the living

533

ferment of the Master's spirit—the very opposite of war—that yet may leaven this evil world to decency, brotherhood and peace, shall be kept vital and potent in our lives and churches; but we will not separate ourselves from our people. Their troubles are our troubles; their sins, alas, have been our sins too; their peril is ours."

Moreover, divided as Christians were on questions of public policy, all could stand together on at least one platform: "A positive, constructive, creative determination that, despite war's accumulated bitterness, all this agony shall not be wasted as it was the last time, but shall issue in a world so organized for cooperation instead of war, that our children shall have a decent chance at life, liberty, and happiness." Further, the churches must minister as never before to the spiritual needs of the people and, no less, to the worldwide physical needs of the millions crushed by war.

Fosdick then reminded the congregation of the stern Oxford Conference condemnation of war—the supreme defiance of the righteousness of God—and asked that they now "not bless war or call it holy, for it never is." He pled that they not be consumed by hatred of the enemy, especially not by hatred of the Japanese based on racial prejudice. Nor should they succumb to a self-righteous nationalism. America is not sinless. "Humility and penitence become us all, and if coming into the Christian church and kneeling before the altar of the Crucified, whom the world is crucifying afresh, we are not reminded of that, then the church has failed in its function." The sermon concluded, "Finally, there is the ancient function of the church that today gains special meaning, namely, keeping clear in man's vision and faith the eternal things amid the tempests of the temporal. Alas for a man who in these times, when the immediate is so noisy and obsessive, has no vision that still can see the abiding stars that were here before this storm arose and will be here afterward!"*

Several months after addressing the question of the churches in a warring world, Fosdick turned to "The Role of the Pacifist Minister," the title of an essay appearing in *Fellowship*, the journal of the Fellowship of Reconciliation. First, the pacifist minister "must recognize that full Christian pacifism is not at this present time within reach of his country as a whole, that it is not among the government's immediate practical alternatives, in view of the ethical convictions of the majority. Nevertheless, he is all the more and not the less constrained to stand for and

---

* Three days after war broke upon Pearl Harbor and lashed American shores the Fellowship of Reconciliation declared in words approved by Fosdick: "Trusting in God, we meet this hour without dismay. Despite the human foolishness and sin which mark us all and which have sundered us into warring nations we are all children of the one Father who is eternal God and whose name is Love. His Kingdom will come and His will will be done on earth as it is in heaven."

bear witness to a way of life and a means of combating evil utterly different from the violence his nation uses, practically unavoidable and relatively justifiable though it be."

Concretely, the pacifist minister will do his best to keep the fellowship of his own congregation unimpaired. He will intensify and extend every humanitarian service in his power to render. He will endeavor to "support the proposition that the church of Jesus Christ is not at war; that she is a super-national institution, universal, catholic, ecumenical; that, as such, she has special functions in war time, far removed from fanning the flames of hatred or turning her services of worship into forums on the prosecution of the battle; that she must not surrender her vision of her Lord, standing above the conflict and passing judgment on all the combatants, nor leave her gospel of the one God to whom all souls belong to echo nationalistic war cries." The pacifist minister will be concerned to maintain and strengthen the pacifist fellowship, a small minority group widely judged to be fools and visionaries, dupes of an incredible faith. Finally, he will throw all his weight into the campaign for a world organized for peace. Such a world will mandate the surrender of national sovereignty, abolition of economic privilege, and the overcoming of racial prejudice and inequality.

In this chapter we shall examine these wartime goals set by Fosdick for the churches and for pacifist ministers.

II

About two hundred of Riverside's young men and women saw active service in the armed forces. Fosdick and the other ministers wrote to each of them at least once annually. They received the *Church Monthly* to keep them in touch. They received a new one-volume edition of Fosdick's devotional classics, *The Three Meanings*, and a little volume, the *Words of Jesus*, with an introduction by Fosdick. They were remembered with Christmas packages.

Riverside maintained a "War-Time Visitors Book" in the narthex for visiting individuals in uniform to sign, asking them to give their home addresses, names of parents, wives, and sweethearts. Over fifteen thousand letters were sent to these loving, anxious folk—and hundreds if not thousands of letters of gratitude were received in return. Countless lonely youngsters stationed in New York were entertained in the homes of Riverside parishioners or at social functions in the church, thanks to the War Service Committee.

Of course, parishioners made thousands of surgical dressings and gave to a blood plasma unit set up by the Red Cross in the church, and Fosdick made a special radio appeal on behalf of the Red Cross. Funds were raised for the China Relief Legion and other organizations. Sandbags were purchased for the Assembly Hall windows at the request of the New York City Air Raid Wardens, the church being designated a shelter. The American flag was flown in the gardens, the trustees authorizing the erection of a flagpole. The church bought government war bonds totaling tens of thousands of dollars.* Fosdick agreed to lend a hand to the Greater New York USO Joint War Appeal. He gave his name and such help as he could to the Manhattan Civilian Defense Volunteers Office. For his "National Vespers" preaching he was awarded a Certificate of Merit in recognition of his contribution to national morale.

Riverside's proximity to Columbia University made it possible to minister to the thousands of young men in the Midshipmen's School headquartered there. For three and a half years these officer candidates used the church's facilities for purposes ranging from band or choir practice to bowling or a workout in the gym. Some elected to attend the Sunday morning worship service and each Sunday evening some two thousand worshipped at the Protestant Vesper Service. When the young men were commissioned and ready to leave for active duty, hundreds of brides came to New York and were married in the church—the record, as Fosdick recalled, being twenty-seven weddings in one day. In gratitude, the commandant, John K. Richards, presented the church with a bronze plaque and a $5000 check, which Fosdick accepted only after making it clear to Captain Richards that the ministry to the midshipmen was considered a high privilege, not in the least a burdensome obligation.

The one point of tension between Fosdick's pacifism and the requirements of the Midshipmen's School came when the Navy petitioned that graduation exercises be held in the church. The church officers granted such permission. Fosdick, on vacation, was consulted by letter and shot back an emphatic protest. "I thought then, and I still think," he informed an interested midwestern pacifist Methodist minister, "that the employment of a Christian church for the commissioning of fighting men is a misuse of the sanctuary of the Prince of Peace. I explicitly declined, however, to have my judgment count for more than one in the group that represented the congregation and had to make the decision." And so the affirmative decision stood.†

---

* At least one pacifist minister, the Methodist Ernest Fremont Tittle, believed that the church he served should not support the war effort to the extent of investing its money in government war bonds.

† In 1943, however, the exercises were moved to the Cathedral of Saint John the Divine to accommodate the six or seven thousand persons in attendance.

Fosdick further reported to this Methodist pacifist that he declined an invitation to offer the invocation at the commissioning exercises, with the implication that he did so as a matter of principle. His letter of declination to Captain Richards, however, expresses deep appreciation for the invitation and concludes that "other commitments make it impossible for me to take advantage of this opportunity." Is there not a tincture of dissimulation in this? This letter contained no hint of Fosdick's convictions. Could Fosdick's pacifism be detected, to cite another example, in a 1944 letter to Major Winthrop Rockefeller that closed: "Here at the church we miss very much those who are gone, but at the same time the war has opened unexpected doors of opportunity for service, and I have never seen the church more active and vigorous than it is today. Some of us are too old to do anything at the front as we tried to do, in however small a way, in the last conflict, but here at home we are trying as hard as we know how."

For one moment only was the Riverside Church accused of being pro-German. In 1942 the carillon played the old hymn, "Glorious things of thee are spoken, Zion, city of our God," to a tune by Haydn. The church telephones began ringing off the walls. What, in heaven's name, angry people in the neighborhood wondered, was the carillon of the Riverside Church doing playing "Deutschland Über Alles"?

III

More than 16 million American youth answered their country's call to the colors. But what of those who could not bring themselves to kill another human being, even one who marched under the brutal banner of the swastika or Rising Sun? There were possibly 100,000 objectors to war of military age. This is only an infinitesimal fraction of the more than 34 million registrants—not more than 0.30 of 1 percent. Another authority states that of the men ordered to report for induction, the government classified as conscientious objectors (C.O.s) 42,973, or 0.42 of 1 percent. Of these war resisters, over 25,000 served as noncombatants in the army and navy. Some 11,868 C.O.s reported for alternative service under the Civilian Public Service (C.P.S.), a program proposed by the historic peace churches, endorsed by the Federal Council of Churches and the major denominations, and rather warmly accepted by the Selective Service Administration, "glad to have the churches shoulder the responsibility for the conduct of persons who could, with infinite firmness, say 'No' to every military demand." In the C.P.S. camps or on detached service these individuals tolled more than 8-million man-days of work, tilling the soil, making roads, fighting forest fires, caring for the mentally ill, acting as "guinea pigs" for medical research. If the government had paid for this labor at the same rate as for its Army, it would have spent over $18 million. As it was, the C.O.s were obliged to work for nothing, while they, their families, and the churches paid for their maintenance. A final group of more than 5000 went to prison, either because they refused to register or because their objection was based on nonreligious grounds inadmissible under the law.

Fosdick anguished much over the fate of these young pacifists who in the words of Justice Holmes took the Sermon on the Mount more seriously than the rest of us. The young idealists in the Riverside fellowship were not cut adrift, and whether in noncombatant service or C.P.S. camps or in prison they, too, received from the church letters, books, the *Church Monthly*, and Christmas gifts. Fosdick testified on behalf of those seeking C.O. status from their draft boards and of those in camps seeking detached service, in hospitals for example. Small worship services were held specifically for those of pacifist persuasion. Alfred Hassler, who in 1944 was sentenced to three years in prison for refusing to register, recalled on Fosdick's ninety-first birthday, "It seems a long while ago that you brought such reassurance and strength to Dot while I was in prison, yet it is the warmth and concern that you brought to that situation that lives most vividly in our memories, even more than the tremendous services that you have made to the cause of peace and human understanding throughout your life." In 1942 Fosdick agreed to serve as honorary chairman (together with Quaker Clarence Pickett) of the Pacifist Research Bureau, the only pacifist organization founded during the war, though he confessed, "I think I have been of mighty little help to you, and my honorary chairmanship has been very honorary indeed." Fosdick further sought to raise funds for the maintenance of the boys in C.P.S. camps, though he failed in his efforts to secure a trifling $1000 from Rockefeller, Jr.*

Much as Fosdick honored those who refused to bear arms, he was well aware of the dissension in many of the C.P.S. camps, the bitterness between different groups of pacifists, the proud and defiant spirit of some of the resisters, with some of the younger radicals scoring the "Pacifist Establishment" for its docile cooperation with the government. Methodist Bishop G. Bromley Oxnam, who had labored to have the conscription law worded to recognize the right of conscience and who was chairman of the Board of Trustees of the National Service Board for Religious

---

* Fosdick's appeal was directed to Rockefeller associate Arthur W. Packard, and it may be the negative decision was made by Packard without Rockefeller's knowledge.

Objectors, confided to his diary concerning the uncooperative objectors, "They are so blessed cock-sure in their assumption of being the only Christians in the nations." Oxnam's anger may have been unconsciously fueled by the fact of having two sons in military service. But the papers of even such firm and veteran pacifists as Ernest Fremont Tittle, A. J. Muste, and John Haynes Holmes reveal a similar exasperation. Holmes became "sick and tired of all the complaints and protests that are coming up from the C.P.S. camps," even to the point of being "tempted to feel that conscientious objectors were not men of good will at all, but men of intolerant spirit and stubborn temper." Fosdick thanked Holmes for facing the question of whether "some of our pacifist friends are really pacifist against war, or anarchist against government."

Remembering World War I, Fosdick did what he could to see that civil liberties were not again washed away by a tidal wave of hysteria. Though he acted in several areas, undoubtedly his greatest concern was for the Japanese-Americans. When he had successfully secured a check made out to the National Japanese American Student Relocation Council from John D. Rockefeller, 3rd, Fosdick accompanied his letter of thanks with an expression of serious concern about the indiscriminate treatment of Japanese citizens and their forcible removal from their homes to internment camps. Riverside Church sought to lend a hand to Japanese-Americans in New York, although one critic of the church's outreach growled that teas and talks and "service jobs" would not cut the mustard, especially since these citizens in the New York area were primarily professional and skilled clerical workers.

While 110,000 Japanese-American civilians suffered oppression because they were suspected of loyalty to the enemy, Japanese and German civilians by the scores of thousands suffered excruciating deaths because they were known to be the enemy. On the day Germany's invasion of Poland and the pounding of Warsaw from the skies began, President Roosevelt, in identical notes to Britain, France, Germany, and Poland, declared: "The ruthless bombing from the air of civilians in unfortified centers of population . . . which has resulted in the death of thousands of defenceless men, women and children, has sickened the heart of every civilized man and woman, and has profoundly shocked the conscience of mankind." After the war, when historians examined the evidence of Allied bombing ethics, it would become clear that Britain did not even pretend to confine its bombing to enemy military targets; the night saturation raids were deliberately designed to demoralize the foe by hitting populated neighborhoods. U.S. Army Air Force generals maintained that to the contrary, American precision daylight raids were surgical in nature, designed to spare civilian centers of population. "Yet when the evidence is examined closely," concluded one careful historian of American bombing in Europe, "it is clear that the ethical codes of these men [the generals] did little to discourage air attacks on German civilians. Prewar American air plans and doctrine and the development of operations during the war reveal that official policy against indiscriminate bombing was so broadly interpreted and so frequently breached as to become almost meaningless. Statements of air commanders that supposedly indicate abhorrence of terror bombing, when analyzed in context, mean something very different. In the end, both the policy and the apparent ethical support for it among AAF leaders turn out to be myths; while they contain elements of truth, they are substantially fictitious or misleading."

Early in 1944 Dr. Cosmo Gordon Lang, former Archbishop of Canterbury, and the Right Reverend George K. A. Bell, Bishop of Chichester, protested in the House of Lords against the indiscriminate bombing of German cities by the Allies. On February 20 fifteen American and Canadian churchmen cabled Dr. Lang the following message: "The appeal of Chichester and yourself in the House of Lords against Allied policy of blotting out whole German cities and nonmilitary areas is welcomed by many American churchmen. Obliteration of historic cities and incineration of masses of civilian victims does violence to professed war aims and standards of Christian faith. Deeply grateful for your courageous stand."* On February 14 Fosdick had been importuned to add his name by Oswald Garrison Villard and John Nevin Sayre. This he declined to do in a letter of February 16 to Sayre.† The heart of Fosdick's position is found in this passage:

> I feel poignantly the hideousness of this mutual bombing of cities. I share the emotional reactions to this shame and horror from which this protest springs, but nevertheless, I must disagree with this way of getting at the matter. This protest is an endeavor to determine a detail of military strategy on the basis of Christian motives. That seems to me a contradiction in terms. As I see it, all military strategy is an utter denial of Christian motives; the whole military business is essentially unchristian. It will not do, then, will it? to pick out one special horror of this devilish process and try to apply Christian motivation to it as this protest does. Do we think that this whole business of war is Christian, that we take pains to cable the Bishop of Chichester our agreement with him that obliteration

---

* Among the American signers were Bishop W. Appleton Lawrence, Walter Russell Bowie, Rufus Jones, John Haynes Holmes, George A. Buttrick, Allen Knight Chalmers, and Ernest Fremont Tittle. All but the first and last individuals were Fosdick's close friends.

† Fosdick does not mention this decision in his autobiography.

bombing does violence to the "standards of the Christian faith"? Of course, we don't. I don't want to be in the position of Luther, taking war in general for granted, and protesting against gunpowder. Well, forgive me! I am horrified and heartsick at what is going on, but this proposal, I am sure, will get us nowhere.

Very shortly Fosdick was to change his mind, although the reason for the volte-face is not found in the records. *Fellowship* published as a supplement to its regular March issue an article by Vera Brittain entitled, "Massacre by Bombing," an eloquent indictment of Allied bombing strategy, a jeremiad especially forceful because it was penned by a sensitive English woman who had witnessed the horrors of the Great War and who had herself endured German bombing in the second conflict. As a foreword to the article there was an appeal to end obliteration bombing signed on March 5 by twenty-eight American clergymen, including Fosdick. The appeal read in part: "Christian people should be moved to examine themselves concerning their participation in this carnival of death—even though they be thousands of miles away. Here, surely, there is a call for repentance; that we have not acquainted ourselves with the verities and realities of what is being done in our name in Europe; and surely Christian obligation calls upon us to pray incessantly to God that He in His own way may bid the winds and waves of war be still."

The appeal touched off what Fosdick termed "an outburst of vitriolic denunciation." Vera Brittain estimated she was condemned in two hundred articles. The *New York Times*'s story stimulated a heavy reader response, the letters running fifty to one in opposition to the protest. Many of Fosdick's clerical friends were numbered among the critics. Dr. Daniel Poling accused the signers of being "mushy" and dismissed the protest as a "squawk." Bishop C. Bromley Oxnam, then president of the Federal Council of Churches, publicly denied that obliteration bombing had taken place and said that in any case war is a "stern, dirty business" and bombing a "revolting necessity" to free the world of fascism.* Bishop William Thomas Manning, Anglophile that he was, naturally rallied 'round the Union Jack.

Secular criticism of the signers was even more severe. President Roose-

---

* It is worth remembering that Dr. Poling's son was killed in the war and that Bishop Oxnam had two boys in service, and, he reported, "I, like other fathers, never open a telegram these days without hesitation." The distinguished John C. Bennett has stated that Reinhold Niebuhr was a critic "of obliteration bombing in the Second World War." Maybe so, since Bennett was close to Niebuhr and in a position to know. All I can say is that I do not recall encountering such criticism in either Niebuhr's published works or unpublished letters, but, of course, I may have missed the item.

velt, through his press secretary Stephen Early, defended the necessity of the Allied bombing. The journalists Walter Lippmann and William L. Shirer argued that the alternative to bombing Germany's cities was "slavery to the Nazis." The novelist MacKinlay Kantor, like many other Americans of Jewish heritage, was understandably bitter about "the tut-tuttings of the American clergy at this time," adding, "Those fecund germs of another war are planted in every squawk against the awful effectiveness of our high-altitude warfare—every wail by prelate or lay 'humanitarian.' "

The signers of course received private as well as public chastisement, Ernest Fremont Tittle, for example, was called (by mail) a "traitor" and "big mouth meddler." Fosdick replied to one critic, a Riverside parishioner, in several long letters, the pith being: "This is still the United States of America my friend, and the free expression of opinion on matters of public importance is still the citizen's privilege and duty. I deeply respect your conviction on the matter in question. I would fight for your right to express it freely. I claim an equal right to the expression of my own conviction. My mail has been about equally divided between warm approval and warm disapproval, but you alone have interpreted my act as a citizen as being within the domain of the church's right to pass judgment. It certainly is not within the domain of the church's right to pass judgment, and no one here at Riverside would seriously consider for a moment thinking of it as such. I should be seriously grieved to have you leave the fellowship of our church, and I earnestly hope that you will not do so. We are a free fellowship, where as it has often been said, No one has to agree with anyone else, least of all with the ministers."

"I take great comfort in God," said one of Fosdick's favorite poets, James Russell Lowell. "I think he is considerably amused with us sometimes, but that he likes us on the whole, and would not let us get to the match-box as carelessly as he does, unless he knew the frame of his universe was fireproof." These comforting nineteenth-century words could not have been uttered after August 6, 1945. On that date a uranium atomic bomb, "Little Boy," was dropped over the inhabitants of Hiroshima. Three days later the people of Nagasaki received the visit of "Fat Man," a plutonium atomic bomb. We may agree that President Truman was not a moral monster and that the bombs were unleashed to bring a quick end to a terrible war, saving ultimately, it was believed, tens of thousands of American *and* Japanese lives.* After all, the presi-

---

* The much-debated question concerning whether Hiroshima and Nagasaki were intended to alert the Soviet Union to the fact that we possessed the bombs and, equally important, were fully capable of employing them against human beings, need not concern us here.

dent reasoned, what could be worse than the B-29 fire-bomb raid of Tokyo the night of March 9–10 that had cremated an estimated one hundred thousand men, women, and children. After all, his predecessor in the White House and the British Prime Minister had seen no alternative to razing Dresden, Hamburg, Berlin, and other German cities. Little wonder that when informed of the "success" of the Hiroshima bombing, Truman on board the U.S.S. *Augusta* rushed to the officers' wardroom and exalted: "We have just dropped a bomb on Japan that has more power than 20,000 tons of T.N.T. It was an overwhelming success. We won the gamble." He then shook the captain's hand and said, "This is the greatest thing in history."

There are other perhaps more appropriate reactions to the atomic bomb:

Robert J. Oppenheimer witnessing on July 16 the first atomic fireball rising from the New Mexico desert and recalling words from the Bhagavad-Gita: "I am become death, the shatterer of worlds."

Oppenheimer's colleague, witnessing the same scene, turning to him and confessing, "Well, Oppie, I guess we're all sons-of-bitches now."

The co-pilot of the *Enola Gay* recording in his flight log as the B-29 turned away from the Hiroshima blast: "I honestly have the feeling of groping for words to explain this or I might say My God, what have we done?"

The philosopher remembering the question of Dostoyevski's Grand Inquisitor: If all mankind could realize eternal and complete happiness by torturing to death a single child, would this act be morally justified?

Raymond Blaine Fosdick pulling his car over to the side of the road and becoming physically ill.

Harry Emerson Fosdick turning to his Bible to find the words of Deuteronomy: "I have set before thee life and death, the blessing and the curse: therefore choose life."

Fosdick became a member of the Hiroshima Peace Center Associates; ill health prevented him from accepting the position of honorary chairman. Carved in the stone of the cenotaph in Hiroshima are the words: "Rest in peace, for the mistake will not be repeated." Perhaps.

IV

General Douglas MacArthur concluded the formal surrender ceremonies of Japan aboard the U.S.S. *Missouri* anchored in Tokyo Bay with the words: "Let us pray that peace be now restored to the world and that God will preserve it always." Of course Fosdick raised up many such prayers, but even before the end of hostilities he expressed forebodings about the postwar world, quoting the lines: "The many men so beautiful, / And they all did dead lie. / And a thousand slimy things / Lived on; and so did I."

Nevertheless, Fosdick was never one to permit forebodings to cut the nerve of action. He continued to be active in the Fellowship of Reconciliation and received many letters of thanks from its officers.* He contributed to the eloquent 1950 document, *The Christian Conscience and War: The Statement of a Commission of Theologians and Religious Leaders Appointed by the Church Peace Commission*. He submitted to the World Council of Churches meeting in Amsterdam in 1948 a manifesto as strong as any to come from his pen:

> From the nature and function of the Church it follows also that the members of the Church cannot participate in war without violating the essential meaning of the Gospel. Christians can never love universally as church members and yet fight each other as citizens. Christian citizens have real duties to the state, but their first duty is to Christ. When they cannot serve both God and country, their first duty is to God. If ever a church member is convinced that as between possible alternatives of national action, war is the least evil choice available, he should still recognize that even so war is the denial of all Christian values, and that all who engage in it are under the judgment of God.

As he had been doing for years, Fosdick continued his endeavors to succor the victims of war and oppression. He actively supported the American Friends Service Committee, sent packages of food and clothing to a German family he had known before the war, and pressed for the wider opening of America's doors to Europe's dispossessed, "especially our Jewish brethren."

Nor will it come as a surprise to learn that he pulled out all stops to prevent the adoption of new conscription legislation. In 1944 he wrote to his congressman protesting a bill that would establish permanent univer-

---

* It is true that he never accepted the absolutist position of that great "Fool-for-Christ" A. J. Muste, but he continued to count him "my friend."

sal military training. If passed, such a measure "will be the severest blow that has ever been struck to the great traditions of our American democracy." It will lead to "an immensely powerful and immensely expensive military system with a permanent military clique." He further sent a statement to every member of the House Committee on Military Affairs, which was printed in the *Congressional Digest*. It contained this warning, "The compulsory conscription and regimentation of American youth in military training is the longest step ever proposed in this country toward the idea and methods of the Fascist state." In 1948 Fosdick joined with other ministers in calling for a Day of Mourning and Repentance as a protest against the peacetime draft. When in the 1950s a Universal Military Training Bill was before Congress, he petitioned General MacArthur to raise his voice against it, explaining that the measure "is one of the most inept, inefficient, inexcusably expensive, and publicly disrupting proposals ever made to an American Congress." He also joined a new organization, the National Council Against Conscription.

Concurrently, Fosdick continued to protect conscientious objectors. He agreed to join John Haynes Holmes in appearing before Judge Harold Medina to plead the case of a young man who could not present a religious basis for his pacifism, but who was a sincere believer in the nonviolent principles of Gandhi.* On another occasion when a judge sentenced a nineteen-year-old Quaker to ten years in prison for failing to register, Fosdick sent that judge a stern demand that the sentence be reduced.

As we saw in Chapter Twenty-Six, Fosdick had few illusions about Stalinist Russia (Stalin, that "pock-marked Caligula," as Pasternak spit out), but neither was he a Cold War warrior. For example, when America still possessed an atomic bomb monopoly, he worried that "There are irresponsible voices saying that we have got to lick Russia, and we might just as well do it now when we have the power to do it thoroughly." Such a war he said elsewhere would be "insane"; and besides, "we had better get hold of ourselves before we complain too much about Russia." The "brinkmanship" of Secretary of State Dulles changed his once admiring mind, holding in 1958 that "Secretary Dulles could make the most outstanding contribution to the peace of the world in this generation, if he would only resign!" When Castro came to power in Cuba, Fosdick hoped "that the United States will be wise enough to manage to keep the peace, so that we do not lose the friendship of that hopeful people." As nuclear weapons proliferated he dreamed the impossible, ap-

---

* Actually, Fosdick was ill on the day of the hearing, but that does not alter the fact that he agreed to appear.

parently, dream of placing them under international control, and he became a national sponsor of the National Committee for a Sane Nuclear
Policy.

At the same time Fosdick signed an appeal for amnesty for political
prisoners in Hungary and informed the peoples of Eastern Europe, over
Radio Free Europe, of the friendship of the Americans for those "who
are under the Kremlin's domination." In 1962 he made a measured assessment of Khrushchev's leadership, saying, "Our problem is not either
to blame or to excuse Khrushchev for being what he is in view of his
heredity or environment, or to wonder if under the circumstances we
would have come out any better—such judgment is God's business."
The communication closed: "Personally, I am hopeful. He does not want
war any more than we do. We are quite as likely to make fools of ourselves as he is—see the Cuban debacle, for example. Only undiscourageable goodwill can ultimately save the world. And, as for the magnificent
achievements in the elimination of Russian illiteracy, etc., they increase
my hope. An educated Russia will not ultimately remain a dictatorship.
Some day what Khrushchev has done to Stalin will be done to Khrushchev."

V

Fosdick was in his eighties when he saw American involvement in Vietnam deepening. Even so, his hatred of war gave him the strength to
write President Kennedy: "United States support of the corrupt and ty-
rannical regime in South Vietnam will become the scandal of the era." It
gave him the strength to inform the American people, in the pages of the
New York Times, that it was a fiction to believe that we were fighting
for freedom and that it was folly to sacrifice "American lives and billions
of dollars to bolster a regime universally regarded as unjust, undemocratic, and unstable."

Of course, even the strongest warhorses in the war against war must
one day die. One of the last things Fosdick wrote, perhaps the last thing
he wrote, was a note of thanks to an old comrade who had remembered
him on his ninety-first birthday, only months before the final summons.
The note contains only four sentences written in a now shaky hand:
"My gratitude to you for your gracious letter! This monstrous war in
Vietnam is one of the most tragic and deplorable mistakes in all our
American history. Strength to all of you who are speaking out against it!
I am powerless to help now and can only pray for you."

Although Harry Emerson Fosdick would not approve, holding as he did that one should think and pray and act affirmatively, on reading this little note one is gripped by an overwhelming sense of sadness. Perhaps, however, Fosdick himself found consolation in the old, stirring words, "It is not necessary to hope in order to undertake, nor to succeed in order to persevere."

Chapter Twenty-eight

The Decision To Step Down, 1946:
Saying Farewell to Riverside and Union

I

To paraphrase a famous line, and not to minimize the nobility of Fosdick's life, nothing in his ministry became him like the leaving of it. It will be the burden of this brief chapter to sustain that statement.

II

The Riverside fellowship flourished during the war years. Fosdick reported to a daughter: "Everything at the church is going with éclat. We have overflow congregations every Sunday, and I have been speaking to an average of 650 to 700 people on Wednesday evenings. Our whole program is going on high gear, and our work, I think, has never been more vigorous and active, or had a warmer or more numerous response." Nevertheless, the very fact that things were going on "high gear" placed ever increasing demands on Fosdick's ever decreasing physical resources; and as his sixty-fifth birthday in May of 1943 approached he happily anticipated stepping down. Not wishing to take the church officers by surprise, on September 1, 1942, he formally submitted his resignation, "to take effect not later than June first, 1943." The letter thanked the church for having given him an opportunity, "of which no man could be worthy, unsurpassed among the churches of this nation." The officers protested at the thought of losing him and suggested that he remain, but on a reduced work schedule. Fosdick thought the idea unwise and insisted that it was time for them to bite the bullet, accept the inevitable, and begin immediately the search for his successor. The officers were not dissuaded, however, and in March, 1943, their persistence prevailed. Fosdick agreed to remain, continuing his Sunday preaching and Wednesday night and communion service duties, but relieved of a large part of his administrative and pastoral responsibilities. This arrangement was renewed in 1944 and again in 1945. In June, 1945, however, Fosdick made it plain positive that under no circumstances would he remain beyond May 1946 when he would turn sixty-eight.

Francis Harmon, an important lay leader in the church, believes that an argument that he advanced before a joint meeting of the trustees and deacons and subsequently presented to Fosdick was crucial in persuading Fosdick to stay on after 1943. The argument was that if Fosdick were to depart from Riverside while the war was still raging, it would be widely believed that he had been sacked. Harmon pictured his business associates commenting sarcastically "that despite all our talk about 'freedom of the pulpit' we had eased out a pacifist preacher because we disagreed with his position." Harmon closed his case by pleading that Fosdick continue until the war was over. It is just possible that Fosdick's mind was in fact changed by Harmon, for Fosdick would do anything to prevent Riverside's reputation from being tranished. Moreover, he would also do anything to prevent harm coming to other pacifist ministers across the country, and if it was believed that he was forced out, official boards elsewhere might be emboldened to fire their pacifist preachers.

Mrs. Dorothy Noyes, Fosdick's longtime secretary, has suggested another possible factor. Elinor Fosdick Downs's husband died in February 1945 and perhaps Fosdick needed a final year's salary to lend his daughter a financial helping hand. In any case and for whatever reason, Fosdick originally intended to retire in May of 1943 and postponed the deed until May of 1946.

The farewell ceremony was held on May 22 and was attended by several thousand parishioners. Many were the warm words spoken by selected parishioners, including Rockefeller, to Harry and Florence, and their replies, if briefer, were equally fervent. Gifts of a Dodge sedan and a painting of sailboats at sunset off Brittany were bestowed. They were gathered, said the presiding officer, simply to honor two dearly loved friends. "It was a strawberry festival without the strawberries."

The following Sunday Fosdick preached his farewell sermon, "Your Present Is the Past of Your Future." After the service, one thousand of the three thousand worshippers filed past the chancel steps to shake his hand.

III

At a congregational meeting on June 27, 1945, a seven-person Pulpit Committe had been authorized to search for a new minister. It started with eighty prospects, including one unfortunate soul in a New Jersey church who, unaware that members of the committee were in the congregation one Sunday sizing him up, preached a Fosdick sermon word for word. Gradually, candidates were eliminated until they came down to a bare half-dozen. "Now the crux of the matter comes," Fosdick reported to a daughter, "and naturally I am keeping my hands off, while I am watching the process with great eagerness."

One of the finalists was Robert James McCracken, barely forty years of age. Born in Scotland, educated at Glasgow University and Cambridge, he had served Baptist churches in Glasgow and Edinburgh, and in 1938 had accepted an assistant professorship of theology and philosophy at McMaster University in Canada. He quickly acquired a splendid reputation in preaching and theological circles. He was first invited to preach from the Riverside pulpit in October. He made a handsome impression, and was asked to preach again in January 1946. On the return visit McCracken and Fosdick spent seven hours together, beginning with breakfast at the Fosdicks' apartment and continuing through lunch at the Century Club. "I found him, as everybody else has, a charming companion and thoroughly liked him; for his personal qualities are altogether attractive and admirable," Fosdick reported to the chairman of the search committee. "We went over, I think, every conceivable aspect of the church's life here, and had a first-rate, frank, confidential talk."

As further letters between Fosdick and chairman Clifford Petitt and also between Fosdick and McCracken make clear, there was only one real stumbling block: Was the Scot too loyal and stiff a Baptist, especially on the question of infant baptism? Was he too conservative in his theology for the free-spirited, free-practicing liberal Riverside congregation? Happily, the church concluded he was not and for his part the Scot concluded that the church was a genuine Christian fellowship. The formal invitation was extended on April 2 and accepted April 5. McCracken would later confess that he trembled at the thought of stepping into Fosdick's shoes and lingered at the point of refusal. "Had I done so," he added, "I am certain that I should have gone through the balance of my life inwardly convicted of cowardice."

The young minister's installation took place on October 2. Among those participating was Bishop G. Bromley Oxnam, who recorded the event in his diary: "Riverside Church, of course, was crowded. I went up to the robing room. Dr. Fosdick, Dr. McCracken, and I came down for the photographs. I was interested to hear a photographer say to Dr. Fosdick, 'I got instructions to take a picture of Mr. Rockefeller, some fellow named Fosdick, and a new preacher here.' It is hard for anyone to believe that there is anyone who does not know Dr. Fosdick, but there it was." "This is indeed one of the great churches of the world," the entry closes.

IV

In late November 1946 McCracken confided to Rockefeller, Jr., his continuing doubts about his qualifications to follow Fosdick in the Riverside pulpit. "The biggest battle I have to fight is in that region, and I ought to say that no one helps me in the struggle more than does Dr. Fosdick. He is a great soul, and I am fortunate in having him at hand for direction and advice." At the onset of the transition the incoming minister had insisted that the outgoing minister remain on board the Riverside ship as minister emeritus, and Fosdick with extreme reluctance consented, saying, "I am . . . your humble servant, and whatever I do or do not do will be done or not done at your request, in the sole thought of backing up your ministry." "I am more thankful than I can say that I had sense enough to retire when I did and that you are to be in my place this fall," Fosdick on another occasion wrote to his young successor. "I can't even imagine anything that I can preach about on September 29th that I haven't said again and again! The old tank is just plain dry and I am saying, Hurrah! about the new man."

And so for a decade* Fosdick extended a hand of help. He preached an occasional Sunday sermon, such as on Budget Sunday to avoid embarrassment to the new pastor. Once in a while he gave the pastoral prayer or scripture meditation. More than once he assumed leadership of the Wednesday evening service, especially during Lent. He assisted in some communion services. He gave of his experience and knowledge to the preparation of a major church survey, the Kimball Report. Perhaps above all, he responded to McCracken's petitions for advice on matters public and personal. For this continuing limited service Fosdick was invited to maintain an office and a secretary at the church and receive a purse of $2500.

It must be emphatically insisted that Fosdick did not press his continuing service; his hand did not need to be pried from the tiller. Indeed,

---

* It will be remembered that Fosdick preached his last sermon from the Riverside pulpit, and indeed from any pulpit, in 1955, his preaching energies at last totally exhausted.

in 1947, after only one year, he absolutely refused to continue to receive an honorarium: "It is not necessary, and the church is being very generous in allowing me an office, and secretarial assistance." Even more significant, in January 1947 he firmly ordered that his name as minister emeritus be no longer printed in the church publications at the top of the list of ministers, expressing regret that he had ever allowed himself to be persuaded to the listing in the first place.

It is well that Fosdick did not disappear immediately and entirely, for McCracken suffered a nervous breakdown during his first Christmas season as Riverside's pastor. Recalled Rockefeller, Jr., in a letter of appreciation to Fosdick: "What you have done for the Riverside Church and for Dr. McCracken during the past twelve months, it would be difficult to overstate. The fact that you were willing, at Dr. McCracken's urgent request, to continue your relation to the church as Pastor Emeritus was a godsend to him and to the church. I do not know what we would have done during the difficult period of Dr. McCracken's absence at the holidays last year had you not stepped into the breach as you did and carried on magnificently. That everything has turned out so well, that Dr. McCracken's health has been completely restored and that he seems to be in such splendid condition now and increasingly in command of the situation, must give you the greatest satisfaction, as it does me."* Fosdick replied: "The credit you give me for what little I have done since Dr. McCracken came is far beyond my deserts; and the outcome of our united efforts, as seen in the present most promising outlook for his ministry, is, as you can easily imagine, a profound satisfaction. For my small contribution the reward, as I watch the church rallying around Dr. McCracken, is a thousandfold."

There was one cruel actuality in McCracken's life beyond even Fosdick's abilities to moderate. In the 1950s Mrs. McCracken, Maude, underwent a heart operation that saved her life, but a blood clot permanently damaged her brain. Thereafter, she suffered from aphasia, paralysis, and irrational rages. Her hell was her husband's hell, who also had an angina condition of his own. It came to the point where McCracken's ministerial associates believed that if Maude was not institutionalized, his own mental and physical health would be shattered. An associate minister, Eugene E. Laubach, went with a small group to Fosdick to seek his interces-

---

* There is a hint of what might have contributed to McCracken's breakdown in a letter from Rockefeller, Jr., to Francis S. Harmon: "Recalling as I do the very delicate situation with which the Trustees were confronted when Dr. McCracken became the pastor of the Church, because the two older ministers of the Church, perhaps not strangely, felt they out-ranked him."

sion. Would Fosdick not use his influence with McCracken to persuade McCracken to place his wife in an institution? This Fosdick could not bring himself to do personally, though he did give Laubach permission to convey to McCracken that this was his recommendation. Maude was placed for a time in a hospital in Scotland. In the end, she returned, the McCrackens moved to Scarsdale to escape some of the pressures of the Riverside ministry, and then in retirement they settled in a retirement community in New Jersey where medical service was at hand.

"Jim" McCracken's admiration and affection for Fosdick was boundless. "To be associated with you has been a prized privilege. No preacher could possibly have been more blessed in his predecessor," he wrote. On another occasion he confessed to "wearing my heart on my sleeve which is something no Scotsman is supposed to do," but he wanted to express his appreciation for Fosdick's "deliberately staying out of things during the first years so as to leave 'the center of the stage' to me." Said McCracken to a reporter of Fosdick: "Always his intention is to commend and support his successor. I cannot recall that he performed any ministerial function without first discussing the pros and cons with me."

For his part, Fosdick never tired of praising his successor. Read one of many notes to McCracken: "I think that service of worship at Riverside yesterday was the most inspiring I ever attended. Everything was right—the hymns, the prayers, the readings of the Scriptures—everything! And that sermon of yours! That was the most magnificent and moving sermon I ever listened to. Please have it printed. I want a copy myself, and I know folk from here to Arkansas to whom I wish to send it." Fosdick sung the Scot's praises to others, from Rockefeller to the person in the pew next to him after a McCracken service. And when age no longer permitted attending Riverside, Fosdick wrote a friend, "No longer able to come to Riverside, Mrs. Fosdick and I listen every Sunday to Dr. McCracken's preaching and thank God for him."

V

The same spring that Fosdick stepped down as Riverside's senior minister he also retired from the Union Seminary faculty,* and this meant giving up the comfortable seminary apartment. Anticipating this, Harry and Florence had purchased a home in Bronxville, a suburb some twenty-eight minutes north by train from Grand Central Station. The handsome

* See Chapter Seventeen.

English-style dwelling, situated on a rising half-acre above the High Road, was spacious enough to shelter the Fosdicks and their daughter, Elinor, and her two children, until the time came fifteen years later to move to an apartment. Here were spent the active retirement years.*

* The home was opened to the McCrackens one summer while the Fosdicks vacationed in Maine. Wrote Rockefeller, Jr., in 1947: "We are happy also in the thought that you have established so comfortable a permanent home in Bronxville. Once before I asked the privilege of having a little part in helping to develop that home and am now hoping that you will permit me to have a further interest in it by the acceptance of the enclosed check, to be used in any way in connection with your home or the well-being and happinesss of its inmates that you may see fit."

Chapter Twenty-nine

"Leisure Is the Time for Doing Something Useful": A Retirement of Activities and Accomplishment

I

Fosdick retired from Riverside and Union the month he turned sixty-eight and for almost a score more years he put into practice the poet James Russell Lowell's Victorian admonition, "leisure is the time for doing something useful." Fosdick was fond of quoting another Victorian, Julia Ward Howe, who in her old age observed that she found all the sugar in the bottom of the cup. Save for periods of ill health, he could honestly say to a friend in 1960, "I think I never was happier than now, and I hope you too are finding rich rewards in the closing years." Anyhow, when at age seventy-eight Fosdick received from John Haynes Holmes a newspaper story referring to "the late Dr. Fosdick" they both had a good laugh for the "lion of Mouse Island" was not only not dead, he was far from toothless.

II

Life was pleasant in Bronxville. The pink stucco house on a small hilltop, shaded by dogwoods and graced by well-tended shrubbery, comfortably housed Harry and Florence and, when not abroad, Elinor and grandchildren Stevie and Patty. Servants eased the household tasks. Here Fosdick spent mornings writing in his upstairs study. At noon he would break for a light lunch, a short nap, and then a walk downtown. Unlike his preretirement walking days, Florence often joined him, and unlike in the earlier days, he broke his stride to chat with villagers and shopkeepers. His erect carriage—"as straight as a drum major," one villager observed—was much remarked, and few were aware that if he bent his back ever so slightly the arthritic pain was agonizing. Afternoons found him at his desk again. Then dinner and before bedtime an hour or two of reading, television, gin rummy, or an occasional movie. Although generally the Fosdicks disliked restaurants, they regularly took their midday Sunday meal at a favorite Bronxville tea room. Harry and Florence had never been avid party goers or party throwers, but they were not recluses and they did receive and extend occasional party invitations. They especially enjoyed "The Little Forum," a dinner-discussion group of forty couples.

Once or twice a week Fosdick broke his daytime schedule and took the train to Manhattan to catch up on the correspondence awaiting him at his Riverside office or to attend a church or secular organization meeting.

Summers, from May to October, found the Fosdicks on their beloved Maine island. Several weeks each winter found them at a favorite Arizona ranch. Florida continued to be visited. Speaking missions called Harry to all points of the compass, Florence joining him on one such mission to California.

Foreign travel had once been a delight, but aside from a preaching mission in the Panama Canal Zone and a trip to Geneva to visit Elinor, the Fosdicks now elected to stay closer to home. Indeed, invitations to spend extended periods in Australia, Shanghai, and Beirut were all turned down.

A reporter who interviewed Fosdick at age seventy-five found him robust, ruddy faced, alert, with eyes shrewd and twinkling. "It is a fact that you never notice his age." On his eightieth birthday another reporter noted his cheeks wore a ruddy, youthful glow and that he looked "a trim sixty." Perhaps Fosdick summed up best the first years of his retirement when he said to a friend in 1954: "What with occasional preaching, lecturing, and fairly steady writing I have found that, blessed with good health, retirement is one of the happiest parts of one's life. Now in my seventy-sixth year I am trying to slow down and act my age, but I still am getting around the country on various speaking missions, and I cannot break the habit of having a book or two to think about and work on in the hope that someday I shall get it written."

Although Fosdick no longer received the thousands of letters that had come to him during the radio-preaching years, his correspondence by no means completely dried up. He was the soul of conscientiousness in answering his mail promptly. Some of his letters he dictated to a Riverside secretary, but many he wrote by hand, the script remaining firm and clear almost to the year of his death. His birthdays brought cards, notes, and telegrams, and these remembrances numbered in the hundreds on the seventy-fifth and ninetieth anniversaries.

III

Said Fosdick to a reporter concerning his grandchildren, "Every night they make me aware of all the things I must do the next day. Life wouldn't be worth living if I went to bed at night feeling there was nothing to be done in the morning." One thing that Fosdick did at his desk in the morning was to prepare sermons and lectures, and this continued for ten years until his doctors ordered him to cease and desist. This is not to say that with retirement he embarked upon an extensive itinerant ministry. On the contrary, he carefully husbanded his energies, accepting only a fraction of the scores of speaking invitations tendered. Moreover, if an invitation was accepted he made a frank appeal that he not "be killed with kindness"—that he not be caught up in a whirl of banquets, luncheons, and teas before or after speaking.

Several of the more significant speaking engagements merit mentioning. In early 1948 he delivered fifteen addresses in ten days in the Panama Canal Zone, and although he admitted to "a certain unholy pride" in pulling off the schedule, despite tropic heat, he vowed never to try such a thing again. In that year also he gave the Shaffer Lectures at the Yale Divinity School, which were the basis of a major book, *The Man from Nazareth, as His Contemporaries Saw Him.* In 1952 he presented the Earl Foundation Lectures at the Pacific School of Religion, which were published under the title, *A Faith for Tough Times.** In that year he gave the Garvin Lecture, a significant statement of his understanding of "The Idea of God as Affected by Modern Knowledge."

As we know, in 1955 "Mother Nature gave him a warning" and his long career as a public preacher and speaker came to a sharp end, save only for such very rare instances as giving in 1958 the closing prayer at the laying of the cornerstone of the massive Interchurch Center across the street from Riverside.

In the 1950s Fosdick permitted himself one other avenue of public exposure. This was appearances on three television interview shows: Alistair Cooke's "Omnibus"; NBC's "Wisdom" series; Arlene Francis's and Hugh Downs's "People at Home" series. And also on one radio program, the Martha Deane show.

---

* Fosdick declined an invitation to join the faculty of the Pacific School of Religion, as he declined other teaching offers.

IV

In addition to *The Man from Nazareth* and *A Faith for Tough Times*
other books appeared bearing his name.* The year of his retirement
Harper & Brothers published the seventh volume of sermons preached
from the Riverside pulpit, *On Being Fit to Live With: Sermons on Post-
War Christianity.* The next volume was an obvious labor of love, *Rufus
Jones Speaks to Our Times, An Anthology.* As he wrote to the famed
Quaker's widow, "I cannot tell you what an inspiration it has been personally to me to read and reread Rufus Jones' writings with the anthology in mind. I am unpayably grateful to him all over again!" The following year, 1952, he compiled and edited a massive work, *Great Voices of
the Reformation, An Anthology.* Although the words of the Reformers
naturally comprise the bulk of the contents, Fosdick's voice is also heard
in the lengthy introduction and in the commentaries on each selection.
Fosdick obviously put a lot of labor into this work, as the bibliographies
reveal. It received favorable reviews and justly so.

In 1955 Harper's brought out an eighth volume of sermons, *What Is
Vital in Religion,* and then in 1958, on the occasion of Fosdick's eightieth birthday, a final volume of sermons, *Riverside Sermons,* appeared
with an introduction by Henry Pitney Van Dusen. No other single volume so fully captures the richness of Fosdick's preaching. Reviewers, of
course, failed to find some of their favorites among these forty sermons,
but *Riverside Sermons,* selected from almost six hundred preached between 1931 and 1946, remains the best introduction to Fosdick's preaching. *A Book of Public Prayers* appeared in 1959, bringing conveniently
under one cover those prayers many worshippers remembered with a
gratitude even greater than for his sermons.

Meanwhile, Fosdick's friend, Bennet Cerf, head of Random House,
asked him in 1956 to write a brief biography of Martin Luther in the
Landmark Series for teenagers. This Fosdick did, followed in the same
series by biographies of Jesus of Nazareth in 1959 and Saint Paul in
1962.

Fosdick's lifelong concern with apologetics found final expression in
Dear Mr. Brown: Letters to a Person Perplexed About Religion published
in 1961. The book enjoyed substantial success selling over sixty-thousand
copies, although it scarcely ranks in sophistication with the little classics
of C. S. Lewis. Concurrently, new editions were brought out of Fosdick's

---

* In retirement the flow of articles for magazines from his pen did largely dry up.

early true classics, *The Meaning of Prayer, The Meaning of Faith, The Meaning of Service* and *The Manhood of the Master.*

Autobiography has been termed the most difficult and dangerous form of fiction. In 1953 Fosdick "with strong reluctance" began the task of writing his. Nowhere does he state the reason for this reluctance, though he hints at a feeling of embarrassment in engaging in such a supposedly egotistical endeavor. In the prologue of *The Living of These Days* published in 1956, the title of which was taken from his glorious hymn at the suggestion of Elton Trueblood, Fosdick reported that he succumbed to the pressure of friends, ministerial colleagues, and his editor at Harper's, Eugene Exmam. Elsewhere, however, he stated that he wrote it only for his grandchildren with no intention of placing it in the public domain. Maybe these statements can be reconciled by the conjecture that he started to write for Stevie and Patty and only when the manuscript was completed did he give in to pressure from others to publish it. The alternative to this dubious hypothesis is that he repeatedly gave the grandchildren and "strong reluctance" explanations to avoid the possible appearance of conceit. As we know, appearances counted strongly with Fosdick.

If the origins of *The Living of These Days* are murky, there is no reason to doubt Fosdick's repeated assertions that it was "the most difficult piece of writing I ever undertook, and I am praying now that I may *not* have a reincarnation and be compelled to write another one." When congratulated by McCracken, Fosdick replied: "I agree with you on one point at least: The *publisher* has done an excellent job. As for the author, I dare not pray for justice; I can only hope for mercy! Anyway I am glad that the book is off my hands."

After the book's appearance, Fosdick expressed gladness that he had consented (if reluctantly) to publication "because my friends are giving it so warm a welcome." Indeed, they did in handsome reviews and in personal letters of appreciation, admiration, and affection. Nor was the public indifferent, buying over thirty thousand copies—not bad for a preacher's memoirs, especially a preacher who had been in retirement for ten years.*

In the prologue Fosdick stated as his main intent "to share with the reader the experience of living through these past threescore and eighteen years, which have radically changed the world." This purpose is fulfilled, as the reader knows when he turns the last page, but such a public purpose is hardly the stuff of the great autobiographies. One won-

* The autobiography was recorded for the blind: the prologue was spoken by Fosdick.

ders if Stevie and Patty learned anything more about their grandfather, as a person, than they had learned from all the days of living with him.

                                   V

Retirement did not terminate Fosdick's concern with the American religious scene. It was a time when the nation was being washed by a torrential surge of piety. Church memberships soared, attendance at worship services became au courant, and vast sums were lavished on building programs. The Norman Vincent Peales spoke to millions who sought peace of mind, the Billy Grahams spoke to millions who sought peace of soul. Presidents and disc jockeys "got religion." Book publishers, Hollywood producers, and recording companies discovered that the "Man Upstairs" handsomely rewarded those who sang His praises—and they continued to sing His praises all the way to the bank. The Pledge of Allegiance was amended to include the phrase "under God," a prayer room was installed in the national capitol, and the president of the United States and the presidents of mighty corporations attended prayer breakfasts. Small wonder that by 1957 more than ninety-five percent of the American people claimed a specific religious affiliation.

One element in this religious renewal was the fresh wave of young people who were entering the ministry. Fosdick of course watched Union Seminary's expansion with interest, lending a helping hand when he could. On invitation of President James B. Conant, moreover, he actively assisted in the revitalization of the Harvard Divinity School, both by fund raising and by serving on the Board of Appointments.

Fosdick was not blinded by the statistics of church growth. He once observed, "Yet, look at us! In one realm after another of personal and public behavior we do not give the impression to ourselves or to anybody else that we are really a Christian people." "Something inside the churches is wrong," he continued, "and one aspect of that wrong is obvious: millions of our church members are secondhand Christians. Their Christianity is formal, not vital; they have inherited it from their families, borrowed it from their friends, taken it over like the cut of their clothes from the fashion of their group. Their churchmanship is part of their respectability."

In 1976 a major study of university divinity schools noted that Billy Graham had replaced Harry Emerson Fosdick "as the best-known American preacher." Unlike Dr. Peale, whom Fosdick knew and liked (although believing that Peale had only one string to his bow), Dr. Graham and Fosdick never met, although Fosdick did watch the evangelist on television. When asked his opinion, Fosdick always replied that he understood that Graham had a gracious and winning personality, that his crusades were managed with great intelligence and efficiency and did some good, and that the manner of his preaching could only waken admiration. Nevertheless, Fosdick found Graham's theology "incredibly fundamentalist" and "dreadful." "I do not think . . . that he represents any serious theological trend that was not here already. Of course, here at Riverside Church it is natural that we should not feel any particular reaction to him one way or another."

VI

As earlier pages have shown, in retirement Fosdick's concern for public issues did not abate—war, segregation, poverty, civil liberties, the planned parenthood and mental health movements. Beyond question, however, two allied enterprises engaged by far the bulk of his time and energy, the Manhattanville Neighborhood Centers, Inc., and Morningside Heights, Inc.

In May 1946 Fosdick invited sixteen individuals representing Morningside Heights' prestigious institutions to join him for lunch in the Riverside dining room. Among them were Dean Harry J. Carman of Columbia, Father George Ford of Corpus Christi Church, Rabbi Moshe Davis of the Jewish Theological Seminary, Charles White of Union Seminary, and the Honorable Stanley M. Isaacs, New York City councilman. "This community is on my conscience," Fosdick confessed as he described the festering conditions, especially for the children, in the densely crowded, deteriorating Manhattanville or Morningside Heights' immediate neighbor in the valley to the north. "After all," Fosdick observed, "from 110th Street to 135th Street we are one community. It cannot be well with any part of that area unless it is well with the whole of it."

Thus was born the Manhattanville Neighborhood Center, building on the fine-spirited but limited Manhattanville Child Care Center for children of working mothers, which had been established during the war. One fine morning in September two members of the steering committee, Union Seminary's Charles White and Mrs. Emilie Speyer, long active in community youth work, journeyed with crossed fingers to Bronxville to put a question to Fosdick: Would he accept the chairmanship of the Board of Directors of the Manhattanville Neighborhood Center? "Yes," came the unhesitating reply. He remained as chairman until 1954, after the center's expansion and change of name to Manhattanville Community Centers, Inc., and then continued in a less arduous capacity as honorary chairman. By the end of the 1950s the centers' programs, now with the coming of new housing projects at several locations, were serving hundreds upon hundreds of Manhattanville's children and teenagers, 49 percent of whom were black, 40 percent Spanish-American; and 11 percent white and nonclassified. Adults, too, were brought within the compass of the centers' concern.

It would require a short book to tell the full story of this enterprise: the sustaining support of thirteen key institutions on "the Hill"; Rockefeller, Jr.'s donation of $100,000 to renovate the vacated old Speyer School as the original center when the $60,000 on hand proved insufficient; the continuing contribution of John D. Rockefeller, 3rd; the sacrificial dedication of the executive directors Charles White and Clyde Murray; the real concern of Columbia's Carman and John Krout; Isaacs's combination of idealism and political moxie; the cooperation of New York's Department of Welfare; the labors of Secretary of the Board Mrs. Carl Goldmark, Jr.; and the labors of Riverside's Mary Downs.

Of course, there were never enough funds adequately to meet the community needs of a teeming area like Manhattanville. Staffing was always a problem, not only because of lack of money, but because of union difficulties. (There is a hint in the records of deliberately disruptive tactics by the Communist-dominated Social Service Employees Union—a union kicked out of the C.I.O.). Vandalism at the centers was not unknown. Above all, all the programs in the world could not have saved all the boys and girls in Manhattanville from becoming strung out on booze or drugs or from becoming trapped in lives of crime or prostitution.

In 1957 Fosdick was honored for his services and at a banquet messages of praise from Mayor Robert F. Wagner and President and Mrs. Eisenhower were read aloud—the Eisenhowers were well aware of the situation from their days at Columbia University; in fact, Mrs. Eisenhower had been a director-at-large.

In throwing himself totally into this enterprise—and it is clear from the full record that that is precisely what he did—was Fosdick free from selfish motives? The obvious answer is that, of course, the weal of "the Hill" mandated healing the woe of the adjacent "valley." So what? Even acknowledging that the enterprise was consonant with the self-interest of the Riverside Church and the other religious, educational, and medical institutions on Morningside Heights and that only a minority of the children of Manhattanville were reached, it is still possible to say that a number of concerned adults gave a lot of themselves to help give a lot of God's children a fighting chance. Remember, until the advent of Fosdick's group the children of the "valley" were truly overlooked, having no

Y.M.C.A. or Y.W.C.A., no gym, no pool, no playgrounds, no proper parks—nothing to lure them off the streets, where they went to escape crowded, smelly, often bathless and even heatless tenements.

Fosdick and other concerned Morningside Heights' citizens recognized that the fate of Manhattanville's children was ultimately bound up with the future of the entire area. Moreover, it did not require much perspicacity to see that Manhattanville's continuing deterioration threatened life on the Heights. Thus was born to join the Manhattanville Neighborhood Centers, the much more extensive, far-reaching, and controversial Morningside Heights, Inc.

Before World War II, conditions in Manhattanville were tough for its inhabitants, primarily Irish Catholic and German family-oriented working-class people, but the area was not yet a slum. The black population north of 135th Street and the black and Puerto Rican population east of Amsterdam Avenue were not so much seen as felt. The war and the immediate postwar years brought not only a rapid growth in population, but also an influx of new groups until by 1950 of the forty-five thousand inhabitants more than one third were black, almost one third were Puerto Rican, and one third divided among twenty-four different nationalities. Studies documented what was evident to the eye: the press of the new populations was hastening the decay of Manhattanville's tenements and pressing hard on the Heights, itself suffering a severe postwar housing shortage. To the surprise of few, the City Planning Commission designated Manhattanville Section M–1 on the Master Plan of Sections Containing Areas for Clearance, Redevelopment, and Low Rent Housing.

Confronted with this situation, early in 1947, the Acting President of Columbia, Frank Fackenthal, and Henry Pitney Van Dusen, President of Union, set in motion a series of actions culminating in a dinner given by David Rockefeller and attended by representatives of the institutions on "the Hill," and at which was formed Morningside Heights, Inc., defined as a nonprofit corporation whose goal was to "promote the improvement and redevelopment of Morningside Heights as an attractive residential, educational and cultural community." David Rockefeller was elected President.*

* Collier and Horowitz in their critical study, *The Rockefellers: An American Dynasty*, find this election sinister and assert that Rockefeller's involvement "was an attempt on David's part to protect the family investment in the area." This is simpleminded in that the Rockefellers' "investment" in, say, Union Theological Seminary, The Riverside Church, and the (future) Interchurch Center did not give them ownership of these properties. The original members of Morningside Heights, Inc., were Columbia University, Corpus Christi Church, International House, Jewish Theological Seminary, Juilliard Musical Foundation, Riverside Church, Saint Luke's

What then transpired is important but too complicated to relate in detail here. Ultimately, working in cooperation with the city and the federal government, and with the creation of the Morningside Heights Housing Corporation,* old buildings were razed and new housing erected. Morningside Gardens consists of six 21-story cooperative apartment houses for middle-income families. Morningside Gardens gave first priority for apartments to those whose dwellings were demolished to clear the site and second priority to the employees of the sponsoring institutions. It was plainly both the moral and legal intent of Fosdick and all those involved that all of the new housing be racially integrated. The Morningside Gardens ratio when opened was 75 percent white, 20 percent black, 4 percent Oriental, and 1 percent Puerto Rican. At least some—perhaps a considerable number—of the black residents now attend nearby Riverside Church.

Immediately north, five buildings of twenty-one stories and immediately east an additional four buildings were erected and named the General Grant Houses.† Built by the City Housing Authority and subsidized by federal grants these low-cost public housing units were originally rented to families with incomes not exceeding $4000. Father George Ford, a linchpin figure in all of this, argued for a quota system that would insure that 50 percent of the tenants would be black and Puerto Rican and 50 percent non-Puerto Rican white and thought he had reached such an understanding with the City Housing Authority. The representative chosen to make selections of the tenants from a long list of applicants abrogated the understanding, and as a result those living in the General Grant Houses when opened were 51 percent black, 38 percent Puerto Rican, and 11 percent non-Puerto Rican white. (Father Ford in his 1969 autobiography estimated the figure for blacks at 90 percent, with most of the other 10 percent Puerto Rican.) Few, if any, of the residents of the General Grant Houses now attend nearby Riverside Church.

The point to be stressed is that Fosdick and his associates did not intend to leave the poor out of their program. In opposition to the slogan "gentrification is genocide," they posited that only a combination of low-

---

Hospital, Teachers College, and Union Seminary. Shortly thereafter, the Cathedral of Saint John the Divine and Barnard College joined. It merits mentioning that in 1947 the rapid influx of blacks and Puerto Ricans into Manhattanville was only just beginning, though in a brief period a dramatic change of population did take place.

  * This corporation, formed by Morningside Heights, Inc., availed itself of Title I of the National Housing Act. This act permitted cities to acquire slum properties and resell them at a markdown to private developers, the federal government making good two thirds of the resale-price difference and the city one third.

  † Still further north in Manhattanville, but yet south of Harlem's Sugar Hill, six Manhattanville Houses for low-income families also soon arose.

cost public housing (such as the General Grant Houses) *and* middle-income cooperative housing (such as Morningside Gardens) could realistically serve and save the community.

Fosdick was engulfed in the activities of Morningside Heights, Inc. Indeed, he flew to Washington with Father Ford and David Rockefeller to obtain additional funding for the General Grant Houses from the Housing and Home Finance Agency. The funds were awarded when Father Ford said to the stern-faced and unresponsive agency members: "Gentlemen, the members of this agency have never been in such mortal danger as they are today. Dr. Fosdick has plenty of Protestant excommunications, and the Catholic Church never runs out of them, so I have more than my friend Dr. Fosdick has, and if you say 'no' to our request, you will all go to hell."

In the midst of these developments a "Save Our Homes Committee" was formed that gave Ford and Fosdick hell. This organization sought, as its name suggests, to block the new housing and prevent the razing of existing dwellings, which, after all, were home to many families.* The organization was spearheaded by Mrs. Guy Barker, Jr., an articulate Stanford University graduate who, incidentally, did not herself live on a condemned site and who subsequently of her own free will moved to Cape Cod. Among her other accomplishments in the fight, she presented a petition with four thousand signatures to the Board of Estimate, and if it had not been for Father Ford's eloquence before the board, she might have carried the day.

Ford believed Communists were behind the "Save Our Homes Committee" and so did Fosdick, who once reported: "We have just had a bitter fight with the communists in the Morningside-Manhattanville area. . . . They tried their best to defeat our now successful endeavors to get new housing and to renovate the deteriorating conditions that were creating a slum. They are detestable public enemies. I am procommunist! Whenever I think of them my hackles rise!" In a later interview concerning the opposition to the housing development, Fosdick said: "The communists stood for the status quo. They apparently wanted the miserable conditions to continue, furnishing fertile soil for the social discontent they thrive on. They desire no change for the better to take

---

* It should be noted that families forced to vacate were offered assistance in locating new residences and received assistance in meeting moving expenses. Robert Caro, the not innocent biographer of Robert Moses, stated in that biography: "The Morningside Corporation had enlisted Orton's [of the City Planning Commission] help to create a humane and compassionate relocation program." Caro further stated: "These liberals began to understand that something terrible was going on in some of the Title I sites, *not the sites turned over by Moses to organizations such as the Rockefeller-backed Morningside Corporation*" (emphasis added).

place under any auspices other than the communist revolution." "I have found myself compelled," he added, "not only to disagree with the communists but to despise them for their tactics."

The charge that the Riverside Church was implicated in efforts to seek the gentrification of its neighborhood has continued down over the years, but as late as 1982 Edward G. Sullivan, Assemblyman, 70th District, Manhattan, could deny the charge: "Riverside Church is not an institution considered by people on the Heights as a threat to their homes or to the heterogeneity of the community."

Chapter Thirty

"Awaiting the Day
of New Beginnings"

I

At age eighty-one Fosdick and Florence moved from their home to an apartment in Bronxville. Before doing so, Fosdick made arrangements for the Evangelical Seminary of Puerto Rico to receive his personal library as a gift. About this time, he declined an invitation from the Library of Congress to provide a permanent home for his papers, preferring instead to give them to his beloved Union Seminary. Although death was not to come for ten years, the last decade inevitably meant a perceptive slowing of the pace of life.

The days of public preaching and speaking were now over. "Now in my eighty-fourth," he wrote a supplicant in 1961, "arthritis is closing in on me, and I can accept no more speaking engagements. Don't think of me as ill or waste any sympathy on me! I am in no serious discomfort and am very happy, but I need a new skeleton! Locomotion is increasingly difficult, so that I have had to give up all public appearances." The last book, *The Life of Saint Paul*, for juveniles, appeared in 1962. Thereafter his writing was confined to letters to the editors and to public officials concerning those social issues that continued to trouble his conscience. And also to answering the continuing moderate incoming flow of letters.

Harry and Florence read, sometimes aloud to each other, listened to the radio and watched television, took an occasional dinner with friends, reminisced, and cherished their memories. At age eighty-four Fosdick reported, "My wife, who is the same age as I am, and I sometimes just burst out laughing at ourselves. We are having a wonderful time." Elinor, then a professor at Columbia University's College of Physicians and Surgeons, lived in an adjacent apartment, and from across the courtyard she could see into her parent's living room and keep a loving eye on them.

Florence died suddenly, in the night, on November 6, 1964, at age eighty-four. Her death was unexpected, for until the end her health had been good. When Jesse Lyons, the Riverside minister whom Fosdick phoned, asked the husband how he was taking it, he replied, "When I think that Florence and I had over sixty years together, gratitude overcomes grief." To a friend he wrote, "Our loss is heavy but we are sustained by priceless memories and eternal hopes." Everyone had anticipated that Harry would go before Florence, and the daughters believe it was a blessing that their mother was spared the loneliness of widowhood, such was her total devotion to her husband. Harry experienced the darkness of loss, but he was determined to practice what he had preached to parishioners and not to succumb to despair or self-pity. The day after Florence's death Fosdick confided to a neighbor: "I'm the one who had ailments, and I was afraid I'd die first and leave her alone. Now she's gone, and *I* will be the one to face loneliness. I'm so thankful for that. That is something I can do for Florence." There are those who say that Fosdick found great comfort in holding daily conversations with the physically departed Florence.

The letters Fosdick wrote while in his eighties suggest an unembittered and mentally alert old age. "I've grown old and lame now, but am happy, contented, grateful for endless blessings, and keeping young in spirit," read a 1964 epistle. Read another from the year 1967: "Now in my 90th year, I am house-bound, crippled by arthritis, with 3 nurses watching me 24 hours a day. But my spirits are high, wide, happy and handsome, and I have far more to be grateful for than I have to complain about." The following year he wrote a former student a fairly long, articulate letter, closing, "Best wishes to you, my friend! In the nineties the body weakens, but my spirits are high, wide, happy and handsome." At almost the very end he scratched the note, "My hand writing betrays my arthritis. I am now in my 92d year, and have reason to be thankful that it is no worse." A final illustration: "I am a very old man, and God has abundantly blessed my life. But I am tired now, and shall not be disappointed when that hour comes when the angels shall sound the trumpets for me, and I shall come over to the other side."

Fosdick's spirits were sustained by the knowledge that in his isolated confinement he was not forgotten. His ninetieth birthday, announced in the *Christian Century* and Riverside and Union publications, brought a flood—perhaps as many as nine hundred—greetings. The printed card of acknowledgement read: "I warmly appreciate your gracious remembrance of me on my ninetieth birthday. Friends are God's choicest gift, and I am more grateful than words can tell for the affectionate goodwill your greeting expresses. Plentiful blessings on you always and always!" The birthday signaled a drive to secure a $250,000 endowment for the library of the Evangelical Seminary of Puerto Rico. And it was the occasion for a grand jollification at the Riverside Church, the proceedings being transmitted to Fosdick in Bronxville. To the assemblage he wrote a note (composed in ten minutes, Elinor reported) which read:

My friends at Riverside Church, my affectionate gratitude goes warmly out to all of you who are using this Strawberry Festival to celebrate my 90th birthday. How much I wish I could be with you! The doctor has retired me from life's normal activities to make my heart behave itself, but could I be with you tonight you would see that I am not as ill as rumor sometimes makes me out to be. I am remarkably free from pain, am content and comfortable, am beautifully taken care of, have infinitely more to be grateful for than to complain about, and my spirits are high, wide, happy and handsome.

I recall a friend of mine who, 104 years old, said: "When I wake up in the morning the first thing I do is to get the newspaper and read the obituary notices. If I am not there, I have breakfast." Well, I can match him in good humor about old age, but I confess that I have breakfast without bothering about the obituaries.

Were I with you tonight my greatest pleasure would be to thank you for all that you have made of Riverside Church since I left my active ministry here over two decades ago. For Dr. McCracken's fruitful ministry I am deeply grateful. For the amazing competence of the ministerial staff you have assembled to lead you, my admiration daily increases. For the faithful service of the laymen and laywomen who have fulfilled my dream that the church would be open seven days and nights a week to serve the community—I cannot adequately express my appreciation. You are a great church. I am proud of you. God bless you! God bless you all!

II

As the end drew near Fosdick's confinement tightened. Hour after hour he sat in a comfortable chair by the window gazing at trees and the skies, lost in rich memories—memories broken, perhaps, by a wave from Elinor from her apartment window across the courtyard. Perhaps he would then turn his eyes to embrace the picture of Florence over the desk. To ease the tasks of the devoted black and Puerto Rican nurses who cared for him, he slept in a hospital bed. On the opposite wall was a painting of his Saviour. Perhaps on awakening he recalled the hymn sung times beyond number: "When morning gilds the sky, my heart awakening cries—may Jesus Christ be praised."

In late September 1969 the great heart again misbehaved. Fosdick entered Lawrence Hospital. After he had taken his great-granddaughter into his arms he was ready to say his *Nunc Dimittis.* He had fought the good fight; he had finished the course; he had kept the faith. From the oxygen tent he said to the youngest daughter, "I'll be waiting for you at the bottom steps to the Pearly Gates." Puzzled, Dorothy asked, "Why at the *bottom* steps?" Her father responded with a wink, "Because you'll need someone to guide you up and by Saint Peter."

III

Death—"Dark mother, ever gliding near with soft feet"—came at 5:30 in the darkening afternoon of October 5. The body was cremated. At the memorial service, after Dr. McCracken's meditation, the congregation, fifteen hundred strong, rose to sing the hymn their pastor had composed at the onset of the great Riverside adventure:

> God of grace and God of glory,
>   On thy people pour thy power;
> Crown thine ancient Church's story;
>   Bring her bud to glorious flower.
> Grant us wisdom, grant us courage,
>   For the facing of this hour.
>
> 2 Lo! the hosts of evil round us
>   Scorn thy Christ, assail his ways!
> From the fears that long have bound us
>   Free our hearts to faith and praise:
> Grant us wisdom, grant us courage,
>   For the living of these days.
>
> 3 Cure thy children's warring madness,
>   Bend our pride to thy control;
> Shame our wanton, selfish gladness,
>   Rich in things and poor in soul.
> Grant us wisdom, grant us courage,
>   Lest we miss thy kingdom's goal.
>
> 4 Set our feet on lofty places;
>   Grid our lives that they may be
> Armored with all Christ-like graces
>   In the fight to set men free.
> Grant us wisdom, grant us courage,
>   That we fail not man nor thee.   Amen.

Essay on Sources

I. LETTERS TO THE AUTHOR

In response to petitions placed in the *New York Times*, Riverside Church publications, Union Theological Seminary publications, and also in response to specific letters of inquiry, the following individuals wrote to me about their associations with Fosdick or knowledge of him. In many instances these individuals included letters they had received from Fosdick and other items, such as in one case lecture notes from Fosdick's Union classes and in another diary extracts. Incidentally, as often as not the enclosed Fosdick letters were handwritten, confirming my hunch that thousands of his letters are irretrievably "lost" because carbon copies were not made and filed.

F. Emerson Andrews; Constance L. Ball; Saul P. Beeser; John C. Bennett; Helen Bevington; Carlton D. Blanchard; Clifford C. Bruck; Frances Buel; C. Roy Burchette, Jr.; Millar Burrows; Robert E. Campbell; Mrs. Everett Case; Edward W. Castner; David D. Coffin; William Sloane Coffin, Jr.; A. B. Coleman; Winifred Craig; Robert H. Crilley; W. J. Cunningham; Warren E. Darnell; Mrs. David Duys; Emily F. Ellis; R. H. Edwin Espy; Dorothy Ganfield Fowler; Jean Dickey Gates; Dorothy Gay; N. Robert Gill; Edwin A. Goldsworthy; Anne S. Goodrich; Charlotte L. Greene; Mildred R. Greenfield; Basil D. Hall; Edward R. Hardy; Francis S. Harmon; Frank S. Harwood; C. Howard Hopkins; Mary Risk Hine; Mary Hoxie Jones; Steward B. Kauffman; Edwin O. Kennedy; Eugene Kennedy; Sylvia Knox; Ann Lacto; Helen B. Large; Everett G. Leonard; Timothy Tingfang Lew; Eugene P. Link; Lefferts A. Loetscher; Robert W. L. Marks; Robert James McCracken; Mrs. Henry R. McLane; William R. McLeRoy; Raymond Mesler; Grace Nutting Miller; Florence K. Moore; Julia P. Morgan; Wilma Mosholder; Mrs. G. Mott-Smith; Mary-Elizabeth Murdock; Gardner Murphy; I. George Nace; Gordon Nelson; E. Marcellus Nesbitt; Ursula M. Niebuhr; Dorothy W. Noyes; Marjorie Clarke

Noyes; Loral W. Pancake; Mary Emily Peck; Thorton B. Penfield, Jr.; Irene H. Perhoc; Edward A. Puff; Martha Halvorsen Rehberger; Margaret Renton; Earl Robinson; Theodore Ropp; Elizabeth Rouse; Hildegard Ryals; Wendy Clauson Schlereth; David H. Scott; Roger L. Shinn; Mrs. Raymond Smith; Ellen Sowchek; T. Guthrie Speers; William A. Spurrier; Janet Stamm; Mrs. F. B. Stannard; Norris L. Tibbetts; Richard Tooker; D. Elton Trueblood; Dale E. Turner; Carl Hermann Voss; James M. Wheeler; Edmund White; Charles Willard; Leland Wilson; H. Davis Yeuell; Frances L. Yocom.

II. PERSONAL INTERVIEWS

A number of individuals shared their memories in interviews and great is my gratitude to them. I confess to a feeling of ambivalence towards oral history. On the one hand, the claims made on its behalf by its more ardent exponents strike me as wildly exaggerated and the resultant "books" often appalling. On the other hand, the critic was too severe who dismissed oral interviews as "mostly gossiped reminiscence, colored by personality, dimmed by time, fabricated by weakness and shaped by self-interest." In my judgment oral testimony is a valid and valuable source if evaluated with the historian's customary critical caution, especially when that testimony can be checked by cross-examination and against the written record. Anyhow, talking with these individuals, often over morning coffee or afternoon tea in a relaxed atmosphere, gave me a "feeling" for Fosdick that the documents alone could not supply; and I am convinced that these conversations (unburdened by the presence of a tape recorder) importantly complemented the written record but in no sense supplemented that record. Inasmuch as Fosdick lived to be ninety-one it is self-evident that many of the key persons in his career were no longer living at the onset of my researches in 1972 or, as in the critical instances of Raymond Blaine Fosdick and Robert James McCracken, died before interviews could be consummated.

Dorothy Beck, N.Y.C.; Cora Bennett, Montclair, N.J.; Mr. and Mrs. Frank Bennett, Montclair, N.J.; John C. Bennett, Wake Forest, N.C.; Lucilla Walker Bergeret, N.Y.C.; Helen Bevington, Raleigh-Durham Airport, N.C.; Bernard Boyd, Chapel Hill, N.C.; Beatrice Byran, Montclair, N.J.; E. Fay Campbell, Chapel Hill, N.C.; Mr. and Mrs. Samuel McCrea Cavert, Bronxville, N.Y.; Harrie Chamberlin, Chapel Hill, N.C.; Elizabeth Cruden, Montclair, N.J.; Elisha P. Douglass, Chapel Hill, N.C.; Elinor Fosdick Downs, N.Y.C.; Frances Eaton, N.Y.C.; R. H. Edwin Espy, N.Y.C.; Eugene Exman (by phone), N.Y.C.; Sophia Lyon Fahs, N.Y.C.; Stephen F. Feke, N.Y.C.; Louis Finklestein, N.Y.C.; Elizabeth Flower, Chapel Hill, N.C.; George Barry Ford, N.Y.C.; William Fore, N.Y.C.; Dorothy Fosdick, Washington, D.C.; Dorothy Ganfield Fowler, N.Y.C.; Ellen French, N.Y.C.; Hazel Goldmark, N.Y.C.; Robert T. Handy, N.Y.C.; Francis S. Harmon, N.Y.C. and Lake Mohonk, N.Y.; Mrs. C. Ivar Hellstrom, N.Y.C.; Samuel Hill, Chapel Hill, N.C.; Paul Hoon, N.Y.C.; Winthrop S. Hudson, Chapel Hill, N.C.; G. Huggins, Boothbay Harbor, Me.; John Jacobs,

N.Y.C.; Irene Jones, N.Y.C.; James Jones, Bronxville, N.Y.; Mary Hoxie Jones, Haverford, Pa.; John G. Kauderer, N.Y.C.; Eugene E. Laubach, N.Y.C.; Gerald E. Lenski, Chapel Hill, N.C.; Calvin Leonard, Monroe, N.C.; Robert Lynn, N.Y.C.; Jesse Lyons, N.Y.C.; Joseph Matthews, Chapel Hill, N.C.; John B. Mcnab, N.Y.C.; Grace Mead, Montclair, N.J.; Virginia Mead, Montclair, N.J.; Mrs. G. Mott-Smith, N.Y.C.; Dorothy W. Noyes, Carmel, N.Y.; Loral W. Pancake, Mt. Lakes, N.J.; Mary Emily Peck, N.Y.C.; Captain "Chick" Pinkham, Boothbay Harbor, Me.; Mr. and Mrs. Cyril Richardson, Lake Mohonk, N.Y.; Mrs. Charles E. Rush, Chapel Hill, N.C.; David H. Scott, N.Y.C.; Mr. and Mrs. Roger L. Shinn, N.Y.C.; Mrs. Dudley Smith, Montclair, N.J.; Elizabeth Leland Smith, Hamilton, N.Y.; H. Shelton Smith, Durham, N.C.; Mary Sockwell, N.Y.C.; T. Guthrie Speers, Baltimore, Md.; Mrs. Philip Stimson, Heightstown, N.J.; the superintendent of apartment in Bronxville, N.Y.; Norris L. Tibbetts, N.Y.C.; Mr. and Mrs. Henry Pitney Van Dusen, Princeton, N.J.; E. Raymond Wilson, Swarthmore, Pa.; Howard D. Williams, Hamilton, N.Y.

III. PERSONAL OBSERVATIONS

Another manner in which a biographer obtains a "feel" for his subject is by visiting those places where his subject lived. This I did in regard to (1) Fosdick's New York boyhood homes in Buffalo (four of the five are still standing), Lancaster, and Westfield; (2) his schools, Colgate in Hamilton, N.Y., and Union in N.Y.C.; (3) his churches, Montclair's First Baptist Church, New York's First Presbyterian Church, New York's Park Avenue Baptist Church (now Central Presbyterian), and New York's Riverside Church; and (4) his residences, the Union apartment, the home and apartment in Bronxville, and his beloved Mouse Island, Maine. Moreover, by prowling Morningside Heights and Manhattanville I got some sense of those far different neighboring communities. I am grateful to Mr. and Mrs. Roger L. Shinn for showing me a Union apartment identical to that of the Fosdicks; to Mr. and Mrs. Samuel McCrea Cavert for guiding me to the Fosdicks' retirement home and retirement apartment in Bronxville and to the superintendent of the apartment (whose name I shamefully have forgotten) for access into it; to Captain "Chick" Pinkham, Fosdick's island caretaker, for a boat ride to and guided tour of Mouse Island.

IV. THE FOSDICK COLLECTION AND OTHER UNION THEOLOGICAL
SEMINARY HOLDINGS, NEW YORK CITY

Such was Fosdick's devotion to Union Theological Seminary, it was inevitable that his old school should be chosen as the depository of his papers, despite a bid for them from the Library of Congress. When I first sought to examine the Fosdick Collection in the summer of 1972 not a single item was as yet available, the vast collection then in the arduous process of being de-acidified, indexed, and calendared. I returned annually, each visit progressively proved more rewarding until by the end of 1975 the entire collection had been culled. At that time the collection consisted of 40 boxes marked "Letters" arranged alphabetically and 40 boxes marked "Sermons," the latter also including manuscripts of books, lectures, and articles.

It is clear that before his death Fosdick winnowed the materials. Time and again he made in pencil such marginal notations as "check thru before discarding" and "keep" and "keep for awhile" and "throw out later" and sometimes he changed his mind by deleting "throw out" and adding "keep." From time to time, also, Fosdick marked an item with the notation "biography," suggesting that he anticipated that one day his biography would be written. Although most certainly a winnowing took place, it is not at all clear that the intent was to expurgate damaging information for the collection contains many very candid items; and it is my guess that in going over his papers Fosdick sought to discard the trivial and save the significant, not to destroy the critical and preserve the laudatory.

In addition to the boxed "Letters" and boxed "Sermons," I also read three large stacks of letters that were then (1974) uncatalogued. The overwhelming majority of these were letters sent to Fosdick on the occasions of his seventy-fifth and ninetieth birthdays. Also separate from the boxed materials are (or were) two large folders relating to the Rockefeller family, one folder containing approximately one hundred letters between Fosdick and John D. Rockefeller, Jr., and also Mrs. Rockefeller, the other containing about fifty letters between Fosdick and the Rockefeller sons. The Fosdick Collection further consists of twelve soft-leather spiral notebooks containing revealing sermonic materials, described more fully in the text.

This Fosdick Collection housed at Union is large, important, and indispensable. Yet it does not fully answer all the questions one would wish to ask about the man. Bluntly, it is where every biographer might begin but where only an innocent biographer would end his researches.

Of course, Union is the location of major materials other than the Fosdick Collection. Helpful are two bound scrapbooks entitled "Dr. Harry Emerson Fosdick and the Fundamentalist Controversy. Newspaper clippings 1923–1926 Collected by Henry Martyn Humphrey and Mounted by Stella Hadden Alexander" and "Fundamentalism Versus Liberalism 1923–1926. A Volume of Clippings To Accompany 'Dr. Harry Emerson Fosdick and the Fundamentalist Controversy.' Collected by Henry Martyn Humphrey an Elder in the Brick Presbyterian Church In the City of New York and Mounted by Stella Hadden Alexander." There is no discernible organization to these scrapbooks and some of the clippings are unidentified; consequently, they are not easy to use. An allied aid is a cardboard box stuffed with "uncatalogued material relating to Dr. Harry Emerson Fosdick's connection with the First Presbyterian Church and controversial material centering around him" (as the label reads), probably collected by Robert Hastings Nichols.

Fosdick's record as a student is found, of course, in the Registrar's Office. His career as a teacher may be traced through various miscellaneous items, such as courses of study, examination schedules, graduation programs, *Minutes of the Monthly Social Meetings of the Faculty,* and *Union Theological Seminary Bulletin.* (The file of *Union Seminary Quarterly Review* is rich with relevant articles; of course, this file is available in many libraries other than Union, and in fact was examined in Chapel Hill.) For those who never had the opportunity to hear Fosdick preach (as I did not), Union has a limited number of his recorded sermons.

Only mildly rewarding *for my purposes* were the papers, usually thin and fragmented, at Union of Henry Sloane Coffin, Robert Hastings Nichols, Henry Pitney Van Dusen, Dietrich Bonhoeffer, William Adams Brown, Arthur Cushman McGiffert, Henry Leiper Smith, and Henry Preserved Smith.

The year and more of research at Union was made less long because of the unfailing courtesies of the librarians Robert F. Beach, Richard H. Pachella, and William Robards and the hospitality of Union professors Robert Handy, Paul Hoon, Robert Lynn, and Roger Shinn.

V. THE ARCHIVES OF THE THREE CHURCHES
SERVED BY FOSDICK

1. First Baptist Church, Montclair, New Jersey

The archives of Fosdick's first parish contain helpful materials, especially *Minutes of the Board of Trustees* and "Minute Book of the First Baptist Church of Montclair, N.J., incl. Ministers, Baptisms, Hand of Fellowship, Death, Marriages, Letters Received, Experiences, Dismissals by Letter, Pulpit Supplies, Dismissals by Erasure." I am grateful to the Reverend Frank W. Koshak for granting unrestricted access to the archives and also for arranging interviews with older parishioners who remembered Fosdick and, not the least, for the hospitality of his home. (Curiously, the Riverside Church Archives possesses a number of items dealing with the First Baptist Church not found in the Montclair church; probably Fosdick carried these items with him on his departure. The items include copies of the church bulletin, the "Messenger," and a descriptive booklet detailing the activities of the congregation during the Fosdick era and a pamphlet entitled "Services for the Installation of Pastor, Rev. Harry Emerson Fosdick" and two printed items, "Program of Services in Dedication of the New Edifice" and "Dedicatory Services of the First Baptist Church, Montclair, New Jersey, January 29th–February 12th, Nineteen Hundred and Eleven.") A secondary work is *The First Baptist Church, Montclair, New Jersey. A Brief Story of Its Beginnings and Its Growth, 1886–1936* (n.d.), author unnamed.

2. First Presbyterian Church, New York City

An examination of the "Old First" archives was crucial, for here are found *Minutes of the Session* in two bound volumes for the period May 31, 1918– June 16, 1932, and a file of the *Church Tower,* a monthly publication detailing the activities of the congregation and invariably carrying a Fosdick sermon, the first issue appearing in December 1923. Equally valuable is a mass of uncatalogued correspondence between Fosdick and key church leaders and between these leaders and national Presbyterian leaders. Further, here are thirty-six typed untitled stenographic reported sermons preached by Fosdick between November 17, 1918, and November 14, 1920, and six titled and dated sermons, a body of early sermons not to be found elsewhere. A large collection of newspaper clippings is here also. A secondary work is Arthur Courtney's *Our Father's Faith and Ours. An Historical Account of the First Presbyterian Church University Place Church Madison Square Presbyterian Church . . .* (1949). I much appreciate being granted unrestricted access to the archives by the ministers Dr. John Mellin and Dr. John Macnab and am indebted to Dr. Dorothy Ganfield Fowler, Professor of History Emeritus, Hunter College, for her guidance through this archival richness. Dorothy Hucke and her office staff made the weeks of research pleasant indeed.

3. *The Riverside Church (formerly Park Avenue Baptist Church),*
   New York City

The Riverside Church holdings are vast and vital to the biographer of Fosdick. In the safe of the business manager are *Minutes of the Board of Deacons* and *Minutes of the Board of Trustees* of the Fifth Avenue Baptist Church and the Park Avenue Baptist Church and The Riverside Church. Deposited also in the safe is the major 1939 survey and report of the consulting economist, Mark M. Jones, entitled "The Riverside Church In The City of New York," with this note attached: "Jones Report. This should be saved—and carefully filed with permanent papers. It is probably the only copy any longer available." Stephen F. Feke, then the business manager, with the authorization of the Board of Trustees, made these materials freely available and provided a desk and typewriter in the business office to facilitate note taking. My appreciation to Mr. Feke and the Trustees is literally beyond measure.

A second location of materials is the Office of Communications, then in charge of Emily F. Deeter. Here is found a cluster of publicity releases, newspaper clippings, magazine articles, photographs, some correspondence—in sum, a variety of items relating to the church and its activities.

A third repository is the "McCracken Room" (my designation) where the papers of Fosdick's successor, Robert James McCracken, are filed. Thanks to Ellen French, who was then at the task of sorting the papers, I was permitted to read a revealing file of correspondence between Fosdick and McCracken, some thirty-six letters and one telegram from Fosdick to McCracken and seven letters from McCracken to his predecessor. (There are additional letters between the two men at Union.)

Significant as the sources in these three Riverside locations are, they do not match the richness of the enormous Riverside Archives. Happily, Mr. Feke provided me with the necessary keys to gain access to the guarded area and alerted the church watchmen to my comings and goings, thus making it possible for me to labor "after hours" and on weekends. The archives contain a bound set of the *Church Monthly,* each issue chock full of parish activities and also carrying both a sermon and a prayer by Fosdick. Here also are found a complete file of worship-service bulletins and the Riverside Guild's *Horizon* and Fosdick's "National Vespers" sermons. Here, further, are scores of typed manuscripts of Fosdick's sermons, addresses, and articles, and scores of Fodick's printed sermons, addresses, and articles. Immeasureably valuable were the clippings of hundreds of reviews of Fosdick's books. Here is the location of numerous clippings about Fosdick and the church and photographs of the church under construction and some correspondence of the lay leaders.

This archival richness is perhaps not unexpected considering Riverside's size and significance. What did come as a joyful surprise was to find in Riverside treasures one presumed to be in Union's Fosdick Collection. For example, in a large folder labeled "Personal Family Correspondence," there are fifty-one letters from Fosdick to his father and three from father to son and additional letters between Fosdick and his brother and several from his daughters to him—letters as revealing as a mirror and as personal as any found in Union. Further, it is Riverside, not Union, that holds the absorbing diary Fosdick kept in France in 1918 and the candid notes he made while in the Holy Land in 1926 and autobiographical fragments of his spiritual growth. Further still, here are excerpts from almost two hundred letters of appreciation he received from "National Vespers" listeners. And here are materials collected by Raymond Fosdick during the Fundamentalist controversy, which Raymond apparently turned over to his brother. Finally, here are honorary plaques and diplomas and certificates of merit and the like.

I cannot pertend to explain why these personal and important Fosdick records were not transferred from Riverside to Union, and can only be grateful that they remain safe and that Lady Luck permitted me to stumble across them. As in the case of the Union holdings, it is clear that the Riverside materials were reviewed by Fosdick before his death because many of the folders are marked in his hand with "Correspondence with Raymond," "Letters to Dr. Alexander," "Correspondence with Coffin," and so forth.

Published sketches of the Riverside Church appeared in many places, including *Life, Time, New York Times, Church Management, Reader's Digest,* and *Christian Century,* but the outstanding secondary source is the sixty-page booklet by Mina Pendo, *A Brief History of The Riverside Church* (1957). Perhaps note should also be made of the eighteen-page *The Riverside Church. One Hundred Years of Historical Background, 1841–1941* (1941), author unknown.

It is with a thankful heart that I remember those at Riverside, in addition to Stephen Feke, Emily Deeter, and Ellen French, who made the months of research there as pleasant as they were profitable: Mary Sockwell, Mary Emily Peck, Mrs. G. Mott-Smith, the Reverend Eugene E. Laubach, and above all, Francis S. Harmon and the Reverend Jesse Lyons. Messrs. Harmon and Lyons both gave hours of their time to lend a helping hand, including opening doors that otherwise might have remained sealed and arranging rewarding interviews with individuals who otherwise might have remained strangers. My thanks, too, to Max Cole, the church's FM radio manager who played for me tapes (against a background of jazz) of recorded church celebrations, including the poignant "Strawberry Festival" celebrating Fosdick's ninetieth birthday and the memorial service. I recall well the faces, but, alas, not always the names, of many others: the electrician who set up and ran the projector and record player so that I might see and hear the television and radio programs on which Fosdick appeared; the secretary who permitted me repeated access to a xerox machine; the watchmen with their unfailing courtesy; the brewers of coffee in the staff lounge. Finally, I am grateful to Dr. Ernest T. Campbell, then the preaching minister, who without any show of exasperation tolerated my prowling about his church month after month. I thank him, too, for the privilege of hearing him preach.

VI. OTHER ARCHIVES AND LIBRARIES WITH A BRIEF DESCRIPTION OF THE HOLDINGS HELPFUL TO THIS STUDY

1. American Baptist Historical Society, Rochester, New York

Among the items examined in the American Baptist Historical Society, a major denominational research center, were the papers, some quite fragmentary, of Samuel Zane Batten, Albert G. Larson, Jasper Cortenus Massee, John Roach Straton, and Cornelius Woelfkin. In addition: *Annual of the Northern Baptist Convention* (1918–1940), *Year Book of the Northern Baptist Convention* (1941–1947), *Minutes of the New Jersey Baptist Convention* (1904–1915), *Minutes of the Southern New York Baptist Association* (1923–1947), "Registry of Ministers and Missionaries of the Northern Baptist Convention." The Historical Society also possesses a quite full collection of Fosdick's printed materials. Curator Edward C. Starr and his assistants were the soul of cooperation.

2. Boston University Library, Boston, Massachusetts

The Boston University library was visited for the sole purpose of examining the papers of Allan Knight Chalmers, a clergyman much involved in pacifism, civil rights, and civil liberties, and the collection contains letters from Fosdick on these matters. The two men were friends and worked closely together.

3. Buffalo, New York, Department of Public Instruction

Various reports in the Department of Public Instruction provide information on the schools attended by Fosdick and also on the teaching career of Fosdick's father, and I thank Gladys Bednarcyck, Pupil Personnel Services, for her guidance to these materials.

4. Buffalo-Erie County, New York, Historical Library

Among other items, the Buffalo-Erie County Historical Library possesses the annually published *Buffalo City Directory*, which enabled me to locate the exact addresses of the Fosdick homes in Buffalo; a file of the *Calendar*, the high school triweekly paper of Fosdick's day; a file of *Masten Park Hill Topics*, helpful for information about Fosdick's father; two histories of Hutchison-

Central High School; files of the *Buffalo Courier* and *Buffalo News;* and a slew of books and journals carrying information about Buffalo's history. The Tenth U.S. Census (1880) and the Eleventh U.S. Census (1890) are packed with statistical data on Buffalo and Erie County.

5. Century Club, New York City

The Century Club is the only one to which Fosdick belonged in New York. Its library contains sketches of both Harry and Raymond and histories of the club.

6. Colgate University Archives and Library, Hamilton, New York

Colgate University is justly proud of her most distinguished graduate and the archives contain not only Fosdick's transcript, but also a large amount of material on Fosdick's later activities. The library houses files of the *Madisonensis*, the school paper, and *Salmagundi*, the yearbook, and the *Annual Catalogue*, all central to an understanding of Fosdick's college experiences, academic and extracurricular.

Dr. Howard D. Williams, Professor of History and University Archivist, assisted me far beyond the call of duty: describing the history of the school as we walked the campus, relating anecdotes about Fosdick and his teachers, arranging interviews with older people who remembered Harry, providing a showing of Alistair Cooke's interview with Fosdick on "Omnibus" (a television episode I was not then aware of); and supplying histories of Colgate, including his own splendid study. (Hamilton Theological Seminary, attended by Fosdick for one year on his graduation from Colgate, subsequently became part of Colgate Rochester Divinity School and the seminary records have been transferred from Hamilton to Rochester. According to Peter N. VandenBerge, Director of Library Services, Ambrose Swasey Library, Fosdick's record is absent. Happily, however, copies are in the Fosdick Collection at Union and also in the American Baptist Historical Society.)

7. Columbia University Registrar's Office and Butler Library, New York City

Among the sources held at Columbia University several were of special significance: the transcript of Fosdick's record as an M.A. candidate, 1907–1908 (made available thanks to the kind intercession of Mr. Charles Hurd, Registrar); Fosdick's M.A. thesis; and *Catalogue and General Announcement*, giving a description of the courses taken by Fosdick. (A. J. Muste, Reinhold Niebuhr, and Norman Thomas are three individuals in Columbia's justly famed Oral History Collection, but their transcripts are available in the University of North Carolina's Wilson Library, and were read there.)

8. Congregation Emanu-El Archives, New York City

During the construction of Riverside Church the Park Avenue Baptist congregation worshipped in Temple Beth-El for a year. To more fully understand this interesting arrangement, I sought to examine the *Trustee Minutes*, Congregation Emanu-El, and permission to do so was graciously given by Mr. Henry

Fruhauf, Administrative Vice-President, Congregation Emanu-El. (Temple Beth-El had been razed following the move to the new edifice, Temple Emanu-El.)

9. Duke Divinity School Library and Duke University Perkins Library, Durham, North Carolina

It is difficult to exaggerate my indebtedness over the years to Mr. Don Farris and his staff of the Duke University Divinity School Library. Suffice to say, when it was necessary to check an article in a religious journal or a denominational record or a published work in church history unavailable at the University of North Carolina, more often than not that item was found in the Divinity School Library. The papers of Bishop James M. Cannon, Jr., though examined in the Duke University Perkins Library, are only slightly relevant to the career of Fosdick.

10. Evangelical Seminary of Puerto Rico Library, Rio Piedras, Puerto Rico

Fosdick gave as a gift the bulk of his personal library, some fourteen hundred volumes, to the Evangelical Seminary of Puerto Rico. Miss Wilma Mosholder, Librarian, graciously provided me with a copy of the acquisitions list. Curious, I then flew to San Juan to spend a week in the seminary library, removing from the shelves every volume (the library is not large), examining the volume for the Fosdick book plate, and on finding such an identification, thumbing the book to see how Fosdick had marked it up, as described in the text. An unexpected bonus was the discovery of the inscriptions in the personal volumes given to Fosdick by many luminary authors. It is a real pleasure to acknowledge here Miss Mosholder's enthusiastic assistance.

11. Garrett Theological Seminary Library, Evanston, Illinois

Here are deposited the papers of the great Methodist minister, Ernest Fremont Tittle, and although Tittle and Fosdick corresponded but rarely, the Tittle Collection is valuable because of the light it sheds on a galaxy of issues that much concerned Fosdick, especially the issue of pacifism. (This collection was examined before I began work on the present study and I did not find it necessary to return to Evanston.)

12. Geneva College Library, Beaver Falls, Pennsylvania

The Geneva College Library houses the papers of Clarence Edward Macartney, leading Presbyterian divine; although there are no letters to or from Fosdick, there is much correspondence between Macartney and major conservative Presbyterians and also some correspondence with liberal Presbyterians concerning Fosdick, valuable to an understanding of the Presbyterian division. Macartney also assembled a collection of clippings on the Fundamentalist/ Modernist struggle. My thanks to Mr. Gerald D. Moran, Librarian, and Miss Helen Fattal, Macartney Collection Librarian, for permitting unrestricted access to these materials.

13. *Harper & Row, Publishers, Inc., Offices, New York City*

Harper published many of Fosdick's books, including the volumes of sermons and the autobiography and *On Being a Real Person,* and I am indebted to Mr. H. Davis Yeuell for supplying me with sales figures, though with the stipulation that these figures be used in a general fashion.

14. *Haverford College Library, Haverford, Pennsylvania*

The Hartford College Library houses the papers of the great Quaker leader, Rufus Jones, whom Fosdick admired ardently. Although the correspondence between the two men was apparently limited, there are additional letters from Fosdick to Jones's wife and daughter and one rare letter from Mrs. Fosdick to Mrs. Jones. Dr. Mary Hoxie Jones not only made the collection freely available, she also shared with me memories of her father.

15. *Hunter College Library, New York City*

Hunter College Library was visited for the sole purpose of reading a very helpful unpublished M.A. thesis by Edith Waldvogel (see p. 590).

16. *Lancaster, New York, Public Library*

As a boy Fosdick lived for a period in Lancaster and the public library possesses works describing the town and the churches attended by Fosdick in that earlier era.

17. *Library of Congress, Washington, D.C.*

Six collections in this great repository were inspected. The papers of Bishop Charles H. Brent are full but unimportant to this study. The papers of Peter Marshall are thin, and the one box of correspondence worthless. It was neither possible nor needful to examine the entire vast William Jennings Bryan Collection. However, Boxes 35 through 40, covering the years 1922–1924, were extraordinarily important to an understanding of the Fundamentalist/Modernist controversy, especially, but not exclusively, as related to Presbyterianism. The papers of New York's unabashed liberal and pacifist preacher, John Haynes Holmes, are located in 243 boxes, and of these I examined the 71 boxes most relevant to my purposes. Generally, the Holmes correspondence is revealing of the concerns of liberal Protestantism shared by Holmes and Fosdick. Specifically, the correspondence includes approximately 60 letters to and from Fosdick. Regarding the Reinhold Niebuhr Collection, Boxes 1 through 13 contain his correspondence and these I examined, though I deemed it unnecessary to look at the additional boxes containing his writings, having earlier encountered much of them in published form. Despite the fact that there are no letters *here* to or from Fosdick, the couple of weeks spent working through the Niebuhr correspondence was not wasted because Niebuhr's perspective on issues both illuminates and corrects Fosdick's angle or vision. The approximately sixteen thousand items in the Bishop G. Bromley Oxnam Collection are found in 137 boxes, and of these 37 were gleaned for information on Fosdick, with fairly rewarding results, especially among Oxnam's diary references.

18. *Montclair, New Jersey, Public Library*

Reading a file of the *Montclair Times,* 1904–1915, in the Montclair Public Library contributed beyond measure to my knowledge of Fosdick's first ministry. Several items of local history were also tapped.

19. *National Broadcasting Company, Inc., Archives, New York City*

Mr. Thomas E. Coffin, Vice President of Research, and Miss Winifred Craig, Administrator, Statistical Records, cooperated to the fullest extent, but only limited materials relating to Fosdick's "National Vespers" program have been preserved in the NBC Archives.

20. *National Council of the Churches of Christ in the United States of America Archives, New York City*

Dr. Irene Jones, Archivist, and Dr. William Fore of the National Council's Commission on Broadcasting and Film, cooperated to the fullest extent, but apparently only limited materials relating to Fosdick's radio ministry have been preserved. I say "apparently" because at the time of my investigations the records of the National Council at the Interchurch Center were being transferred to the Presbyterian Historical Society in Philadelphia for permanent deposit. As I write plans are underway to organize and arrange the materials and prepare guides so that the "materials will be accessible for reference and research." Therefore, in time future scholars might find in the records of the National Council Fosdickian items I failed to discover.

21. *New-York Historical Society, New York City*

The holdings of the New-York Historical Society include works helpful in a general sense to an understanding of the history and nature of the neighborhoods in which Fosdick's New York churches were located, especially an unpublished study by John Van Dusen of Morningside Heights, Inc.

22. *New York Public Library, New York City*

The papers of five individuals deposited in the great New York Public Library contain nothing to or from Fosdick: Walter Russell Bowie, William Adams Brown, Carrie Chapman Catt, Bolton Hall, Albert Shaw. The papers of Alfred Williams Anthony and William H. Matthew contain, respectively, nine and twelve unimportant letters from Fosdick. However, one folder in the John Houston Finley Collection contains significant correspondence to and from and about Fosdick. The papers of Stanley M. Isaacs are illuminating, for he and Fosdick shared civic concerns, especially in the area of housing, and it is clear Fosdick much admired this New York politician. The library also possesses a file of the annual "Report of the Executive Director To the Board of Directors of Manhattanville Neighborhood Centers, Inc." and "Manhattanville Community Centers, Inc." and studies made of Morningside Gardens and Morningside Heights, Inc., all deeply engaging Fosdick's interest and energy. This library also has several books and pamphlets relating to Fosdick's career not found in Chapel Hill or available on loan.

23. *New York University Library, Washington Square, New York City*

New York University Library was visited for the sole purpose of reading a not very helpful (as it turned out) unpublished Ph.D. dissertation.

24. *Presbyterian Historical Society, Philadelphia, Pennsylvania*

Among the items examined in the Presbyterian Historical Society, a major denominational research center, were *Minutes of the General Assembly of the Presbyterian Church in the U.S.A.* (1923–1925), *Minutes of the Presbytery of New York* (1916–1926), *Minutes of the Philadelphia Presbytery of the Presbyterian Church in the U.S.A.* (1918–1925). Also, and most important, a box of materials, Presbytery of New York, "Correspondence, Minutes and newspaper clippings, concerning the Fosdick case: 1920–1924"; a box of materials, "Clippings and Articles on the fundamentalist controversy in the Presbyterian Church"; a folder of materials, "Papers and extracts relating to the Rev. Harry Emerson Fosdick's relations to the First Presbyterian Church, New York, N.Y." Scattered among these materials are a number of most significant letters between Presbyterian leaders. My thanks to Mr. Gerald Gillette of the society for his cordial assistance.

25. *Princeton Theological Seminary Library, Princeton, New Jersey*

Setting aside a cluster of printed works, the only papers I examined at the Princeton Theological Seminary Library were those of Robert E. Speer. If Speer and Fosdick ever corresponded, the letters are not in this collection. However, Speer did correspond with others concerning the Fosdick controversy and he compiled four folders of clippings dealing with that controversy.

26. *Princeton University Firestone Library, Princeton, New Jersey*

At the Princeton University Firestone Library may be found the papers of Raymond Blaine Fosdick and Ivy L. Lee, both collections being important to this study.

27. *Rockefeller Family and Associates Archives, New York City*

The Rockefeller Family Archives proved to be for the biographer of Fosdick the most rewarding of all holdings, excepting only those at Union Seminary and Riverside Church. Here are found thousands of items dealing with every aspect of the Park Avenue Church enterprise and The Riverside Church adventure, and also with John D. Rockefeller, Jr.'s relationships with his many other denominational, interdenominational, and missionary concerns. My researches, centering of course on Fosdick, were limited to Boxes 8–9, 36–39, 62, 69–94, with occasional forays into other boxes seeking specific items. My affirmative assessment of John D. Rockefeller, Jr., derives largely from the record as found here. The archives are wonderfully organized, thanks to Dr. Joseph Ernst and his staff, and it was a joy to spend many weeks in the research rooms at Rockefeller Center.

28. *Swarthmore College Library, Swarthmore, Pennsylvania*

The Swarthmore College Peace Collection is justly famous. Here are found the records of the Fellowship of Reconciliation, the Emergency Peace Campaign, the Committee on Militarism in Education, the New York Metropolitan Board for Conscientious Objectors, and other groups involving Fosdick. A. J. Muste and Fosdick corresponded but lightly; Ray Newton and Fosdick heavily. The Jane Addams papers contain only one letter from Fosdick, and that not addressed to her. There is one folder specifically of Fosdick items, all printed and all available elsewhere. My thanks to librarian Bernice Nichols.

29. *T. J. Ross & Co. Offices, New York City*

T. J. Ross & Co. is the successor to the Ivy J. Lee public relations firm, and although the present records do not touch on Fosdick's relations with Lee, I am grateful to Mr. Richard Govan for directing me to Lee materials elsewhere; therefore, the visit to the Ross offices was not in vain.

30. *University of North Carolina Southern Historical Collection and Wilson Library, Chapel Hill, North Carolina*

The Southern Historical Collection houses the papers of a number of churchmen, and although I looked at perhaps a dozen collections, the only one that merits mention in a biography of Fosdick is that of the Southern Baptist liberal, E. McNeill Poteat. The Louis Round Wilson Library is where naturally I first turned to check reference works, monographs, files of periodicals and newspapers, and to obtain interlibrary loan volumes. I hope that over the years I have made clear my deep appreciation to the staffs of both the Southern Historical Collection and the Wilson Library.

31. *Westfield, New York, Public Library*

As a boy Fosdick lived for a period in Westfield and the public library possesses works describing the town in that earlier era.

32. *Westminster Theological Seminary Library, Chestnut Hill, Pennsylvania*

The Westminister Theological Seminary Library is the home of the papers of J. Gresham Machen, respected conservative Presbyterian theologian, and although there are no letters to or from Fosdick, there is much correspondence between Machen and Presbyterian leaders with blunt references to Fosdick and also a revealing file of letters between Machen and his mother. Mr. Arthur Kuschke, Westminster Librarian, has my full gratitude.

33. *Young Men's Christian Associations Library, New York City*

Fosdick's wartime record with the "Y" is in the Y.M.C.A. Library in New York City, but that record is factual and unadorned. Fosdick's article in *Association Men* is found here also.

VII. OTHER ARCHIVES AND LIBRARIES NOT VISITED BUT WHOSE HOLDINGS WERE TAPPED BY MAIL

I received, thanks to Mr. Carl F. Miller, from the American Philosophic Society copies of letters between Fosdick and H. Amoss, Franz Boas, Rufus Cole, and Simon Flexner. From the Andover-Harvard Theological Library I received, thanks to Mr. Alan Seaburg, informal photographs of Fosdick, originally assembled by William R. Hutchison. From Drew University, thanks to Mr. Kenneth Rowe, I received copies of letters from Herbert Welch to Fosdick. Copies of letters involving Fosdick and Martin D. Harbin, Jared T. Newman, and Andrew D. White came to me from the Department of Manuscripts and University Archives, Cornell University. The librarians of the Elmira, New York, Public Library kindly sent me articles appearing in the *Chemung Historical Journal* and the *Elmira Sunday Telegram,* describing the Gleason Sanitarium where Fosdick was institutionalized in 1902, and I never otherwise would have come across these rewarding items. Gerald Grob alerted me to Fosdick correspondence in two places and I received copies of his letters from the Dr. Thomas W. Salmon Collection, American Foundation for Mental Hygiene Papers, Library of the New York Hospital-Cornell University Medical Center and from the Association for Voluntary Sterilization, Social Welfare History Archives, University of Minnesota Libraries.

VIII. A WORD ABOUT THE PAPERS OF SOME OTHER PROTESTANT CHURCHMEN IN FOSDICK'S ERA

A fairly extensive correspondence with scholars and librarians and relatives of key individuals has convinced me that important collections have either disappeared or were not preserved initially, such as those of Henry Sloane Coffin and Charles W. Gilkey, although I found some of their letters scattered in various places. (The Coffin papers at Union are not complete.) Further, I have been informed that several collections, those of John R. Mott and Washington Gladden, for example, contain no Fosdick correspondence.

IX. BOOKS BY FOSDICK

Between 1908 and 1962 Fosdick's name appeared on the cover of over forty volumes if one includes the collections of sermons, lectures, and articles brought together between hard covers, works for juveniles, the early devotional classics, the Biblical studies, the psychological guides, the works he compiled and edited, and the autobiography. The titles of these volumes are cited in appropriate places in the text and the major works are examined at some length.

X. SERMONS, PRAYERS, HYMNS, PREFACES, INTRODUCTIONS, ADDRESSES, ARTICLES,
CHAPTER CONTRIBUTIONS TO VOLUMES BY OTHER AUTHORS, BOOK REVIEWS,
AND OTHER MISCELLANY BY FOSDICK

In a moment of excessive zeal I once made an alphabetical listing by title of
over one thousand items in this mixed category of works coming from Fosdick's pen in the foolish thought of presenting here a critical, annotated
bibliography. Common sense prevailed and the reader will be spared perhaps
one hundred further pages. Let me illustrate by reference to a single hypotheti-
cal sermon preached from the Riverside pulpit. The typed stenographic report
of the sermon might be found at Union or Riverside or both locations. The
sermon might well have been printed in pamphlet form and also published in
the *Church Monthly*. It might further have appeared in one or many periodicals, such as the *Christian Century* and the *Pulpit*. The sermon might have
been picked up by a secular magazine as well. Quite possibly major extracts
were carried by the newspapers, especially the *New York Times;* if so, quite
possibly the extracts were garbled—to Fosdick's voiced dismay. The sermon,
slightly abridged, then might have been preached over the radio a week or a
month after its presentation at Riverside and printed and supplied on request
to listeners. The sermon ultimately might have appeared in an anthology and
also in one of the eight volumes of Fosdick's sermons published by Harper &
Brothers and then again perhaps in the collection ranging over his entire
Riverside ministry, *Riverside Sermons*. Further, a recording of the sermon
might have been made, the record now in one of several depositories: Union,
Riverside, or the major collection of recorded sermons at Union Theological
Seminary, Richmond, Virginia. In sum, a single sermon might require as many
as ten or fifteen citations to where it could be found.

But the complications of presenting an annotated bibliography do not end
here. In some instances essentially the same sermon was given different titles.
In other instances a sermon was preached a second or third time with the title
unchanged and the content either slightly revised or markedly altered. Further,
on occasion the editor of a journal would reprint a sermon verbatim while supplying a new title, one presumably deemed more "peppy." Much to Fosdick's
understandable anger, on occasion an editor would reprint his material without
permission—and worse, in so doing altering or abridging the content.

In sparing the reader a listing of over a thousand titles, I do not wish totally
to duck my responsibility, and if some scholar is interested in finding the location, or many locations, of a particular item, I will be happy to lend an assist.
However, it should be noted that few of the sermons Fosdick prepared during his first ministry, 1903–1915, have survived; according to his secretary,
Mrs. Dorothy Noyes, he had most of them burned.

XI. PUBLISHED WORKS ABOUT FOSDICK

Excluded from this listing are the many references to Fosdick in volumes dealing with various aspects of American church history, although in a few in-

stances where the discussion is substantial, the book is cited with the appropriate chapter title. Omitted, too, are the brief sketches found in biographical dictionaries and religious encyclopaedias and also the scores of thumbnail newspaper portraits.

Abbot, E. H. "Dr. Fosdick's Religion," *Outlook,* March 11, 1925.

Alger, Edwin. "The Minister Who Doesn't Preach," *Radio Digest,* April 1931.

Bagnell, Kenneth. "This Is Fosdick," *United Church Observer,* March 1, 1962.

Baldwin, Arthur. "The Ministry After Fifty Years," *Chronicle,* January 1953.

Ban, Joseph. "Two Views of One Age: Fosdick and Straton," *Foundations,* April–June 1971.

Barton, Bruce. "Does Anything Come After Death?," (an interview with Fosdick) *American Magazine,* March 1923 and *Reader's Digest,* March 1923.

Beecher, Tex. "Harry Emerson Fosdick," *Christian,* June 20, 1931.

Beverly, Harry, Jr. *Harry Emerson Fosdick's Predigtweise, Its Significance (for America), Its Limits, Its Overcoming.* 1965.

Blackwood, Andrew. "Preaching in Time of War: The Discussion of a Live Problem: Harry Emerson Fosdick," *Pulpit Digest,* May 1945 from Blackwood, *The Fine Art of Preaching.* 1937.

Blassingame, Lurton. "Profiles: A Twentieth Century Puritan," *New Yorker,* June 18, 1927.

Bosley, Harold. "The Best Is Yet to Be!," *Christian Century,* May 21, 1958.

Bowen, T. Hassell. "Dr. Harry Emerson Fosdick—An Interpretation," *College of the Bible Quarterly,* October 1952.

Calkins, Harold. "Harry Emerson Fosdick," in *Master Preachers.* 1960.

Campion, Nardi Reeder. "Unforgettable Harry Emerson Fosdick," *Reader's Digest,* January 1971.

———. "Whose God Is Dead?," *Reader's Digest,* October 1966.

Cauthen, Kenneth. "Personality-Centered Christianity: Harry Emerson Fosdick" in *The Impact of American Religious Liberalism.* 1962.

Chapin, Lloyd. "Preacher to America: Harry Emerson Fosdick," *Colgate University Publication,* April 1970.

Christian Century editors. "Harry Emerson Fosdick," *Christian Century,* May 21, 1958. The *Christian Century* editors followed closely Fosdick's career for literally a half-century and carried many editorials about him. I am citing this one for its perception and also because this is a "special issue of recognition and gratitude" carrying three additional articles about him. See also "Honor to Dr. Fosdick" in May 20, 1953, issue.

Crocker, Lionel, compiler and editor. *Harry Emerson Fosdick's Art of Preaching: An Anthology.* 1971. This helpful anthology brings together seven essays on preaching *by* Fosdick and fourteen essays *about* Fosdick's preaching, most of them earlier published elsewhere, by Samuel Miller, Eugene May, Erdman Harris, Edgar Jones, Roy McCall, Robert Clark, Edmund Linn, Gilbert Macvaugh, Charles Kemp, and Crocker himself.

Davis, Jerome. "Dr. Harry Emerson Fosdick" in *World Leaders I Have Known.* 1963.

Dugan, George. "Fosdick, 80 Today, Is Still Writing," *New York Times*, May 24, 1958.

Eppinger, Paul. "Four Great Baptist Preachers and the Theology of Preaching," *Foundations*, April–June 1968.

Exman, Eugene. "Fosdick as Author," *Christian Century*, May 21, 1958.

F.A.A. "Harry Emerson Fosdick. A Character Study," *Christian World* (London), October 13, 1927.

Fagley, F. E. "Harry Emerson Fosdick's Preaching," *Congregationalist*, April 26, 1923.

Fant, Clyde, Jr., and William Pinson, Jr. "Harry Emerson Fosdick" in Fant and Pinson, *20 Centuries of Great Preaching*, Volume 9. 1971.

Fields, Sidney. "Making Retirement an Art," *New York Mirror*, May 23, 1958.

Fiske, Edward. "Harry Emerson Fosdick's Obituary," *New York Times*, October 6, 1969.

Glass, J. P. "Discoveries of Genius," *New York Evening World*, May 4, 1925.

Gordon, James. "One HEAVEN of a Fellow," *Coronet*, December 1947.

Handy, Robert. "Dr. Fosdick's Use of History," *Union Seminary Quarterly Review*, May 1953.

Harper, John. "God of Grace and God of Glory," mimeographed sermon preached April 1, 1973.

Haywood, Percy. "Harry Emerson Fosdick—Christian Minister" in Philip Lotz, editor, *Vocations and Professions*. 1940.

Hiltner, Seward. "The Man of the Month," *Pastoral Psychology*, December 1958.

Hodges, Graham. "Fosdick at 90," *Christian Century*, May 22, 1968.

Hudnut, William, Jr. "Fosdick as Teacher," *Christian Century*, May 21, 1958.

Hutchison, William. "The Great War and the Logic of Modernism" and "The Odd Couple" in *The Modernist Impulse in American Protestantism*. 1976.

Irwin, Virginia. "Dr. Fosdick—Fighting Rebel All His Life," *St. Louis Post Dispatch*, October 29, 1953.

Lemmon, Clarence. "Dr. Fosdick in Missouri," *Pulpit*, October 1946.

Linn, Edmund. *Preaching as Counseling: The Unique Method of Harry Emerson Fosdick*. 1966.

Loetscher, Lefferts. "A New York Pulpit" and "The Special Commission of 1925" in *The Broadening Church: A Study of Theological Issues in the Presbyterian Church Since 1869*. 1957.

McCracken, Robert James. "Harry Emerson Fosdick," *The Century Association Year-Book*, 1972.

Macnab, John. "Fosdick at First Church," *Journal of Presbyterian History*, Spring 1974.

Meyer, Donald B. "The Empty Adventure" in *The Positive Thinkers*. 1965.

Mingos, Howard. "Fosdick, Liberal Preacher," *World's Work*, October 1925.

Newsweek writer, unnamed. "Dr. Fosdick at Eighty," *Newsweek*, May 5, 1958.

Niebuhr, Reinhold. "The Significance of Dr. Fosdick in American Religious Thought," *Union Seminary Quarterly Review*, May 1953; reprinted with title "Fosdick: Theologian and Preacher," *Christian Century*, June 3, 1953.

Phillips, Robert, Jr. "Fosdick and the People's Concerns," *Foundations*, July–September 1970.

Potter, Richard. "Popular Religion of the 1930's As Reflected in the Best Sellers of Harry Emerson Fosdick," *Journal of Popular Culture*, Spring, 1970.

Riverside Church Congregation. "In Appreciation of Dr. and Mrs. Harry Emerson Fosdick," *Church Monthly*, Summer 1946.

Root, Edward, "The Power of Faith," *American Magazine*, May 1926.

Rusterholtz, Wallace. "Harry Emerson Fosdick: Emerson Again" in *American Heretics and Saints*. 1938.

Samuels, Gertrude. "Fosdick at 75—Still a Rebel," *New York Times Magazine*, May 24, 1953; reprinted at request of the Honorable Henry M. Jackson in *Congressional Record, Appendix*, June 1, 1953.

Schaick, John van, Jr. "Cruisings Casual and Careful: A Truly Great Preacher," *Christian Leader*, January 19, 1929.

Shepherd, William. "Harry Emerson Fosdick" in *Great Preachers as Seen by a Journalist*. 1924.

Shinn, Roger. "Harry Emerson Fosdick, Religious Reformer" in Paul Sherry, editor, *The Riverside Preachers*. 1978.

Smith, Helena. "Respectable Heretic," *Outlook and Independent*, October 9, 1929.

Sockman, Ralph. "Forty Years of Fosdick," *Religion In Life*, Spring 1957.

Spencer, Marcus. "Harry Emerson Fosdick: Teacher and Preacher," *Outlook Magazine* (England), December 1969.

Stevenson, Dwight. "Fosdick on Preaching," *College of the Bible Quarterly*, October 1952.

Strong, Sydney. "Harry Emerson Fosdick," *Unity*, December 8, 1930.

Thwing, Charles. "American Pulpit Leaders," *Review of Reviews*, March 1925.

Time writer, unnamed. "Ave Atque Vale," *Time*, April 8, 1946.

———. "The Liberal," *Time*, May 25, 1953.

Uren, A. R. "Rev. Harry Emerson Fosdick, D.D.," *Presbyterian Messenger* (Australia), undated.

Van Dusen, Henry Pitney. "Introduction," *Riverside Sermons*. 1958.

Wilkie, Katharine. "A Preacher Unafraid," *Classmate*, August 8, 1948.

Williams, J. Paul. "Why Fosdick Appeals to Youth," *Epworth Herald*, January 19, 1929.

Wilson, Leland. "For the Facing of This Hour," *Gospel Messenger*, May 26, 1962.

Worthington, W. C. "Dr. Fosdick Resumes the Experiment," *Delta Upsilon Quarterly*, July 1925.

Woolf, S. J. "A Religion to Fit the Life of Today," *New York Times Magazine*, October 5, 1930.

XII. UNPUBLISHED WORKS ABOUT FOSDICK

Manifestly the following unpublished works vary markedly in merit. Several were of little or no help to me. A number, however, are splendid studies of impressive scholarship. In truth, several probe specific areas of Fosdick's thought with greater depth and sophistication than I was able to do in the present broader study. Although almost all of them attempt biographical sketches of Fosdick's life, it is not unfair to observe that none of them may properly be termed biographies. Moreover, none of them derive from research in Fosdick's papers at Union or Riverside. This list does not pretend to be definitive and might be augmented by at least a dozen titles that I judged unnecessary to obtain in microfilm or xerox form or on interlibrary loan and by at least a dozen titles too insignificant to mention.

Bonney, Katharine. "Harry Emerson Fosdick's Doctrine of Man." Unpublished Ph.D. dissertation, Boston University, 1958.

Boyer, Ralph, III. "Interrelatedness of Pastoral Counseling and Preaching with Special Emphasis upon the Ministries of the Rev. Dr. Harry Emerson Fosdick and the Rev. Dr. Leslie Dixon Weatherhead." Unpublished S.T.D. dissertation, Temple University, 1960.

Brister, C. W. "The Ethical Thought of Harry Emerson Fosdick—A Critical Interpretation." Unpublished Th.D. dissertation, Southwestern Baptist Theological Seminary, 1957.

Burtner, Elmer. "The Use of Biblical Materials in the Sermons of Harry Emerson Fosdick." Unpublished Th.D. dissertation, Boston University School of Theology, 1959.

Clemons, Hardy. "The Key Theological Ideas of Harry Emerson Fosdick." Unpublished Th.D. dissertation, Southwestern Baptist Theological Seminary, 1966.

Eberts, Harry. "The Relevance of Preaching. A Study of the Preaching and Theology of Harry Emerson Fosdick." Unpublished essay, undated, written at San Francisco Theological Seminary.

Firth, Robert, "Harry Emerson Fosdick and His Impact on Liberalism in Religion in the United States." Unpublished M.A. thesis, University of Southern California, 1957.

Kovar, Leonard. "An Analysis of Selected Sermons of Dr. Harry Emerson Fosdick." Unpublished B.D. thesis, Andover-Newton Theological School, 1953.

Landry, Fabaus. "The Preaching of Harry Emerson Fosdick: An Analysis of Its Intent, Style, and Language." Unpublished D.D. dissertation, Divinity School of Vanderbilt University, 1972.

Lawson, Douglas. "The Idea of Progress in the Theology of Harry Emerson Fosdick." Unpublished Ph.D. dissertation, Duke University, 1963.

Leininger, Charles. "The Christian Apologetic of Harry Emerson Fosdick." Unpublished Th.D. dissertation, Southern Baptist Theological Seminary, 1967.

Le Vander, Theodor. "A Critical Study of Selected Radio Addresses Delivered by Dr. Harry Emerson Fosdick on National Vespers, 1939–1940." Unpublished M.A. thesis, State University of Iowa, 1940.

Lindsay, John. "Harry Emerson Fosdick's Views on Religion." Unpublished Th.D. dissertation, Boston University School of Theology, 1941.

McDiarmid, Allan. "A Critique of Harry Emerson Fosdick's Concept of Preaching as Personal Counseling on a Group Scale." Unpublished Th.D. dissertation, Pacific School of Religion, 1961.

McLeRoy, William. "Sackcloth and Ashes: The Struggle of Harry Emerson Fosdick with War and Peace, 1914–1941. Unpublished M.A. thesis, Texas Christian University, 1968.

Pancake, Loral. "Theological Liberalism in the Life and Ministry of Harry Emerson Fosdick." Unpublished M.A. thesis, Drew Theological Seminary, 1946.

Shelton, Robert. "The Relationship Between Reason and Revelation in the Preaching of Harry Emerson Fosdick." Unpublished Th.D. dissertation, Princeton Theological Seminary, 1965.

Waldvogel, Edith. "Harry Emerson Fosdick, First Presbyterian Church, and Riverside Church: A Chapter in the Fundamentalist-Modernist Controversy, 1919–1935." Unpublished M.A. thesis, Hunter College, The City University of New York, 1971.

Weaver, Samuel. "The Theology and Times of Harry Emerson Fosdick." Unpublished Th.D. dissertation, Princeton Theological Seminary, 1961.

XIII. TELEVISION AND RADIO PROGRAMS

On three occasions Fosdick was the subject of television interview shows: Alistair Cooke's "Omnibus" program; NBC's "Wisdom" series; and Arlene Francis's and Hugh Downs's "People at Home" series. Fosdick was also the subject of several radio interviews on the WOR Martha Deane show. Additionally, Mary Sockwell kindly loaned me a tape of the interview she conducted with three individuals intimately involved in Riverside's history, Dr. and Mrs. Norris Tibbetts and Mr. Bettis Garside.

XIV. A WORD ABOUT REVIEWS OF FOSDICK'S BOOKS

Fosdick's many books were widely reviewed. A search for these reviews was made in ten secular publications and sixty-two religious journals available in North Carolina's Wilson Library and Duke's Divinity School Library. In addition, and conveniently, clippings of scores of reviews are found in the Riverside Church archives, and I must confess that a number of these reviews I would never have tracked down independently, especially those from British publications.

XV. A WORD ABOUT THE RELIGIOUS AND SECULAR PRESS

My earlier books, especially *American Protestantism and Social Issues, 1919–1939*, rested heavily on an issue by issue examination of several score religious and secular publications. That enormously tiring and time-consuming task did not seem worth repeating for this biography, or so I rationalized. May I in extenuation plead four compensating factors. I did con complete files of the *New York Times* and the *Christian Century*. I did tap my earlier press and periodical researches. I did engage in fresh researches in these sources for limited periods and on specific topics. And I drew frequently on thousands of clippings compiled by others and found in the archives and libraries named earlier.

XVI. A WORD ABOUT PILFERING FROM YELLOWING NOTES

My earlier books rested heavily on an examination of official denominational records, Federal Council of Churches records, the records of such secular bodies as the Socialist Party of America and the American Civil Liberties Union, some unpublished papers of churchmen, a raft of sermon collections, autobiographies, biographies, monographs, and three score unpublished dissertations and theses. Where appropriate, I drew for this biography shamelessly from my old yellowing notes.

XVII. A WORD ABOUT SECONDARY LITERATURE

Each of the thirty chapters, with the exceptions of Chapters Twenty-eight and Thirty, required a plunge into a sea of secondary works: unpublished dissertations (in addition to those already cited dealing directly with Fosdick), magazine and journal articles, biographies and autobiographies, and monographs. Probably in no chapter (aside from Chapters Twenty-eight and Thirty and perhaps a few others) would the number of secondary items consulted total less than one hundred, and for several chapters the total was much larger. To list the titles here would be a hopelessly long enterprise and an unconscionably pretentious one.

Index

70279